Ghosts could walk freely tonight, without fear of the disbelief of men; for this night was haunted, and it would be an insensitive man who did not know it.
John Steinbeck

Every small town has at least one house the children whisper about; the type of house that has always been abandoned; where the once pristine white paint has faded to a grimy gray; where the windows are boarded, and the lawn never grows; where children hold their breath and close their eyes as they pass by. A house that sounds like it contains an army of whispering spirits when the wind whistles through the nearby trees.
The Blood Brothers

Death doesn't exist. It never did, it never will. But we've drawn so many pictures of it, so many years, trying to pin it down, comprehend it, we've got to thinking of it as an entity, strangely alive and greedy. All it is, however, is a stopped watch, a loss, an end, a darkness. Nothing.
Ray Bradbury

It's easier to dismiss ghosts in the daylight.
Patricia Briggs

I don't suppose you have to believe in ghosts to know that we are all haunted, all of us, by things we can see and feel and guess at, and many more things that we can't.
Beth Gutcheon

Yet, despite all, it is a difficult thing to admit the existence of ghosts in a coldly factual world. One's very instincts rebel at the admission of such maddening possibility. For, once the initial step is made into the supernatural, there is no turning back, no knowing where the strange road leads except that it is quite unknown and quite terrible.
Richard Matheson

Look, I know the supernatural is something that isn't supposed to happen, but it does happen.
Dr. John Markway — The Haunting

GHOSTS OF THE PRAIRIE

HISTORY & HAUNTINGS OF CENTRAL ILLINOIS

TROY TAYLOR

Original Cover Artwork Designed by
© Copyright 2016 by April Slaughter & Troy Taylor

This Book is Published By:
Whitechapel Press
American Hauntings Ink
Jacksonville, Illinois | 217.791.7859
Visit us on the Internet at http://www.whitechapelpress.com

First Edition – September 2016
ISBN: 978-1-892523-07-5

Printed in the United States of America

INTRODUCTION

Ghosts of the Prairie

The book that you are now holding in your hands is not the book that I originally intended to write. Yes, at least some of what is contained between these covers would have ended up within the original project, but not all of it. My intention was to write a fourth edition of my earlier book, *Haunted Illinois*. It had been almost 12 years since the last edition was written and, needless to say, much has changed. A score of other books have been written since then – my own books and those by other authors – chronicling the many ghosts of Illinois. When I wrote the first edition of *Haunted Illinois* back in 1999, it was the first book that had been written about the haunted places of the state. Today, there are a couple of dozen such books, but I knew that I needed to update my earlier work. There were new stories about old places, old stories about new places, and places that had never appeared in any of my other books. As I had written back in 1999, Illinois is a state that is always revealing its history in new ways – along with its hauntings.

Obviously, a fourth edition of *Haunted Illinois* would not have been my only foray into the haunts of Illinois. I have written more than a dozen volumes about various parts of the state and every region's resident ghosts, from Alton to Chicago, Decatur, Jacksonville, and beyond. I had never made the claim that I'd tracked down every story that Illinois had to tell. Every town in the state, no matter how small, has at least one or two ghost stories that are known only to those who call the place home. Some of these tales will never be known to outsiders, but if I could pry them loose, I did so.

And that became part of the problem.

As the new *Haunted Illinois* project came together, it began to spin out of control. As more and more stories were inserted into the book, it began to grow – and grow. It wasn't long before I realized that the book would be so large, so unwieldy, and so expensive, that no one would take the time to actually read it, let alone want to pay for it. So, that one updated volume turned into several updated volumes. The first of them, *Ghosts of the Prairie*, is the one you're holding in your hands right now. Rather than try to cram an updated and revised history and hauntings of Illinois into a single book – and have to cut, slice, and leave out a lot of good material – I decided to turn it into a complete project with a number of books about various portions of the state. In this way, the reader will have access to not only classic stories of the region, but little-known history and hauntings that might never have appeared in my earlier books – and certainly would not have been included in the planned fourth edition of *Haunted Illinois*.

I hope that you will understand the reason for this new plan. Illinois is a state where ghost stories have been shaped by the past, and I just couldn't bear to leave any of them out. I needed to tell the story of how Illinois was quite literally born in violence, fire, and blood. From the days of the first pioneers to the Indian massacres during the War of 1812, it is a place that became infamous for murder, mystery, and mayhem. It was a place that was home to the most brutal gangsters of the Prohibition era and some of the most deranged killers in history. Illinois has a past that is often frightening, disturbing, and filled with cruel events that left a bloody mark on its haunted landscape. Is it any wonder that Illinois has so many ghosts?

Even if you comprehend my reasoning, you likely still have questions. Why start in the middle of the state? Why not start at either the northern or southern ends of the state and tell the stories in subsequent books, from one region to the next? The reason is simple – I decided to begin this collection of updated *Haunted Illinois* books where my own story began. For the most part, I was raised in Central Illinois and I have lived in the region – in one city or another – for a large part of my life. I can call the rolling prairie, corn fields, woods, pastures, and creeks my home. When I first began writing about Illinois and its history and hauntings in 1993, I began writing about Central Illinois. In this way, a book like this sort of comes "full circle," especially when you include the fact that I also published a magazine for several years, starting in 1996, that was called *Ghosts of the Prairie*. The title of this book is a nod to those early days.

But my fascination with ghosts started much earlier than the 1990s. It began while living in Central Illinois and, I have to admit, it began because of a cereal box. It was a box of Honeycomb cereal that my mother purchased one Halloween season in the late 1970s. That October, the cereal maker decided to manufacture boxes with three different 45-rpm records pressed into the cardboard. Each of the records had a different story on it, and once you finished eating all of the cereal, you could cut it out of the box and play it on your record player. I don't remember what one of the stories ("The Miser's Gold") was about, but I do remember that one of them was a dramatized version of "The Legend of Sleepy Hollow" and the other was "The Vanishing Hitchhiker."

I remember sitting transfixed in front of the record player in our basement, listening to the scratchy sounds of the "vanishing hitchhiker" record. The quality was not great (what do you want from a record that used be part of a cereal box?) but I can remember my hair standing on end when the narrator went out to the cemetery the next morning and found... Well, I won't ruin the story for you, but let me just say that this record is likely the reason that I chose my peculiar career path. My fascination with the story led to tales of real vanishing hitchhikers (like Chicago's Resurrection Mary), which in turn led to seeking out ghosts, haunted houses, cemeteries, and strange tales of the unexplained.

And after all of these years, my fascination with ghosts and scary stories is just as strong as it was then. I can't help collecting them, tracking them down, and, most of all, writing about them. And with that said, I hope you enjoy the stories in this book – both the old and new tales -- as much as I enjoyed writing them. I wish I could tell you that no ghost stories of Central Illinois have managed to elude me, but that's not the case. There are haunted places out there that have remained unknown almost since the first settlers came to our "seas of prairie grass" and will never be told. Even so, while I may never uncover every ghost story the state has to offer, I think you'll be startled, intrigued, and, hopefully, unnerved by the stories in this book.

And I hope that at least some of them – preferably, many of them – will have you leaving the light on when you go to bed at night.

Troy Taylor
Fall 2016

1. THE BUILDING OF ILLINOIS
Murder, Mayhem, History & Hauntings

Illinois is the hiding place for villains from every part of the United States, and indeed, from every quarter of the globe. A majority of the settlers have been discharged from penitentiaries and jails or have been the victims of misfortune or imprudence. Many of those will reform, but many, very many, are made fit for robbery and murder.
Milo M. Quaife

Illinois has always been a mysterious place. I have always said that it was "born in blood," steeped in the violence and death in its past. The tragedies of yesterday so often become the ghost stories of today. From its very beginning, Illinois was a place where death was commonplace and unsolved mysteries thrived.

The land that would someday become "Illinois" was a place of legend, lore, and the rolling "prairie seas of grass." It was a rich land, and one that would be coveted by the settlers and frontiersmen who traveled west from the original American colonies. The recorded history of Illinois began in 1673 when the first French explorers came to the region, but men walked the prairie centuries before that. The explorers who first encountered Native Americans living in the woods and along the rivers of the land, found scattered tribes with no written language and no central communities and culture. But they also discovered strange mounds, altars, burial sites, and ruins where towns and cities had once stood. It seemed that a civilization, far advanced of the current natives, had once lived in the Mississippi River Valley. Who these mysterious dwellers might have been remains a mystery. They have been dubbed the "Mound Builders," thanks to the monuments of earth they left behind, but the people so utterly disappeared that their true identities will never be known. They left only silent graves, enigmatic mounds, and unanswered questions in their wake.

The Mound Builders were followed by the hunters and wanderers, who were the sole occupants of the land when the explorers arrived. Their small villages were scattered across the prairie and nestled close to the rivers and water sources. They hunted the deer and bison, fished the rivers, and traded with and fought the neighboring tribes.

When the Native Americans of the region encountered the first French explorers at the mouth of the Des Moines River, they referred to themselves as "Illiniwek," a word that simply meant "the men," which was how they referred to their tribe. This designation was meant to separate them from the Iroquois Indians, who were their mortal enemies and called "animals." From that time on, this branch of Algonquin Indians was known as the "Illinois" confederation and it would be from this band that the territory – and later, the state – would take its name. The confederation was made up of several tribes who had banded together for the purpose of defense. They held a large portion of the state, which they shared with several other tribes, including the powerful Kickapoo Indians.

"The Old Northwest"
Conquering the Illinois Territory

No one will ever know the name of the first white man to set foot in Illinois. It is possible that some adventurer, trader, or wanderer arrived first, but recorded history begins with the arrival of Louis Jolliet and Father Jacques Marquette in June 1673.

Jolliet was a young French-Canadian explorer and map-maker and Marquette was a Jesuit priest who longed to bring his faith to the native people of the American wilderness. The two men, along with several Indians and 19 white men, took a treacherous journey down the Mississippi River, which, to their surprise, did not end at the Pacific Ocean.

The expedition had reached the Mississippi by way of the Illinois River, which Marquette noted for its "peaceful current." He wrote of the strange rocks and bluffs on the eastern banks and on old French maps of the region, they were later referred to as "ruined castles." For several weeks, the expedition traveled south on the Mississippi, encountering new lands, fish, plants, and animals. Marquette wrote, "From time to time, we came upon monstrous fish, one of which struck our canoe with such violence that I thought it was a great tree, about to break the canoe into pieces." He also recording seeing and eating bison, which he referred to as "wild cattle."

On June 25, Marquette wrote that the explorers came into contact with members of the Illinois tribe. They had seen tracks on a well-traveled path along the shore and Marquette and Jolliet decided to follow them. The encounter went well, and the two sat down with representatives of the tribe and smoked tobacco pipes as a token of peace. Afterward, the explorers were invited to the tribe's village, where they met a man that Marquette called "the great captain of all the Illinois." They enjoyed a meal with him, stayed the night, and returned to the Mississippi the following day.

As the expedition continued, they rounded a sharp curve on the river and got their first glimpse of the future site of Alton, Illinois. On the smooth face of a high bluff were two depictions of a strange monster that had been painted in red, black, and green. According to Marquette's journal, they were painted monsters "upon which the boldest Indians dared not long rest their eyes." The creature, known as the "Piasa" by the native populace, would later be described by other explorers and would serve as a river landmark for decades to come. River tradition has it that as Indian delegations passed the bluff, they "attacked" the creature with well-aimed arrows from the river.

The sight of such a creature, even a painted rendition of it, unnerved Marquette. He had been told by the Indians of strange creatures that awaited them downstream. According to the explorer's journal, the men had scarcely recovered from the terrifying sight of the Piasa when they were plunged into real danger. A torrent of yellow and muddy water gushed into the quiet stillness of the Mississippi River, threatening to overturn the expedition's canoes. They turned to the eastern shore to avoid the strong current, desperately hoping to avoid the huge masses of driftwood and uprooted trees that coursed toward them. This was the mouth of the Pekistanoui (Missouri) River and Marquette wrote that he "never saw anything more terrific."

In time, they reached the mouth of the Arkansas River, where they met members of the Quapaw tribe. They were told they were only one week from the sea, but that the natives farther south were hostile. Marquette and Jolliet also saw European trade goods among the Quapaw and realized they would encounter the Spanish if they continued on downriver. Not wanting to be captured by the Indians or the Spanish, they decided to turn back. The return journey was more arduous because the group had to paddle against the river current.

In late August 1673, they reached the mouth of the Illinois River, coming ashore at a spot near modern-day Grafton, Illinois, which is now marked by a stone cross. A few weeks later, the expedition arrived at an

Illinois tribal village, near modern-day Utica. From there, they paddled the Des Plaines River and traveled by land to reach Lake Michigan. After arriving safely, Marquette vowed to return to Illinois to establish a mission.

Marquette and Jolliet parted ways at the Des Peres mission at the mouth of Green Bay. The priest had fallen sick and stayed behind while his friend continued on to Montreal. When he was almost home, Jolliet's canoe capsized and his maps and journals from the Illinois trip were lost. Because of this, only Marquette's notes remain about the discovery of the region. He returned to Illinois in the latter part of 1674 to keep his promise of returning to set up a mission. By the time he arrived at the Chicago portage, though, he was seriously ill. He spent the winter in a small hut, becoming increasingly weak as the months passed. When spring arrived, he was well enough to direct the building of the mission, but soon became bedridden again. In May 1675, he died on the eastern shore of Lake Michigan, where a river was later named in his honor.

Marquette opened the way for other priests, many of whom would meet danger and death in the wilderness. They were some of the earliest residents of the state and perhaps met with greater hardships than any of those who followed. Sadly, however, most of their names have been forgotten today.

Marquette and Jolliet's expedition began the French exploration of North America. In that era, the British claimed most of the eastern seaboard, while the French claimed the southern and eastern reaches of Canada and the Great Lakes. The Spanish controlled Mexico, the Southwest, and California. All of these European powers battled to claim more territory in the New World and to find a water passage across the continent that would make for faster travel to the Far East.

One of the great explorers to attempt to conquer Illinois was Robert Cavalier, who was better known as the flamboyant self-promoter, Sieur de LaSalle. He was the first of the early arrivals to understand the economic importance of the territory and also became the first to explore many of the waterways and forests of the region. In spite of his courage and his brilliance, LaSalle was regarded by most as haughty, arrogant, and rude. He was often referred to as a "man of magnificent failures." He made a dark mark on the region's history as he brutalized the Indian tribes, borrowed huge sums of money, and squandered fortunes. Somehow, though, he managed to gain the respect and loyalty of a true adventurer. Henri de Tonty was an Italian soldier of fortune who became a character in his own right. He was both admired and feared by the Native Americans, largely thanks to the wicked metal hook that replaced the hand that he had earlier lost in battle. Tonty became LaSalle's boon companion and perhaps his anchor of sanity, as well.

LaSalle had been born into a noble French family in 1643. He came to America two decades later and took up exploration as a means of creating his fortune. On his first trip, seeking the Ohio River, he encountered the explorer Louis Jolliet, who was returning from Illinois. Jolliet's fortunes would never be made, LaSalle believed, because he was unable to get land grants from the French government. In addition, because of his friendship with Marquette, the explorer would always be hampered by his links to the Jesuit order of the Catholic Church. LaSalle did not have such problems. He despised the Jesuits and managed to avoid any political connections that would drag him down. He was able to gain a grant that gave him control of the fur trade south of the Great Lakes. In return for it, he agreed to explore the lower Mississippi Valley and try to discover a water passage to the Pacific Ocean.

LaSalle, based in the north, began building a ship called the *Griffon*, which became the first sailing ship on the Great Lakes. He planned to use it to take his cargoes of furs to the east and then on to Europe. The vessel set sail with a full crew and a hold filled with cargo, and then disappeared without a trace. To this day, no trace of it has ever been found. Luckily for LaSalle, he wasn't aboard when the ship went down.

LaSalle was busy making a winter trek across Illinois. He pioneered the St. Joseph - Kankakee River route and built a shelter called Fort Crevecoeur at present-day Peoria in 1680. It was a crude, wooden structure, but it was the first building erected by the French in the west. It did not last long. While LaSalle was in Canada, preparing supplies for a journey down the Mississippi, the men who remained at the fort mutinied and burned down the building. It was never rebuilt.

In the spring of 1682, LaSalle and his companion, Tonti, made the first journey down to the mouth of the Mississippi River. When they arrived, LaSalle claimed all of the land for France and dubbed the region "Louisiana," in honor of the king. In so doing, he created a vast territory that stretched from the Appalachians to the Rocky Mountains.

After that, they returned to Illinois and LaSalle built another fort, this one called Fort St. Louis, on Starved Rock, which was located on the Illinois River in the northern part of the state. On this site, the men erected a blockhouse, a storehouse, and a dwelling on the summit of the rock. It was impassable on three sides and had only a narrow trail to defend on the fourth.

LaSalle left Illinois after only five years. He returned home to France, where he was considered a hero. He was asked again to serve his country, as France was now at war with Spain, and LaSalle promised to set up a base of operations at the mouth of the Mississippi River. He departed with 200 colonists but somehow managed to sail past Louisiana and landed in Texas instead. He conducted several expeditions in search of the Mississippi, but he never found it again. While on the fourth mission, he was shot and killed by one of his own men. It was a rather strange, but somehow fitting, end for someone known as the "man of magnificent failures."

In the years that followed LaSalle's departure, Tonti became a well-known figure on his own. Being less adversarial than LaSalle, he made many friends and allies and spent more than 15 years guiding French settlers to Illinois. Despite LaSalle's many faults, Tonti remained loyal to him, and after his expedition vanished (no one knew yet that he had been killed), Tonti led a search party to find him. A mystery still surrounds the death of Tonti. Some say he died while searching for LaSalle in Alabama, but local natives claimed that he returned to Starved Rock to live out his final years. What truly happened to him will never be known.

From 1698 to 1722, the French expanded throughout the Lower Mississippi Valley. In 1700, Jesuit missionaries briefly established a village with some Kaskaskia Indians north of River Des Peres. Aside from this settlement, though, the French stayed mostly in the south for many years, founding Mobile, Alabama, in 1702 and New Orleans in 1722. A few years later, more settlements began to appear in the north at Kaskaskia, Cahokia, St. Genevieve, and Fort de Chartres. In 1763, the city of St. Louis was founded and not long after settlers, explorers, and fur traders flocked to the region.

Americans first arrived in Illinois with an "invasion" that was launched by George Rogers Clark during the American Revolution. By mid-1878, the war between Britain and her upstart colonies was badly stalled. During the previous fall, the British had captured Philadelphia and, a month later, repelled an American counterattack at Germantown, Pennsylvania. Washington and his troops had barely survived their winter at Valley Forge. In February 1778, the French had signed a treaty with the Americans to supply troops, ships, and goods for the war effort. In June, the British abandoned Philadelphia to solidify defenses in New York. A major battle in New Jersey had been fought to a standstill. The Americans were badly in need of a victory.

Washington placed his faith in George Rogers Clark, one of five brothers from Virginia who became an officer during the war. Clark was only 26, but had earned a reputation as a solid military leader and was a militia major in Kentucky, which was then part of Virginia. In 1777, the British commander at Fort Detroit had begun encouraging British-friendly Native Americans to harass and attack settlers in Kentucky. Clark decided that the best way to stop the attacks was to capture British posts on the Ohio River. He was given permission by Virginia governor Patrick Henry to lead a secret war party to attack the British in what would become the state of Illinois.

In July, Clark and a small force of about 175 men crossed the Ohio River at Fort Massac (near modern-day Metropolis) and marched on the former French settlement of Kaskaskia, which had been taken over by the British. He caught the British by surprise and, with the support of the French and Native American settlers, seized the city without firing a shot. A messenger was sent to other British posts in the region, including Cahokia,

Prairie du Rocher, St. Phillip, and Vincennes, and offered terms of surrenders. The terms were accepted without resistance, but the British commanders were not going to give up without a fight. Lieutenant Governor Henry Hamilton, the Detroit commander, retaliated by mustering a force of British troops and Indian allies, and they marched from Detroit to Vincennes. After recapturing the city, Hamilton encamped there for the winter. He planned to gather additional troops and then re-take the cities taken by Clark in the spring. But the British underestimated Clark. He and his men marched through almost 240 miles of flooded wetlands and surprised the British at Vincennes. Trying to keep the British off guard, he ordered his troops to hide behind a slight rise and had his flag bearers march back and forth so that the British would believe his force was much larger than it was. The fighting lasted for three days, but Clark prevailed. Hamilton surrendered and Clark claimed the region for Virginia.

The victories in this region, known as the "Old Northwest," were welcome news to Washington and the commanders in the east. In addition, Clark's claims to the northwestern frontier cemented America's hold on the region, which encompassed most of what would become the Midwest. Those gains were formally recognized when the British ceded the area to the Americans in the Treaty of 1783.

Sadly for George Rogers Clark, the victories in Illinois were the highlights of his career. After the war, he was named superintendent-surveyor of public lands granted to men who had served in the Virginia militia. In response to Native American hostility toward white settlers in the region, Clark agreed to lead an expedition of 1,200 men against the Indians in 1786. The campaign fell apart when more than 300 of the men refused to continue after a dispute over food and supplies. It was also reported that Clark was heavily drinking while on duty. He attempted to combat those claims by demanding a formal inquiry to clear his name, but his request was denied and Virginia politicians publicly chastised him.

To make matters worse, Clark had assumed personal responsibility for many of the expenses that were incurred during his campaigns and was never reimbursed by the state of Virginia or the U.S. government. Creditors hounded him. He lost most of his extensive land holdings in Indiana that had been granted to him for his military service, and by 1803, his estate had dwindled to only a grist mill, a two-room cabin, and a small plot of land in Clarksville, Indiana. Ironically, the town had been named in his honor. By 1809, Clark was a physical wreck. Angry about his mistreatment by government officials, he had become a heavy drinker. After suffering a stroke, he had an accident at the mill, which cost him his right leg. He sold everything he had left and moved to Kentucky to live with his sister and her husband. After another stoke, he died on February 13, 1818.

Too late to matter, Clark became regarded as a hero after his death. The state of Virginia finally repaid his estate for his war expenses, a memorial was erected in his honor, and he is lauded today as the man who conquered the west during the American Revolution.

Across the Mississippi River, the French remained in control until 1803, when news arrived that the United States had purchased the entire region from France for $15 million. The French settlers on both sides of the river were outraged. They had been all but forgotten by their own county, and now had been sold to the United States without their knowledge or consent. The American flag was raised over the Louisiana Territory on March 10, 1804. It was a time of great uncertainty for the settlers, who feared being invaded by the "Bostons," a local slur for the Americans from the east. But President Thomas Jefferson issued orders that changed little for the inhabitants and the transition went smoothly.

Meanwhile, Jefferson was anxious to discover just what he had acquired for the United States and what was located between the Mississippi and the Pacific Ocean. He soon authorized an expedition to the west to be led by his secretary, a young man named Meriwether Lewis. Lewis eagerly accepted the commission and began buying scientific instruments, studying medicine, and even ordered the Harper's Ferry arsenal to build him a collapsible iron boat. Most importantly, Lewis requested the help his friend William Clark to accompany him on his journey. Clark knew the wilderness and was good with a drawing pencil and would make a perfect companion for the expedition. His brother, George Rogers Clark, had become famous for his expedition to the Illinois frontier during the American Revolution. Clark quickly accepted and replied in a letter to Lewis that "no man lives with whom I would prefer to undertake and share the difficulties of such a trip than yourself. My friend, I join you with hand and heart." With that said, the two men began to embark upon a journey that changed the entire course of our history.

St. Louis became the base of operations for the expedition. It was the largest city in the region and was the place to find mountain men and trappers like Manuel Lisa, who were full of information about the wilderness of the west. Many of them had traveled far up the Missouri River and had lived among the Indians. During the journey west to St. Louis, the captains recruited a number of young men to the party and a camp was needed for them to prepare for the journey. They made the camp east of the river in the Illinois Territory. The site that was chosen was called Camp Dubois, which was located near the present-day towns of Hartford and Wood River in Illinois.

Lewis and Clark's Corp of Discovery stayed in Illinois for the five winter months prior to their journey. They organized their supplies, drilled the men, hunted for food, and spent long days in endless routine. They finally departed Illinois in May 1804, steering their boats up the Missouri River to St. Charles. When they arrived, Clark met with famous frontiersman Daniel Boone, who lived nearby and with whom Clark had consulted over the previous months. The expedition finally departed a few days later.

The adventures of the Corps of Discovery as they blazed the way to the west is another story altogether but, suffice it to say, their return to St. Louis more than two years later marked the beginning of a new era for the city and the surrounding region. The Illinois Territory became a place of national importance and the climate of the entire region rapidly began to change.

"Where Blood was Spilt..."
Indian Massacres, War & Bloodshed

The birth of Illinois is a history that has been written in blood. The early years of the nineteenth century was a time of lawlessness and a lack of order in the region. Outlaws, fleeing in desperation from the restraints of civilization, where the law was strictly enforced, found the wilderness to be a place where they could carry on their lawless ways. The settlements in those days were small and widely scattered, with broad spaces of unknown forest and prairie lying in between. The beleaguered upholders of the law were unable to be everywhere at once, if they existed at all. It was easy in those days to operate in secrecy, while the very life of the frontier bred a class of rough and desperate men, capable of committing almost any crime.

There is no part of Illinois that does not have its local traditions of outlawry during its period of early settlement. There are locations that even today are pointed out as weird and gruesome murder sites, or places where gangs of outlaws once hid out. Often these tales are so filled with legend that it is hard to tell where truth ends and fiction begins. Regardless, they paint a vivid portrait of how Illinois came to be and why it gained such a reputation as a lawless place.

One of the first bloody periods of Illinois history came soon after Illinois became a territory in 1809. By this time, settlers from the east had started to arrive in the area in greater numbers, which was understandably perceived as a great threat to the life and lands of the Indian populace. The unwanted arrivals, mixed with another war with England, led to the first blood being spilled in Illinois.

When the War of 1812 began with Britain, the Illinois Territory became an integral part of the fighting. Along the east coast and the Canadian border, the American forces fought against British invasion. Illinois, on the far western frontier, was torn apart by massacres and bloody battles with the Indian allies of the British. They wreaked havoc on the Illinois settlers, burning homes and slaughtering pioneer families in more barbaric ways than the British could have ever imagined. Shortly after the war began, the infamous Fort Dearborn Massacre took place at the site of present-day Chicago. This terrifying incident took the lives of scores of settlers and soldiers, including women and children.

Soon after the massacre at Fort Dearborn, British commanders started down the Mississippi River spreading discontent among the Indians and bribing them with trade goods and liquor. In retaliation, the territorial governor of Illinois, Ninian Edwards, mustered a group of volunteer frontiersmen at Camp Russell, which was near present-day Edwardsville. They were reinforced by three companies of United States Rangers under the command of Colonel Russell. The mounted riflemen advanced north along the Illinois River, burning native settlements and killing any of the inhabitants who resisted them.

By 1813, Illinois had fortified and settlers prepared for the worst. Blockhouses and forts had appeared along the frontier and settlers in remote locations were evacuated to safety. New companies of rangers were formed and posted in positions all over the territory, but this was not enough to stop the marauding Indians. Slipping past the forts, Native Americans attacked the Lively family, who lived four miles south of Covington, in present-day Washington County. The attackers offered no mercy. Lively was mutilated and murdered and his wife and daughter were raped, savaged, and slain. One of Lively's sons, a child of seven, was dragged from the house and beheaded. Another of his sons, along with a traveler who had been invited to supper with the family, escaped and summoned help. A company of rangers under Captain Bond pursued the Indians, but they vanished into the wilderness.

A few days later, two men were murdered near what is now Carlyle. Several more attacks and murders followed on the Cache River, near the present-day town of Albion, and on the Wabash River, where a woman and her four children were slaughtered. Another military expedition was formed in response and marched north to the area around Peoria Lake, where a large number of Native Americans had gathered and were using the area as a staging point for attacks across the territory. A group of 900 soldiers were sent under the command of General Howard of the U.S. Army and they rendezvoused with troops from Missouri under Colonel McNair. The troops, now banded together, continued their northward march.

Near present-day Quincy, they turned east and headed to the mouth of the Spoon River, and then followed the Illinois to Peoria, where they found a small stockade commanded by Captain Nicholas. The stockade had been attacked just two days before, but Nicholas and his men had managed to fight off the Indians. The expedition continued on but found only deserted villages as they marched. The raiders had apparently moved on to another location. The entire expedition turned out to be bloodless, but it did manage to temporarily halt the attacks on the Illinois settlers.

Despite the best efforts of the rangers and the frontier defenders, the atrocities and attacks continued. The war was beginning to turn against the British by the early months of 1814, and after their defeat at the Battle of Thames, most of the hostile Indians were driven south of the Canadian border. This was a good sign for overall victory in the war, but it had dire results for Illinois settlers. Indians began to gather along the upper Mississippi and started attacking small Illinois settlements.

In July, Indians attacked the homes of two families between the forks of the Wood River, near the present-day site of Alton. The attacks occurred on Sunday, July 10, while Reason Reagan was away at church. He left his wife, Rachel, and two children, Elizabeth and Timothy, at the home of neighbor, Abel Moore. Late in the day, Rachel returned home and took all of the children present with her, including two children of Abel Moore, and two children of his brother, William. Another young woman, Hannah Bates, planned to accompany her but turned back because her feet were hurting from a new pair of shoes. Tragically, the rest of the party never made it to the Reagan home.

Shortly after nightfall, William Moore began searching for his missing children. He and his wife took separate routes in their search. Moore stumbled over a body in the darkness, but could not identify it. His wife was not as fortunate. She found the bloody corpse of Rachel Reagan and her son, Timothy, and ran home crying hysterically. At dawn, a party from a nearby military encampment took up the search and found the bodies of the missing settlers less than a mile from the safety of the camp. They wrapped them all in sheets, since there was no one available to build coffins, and buried them in a common grave.

Captain Samuel Whiteside, along with a company of rangers, pursued the Indians who had slaughtered the woman and the children and followed them north to the Sangamon River. They caught up with them near the present-day site of Virden, but only one of the Indians was killed. Tucked into his belt, they found the blood-soaked scalp of Rachel Reagan. The rest of the killers vanished into the forest.

The victims of what came to be called the "Wood River Massacre" were buried at what is now Vaughn Hill Cemetery, in present-day Wood River. Not surprisingly, the graveyard has gained a reputation for being haunted over the years. Many visitors claim to have experienced frightened or uneasy feelings at the edge of the burial ground. Others have heard the sounds of cries and weeping and have seen eerie lights among the gravestones and markers. Even those who do not believe in ghosts will admit that this is a spooky place.

Another Indian attack occurred about 20 miles from present-day Vandalia in August 1814. An encampment had been constructed there to protect the local settlers and was under the command of a Major Journey. One day, Benjamin Henson, a resident of the camp, was out hunting and returned to report seeing Indians in the area. He told the commander that he believed they were in danger of an attack. For whatever reason, the officers and soldiers refused to believe him. One of the officers called him a liar and laughed at any suggestion of danger. But Henson refused to back down. He was so insistent that finally, the commander grudgingly agreed to send out a squad of men the next morning to look for Indians.

The next morning, Major Journey and all of the available rangers left the fort to search for any sign of the Indians that Henson had reported. They left the camp defenseless, with the gates open, and the women milking the cows. The rangers followed a narrow path into a ravine, where they were ambushed by Indians on both sides of the trail. Major Journey, Captain Grotz, and two privates, Lynn and William Pruitt, were instantly killed. A fifth man, Thomas Higgins, was shot in the leg and fell from his horse, which ran off. The other soldiers left the path and scattered in different directions, trying to find places from which they could fight back. Having seen Higgins fall from his horse, they assumed that the man was dead and slowly retreated toward the camp. As they drew near, several Indians appeared out of a small corn field to the north. They had been planning to attack the women who had been left behind in camp, but the sudden reappearance of the soldiers caused them to flee.

Meanwhile, Thomas Higgins was fighting for his life. He was wounded, but still very alive. Pulling himself to his feet, he cocked his rifle and held several attackers at bay. The Indians were uncertain whether his gun was loaded or not, and were afraid to rush him. They slowly closed in, circling around him, stabbing at him with spears. Higgins writhed with pain, but he kept his attackers at a distance. He waited to fire his rifle, knowing that he would only get one shot. He needed to make it count. If he could kill one of the leaders, he knew, he might survive. Suddenly, one of the Indians thrust a spear at him, striking him in the mouth and jaw. Higgins cried out in agony and fired at the man who had stabbed him, killing him on the spot.

The other attackers, knowing that his gun had been fired, advanced on Higgins. He was not giving up. Grabbing his rifle by the muzzle, he swung it around just as several of the Indians rushed at him with loud and triumphant yells. Higgins struck the first one over the head, splitting his skull and killing him. The force of the blow broke off the gun at the breach and the barrel flew out of his hands. Exhausted, he collapsed, and being unable to stand, he crawled toward the gun barrel, his only means of defense. But one of his attackers reached it first, swinging it around and crying out as he charged toward Higgins. The soldier had reached a small tree, pulled himself to his feet, facing what he knew was certain death.

As he prepared to die, he saw two soldiers on horseback – William Pursley and David White – coming to his rescue. They were coming up behind the Indian, who was too focused on killing Higgins to see them, and opened fire, killing him before he could club the wounded man with his own rifle barrel.

Higgins eventually recovered from his wounds and lived out the rest of his life in Fayette County, Illinois, eventually serving as the assistant door-keeper of the state House of Representatives.

Throughout the rest of 1814, attacks continued to occur and dozens of settlers were killed. In late summer, the rangers struck back and attacked an Indian war party near the site of the Lively massacre, which had occurred the previous year. All of the Indians were killed and one soldier was lost in the skirmish.

The end of the year also brought an end to the war. In the days and months that followed, a strong movement began to bring more settlers to the region and to move the Native Americans out. The white men were rarely honest when it came to business dealings with the Indians and large portions of land were purchased for small amounts of money through disreputable treaties. In many cases, the Indians were driven out and given nothing in return. By 1818, the federal government had decided to turn the Illinois Territory into a state, but the problems with the Native American populace was not yet at an end.

Trouble had been brewing for more than three decades. When the number of white settlers in the Illinois country began to grow, it was only a matter of time before the native people who already lived in the region – the Illinois, Ho-Chunk, Fox, Sauk, and Miami – began to have a conflict with the new arrivals. To pacify the Indians, they were presented with various treaties that were designed, in most cases, to relocate them, usually across the Mississippi River. Between 1804 and 1824, a series of 14 controversial documents, referred to as the Treaty of St. Louis, gave all of the Sauk and Fox lands east of the Mississippi to the United States government. There were problems with the first treaty in 1804, when many of the Sauk and Fox refused to recognize the treaty. The most outspoken of them, a prominent war chief named Black Hawk, opposed it on the grounds those who signed the treaty had not been authorized by the tribal councils to do so.

It was the anger raised over the Treaty of St. Louis that caused Black Hawk, along with the majority of the Sauk, Fox, and Ho-Chunk, to side with the British during the War of 1812. The British promised Black Hawk that if the Americans were defeated, they would create an Indian-controlled buffer between the eastern states and the western frontier. This would keep the Americans from expanding any further to the west if, of course, the British won the war. As it turned out, they were defeated a second time by the young, upstart nation and the Treaty of St. Louis remained in effect. In fact, in 1828, restrictions were stepped up and the government gave the Sauk and Fox one year to vacate all of their lands in Illinois.

By the spring of 1829, nearly two dozen white families decided that they had waited long enough and moved into Indian lands at Saukenuck, Black Hawk's home village, which was located near present-day Rock Island. In the process, they tore down Indian lodges and put fences around Sauk farm fields. The Sauk reported the invasion to U.S. officials, but were ignored. In September, a young Sauk chief, Keokuk, decided that it was best to avoid the conflict and led most of the remaining Sauk to lands west of the Mississippi.

Black Hawk, meanwhile, remained angry over the treaties and the indignities suffered by the Sauk. In the spring of 1831, he led a group of about 300 of his people back to Saukenuk and ordered the squatters to leave. His warriors burned a number of cabins, and word spread that the Sauk had declared war on the white settlers. Illinois Governor John Reynolds called up a militia of 700 men, and they were later joined by about an equal number of regular troops. The newly assembled army marched against the Indians, and facing this much larger adversary, Black Hawk agreed to return to Iowa. He even signed a treaty that promised he would not return to Illinois without permission.

But nature made it impossible for him to keep this bargain. The winter was bitterly cold and the Sauk had no fertile grounds for planting, as they had in Illinois. Hunting was poor and Black Hawk's people were starving. Believing he had no choice, he led 500 men and nearly 1,000 women and children back home, across the

Mississippi in April 1832. He planned to plant corn with the Winnebago near Prophetstown, about 50 miles up the Rock River, trying to stay away from the settlers in the region. But word spread and eventually reached Governor Reynolds, who again called up troops, including a young Abraham Lincoln, who was captain of a company from New Salem. This time, 1,000 soldiers and nearly 2,000 militia volunteers marched against Black Hawk.

Black Hawk began negotiating with other tribes in the region, trying to gain support from them to help fight the approaching army, but his efforts failed. He decided to withdraw to Iowa, and sent a handful of his men, under a white flag of truce, to meet with the U.S. troops, hoping to reach an agreement that would avoid bloodshed. Black Hawk believed that the nearest company of troops was under the direct command of General Henry Atkinson, leader of the Illinois army. The company, however, was a batch of newly recruited militia members under Major Isiah Stillman. When the Sauk envoys reached the encampment, the undisciplined militiamen attacked them, killing several of the Indians. Black Hawk, who was close by with about 40 warriors, decided to counterattack. Although greatly outnumbered by the disorganized militia, the braves fiercely charged them and the surprised soldiers turned and fled.

This rout, followed by several subsequent attacks on settlers and the militia, emboldened Black Hawk and he became determined to outlast the soldiers. By June, the frustrated U.S. command called up a new army of about 4,000 soldiers and militia volunteers and began a dogged pursuit of Black Hawk and his people through Illinois and into southwestern Wisconsin. In August, the army finally caught up with Black Hawk at the Battle of Bad Axe. The Sauk and Fox were overwhelmed by numbers and, soundly defeated, Black Hawk surrendered. But even in surrender, he remained defiant, blaming the short-lived war on a government that lied and cheated the Indians.

Black Hawk and several of his chiefs were taken east and placed in prison in Virginia, where he met with President Andrew Jackson and Secretary of War Lewis Cass. He was eventually released, but then was forced to take part in parades through several American cities, where huge crowds turned out to see the exotic captives. Jackson and Cass had an underlying reason for sending Black Hawk on tour: they wanted him to see the size of resources of the United States, and to realize that the Indians had no choice but to surrender.

After returning to Illinois, Black Hawk was again imprisoned, this time at Fort Armstrong, near Rock Island, where he told his story to an interpreter and writer. It became the first Native American autobiography published in the United States.

The Black Hawk War marked the end of the major conflict between Indians and white settlers in Illinois. The surviving Sauk and Fox, including Black Hawk, were sent to a reservation in southeastern Iowa, where Black Hawk died in 1838.

"They Bathed in Buckets of Blood..."
Bandits, Thieves & Killers of Early Illinois

The greatest danger to travelers and settlers during the days of early Illinois was the threat of robbery and murder. Bandits and highwaymen prowled the roadways of the state, especially in the sparsely populated areas. In 1819, a western traveler wrote, "Illinois is the hiding place for villains from every part of the United States and, indeed, from every quarter of the globe. A majority of the settlers have been discharged from penitentiaries and jails or have been the victims of misfortune or imprudence. Many of those will reform, but many, very many, are made fit for robbery and murder."

This may have been a bit of an overstatement, but it is clear that throughout the early days of Illinois, crimes of violence were alarmingly prevalent. The chief crime among them was robbery, and during the 1840s and 1850s, Illinois was infested by organized bands of cutthroats who brought terror to travelers and law-abiding citizens throughout the region. The two things most commonly sought were horses and money. For the most part, horse theft was a bloodless crime. Horses were easily stolen and passed off to confederates who could whisk them away to a place where the animals and their unlucky owner was unknown. A victim of such a crime knew that he had been robbed, but there was little chance of tracing his property back then, and almost no way of proving ownership if he did manage to find his missing stock.

Burglaries were also common – and fruitful. In those days, few settlers trusted banks, or more likely, there was no local bank where they lived. For this reason, most hid their money at home. This was likely known, or suspected, by neighbors, who also knew the layout of the house and the members of the potential victim's family. A neighbor with criminal intentions, which was easy to find, could pass the information on to a professional thief, who could commit the robbery and depart the area, after paying off the helpful neighbor for his part in the crime. If all went well, the crime would be a case of simple burglary. If the crime was interrupted, though, someone was likely to end up dead.

Crime obviously affected everyone in the region, but strangers and travelers were in the most danger. A man might be robbed and killed in the town where he lived, but those kinds of murders were usually quickly solved as crimes of passion or revenge – although not always.

There was one murder in Jacksonville, that of Murray McConnell, that affected the entire history of the city. McConnell was no stranger to crime. During Jacksonville's pioneer era, he was involved with vigilantes who attempted to keep order in the area before organized law enforcement was established. He was the first attorney to ever practice in Morgan County – he was a law partner of Stephen Douglas -- and one of the most prominent residents of the town. When he was murdered on February 9, 1869, it shocked the entire city.

McConnell was in his office at home on North Main Street when he was attacked by a perpetrator who still remains unknown. His death was caused by five "mental wounds" caused by blows to the head by an unknown object. He was found, in a pool of his own blood, on the floor of his office by Mary Ryan, a household servant. She had gone into his office – also his bedroom – and found him on the floor. She testified later that she had just been in his room to make up the bed and then had gone upstairs. A few minutes later, she heard a loud, sudden sound like a heavy fall. She hurried back downstairs and found that McConnell had been killed. Although it was in broad daylight, the family saw no one entering or leaving the room. The force of the blows had been so vicious that McConnell's jaw was broken and his skull was fractured in several places.

Whoever had killed him certainly seemed to have a grudge against the attorney.

Murray McConnell had been born in September 1798 in western New York. He left home at the age of 15 and headed west, intent on settling on the frontier. By 1815, he had reached Illinois but did not settle in what would become the city of Jacksonville until about 1821. He had been a resident of the city for nearly 50 years at the time of his death and had been deeply interested in almost every facet of the growing community. He was a well-regarded attorney and a fervent Democrat who had been part of county, state, and national nominating committees. He was a member of the lower house of the Illinois Legislature, held the office of commissioner of internal improvements, and he also served as fifth auditor of the treasury during the administrations of Presidents Pierce and Buchanan. His last service in political life was the filling of a term of two years in the Illinois Senate, representing the Jacksonville area. He held the title of "general" for his time in the state militia and he also served as a volunteer during the Blackhawk War. Although he was too old to serve during the Civil War, he stayed true to the Union, and following the example of Stephen Douglas, spoke with eloquence on many occasions about the need to sustain the government during those trying times. Some came to believe that it was McConnell's political beliefs that got him killed.

A coroner's inquest was held two days after McConnell's death and the jury returned a unanimous verdict against William A. Robinson, a 28-year-old grocery store owner who had borrowed money from McConnell. He had apparently been spotted going into McConnell's house that morning by milkman, W.H. Worrell. And while this seems to be rather shaky evidence on which to indict a man for murder, Robinson was arrested and the case went to trial on May 26, 1869.

The trial itself, due to intense public attention to the case, had to be held in the jam-packed Strawn Opera House on the square, with the judge presiding over court from the stage. The prosecutor and the defense attorney interviewed 130 citizens before the jury could be selected. Shortly before the trial began, the local newspapers noted that the public seemed to believe that Robinson was innocent of the crime.

The evidence was, as noted, very circumstantial. Robinson did owe McConnell money. He had borrowed $420 in gold from the attorney to make a start of his grocery business. When McConnell's body was discovered, the books in his office were open to a page of interest rate calculations. There was a black mark in the book next to a set of figures that would have applied to Robinson's debt. In addition to the eyewitness account of the milkman on the morning of the murder, several other people testified that they had seen Robinson in the neighborhood that same day. Also, a few days before the murder, Robinson sold a good chunk of his property and sent his wife and children to his father's house in Lawrence County.

The most damning evidence against the grocery store owner, though, was his own ledger book. It appeared that he was copying his finances into a new book and the new figures showed that the loan from McConnell was paid off, even though it wasn't.

All in all, it was pretty flimsy evidence and the eyewitnesses at the trial didn't help matters. During cross-examination, the milkman was forced to admit that he would have had to identify Robinson from a distance of about 60 feet and couldn't say for sure what kind of clothes he was wearing. Another witness admitted that she was on the other side of the street when she allegedly saw the suspect. The defense produced a string of witnesses that gave Robinson an alibi. The time of death had been estimated between 8:50 and 9:10 a.m. – when five witnesses stated that they were with Robinson at his store.

The trial went on for a month and ended with Robinson's acquittal. The jury's verdict, according to court records, stated that the evidence was circumstantial and "it is from the evidence that it is possible that some other person may have committed the murder." But was this the case? Could the witnesses have been lying about where Robinson was that day? Or could Robinson have hired someone to commit the murder? We will never know. The case remains unsolved today. Seven years later, a Bloomington man allegedly "confessed" to the murder, but he wasn't taken seriously. By then, public opinion had shifted and many believed that Robinson had, in fact, killed General McConnell after all. But it was too late by then. He had already been acquitted and Robinson had since vanished into the pages of history – leaving the mystery of Jacksonville's most sensational murder in his wake.

During the frontier days of Illinois, the greatest danger seemed to be for strangers and travelers. A traveler was cut off from everyone who knew him. If his appearance, or perhaps his conversation, caused someone to believe that he had money, he made a promising potential victim to the criminals who frequented the taverns and highways. A wealthy traveler might vanish without explanation and no one would be the wiser. It could happen, and it often did, as the records of the era make painfully clear. One gang of outlaws, which operated for a time, eventually fled the region, but left a number of chilling items behind. Among the effects found abandoned in the house they used as a headquarters were a suspiciously large number of trunks, cases, and empty containers that had once belonged to travelers, peddlers, and businessmen. This discovery was generally believed to account for the fate of salesmen and other travelers who, at various times, had been known to come into the community and had mysteriously vanished from sight.

A local sheriff later wrote, "Organized bands of counterfeiters, horse thieves, and desperate men, versed in crime of every character abounded. For every head of the serpent crushed, another was raised. Every grove to the Wabash might have been said to contain caches of stolen goods and horses, and the cellar of many a tavern, the bones of murdered men."

During the 1840s and 1850s, outlaw gangs were so rampant in Illinois that they set up regular routes of travel along the entire length of the state, using trails where they knew they could pass unmolested by the few lawmen that existed. For many years, the legal authorities were utterly powerless to convict them, even if they were suspected of committing crimes. Most of the outlaw leaders had great influence in the towns where they lived because that was where they freely spent their ill-gotten gains. The law and the courts rarely touched them. Lawmen and witnesses were murdered and courthouses were burned to destroy evidence. Many regions lived in a literal state of terror as counterfeiters, horse thieves, highway robbers, and killers operated unchecked. Finally, unable to count on the few lawmen that existed in the state, the citizens began to take the law into their own hands. The people formed what Governor Ford called banks of "Regulators," vigilante societies that shot, hanged and drove out the worst offenders.

As early as 1816, these vigilante groups began to appear in every part of the state, including Central Illinois. Their sole purpose was to rid the state of undesirable characters. Even those who counseled against civilians taking the law into their own hands agreed that the vigilantes were justified by the circumstances. Things had become so bad that no traveler was safe, no homeowner could leave a door unlocked, and no farmer could go to bed at night and be sure that his cattle would still be in his field the next morning. A number of small towns were actually invaded by bandits seeking plunder and isolated roadside taverns were almost guaranteed to be robbed. In many counties, the outlaws were so numerous and well-organized that they could openly defy the law. Sheriffs, justices of the peace, judges, and constables numbered among the law-breakers and shielded their confederates from punishment. When any of the bandits were arrested, they easily escaped from poorly-constructed jails, bribed jurors, or used lying witnesses to prove themselves innocent. Conviction, by any normal procedure, was practically impossible.

It was under these conditions that the vigilante groups began to seek their own justice. The governor, as well as most of the honest judges in the region, realized the necessity of the action and largely ignored what was going on. With night raids, brutal attacks, tarring and feathering, whippings, and even secret hangings, the Regulators purged a great deal of crime from the state. Governor Ford described the Regulators as being in numbers about equal to a company of soldiers, with officers elected as in the militia. They operated mostly at night, keeping their identities secret, and they were armed and equipped as if for war. When they targeted a lawbreaker, they went to his residence or hideout and arrested, tried, and punished him on the spot. The punishments were usually whippings or banishment from the region, but a few men were killed outright, although only if the cause of what they considered justice was served.

Various Regulator groups operated throughout the state, especially in Southern Illinois, where outlaws almost completely controlled Pope, Massac, and other counties along the Ohio River for several years. Honest settlers eventually banded together and drove them out, using a borrowed military cannon and sheer brute force.

Well-organized bands of outlaws operated for many years along the Illinois River, engaging in murder, horse stealing, robbery, and counterfeiting. Several large groups operated in Ogle, Winnebago, Lee, and DeKalb Counties and were so well-connected that any chance there might have been to convict them at trial was rendered impossible. In the spring of 1841, several well-known outlaws were locked up in the Ogle County Jail and their friends actually set the building on fire in hopes that they could escape in the confusion. The jailbreak failed, but the courthouse was destroyed. The public was outraged and taking advantage of this sentiment, the court convened and three of the prisoners were tried, convicted, and sentenced to the penitentiary. During the trial, one of the outlaws' confederates managed to get onto the jury and refused to agree on a verdict until the other jury members threatened to hang him in the jury room. The four other prisoners obtained changes of venue and were never brought to trial. They managed to break out of jail and escape. The entire affair so aroused the people in the region that a vigilance society was organized with the sole purpose of hunting down criminals, punishing them, and forcing them out of the area.

Among the banished were a man named Driscoll and several of his sons. They were determined not to be forced out and, banding together with other bandits, vowed to retaliate against the Regulators. They soon threatened death to one of the Regulator's leaders, a man named Campbell. Several of the bandits, pretending to be travelers who were lost, went to Campbell's home one night. After luring him outside, they shot Campbell to death in front of his wife and children.

By daybreak, the news of the murder had spread throughout the region. Regulators, and men sympathetic to their cause, made plans to avenge Campbell. They tracked down Driscoll and one of his sons and placed the two men on trial before an assembly of 300 Regulators. They were sentenced to death, blindfolded, and forced to kneel in front of the entire company. Every man present fired his rifle at the condemned, so that none of them could be legal witnesses to the deed. The execution served its purpose, sending scores of bandits fleeing from the region.

In February 1832, a vigilante society formed to deal with a group of renegades that were preying on law-abiding settlers in the Jacksonville area. The trouble began years before, in 1820, when a man named Abraham Williams settled near what would soon be Jacksonville. He carved a home from the fields and forests along the Mauvaiseterre Creek and broke ground for planting. Williams' trail was followed by others and soon, about six families made up a small settlement. Cabins were constructed, grain was planted, and the woods were hunted for food. The following season, more families came, and the settlement grew. But with the settlers came the unsavory and the lawless. Three men – John Cotrill, Henry Percifield, and his brother, Jerry – settled near Williams and in a short time became his friends and associates.

During that autumn, Jerry Percifield, the oldest and the worst of the lot, brought the first two barrels of whiskey into the new settlement. Abraham Williams took possession of it and opened up his home as a tavern of sorts, attracting all of the men of the fledging settlement.

Robberies began occurring in the area and in neighboring counties and goods from plundered stores were rumored to be hidden near Williams' grove, which made him and his three cronies suspected as the perpetrators of the crimes. The law-abiding settlers were anxious to have their settlement retain a fair name for honesty and good order, and so warrants were issued, the suspected parties searched, and some of the stolen goods recovered. When the men were brought before the magistrate, though, they were allowed to testify on each other's behalf, so all were acquitted.

Soon after, horse theft, house breakings, armed robbery, store thefts, and other crimes began to multiply. Williams suddenly became rich, having horses, cattle, and more household goods than he could have possibly been able to buy under ordinary circumstances. Shady-looking men began hanging around his property, drinking, gambling, and horse racing during the day and committing crimes at night. Williams, Cotrill, the Percifield brothers, and their assorted ilk soon had the run of the area, beating, and bullying the other men of the settlement into going along with their crimes.

Around this time, two new characters emerged on the scene, one of whom was a respectable old gentleman named Lewis G. Newell, who settled south of the Mauvaiseterre. He built a fine home, which, of course, caught the attention of Williams and his men. Assuming he had a lot of money hidden away inside, they went to look the place over and ascertain how much money Newell might have, where he might hide it, when he left home, and when he might return. Williams began calling on Newell several times each week. The old man likely assumed that he was being friendly, never realizing that Williams had sinister intentions.

The other new arrival to the area was a Kentucky man whose name was never revealed. He was a backwoodsman and hunter, armed with a knife and a long rifle, his movements were mysterious and he visited every house in the settlements – except that of Williams. No one knew his name but several referred to him as the "wild hunter of the prairie."

One night as Williams and Jerry Percifield were returning from a visit at Newell's home, they saw by the light of the moon that the form of a man was moving toward them on the path. Percifield nudged his friend, asking him if he had seen the "wild hunter." But before Williams could answer, the frontiersman stepped right up to the two men and called on Williams, asking if he recognized him. Williams flinched at the man's voice and cowered behind Percifield.

The hunter spoke again: "Abraham, you know me well; you know too, that I am acquainted with your unnatural deeds, your ill-gotten wealth shall avail you little. Before many days pass by I will see you again, when circumstances are different, and times more favorable than now." Then the man vanished from sight, slipping silently into the forest.

Percifield was unnerved by the encounter, but nowhere near as frightened as Williams, who refused to speak about the stranger or his identity. Over the course of the next few days, he began selling off his property and he packed up his family and moved to the west side of the Illinois River – very close to the spot where he would soon be buried.

A short time before Williams moved away, Newell left home on business, leaving his wife and young son behind. Two nights after he departed, his house was broken into and all of his money and valuables were stolen. This bold robbery alarmed the citizens of the settlement. A public meeting was held and a company was formed, consisting of 10 well-armed men and they bound themselves together under the name "Regulators of the Valley." They were determined to rid the area of horse thieves and robbers and not to cease their operations until the outlaws had fled or had been killed. They drew up papers and each of the men signed his name to the contract. After all of this was completed, the party resolved to make Abraham Williams their first target.

The plan was to go to his house in disguise, seize him by force, tie him to a tree, and scourge him with whips until he surrendered the money and goods that had been stolen from Newell and others. They also wanted him to reveal the names of his associates and accomplices, but they had no intention of taking his life. With this plan in mind, the Regulators rode toward Williams' home across the Illinois River. They crossed the river near the mouth of the Mauvaiseterre and rode quietly toward his cabin. As they drew near, a voice whispered to them from the woods. It was a friend, the voice said, and the hunter stepped out from the trees. He told the men that he knew their intentions and that Williams was his enemy, having committed a crime against him that he needed to avenge. He asked the Regulators to accept him as their captain, which they did, and then he led the way to Williams' house.

They surrounded the cabin and then the hunter, along with two of the other men, prepared to break open the door and bring Williams outside. Before they could do so, the ferocious barking of Williams' dogs echoed in the night. A light flared to life inside of the cabin and the door opened a little, allowing one of the household to peer outside. Williams, perhaps believing that someone was stealing his property, seized his rifle and rushed outside and the first thing he saw was the mysterious captain. He immediately cried out for the man to stand back or he would shoot him dead. He pulled the trigger and by some unaccountable accident, the weapon snapped but misfired. He was again making ready to shoot when cries went up all around the yard – "Fire! Fire!" A single rifle shot rang out and Williams fell. The other Regulators rushed to the door and found the man they had come to question lying on the ground in his own blood.

They did not stand in silence for long. A woman's screams resounded in the cabin and Williams' wife rushed forward, scratching and clawing at the men, attempting to get to her husband. One of the Regulators fired off a shot into the air, hoping to scare her, but it was in vain. She pressed on until she was stopped by the hands of the hunter – a man she had also seen before – and he forced her into the house and closed the door.

The Regulators – who were farmers and tradesmen with no knowledge of the law – were frightened and unsure of what to do. They left the house and rode off into the woods. The hunter called a halt. He spoke to them, "My friends, the deed is done. I did it in self-defense. I have rid the world of a monster and myself of an inveterate foe. My conscience acquits me; so I will not regret the act. My advice is for each of you to go your way and I will go mine. You will never see me again. Let every man guard well his secret, and none other will know you were here."

After that, the hunter rode off and vanished into the darkness, leaving the other men behind. The news of Williams' death made the rounds, but there were none who could claim that they knew who had fired the fatal shot, or even who had been there that night. Cotrill, Percifield, and the others soon left the area and Morgan County was never troubled by such outlaws again. Williams was buried on the left bank of Magee's Creek in Pike County, but no one knows where his grave lies today.

"Winter of the Deep Snow"
The Dangers of Pioneer Life on the Prairie

Starting in the middle part of the nineteenth century, farming became a standard way of life in Central Illinois. However, it was not always that way. When the early settlers first came to the region, they chose to live in the shelter of the forests that grew along the nearby sources of water. The vast prairie land that stretched before them seemed daunting. It would be years before the waves of grass and rich ground would be broken to eke an existence out of the soil. These first settlers were largely hunters, making their homes on the edge of the timber. It would be some time before they realized there was nothing wrong with the soil. They didn't understand how earth that grew prairie grass, yet no trees, could possibly be fertile. In addition to that, the trees were essential for survival, providing wood for fires, tools, and homes. When much of the populace turned to farming, they found that wooden split rail fences would protect the fields and would keep the livestock from roaming into the forest and being killed by wolves.

The farmers soon found that corn was an ideal crop for the prairie. It was easy to sow and to cultivate and was easily turned into many food products and a marketable whiskey. Many farmers owned stills that converted corn mash into a clear but potent whiskey, which could then be transported to market via pack horse or river barge. This corn alcohol became a popular western drink and the jug would circulate freely at social events like dances, barn-raisings, and at election time.

The secondary crop became wheat, which could be converted to flour, but only at a mill. The mills came a little later, following the small settlements, and bringing rudimentary mechanics to the frontier. The mills were built along rivers for power but where dams could not be built, horses and oxen provided the power for the grinding stones. Soon, the mill became the leading establishment in many of the settlements, and other businesses followed, like blacksmith shops and general stores.

In those days, almost no one on the prairie had money. The settlers made their own clothing by tanning the hides of deer and cattle for shoes while women with spinning wheels and looms produced trousers, shirts, and dresses. They grew their own food, or hunted in the forests, and the small farms provided eggs, milk, and butter. In the general stores, the settlers could trade any surplus goods for whiskey, sugar, salt, tools, crockery, or coffee.

But as idyllic as this all sounds, the frontier was not without its dangers. In the early years, much of that danger came from the Native American populace. The Kickapoo, and other tribes, would keep the settlers in a constant state of alarm for many years. The pioneers died from the many diseases that plagued the region, as well as from the often extreme weather conditions. Terrible thunderstorms on the open plains were not uncommon and fires were frequently started by lightning strikes, which could burn whole fields, stands of woods, or even entire towns. There were no fire departments to battle these blazes in those days.

And there were plenty of other dark events that gave rise to tales of ghosts. One such story was discovered in the early records of Macon County. According to the old account, a man named Thomas Nelms came to Central Illinois from Logan County, Kentucky, in 1829. A year later, in August, he died during a woodcutting accident when a tree that he was working on fell and struck him. The older settlers stated that after the tree was cut down, but before it was split into rails, a number of witnesses reported a curious "tingling" sound that came from the tree. They described these sounds as being like those of an ax striking a particularly tough piece of wood. Apparently, the unexplained sounds continued even after the tree was spilt into rails and turned into a fence. Travelers who passed the fence were often attracted by the strange noise and despite a number of investigations, no one could discover a cause for it. Most came to believe that it was the ghost of Thomas Nelms, still connected to the tree that had taken his life.

In the winter, many settlers died from the extreme cold, having little protection from it. Over the winter of 1830-31, Central Illinois was hit with disaster. This terrible season would be remembered for many years as the "Winter of the Deep Snow."

Early that winter, following several torrential rains, snow began to fall and continued to come in intervals, sometimes alternating with sleet and freezing rain. This treacherous mixture formed a layer of snow and ice that blanketed the state with frozen drifts that were as high as four and six feet. Storms with high winds continued for 60 days in a row. Many settlers had depended on going into the nearby forest for firewood, but found themselves trapped in their homes, and froze to death. Corn and wheat, food for man and animal, had been left stacked in the fields, but could not be found under the layers of snow and ice. Paths that were cut through the snow were filled in by the wind in minutes. Travelers remained wherever they happened to be when the snow first started. Those who tried to continue their journey often perished. One newspaper report told of "Cold Friday," when a man, his wife, and six children froze to death, huddled about their half-burned wagon on the prairie.

The snow drifted so high that loaded wagons could be driven over the top of fence rails. Livestock perished and soon game became scarce. At first, the deer became trapped in the snow and were easily caught, but as time wore on, they were eaten by the settlers and the wolves, causing the population to dwindle almost to nothing. Herds of buffalo floundered in the deep snow and starved. It has been said that the Winter of the Deep Snow took the last of the buffalo from east of the Mississippi River. It would be years before the squirrels and prairie chickens could be found to hunt again. It was a calamitous season and one that would be remembered for many decades to come.

One resident of Central Illinois almost didn't survive the winter. In 1830, Abraham Lincoln was a young man living with his family west of Decatur. He worked as a farm hand for several local settlers, including Sheriff William Warnick, who lived about two miles from the Lincoln cabin. During the Winter of the Deep Snow, Lincoln was walking to the Warnick home when he fell through the ice into the Sangamon River. He convalesced with the Warnicks for more than a week as he recovered from frostbite and severe cold. According to legend, Lincoln read through the sheriff's copy of the Illinois Statutes while in his sickbed and this is how he first became interested in the law.

But many settlers were not a lucky as Lincoln. Many died in the bitter cold and snow. Some people simply vanished. Many bodies were found when the shows finally melted with warmer weather. A lingering cold hurt the spring corn crop, game was scarce for years, and the cotton fields in Southern Illinois perished and never returned. When spring arrived, the snow and ice melted and turned creeks into impassable torrents. Cholera epidemics, caused by the wet conditions, sent many of the survivors of the Winter of the Deep Snow into their graves.

The terrible winter, along with the deadly cholera epidemic, gave birth to a number of mysterious legends about ghosts, hauntings, and sometimes, even darker things. According to one story, there was once a small settlement that existed south of Decatur, near a Native American burial ground along the Sangamon River. In later years, it would become Greenwood Cemetery but, in those days, it was a place avoided by the white settlers and held in superstitious awe.

The settlers survived in their secluded cluster of cabins until the bitter winter of 1830. As snow fell throughout the winter, freezing into large drifts, livestock perished and game became scarce. Many settlers died all over Central Illinois, but things became very dire in the small settlement. The lack of food struck there the hardest because it was cut off from the rest of the pioneers in the area. At first, wild game approached the cabins without fear. Food was so scarce that the animals hoped for handouts of grain, but were instead captured and ended up in the stew kettle. As the cold months wore on, the deer, turkey, squirrels, and prairie chickens were eaten up, and soon, the stores of flour and dried meat also disappeared. As things grew more hopeless, it began to look as though the settlers would starve to death before spring arrived. They made do with what they could forage, boiling the bark from the trees into a bitter soup and then eating shoe leather and rawhide to stay alive. Finally, the legends say, there were no other choices left to them. They had no option but to turn to the only food supply that was still available – each other.

In the early months of the winter, one of the older members of the community had passed away and the body had been stored in an outbuilding so that he could be buried when the ground thawed. This was the first of two corpses that the settlers were forced to eat that winter.

When the weather finally broke, and contact with the outside could be achieved again, the bodies were secretly buried on the hill and the cannibals were sworn to secrecy. No one was ever to know under what conditions the community had survived. A few months later, though, a tinsmith with goods to sell ventured through the woods to the settlement, only to find that everyone had vanished. The homes had been abandoned. Some believe that an outsider discovered the horrible secret of what had occurred there during the long winter and the settlers fled from the area, leaving no trace behind.

The strange story is believed to have been the first bizarre event in this part of Central Illinois – and area that was later nicknamed "Hell Hollow" – but it was certainly not the last.

The seclusion and ruggedness of the small valley where the settlement had been began attracting a criminal element from the region. It became known as a bandit hideout, where few police officers dared to venture. Stories claimed that more than one sick or wounded criminal died in the woods, only to be buried secretly and under the cover of darkness. For years, it was dotted with unmarked graves, which remain lost today.

At some point in the middle years of the nineteenth century, the woods near Greenwood Cemetery became the territory of a gang called the "Biscuit-Necks" by the local authorities. They specialized in extortion and robbery, angering the townsfolk. One night, a vigilante group invaded the woods, searching for the gang. It is believed that the lynch mob was forced into action after the gang robbed a store and killed the owner. The gang members were captured and hanged on the spot. As a message to other lawbreakers, the bodies of the Biscuit-Necks were left hanging in the trees until they rotted away.

The woods, which surrounded the Sangamon River, claimed many victims over the years and they were the scene of a number of mysterious deaths and puzzling disappearances. In August 1896, a young boy named Frankie Ackerman drowned near where the river entered the woods. Frankie and another boy, Guy Stevens, were wading in the water when a strong undercurrent swept them off their feet and carried them downriver. Guy Stevens was rescued by some fisherman, but Frankie vanished and was never found.

A few months later, in October 1896, a boy who was hunting in the woods found the badly decomposed body of a man, lying just a few feet from the river bank. Scared, he ran to a grocery store a short distance away and called the police. Officers were unable to get a wagon into the woods, so they had to carry out the remains in a canvas tarp. The man had been badly beaten. He was never identified but the police did find a knap-sack nearby that contained a pen knife, five keys, three bottles, and an account book that contained the address of several stores in town. Unfortunately, the bag was so wet from a recent rain that the man's name could not be found.

In August 1905, brothers Acy and Luster Woody decided to try and make a trip downriver on the Sangamon in a homemade boat. They were last seen entering the woods – and were never heard from again.

An 11-year-old boy named Willie Godwin drowned in the river at the edge of the woods in September 1905. Willie, along with several friends, was playing in the woods and decided to cool off on that hot afternoon by going for a swim. He vanished under the water and did not come back to the surface. His friends ran to a nearby waterworks and called for help. Workers on duty ran down to the river, while another telephoned the police. There was no sign of the boy in the water. Police officers soon arrived with a local doctor, T.C. Hunt. They searched frantically for more than two hours before Willie's body was finally discovered using long poles. Somehow, the corpse had managed to travel upriver, against the current. No explanation for this strange feat was ever offered.

In June 1910, an "aged Negro" named Perry Orr committed suicide in the Sangamon River in Hell Hollow, after first taking off all of his clothes and singing a religious hymn on the river bank. The drowning was a mysterious one. Although Orr had been in poor health for some time, he gave no indication that he would commit suicide. Orr was last seen alive by Mrs. Anna McCoy, who was fishing on the banks of the river. She looked up when she heard someone singing, saw the old man remove his clothes, and sink beneath the water. Mrs. McCoy raised the alarm and two other men who were nearby responded. As they looked for any sign of Orr, Mrs. McCoy left to summon the police. The river was searched for hours and Orr's body was eventually found. His identity was learned from the clothing that he left on the river bank. Orr left behind a devoted wife, two step-children, and many friends. He was known all over the city as a hard-working, industrious man and he was an active member of the Antioch Baptist Church. Everyone who knew him was shocked by his death and found it impossible to believe that he had killed himself.

The years passed and the woods became known as a "hobo jungle," where transients and small-time criminals camped and lived. The railroad tracks passed close to this area and it was convenient for the hoboes to hop a freight train from one town to the next.

It was in the 1930s that the woods gained the name of "Hell Hollow," thanks to a creative newspaper reporter from Chicago named Robey Parks. Looking for a lurid story, he connected a number of unsolved murders in the city with a bootlegging operation and several incidents of grave robbery in Greenwood Cemetery to concoct a criminal gang he dubbed the "Hounds of Hell Hollow." The story shocked the locals, thrilled readers, and created an enduring legend around the many years of strange incidents that had occurred in the woods.

The weird stories – from cannibalism to murder, suicide, and disappearances – had already marked the woods on the south side of town and Robey's series of articles cemented them as a terrible place, where ghosts and strange events were common. Even as the woods became smaller in the years that followed, their reputation refused to fade. For a long time, the remaining stretch of trees loomed over a narrow gravel road that twisted and turned along the river. To area residents, this was all that was left of "Hell Hollow" and it served as the last reminder of the violence of years gone by. But the legend was not quite dead yet.

In the 1960s, the woods earned a new notoriety with teenagers as a spooky place for a romantic rendezvous. A new collection of stories started to be told about killers with hooks for hands and horrifying murder that usually involved teenagers in parked cars. However, not all of the stories told about the woods could be passed off as rumors and urban legends. Every once in a while, someone encountered something truly unexplainable in Hell Hollow. Were the stories true or merely the result of wild imagination?

One particular story involved a couple who had gone down to the Hollow for a romantic interlude one night and were surprised to hear and feel what seemed to be open hands slamming down on the trunk of their car. Thinking that someone was playing a trick on them, the young man jumped out of the car and looked around. To his surprise, no one was there. He heard a movement over to his left and turned to see the tall grass alongside the road being pushed aside, as if some invisible presence was passing through it, he later recalled.

He quickly returned to the car and something caught his eye. There, on the dusty trunk, were the clear impressions of handprints, even though he had seen no one standing behind the car.

The woods remained a popular and spooky place for some time. A few short years ago, the road that ended in Hell Hollow was closed off and city crews cut and cleared away the thick growth of trees that once filled the valley. A couple more years passed and another road was closed. This time, Lincoln Park Drive, which skirted the edge of Hell Hollow and Greenwood Cemetery, was closed off and turned into a bike trail that is off limits after dark. The official word was that the road was closed to keep trespassers out of the cemetery at night, forgetting that there were plenty of places where people could enter the cemetery if they wanted to do so. What was the real reason? Oddly, the woods had been the scene of several recent deaths and a brutal double murder that had shocked the city. It seemed that the violence of the woods had returned, again casting an ominous shadow over the region that stretched all the way back to the "Winter of the Deep Snows."

"As a Lamb to the Slaughter"
The Murder of Joseph Smith

In June 1844, Joseph Smith, the founder of the Mormon religious movement, was shot to death at the jail in Carthage, Illinois. Smith, along with this brother, Hyrum, had surrendered themselves to the authorities in Carthage after being promised sanctuary by Illinois Governor Thomas Ford. But things did not turn out as promised. A mob appeared at the jail one night and the Smith brothers were murdered for their beliefs. How had things gone so badly for a group that had been welcome to Illinois just six years before?

The story that ended in a bloody stone cell at the Carthage jail began with the birth of Joseph Smith in Vermont in 1805. Years later, when Smith was 15, he moved with his father, mother, and eight siblings to Western New York. His father was a farmer and Smith grew up in an area that was known for its religious zealotry. The local climate had become so bad that it had been given the derogatory nickname of the "Burned-Over District" because the people of the region had been subjected to so many evangelists, revival meetings, and religious renewals that all the religion had been "burned out of them."

But religion had not been burned out of young Joseph Smith.

One day, while praying in his upstairs bedroom, a 17-year-old Smith claimed that he was visited by a figure that was bathed in light that was "as bright as the midday sun." The figure, an angel named Moroni, told Smith that God had work for him to do. The angel returned to visit Smith several more times in the years that followed and eventually led him to discover a set of golden tablets upon which had been engraved the words that would form the foundation of the Mormon Church. Smith was the only person who ever saw these golden tablets – which could only be read using a pair of "magic spectacles – but by 1832, he had translated the inscriptions as the *Book of Mormon*. The book claimed that two tribes of Israelites had been brought by God to North America 600 years before the birth of Christ. These people had built a powerful civilization, but then had turned away from God and had fallen from grace, regressing into the Native American tribes that the Europeans found living on the continent centuries later. The Angel Moroni was the last of God's true prophets in North America, and he had hidden the golden tablets until Smith could reveal the Mormon story to the world.

Perhaps unsurprisingly in an era of bizarre religious beliefs, the fantastical tales in the *Book of Mormon* met a receptive audience and the ranks of the movement that Smith was calling the Church of Jesus Christ of the Latter-Day Saints began to swell. But not everyone was a believer, of course. The majority of people, usually farmers and tradesmen of simple religious beliefs, met the new church with resistance and began persecuting the Mormons for their unorthodox teachings.

Smith and his followers were driven out of Western New York by Christians who felt they were blasphemous and they moved to Kirtland, Ohio, on the southern shores of Lake Erie. After arriving, they made plans to start a new Mormon community. The Saints believed that it was essential that a new Zion be built in the American wilderness so that they could create a Mormon paradise on Earth that would be duplicated in Heaven.

At first, the 2,000 Mormons were met with open arms by the people of Kirtland, but it wasn't long before they wore out their welcome. Smith, a handsome, charismatic man, began to spread the philosophy of polygamy (he would eventually take on 49 wives of his own), although he called it "celestial marriage." He justified it by pointing to the great characters of the Bible, who all had many wives. Polygamy became a source of conflict both in and out of the Mormon Church, especially in a frontier community where the men greatly outnumbered the women. The general public was horrified and fascinated with the practice and it would plague the church for many decades to come. Even today, fundamentalist Mormons are seen as radical zealots, even by other Mormons.

But it would be money that would drive the Mormons from Ohio. As the bank panic of 1837 hit the United States, a bank that Smith had opened spread useless paper currency around the area. Facing criminal charges, he fled Kirtland in the middle of the night and traveled to Missouri.

Unfortunately, the story was the same everywhere. As the ranks of Mormons grew larger, people began to resent them and Mormon settlements were targeted with violence. The lieutenant governor of Missouri even stated publicly: "Mormons are the common enemies of mankind and ought to be destroyed." There were those who followed his suggestion. A band of vigilantes attacked a Mormon settlement at Haun's Mill, Missouri, in 1838 and gunned down an entire family, including a 10-year-old boy, in cold blood. "Nits grow lice," one of the men reportedly said before he put a bullet into the boy's head.

Soon after this incident, the Mormon community fled to Illinois. Initially, the Mormons were welcome as "potential taxpayers and voters at a time of slow economic growth in the state." They purchased land in Hancock County and established a settlement they named Nauvoo, which meant, according to Smith, "beautiful place."

Within a few years, Nauvoo was the largest community in the state with more than 11,000 residents. Thousands of Mormons and new Mormon converts arrived in the city from the eastern United States, Canada, and England. To accommodate the new city, the Illinois General Assembly approved a formal charter for Nauvoo in December 1840. Smith and his closest followers established a city council, as well as an independent militia known as the Nauvoo Legion. It boasted 2,000 troops, which was a quarter of the size of the standing U.S. army at the time.

It didn't take long for things to sour. In November 1840, former attorney Thomas Coke Sharp had become a co-owner and editor of the *Warsaw World* newspaper, published in Warsaw, Illinois, a little south of Nauvoo. Sharp renamed the paper the *Warsaw Signal* and began publishing stories and editorials that were critical of the Mormons. He kept his readers informed about Mormon activities and carefully agitated for action about Smith and his followers.

Sharp, like many long-time residents of the county, resented the growing power of the Mormons, who were starting to influence local and regional elections because they voted in a block, which was directed by Smith. Sharp also called for the creation of an anti-Mormon political party in 1841. Tensions escalated a year later when a former Mormon church leader named John C. Bennett split from Smith and started spreading the word about how the Mormons were practicing polygamy.

In June 1843, Smith was arrested while riding outside of Nauvoo by two lawmen who wanted to return him to Missouri, where he was wanted on charges of committing treason against the state. But members of Smith's militia – who were more likely part of the secret "Sons of Dan," or "Danites," who did all of Smith's dirty work for him – intervened and returned him to Nauvoo. The arrest was a sign that legal and political pressure on the Mormons was increasing and Smith reacted. The city council soon passed a law authorizing the mayor, who happened to be Joseph Smith, to review any "foreign" legal paperwork issued from outside of the city and decide whether or not to honor it. Smith had essentially set up his own little kingdom inside of Illinois.

A year later, in June 1844, critics of the Mormons established the *Nauvoo Expositor,* a newspaper with a clear anti-Mormon agenda. The paper stated that its mission was to expose the "abominations and whoredoms" of the religious movement established by Smith and show that it was not in accordance with the teachings of Jesus Christ and his apostle. The newspaper also claimed that Smith was using religion as a pretext to bring innocent women to Nauvoo, where they became part of the growing harems of Mormon wives.

Immediately after the first issue of the newspaper was published, the city council met to discuss the threat that it posed to the community. Smith persuaded the council to declare the newspaper a public nuisance and to destroy its printing press. Later that same day, Smith ordered the city marshal to have the militia carry out the order.

This was the biggest mistake that Smith could have made. The destruction of the printing press incited anti-Mormon sentiment throughout the entire region, inviting criticism from newspapers all over the state. Some took it further than others. In his paper, Thomas Sharp wrote that he and other anti-Mormon factions were ready to "exterminate, utterly exterminate, the wicked and abominable Mormon leaders," and called for an attack on the city of Nauvoo. Some of Smith's enemies acted with a bit more subtlety. Legal charges were filed, claiming that Smith and other Mormon leaders had promoted a riot. A constable was sent to Nauvoo from the county seat of Carthage to arrest Smith, but he refused to leave with him. In response, anti-Mormon factions sent out messengers to surrounding communities and asked for armed men to come to Carthage and see that Smith was taken into custody.

Faced with what seemed to be an armed action against the Mormons, Smith declared Nauvoo under martial law and called out the militia. This action later resulted in his enemies filing charges of treason against him. On June 21, Governor Ford learned of the impending conflict and traveled to Carthage to try and defuse the situation. He asked Smith to submit evidence justifying his actions against the *Expositor,* the newspaper he had destroyed. After reviewing the documents, Governor Ford wrote to Smith and told him that his actions had been illegal and demanded that he turn himself over to authorities in Carthage. He told Smith that if he did not comply, he feared an attack on Nauvoo.

Smith sent a letter in reply. He feared for his life if he left Nauvoo, he wrote, and wouldn't feel safe until the armed mobs in Carthage were dispersed. Soon after, fearing that the situation was out of control, Smith and his brother, Hyrum, fled across the Mississippi to Iowa. He wrote to his wife, Emma, asking her to bring his other wives and his children and join him, with the plan of going west. The letter alarmed Smith's followers in Nauvoo, many of whom felt he was abandoning the church at the time they needed him most. Several church leaders persuaded Emma to write him a letter that urged him to return. Stung by the criticism, Smith and his brother returned to Nauvoo and agreed to surrender to the authorities in Carthage. Despite assurances from Governor Ford that he would be safe, Smith told his followers before he left, "I go as a lamb to the slaughter."

When they arrived in Carthage on June 24, Joseph and Hyrum Smith spent the night at the Hamilton House, the same hotel where the governor was staying. The next day, the Smiths surrendered to the constable and were incarcerated in the prisoner's quarters on the second floor of the jail, a two-story stone building on the north side of town. They were ordered held without bail until June 29, when a material witness would be able to appear.

On the third day of their incarceration, an armed mob gathered at the jail. They broke into the building and rushed upstairs to where the prisoners were being kept. Hearing the commotion and the shots that were fired, the Smiths attempted to barricade the door. As Hyrum Smith blocked it with his body, shots were fired through the wooden barrier and struck him in the face. He was instantly killed. Enraged, Joseph, who had been smuggled a small pistol by a sympathizer, flung open the door and began firing into the crowd. After emptying the gun, he ran to the window, where he was spotted by men outside. They began firing at him. Smith was struck four times: twice in the back, once in the right collarbone, and once in the chest. Mortally wounded, he fell from the second-story window. According to several eyewitnesses, he was still alive after he fell and apparently "raised himself up against the wall curb, drew up one leg and stretched out the other and died immediately."

With Smith dead, the mob quickly dispersed. When the news of the murder reached Artois Hamilton, proprietor of the Hamilton House, he drove a wagon to the jail to secure the bodies of Smith and his brother, which he hid away at his hotel. The next day, they were taken to Nauvoo, where they were eventually buried.

The murder of Joseph Smith marked the beginning of the end for the Mormon settlement in Illinois. In the aftermath, Mormon leaders bickered over the issue of secession, causing a deep divide within the church that caused it to splinter into several alternate movements. In August of the following year, the ruling council chose Brigham Young as their new leader. He was a dynamic speaker and natural leader, but he knew the Mormons could not stay in Illinois and prosper. He still needed to create the new Zion that Joseph Smith has espoused and Young knew it needed to be far to the west in an unpopulated territory. With that decision made, Young led his people on a terrible journey in 1847 and settled them in the arid country around the Great Salt Lake in present-day Utah. It was not the biblical paradise that Smith had envisioned, but Young insisted that they begin irrigating the country on the day they arrived and gradually, Salt Lake City began to grow.

In Illinois, the community of Nauvoo began to fade into history. Once a large and thriving town, it lost most of its commerce and population when the Mormons migrated west to Utah. The population of Nauvoo, which once was well over 12,000, is now home to less than 1,000 souls. While it still holds onto its Mormon roots, it is a much different place than it was in the middle years of the nineteenth century.

Strangely, Nauvoo's history tells of a bizarre ghost sighting that occurred in town when a frightening phantom with no eyes or mouth, spouting rays of glowing light through holes in its face, appeared to two boys and a prominent Nauvoo attorney. The ghost displayed a deep gash in its side and moaned to them about Joseph Smith's Danites, the secret society that he formed as a vigilante group to protect Mormon interests during the conflict of the 1840s.

The ghost sighting appeared in newspapers on August 18, 1894, and told of how attorney George A. Ritter and two young boys saw the frightful apparition as they were driving some cows toward home. Ritter admitted that he had previously been told of the phantom by some neighbors, who claimed that it had been seen it in his pasture, but that he had ridiculed the idea.

As Ritter entered the field, he saw something white crouching on the ground. At first, he thought it was one of his cows. He called to the animal to get it moving toward home, but instead of a cow, he saw a figure rise from the ground. It was dressed in long, white, flowing robes and as it stood up, it stretched out its arms. Ritter said the most horrible part of its appearance was its face. It had absolutely no eyes, nor nose, and only holes in the head "from which gleamed a sort of sulphurous light. The form was arrayed in a shroud, and yet it was white, having long, matted locks of hair that hung down almost to its waist. Its arms were long and bony and its hands "resembled more those of a beast or a great bird of prey."

According to the *Chicago Times*, as the creature rose, the boys who worked for Ritter yelled and fled from the pasture. Ritter admitted that he was not feeling too well himself at the time. He did summon up the courage to speak to the ghost and as he did so, it shook its head and pulled aside its white robe to expose a horrible gash in its right side. The ghost kept moving its lips and then Ritter said that the expression on its eyeless and noseless face was "simply dreadful." He said that he heard the phantom hiss or moan the words "Danites! Danites!" at him.

Newspaper writers surmised that the ghost – which remained in site an amazing 10 minutes, according to Ritter's account – was anti-Mormon who had been murdered by one of the members of Smith's secret militia. Ritter admitted that he had no idea what the ghost was or why it appeared in his field – but was convinced that he had seen something supernatural. The article went on to say that Ritter was not a believer in spooks or spirits, and was not anxious to have his name used freely in connection with the apparition "unless his position upon the subject could be thoroughly explained."

A band of men were selected to keep a watch for the reappearance of the horrible apparition and, if possible, to capture it. As far as we know, though, it never returned.

"The Liberty Line"
Central Illinois and the Underground Railroad

In the years that led up to the Civil War, a number of homes and farms in Central Illinois served as stations on the Underground Railroad, the network of hiding places for escaped slaves on their way to freedom in the north. Some of the locations were rural homes, barns, stagecoach stops, churches, and even college buildings – or so the stories say. Very few stations on the Underground Railroad offer documented evidence of the purpose they once served because secrecy was necessary for the stations to survive. Their owners were breaking the law, essentially helping to "steal" another man's property, when they helped the slaves seek freedom in the northern states and Canada.

Starting in the early 1800s, thousands of slaves used the Underground Railroad to reach freedom. Traveling mostly at night, scores of them moved secretly through Sangamon, Adams, Macon, Menard, and Morgan counties, along with other parts of Illinois.

The term "Underground Railroad" is a bit of misnomer. It originated in 1840, when a Kentucky farmer lost track of one of his runaway slaves. He reportedly said that the man must have gone "off an underground road." The name was changed to Underground Railroad because slave escapes increased after the railroads were built, and some of the secret routes paralleled actual railroad lines.

Illinois was a major link in the Underground Railroad because of its location. By law, it was a free state – although many slaves were held throughout Illinois history and free blacks were often kidnapped and enslaved – but its importance lay in the fact that it was easy to reach. Since it bordered the slave states of Missouri, Kentucky, and Tennessee, slaves could cross the Mississippi or the Ohio River and be one step closer to freedom.

At least five Underground Railroad routes existed in Illinois, stretching from Alton, Chester, Cairo, and Quincy in zigzag lines to the Chicago area. The Springfield and Jacksonville areas were heavily used by slaves traveling on the Underground Railroad. One route that began in Alton passed through Jerseyville, Waverly, Jacksonville, Springfield, Delavan, Varna, and Chicago. Another route that passed through Springfield began in Chester, included Sparta, and branched from Springfield to towns like Galesburg and Ottawa. There are believed to be former Underground Railroad stations in Chatham, Rochester, Beardstown, Carlinville, Berlin, and Waverly.

Samuel Pond of Greenview used to pick up slaves from homes in Farmingdale (then called Farmington) by wagon and take them to his home. He hid the slaves in his barn until he considered it safe to take them by wagon to Forrest City in what is now Mason County. A neighbor of Pond's, Asa Cleaveland, reportedly kept runaway slaves in his cellar or his barn until they could be taken to the next station to the north.

In Decatur, a rural estate known as "The Pines," was used as an Underground Railroad station. Built by Colonel J.M. Clokey, the brick home was fitted with an outer wood structure and escaped slaves were hidden between the two walls until they could be taken to safety. Another local Underground Railroad home, located at 409 South Main Street, was built by the Charles Imboden family in 1855. The house was built with a secret cellar and a hidden passageway that opened outside from the basement. It allowed the slaves to slip out under the cover of darkness.

Slave owners often tried to recapture their escaped slaves, or hired "slave-catchers" to do their dirty work for them. Advertisements were often placed in newspapers like Springfield's *Sangamo Journal* in search of runaways. The Underground Railroad had to be kept secret because the participants took such enormous risks. Those who were discovered faced official and vigilante justice, even death. The slaves that were recaptured faced even greater hardship when returned to their masters. For these reasons, the abolitionists who operated the Underground Railroad and, as a result, they often went to extreme measures to avoid detection and to try and get the slaves to safety. They often dressed them in fancy clothing and heavy veils so that no one could tell whether they were white. Deacon Nathan Jones, from Canton, had some friends help him create a mock funeral procession to take slaves from Canton to Farmington. A Farmington man named Pomeroy Wilson, when he became convinced that he was being watched by slave-catchers, wrapped his wife and children in blankets to pose as runaway slaves. While the pursuers followed Wilson to a neighboring farm, another abolitionist whisked the slaves away to another hiding place.

Springfield, Illinois' capital city, was an important station on several Underground Railroad lines through the state. Slaves usually came to Springfield from Jacksonville or Farmington. Both towns were known for their abolitionist views.

At dawn one morning in the middle 1840s, Benjamin Henderson of Jacksonville was preparing to deliver some cradles to Springfield. Henderson, a black man, was a former slave who paid his master $250 for his freedom before settling in Jacksonville. But before Henderson could load his wagon that morning two runaway slaves – a man and a woman – came to his home and asked him to help them travel north. A bounty of $1,000 had been offered for the man. Henderson agreed. He put some hay in the bottom of his wagon and had the couple lie down on it. He spread a wagon cover over them, then placed more hay and the wooden cradles on top. That day, Henderson drove around the Springfield city square, stopping and talking to people, before taking the fugitives to the home of a local man who could help them continue their journey to freedom.

Henderson later recalled, "I became so well known to the slave catchers, who used to congregate about St. Louis, that for years I would not have visited that city for any amount of money. It is now rather a matter of pride to be reckoned among the abolitionists of those days, but it was not so then."

During the winter of 1853-1854, another African-American from Jacksonville, David Spencer, transported eight escaped slaves to Springfield by way of the Great Western Railroad. They brazenly boarded the train in Jacksonville just before daylight, believing it best to hide in plain sight. Spencer was asked several times who his friends were and he replied that they were friends from Chicago who had been visiting him over the holidays. Soon after the train left the station, one of the runaways leaned over and whispered in Spencer's ear that his old master was in the same railroad car, just a few seats in front of them. Spencer told him not to be afraid, that he had a pistol with him and he would use it if he had to. Spencer later told author Charles M. Eames, "To our great relief, the slaveholder left the train at Springfield, little thinking who had been riding with him."

According to historian Dick Hart, there were a number of "conductors" who took care of the escaped slaves when they reached Springfield; at least two white and four black men. The white men included Luther Ransom, who had been active in the Underground Railroad in Farmington before moving to Chatham, and then Springfield. He ran a boardinghouse near the Globe Tavern, where Abraham and Mary Lincoln lived when they were first married. Another was Erastus Wright, a teacher, Sangamon County school commissioner, and member of the Second Presbyterian Church, which was known as the "abolitionist church" in Springfield. Of the four black Underground Railroad conductors, Hart found that three of them had ties to Abraham Lincoln. Jamieson Jenkins was a neighbor, living just south of the Lincolns on Eighth Street. Jenkins was a wagon operator who used his profession to transport slaves to safety. The Rev. Henry Brown worked for the Lincolns as a laborer and led Lincoln's horse in his Springfield funeral procession. Hart found that he had helped escaped slaves in

Quincy and Springfield. Aaron Dyer didn't have any connections to Lincoln, but as a blacksmith and wagon operator, he also drove his horse and wagon at night, taking slaves to the next Underground Railroad station.

William Donnegan is perhaps the most tragic of the Springfield Underground Railroad operatives. He was a shoemaker, and Lincoln was a customer. In 1898, a Springfield literary magazine, *Public Patron*, published an article that was written by Donnegan about some of his experiences. He wrote that in 1858, "I lived on the north side of Jefferson, between Eighth and Ninth Streets, in a story and a half house, and I could show you the garret yet in which many a runaway has been hidden while the town was being searched. I secreted scores of them. When a man unloaded one or more Negroes at my house or at any other station in the night, it was done then, his name was not asked."

Donnegan described a harrowing experience helping a young woman who had escaped from slavery. She wouldn't follow directions and narrowly missed being spotted by her master, who had followed her to Springfield. Donnegan wrote, "I knew the house would be watched all night. I heard in the afternoon that about thirty men had been engaged about town for that night. A full description of her had been given in the *Springfield Register* with an offer of, I think, $500 for her capture." He bought the girl white gloves and "a white false face, told her what to call men and what to talk about" and how to alter her voice, "so if her master heard her, he would not know her." During the night, he slipped the girl out of the house, but her master and a group of armed slave-catchers tracked the two of them and cut off their escape. Donnegan outsmarted them by sneaking into a church, then his brother's house. There they dressed the young woman as a boy and sent her out with a work gang the next day to the home of a nearby abolitionist. She was eventually able to make it out of Springfield to safety.

In the late nineteenth century, Donnegan enjoyed a brief notoriety for his exploits on the Underground Railroad, but only a few years later, he was lynched during Springfield's race riots, one of the most terrible events to ever occur in the region.

Springfield was an important Underground Railroad stop in Central Illinois, but there was no city more closely tied to the secret route, or the entire abolitionist movement, than Jacksonville. The city was greatly influenced by the abolitionists in 1829, when just five years after its founding, the "Yale Band" arrived in the city to establish what would become Illinois College. The Yale Band was influenced by Reverend John M. Ellis, a Presbyterian minister who felt that a "seminary of learning" was needed in the frontier town. His plans came to the attention of a group of students at Yale University in New England and seven of them – who became known as the Yale Band – came west to help establish the college. The men from Yale were fervent abolitionists and greatly influenced the college and the city, making it an important part of the Underground Railroad movement.

The abolitionist movement was first publicized in Jacksonville during a legal case in 1837. The court case started when Marcus A. Chinn, who surveyed the Northern Cross Railroad from Jacksonville to Springfield, and Lucy Jane Hardin Chinn, his wife and the sister of local politician John J. Hardin, arrived in town. They had brought with them their two slaves, Robert and Emily Logan. The presence of the two slaves in the community aroused local abolitionists and they informed the Logans that they had been emancipated since Illinois was a free state. When the slaves left the Chinns, they were hidden in town by sympathizers. At some point, Robert was out running an errand and was kidnapped and sent down the Illinois River by slave traders. Left behind, Emily Logan sued for her freedom. On December 1, 1840, after a trial in which Edward D. Baker and Ninian W. Edwards represented Emily, and John J. Hardin represented the Chinns, Emily was declared a free person. The case attracted a lot of attention, even though Jacksonville was already secretly known in abolitionist circles as a safe haven.

During the 1830s, most Illinois people regarded abolitionists as a fanatical and unpopular minority, radical Yankees who were unwanted in a state that still allowed for slavery in the southern sections of the region. At that time, the French still had slaves and indentured servants along the Mississippi River, and southern slaves were leased to work the salt mines in the southeastern counties. Southern Illinois, with its close ties to the South, was still the most populous part of the state and the average person had little interest in allowing New England extremists to upset the status quo and attack an institution that was legal in the neighboring states of Kentucky and Missouri.

Going along with the majority sentiment, the Illinois legislature adopted resolutions that denounced abolitionism in 1837. Senate action was unanimous. Among six dissenting state representatives, Abraham Lincoln and Daniel Stone later recorded a protest in the official journal. They raised a moral point by condemning slavery as both unjust and bad policy, but they agreed with the majority that the "promulgation of abolition doctrines tends rather to increase than abate the evils." Despite the delay and the backpedaling, their protests showed political courage.

There were other exceptions. Many in the southern counties of the state were descendants of men who had left the South because of their hatred of slavery, either on philosophical grounds or because they could not compete economically with the plantation owners. They had come north because Illinois, after 1824, was the only free state with cheap land. Outnumbered and unorganized, they were a silent abolitionist minority that had only a few reinforcements from New England, like the Yale Band in Jacksonville.

The Yale Band, or the "Illinois Association," had organized at Yale University on February 21, 1829 to establish a school and preach in Illinois. A short time later, they combined their efforts with Reverend Ellis. Julian M. Sturtevant, the Yale Band's advance agent, arrived in Jacksonville on November 15 and began organizing Illinois College. Very soon after, construction began on Beecher Hall, the new college's first building. The college was open on January 4, 1830.

The Yale Band was not alone in its support of the abolitionist movement. The American Colonization Society also had a few branches in Illinois. Its members advocated for slaves to be freed, but then to be returned to a colony in Africa. Others were more radical, stating that slavery should be abolished altogether. Perhaps the most outspoken of these men in Illinois was Elijah P. Lovejoy, a Presbyterian minister and newspaper publisher.

Lovejoy was born in Maine and came west as part of a New England movement to uplift the morality and culture of the newly-settled states. In St. Louis, he established a classical high school and then edited a political newspaper that covered many reform causes, but ignored slavery. After five years, he experienced a religious conversion, entered Princeton Theological Seminary, and obtained a license as a Presbyterian minister. In 1833, he returned to St. Louis and started a newspaper called the *St. Louis Observer*. In it, he opposed Catholics, Baptists, liquor, and slavery with equal intolerance. He came to believe that slavery was a sin and "must cease to exist." Fanatical and stubborn, often in physical danger, he refused to stop his anti-slavery sermons and editorials. Amid growing hostility (Missouri was a slave state, after all), he became an unpopular champion of civil rights, including the right to publish, to speak, to petition, and assemble. Editorials that he wrote denouncing the burning at the stake of a free black man in St. Louis resulted in mob action and damage to his printing press. To protect his wife and infant son, Lovejoy moved across the river to Alton, then the largest and most progressive city in Illinois. He brought along his printing press, but when it arrived on the Alton docks on Sunday, the unguarded press was destroyed and dumped into the river.

Alton, like Jacksonville, was then dominated by businessmen from New England and as a progressive and comparatively enlightened city, it competed commercially with St. Louis. During the 1830s, it grew steadily as a steamboat and packing center with commission houses that dealt in beef, pork, lard, whiskey, furs, flour, and lead. Much of the town's business was with southern states and new laborers who arrived during that decade's boom years, displayed a not uncommon hostility toward blacks. Nevertheless, Alton city leaders offered moral and financial support to Lovejoy, who planned to call his newspaper the *Alton Observer*. Even though he was now in a free state, he made it clear that he would practice the freedom of the press and continue to fight for the abolition of slavery. And fight he did, angering local residents and even causing some of his supporters to withdraw because of his intolerance. Even so, many admired the raw courage of a man who several times faced down mobs with plans to tar and feather him – or worse. On August 21, 1837, a mob broke into Lovejoy's newspaper office and destroyed his printing press. Contributions from the east helped pay for a third press, which arrived one month later and was immediately hauled out of a warehouse and dumped into the Mississippi.

In September 1837, Lovejoy and Lyman Beecher attended the Illinois College commencement in Jacksonville. They had come to town to rally support for an abolitionist society that he wanted to form in Alton. Edward Beecher, another New England reformer and president of Illinois College, helped to organize the Illinois Anti-Slavery Society, which met in Alton on October 28. Lovejoy had issued a call, signed by 255 men, including 25 from Alton, for the convention. Beecher unwisely broadened the call by inviting any "friends of free discussion." Sympathetic delegates came from Quincy and Galesburg. Elihu Wolcott of Jacksonville was chosen as the society's president and delegates from Morgan County were Beecher, Wolcott, William Carter, Jonathan B. Turner, Elijah Jenney and A.B. Whitlock. Unfortunately, the meeting was taken over by a group of slavery supporters that included Usher F. Linder, the young and brilliant attorney general of Illinois. Compromises failed and Linder and Cyrus Edwards won majority support for a rejection of Lovejoy's constitutional right to publish his newspaper. He was asked to leave Alton, but he refused. He stated before the room, "You can crush me if you will; but I shall die at my post, for I cannot and will not forsake it. The contest was commenced here; and here it must be finished. Before God and you all, I here pledge myself to continue it, if need be, till death. If I fail, my grave shall be made in Alton."

One of Lovejoy's backers was Winthrop S. Gilman, who along with Benjamin Godfrey, was the owner of a massive warehouse on the Alton riverfront. Lovejoy decided that his fourth printing press would be protected there by an armed force of supporters. It arrived by steamer at 3:00 a.m. on November 7. The next night, a mob gathered and gunfire rang out. A man in the crowd fell mortally wounded. Someone carried a flaming torch up a ladder to set fire to the roof. Lovejoy ran out of the warehouse to stop him and was shot five times, falling to the ground and dying almost immediately. His friends fled and the mob put out the fire and destroyed the printing press.

Lovejoy's murder made headlines across the country, even in the South, where his politics were ignored and he became a martyr to freedom of the press. During the wave of indignation that followed, anti-slavery societies gained new members, but the mob leaders went unpunished and State's Attorney Linder even went to the extreme of trying to prosecute Gilman on a charge of starting a riot. Lovejoy, a failure as a reformer in life, had managed to ignite a movement in death that would lead to a civil war just over two decades later.

In the meantime, as slavery continued, the Underground Railroad gained importance and men from Jacksonville were involved almost from the beginning. Helping slaves escape involved great danger, as well as legal problems. In 1843, Owen Lovejoy, brother of the slain newspaper publisher, was indicted for helping two women escape from slavery. Dr. Richard Eells of Quincy was arrested that same year for aiding a fugitive. Judge Stephen A. Douglas fined him $400. Eells later became the president of the Illinois Anti-Slavery Society and, in 1844, the candidate for governor of the Liberty Party. In March 1842, Julius Willard and Samuel Willard were indicted in the circuit court for hiding a black woman who had escaped from slavery. Elihu Wolcott signed their bonds. Julius was found guilty of the charge and fined $25, but Samuel's case never went to trial.

The murder of Elijah Lovejoy and the presence of the Chinn slaves in Morgan County added fuel to the flames of abolitionism in Jacksonville. Reports say that fugitive slaves were safely passed through the county toward Canada as early as 1823. The Underground Railroad in the area was kept very secret, but after the Lovejoy murder and the Logan affair, the abolitionists of Jacksonville became much bolder and very active. The city became an important stop on the Underground Railroad in Illinois with fugitives passing through the area almost continuously until the start of the Civil War. During the 1830s, Elihu Wolcott and Ebenezer Carter were the local leaders of the Underground Railroad, and they were assisted by many other prominent businessmen, as well as professors and students at Illinois College.

Occasionally, the abolitionists met with resistance from some elements in Jacksonville. In 1843, Sarah Lisle of Louisiana came to Jacksonville to visit two of her sisters and brought a slave girl with her. When the girl was advised that she was free after coming to Illinois, she went to local abolitionists for help and they attempted to send her off to Canada. Before they could do so, however, she was intercepted by a number of pro-slavery men from the community. They were outraged and rallied a number of other pro-slavery residents to their cause. A public meeting was held and handbills were printed calling for a protest against the conduct of the abolitionists. The meeting was held on February 23, 1843, and a resolution was adopted condemning Julius Willard, Samuel Willard, Ebenezer Carter, Chauncey W. Carter, and others for their part in the affair and they promised in the future to protect the property of their acquaintances in the South. They planned to form an Anti-Negro Stealing Society and urge Missouri newspapers to print their resolutions so that slaveholders would know that there was an opposing force at work in Jacksonville.

In the end, the Anti-Negro Stealing Society had little effect on the work being done by local abolitionists and the Underground Railroad continued to operate in the city and in the surrounding area.

There were a number of homes that were used as "stations" on the Underground Railroad in the city. Many of the fugitive slaves that came to Jacksonville, came north from the Alton and Chester areas, with Benjamin Henderson and David Spencer frequently driving the wagons filled with fugitives. They traveled at night and took the escaped slaves to whatever location in town was safest at the time.

Dr. Bezaleel Gillett was a staunch abolitionist and one of the founders of the Trinity Church, the first Episcopal Church in Illinois in 1832. He was also an original trustee of the Jacksonville Female Academy, which later merged with Illinois College. As a member of the first board of trustees of the Illinois State Hospital for the Insane, he was also a recognized hero for his tireless efforts serving both rich and poor during the cholera epidemic of 1833. Fugitive slaves were often kept in a large shack that was once located south of the house.

Located on Grove Street was the home of Asa Talcott, an abolitionist and one of the founding members of the Congregational Church. The house was built in parts beginning in 1833 and was added onto in 1844 and 1861. Benjamin Henderson, one of Jacksonville's most important Underground Railroad conductors, stated that Talcott was among those he could count on for help when he needed supplies for the fugitives. Talcott was a brick layer and plasterer and it was reported that he provided refuge for runaways in his barn. One incident that was recorded occurred in February 1844, when Illinois College students brought a fugitive to Talcott after word spread that he was hiding in Jacksonville. Probably like many other escaped slaves, the slave was hidden under the hay in Talcott's barn.

Located on the Illinois College campus is Beecher Hall, the first building constructed on campus in 1829. According to legend, the building was a frequently used station on the Underground Railroad and a number of school officials and students assisted escaped slaves and hid them in Beecher Hall until they could be moved to safety.

Over the years, Beecher Hall has gained a reputation for being one of the college's most haunted sites. It was once used as a medical building and during the early years, cadavers were stored on the upper floor. During a time when it was illegal for students to possess corpses for medical corpses, the bodies had to be hidden away – in the same secret spots where escaped slaves were sometimes kept. There are some who believed that the cadavers may explain the hauntings at Beecher Hall, but it's more likely that the activity is connected to the slaves who passed through the building during the days of the Underground Railroad. There were a number of tragedies that took place during the years when the secret line was passing through Jacksonville, when slaves were killed, never making it to freedom. The Underground Railroad was filled with peril, death, danger of capture, sickness, and hunger. In many former stations, hauntings have lingered in the Underground Railroad's wake.

Beecher Hall is a place where the past returns to life in the form of phantom footsteps, incessant pacing sounds of boots that go back and forth, often on the upper floor. Voices have also been heard, along with whispers, and an eerie whistling sound that seems to come from nowhere. There have also been students and staff who claim to have seen apparitions in the hallways and rooms. The shadowy, ethereal figures are present one moment, and then gone the next.

Located about three miles east of Jacksonville is Woodlawn Farm, another important station on the Underground Railroad. The farm was established by the Michael Huffaker family in 1824 and soon began to play a prominent role in the development of modern agricultural practices in the region. Huffaker was also an abolitionist and allowed the farm to serve as a hiding place for fugitive slaves. In addition, he was one of the first Morgan County farmers to employ free blacks.

Like many other Underground Railroad sites, Woodlawn Farm has been plagued by rumors of ghosts over the years. Stories passed on by visitors to the historic site recount eerie sounds, voices in empty rooms, and the overwhelming presence of a man on a staircase in the house. One woman stated that she was visiting the farm on a bus tour several years ago and clearly saw the image of a man looking at her from one of the upper windows of the house. He appeared to be dressed in period clothing and so she assumed that he was a re-enactor who was present at the house that day. When she asked about him, she was told that not only was no one upstairs in the house, but that there were no re-enactors working at the farm at that time. She was very clear about what she'd seen, but who the man might have been remains one of the many mysteries of Central Illinois.

"An Engine of Steam and Terror" The Coming of the Railroads to Central Illinois

Aside from the introduction of farming on the open prairie, perhaps the greatest event to shape the history of Central Illinois was the arrival of the railroads in the 1850s. The railroads completely changed the lives of the residents of the farm communities that were spread across the region. All at once, goods from the east could be purchased in local stores and products from the prairie, like grain and cattle, could be shipped to expanding markets all over the country.

One of the greatest railroad hubs in Central Illinois was the city of Decatur. All of the major rail lines that came through Illinois had headquarters and rail service through this small Midwestern town. The arrival of the railroad in Decatur in 1854 changed the future of the city forever. The first railroad to establish service in Decatur was the Great Western Line, which eventually became a part of the Norfolk & Western Railroad, but many others followed, including the Illinois Central Railroad and the Wabash Railroad.

The Illinois Central Railroad built their first line into the city in October 1854. A Union Station was built in 1856 to serve the IC and Wabash passenger trains. It was used until 1903, when both railroads built their own stations. The old Union Station included the Central House hotel, which offered sleeping quarters, offices and a dining room. Abraham Lincoln stayed the night at the hotel while attending the Republican convention here in 1860. The new Illinois Central Station was built in 1900 and was the loading point for 27 daily passenger trains. Decatur was once the main stop between Chicago and St. Louis, but eventually the passenger service died out and the station was razed in 1951, leaving only memories behind.

The Wabash Railroad became one of the area's largest employers. In 1869, they built their first roundhouse in the yards, which could service eight locomotives at a time. The Wabash shops were moved to Decatur in 1884 and operations were expanded. Decatur became the hub of all of the railroad's operations and, in 1925, had a peak employment of 3,500 men, making it the largest employer in the city. Eventually, the railroad died out in the city and the Wabash merged with Norfolk & Western in 1964. A heavy loss in passenger service was cited as the main reason for the merger, and most of the service was finally abandoned. At one point, at its peak, the Wabash Railroad operated 25 passenger trains out of Decatur every day. Today, the old Wabash station still stands. It is now a large antique store, but not all of the memories of the past have faded completely – as the reader will learn in the next chapter.

During the heyday of the railroads, thousands of people came and went through the local railyards, used the passenger service, crossed the tracks, and labored in an industry that could often be hazardous. It's no surprise that the railyards saw scores of deaths and injuries over the years – some of which, led to tales of ghosts.

In March 1895, a Springfield man was run over by a Wabash freight train. Ironically, the same train had brought him to town. He was in charge of a shipment of horses, on their way to Lafayette, Indiana, and was last seen alive on the front platform of the caboose. It was surmised that when more cars were added to the train, he lost his balance and fell down onto the tracks. The cars only moved a few feet – but that was enough to kill him. The wheels passed over his body, severing it at the abdomen, and he was instantly killed. In the dead man's coat pocket, railroad workers found a nearly empty bottle of whiskey, which likely explained how he lost his balance in the first place.

In October 1895, the engineer of a Peoria, Decatur & Evansville Railroad train struck a suicidal man about a quarter-mile from the railyard. The man, John Waterlin, had been walking down the tracks and even though the engineer tried to stop, he spotted the man too late to avoid the collision. Waterlin ignored the train's whistle and made no effort to avoid the locomotive. It struck him and he was thrown to the side of the tracks. When railroad workers rushed to the scene, they found Waterlin bleeding badly, but conscious enough to gasp out his name. A doctor was summoned and Waterlin was taken to his father's home, which was nearby. He had a broken, jaw, his shoulder was broken in three places, and had numerous internal injuries that could not be treated. Police officers learned that Waterlin had been living in Peoria, but after his wife had left him, his health had declined and his father said he "had been out of his head." He lingered for two days in agony before he died.

In November 1895, a local man named Billy Barnett was planning to take a train out of town and while waiting, crossed the tracks to have breakfast at a nearby café. When he returned, he crossed the tracks behind the depot and was startled by a swiftly approaching train. Unable to get off the tracks in time, he attempted to jump onto the footboard – and slipped off. The wheels passed over him, crushing his skull and cutting off both of his legs.

In September 1896, a Wabash train struck a buggy driven by Mrs. Jud Thomason at the Water Street crossing. She was returning from an evening drive, and crossing the tracks, when the train stuck her. The buggy was demolished and her horse was killed. Frank Durendo, a tramp who had been riding in freight cars, was standing on the steps of a baggage depot when the accident occurred. Mrs. Thomason's buggy was flung into the air and Durendo was struck by it. His was badly hurt and his left foot was so mangled that it had to be amputated the following day. Mrs. Thomason's skull had been crushed in the accident. She was taken to St. Mary's Hospital, but died a few hours later.

Later that same month, a 17-year-old boy named Clarence Eberly was walking down the tracks with a friend, planning to go hunting outside of town. They were walking through the railyards when an eastbound train overtook them. As a lark, Eberly reached out and grabbed a ladder on the side of a freight car. He planned to ride a short distance and let go – but instead, he slipped off and fell onto the tracks. The wheels of the next car passed over his legs. The train crew saw what had happened and, after improvising a stretcher, took the boy to a nearby house and summoned a doctor. When the physician arrived, he pronounced his wounds to be fatal. He was right – Eberly died a few hours later.

On October 23, 1905, a Wabash employee named John S. Early was killed in the yards when he stepped between two cars and was crushed to death. He had only worked for the railroad less than a year and, apparently, didn't realize the danger of stepping between two cars that were coming together on the tracks. He was caught between them, crushed, and pinned into place until the cars were moved. He died almost instantly.

In January 1906, a Wabash brakeman named Albert T. Brown was killed as a result of a freak accident. Brown was assisting in moving a car of cinders from one track to another and stepped backward to avoid blowing dust that was coming off the car. Brown wiped at his eyes and looked up to see that he had stepped onto tracks that were directly in the path of Engine No. 754. He had plenty of time to get out of the way but, unfortunately, his foot got caught in a frog, which is a railroad switch that enables trains to be guided from one track to another at a junction. Unable to pull it out, the engine slammed into the unlucky brakeman and he was thrown several feet in the air. Horribly, his foot and a part of his leg were left behind, snagged in the frog. The engine was going so fast that the engineer was unable to stop immediately. When workers arrived at the scene, they gathered the pieces of Brown's body – after first wrestling his leg and foot out of the railroad switch.

Another freak accident occurred in the Wabash yards on January 17, 1910, which resulted in the death of one railroad worker and injured another. John W. Trammel and Elmer Mills, both switchmen, jumped onto the footboard of a Wabash switch engine as it was traveling through the yards. Suddenly, the footboard broke under the weight of the two men and threw them both under the wheels of the engine. Trammel's legs were instantly severed and although he survived for a short time, he died a few hours later at St. Mary's Hospital. Mills' escape was nothing short of a miracle. He fell down between the wheels and managed to end up in the middle of the tracks. Even though he was reported to be a very large man, the train passed over him.

On February 2, 1927, a Wabash shops worker named Lafe Schultz was instantly killed at the Seventh Street crossing when he walked out onto the tracks behind an eastbound passenger train – and stepped into the path of a string of freight cars being moved by a switching crew. He was solidly struck and dragged for more than 50 feet before the train could be stopped. His body was, according to newspaper reports, badly mangled.

And the incidents of death, violence, and even murder in the railyards of Decatur goes on and on. Is it any wonder that the area has come to be regarded as very haunted?

One of the most colorful accounts of railroad ghosts appeared in newspaper stories in April 1906. Stories had been circulating for some time that the boiler room of the Wabash shops was haunted and by the spring of that year, even the newspapers were taking notice. According to the account of the two men who experienced the ghost, Charles Brown and W.H. Giles, they were working in the boiler room one morning when they experienced the haunting. The men were holding a large rubber hose, while Brown washed out a boiler. Suddenly, in a space of about two feet between where the men were holding the hose, a third set of hands appeared. The spectral hands ended at the wrist and firmly grasped the hose for only a few moments and then vanished.

As startling as the encounter was to the two men, this was not the first report of a phantom occupant in the boiler room. So many of the workers had encountered the spirit that they had nicknamed the ghost "Mr. Auburn." Up until that day, W.H. Giles had not been a believer. "I never believed in ghosts, but I can't explain what I saw this morning," he later said. "I never say, and never thought I saw, a ghost or anything of that kind until today."

Charles Brown, however, believed that he had seen the ghost before. One afternoon, he was working in the back of the boiler room and had climbed up on a ladder to do some repairs on an electric light. The room was dimly lit since the light was out. He happened to glance down and saw a figure appear from behind one of the boilers. He walked through the shadows to the foot of the ladder and Brown thought that one of his co-workers had slipped in and was going to shake the ladder to frighten him. He laughed and called out a good-natured warning and the figure vanished. Brown hurried down from the ladder and looked around the room, but there was no one in sight. Anyone leaving the room would have been between Brown and the light outside of the room and would have been plainly seen. He was sure that no one had left the room – but the place was completely empty.

Charles Mitchell, the foreman of the machine shop, came into the boiler room as Brown was standing in the doorway looking around. He saw no one else leave the place, but he stated that it was clear that Brown was disturbed by something. "His eyes were as big as saucers," he recalled.

In the only newspaper account of the haunting, it mentioned that some of the shop men had declared that the boiler room had been haunted for months. There was even one story told that a man who worked in the boiler room at night actually quit his job after encountering the ethereal "Mr. Auburn."

The most enduring railroad ghost story of the area, though, involves a mysterious light that has been seen traveling through the open ground behind the old Wabash station. The station no longer sends travelers off to their destinations and the railyards behind it haven't been used in years. What was once one of the most bustling parts of the city is an overgrown field that is broken only by rusted railroad tracks, worn-out gravel roads, and the remains of the Wabash shops and roundhouse. The heyday of the railroad is gone, but the light remains. It's not a random reflection or glare of light, but a solid yellowish-white lamp that moves with purpose as if searching for something – or someone. It passes through the field, following the lines of tracks that once existed and then it vanishes without a trace.

The light is no mystery. It's true that the complexities of how a ghost manages to return from the other side remains unexplained, but as to the identity of the ghost, or why he still walks there, that's been a poorly-kept secret since the 1930s.

The Wabash ghost light dates back to October 1935 and can trace its origins to one of the most sensational unsolved murders in Decatur history. On a chilly evening in that year, former city police chief Omer E. Davenport was brutally slain by two unknown men just north of the Wabash station. At the time of his death, he was on duty as a special patrolman for the Wabash Railroad.

Major Omer Davenport was one of the respected and well-liked men in the city in 1935. He had distinguished himself in the military and had become the commanding officer of the 130th Infantry of the Illinois National Guard. After serving during World War I, he returned to Decatur and became the chief of police for three years. He was the youngest chief to ever serve, taking over the position at the age of 26. Davenport left the police department in 1927 and became a special patrolman for the railroad. After surviving a war, he probably never imagined that this important, high-paying job would be the one that would lead to his death.

During the early morning hours of October 8, the Wabash Passenger Train No. 17 arrived in Decatur from Chicago and Davenport was nearby as it pulled to a stop just west of Morgan Street. In the dim light, he saw two black men jump from the train and dodge behind a flagman's shack. Davenport started in their direction to investigate, but before he could get very far, both of them drew revolvers and began firing at him. One bullet struck Davenport in the left leg, just above the knee, and the other passed through his neck, grazing his windpipe. He fell beside the tracks, bleeding badly, while the two men turned in the opposite direction and disappeared.

Noah W. Deyton, the fireman on train No. 17, was the only witness to the shooting. He told the police, "After Officer Davenport fell, several men ran to him and he was taken to the hospital. The two Negroes ran south toward Cerro Gordo Street. I was too far west of the crossing to tell whether they turned on reaching the street or kept on going south."

Railroad patrol officers began searching the area and after a phone call, the Decatur police force joined in the hunt. Unfortunately, the description of the two men was sketchy, but the police had other clues to work with. The gun that killed Davenport had been stolen earlier that night from the home of Isaiah "Doc" Taylor, an employee at the Wabash roundhouse. Several items of clothing that had also been stolen were found on the ground near the watchman's shack.

Police detectives searched the area and officers from all over the city and county worked overtime on the case. The night shift worked all through the next day as they scoured the city for leads. The local highways, railroad yards, and freight cars were searched and one group of officers walked almost 10 miles from the Wabash yard to the town of Elwin, south of Decatur, in hopes that some lead might be found. Trains were stopped and cars searched. Trucks were stopped on the highways and deputies went to nearby towns to search the railroad depots. The state police aided in the search and broadcast the description of the suspects all over Illinois.

Meanwhile, Omer Davenport had been rushed to the nearby Wabash Employees Hospital, which was located on East Grand Avenue, a short distance from the station. He was still alive when he arrived there, but he was struggling to stay alive. The doctors stated that his chances for survival were grim. The bullet that had struck his throat had worked itself into one of his lungs. It had caused serious complications and if they tried to operate, they were convinced that it would kill him. He died later on that night.

A few days later, the manhunt began to slow down. Detectives traveled as far as St. Louis and Chicago in pursuit of some sort of lead, but they found nothing. A reward was offered by the railroad in exchange for information about the killers, but it was never paid. Whoever the two men were, they vanished into history, leaving behind no clues as to their identities.

Omer Davenport was buried with full military honors, but there are many who believe that he has never rested in peace. For years after his death, there were those who believed that his ghost haunted the Wabash Employees Hospital where he died. There were many reports of a man fitting his description who was seen walking the hallways and vanishing without explanation. The hospital closed down in 1972 and was used for a time as a community health improvement center before being abandoned. During its final years of operations, staff members spoke of the ghost of a man who wandered the building as if lost and then faded from sight. Could this have been the lingering spirit of Omer Davenport? The old hospital was demolished in 1996, leaving that question unanswered.

Davenport's most often encountered haunting, though, was not at the old hospital. It was his manifestation as the strange light that has long appeared behind the Wabash station, where he was shot in 1935. For many years after his death, Wabash workers, station crew members, police officers, and local residents reported the weird light and came to believe that it was the flashlight of the slain patrolman, still walking the line, perhaps looking for some clue as to the identity of the men who took his life.

The Wabash ghost light still appears in the open field behind the station today, a lingering reminder of the heyday of the railroads in Central Illinois and of the fallen hero who once tried to keep this area safe for the railroad men and the passengers who worked and traveled in and through this part of the city.

The Chatsworth Disaster

Decatur was not the only railroad city in Central Illinois to experience death and horror. One of the greatest railroad disasters in the state's history occurred near the small town of Chatsworth in 1887.

It had been a dry, brutally hot summer that year. A severe drought held the entire state in its grasp. By August, newspapers were reporting that stream beds were dry, wells were running out of water, and that cornfields were scorched beyond recovery. It was so bad that even sporadic showers and thunderstorms became newsworthy events. According to the news reports of the time, railroad section workers were kept busy putting out fires that had been caused by sparks from passing locomotives. For some reason, supervisors on the line thought the dry weather was a good time to put the men to work burning the dry weeds that grew along the tracks – it was a poorly thought out plan that would become deadly.

On August 10, 1887, workers along a section of the Toledo, Peoria & Western line near Chatsworth spent most of the day burning weeds and brush. The men would later state that all of their fires had been extinguished when they left for the day, but during the night, a small bridge that was close to where the men had been working managed to catch fire. Whether it burned because of the weed clearing or as a result of sparks from a passing locomotive will never be known. Whatever the cause, by midnight, the fire had burned through the wooden trestle that was just west of the Ford-Livingston County line. Just as the clock struck the hour, an excursion train roared toward the smoldering bridge.

The excursion train that raced toward its doom that night was one of the hundreds of such trains that traveled each year during the latter part of the nineteenth century. Trains like this one provided a welcome respite for hardworking Midwesterners. For a small fee, they could get away from home for a few days and enjoy scenic and natural sites that they might not otherwise see. Some of the most popular places to visit for the excursion trains were Mammoth Cave in Kentucky, Hot Springs, Arkansas, and Niagara Falls. It was to that New York natural wonder that the train was heading when it crossed Illinois in August 1887. When the railroad had posted handbills about the excursion to Niagara Falls that summer, hundreds of people eagerly responded. A round trip ticket only cost $7.50.

The 239 miles of the Toledo, Peoria & Western line stretched across Illinois from Warsaw on the Mississippi, through Peoria, to a town called State Line (now Effner) on the Indiana border. In 1887, the Toledo, Peoria & Western company was a thriving and important railroad and provided a valuable east – west service across the state. As it was advertised, the Niagara Special started at LaHarpe in Hancock County. A large crowd of excited travelers, mostly from Galesburg and from neighboring Iowa, was on board the train. Fatefully, or perhaps it seemed so in hindsight, the train was being pulled by Engine No. 13. Even those who were not superstitious could agree that the engine turned out to be unlucky for those on board the train.

The train traveled eastward after departing from LaHarpe, picking up passengers from many of the small towns along the way. The train steamed into Peoria in the early evening hours with 15 coaches. At the Peoria station, switchmen added several more coaches and dozens of additional passengers climbed aboard. After the train crossed the Illinois River, Engine No. 21 was coupled to the front of Engine No. 13. The train now consisted of two locomotives, pulling at least 20 cars with about 800 passengers on board.

With all of the stops and the addition of more cars, the train had fallen about two hours behind schedule. It was nearly midnight by the time that it arrived in Chatsworth. After a brief stop, the train left the depot and began to pick up steam. About two miles east of town, the lead locomotive crossed a small hill and from this vantage point, the engineer spotted flames ahead on the rails. Horrified, he realized that a wooden trestle ahead of them was burning. There was no possible way, he knew, to stop the train.

The engine roared ahead, despite his immediate attempt to apply the brakes, and as No. 21 passed over the trestle, the engineer "felt the engine sink a little and felt a shock." The locomotive rumbled across the bridge. Engine No. 21 was safely across but as No. 13 began to shudder its ways across the treacherous bridge, the trestle began to collapse. The engine tipped over on its side, as it was still moving forward at a speed of about 25 miles an hour, it skidded along the ground, churning up rock, sand, dirt, and wood.

As the heavy coaches, filled with passengers, collided with the overturned engine, they slid sideways off the tracks. The coaches plowed into the engine, ramming into one another with a metallic fury. Metal screamed with a horrific grinding noise and wood splintered and broke. Even in the darkness, many would recall a rolling cloud of soot, cinders, ash, and dust. The railroad cars slammed together with a telescoping effect, each coach slicing into the one in front of it. The flying metal whirred like the blades of a saw, producing a grisly death toll. Many of the passengers were cut into pieces, their bodies savagely sliced apart. Many more of them were crushed and died instantly.

As the wreck finally ground to a halt, 11 of the railroad cars now occupied the space that was once occupied by two. The sound of the tearing metal faded and was immediately replaced by a chorus of human screams and wails. The survivors of the disaster began to stumble about, looking for family members, friends, and anyone else who might have lived through the terror.

The engineer of locomotive No. 21 climbed down from his cab and stared in awe at the unbelievable wreckage that loomed behind him. Only the dim light of burning fires illuminated the scene, but the flames showed him more than he wanted to ever see. The scene would live on in his nightmares for many years to come. Two firemen from No. 21 took over the controls of the engine and rushed east to Piper City. They blew their whistles, hoping to alert as many people as possible to the awful news about what had happened. A brakeman from the train ran off in the opposite direction, following the tracks back to Chatsworth. As he ran, he began to see flickers of lightning in the dark sky. A storm was coming.

Almost impossibly, the horror at the crash scene became worse. The wreckage of the train caught fire, trapping many of the injured survivors inside. As screams filled the night, other survivors, who had managed to make it out of the ruined cars, began to throw handfuls of dirt onto the flames. As rescuers began to arrive from Chatsworth, and from small farms nearby, they joined them and clawed at the dirt with their bare hands to keep the blaze from spreading. Meanwhile, telegrams were sent out from Piper City and Chatsworth and rescue trains began steaming toward the accident.

Then, around 3:00 a.m., the summer drought finally broke and torrents of rain began to fall from the sky. The storm, which had been only flickering lightning in the distance at the time of the wreck, reached the awful scene and unleashed its fury on the survivors, the rescuers, and the dead. The rain managed to put out the remains of the fire but it also turned the nearby fields and dirt roads into a muddy swamp, making them nearly impassable.

By sunrise, Chatsworth was swarming with both volunteers and curiosity-seekers. People came from all over the region to provide comfort and aid and to see the carnage for themselves. Over the days that followed, the gruesome task of removing and identifying the dead was carried out. The twisted metal coaches made this job nearly impossible and newspapers repeatedly used the word "pulp" to describe the condition of the human remains.

Many of Chatsworth's buildings were turned into temporary morgues and the crowds who came to view the remains became so troublesome that armed guards had to be posted at the doors. One newspaper account noted, "Charnel houses and hospitals make up tonight what has been the peaceful village of Chatsworth."

Fanned by sensational newspaper reports and wild rumors, terrible stories spread through the area. The rumors included reports that belongings had been stolen from the dead and that the bridge fire had been set on purpose. Responding to public anger, a section foreman was arrested and blamed for the fire, but he was later released. To this day, much about that night remains a mystery, including the cause of the fire and the number of people who died. Some accounts claim 81, others place the tally at 85. Regardless, it was one of the worst disasters in Illinois and one of the greatest losses of life for railroad crashes in American history.

Four days after the disaster, the railroad gathered most of the debris into an enormous funeral pyre. A Bloomington newspaper described the scene: "A match was touched to the mass and in a few hours heaps of ashes hid whatever secrets the wreck still contained. A smell of burning flesh from time to time filled the air."

It should come as little surprise that the horrific disaster has inspired a few ghost stories over the years. Locals often told tales about the sounds of screams and moaning at the site of the crash and teenagers often claimed to see eerie lights that appeared near where the train had burned. Some said that they were the spectral lights of rescuers, hurrying to the grisly scene with lanterns in their hands. Many years later, when a freight train derailed in Chatsworth on the anniversary of the disaster, a local resident quipped, "I guess the ghosts are still out there."

But the most enduring ghostly tale that was connected to the crash did not occur in Chatsworth, but rather in the LaSalle Cemetery, just outside of Chillicothe, Illinois, near Peoria. According to the accounts, one of the survivors of the crash was a man named Ira Hicks. He and his wife, Nancy, were traveling to Niagara Falls aboard the excursion train. After the wreck, Hicks searched in vain for his wife. Amidst the carnage at the scene, he stumbled about calling her name, but she did not answer. The days that followed were bloody and chaotic. The injured and the dead were scattered about in makeshift hospitals and Hicks was unable to find her. In hopes that she might also be looking for him, he returned to his home in Chillicothe, believing that, if she was alive, she would look for him there.

Sadly, nearly two weeks passed with no sign of Nancy, so Hicks returned to Chatsworth. When he arrived, he was met with terrible news – his wife was dead. To make matters worse, she had been incorrectly identified as the wife of a man named Henry Clay. Her body had already been taken to Eureka, Illinois, where she had been buried in the Clay family plot. Nancy's body was exhumed a short time later and she was reburied at the LaSalle Cemetery in Chillicothe.

And, after that, things started to get strange.

Years later, stories began to circulate in the community that the gravestone of Nancy Hicks was behaving in a very odd manner. People who passed by the cemetery at night began reporting that the stone was giving off an eerie glow in the darkness. Some even claimed that it looked like the light of a steam locomotive. Scores of curiosity-seekers flocked to the graveyard after dark to witness the glowing stone. No one could explain what caused the stone to glow. Tests were made on the stone of the monument to see if it had any special reflective qualities, but it seemed to be ordinary granite. Could the phantom light be a sign from the ghost of Nancy Hicks, still making her presence known after all of these years?

Unfortunately for ghost enthusiasts, the story was debunked in the late 1980s when burlap bags were used to form a barrier between the gravestone and the headlights on the road next to the cemetery. Somehow, with a number of bizarre angles that could not easily be seen, auto headlights were bouncing reflections off the stone, making it appear to glow. A few years later, homes were built between the road and the cemetery, permanently blocking the auto headlights.

The "ghost" of Nancy Hicks had finally been laid to rest.

The Haunted President
Abraham Lincoln and the Supernatural

There is no American president more closely connected to the supernatural than Abraham Lincoln. The unusual, often melancholy man, was a great believer in signs and portents, toyed with Spiritualism after the death of one of his sons, and believed that dreams foretold his presidency – and his death. He forever changed the face of America and his legacy is an integral part of the ghost stories and strange tales of Central Illinois.

Abraham Lincoln was born in Kentucky in 1809. His father, Thomas Lincoln, had married Nancy Hanks, a tall, pretty, uneducated girl, three years before and they had built a log cabin at a place called Sinking Springs Farm. Thomas was a well-liked man, a good storyteller, and a man adept at many things, although he rarely settled down to try any one thing in particular. Abraham was likely to follow in his footsteps, despite his obvious intelligence. He was a thin and spindly-looking boy who showed remarkable curiosity about everything and would always be the best reader in his school class.

The Lincoln family later pulled up stakes and moved across the Ohio River to Indiana, where they settled on Little Pigeon Creek. Abraham soon learned the ways of the outdoors and hard work, helping to clear land around their new home. He became known as an honest and self-reliant boy, but lonely and withdrawn too, sometimes vanishing into the woods for hours at a time.

In 1818, Lincoln's life changed abruptly when the family was struck by a terrible frontier disease dubbed "milk sickness." It was mysterious and incurable at the time, but was later traced to cattle eating a poisonous plant and passing it to humans in their milk. The nearby community was plagued by the sickness, killing the Sparrows, close friends of the Lincolns. A short time later, Nancy Lincoln also grew sick and died. With his own hands, Abraham helped to fashion his mother's coffin and then helped place her in the ground. It was later said that he held his head in his hands and wept for hours. At that point, his father and sister forgotten, Lincoln later said that he felt completely alone in the world.

In 1819, Thomas Lincoln traveled back into Kentucky and returned with a new wife, Sarah Bush Johnston, the widow of an old friend. She was raising three children of her own, along with an orphaned cousin, Dennis Hanks. With the cabin now jammed to capacity, Abraham later recalled escaping into the woods with his books for peace and quiet. On other occasions, he stayed up late into the night, reading by the dying embers of the fire, while everyone else in the house slept.

A short time later, an accident occurred that may have shaped young Abraham's life. The boy enjoyed taking corn to the local mill for grinding and, as always, he hitched his old mare to the gear arm that day, urging her forward to turn the millstone. He whipped the horse to get her moving and the horse kicked backward, striking Lincoln in the head, and knocking him to the ground. Bleeding and senseless, a neighbor rushed the boy home. The family was convinced that he would die. Over the next few days, though, he slowly recovered, but some believed he was never completely himself again. Friends said that he sometimes seemed "in a world by himself," ignoring his surroundings and those around him. He often sat for long minutes in complete silence, staring straight ahead, noticing visitors "like one awakened from sleep." One of his closest friends and long-time law partner, William H. Herndon, stated that Lincoln was "a peculiar, mysterious man with a double consciousness, a double life. The two states, never in a normal man, co-exist in equal and vigorous activities though they succeed each other quickly."

Lincoln's odd behavior never stopped him from excelling in school, though. He stood out among other students, composing poems and essays, and sometimes mounting a tree stump to give speeches about things that moved him. He was very physically strong, an expert log-splitter, skilled butcher, and mastered a field plow. By age 17, he was nearly six-feet-tall and could outwrestle anyone in the surrounding communities. He was also an insatiable reader, devouring anything he could get his hands on. Local ministers and teachers admitted that the young man was better read than they were and doubted that a life of hard labor on a farm would ever suit him. He went about his day with a book in his back pocket, but began to resent the life that he felt trapped in.

In the late 1820s, Thomas Lincoln moved his family again, this time to Illinois. They arrived in Decatur in March 1830 on the advice of John Hanks, a relative of Abraham's mother, who suggested they settled at a site along the Sangamon River. The family built a cabin and Abraham kept busy working his father's land and hiring out to other local farmers. He became proficient at splitting wooden rails, working for William Warnick, the Macon County sheriff. Lincoln was on his way to Warnick's home during the "Winter of the Deep Snow" when he fell into the river and almost died from frostbite. Legend has it that he read Warnick's law books during his recovery, which led to him taking up law as a career.

In the spring, Thomas Lincoln decided to leave Decatur and took his wife and stepson to Coles County, where they lived out the rest of their lives. Abraham, now 22-years-old, decided not to follow. He was unsure what he wanted to do with this life, but he was ready to be on his own.

In February 1831, Denton Offutt from Kentucky came to Decatur to see John Hanks, who had formerly operated flatboats on the Ohio and Mississippi rivers to New Orleans. Offutt proposed a similar operation in Illinois. Hanks was interested and suggested that Abraham Lincoln and his stepbrother, John Johnston, join him in the enterprise. A few weeks later, around the middle of March, the three men paddled a canoe down the Sangamon River on the first leg of their journey to New Orleans.

Lincoln was soon working on a flatboat that was hauling farm produce down the Ohio and Mississippi Rivers to New Orleans. At the end of his journey, he found the promise of a new life in the village of New Salem, Illinois. He went to work running a small store for Denton Offutt and became popular in the village for this humor and storytelling ability. He was a hard worker and powerful wrestler, which earned him both friends and admirers. He studied, borrowed books, and joined the local debate society, all with plans of becoming an attorney. Before that, though, he was convinced by friends that he should run for the state legislature. His campaign was interrupted by the Black Hawk War and he spent two months in the state militia. He was delighted when his fellow soldiers asked him to serve as captain, but often complained about there being more mosquitoes to fight than Indians. He was mustered out after the campaign and set out for home, only to have his horse stolen. Lincoln ended up walking most of the way back to New Salem from the Wisconsin border. By the time he arrived back home, he had only two weeks left to campaign. He lost the election, coming in eighth in a field of 18.

Lincoln's return to New Salem brought him other disappointing news. The store where he had been working had closed down, so he took the position of New Salem's postmaster. He took the liberty of reading dozens of newspapers every week before delivering them and soaking up the information they contained. He also became a deputy surveyor and used both jobs as a way to campaign again for the legislature in 1834. He drummed up votes at dances, barbecues, cock-fights, and wrestling matches, where he normally served as referee since everyone refused to fight him. This time, he won the seat and at the age of 25, left for Vandalia to serve in the legislature. He left home wearing the first suit he had ever owned.

Lincoln served out his term in Vandalia, and in 1836, he was elected again. This time, he went to the new capital of Springfield, where he also practiced law. He had read all of the books required and in March of 1837 passed the exam that made him an attorney. He borrowed a horse and bid goodbye to the fading town of New Salem.

When Lincoln moved to Springfield, he was already well-known. He had made a name for himself in the legislature and became sought after as an attorney. Lincoln, although friendly, was a hard man to know. He was quiet and introverted and while he had a few close friends, he was a lonely man. Springfield was then on the verge of becoming a real city, despite its unpaved streets, lack of sewers and sidewalks, and the packs of wild hogs that had been roaming the streets for almost a decade. It also had a social circle that Lincoln, despite his quiet manner, was drawn into, largely thanks to his political status and the friends that he had managed to make. One of those friends was Ninian Edwards, the son of a prominent politician. His wife, Elizabeth Todd Edwards, was a born matchmaker and delighted in finding husbands for her sisters among Ninian's friends. Her sister, Mary Todd, came to visit in 1839. Mary was described as being "high strung" but was said to have an engaging personality and a quick wit. She became the center of attention among Springfield socialites and had plenty of potential suitors to choose from, including Stephen Douglas, who was the most insistent.

In December 1839, during the grand Christmas cotillion, Mary met Abraham Lincoln and they were attracted to one another from the start. They eventually became engaged and their relationship dragged on for more than a year before Lincoln suddenly broke it off. Lincoln didn't eat, didn't sleep, let his work slide, and acted, in the words of his friend and law partner William Herndon, "as crazy as a loon." He fled Springfield for the Kentucky home of his friend, Joshua Speed, who was also in the midst of a turbulent relationship of his own. It was Speed who convinced Lincoln to return to Springfield and reunite with Mary, which he did in the summer of 1842. The two were married in a hastily arranged ceremony on November 4. Their first child, Robert, was born just three days short of nine months after the wedding.

During the early years of their marriage, Lincoln and Mary lived at the Globe Tavern in Springfield, but in 1844, Lincoln purchased the only home that he would ever own. The house, located at Eighth and Jackson Streets, was not far from Lincoln's law office. Over the next few years, it was renovated and enlarged to provide room for a growing family. Their son, Eddie, was born in 1846, following by Willie in 1850, and Thomas, or "Tad," in 1853. Tragically, Eddie died just one month after his fourth birthday on February 1, 1850.

According to relatives, Lincoln had an eerie dream on the night before Eddie died. He had experienced it before and knew that something unusual was about to happen. In the dream, he was in a ship that was sailing quickly into the night, carrying him into darkness and oblivion.

Lincoln would have the dream again shortly before his own assassination.

Lincoln's law practice was based in Springfield, where most people in Central Illinois brought their grievances for settlement. However, twice each year, a judge took justice out to the people. At fixed sessions of two days each week, this special magistrate sat at county seats that were scattered all over the prairie and tried to mete out rulings on the crimes and cases in what was known as the Eighth Circuit. Joining the judges were lawyers who "rode the circuit," defending clients in the various communities. Lincoln's love for travel and the law often kept him away from home, but he eagerly welcomed the adventure. In those days, few of the county seats could be reached by the new railroads. Most were only accessible by muddy tracks that passed for roads, across bridges that often washed out, and along wooded trails that were traversed on horseback. Lincoln and his fellow attorneys slept in farm houses, barns, hotels, and tavern beds. The courtrooms were primitive and defense strategies often had to be created on the spot.

When the work days ended, the lawyers usually gathered around the fire at the local tavern to play cards, swap stories, and sing songs. Lincoln was usually the center of attention, whether he was laughing about the day's activities, telling jokes, good-naturedly mocking his opponents. He also mingled with the people that he met in the small towns and backwoods communities, visiting their homes, talking about their crops and livestock, discussing politics or bouncing their children on his knee. Lincoln was becoming widely known across the Illinois prairie. He was a man who listened when people talked and, in turn, they turned a receptive ear to his often strong opinions.

Lincoln's life as a nomad attorney continued for some time. Even after his term in Congress in the late 1840s, his law practice kept him too busy to consider returning to political life. However, the institution of slavery, and his empathy for the people who suffered from it, began to slowly alter the course of his career.

When Thomas Lincoln had moved his family from Kentucky to Indiana in 1816, part of the reason for it was his desire to get his family away from the ugly presence of slavery. But Lincoln had little experience with people of color until 1828, when he took a cargo of produce down the Mississippi to New Orleans and saw the slave markets for the first time. He was so bothered by the experience that he never forgot it. Years later, he and his friend, Dan Stone, were the only state legislators in Illinois to take a stand against slavery. They called it an "injustice" but, even then, Lincoln was content to believe that slavery would eventually die out on its own, and while he hated the practice, he did not endorse it being abolished. Instead, Lincoln was opposed only to the further spread of slavery in the country. He believed in the Missouri Compromise, which outlawed slavery in the west, because he believed America's future would be built in the western states. In 1854, though, a congressional act, provoked by Lincoln's long-time rival, Stephen Douglas, threatened to allow slavery in the territories. This made Lincoln angry enough that he decided to put his law practice on hold and return to the political arena.

That summer, Lincoln decided to campaign for a seat in the Illinois State Assembly. He easily won the election, but resigned because he really wanted a spot in the U.S. Senate. It was there, he believed, where he could really make a difference for the country. In February 1855, he sought, but failed to get the coveted seat. Things started to change in early 1856, however, as a new political party was created called the Republican Party. The first political move by the party was to try and keep Democrat James Buchanan out of office. They failed, but were gaining attention.

Buchanan's term in the White House pushed back the anti-slavery movement by years. During his time in office, the U.S. Supreme Court ruled in the Dred Scott case, effectively deciding that blacks would never be considered as American citizens. Passions were beginning to ignite in the nation and dire predictions began to be made about the possibilities of secession and Civil War. Stephen Douglas abruptly changed his mind and now announced that he was, despite his earlier concessions, now completely against allowing slavery into the western territories. In spite of this change, Illinois Republicans nominated Lincoln to run against Douglas for a seat in the Senate.

On the night of the nomination, in a speech before the excited convention, Lincoln made his famous "House Divided" speech, declaring that the country could not endure as a divided nation. "A house divided against itself cannot stand," Lincoln told the assembled Republicans. "I believe this government cannot endure permanently half slave and half free. I do not expect the Union to be dissolved -- I do not expect the house to fall -- but I do expect it will cease to be divided. It will become all one thing, or all the other."

On July 24, Lincoln proposed that he and Douglas meet in a series of debates before audiences all over the state. His opponent agreed and the two men began a series of volatile appearances across Illinois. "The prairies are on fire," wrote one reporter, after witnessing a clash between Lincoln and Douglas. The debates were bitter and powerful between the two long-time rivals. Lincoln argued that slavery must be abolished, while Douglas insisted that it could be contained and allowed to flourish in the South, as long as the states there wished it. After a whirlwind of appearances and hundreds of miles traveled, the debates ended in October 1858. In the end, Lincoln lost the election to Douglas, but a bigger future was waiting for him. Political analysts, on both sides, had watched the race closely and had seen the way that the debates captured the attention of the entire country. Word spread that the Republicans had begun to favor Lincoln as their choice for president in 1860.

Lincoln began to travel all over the country, backed by the Illinois Republican contingent, making his name known and becoming a recognizable entity. It would be at home in Illinois; however, that Lincoln would earn his first presidential nomination. In 1860, Decatur was chosen as the site of the Illinois State Convention for the Republican Party. The convention attracted more than 700 delegates to the city, along with party leaders, candidates, newspaper reporters, and scores of interested citizens. A temporary hall, dubbed the "Wigwam," was erected, where Republican candidates for state office would be named. But supporters of Lincoln had other plans in mind. On the afternoon of May 9, they entered the Wigwam with two wooden rails and a banner stretched between them that announced Lincoln's candidacy for president in November. The incident was met with shouts of approval and thunderous applause. Hats, canes, and books were thrown into the air and the assembly jumped and screamed until the canvas roof of the hall fell down onto their heads.

A week later, at the Republican's national convention in Chicago, Lincoln's supporters began working to ensure that his name went on the ballot for the entire country. They rushed fellow supporters into the city and began working behind the scenes to pack the hall with delegates for Lincoln. In the first roll call of states, William Seward – who was expected to win – had 173 votes; while 236 were needed to win. Lincoln followed with 102 votes, with Simon Cameron of Pennsylvania, Salmon P. Chase of Ohio, and Edward Bates of Missouri each received about 50 votes. Recognized that Pennsylvania would be crucial in winning the nomination, Lincoln's supporters arranged for delegates of the state to be seated between Illinois and Indiana, which both backed Lincoln. They then convinced the Pennsylvania delegates that if Seward won the nomination, the party would lose the election. As a result, Cameron withdrew.

When the second ballot was called, it offered a stunning surprise. Seward had gained only 11 votes, but Lincoln's total had increased by 79. This left Chase in third place with just 42 votes.

Workers in the Lincoln campaign had been busy contacting delegates from every state, using a deceptively simple strategy. Instead of asking for votes on the first ballot, they persuaded as many men as possible to make Lincoln their second choice. They also stressed the contrast between Lincoln and Seward. Lincoln had been guarded in his campaign so far and had been careful not to offend anyone. Seward meanwhile, had made his position clear on most national issues. Seward was the only nationally known Republican who had allegedly praised John Brown's recent attack on Harper's Ferry and had hinted at a civil war by warning that an "irrepressible conflict" seemed to be coming because of slavery. Lincoln, on the other hand, was on record as opposing the extension of slavery into the territories, but he also underscored the conviction that slavery where it existed was lawful and that it should not be challenged. He believed that the institution would die out on its own.

But what truly decided the nomination will never be known. Mysterious things occurred in Chicago's famous "smoke-filled rooms" for during the third ballot, Seward lost four votes, which Lincoln had gained 53. He was only a handful of votes away from the nomination. When the news swept through the hall, swirling amidst the shouts, cries, and laughter of the assembly, five of the delegates from Ohio announced that they wanted to change their votes in favor of Lincoln. He was now the official Republican Party candidate for president.

No one can say how Lincoln pulled off this victory, but one thing is clear: many of those who stepped aside for Lincoln, or who worked for him behind the scenes, were chosen for important posts. Seward became Lincoln's Secretary of State; Chase headed the Treasury Department; Cameron became Secretary of War; and Edward Bates became Lincoln's Attorney General. And the list went on.

News of Lincoln's nomination was met with skepticism in some cities, but when the news reached Springfield, it was immediately greeted by a 100-gun salute. A huge crowd gathered at Lincoln's home that evening. He spoke to them from the front steps, inviting as many into the house as could crowd inside.

Outside of Illinois, Lincoln was not thought of so warmly. He was a "county lawyer" and a "yokel." The abolitionists predicted he would lose the election and one even declared that the gangly man was "half horse and half alligator," and a "backwoodsmen" from the frontier.

By the summer of 1860, the nation's attention was focused on Springfield. Politicians from all over America were traveling to the city to visit with Lincoln. He had become a real threat to southern politicians, who feared that if he won the election, it would be the end to their way of life. They came to Illinois, as did northerners, who wanted to see what the man was really like. Lincoln's advisors suggested that he remain at home during the campaign. He had others traveling the country and speaking on his behalf. Lincoln was told that this way he could just focus on the issues, but in reality, it was to keep him hidden away. While the Republican leaders had great faith in Lincoln as a candidate, they hesitated to let the public see his lanky frame in his wrinkled suits, frumpy hat, and sweat-stained shirts. He was not exactly the picture of a future president, they decided.

The city of Springfield had a carnival-like atmosphere about it that year, highlighted with a Republican rally at the fairgrounds during the hottest days of the summer. The parade took more than eight hours to pass the Lincoln home and ended with a picnic, where tubs of lemonade and whole cooked steers awaited the revelers.

Election Day in the city dawned with rousing cannon blasts, with music and contagious excitement. Lincoln spent the day and evening with friends at the telegraph office. By midnight, it was clear he had carried the election. A late dinner was held in his honor and then he returned to the office for more news. Guns fired in celebration throughout the night.

Lincoln won the day in the Electoral College, but fared poorly in the popular vote with only 40 percent of the vote among the people. He became a minority president with no support in the southern states. Rumors of secession spread through Washington and beyond. Lincoln was even hanged in effigy on Election Day in Florida.

In the early morning hours, Lincoln finally returned home, although news of his victory and messages of congratulations were still being wired to the telegraph office. He went into his bedroom for some much needed rest and collapsed onto a settee. Near the couch was a large bureau with a mirror on it and Lincoln stared for a moment at his reflection in the glass. His face appeared angular, thin, and tired. Several of his friends suggested that he grow a beard, which would hide the narrowness of his face and give him a more "presidential" appearance. Lincoln pondered this for a moment and then experienced what many would term a "vision" --- an odd visitation that Lincoln would later believe had prophetic meaning.

He saw in the mirror that his face appeared to have two separate, yet distinct, images. The tip of one nose was about three inches away from the tip of the other one. The vision vanished, but appeared again a few moments later. It was clearer this time and Lincoln realized that one of the faces was actually much paler than the other, almost with the coloring of death. The vision disappeared again and Lincoln dismissed it as nothing more than lack of sleep.

The next morning, he told Mary of the strange vision and attempted to conjure it up again in the days that followed. The faces always returned to him and while Mary never saw them, she believed her husband when he said that he did. She also believed she knew the significance of the vision. The healthy face was her husband's "real" face and indicated that he would serve his first term as president. The pale, ghostly image of the second face, however, was a sign that he would be elected to a second term --- but would not live to see its conclusion.

Lincoln spent the remainder of the year in Springfield, growing a beard and preparing for the move to Washington. His daily mail, which secretary John Nicolay carried into the office by the basket load, was starting to be liberally sprinkled with hate letters. Other letters warned of danger and conspiracy. He was concerned by the outpouring of hatred, largely from southerners, but he refused to show his worry. He met with people every afternoon at the capitol building, talking, laughing, and letting them know that he was still one of the people. Days passed and the crowds never stopped coming, so John Nicolay cut the visiting down to only an hour or so each day. Lincoln was becoming exhausted and worried about the future.

Mary went east to New York in January and returned home for the last open house in their Springfield home. By this time, their belongings had all been packed away and their steamer trunks had been moved to a local hotel to await their departure.

Lincoln bid goodbye to Springfield on a rainy morning. He rode alone in his carriage to the train station. He had requested that there be no public demonstration over his departure, but several hundred friends and well-wishers lined the streets near the station anyway. His voice was thick with emotion as he said farewell and then boarded the train. He didn't look back as the train steamed away, likely because he had no idea that he would ever see his beloved city again.

Lincoln's life was in danger when he departed Springfield. The threats against him were now being taken seriously and those who vowed to protect him took great care in mapping out Lincoln's train route across America. Unfortunately, not even the presence of his wife and children prevented disaster from almost striking several times. One assassination attempt was averted when guards discovered a grenade in a satchel near the President's seat.

The train traveled across the country to New York, where newspapers and critics mocked Lincoln's awkward gestures and western mannerisms, and then south through New Jersey to Philadelphia. The family checked into the Continental Hotel, where the nearly exhausted Lincoln surrendered to another crowded and noisy reception. Late that evening, Chicagoan and friend Normal Judd called Lincoln to his room for a secret meeting with Allan Pinkerton, another Chicagoan and the head of the detective agency that was now working for the Philadelphia, Wilmington and Baltimore Railroad. Pinkerton informed Lincoln that his detectives had uncovered a well-organized plot to assassinate the President-elect in Baltimore, a rabid secessionist city. Lincoln was scheduled to change trains there and the plotters intended to kill him as he took a carriage from one station to another.

An intricate plan was devised that had Lincoln leaving the city by train, then slipping away to return to Philadelphia on a special train. In disguise, he would board a sleeping coach and a night train would take the coach to Baltimore. He would then take another train into Washington. The next morning, the regular presidential train would go on to Baltimore as scheduled, with a military escort on board to protect Lincoln's family and staff. Lincoln reluctantly agreed to the plan, upset about being forced to sneak into the capital. That night, disguised in a large hat and overcoat, he departed on the special train. He was accompanied by his friend, Ward Lamon, who was armed with two revolvers, two derringers, and two large knives. The sleeping car, with bunks much too short for the gangly Lincoln, was reserved under a false name, supposedly for an invalid who was being accompanied by his sister. The "sister" was in reality a Pinkerton agent named Kate Warne. It was an inauspicious arrival into Washington, but at least Lincoln was safe and alive.

Lincoln reached the capital at dawn on February 23 and went straight to the Willard Hotel. Mary arrived with the boys that afternoon, still shaken from an ordeal in Baltimore, where frenzied crowds had greeted the presidential train and had shouted for Lincoln. No violence had occurred, but Mary had been terrified. She collapsed at the hotel with one of her legendary headaches and did not stir again until late in the evening.

Inaugural week was a nightmare for Lincoln. Rabid and persistent office-seekers refused to leave him alone and, to make matters worse, endless delegations from the office of outgoing President James Buchanan were in and out of his hotel suite. Lincoln was also plagued by groups of congressmen and senators who harassed him about his Cabinet choices and his policy for dealing with the South. In the midst of all this commotion, Lincoln had to complete his cabinet, even with rival factions fighting with him down to the last appointment. He clashed repeatedly with William Seward, who believed himself a better politician than Lincoln, until Lincoln hinted that he might replace him, which seemed to cool the tension somewhat.

The morning of the Inauguration brought dark skies and an ominous mood to the city. Soldiers patrolled the streets, wary of would-be assassins. For every man who feared for Lincoln's safety, there was another who waited for terror to strike. Lincoln remained in his hotel suite until the time for the event arrived. Dressed in a black suit, he put on his stovepipe hat at noon and adjourned to the lobby, where President Buchanan called on him for the traditional carriage ride to Capitol Hill. The two men said little during the journey. By now, the clouds had lifted over Washington and the sun was shining brightly on the military bands, the marching soldiers, and the ranks of cavalry who honored the new President with their parade. General Winfield Scott had deployed officers throughout the assembled crowds, on the lookout for trouble. At the Capitol Building, Pinkerton detectives paced about, watching windows and rooftops for signs of gunmen. On a nearby hill, artillerymen manned a line of cannons, prepared to fire on the streets below at the first sign of assassins.

Lincoln stood on a giant platform, flanked by nearly 300 dignitaries. In the face of a brisk wind, he stepped to the podium and looked out on the sea of faces below. He began to speak, addressing the greatest worries for the nation – those of war, slavery, and secession. He spoke at length to southern interests, assuring them peace and prosperity and promising not to endanger their way of life or to try and end slavery because he had, according to the Constitution, no right to do so. But Lincoln also spoke about the powers of the national government and he vowed to enforce federal law equally in all of the states. The Union could not be destroyed, he said, and he promised to shed no blood in its defense unless he was forced to do so.

Despite these proclamations to use whatever force necessary to save the Union, Lincoln went on to say, "We are not enemies, but friends. We must not be enemies. Though passion may have strained, it must not break our bonds of affection. The mystic chords of memory, stretching from every battlefield and patriot grave, to every living heart and hearthstone, all over this broad land, will yet swell the chorus of the Union, when again touched, as surely they will be, by the better angels of our nature."

Lincoln then took the oath as the sixteenth President of the United States and began one of the most troubled periods in American history. Within weeks, with the southern states condemning Lincoln's inaugural address as nothing short of a declaration of hostilities, they began leaving the Union and declaring themselves a Confederacy. Fort Sumter was surrounded by rebel troops and artillery and then was fired upon on April 13. The following morning, Lincoln, who had been agonizing over the situation for weeks, declared that the Union could not fall. Officially, he announced that he would not view the conflict as a war between the states but as an insurrection against the government. Since secession was constitutionally illegal, he refused to concede that any of the states had left the Union. Rather he contended that rebellious citizens established a false, Confederate government that Washington would never recognize. Lincoln's objective now was to suppress the southern rebels as quickly as possible and restore order in the sections of the country they had seized.

Lincoln put out a call for 75,000 militiamen and those in the North and the South who had been undecided before to choose sides. In the border states, secession conventions sprang into action, for the thought of invading armies from the North, attacking rebels and freeing slaves was more than even the Southern Unionists could stand. On April 17, the Virginia convention adopted a secession ordinance that was approved by the voters. Virginia joined the Confederacy and the rebels moved their capital to Richmond. Within the next two months, Arkansas, North Carolina, and Tennessee also seceded and became Southern states with Maryland, Missouri, and Kentucky threatening to go, as well.

America was truly coming apart.

In the days, months and years that followed, the personality of Abraham Lincoln was altered considerably. Although he had long been prone to moodiness and "spells," his periods of reflection became longer and more pronounced. As the death toll of the war mounted on both sides, Lincoln became more and more obsessed with God and his divine plan for America – and for the President himself. Lincoln became convinced that he had been born to guide America through the War Between the States. His leadership during this period, although often questioned, never faltered and the events of the early 1860s both strengthened and destroyed the man that Lincoln was.

The great loss of life and the bitter turmoil of the war took their toll on him. He changed and he became more bitter and dark. Gone was the humorous man who was apt to take off his shoes during staff meetings to "let his feet breathe." In his place was a sad, gloomy leader who was prone to severe depression. It was as if the weight of the entire nation had fallen on his shoulders.

Lincoln's times of prayer and contemplation became much longer and he seemed to turn inward. He spoke more and more often of the "hand of God" in certain battles and it was almost as if an uncanny perception somehow strengthened as the war raged on. By this time, Lincoln had truly taken on the mantle of America's military commander. Few realize today just to what extent Lincoln actually orchestrated the Union Army during the bloodiest points of the war, enduring complaints and barbs by often ineffectual generals about his "meddling." The once inexperienced soldier who had looked for help from his aging generals was gone and had been replaced by a Commander in Chief who sometimes claimed supernatural insight into events that were occurring hundreds of miles away.

Documents of the War Department contain one occasion when Lincoln burst into the telegraph office of the department late one night. He had visited earlier, looking for the latest news, but when he came back, he was in a panic. He ordered the operator to get a line through to the Union commanders. He was convinced that Confederate soldiers were just about to cut through the Federal lines. The telegraph operator asked where he had obtained such information and Lincoln reportedly answered, "My God, man! I saw it!" He had been dozing in his office, he stated, and the vision had been sent to him in a dream. Much to the telegraph operator's surprise, a return message that was sent to him some time later informed him that Lincoln's vision had been true. When soldiers in the field asked him where he came by such knowledge, the operator was unable to provide them with an answer that he thought they would believe.

The war took a terrible toll on President Lincoln, but there is no doubt that the most crippling blow that he suffered in the White House was the death of his son, Willie, in 1862. Lincoln was nearly shattered over Willie's death and it was probably the most intense personal crisis in his life. Some historians have even called it the greatest blow he ever suffered. Even Confederate President Jefferson Davis sent a letter to Washington to express his condolences over the boy's death.

In the midst of a terrible war, Lincoln had depended on his two young sons, Willie and Tad, to provide him with comfort and solace. They were his only antidotes to depression and anxiety. He treasured the moments that he could spend with them, reading stories, and reveling in their antics. He loved to beleaguer his visitors with tales of his "two little codgers" and bragged about them to anyone who would listen. The boys had turned the White House into their playground. They ran and shouted in the corridors and burst into Lincoln's office during meetings, chasing one another around stiff politicians who were not amused. Tad, who instigated most of the mischief, once fired his toy cannon at a Cabinet meeting and also liked to stand at the front of the grand staircase and collect a nickel "entrance fee" from those who came to see his father. Also, with Lincoln's help, the boys converted the White House lawn into a zoo, with animals consisting of ponies, kittens, white rabbits, a turkey, a pet goat (which often slept in Tad's bed) and a dog named Jip, who had a habit of sleeping in Lincoln's lap during meals. One day, Tad discovered the White House bell system, which had cords running to various rooms so that Lincoln or the staff could summon servants whenever they needed anything. Tad set all of the bells clanging at once, sending the White House into bedlam. It took a few minutes for them to figure out what was going on, but eventually members of the staff climbed into the attic and found Tad yanking all of the bells and giggling madly. Imitating the soldiers who were encamped in the city, the boys waged mock battles with neighborhood children on the White House lawn and held parades through the building, with the boys and their friends blowing tin horns and banging on drums. Lincoln often took them along when he went to visit General George McClellan's camps across the Potomac. They looked up to the soldiers with wide-eyed reverence and watched the marching bands and the drilling regiments in awe. When Lincoln was presented to the troops, the boys rode with him in his carriage and tipped their hats to the troops just as their father did.

In spite of how it sounds, though, life for the Lincoln boys was not all play. Tad was a nervous boy, like his mother, and a hyperactive child with a speech impediment. He was slow to learn and many did not believe that he could read. Mary hired tutors for the boys, but Tad had "no opinion of discipline" and teacher after teacher resigned in frustration. But Lincoln refused to worry about Tad, insisting that he would learn his letters over time. The boys might be a little spoiled, but he was determined to let them have as much fun as they could. They would have to grow up far too soon.

In contrast to Tad, Willie had a very serious side and often behaved like an adult. He had turned 11 in December 1861 and many of the Lincoln's friends and staff members commented on his precociousness. The young man would sit in church, listening to the minister with rapt attention while Tad played with a jackknife on the floor of his mother's pew. When he was tired of romping with this younger brother, Willie liked to lock himself in his room, where he would curl up in a chair and read a book or write stories on a pad of paper, just as his father used to do when he was growing up. Willie was much like his father in so many ways and because of this, the two were very close. He and Willie shared many interests, especially reading, humor, and a love for animals. Lincoln had bought Willie a pony for his birthday and it became the pride of the boy's life. Mary loved Willie's gentleness and he was so affectionate that she often counted on him desperately for family companionship. He would, she prayed, "be the hope and stay of her old age."

Tragically, this was not meant to be.

In late January 1862, both Tad and Willie became sick. The boys had been out playing in the snow and both developed serious colds with fevers. Tad's illness soon passed, but Willie seemed to get worse. He was kept inside for a week and finally put into bed. A doctor was summoned and he assured Mary that the boy would improve, despite the fact that Willie's lungs were congested and he was having trouble breathing. Day after day passed and Willie grew more and more sick. He shivered under blankets, unable to ward off chills, and his fever soared out of control. Staff members later spoke of hearing the poor boy as he cried through the night. Willie's ailment remains a mystery. Some believed he suffered from consumption, or from a malarial infection, or typhoid. Whatever the case, the lack of proper sanitation was likely a factor. During this time period, Washington had open sewers and a filthy canal for drinking water. The city's garbage was dumped into the river just a short distance from the White House.

Before Willie's illness, the Lincolns had scheduled a reception at the White House with over 800 people in attendance. The lavish affair included dinner, music, and dancing. The invitation had already been mailed and Mary had no way to cancel, so it went on as planned. It turned out to be a dismal night for the Lincolns, though, as they worriedly took turns climbing the stairs to check on Willie.

The boy did not improve. More doctors arrived and by then, everyone in the household and in the offices knew that Willie was dangerously ill. Soon, word of the condition reached the newspapers, prompting speculation about his illness. One parent stayed with the sick and frightened boy at all times and nurses from the local hospital volunteered their time to stay with him. After a week of this, Mary was too weak and exhausted to rise from her own bed, but Lincoln rarely left Willie's side, sleeping and eating in a chair next to his bed. All he could do was to bathe the boy's face with a wet cloth and look on helplessly as his son's life slowly slipped away. As he grew worse, the doctors offered no hope for his recovery. Willie became so ill that he was unable to recognize anyone in the room, including his beloved father.

Death came for Willie on the afternoon of February 20, 1862. Lincoln covered his face and wept in the same manner that he had for his mother many years before. He looked at Willie for a long time, refusing to leave his bedside. Mary collapsed in convulsions of sobbing and her closest confidante, seamstress Lizzie Keckley, led her away to comfort her. Mrs. Keckley, a former slave, had become an almost constant companion of Mrs. Lincoln after completing her ball gown for the Inauguration. She was one of the few people who possessed the patience and strength needed to deal with the high-strung First Lady. Mary trusted her implicitly, confided in her, and called the woman her best living friend. Keckley listened to Mary, sympathized with her, and advised her as best she could. She would soon influence Mary greatly when it came to her beliefs in Spiritualism. After Willie's death, it was Lizzie who washed the boy's body and dressed him in a plain brown suit of clothes for the funeral. She herself had lost her only son and understood Mary's pain at the loss of Willie.

President Lincoln was devastated by Willie's death. He barely managed to stand after Mary was led away by Lizzie Keckley, but stumbled into John Nicolay's office to share the horrible news. Then, sobbing, he walked to Tad's room. He sat down with the boy and tried to tell him that Willie would not be able to play with him anymore. When he said that Willie had died, Tad refused to believe it at first, and then he began to weep.

Orville Browning, Lincoln's old friend from Illinois, and his wife, Elizabeth, immediately came to the White House when they heard the news. Elizabeth stayed with Mary throughout the night and Orville began taking care of funeral arrangements. According to the tradition of the day, the mirrors in the White House were covered and the mansion was draped with black crepe. The Lincolns hardly stirred from their rooms. If not for their friends and Lincoln's most trusted staff, the White House would have come to a standstill.

A funeral was held in the East Room on February 24. Willie's body was placed in a metal casket in the nearby Green Room and mourners filed past him. Robert Lincoln offered comfort to his father, both of their faces twisted with grief, but Mary did not attend the service. She was in such a state of shock that she was unable to leave her room. Most of official Washington was there, including William Seward, who wept openly. He was joined by cabinet members, scores of politicians, and General McClellan, with whom Lincoln frequently battled. He was so moved by the President's suffering that he later sent Lincoln a compassionate note that expressed his sorrow and gratitude that Lincoln had stood by him after his many failures. When the service was concluded, the pallbearers and a group of children from Willie's Sunday school class carried the coffin outside and to the waiting hearse.

The funeral procession traveled to Oak Hill Cemetery in Georgetown in pouring rain and strong winds. The service was short. Willie had been embalmed to make the trip back to Springfield to be buried beside his brother, Eddie, but Lincoln changed his mind about that at the last minute. He accepted an offer made to him by a friend, William Thomas Carroll, to place the body of Willie in one of the crypts in the Carroll family tomb. The body would remain there until Lincoln retired from the presidency and returned to Illinois. He could not bear the idea of having Willie so far away from him just yet.

In fact, Lincoln returned to the cemetery the next day to watch the body as it was moved from the cemetery chapel to the crypt itself. The tomb was located in a remote area of the cemetery and was built into the side of a hill. It was a beautiful and peaceful spot, but Lincoln wouldn't be able to leave his son unattended there for long. Word spread that Lincoln returned to the tomb on at least two occasions and had Willie's coffin opened. The President claimed each time that he opened the casket that he wanted to look upon his boy's face just one last time.

Soon, the need to see his dead son's face was overshadowed by the possibility of actually speaking to him one last time – from beyond the veil.

After the funeral, Lincoln tried to go on about his work, but his spirit had been crushed by Willie's death. One week after the funeral, he closed himself up in his office all day and wept. Lincoln treasured small items and drawings that had been given to him by Willie, sometimes putting them all over his desk while he worked, hoping to capture his essence. Small toys that had belonged to Willie were placed on his fireplace mantel, along with a framed picture that Willie had done for his father. Lincoln would tell visitors that it had been painted by "my boy, who died." His friends stated that Lincoln would often watch the door while he worked, as if expecting the boy to run through it and give his father a hug, as he often did in life.

Willie's death left a permanent hole in Lincoln's heart. Often he would dream that Willie was still alive and would see the boy playing in the leaves on the White House lawn and calling out to him --- only to awaken in his darkened bedroom and realize that it was only a dream.

More eerie to members of Lincoln's staff was his claim that Willie's spirit remained with him and how he could sense his presence in his home and office. Some mediums theorized that Lincoln's obsession with the boy's death may have caused Willie's spirit to linger behind, refusing, for his father's sake, to pass on to the other side.

It was at this time, according to a number of sources, that Lincoln became involved with the Spiritualist movement in Washington. At that time, Spiritualism had been around for less than two decades, springing to life in the 1840s in New York when two sisters began to make claims that they could communicate with the dead. The popularity of the movement swept across the country, even to the White House.

Mary Lincoln openly embraced the idea of communicating with her dead son. This is not surprising considering that the White House was a place of tragedy and grief. The President was deeply in pain. Tad rarely played and often broke into bouts of weeping. But Mary was even more deeply affected by Willie's death. Always high-strung and emotional in the best of times, she suffered what was likely a nervous breakdown and she shut herself in her room for three months. She stayed in bed, crying and begging Willie to come back to her. Lizzie Keckley would later recall how tender President Lincoln was with his anguished wife, but he worried about her as well, fearful that she would lapse into insanity.

With care from her husband, and Lizzie's friendship and kindness, Mary began to slowly improve, although the mention of Willie's name or a reminder of him would send her into violent sobs. Unable to bear any memory, she gave away all of his toys and anything that might make her think of him. She never again entered the guest room where he died or the Green Room where he had been laid out in his coffin. She canceled all but the most important social functions and lived in veritable seclusion for some time, trying anxiously to hold on. Five months after her son's death, she was still so shaken that she could barely write to her friends in Springfield about "our crushing bereavement."

As time wore on, Mary began to find small ways to alleviate her grief. Following Lizzie Keckley's advice, she began visiting the military hospitals in Washington, distributing food and flowers to the wounded soldiers. She also developed a deep compassion, thanks to her own suffering and her friendship for Lizzie Keckley, for all of the "oppressed colored people." She helped Lizzie to care for "contraband" blacks who were now streaming into Washington and even convinced President Lincoln to donate $200 to her cause. Mary also did everything that she could to find jobs for the refugees.

All of this did only so much to ease her pain, though, and Mary remained unstable. Her mood swings, headaches, and explosive temper were worse than ever. In addition, she began to see political conspiracies against her husband everywhere, especially on the part of William Seward, the "dirty sneak" who had tried, and was still trying, she believed, to take her husband's job. She believed that all of the Cabinet members were evil and was bothered by the fact that her husband seemed to be so unaware of it. Mary also fretted about his safety, begging Lincoln to take guards along when he went out on his nocturnal walks to the War Department. She begged him to be careful and worried about him so much that it seemed to Lizzie that Mary "read impending danger in every rustling leaf, in every whisper of the wind."

Perhaps the only thing that really provided Mary with any comfort at all was her embrace of Spiritualism. The Lincolns were no strangers to ghosts and contact with the dead. Lincoln knew several Spiritualists in Springfield, and Mary had been raised by slaves in Kentucky and their spiritual beliefs were familiar ones to her. Mediumship among the African-Americans of the time was commonly reported and it was said that many "see spirits, foretell events, and recognized influences... often describing the spirits of their deceased friends." The maid who cared for Mary when she was young used to tell her tales of spirits and stories of the dead returning for friendly visitations.

By the summer of 1862, Mary was meeting with a number of different Spiritualist mediums and invited many of them to the White House, as each claimed to be able to "lift the thin veil" and allow Mary to communicate with Willie. She was also introduced to the Lauries, a husband and wife medium team who lived in Georgetown, and to the woman who became her closest Spiritualist companion, Nettie Colburn Maynard. Lincoln also knew Nettie and met with her many times. In 1863, he was present at a séance in which a piano levitated off the floor. Lincoln and Colonel Simon Kase both climbed onto the piano, only to have it jump and shake so hard that they climbed down. Lincoln was said to have referred to the levitation as proof of an "invisible power." When word spread of his interest in the spirit world, a piece of sheet music was published that portrayed him holding a candle while violins and tambourines flew about his head. The piece of music was called "The Dark Séance Polka" and the caption below the illustration of the President read "Abraham Lincoln and the Spiritualists."

Stories are still told concerning the fact that Lincoln consulted with these mediums and clairvoyants to obtain information about future events in the war. He found that sometimes they gave him information about matters as mundane as Confederate troop movements --- information that sometimes matched his own precognitive visions. There is much written about Lincoln and the Washington Spiritualists of the day in the accounts and diaries written by friends and acquaintances. One such acquaintance would even claim that Lincoln's plans for the Emancipation Proclamation, which freed the southern slaves, came to him from the spirit of Daniel Webster and other abolitionists of the spirit world.

Most of the information about Lincoln and his interest in Spiritualism came from an 1891 manuscript written by Nettie Colburn Maynard, who had first manifested psychical abilities as a teenager in the 1850s. During the war, Nettie lived in Washington with her friend, Mrs. Anna Crosby, who introduced her to other mediums, as well as prominent residents of the city. She gave private and public séances for many of these people, and through Spiritualist circles, became acquainted with Mary Lincoln.

Nettie first met President Lincoln on February 5, 1863, during a séance in Georgetown. During the sitting, Lincoln was allegedly contacted by the spirit of an "old Dr. Bramford," who was said to have provided him with information about the war, including the state of morale at the front, where General Hooker had just taken command. The spirit claimed that the army was demoralized and in a state of disarray. The remedy for the problem, he told Lincoln, was for the President to pay a visit to the front lines. Seeing Lincoln in person would unite the soldiers again. In April, Lincoln paid the Army of the Potomac a lengthy visit, arriving at Aquia Creek and traveling by train to Falmouth where Hooker's men were camped. From there, Lincoln could see with a spy glass across the Rappahannock to Fredericksburg, where Robert E. Lee's Army of Virginia waited, less than a half mile away. A short time later, the overconfident Hooker led the Union to one of the costliest defeats of the war at Chancellorsville. In the midst of this disaster, though, his men followed him bravely into battle. It was believed that their courage had been restored by the visit from President Lincoln.

While Nettie Maynard was able to provide spiritual relief to Lincoln on a number of occasions during the war, the President still came to believe that a portent of doom hung over his head. The constant threats of death and violence that he received kept his personal bodyguards on edge at all times. It is also believed that some of his Spiritualist friends felt the end was near. They sent frequent letters, warning him of danger.

That feeling of dread remained with Lincoln, leading to the most famous supernatural incident that has been linked to him – the prophetic dream that he had on the eve of his assassination. In truth, Lincoln had many dreams that he considered to be prophetic in his life, including the often repeated nightmare of sailing off into a dark sea, which reportedly occurred just before the death of his son, Eddie, in Springfield. He also dreamed of his own death, which he felt was looming over him. Unfortunately, though, Lincoln was almost impossible to keep safe. Even as the war dragged on, and threats of death and murder seemed to multiply, Lincoln's bodyguards, as well as the soldiers assigned to his protection, were constantly thwarted from their duty by Lincoln himself. He often slipped out of the White House at night for solitary strolls and refused to take precautions that were necessary to keep him protected. Many felt that it was only a matter of time before the assassin's bullet caught up with the President.

One of Lincoln's old friends from Illinois was a lawyer with whom he had ridden the legal circuit named Ward Hill Lamon. He was the same man who had assisted Lincoln in slipping into Washington before his first inauguration. Lincoln had later appointed him to a security position in the White House and Lamon worried constantly over Lincoln's seeming indifference to threats and warnings of death. Lamon often resigned his position because his friend did not take the danger seriously. Lincoln always convinced him to stay on, promising to be more careful before slipping out of the White House at night or attending the theater without protection. Lamon became obsessed with watching over Lincoln and many believe that the President would not have been killed at Ford's Theater had Lamon been on duty that night. As it turned out, the security chief was in Richmond, Virginia, on an errand for the President, when disaster struck. He never forgave himself for what happened, especially since he believed that he had a forewarning of the event, from Lincoln himself.

Years later, Lamon would remember that Lincoln had always been haunted by the strange vision that he experienced in the mirror in 1860. Several years after that, it was to Lamon and Mary Lincoln to whom the President would recount an eerie dream of death, just shortly before his assassination.

"About ten days ago, I retired late. I soon began to dream. There seemed to be a death-like stillness about me. Then I heard subdued sobs, as if a number of people were weeping. I thought I left my bed and wandered downstairs. There the silence was broken by the same pitiful sobbing, but the mourners were invisible. I went from room to room; no living person was in sight, but the same mournful sounds of distress met me as I passed along.

"It was light in all the rooms; every object was familiar to me, but where were all the people who were grieving as if their hearts would break? I was puzzled and alarmed. What could be the meaning of all this? Determined to find the cause of a state of things so mysterious and so shocking, I kept on until I arrived at the East Room, which I entered. Before me was a catafalque, on which rested a corpse wrapped in funeral vestments. Around it were stationed soldiers who were acting as guards; and there was a throng of people, some gazing mournfully upon the corpse, whose face was covered, others weeping pitifully.

"'Who is dead in the White House?', I demanded of one of the soldiers.

"'The President', was his answer, 'He was killed by an assassin.'

"Then came a loud burst of grief from the crowd, which awoke me from my dream. I slept no more that night; and although it was only a dream, I have been strangely annoyed by it ever since."

Lincoln was murdered just a few days later and his body was displayed in the East Room of the White House. Mary recalled this dream of her husband's quite vividly in the days that followed. It was said that her first coherent word after the assassination was a muttered statement about his dream being prophetic.

On April 14, 1865, a few days after the horrifying dream and on the night he was to attend a play at Ford's Theater, Lincoln held a cabinet meeting. Edwin Stanton, Lincoln's Secretary of War, arrived late and the meeting began without him. As Stanton and Attorney General James Speed were leaving the meeting, Stanton commented to him that he was pleased about how much work was accomplished.

"But you were not here at the beginning," Speed said. "When we entered the council chamber, we found the President seated at the top of the table, with his face buried in his hands. Presently, he raised it and we saw that he looked grave and worn."

The President spoke to them, "Gentlemen, before long, you will have important news. I have heard nothing, but you will hear tomorrow. I have had a dream. I have dreamed it three times before -- once before the Battle of Bull Run, once on another occasion, and again, last night. I am in a boat, alone on a boundless ocean. I have no oars, no rudder, I am helpless. I drift!"

He spoke no more of it, but that same night, while attending a performance of the play "Our American Cousin" at Ford's Theater, Lincoln was shot to death by the assassin, John Wilkes Booth.

One member of his staff who would never forget Lincoln's eerie prophecies was Colonel W.H. Crook, a member of the White House security team and one of Lincoln's personal bodyguards. Crook took his task seriously, often staying awake at night and sitting outside Lincoln's bedroom while the President slept. Crook even refused to read a newspaper while on duty so that he would be ready in case of an emergency.

Crook was on duty the evening of April 14, and that same afternoon, Lincoln spoke to him about the strange dreams that he had been having. Crook pleaded with the President not to go to the theater that night, but Lincoln dismissed his concerns, explaining that he had promised Mary they would go and that he needed a night away from the problems of the country. Crook then asked to accompany the President, but Lincoln again refused, insisting that Crook could not work around the clock.

Lincoln had a habit of bidding Crook a "good night" each evening as he left the office and went to his bedroom. On that fateful day, according to Crook, Lincoln paused as he left for the theater and turned to the bodyguard. "Good-bye, Crook," he said significantly.

"It was the first time that he neglected to say 'Good Night' to me," Crook later recalled. "And it was the only time that he ever said 'Good-bye'. I thought of it at that moment and, a few hours later, when the news flashed over Washington that he had been shot, his last words were so burned into my being that they can never be forgotten."

On that night, April 14, 1865, Lincoln was shot in the back of the head while seated in a private box at Ford's Theater. His assassin, popular American actor John Wilkes Booth, was a Confederate sympathizer who was enraged by the recent surrender of the southern military and the fall of Richmond, the Confederate capital. The Civil War was almost over, but Booth and a group of conspirators were determined to continue the hostilities.

After the shooting, Lincoln was rushed to a nearby boarding house, and while everything possible was done to save his life, he died in the early morning hours of April 15. The nation was shattered by its loss. Although a controversial president who never even won the majority of the vote when he first took office, Lincoln had managed to win the love and devotion of the American people through the horror of the war. He was a revered figure at the time of his second inauguration, but his death would make him a national martyr.

Two days after his death, Lincoln's coffin was made ready and soldiers carried it to the second floor guest room in the White House, where his corpse had been resting since Sunday afternoon. The soldiers lifted the President from the table where he lay and placed him into the coffin, which was only two inches longer than the lanky man. If they had tried to bury him with his boots on, he would have been too tall. The soldiers lifted the casket and carried it down the stairs.

Gaslight illuminated the silent, eerie journey to the famous East Room, where so many public receptions and events had been held. The coffin was taken to the center of the room and placed on the catafalque. It was a magnificent casket, more impressive than any Abraham Lincoln had ever seen. In life, Lincoln had dismissed his wife Mary's love of frills and finery. He never would have chosen such a stately and expensive coffin for himself. It had cost almost as much as he had paid for his house back home in Illinois. He would have preferred a simple pine box, like the one he had helped build for his mother when he was a boy.

And the decorations in the East Room. Lincoln had always laughed about Mary's obsession with decorating the White House. But no one who entered the East Room over the next two days mocked its lavish vestments of death. When the public and press saw it, they were so impressed that they named it the "Temple of Death." Lincoln had foreseen this stark tableau in the prophetic dream that he had related to Mary and his friend, Ward Lamon.

When Mary heard about the troublesome dream, she had recoiled. "That is horrid! I wish you had not told it. I'm so glad that I don't believe in dreams, or I should be in terror from this time forth."

"Well," replied the President, "it is only a dream, Mary. Let us say no more about it, and try to forget it."

Days later, Lincoln's body was on display in the East Room, just as he had dreamed it.

The funeral display in the East Room had been hastily arranged, just like everything else that took place in the wake of the President's death. Washington was a scene of chaos in mid-April 1865. In the midst of the search for Lincoln's killer, and the matter of getting a new president into office, there was another matter that needed to be attended to – the funeral of President Lincoln. The initial details of the proceedings were decided and arranged by Secretary of War Edwin Stanton, who was embroiled in just about everything that was going on in Washington at the time. Unfortunately, there was little choice in the matter. Mary Lincoln had locked herself in her room and young Robert Lincoln was still too stunned by his father's death to be of much assistance.

Stanton dealt with Lincoln's embalming and even supervised the dressing of the corpse. But once his corpse was ready for burial, it became unclear where that would occur. Mary had the right to choose the site, but given her mental state, she was in no condition to discuss the subject only hours after her husband's death. Stanton would confer with her and Robert Lincoln later. In the meantime, whatever the final destination of the President's remains, official funeral events would have to take place in the nation's capital within the next few days. Stanton did not have time to plan and supervise a major public funeral, the biggest, no doubt, that the District of Columbia had ever seen. He needed to delegate this responsibility and had to choose between several candidates, including Ward Hill Lamon, Benjamin Brown French, who had great experience with past historic events in Washington, and General Montgomery Meigs, the Quartermaster General of the Army. But the war was not yet over and Meigs was still needed in the field. He also considered another military man, Brigadier General Edward D. Townsend, the assistant adjutant general of the army, but Stanton had Townsend in mind for a special duty of utmost importance, one even more critical than planning the President's funeral in Washington – getting the President home to Illinois.

In the end, Stanton chose George Harrington, assistant secretary of the Treasury. Harrington was experienced in the ways of Washington, was well-known and liked by both Lincoln and Stanton, and Stanton believed him to have the keen, quick, and organizational mind that was essential for the assignment. He was soon in charge of all of the Washington events to honor the late President. Harrington accepted the appointment and quickly went to work.

On April 17, the decision was made on where President Lincoln's body would be laid to rest. Arguments ranged from the capitol building to Kentucky, Chicago, and to Springfield, Illinois, which Lincoln considered his hometown. Friends of the late President, as well as his son, Robert, urged the grief-stricken Mary through a locked bedroom door to return Lincoln to Springfield.

Mary, however, was torn. She had quarreled with old friends and family in Springfield and never wished to return there. She decided first that the President would be buried in Chicago. Lincoln had promised her that after his presidency, they would tour Europe and then retire in Chicago. But Mary also looked back at her last days with her husband and realized again that he had a foreshadowing of his own death. "You will see Europe, but I never shall," he told her. She also remembered her husband's dream to live once more in Springfield. She also recalled his saying, just a few weeks before his death, that he wanted to be buried in "some quiet place." He also said, back in 1860, that the new Springfield cemetery, Oak Ridge, was one of the most beautiful spots that he had ever seen.

After agonizing over her decision, Mary finally decided that Oak Ridge was the "quiet place" that Lincoln would have wanted and directed that his coffin be placed in the public receiving tomb until a proper site could be chosen for his monument. Her decision was telegraphed to Springfield and days and nights of frantic preparation were made. Mary wanted Lincoln to be buried at Oak Ridge --- but the city of Springfield had other plans.

As it happened, when the body of President Lincoln eventually arrived in Springfield, he actually had two different graves waiting for him. One of the graves was a temporary vault at remote and wooded Oak Ridge, which Springfield officials believed was no place to bury a fallen hero, and the other was a small hill located in the heart of the city. This spot was called Mather's Hill and it had been the site of the magnificent stone house that was owned by Thomas Mather. Builders were employed to work around the clock and convert the house into a tomb, complete with a handsome vault and stone urns on either side of the entrance.

Mary learned of the downtown tomb through "troublemakers" and sent a telegram stating that her husband absolutely was to be buried at Oak Ridge. Springfield officials remembered the Mrs. Lincoln of old and recalled her erratic nerves and fits of temper, so they tried to be very diplomatic with the widow. They telegraphed Edwin Stanton and told him that her wishes would be respected --- but continued the work at the Mather tomb. They simply could not believe that Mary would want her husband buried out in the woods, and even if she did, they were sure that they could change her mind when she arrived in Springfield.

Regardless of this, they did make the other preparations that she and Robert asked for, namely moving Eddie Lincoln's body from Hutchinson's Cemetery and placing it in the vault at Oak Ridge. When the funeral train finally arrived in the city, Lincoln's body, along with Willie's, was also securely locked into the vault.

Although Springfield officials had placed Lincoln at Oak Ridge, they still had no intention of leaving him there. In Washington, Mary's friends were urging her to return Lincoln to the Capitol dome, while in Springfield, plans marched ahead to place the President in the Mather tomb. In fact, plans had already been started for a huge ceremony to mark the occasion.

Mary was furious when she read in the newspapers of Springfield's intentions. Immediately, she sent word and threatened to remove Lincoln's body from the city if a monument was not built at Oak Ridge. She claimed that she would further have him removed back to Washington if they did not cooperate. Oak Ridge, she declared, was where her husband would have wanted to rest.

In the summer of 1865, Mary moved to Chicago and a delegation from Springfield went up to plead with her again. She refused to see them and at last, they surrendered to her wishes. A temporary vault was built for Lincoln at Oak Ridge and in seven months, on December 21, he was finally placed inside.

But that was still in the future. In April 1865, Stanton needed to get the President's remains to Springfield, traveling all the way across the country to do so, and still needed to plan a Washington funeral in two days. He decided to follow the same route that Lincoln had used to get to Washington four years earlier, a circuitous route that passed through several major northern cities. Along the way, Lincoln had stopped many times. He offered impromptu, unscripted speeches; mingled with the people; accepted tributes and well wishes; and participated in public ceremonies. Lincoln presented himself to the people as a simple man who had been elevated temporarily to higher office. The inaugural train came to symbolize a living bond between Lincoln and the American people.

Now, with their beloved leader dead, the nation cried out to see the fallen President. Never had any nation so mourned a fallen leader. Lincoln's friends and admirers were heartbroken and even his numerous critics, who had mocked him in life, had ridiculed him as a baboon, and had damned him as an ignorant backwoodsman, now lamented his death and grieved for the country. It was the first time in the history of America that a President had been felled by an assassin's bullet and this was seen as a tragic event in every corner of the Union.

Telegrams began to pour into the War Department from the cities and towns that had wished him well on his journey four years before. Now they begged Stanton to send Lincoln back to them. Once the news spread that the President would make the long westward journey home to Illinois, a groundswell of public opinion clamored for his inaugural trip to be re-created in reverse. The assassination of the President was a national tragedy and yet the American people could not come from all over the country to see Lincoln's body and attend his funeral – so why couldn't Abraham Lincoln come to them?

It was possible to do what they wanted. It would require a special train properly fitted to transport the body, a military escort to guard Lincoln's corpse around the clock to make sure that the remains were treated with utmost dignity; coordination between the military, railroad, and the major commercial lines; cooperation between the War Department and state and local governments; and the resources and will to do it. Stanton believed it could be done. There was only one obstacle – the President's grieving, tightly wound, and unpredictable widow. The plan would be impossible without her explicit consent.

Stanton carefully broached the subject with Mary. He outlined the plan, asking her to try and assuage the people's profound sadness by allowing the President's body to take an extended route that would take him through Maryland, Pennsylvania, New Jersey, New York State, then turning west through Ohio, Indiana, Illinois, Chicago, and across the prairie to Springfield. The route would take many days. The exact duration of the extended trip would depend on the number of times the train stopped for water, fuel, and public ceremonies along the way. Stanton promised that if she agreed, he and his aides would handle all of the details.

There was one more thing. The people wanted to see their President, not just his closed coffin. They wanted to look on his face, which meant an open casket. Mary had consented to this at the Washington ceremonies, but an open casket all the way to Springfield, a trip of more than 1,600 miles? In warm weather, without refrigeration, it would test the limits of the embalmer's art. Mary thought the idea seemed morbid and ghoulish, but a grand, national funeral pageant that affirmed her husband's greatness appealed to her. She consented to the trip.

Plans for the epic journey – unlike anything America had seen before – began immediately.

Lincoln's funeral services were planned for Wednesday, April 19, but the President's adoring public was allowed to view the body the day before. When the doors of the White House were opened, people crushed inside, inching past the body, weeping, and speaking to the President, whose head lay on a white pillow with a faint smile frozen on his pale and distorted face. By the end of the day, an estimated 25,000 people had crowded past the mahogany coffin.

As final visitors filed past the coffin, carpenters anxiously loitered nearby, anxious to get started on their work. They impatiently watched the public file past, waiting for the last one to leave so that the doors could be closed and locked behind them. If the public had its way, the viewing would have continued through the night. Thousands of people were turned away so that crews could begin preparing the East Room for the funeral. Disappointed mourners would have one more chance to view the remains, after they were transferred to the capitol.

A seating dilemma had presented itself for the funeral. There was no way to fit enough chairs into the room for everyone that had to attend, so they decided not to have chairs at all. Only a few important guests, along with the Lincoln family, would have chairs. The rest of the assembly would be seated on hastily built bleachers, which meant that at least 600 guests could be packed into the East Room. The White House thrummed with activity after the viewing as men carried stacks of lumber into the East Room, where carpenters sawed, hammered and nailed them into bleachers.

On Wednesday, Lincoln's body rested in the East Room, which was now hushed and dim and draped in hundreds of yards of black crepe. Upstairs, Mary was locked in her room, too deranged from grief and hysterical weeping to attend the services. Tad tried to console her. Though stricken himself, Tad would throw his arms about his mother's neck and plead with her not to cry, but it was no use. Mary was simply too crazed to be able to pull herself together, even for her son.

Services began around 11:00 a.m. To thwart gate-crashers, funeral guests were not allowed direct entry into the Executive Mansion. Instead, guards directed the bearers of the 600 coveted tickets, printed on heavy card stock, next door, to the Treasury Department. From there, they crossed a narrow, elevated wooden footbridge, built just for the occasion, which led into the White House. As guests entered the building, none of them knew what to expect. The East Room overwhelmed them with its decorations, flowers, and the catafalque.

The scene lives on today only in the written accounts of those who were there and a few artists's sketches and newspaper illustrations. No one took a photograph, before or during the funeral. It could have been done. Alexander Gardner had photographed more complex scenes, including the second inaugural, where he took close-ups of the East Front platform and one of his operators had managed to take a long view of the Capitol dome while Lincoln was reading his address. Edwin Stanton had failed to invite Gardner, or his rival Matthew Brady, to preserve the history of Lincoln's funeral.

The guests crowded into the East Room. Robert Lincoln, his face ashen and grave, was wearing his military uniform and he stood at the foot of the coffin. He tightly held the hand of his little brother, and Tad trembled, his face swollen with tears. General Ulysses S. Grant, a black mourning band on one arm, sat alone at the other end, staring at a cross of lilies. He began to cry, unable to believe what had happened. He would always maintain that this was the saddest day of his life. By now, nearly all of Washington was there, including President Andrew Johnson and his Cabinet, Charles Sumner and his congressional colleagues, numerous military officials, Lincoln's personal cavalry escort, his secretaries and bodyguards, and mayors and government delegates from across the country.

Four different ministers spoke and prayed for Lincoln and after that, 12 reserve corps sergeants carried his casket out to the funeral car. As they stepped out into the bright, sunlit day, church bells all over the city began to toll. From the forts that still surrounded the city, cannons began to boom. Throngs of people lined Pennsylvania Avenue and thousands more peered from windows and roofs along the parade route. Many of these people had been there for hours, waiting for Lincoln's casket to appear. Federal troops moved into formation to accompany the hearse, which now waited outside the White House. The coffin was placed on a high platform, surrounded by glass and elevated so that everyone could see. Soon, the hearse moved forward, pulled by six white horses, all festooned with black cloth and decoration.

The procession moved in a slow, measured cadence, a detachment of African-American troops in the lead. The hearse was followed by a rider-less horse, befitting a fallen general, and all walked to the steady muffled beat of drums. The lines swelled with wounded soldiers, who left their hospital beds and marched along, ignoring their pain as they hobbled after their slain leader. There was a procession of colored citizens, walking in lines that stretched from curb to curb, holding hands as they walked along.

Lincoln's body was then carried to the Capitol building and placed in the rotunda. An honor guard took up position around it and remained in place until the next morning. Shortly after the sun appeared, wounded soldiers were allowed to file past the casket and pay their final respects. After this, the viewing was opened to the public once more. The crowds were so large that the soldiers outside had to remove wooden barricades around the building so that no one would be injured. It was said that more than 3,000 people per hour filed past the coffin before the doors were finally closed at midnight.

On Friday, April 21, one week after the assassination, Edwin Stanton, Ulysses S. Grant, Gideon Welles, Attorney General James Speed, Postmaster General William Dennison, several senators, members of a delegation from Illinois, and various army officers arrived at the Capitol at 6:00 a.m. to escort Lincoln's coffin to the funeral train. Soldiers removed the coffin from the catafalque in the rotunda and carried it down the stairs of the East Front. Four companies of the Twelfth Veteran Reserve Corps stood by to escort the hearse to the train. This was not meant to be a grand procession. There were no drums, no band, and no cavalcade of thousands of marchers. It was a short trip from the Capitol to the Baltimore & Ohio Railroad station, just a few blocks away, but this did not deter the crowds. Several thousand onlookers lined the route and crowded the station's entrance.

Earlier that morning, another hearse had arrived at the station. It had come from Oak Hill Cemetery in Georgetown and carried the body of Willie Lincoln, the president's son. When the soldiers carried Abraham Lincoln about the private railroad car at 7:30 a.m., Willie was already there, waiting for him. Lincoln had planned to collect the boy himself and take his coffin home when his term in office ended, but now two coffins shared the presidential car.

The railroad car that would transport Lincoln's body across the country was never meant to be a funeral car. It had been built to be a luxurious vehicle intended for the living president's use, but Lincoln never saw it or rode in it. The elegant interior, finished with walnut and oak, and upholstered with crimson silk, contained three rooms – a stateroom, a drawing room, and a parlor or dining room. A corridor ran the length of the car and offered access to each room. The exterior was painted a dark brown, hand-rubbed to a high sheen, and on both sides of the car hung identical oval paintings of an eagle and the coat of arms of the United States. As soon as Stanton knew that Lincoln's body would be carried home to Illinois by railroad, he authorized the military to modify the car, decorate it with symbols of mourning, and build two catafalques so that it could accommodate the coffins of the President and his son.

Before the train could leave the station, members of the honor guard took their places beside Lincoln's coffin. Under protocols established by Stanton and General Edward Townsend, the president was never to be left alone. The hearse and the horses that had carried Lincoln's body to the train were not boarded. Instead, in every city where the train was stopping for funeral services, local officials were required to provide a suitable hearse to transport the coffin from the train to the site of the ceremonies.

A pilot engine departed the station 10 minutes ahead of the funeral train to inspect the tracks ahead and then, with five minutes to spare, Lincoln's secretaries, John Nicolay and John Hay, arrived from the White House and boarded the train to be sure that all was in order. In all, about 150 men were on the train that morning, including 29 men from the Veteran Reserve Corps who would serve as the guard of honor. There were also a number of military officers, senators, congressmen, delegates from Illinois, four governors, seven newspaper reporters and David Davis, an old friend of Lincoln's and a justice on the U.S. Supreme Court.

With so many dignitaries arriving at the station, two of the train's most important passengers went unnoticed. In the days to come, the success of the funeral train would depend on their work. To make sure that all ran smoothly, they had to have unfettered access to the President's corpse at any time day or night. Those two men were embalmer Dr. Charles Brown and undertaker Frank Sands. For the next 13 days, they had to try and control the decomposing flesh of Abraham Lincoln.

The train left the station in Washington at exactly 8:00 a.m. Over the course of the next two weeks, the train steamed north and then westward, passing through the greatest crowds ever assembled in America at that time. Reporters followed its passage, telegraphing details to their newspapers back home of the strange, circus-like atmosphere surrounding the funeral train. It is believed that seven million northerners looked upon

Lincoln's hearse or coffin and that at least one million actually looked upon his silent face. Ninety different funeral songs were composed in his honor while thousands (or even millions) cried, fainted, took to their beds, and even committed suicide in the frenzy of Lincoln's passing

The first stop for Lincoln's funeral train was Baltimore, where officials feared that a southern influence in the city would mar the events, but they did not. It was scheduled to stop many times for official honors, processions, ceremonies and viewings, but, for the most part, those plans were merely words and timetables printed on paper. The official documents said nothing about the things to come – the spontaneous bonfires, torches, floral arches, hand-painted signs, banners, and masses of people who haunted the tracks at all hours of the day and night. No official in Washington had ordered these strange public manifestations. Edwin Stanton never expected the train to literally take on a life of its own.

At each stop, it took on the tone and temper of the town and its people. The train was almost like a battery, soaking up the energy of the place. The more time that it spent on the road, and the greater distance it traveled, the more it absorbed the emotions of the nation's pride and grief. It became more than the funeral train of just one man and evolved into a symbol of American sorrow – about the death of a president and the cost of the great Civil War. It came to represent a mournful homecoming for all of the lost men. In the hearts of the grief-stricken American people, an army of the dead -- and not just its Commander-in- Chief – came home aboard that train.

After Baltimore, the train passed into Pennsylvania and people began to line the tracks and watch it pass. Little towns were filled in honor of the President and local bands played funeral dirges as the train went by. The old and sick were carried to the stations to see the train pass by and babies were held up high to get a glimpse of it.

In Harrisburg, thousands waited all night in the rain for a glimpse of Lincoln the following morning. Unfortunately, violent thunderstorms had descended on the city, but despite the rain, the massive crowds still came. The crowds followed the hearse and its military escort to the House of Representatives at the State Capitol, where a black-draped catafalque was waiting. The procession took so long that the casket was not opened for viewing until late that evening. Thousands passed in a double line until the next morning when the funeral train once again prepared to leave. Before the casket was closed, though, the undertaker was forced to re-chalk Lincoln's face to hide the growing discoloration. Lincoln had become America's first public embalming and it would be some time before the methods of preservation would be perfected.

In Philadelphia, more than 500,000 people were already waiting at Independence Hall when the train arrived on Saturday, April 22. It was in Philadelphia that a new aspect was added to the viewing of Lincoln --- violence. For the first time, people were actually hurt in the frantic crush to get into Independence Hall and see the President's body. The trip into the city had been orderly.

Thousands had come out beside the tracks to stand in silence, or kneel, while the train passed. All the shops had closed and farms stood silent and deserted in Lincoln's honor. For miles before the Philadelphia station, there were no gaps in the crowd, just solid lines. The train arrived at Broad Street station in late afternoon, more than two hours ahead of schedule, but then the careful organization of the city officials began to go to pieces.

It took nearly two hours to get the procession under way and afterward, the city would claim that it offered the most gigantic display of all. Eleven military divisions marched to the inevitable booming of cannons, tolling of bells, firing of guns, roll of muffled drums and eerie funeral dirges. At the square, when the Old State House was passed, a large transparency was uncovered --- a picture of Lincoln with a background of a huge coffin, spectacularly lighted by gas jets that formed letters that spelled out "He Still Lives." The coffin was carried to the East Wing of Independence Hall, where the Declaration of Independence had been signed. The hall was filled with flowers, emitting what the newspapers called a "delicious perfume." Those accounts failed to describe the practical purpose of the sweet-smelling flowers, but they were there for a reason. Lincoln had been dead for a week and the embalmers were fighting against a ticking clock. They had slowed but they could not stop the decaying flesh – and fragrant flowers masked the odor.

The viewing that night was by invitation only and handpicked people had been given cards by the mayor. As these special guests departed during the early morning hours, they passed long lines of the general public, which were already forming to be admitted hours later. The exhausted throngs waited all night and by Sunday morning, the entire city was on edge. When pickpockets began to terrorize a portion of the line, it surged into a mob, pressing against the guide ropes. Then the ropes were cut --- by "villains" the newspapers later said --- and bedlam broke out. People who had been almost to the doors were sent back by the police to the end of the nearly three-mile-long double lines to wait for another six or seven hours. The crowd surged out of control and the police fought to keep order. Bonnets were pulled from women's heads and their hair turned loose, dresses were torn away and ripped, all to a chorus of women's screams. As many of the young women fainted, they had to be extricated from the lines and passed over the people's heads. One woman had her arm broken and word got out that two little boys were dead but were finally revived. The closer people got to Lincoln, the more impassioned they became. The police refused to let people stop for even a second to view the body, insisting that they keep moving at all times. Even with these precautions, a number of women tried to climb over the wooden barricade to touch the president or to kiss his face.

It was all finally over early on Monday morning and the casket was returned to the train. It steamed on toward New York, where ceremonies had begun the day before. The entire city, it seemed, had been draped in black and in the hours before the train's arrival, the streets of the city became impassable. The police and military fought to keep them open, but it was no use.

Thousands of people lined the tracks on the journey to New York City. In the early morning darkness of Monday, April 24, the train passed through New Jersey, stopping briefly in Trenton and Newark. The train arrived in Jersey City a few hours later. Crowds had been gathering there since early morning. Only ladies and their escorts were allowed into the gallery at the depot, where the large clock had been stopped at the precise moment of Lincoln's death. When the train arrived, a German singing group thundered forth with a funeral dirge. The bodies of the President and his son were ferried across the river to the magnificent hearse that had been built by New York.

Lincoln's body was taken to City Hall and more than 600,000 spectators accompanied it while more than 150,000 stood in line for a glimpse of the president. The honor guard had a full-time job on their hands trying to keep people from touching Lincoln and trying to keep women from kissing his face and hands. Although no rioting broke out, as it did in Philadelphia, the police had their hands full with surging crowds, most of whom were beaten back with clubs, and with pickpockets, who freely roamed the area, stealing at will.

During the viewing at City Hall, some people tried to do more than touch Lincoln. Some of them actually wanted to place mementoes in the coffin. Such practices, if tolerated, would have turned Lincoln's coffin into a traveling cabinet of curiosities that would have weighed more than the President's corpse.

That night, after the doors were closed, the embalmer brushed a heavy coating of dust from Lincoln's face, beard and clothing. He also rearranged his facial features, which had become twisted from exposure.

The coffin was closed at 11:00 a.m. on Tuesday. The final procession back to the train became New York's moment of glory. Lincoln's newly built hearse, pulled by 16 gray horses, was said to have nearly paralyzed all who saw it. Its platform was huge --- 14-feet long and almost 7-feet wide --- and on the roof of the canopy was a gold and white Temple of Liberty with a half-masted flag on its crown. Inside of the canopy was white fluted satin that matched the inside trimmings of the coffin, and hanging down from it, so that it would hang directly above the casket, was a glittering gilt eagle with its wings spread. It was an amazing work of art and would remain the most elaborate creation on the funeral route.

Led by a squad of mounted police, who made sure the route was clear, it started off with 100 dragoons with black and white plumes and red, yellow and blue facings on their uniforms. They were followed by military officers and their staffs and then the magnificent hearse. Behind that were more than 11,000 soldiers, Irishmen in bright green with black rosettes in their lapels, Zouaves with baggy red trousers and black ribbons on their chests, military and government representatives from foreign countries and eight divisions of civilians. One of them was made up from the trades --- cigar-makers, waiters, cooks clerks, carpenters and others --- and there were divisions of medical men, lawyers, members of the press, the Century Club, the Union League, Freemasons, Civic Societies and finally, nearly 300 African-Americans.

The procession took nearly four hours to pass each point on its route. The streets were jammed with spectators, and it was said that window seats could be rented for $50 from those who lived in the apartment buildings along the path. All through the afternoon, church bells and fire bells tolled, bands wailed, guns boomed, and people wept for the great and fallen leader. Eventually, the train moved on to Albany, leaving thousands disappointed. Many who did not get a chance to see the President boarded trains and planned to try again in Chicago or in Springfield. The Springfield delegates, who were accompanying the train, realized in horror just how many people could be descending on the small city. One of the delegates hurried to Springfield to prepare for the worst.

After leaving the city, the train steamed across the countryside toward Albany. It passed scores of small towns along the way, where people gathered to watch it pass. Each of the towns had gone to enormous trouble to build a display, an arch or to inscribe a huge motto for the train as it passed. At towns where there was no station, there was often a minister and his parishioners, kneeling or singing a hymn. At Yonkers, the people lined up and the men all raised their hats. At Tarryton, a gathering of young women appeared, all dressed in white, save for black sashes, creating an effect both chaste and mournful. At Peekskill, the train stopped as a band played a dirge and guns fired. At Poughkeepsie, the train made another stop. The hilltop there was black with people, guns were fired, and church bells and fire bells clanged with a fury. The train also stopped at Garrison's Landing, opposite the U.S. Military Academy at West Point. The corps of cadets assembled to honor their fallen commander in chief. They passed through the funeral car and saluted. It was now growing dark and as the train continued on toward Albany, torches and bonfires illuminated the tracks.

At Hudson, thousands of people gathered to see the train. General Townsend described the scenes as "one of the most weird ever witnessed." Along the Hudson River, people assembled with torches, illuminating the bizarre tableau they had created. Beneath an arch, hung with black and white drapery and evergreen wreaths was a scene that represented a coffin resting on a dais. A female figure in white, mourning over the coffin, stood on one side while a soldier and a sailor stood at the other end. While a band of young women dressed in white sang a dirge, two others entered the funeral car, placed flowers on the President's coffin, knelt for a moment of silence and then quietly withdrew. Townsend noted that the solemnity of the scene was "intensified by the somber lights of the torches, at that dead hour of night."

It was approaching midnight when the train entered Albany, marking an end to one of the strangest legs of the trip.

At noon, April 26, Albany's grand parade got under way with a specially built catafalque, marchers, bands, tolling bells, and huge crowds of people.

It was while the funeral train was in Albany that a disquieting incident that had occurred in New York City reached the ears of Edwin Stanton. As was the usual, General Townsend had telegraphed Stanton when leaving the city to let him know that all was well. But his telegram did not mention what had taken place while Lincoln's remains were on view at City Hall. When Stanton learned of the incident by reading newspapers later that night, he became enraged and dispatched an angry telegram that threatened to ruin the reputation and military career of the man he had personally chosen to command the funeral train.

Stanton wrote: "I see by the New York papers this evening that a photograph of the corpse of President Lincoln was allowed taken yesterday at New York. I cannot sufficiently express my surprise and disapproval of such an act while the body was in your charge. You will report what officers of the funeral escort were or ought to have been on duty at the time this was done, and immediately relieve them and order them to Washington. You will also direct the provost-marshal to go to the photographer, seize and destroy the plates and any pictures and engravings that may have been made, and consider yourself responsible if the offense is repeated." Stanton ordered Major Eckert at the War Department to make sure that it was sent and hand-delivered to Townsend that very night.

Stanton had assumed, no doubt, that close-up images had been made of Lincoln's face. That was not an unusual custom in the nineteenth century. But Stanton was likely thinking about the condition of Lincoln's body. By the time he was photographed in New York, he had been dead for nine days. Mortuary science of the era could not preserve his body indefinitely. The undertakers attended to the body aboard the train, but there were limits as to what they could do. Stanton undoubtedly feared that horrific images depicting Lincoln's face in a state of gruesome decay would be distributed to the public.

Stanton's telegram did not reach Townsend until the morning of April 26. He was stunned by its contents and knew how angry Stanton had to be. It was Townsend himself who had allowed Lincoln's corpse to be photographed. He decided, before others could report the details of what he had done, to confess and accept the consequences. He immediately telegraphed Stanton and took responsibility for the well-meaning blunder. Stanton calmed down and left Townsend in command. The train was on the move, in the middle of a complicated cross-country journey, and no one on the train possessed greater organizational skills than Townsend. He sent him a reply and filled the man with guilt by stating that the taking of photographs had been expressly forbidden by Mrs. Lincoln. Stanton added, "I am apprehensive that her feelings and the feelings of her family will be greatly wounded."

Townsend was upset that it appeared he had disobeyed an order from the martyred President's widow, but even so, he had not admitted to all he had done. It was bad enough that he had allowed the photographs. It was even worse that he had posed in the pictures while standing next to President Lincoln's body. Stanton might have considered this perceived attempt at personal publicity unforgivable. But Townsend did not see it that way. The remains had been arranged at City Hall at the head of a stairway, where the people could ascend on one side and descend on the other. The body was in an alcove, draped in black, and just at the edge of a rotunda formed of American flags and mourning drapery. The photographer was in a gallery 20 feet higher than the body and forty feet away from it. There was no equipment to make the camera seem closer than it was in those days. It offered a distant view. Townsend stood at one end of the coffin and Admiral Davis stood at the other. No one else was in view. The effect of the picture was taking in the scene as a whole, not offering the features of the corpse.

General Townsend was not the only one worried about the situation. The man who had photographed Lincoln, Thomas Gurney, proprietor of one of Manhattan's most prominent studios, T. Gurney & Son, was also concerned. He had taken unprecedented, newsworthy and commercially viable photographs. No other American president had been photographed in death and no one – not the famous Mathew Brady nor Alexander Gardner nor any of the photographers along the funeral train route – had succeeded in photographing the President in his coffin.

Gurney hoped to gain publicity by distributing prints of the photograph to the press as newspaper woodcuts and to reproduce the photo for sale to the public. On April 26, Gurney sent an urgent telegram, not to Stanton, but to a man he thought might be more sympathetic, assistant secretary of war, Charles A. Dana. Gurney also reached out to Henry Ward Beecher, the widely-known clergyman, abolitionist and author, as well as Henry Raymond, the famous editor of the New York Times. He asked them to lobby Stanton and prevent the seizure and destruction of the glass-plate negatives. They agreed and Beecher and Raymond both telegraphed the War

Department. It earned Gurney a temporary reprieve, of sorts. A telegram from the War Department arrived at Gurney's studio, saving the negatives from destruction for the time being, but only if Gurney surrendered all the glass plates and agreed to abide by Stanton's decision once he determined whether or not to smash them.

Gurney surrendered the glass-plate negatives, plus all of the photographs that he had already printed from them. He had no choice. In the aftermath of Lincoln's assassination, emotions in the country were running high. Scores of people had been arrested, shot, stabbed and lynched for making Anti-Lincoln statements. During this turbulent time, Gurney had no legal avenue to pursue. If he failed to surrender them voluntarily, the War Department would have raided his studio and seized them. He complied. The next day, an army general notified Stanton from New York that the offending images were in government custody.

Stanton's suppression of the photographs did not succeed entirely. He had wanted to prevent Gurney's images from surfacing in any form, but the photographer had already gotten the prints into the hands of a few artists. At least two newspapers printed front-page interpretations of the scene and Currier & Ives published a fine engraving based partly on Gurney's work. But Gurney's negatives were never seen again. Perhaps Edwin Stanton had them brought to his office in Washington and, after viewing them, smashed them into pieces. Perhaps he put them away in some secret place, where, to this day, they languish in some dusty and forgotten War Department file box, never to be seen again.

Stanton could not resist preserving one image of Lincoln's corpse for himself. Almost a century after the President's death and burial, a sole surviving photographic print made from one of Gurney's negatives was discovered by a student in an old archive. It was traced back to Stanton's personal files. Perhaps he saved it for history. Or perhaps he never intended for it to be seen and to remain his private memento – a vivid reminder of the spring of 1865.

On Wednesday afternoon, the funeral train left Albany and steamed through New York state. Late in the evening, the train made a short stop at Syracuse, where veteran soldiers paid honors, a choir sang hymns, and a little girl handed a small bouquet to a congressman on the train. A note attached to the flowers read: "The last tribute from Mary Virginia Raynor, a little girl of three years of age."

At Rochester on April 27, military men, local officials, and former President Millard Fillmore met the train. The former president rode to the next stop, which was Buffalo, where Lincoln's casket was taken from the train for more services. Thousands filed past the coffin, but between the dirges, the silence was oppressive and the "utter decorum" and "remarkable order" were somehow not as much of a tribute as the wild straining to get near the coffin or to touch the President's hand, as had occurred in other cities.

The coffin was closed that evening and Lincoln's body was returned to the train. It steamed on through New York and into the darkness of the night. Townsend knew that the train had begun to leave behind waves of emotion that swelled by the hour. He later wrote, "As the president's remains went farther westward, where the people more especially claimed him as their own, the intensity of feeling seemed if possible to grow deeper. The night journey of the 27th and 28th was all through torches, bonfires, mourning drapery, mottoes and solemn music."

The train pushed on through North Hamburg, Lakeview, Angola, and Silver Creek. Just after midnight, the train passed through Dunkirk on Lake Erie. There, 36 young women, representing the states of the Union, appeared on the railway platform. They were dressed in white, and each wore a broad, black scarf on her shoulder and held an American flag in her right hand. The tableau was so irresistible that when officials in other cities read about it in the newspapers, they copied the idea for their local tributes.

The train later passed through Brocton and then stopped in Westfield, where, during Lincoln's inaugural journey, he visited with Grace Bedell, a little girl who during the 1860 campaign had written him a letter that encouraged him to grow a beard. She told him that it would make him more appealing to women, who would then, Grace promised, make their husbands and brothers vote for him. Lincoln grew the beard and won the election. Now, four years later, a delegation of five women, led by a woman whose husband had been killed the previous year during Grant's futile assault at Cold Harbor, came aboard bearing a wreath of flowers and a cross. Sobbing, they approached Lincoln's closed casket and were allowed to touch it. They "considered it a rare privilege to kiss the coffin." They knelt and each in turn kissed the coffin. Kissing the coffin, with its solid barrier of wood and lead, was a desperately futile gesture, but it never failed to move those who watched the action to tears.

The train crossed the Ohio state line and passed through Kingsville, Ashtabula, Geneva, Madison, Perry, Painesville, and Wickcliffe, where Governor John Brough received the funeral party. General Joseph Hooker, now commanding the Northern Department of Ohio, also boarded the train there. Although Lincoln had once given command of the Army of the Potomac to the boastful general, Hooker failed him several times. After the disaster at Chancellorsville in May 1863, Lincoln fired him, but Hooker never lost his personal affection for the President. When the funeral train crossed the Ohio line into Indiana, Hooker did not disembark. He stayed with Lincoln all the way to Springfield.

Vast crowds stood on the hills outside of Cleveland as the train passed beneath prepared arches that bore sad inscriptions. Of all of the funerals held, Cleveland's was the strangest so far. The funeral was both a solemn wake and a theatrical pageant of flowers, with the city showing its appreciation for the President by introducing an Oriental note to the proceedings. In the city park, a huge Chinese pagoda was erected for Lincoln's coffin to be displayed on for what turned out to be more than 100,000 mourners.

Thirty-six cannons fired a national salute to the president. At that moment, noted the reporters who looked out of the window of the car, a bizarre scene was taking place – perhaps the strangest of the journey so far. A woman, identified in the press only as "Miss Fields of Wilson Street," had erected an arch of evergreens near the tracks. As the train passed, Miss Fields, wearing a costume, stood under the arch and struck poses and attitudes of the Goddess of Liberty in mourning.

The train arrived on the outskirts of Cleveland in the early hours of Friday, just one week after leaving Washington. As it moved slowly into the city, officials on board the train saw crowds of people on the hillsides and high up, a young girl draped in a flag under an archway that read "Abraham Lincoln." People had flocked to the city from all over northern Ohio, western Pennsylvania and eastern Michigan and boatloads of them had arrived by water from Detroit. All of the ladies in attendance had been warned to leave the hoops for their skirts at home --- the breakage of such attire by the throng, officials said, would be swift and total. With the thousands in attendance, standing in the pouring rain, there was not a hint of disorder.

Legions of marchers and mourners descended on the city park, with its Chinese Pagoda, built for the President. The wooden structure was eccentric, to say the least. It was an amazing confection of wood, canvas, silk, cloth, festoons, rosettes, golden eagles bearing the national shield at each end, and "immense plumes of black crepe." As with all of the other venues along the journey, the interior was stuffed with flowers. Evergreens covered the walls, and thick matting carpeted the floor to deaden into silence the sound of all footsteps. Over the roof, stretched between two flagpoles, was a motto from Horace: "Extinctus amabitur idem" (Dead he will be loved all the same).

The embalmer opened the coffin and judged the body ready for viewing. The journey was taking its toll on the corpse. Lincoln's face turned darker by the day and the embalmer tried to conceal this with a fresh application of chalk-white potions.

All through the day and night, people came, thousands upon thousands of them, before the gates to the park were closed at 10:00 p.m. An hour later, the coffin was carried by hearse back to the train.

The rain continued to fall as the train traveled from Cleveland to the Ohio state capital, Columbus. But the foul weather did not keep people from coming to watch the train pass along the route. Bonfires and torches were lit, buildings were draped in mourning, bells tolled, flags flew at half-mast, and the sorrowful inhabitants stood in groups, rain and tears streaming down their faces, as the cortege moved slowly by.

The city of Columbus also offered a funeral of flowers. People had roses in their hands, which they tossed under the wheels of the hearse as it passed, and invalid soldiers from the Soldier's Hospital had literally covered the street near the hospital for several hundred yards with lilac blossoms.

The Columbus hearse was a somber vehicle, drawn by six white horses, but it did have one aspect to it that would have amused Lincoln himself. On one side of the dais, in silver block letters, was the name "Lincoln." The President tried, whenever possible, to avoid the obvious. When, in the spring of 1864, he had been asked to sign a letter presenting a sword to General Dix, Lincoln signed his name and then was asked to add "President of the United States." His answer, putting down his pen, was, "Well, I don't think I'll say 'this is a horse'." When the coffin was placed on a dais at the State Capitol building, the platform was noticed to have been also fitted with the same helpful identification. Lincoln would have gotten a chuckle out of this bit of tragic absurdity.

The Columbus procession moved through drapes and flowers and mottos from the city to the sounds of guns firing, bells ringing, and the muffled beat of drums. The hook and ladder car of the fire department carried 42 young ladies on it, all singing hymns. The coffin was placed on the dais, which had no canopy and no flags. However, instead of black velvet, the surface of it was a carpet of moss and tender green leaves, which let off a fragrant aroma as the casket sank into it. The people gathered in the rotunda watched in awe as the undertaker unscrewed the coffin lid, made a slight adjustment to the position of the body and then made a motion that the viewing could begin. People began to stream by and their passing was in complete silence. A carpet had been laid in the hall so that the shuffling of feet and the click of shoe leather would not be heard. For the eighth time, thousands of Americans said goodbye to their fallen President.

In the press accounts of the funeral train, little mention was made of Willie Lincoln. His coffin was never unloaded from the train. He did not ride in the hearse with his father in any of the funeral processions. His closed casket – he had been dead for three years – did not lie next to his father's at the public viewings. But in Columbus, Willie was not forgotten. General Townsend was the recipient of the gesture: "While at Columbus, I received a note from a lady, wife of one of the principal citizens, accompanying a little cross made of wild violets. The note said that the writer's little girls had gone to the woods in the early morning and gathered the flowers with which they had wrought the cross. They desired that it might be laid on little Willie's coffin, 'they felt so sorry for him.'"

From Columbus, the train steamed on toward Indiana, crossing the state line in the middle of the night. More scenes appeared along the line while in Ohio. At Woodstock, there were 500 citizens waiting beside the tracks and a contingent of young women was allowed to board the train and lay flowers in the funeral car. At Urbana, more than 3,000 people surrounded a huge, floral cross as the train steamed on toward Indiana.

At Richmond, Indiana, the first town across the border, the church bells of the town rang for an hour as the train arrived and over 15,000 people greeted the funeral with pantomimes, scenes, and stage effects that must have looked both ghastly and somewhat horrifying to the party looking out from the railroad car windows. One such display featured a beautiful young woman who was illuminated by red, white and blue lights over a mock coffin, creating one of the most eerie displays on the funeral train's journey.

The funeral train reached Indianapolis near midnight, arriving during a torrential rainstorm. At first, it was hoped that if the rain stopped, the procession could go on during the afternoon. However, the rain continued to fall, increasing in power from minute to minute, until the black decorations on every house hung soggy and the black dye formed dark streaks on the front of stone buildings. Reluctantly, the huge Indianapolis procession had to be canceled and the time devoted to it was set aside for viewing instead.

All of the way from the train depot to the State House, soldiers were lined up at attention, forming two long lines of blue uniforms and drawn swords. The hearse was pulled by eight white horses, six of which had pulled Lincoln as the President-elect a few years before. They took the coffin into State House square and under a large arch to which portraits of Lincoln, Indiana Governor Oliver Perry Morton, General Grant, General Sherman and Admiral Farragut had been affixed. On the points of it were busts of George Washington, Daniel Webster, Henry Clay, and Lincoln. The busts were all crowned with laurel wreaths.

The first to view Lincoln were 5,000 Sunday School scholars and the last were the Colored Masons and hundreds of African-American citizens who each carried a copy of the Emancipation Proclamation. The casket lay under a black velvet canopy, which was sprinkled with golden stars. The mourners all saw a coffin that was heaped with flowered crosses and wreaths, which is interesting in itself. There, on this epic cross-country journey, an American tradition was created. Prior to Lincoln's funeral, it was not customary to send flowers to funerals. With the death of a beloved President, many people searched their hearts about the best way to express their sympathy and thousands of them decided upon flowers. Although with the best of intentions, the sheer numbers of flowers sent to Lincoln were greatly overdone, emptying the contents of each city's hothouses. The colors ran heavily to red, white and blue, which would have pleased a President who stated that he felt emotional each time he looked at the flag. In Springfield, there would be a tremendous red heart, covered with thousands of red roses, that would travel with the coffin all of the way to the tomb.

When the viewing was completed, the coffin was escorted back to the train with Governor Morton and most of the population of Indianapolis following behind. The governor had greeted and entertained Lincoln when he was traveling to Washington as the President-elect and he watched his casket leave the state with great sorrow.

With Indianapolis behind, the train steamed on toward Illinois. There was a massive funeral planned in Chicago and then, it would go on to Lincoln's home town in Springfield. But due to an unexpected delay, there was to be one more funeral, an impromptu service at the depot in Michigan City, Indiana. The funeral train was supposed to travel straight through and arrive in Chicago during the late morning hours of Monday, May 1. But it was forced to wait for one hour in Michigan City for a committee of more than 100 important Chicagoans who were coming out to escort the train into the city. The residents of Michigan City made the most of the unexpected stop, especially since the rain of the past few days had cleared to brilliant sunshine. Now, the occupants of the train were greeted by the depot arch of evergreens and roses, decorated with black ribbons and "tasteful" portraits of Lincoln.

The 300 weary mourners that traveled with the funeral were taken off the train for a large breakfast in the station. After that, the rule was broken about not opening the coffin except in the cities that were putting on funerals. The townspeople were allowed to pass through the car and view Lincoln and then a small funeral service was held with young women singing hymns.

Abraham Lincoln had always been among the first to alter procedures and break rules on the spur of the moment for something better. His office hours were always flexible and he often received people at all hours of the day and night. He was the bane of all who tried to protect his time from the people. The people wanted so little, he often said, and there was so little that he could give – he must see them. Because of this, the Michigan City meeting with the people would have gladdened Lincoln's heart.

Over the course of May 1 and 2, 1865, one of the grandest funerals of the entire route was held in Chicago when the train arrived in the city and thousands turned out to see the body of the slain President. It was in Chicago where ghost remnants of the Lincoln train are still believed to manifest on the anniversary of its arrival in the city.

Chicago spent more than $15,000 to create a spectacular arch, design a hearse, and build decorations for the funeral. When the casket was taken off the train, 36 young women walked beside it and they showered flower petals in all directions. The streets were packed with over 100,000 people as excursion trains had been coming into the city for more than 24 hours, carrying curiosity-seekers from the east. Thousands lined up at the courthouse in the rain and mud to see Lincoln. Exhausted soldiers and police officers recalled that the lines moved less than one foot per hour on Monday and Tuesday. More trains arrived, bringing more people to add to the chaos as at least 125,000 lined up to view the casket. Ambulances came and went, carrying injured onlookers and women who fainted from grief and exhaustion. At one point, a section of wooden sidewalk gave away and plunged hundreds into the mud and water below.

The route of the funeral procession ran through what was the most elegant section of town. It passed down Michigan Avenue first, then along Lake Street, then along Clark to Court House Square, avoiding the world's largest stockyards, the McCormick Reaper Works, and the flour mills. The procession included a legion of clergy with white crosses adorning their black armbands and a division of Zouaves in baggy red pants. There was also a group of captured Confederate soldiers who had taken the oath and now belonged to the Union Army. They were followed by a troop of more than 10,000 schoolchildren, walking with saddened faces and wearing black ribbons in their hair, along with sashes, armbands and badges. In the procession were also immigrants from Germany, France, Ireland and Eastern Europe. They were butchers, bricklayers, tailors, and carpenters, all carrying banners with clumsily worded but unmistakably heartfelt messages about the President. The parade was followed up with a humble, yet unwanted, procession of "colored citizens."

When the hearse finally arrived at the city's Court House, the great bell in the tower began to ring so loudly that it could be heard in the farthest reaches of Chicago. It was not until early evening that the doors were opened to the public and the viewing went on all night long and all through the following day. It was believed that more than 7,000 people per hour passed by the coffin for a quick viewing of the President.

On the evening of May 2, the great procession formed again and by the light of 10,000 torches, the eight black horses drew the hearse with Lincoln's coffin on it back to the railroad depot. The train finally began the last leg of its journey on that night, leaving Chicago and passing under arches which were illuminated with bonfires and decorated with sentiments like "Coming Home," "Bear Him Home Tenderly," and "Home is the Martyr."

The train steamed out of Chicago – and into legend. Over the years, the stories associated with the great funeral train have included a number of ghostly tales from parts of the country that it passed through in 1865. The first sightings of a phantom recreation of the gloomy train were in New York, but they soon spread westward into Ohio, Indiana, and Illinois. One of the earliest reports of the ghost train appeared in New York's *Albany Evening Times*. An article appeared that stated:

Regularly in the month of April, about midnight, the air on the tracks becomes very keen and cutting. On either side of the tracks it is warm and still. Every watchman when he feels the air, slips off the track and sits down to watch. Soon the pilot engine of Lincoln's funeral train passes with long, black streamers and with a band of black instruments playing dirges, grinning skeletons all about.

It passes noiselessly. If it is moonlight, clouds come over the moon as the phantom train goes by. After the pilot engine passes, the Funeral Train itself with flags and streamers rushes past. The track seems covered with black carpet, and the coffin is seen in the center of the car, while all about it in the air and on the train behind are vast numbers of blue-coated men, some with coffins on their backs, others leaning upon them.

If a real train were passing its noise would be hushed as if the phantom train rode over it. Clocks and watches would always stop as the phantom train goes by and when looked at are five to eight minutes behind. Everywhere on the road about April 27, watches and clocks are found to be behind.

More sightings of the phantom funeral train began to enter the regional lore of the places where the train had once passed. Many of the stories are still told, even in areas where the railroads have since faded into oblivion, disrepair, and abandonment. The stories still speak of a phantom train, draped in black, that steams along tracks that are no longer in operation, or have been taken over by companies that did not exist back in 1865.

One such place is Chicago. Many still believe the train makes an appearance each year at the beginning of May, the anniversary of the trains arrival and departure to and from the Windy City. The old tracks, part of the Illinois Central line in the 1860s, is now used by Metra, which brings commuters back and forth to the city from Indiana, skirting along Lake Michigan. In early May, it is not uncommon to find history buffs, Civil War enthusiasts, and ghost hunters camped out around the tracks. The historians are remembering the history that once passed by this place, but the ghost enthusiasts are hoping that history will repeat itself in spectral form. Occasionally, they do not go away disappointed and, according to tradition, if the train does pass by, clocks and watches along its route will cease to work, perhaps never keeping correct time again.

As the train passed out of Chicago, the excitement on board increased. This was the last night of travel. In the morning, the funeral train would reach its destination and the journey would come to an end. Lincoln was in his home state now and the grief of the people huddled around fires along the tracks reached a fever pitch. The passengers on the train saw more signs as they passed in the darkness. "Illinois clasps to her bosom her slain but glorified son, come home," read a sign posted on a house in Lockport. "Go to thy rest," said a sign atop a large arch in Bloomington.

The sun came up on the funeral train as is reached Atlanta and then steamed on towards the south. Emotions ran high aboard the train as it reached Lincoln, a town that had actually been named for the President when he was still a young lawyer. In 1853, Lincoln had been called upon to draft the town's incorporation papers and the founders decided to name the place in his honor. Lincoln responded to the suggestion with his usual humility. "I think you are making a mistake," he said. "I never knew of anything named Lincoln that ever amounted to much." Lincoln then presided over the town's dedication and on April 27, the official story has it that he poured out juice from a watermelon to christen the ground, but other stories say that he spit out a mouthful of seeds as a christening instead. Knowing Lincoln's sense of humor, the latter is probably correct.

During the night of May 2 and during the early morning hours of May 3, the residents of Springfield were restless. They had anticipated Lincoln's homecoming since they had heard the news of his death. After the initial battles with Mary Lincoln about her husband's burial site, it was not clear that Lincoln would return to Springfield at all. But once the citizens knew that Springfield would be his final resting place, they began frenzied preparations.

They had finished hanging the decorations and painting the signs. Crepe and bunting blackened the town. The townspeople had waited 20 days since Lincoln's death and 13 days since the train had left Washington. Beginning on May 3, Springfield would show the nation that no town loved Abraham Lincoln as much as they did. Springfield would be the final stop in the "carnival of death."

On May 3, 1865, the Lincoln Funeral Train, which carried the body of the slain President, arrived in his hometown of Springfield. It was greeted by a mass of people at the station and on the surrounding rooftops. They met the train in silence. Only the sound of weeping could be heard. It seemed the entire city of Springfield had been draped in black but two of the most important buildings to be decorated with mourning weeds were the old State House in the center of the town square, where the body would be placed for public viewing, and the home that Lincoln had owned and lived in for nearly 16 years.

The house now belonged to the Tilton family. Lucien A. Tilton was the president of the Great Western Railway and over the four years of their occupancy, had been kept busy by an estimated 65,000 people who had visited the home and had asked to tour it. Mrs. Tilton was rather apprehensive about what might happen during the Lincoln funeral, but she was a kind-hearted person and had already resolved herself to the fact that she was going to allow people to take grass from the yard, flowers from her garden or leaves from the trees. She had no idea what was coming --- by the end of the funeral services, her lawn and gardens had been stripped, paint had been scraped from her house, and bricks had been carried away from her retaining wall as souvenirs.

The rotunda of the State House had been draped in black cloth and the second floor House of Representatives, where Lincoln was to lie in state, had been renovated with the speaker's podium being removed to allow more people to pass through it. The columns inside had been draped with black, and banners and signs decorated the interior. At the center of the room, a catafalque had been built to hold Lincoln's coffin.

On the morning of May 3, the public viewing was scheduled to begin and thousands of people began to gather outside of the State House. Long before the imposing procession arrived from the station, huge, motionless lines began to form at the north gate. Time ticked by and soon, people began to grow restless --- but there was an unavoidable delay inside. When the undertakers had opened the coffin upstairs, even these hardened professionals were shocked. Thomas Lynch was a courtesy undertaker for the occasion and he had been invited to assist Dr. Charles D. Brown, Lincoln's embalmer. The doors of the room were locked and Dr. Brown, in great distress, informed the other man that he had no idea how to remedy the condition of Lincoln's face – which had turned totally black.

Lynch later wrote, "I asked to have the body turned over to me and the other undertaker readily consented. Making my way with difficulty through the crowds which thronged the corridors of the State House, I called at a neighboring drugstore and procured a rouge chalk and amber, with such brushes as I needed, and returned to the room. I at once set about coloring the President's features, placing the materials on very thick so as to completely hide the discoloration of his skin. In half an hour, I had finished my task and the doors were thrown open to the public."

The crowds were admitted and they walked upstairs to the House of Representatives, where they were sorted out by guards and were sent in groups past Lincoln's casket. Everyone was afforded a few moments to look inside and then they were ushered out through the exit and down the stairs. Very few of those who filed past the coffin shed any tears. They were too shocked by what they saw. But outside on the street, they broke down and wept.

Over the next 24 hours, thousands streamed past the coffin, but these were not the hysterical crowds of New York and Chicago, these were the folks that Lincoln had known and loved in life. They were the people he talked to in the street, laughed with, ate with, and the people he had missed while living in Washington. They were now the people who wept in the streets of the city that he had called home.

On the morning of May 4, the last service was held in Springfield. Robert Lincoln had arrived. His mother and Tad remained behind in Washington. She was still refusing to leave her room – and the White House. Andrew Johnson, Lincoln's successor, was unable to take up residence there because Mary was too distraught to leave.

Shortly before the service, Dr. Charles Brown worked to make Lincoln presentable for one last occasion, dressing him in a clean collar and shirt and applying more powder to his face. He finished just before the procession formed outside. The procession included Robert Lincoln, who rode in a buggy with members of the Todd family; John Hanks, one of Lincoln's only remaining blood relatives; elderly Sarah Lincoln; Thomas Pendel, Lincoln's door man from the White House and a representative of the household servants; and Billy, Lincoln's barber and friend.

The final parade was presided over by General Joseph Hooker and he led "Old Bob," the tired and rider-less old horse that Lincoln had ridden the law circuit on. The parade, like the others before it, was long and marked with music, banners and signs. The journey was to end two miles away at quiet Oak Ridge Cemetery, traveling over what were then rough, country roads.

From time to time, bands broke out in dirges, including four newly composed "Lincoln Funeral Marches." When the music was silent, all that could be heard was the unbroken and ominous roll of drums. Finally, the procession wound under the evergreen arch at the cemetery's entrance, down through the little valley between two ridges, along the small stream and to the receiving tomb that was half-embedded in the hillside. It stood with its iron gates and heavy new vault doors open to receive the President. With no delay, the coffin was carried from the hearse and placed on the marble slab inside of the vault. As soon as the hearse and horses moved away and let the people come close, it could be seen that there were two coffins on the slab. The small casket of Willie Lincoln had been brought to the vault first and was waiting for his father's casket to arrive.

People were standing and sitting behind the tomb on the hillside and along the valley in front of it, with the brook, swollen by the spring rains, dividing the audience. Robert Lincoln stood grimly on one side of the tomb and Ward Hill Lamon, stood nearby. Lamon had stayed close to the President's body all of the way west, skipping meals, and still protecting his old friend from danger. He alternated between helpless weeping and helpless rage over the fact that he had not been present that night at Ford's Theater. On this day in May 1865, Lamon cried unashamedly at the fate of Abraham Lincoln.

As the service began, Reverend A.C. Hubbard began to read Lincoln's words from his second inaugural address. As it drew to a close, Bishop Matthew Simpson of the Methodist Church rose to give his funeral oration. The Bishop's voice was shrill and harsh and people found it unpleasant, but the sound was forgotten when they listened to the words that he spoke of their friend and fallen leader. He spoke so eloquently that people applauded parts of the sermon. When he was finished, a hymn was sung and then Dr. Gurley, who had officiated at the funeral in Washington, delivered the benediction. A final hymn was sung, the words printed on black-edged cards that were distributed throughout the audience, and then the gates to the tomb were closed and locked. The key to the tomb was handed to Robert Lincoln, who passed it to his cousin, John Todd Stuart, who would become the guardian of the President's body for many years to come.

When the key turned in the lock of the President's tomb, the seemingly endless days of travel and the grand spectacles were finally over. Lincoln was laid to rest in Oak Ridge Cemetery in the holding crypt while his tomb and monument were constructed.

Carl Sandburg wrote about those last moments at the crypt better than any witness who was present that day. He wrote:

Evergreen carpeted the stone floor of the vault. On the coffin set in a receptacle of black walnut they arranged flowers carefully and precisely, they poured flowers as symbols, the lavished heaps of fresh flowers as though there could never be enough to tell either their hearts or his.
And the night came with great quiet.
And there was rest.
The prairie years, the war years, were over.

The 20-day "carnival of death" changed Abraham Lincoln from a man to a legend. On the day he was assassinated, he was not universally loved – even in the North. His traveling corpse became a touchstone that offered relief from the pain that the American people had been suffering from during the four bloody years of the war. They mourned for the President and yet, the outpouring of sorrow was greater than for just one man. They mourned for every husband, father, son, and brother who died during the war. It was as though, on that train, all of them were coming home. The frenzied death carnival for Abraham Lincoln was a glorious farewell to the President and to the hundreds of thousands of men of the Union who, like Lincoln, had perished for cause and country.

The story of Abraham Lincoln and the supernatural does not end with his entombment at Oak Ridge Cemetery in 1865. There are other parts of this story to tell in the chapters ahead.

A Lynching & a Race Riot
Unrest that Bloodied Central Illinois

In May 1893, a hanging that occurred in the prairie town of Decatur terrified the African-American population of the city. This was not the public execution of a man who had been tried and convicted of murder, but a brutal lynching that was tragically allowed to happen by the city authorities.

A lynching is simply a public murder by a mob. They were often racially motivated and were used as humiliation for crimes alleged, but not tried in a court of law before a judge or jury. The victims were mostly always black and lynchings dated back to the turbulent days after the Civil War. In the Reconstruction-era south, members of night-riding groups who disguised their identities, especially members of the Ku Klux Klan, carried out all-too-frequent lynchings of African Americans.

Lynchings were not limited to the South; the New York Draft Riots were sparked in part by job competition between Irish-American immigrants and free blacks, and during the riots, 11 blacks were murdered, with many more beaten, and their property destroyed. The riots led to a brief exodus of blacks from New York, and helped establish Harlem as the center of African-American society in the city. Around the turn of the last century, race riots broke out in cities all over Illinois and many either started, or ended, with lynchings. Decatur was fortunate in that it was not the scene of a race riot, but what did occur in 1893 remains a blight on the city's history.

On May 29, a woman who resided south of Decatur reported that a black man had assaulted her. This report was followed the next day by another alleged assault, this time involving a Mt. Zion woman. On June 2, Samuel Bush, who fit the general description given by the two woman, was arrested near Sullivan and brought to the Macon County Jail in Decatur.

Anger simmered in the community and a few days later, around midnight, an armed mob appeared at the jail. According to accounts, several thousand people turned out and the crowd included many women and children. Despite the lateness of the hour and a soaking rainstorm, the mob refused to leave. No efforts were made by the police to clear the streets or disperse the crowd. They stood, waiting for something to happen, for nearly two hours. Just after 2:00 a.m., a group of about 100 men marched on the jail from Wood Street. They were followed by about 20 riders on horseback. None of the men wore masks, but collars were turned up on long coats and most of the men wore their hats pulled down low on their foreheads. Rain could be seen glistening off the barrels of shotguns and rifles and off the long blades of corn knives.

The group approached the jail and demanded that Samuel Bush be turned over to them. Deputy Sheriff Midkiff, who commanded a troop of special guards inside of the jail, refused. The mob broke open the outer doors and pushed into the jail offices. Police Chief William Mason, who tried to reason with the men, was badly beaten and the mob rushed at the jail door. They had come prepared for the task, swinging sledgehammers and iron bars. They punched a hole through the concrete wall near the hinges of the iron gates, removed the heavy door, and pushed their way into the cell block. The few guards who attempted to stop them were quickly subdued and the rest disappeared, leaving the mob to wreak havoc.

The first cell the men reached was occupied by a black man named John Caldwell. He had convinced one of the guards to give him a candle so that he would not be mistaken for Samuel Bush in the darkness. One of the men took his candle from him and used it to light the way to Bush's cell. Using keys that had been taken from the guards, the cell was opened and Bush was pulled out from under the cot where he was hiding. He was stark naked, weeping, and shaking with fear. He was dragged out of the cell, protesting his innocence as he was taken. The mob hauled him outside and when they reached the street, cries began to erupt from the hundreds of people who were still milling about. "Hang him!" they called. "Hang him!"

Bush continued to cry that he was innocent of the crimes he was accused of, but no one was listening. He was allowed to pray and newspapers reported that "he began to sing and pray in plantation style." He said that he hoped he would meet the people putting him to death in heaven.

The mob had failed to bring a rope with them and since none could be obtained, they tied together horses' halters and fashioned the leather into a noose. It was thrown over a light pole at the northeast corner of Water and Wood Streets. A cab driver was forced to bring his cab close to the pole, the doomed man was shoved atop it, and the noose was roughly forced over his head. Bush's feet were left dangling in the air as the cab was driven out from underneath him. He slowly strangled and witnesses later claimed that it took him nearly 15 minutes to die.

The mob gave three cheers for Decatur and for Mt. Zion, where many of the members of the party had come from, and then dispersed into the night. An hour or so later, Coroner Bendure received a telephone call, informing him that a "naked Negro" was hanging from a light post downtown. The remains were retrieved and taken to Brintlinger's undertaking parlor. Once the body was taken down, pieces of the hanging rope were cut away as gruesome souvenirs by people on the street. It was said that Brintlinger handed out pieces of the rope at his undertaker's parlor for several days afterward.

While many would later claim that the lynching was a spontaneous event, it was anything but that. The rumbles of the angry public had been building since the prisoner had been brought to Decatur by train a few days before. Curious crowds surrounded the train during its journey and 18 men had actually tried to stop it near Bement, but they had arrived too late. Several hundred onlookers had met the train when it arrived in Decatur and they followed Bush as he was brought to the jail. Decatur's police chief had been given responsibility for the prisoner since the Macon County Sheriff, Peter Perl, decided that the arrival of Samuel Bush would make the perfect time to visit the World's Columbian Exposition that was being held in Chicago at that time. He preferred the wonders of the World's Fair over the political millstone of a vigilante lynch mob. When he returned to Decatur, he admitted that he had read about the lynching in the Chicago newspapers, but didn't see the point in returning home and cutting his vacation short since the excitement was already over. Many in Decatur shared his opinion. There were few who seemed to regret the tragedy, as evidenced by the fact that a grand jury failed to indict anyone for Bush's murder.

Illinois' governor, Peter Altgeld, was stunned by the incident, though, and called the lynching "a diabolical murder and an outrage to the state." He offered a reward of $200 for the arrest of any man involved in the crime but no one was ever charged and not a single dollar of the reward was ever collected.

The lynching of Samuel Bush was dismissed as a minor incident of violence at a time when African-Americans were shamefully regarded as second-class citizens. The event has never been commemorated and is mostly forgotten in Decatur today.

More racial problems occurred in Illinois in the years that followed. A riot occurred in Cairo in 1909 with the lynching of a man named Will James. Postcards were printed of the lynching and mailed out all over the United States. More riots, this time over labor disputes, occurred in East St. Louis in 1917, and two years later, riots also occurred in Chicago, causing an even higher death toll.

In the summer of 1908, the city of Springfield was rocked by racial violence, leading to a number of deaths and also to the formation of the National Association for the Advancement of Colored People (NAACP). It was one of the worst race riots in Illinois history, and to this day, historians have a hard time explaining just why the rampage that resulted in lynchings, shootings, and fire-bombings ever took place at all.

Some believe that the roots of the violence could be found in the fact that, despite being the hometown of the Great Emancipator, Abraham Lincoln, Springfield, like many northern communities had never been fully integrated. Black residents were not allowed to eat in many restaurants, stay in many hotels, or socialize in many local public places. Additionally, the city's worst vice districts of saloons, gambling parlors and brothels were concentrated in the poorest black neighborhoods, like the downtown Levee and the area known as the Badlands. These areas had the highest crime rates in the city. In the early twentieth century, Springfield had the reputation of being one of the most corrupt cities in the Midwest. Vice was a business that was protected by the authorities and overlooked by respectable citizens. It has been suggested that the riots grew out of white frustration with corrupt city officials, who allowed vice to flourish in black neighborhoods. It may have been the reason behind what happened that summer, but it was no excuse for what occurred.

The event that seems to have set the stage for the riot was the allegation that a young black man, Joe James, had murdered Clergy A. Ballard, a white mining engineer, after Ballard had supposedly discovered James trying to rape his 16-year-old daughter in her bedroom. According to the reports, Ballard had chased the rapist, who slashed him with a straight razor. He fled and Ballard died from his wounds a few hours later. Before he died, apparently, Ballard and his daughter had identified James, a vagrant from Alabama, as the attacker. The police took James into custody after he was attacked by a mob and badly beaten.

About a month later, Springfield residents were angered by newspaper reports of the second assault on a white woman by a black man. The police quickly arrested George Richardson, who was identified by the alleged victim based on his voice.

The two crimes led to calls for vigilante justice. On the night of August 14, about 4,000 people gathered at the jail that held both James and Richardson. Concerned that the two men would be killed, law enforcement officials snuck them out the jail's back door and hurried them away to Bloomington. When the mob discovered that the two men were gone, they turned their fury on nearby businesses, including a restaurant owned by Harry T. Loper, who was suspected of helping to hide the prisoners. The mob began attacking other businesses in the predominately black neighborhood, wrecking almost every building on Washington, Jefferson, and Madison Streets, between Eighth and Twelfth Streets. For the most part, they were careful to burn only homes and businesses that were owned by or served African-Americans.

By early the next morning, a large part of the east end of Springfield was on fire. After looting local gun shops, some of the rioters began beating and shooting any unfortunate black person they encountered. Four white spectators were shot and killed by stray bullets. Around 2:00 a.m., the mob set fire to the home of Scott Burton, an elderly black barber. When he tried to defend his home, with shotgun in hand, he was shot four times and lynched from a nearby tree. As his body hung, vigilantes began mutilating his corpse, only stopping when a company of armed Illinois state militia appeared on the scene and cut down the body.

One of the mob's other victims was William Donnegan, an elderly black man who was mentioned earlier in this chapter as one of the heroes of the Underground Railroad. Donnegan's "crime" was that he had been married to a white woman for more than 30 years. The mob found him sleeping in his backyard, trying to protect his home, and they lynched him from a tree across the street from his house. Before he strangled to death, someone slit his throat, and several men hacked at his body with knives. The militia arrived to disperse the crowd and found that he was still alive. He died in the hospital the next day.

By the next morning, most of the rioters had grown tired and gone home. By then, nearly 4,000 state militia members from other towns had arrived in Springfield to try and maintain order. Crowds of soldiers patrolled the streets and entire battalions were dispatched to black neighborhoods. In the midst of the unrest, black residents fled the city, most heading to Chicago and St. Louis.

The riot ended with 40 homes and 24 businesses in ruin. Five white men and two black men were killed. There were 107 indictments returned against 80 individuals who took part in the violence and three suspects – Kate Howard, Abe Raymer, and Ernest "Slim" Sullivan – were indicted as the ringleaders for the worst of the riot. Additionally, a man named Roy Young confessed to initiating the attack on Loper's restaurant and to starting a number of fires. In subsequent trials, Raymer was acquitted on all counts and charges were dropped against Sullivan and most of the others. Roy Young was convicted of burglary, arson, and rioting. A man named Joe James was convicted of the murder of one of the black men and was hanged in the Sangamon County Jail on October 23, 1908. Kate Howard, the woman who had directed much of the violence, was found guilty but committed suicide by drinking poison before she could serve her time.

It is worthy of note that George Richardson, who had insisted from the beginning that he was innocent of the rape charges filed against him, was completely exonerated when his alleged victim confessed that her assailant had actually been a white man who was known to her.

The terrible events of August 1908 soon faded from public memory, but they did resonate among early civil rights activists. On February 12, 1909, a group of reformers met in Springfield to discuss the creation of a permanent association of black and white activists devoted to protecting the rights of African-Americans. Those in attendance included educators like W.E.B. DuBois, as well as prominent social workers, religious leaders, and jurists. The result was the creation of the NAACP, which was incorporated the following year.

Capitol Hauntings
History, Mystery & Malfeasance in Illinois' State Capitals

Strange tales from the capitol buildings of Illinois date back all of the way to the very first capital, Kaskaskia, one of the oldest communities in the state. In the early days of the region, Illinois was settled by French pioneers, who colonized the fertile plain along the Mississippi River and started a settlement called Kaskaskia in 1703. For more than a century, it was the commercial and cultural center of the region. Little of the city remains today, although it was once a prosperous and thriving settlement. Strangely, many believe that the city was destroyed because of an old curse, leaving nothing but a scattering of houses -- and ghosts -- behind.

Many years ago, Kaskaskia was a part of the mainland of Illinois, a small peninsula that jutted into the river, just north of the present-day location of Chester. Most of what remains of the city is now an island, cut off from Illinois by a channel change in the Mississippi that took place decades ago. Much of the area was flooded at that time and it is now largely a ghost town, consisting of a handful of residents. The remains of the town, while still considered part of Illinois, can now only be reached from Missouri. There is an ancient bridge between St. Genevieve and St. Mary's that crosses the Mississippi to the island. It is the only physical link this desolate spot has to either state. There are only a few scattered buildings that remain as evidence that Kaskaskia ever existed at all.

During the days of the French regime, Kaskaskia was the main rendezvous point for the territory and one of the most important sites of the Mississippi Valley. Dozens of expeditions to the west were launched from Kaskaskia and, in 1809, it became the territorial capital – and later the state capital-- of Illinois. The territory's land office was located in the city, making a place of great importance, and it was made up of stone mansions and houses of typical French architecture. Most of the inhabitants were French, or French-Indian mixtures, who raised cattle, horses, and hogs, and worked small farms. The territorial post office was located there, along with dry goods and general stores, a hat shop, three tailor shops, but only a single tavern. It was said that the town was constantly overcrowded by state officials, politicians, soldiers, adventurers, and land speculators.

In 1818, the state capital was moved to the new city of Vandalia, in the central part of the state. Illinois had just gained its statehood and legislators began searching for a place that was more centrally located than Kaskaskia. The move was made with some regret, but of course no one knew that the river city would ultimately be destroyed by the rising river waters. As the Mississippi shifted in its channel, small sections of Kaskaskia vanished, followed by more land and farms, houses, and buildings. By 1881, the peninsula was completely cut off by the river and the city had nearly ceased to exist.

What changed the fates of this once marvelous city? Was it simply nature taking its course, or was there, as some believed, something supernatural behind the demise of Kaskaskia? Legend states that a terrible curse was placed on the town and that it predicted the land around it would be destroyed and that the dead would rise from the graveyard in horrific torment. Sound hard to believe? As it happened, these events actually took place.

The story of the curse dates back to 1735, when Kaskaskia was a thriving community of French settlers. There was a wealthy fur trader who lived there and who is remembered only by the name of Bernard. He lived in a luxurious stone home in the company of his daughter, Maria, a beautiful young girl who was the pride of his life. Bernard owned a trading post on the edge of the city and he frequently hired local men, both French and Indian, to work for him. Most of the Indians were hired to do the menial work, as Bernard cared little for them and considered them a "necessary evil." At some point, he hired a young Indian to work for him who had been educated by French missionaries. As the two spent time together, Bernard actually began to become fond of the young man -- until he realized that his daughter had also become fond of him. Maria and the young man had fallen in love.

When Bernard learned this, he became enraged. He immediately fired the young man and spoke to friends and other merchants, who then refused to put him to work. Eventually, the young man left town. Before he left, he promised Maria that he would return for her.

Maria was heartbroken by her father's actions. She pretended that nothing was wrong, so as to not arouse her father's curiosity, but deep down, she secretly hoped, waited, and watched for the return of her lover. Several local men attempted to court her, and while she feigned interest in their attentions, she secretly pined away for the young Indian.

A year passed and one day, a group of unknown Indians visited Kaskaskia from the west. Among them was Maria's lover, wearing a disguise so that he would not be recognized by Bernard. The young man and Maria arranged to meet in secret and, together, they fled Kaskaskia to the north.

When Bernard learned what had happened, he vowed to seek vengeance on the young man. He gathered several of his friends and began hunting his daughter and her lover. They were captured near Cahokia. Maria begged her father to understand, but he refused to listen to her pleas. He decided to kill the young man by drowning him. The young man was silent as several trappers tied him to a log and then set him adrift on the Mississippi. Just as they placed him in the water, he uttered a terrible curse. He swore that Bernard would be dead within the year and that he and Maria would be reunited forever. Kaskaskia was damned and would be destroyed, along with all of the land around it. The altars of the churches, the buildings, and the homes would be destroyed – and even the dead of Kaskaskia would be disturbed in their graves.

The river then swallowed the young man beneath its muddy water. His voice became silent, but the prophecy eventually came to pass. Within a year, the curse began to prey on all of those involved. Maria was distraught over her lover's fate and refused to leave the house or eat. She soon died and rejoined her lover on the other side. Bernard became involved in a bad business deal and challenged the man who cheated him to a duel. Bernard was killed by the other man.

And the Mississippi began to seek the young man's revenge on Kaskaskia. The river channels shifted and flooded the peninsula over and over again until, by 1881, Kaskaskia was completely cut off from the mainland. The homes and farms were abandoned and people began to slowly leave the island. The church was moved over and over again, but it did no good. The altar was eventually destroyed in the 1973 flood. By this time, Kaskaskia had become a desolate ghost town, but not before the Kaskaskia cemetery was washed away and the bodies of those buried there erupted to the surface and then vanished beneath the river.

The dead of Kaskaskia truly had risen from their graves.

Chosen as the site of the state's second capital, the town of Vandalia was impressively located on the bluffs that overlooked the Kaskaskia River. From a remote spot in the wilderness, it grew into a thriving city and played witness to the early struggles of Illinois, to the careers of two young men -- Abraham Lincoln and Stephen Douglas -- as they came into the national spotlight, and saw the westward migration of thousands on the old National Road that stretched from Cumberland, Maryland, to Vandalia.

The site that later became Vandalia was first settled by the Kickapoo Indians, who had journeyed to the region from Wisconsin in 1765. In 1819, the peaceful tribe ceded their lands to the state of Illinois and was moved into Missouri. Unfortunately, Missouri was already occupied by their enemy, the Osage, and so many of the Kickapoo returned to Illinois and lived side-by-side with the white settlers, who had arrived in the area a few years before.

The settlement was founded by Guy Beck, a Kentuckian, who had first settled in St. Clair County in 1809. After service during the War of 1812, he moved to the Kaskaskia River area and built a cabin in what was to become Fayette County. He opened a blacksmith shop and served the settlers and travelers who followed. The settlement became known as Vandalia, although legend has obscured the meaning behind the name. Some say that it was taken from the name of a local Indian tribe, the Vandals, or that it was a combination of the words "van," an abbreviation of "vanguard," which means an advancing body of individuals, and "dale" from the river valley below the hills. Others maintain that it remained from the "Vandalia Colony," an aborted pre-Revolutionary War land grant scheme that originated in England and was granted a royal charter for land that extended into Illinois.

No one knows the origin of the town's name, but it was among the first mentioned in Kaskaskia in 1818 when Illinois achieved statehood. At that time, a delegation was appointed in the failing French settlement to choose a new site for the state capital, preferably "on the Kaskaskia River and near as may be east of the third principal meridian on said river."

The choosing of Vandalia is as mired in legend as the name of the city. Some say the site commissioners -- Samuel Whiteside, Levi Compton, William Alexander, Thomas Cox and Guy Smith -- killed a deer beneath a large white oak tree on the spot where the old capitol building now stands and during the drunken feast that followed, chose the site as Illinois' capital. Others claim the place was chosen on the suggestion of a noted hunter and trapper named Reeves, who told the commissioners that the site was more beautiful than the one they were considering at Carlyle. Whatever the method, the second capital of Illinois was chosen and on four sections of land granted by Congress, a town was laid out. Streets were designed and building lots sold at prices that showed the optimism of those who chose Vandalia to be their new home.

The first statehouse in town was nothing more than a plain, two-story frame building with a stone foundation. It was located in the center of the square and, in December 1820, became home to the Illinois archives that were moved from Kaskaskia. The records were transported by ox wagon, driven by a slave and accompanied by Sidney Breese, who was then assistant to the Secretary of State. His task was to cut a path through the woods at any point when the wagon could not make it on the trail.

Vandalia became a bustling place in the months that followed. The General Assembly met and plans were made to build a bridge over the Kaskaskia River east of town, to build several new roads, and to make the city more appealing to new settlers – and to the prominent families and state officials who had arrived from Kaskaskia with the state archives. City organizers felt the need to bring culture to the city, but to do so, they also had to manage the frontier element of the earlier settlers. They started by banning horse racing in the streets.

The city grew by leaps and bounds, attracting many new settlers who were coming to Illinois. Vandalia became the final stop on the Cumberland Road, later known as the National Road, which came west from Maryland and brought thousands of pioneers to the area.

When the General Assembly, composed of 14 senators and 29 representatives, met again in a small frame building at the northwest corner of Johnson and Fifth Streets, Shadrach Bond was the Governor. Other officers of the state were Pierre Menard, the Lieutenant Governor; Elias Kent Kane, a New Yorker who had been an attorney in Tennessee and Kaskaskia, the Secretary of State; Robert K. McLaughlin, Treasurer; and Elijah C. Berry, the Auditor of Public Accounts.

They met in the wooden house until December 1823, when it burned to the ground. Vandalia citizens built a two-story brick building to replace it, but it was torn down in 1836 and some of its wood and brick was used in the capitol building that took its place. Local residents raised $16, 000 for the construction of the new building and the Legislature first convened there on December 5, 1836. Much remained to be completed, though, and as noted in a letter that Abraham Lincoln wrote to his friend, Mary Owen: "The new State House is not yet finished and consequently, the legislature is doing little or nothing."

Even when the statehouse was finished, it was still considered very plain. It was not until 1859 that the eight Doric columns were added to the front. This building, which was erected with such high hopes, was only briefly used as the capitol for the state. When it was decided to move the capital to Springfield, the Legislature voted to refund to Vandalia the amount of money the city used to construct the statehouse.

Springfield was not the original choice for Illinois' new capital. By 1833, there was already talk of moving the capital to a more populated area. When the question of the new location was put to voters, Alton received the highest number of votes. Springfield was a distant third. The question was put on the back burner for a time as the legislators dealt with other state improvements, like the Illinois-Michigan Canal. By the time that the question of the capital was brought up again, Sangamon had become the most populated county in the state. It had two senators and seven representatives, known as the "Long Nine" because the men all averaged more than six feet in height, and their goal was to see the capital in Springfield. Led by Abraham Lincoln, they voted together and were able to convince others to vote with them. The Legislature appropriated $50,000 for the erection of the state house if Springfield citizens would raise a matching fund. It was agreed and Springfield became the third capital of Illinois.

When the capital moved to Springfield, the population of Vandalia declined to only about 300 people. Businesses closed and homes were boarded up. With the city's decline, the old statehouse fell into disrepair. The state gave part of the building to Fayette County to be used as a courthouse but only a portion of it was ever used. One section was turned into a school for a time, but it was also abandoned. Repairs were not made, broken windows were not replaced, and birds and animals roamed freely in the hallways and state chambers. The building crumbled for decades, until it was purchased by the county in 1889. The brick columns that had been added years before were replaced by iron pillars and a balcony was added. In 1930, after a fire, the cupola was rebuilt and three years later, the state began restoring the building to its former glory. It remains in preserved condition today and an integral part of old Illinois history.

It is a place filled with history, legend, and, some say, with ghosts.

There are stories that say that Abraham Lincoln once jumped from a high second-story window to keep from voting on a measure before the Legislature and that Stephen Douglas once rode a donkey up the stairs to the upper floor to celebrate a Democratic victory. It was in Vandalia that these two men first met.

At that time, Stephen Douglas, a native of Vermont who had also lived in Ohio before coming to Illinois, was teaching school in Winchester while he studied law. From his law office in Jacksonville, Douglas went to Vandalia to ask the Legislature for the post of State's Attorney, which was an appointed position in those days. In 1835, when Douglas was named to the position, Lincoln, who had come to Vandalia in 1834 as a representative for Sangamon County, voted against him. The two men would continue to clash over the years. Douglas had been one of the first suitors of Lincoln's future wife, Mary Todd, and the men would also battle for a hotly contested Congressional seat in 1858 with a series of debates throughout Illinois. But Douglas was always a gallant man and a gracious one. Although historically overshadowed by Abraham Lincoln, he helped shape the destiny of the United States when he split the Democratic Party with his stand against succession and assured Lincoln's election as President in 1860.

In addition to these famous figures, there were seven Illinois governors who served while the capital was located in Vandalia. Shadrach Bond was the first Governor of the state and he also briefly served in Kaskaskia. He had come to the region in 1806 and had been in the military during the War of 1812. After the war, he was sent west to settle portions of Southern Illinois. Bond led as Illinois sought to establish itself as a state but many of his initial policies failed miserably, including a disastrous state bank. However, Bond did establish seven counties in the state, including Lawrence, Greene, Sangamon, Pike, Hamilton, Montgomery, and Fayette. Pike County, which now has Pittsfield as its seat, was once so large that it included Chicago, which was then a tiny settlement on Lake Michigan.

Illinois' second Governor was Edward Coles, who led the state's first anti-slavery movement. A former slave owner in Virginia, he granted freedom to each of his slaves when he arrived in Illinois, via the Ohio River. Coles was a graduate of William and Mary College and served as a personal secretary to President James Madison before coming to Illinois.

Ninian Edwards was the third Governor of the state but had already been Governor of the Illinois Territory, named by President Madison, in 1809. In 1819, he became a U.S. Senator from the new state, serving until he accepted the post of Minister to Mexico in 1824. After a hint of scandal, it was necessary for him resign and return to Illinois politics. A break in the Edwards and the anti-Edwards factions in Illinois led to the formation of the Whig and Democratic parties, but despite all of this, Edwards did work for the establishment of several schools like McKendree College in Lebanon and Shurtleff College in Alton.

John Reynolds is remembered today as the state's "frontiersman governor." He was raised in Tennessee, lived at Kaskaskia, and then served in the War of 1812 before becoming a young judge and a member of the General Assembly. Under Reynold's call, young men joined the militia to drive the Sauk and Fox Indians from the Rock River area during the Black Hawk War of 1832. Reynolds was also strongly in favor of slavery, and in fact, even fined former Governor Coles for illegally releasing his slaves while Reynolds was still a judge.

From November 17 to December 3, 1834, William Lee Davidson Ewing, Lieutenant Governor under John Reynolds, was Illinois' Governor. This period was from the time of Reynold's resignation upon election to Congress until the time when new Governor Joseph Duncan took office. Ewing was a trustee for the town of Vandalia and a clerk for the House of Representatives. In 1830, he was elected to the House and later advanced to the state Senate. He was described as a high-spirited man and became a bitter enemy of Abraham Lincoln. It is said that only the intervention of some friends prevented a duel between the two men over the matter of moving the capital from Vandalia to Springfield.

The last governor to serve his entire term at Vandalia was Joseph Duncan, a Kentuckian who served during the War of 1812. Although he never attended school, Duncan became one of the state's greatest proponents of education when he became governor. In 1825, Duncan submitted a bill for the establishment for free public schools in Illinois. Although he was in favor of state improvements, Duncan and Stephen Douglas refused to support the plans of the Lincoln and the "Long Nine," believing they would ruin the state.

Thomas Carlin, successor to Duncan, continued Duncan's cause for good education in Illinois and served in Vandalia from his inauguration on December 7, 1838 to July 1839, when the capital was moved to Springfield.

But who among these legendary men haunt the old statehouse in Vandalia today? Could it be one of the lingering legends like Ninian Edwards, Shadrach Bond, or perhaps even Abraham Lincoln himself? Although the idea that it might be the shade of a young Lincoln at the old capitol building seems a far stretch, there are some who have continued this story for many years. Who better to haunt the place than its most famous former occupant? But Lincoln or not, stories maintain that the building is haunted and many have had strange experiences here over the years.

As far back as the 1960s, visitors at the old State Capitol claim to have heard voices in empty rooms, footsteps pacing back and forth, and have also seen glimpses of figures in hallways and standing in doorways. A second glance finds these figures always disappear from sight, as if they had never been there at all. According to one witness, who visited the statehouse in 1992, he was walking through the otherwise empty building one day and glanced up to see a tall, thin figure looking down at him from an overhead balcony. Startled, because he was unaware that anyone else was present in the building, he looked again to see the man was gone. He explained that he had searched through the place, but there was no one there. He badly wanted to see who the person had been because he thought the mysterious man looked very much like Abraham Lincoln. He later said, "I thought maybe there was a re-enactor there that day playing a young Lincoln or something. He looked just like him, but without the beard. I looked everywhere, though, and there was no sign of him."

Was it the ghost of Abraham Lincoln? Perhaps it was or perhaps it wasn't --- but this phantom, as well as the others that have been seen, appear to have been men linked to this place in the past. The old statehouse may be one of those places where Illinois history still echoes into the present.

In 1839, the state capital of Illinois was moved to Springfield, which was then a rough, frontier town in the central part of the state. The first settlers had arrived in the region just two decades before. The Native Americans had called the place "Sangamo," after the "Saquimont" River that ran through it. The settlers would dub it the Sangamon.

Henry Funderburk of South Carolina was the first to settle at what would someday be the capital city. He had come north through the Cumberland Gap in 1808 and purchased land holdings belonging to Andrew Jackson in Tennessee. In 1815, he continued on north and west to Illinois, settling in St. Clair County, just east of St. Louis. Two years later, he moved his family north to the Sangamon River region and built a home in the Cotton Hill Township. Soon, other settlers followed, including William Nelson and Robert Pulliam, from Alton. Several other families followed them and a small settlement was started. The first church, which doubled as a school, was built in 1821. The first blacksmith shop was built that same year and a grain mill followed, turning the small settlement into a thriving community of log cabins and muddy roads. In 1821, it was chosen as the new county seat for Sangamon County. The exact site of the town was chosen when a wooden stake was driven into a field belonging to John Kelly. It lay close to Spring Creek, so they chose the name of "Springfield."

The city grew slowly through the 1820s, mostly because of a struggle with inadequate transportation. There were no bridges built in the county until 1835 and farmers were losing money trying to transport grain to market. The roads were nearly impassable and Springfield was virtually cut off from outside markets.

In January 1832, though, the answer to the city's transportation problems arrived and Springfield became a booming river town -- at least for a very short time. In March, a steamer called the *Talisman* came slowly up the uncharted Sangamon River. It was owned by a local man named Vincent Bogue and his plan was to create a water route between Springfield and St. Louis. Citizens lined the riverbanks and parties were held in honor of Bogue and the steamer's captain, J.W. Pollock. Unfortunately, before the steamer could be unloaded, the water level of the river dropped and the boat could not be turned around. The *Talisman* was forced to back downstream and a small dam had to be destroyed to make room for the steamboat to pass. Mysteriously – or perhaps not – the *Talisman* burned shortly after arriving back in St. Louis and Pollock and Bogue vanished without a trace, leaving their creditors with nothing. The two men hadn't spent a dime of their own money on the scheme.

The people of Springfield were crushed by this turn of events and their dreams of riverboats and prosperity were dashed. Over the next few years, though, things began turning around as the first railroads began to be planned for the community, as well as new roads and bridges.

Springfield was officially incorporated on April 2, 1832. By this time, Illinois was becoming a largely settled state and a great effort was started to move the state capital, which was then located in Vandalia, to a city that was further north. The city of Illiopolis, which claims to be exact center of the state, was considered as were Alton, Jacksonville, and Peoria. After much debate, Springfield earned the title.

From that point on, all of the politics in Illinois began to center around Springfield. Leading lawyers arrived to use the local court systems, lobbying for power and upward mobility. Many new businesses came to the city, including fine hotels and restaurants, and new construction began to spread wealth to all corners of the city. Springfield soon became the most influential city in the state, rivaling all others for news, grand parties, and inside political information. The days of Springfield being nothing more than a frontier settlement were finally over.

Over the course of the next two decades, Springfield took its place among the major cities of the prairie. In 1849, a new city government was formed and the community's leaders found they had much to contend with, including cholera outbreaks, unpaved streets, and a legion of wild hogs that would remain a constant nuisance for years to come. Apparently, these once domesticated animals had gone wild and they began breeding in the streets like alley cats. They would plague the city for another 50 years, despite their presence being outlawed in 1852.

The city grew in importance and while many improvements were made, it remained an unattractive and troublesome town. None of the streets were paved and in warm weather, a coating of dust settled on everything in their vicinity. When it rained, the streets became a wet, muddy morass and, while dodging stray hogs, were impossible to navigate. Unbelievably, they would not be paved until the 1880s.

Springfield became the center of the nation's attention in 1860 when two of Illinois' most famous politicians squared off for the country's highest office. The campaign of 1860 pitted Abraham Lincoln against Stephen Douglas and their debates rocked the city and state, just as they had done during the Senate race two years before. Local sentiment was divided equally between the two men and while Lincoln won the election, he lost in Sangamon County and only carried the city of Springfield by 69 votes.

When the Civil War broke out, Governor Richard Yates began recruiting troops from all over Illinois and Springfield soon exceeded its quota of volunteers. Camp Yates was established at the old fairgrounds and enlisted men arrived regularly. The camp was so close to the city that local residents soon asked to have it moved to a more peaceable distance. The new military base was set up near Clear Lake, about six miles away. The camp was named for State Treasurer William Butler and became a cash source for liquor dealers and prostitutes. In fact, a nearby brothel run by Lucinda Taylor became known as "Camp Taylor," thanks to the fact that it catered almost exclusively to soldiers. In 1862, Camp Butler was turned into a prison camp for Confederate soldiers. The prisoners were eventually moved, thanks to protests from local southern sympathizers, but not before the camp became a national cemetery. There were hundreds of prisoners buried on the grounds before the war ended. The Civil War ended in 1865, but Springfield's relief turned to dismay when word arrived that President Lincoln, the city's native son, had been assassinated.

Springfield continued to grow after the war and with this growth came new demands for housing outside of the city limits. The city implemented mule-drawn streetcars to connect the downtown area with the new housing districts. Later, electric streetcars replaced these slow-moving vehicles. There were also demands for refinements and entertainment. Fashionable dinners at the Leland Hotel or an evening at Chatterton's Opera House became socially acceptable for members of the upper class, while those of more modest means enjoyed the taverns, dance halls, traveling theater groups, and skating rinks.

Not surprisingly, the high times of wealth and growth in Springfield brought new problems to the city in the form of crime, corruption, and vice. Before a massive reform movement would change the city government in 1911, Springfield would be known all over the state for its political corruption and crime. It would also gain national attention for one of the bloodiest race riots in history, largely brought on by the volatile mix of the conditions and the segregation of the city's neighborhoods.

The city endured World War I, the stock market crash of 1929, and the Great Depression that followed. It was a bleak time in Springfield. Many citizens were at poverty level already, but turned out to see President Herbert Hoover when he visited Springfield, hoping for some comfort. Unfortunately, his speech did little to assure them that better times were ahead, thanks to the fact that there were simply no jobs to be had in Central Illinois. The unemployment office was unable to keep up with the 850 new claims it was receiving each month. Lines of people were reported to circle St. John's Hospital when it began providing a "soup kitchen" for breakfast and dinner. Finally, the election of Franklin Delano Roosevelt as president brought a glimmer of hope, especially to local charities that began to receive some federal aid.

In 1932, however, disaster nearly struck with the closure of the Ridgely Farmer's Bank, the most prominent banking establishment in the city since 1859. There had been a panic run on area banks and the Farmer's Bank was unable to come up with enough cash to cover the record number of emergency withdrawals. And this was not only happening in Springfield. Banks were shutting down all over the country, so President Roosevelt declared a "bank holiday," effectively stopping what could have crippled the entire nation. A special council of Springfield bankers, city officials, and businessmen averted the disaster in the city by issuing a special "scrip" that could be used as money until the banks opened again.

The bank disaster was not the only shocking event of this period. The county had also been hard hit by the decline in the coal market. As industry dwindled, so did the demand for coal. Area miners soon found themselves out of work, as cheaper coal was brought in from non-union mines in other parts of the state.

John L. Lewis, president of the United Mine Workers of America, urged the miners to sign new contracts, which offered lower pay but insured their jobs. Most of them did but the strongest opposition to this was in Springfield, ironically the union president's home district. He traveled to Central Illinois to speak to the miners and negotiated with them throughout the summer of 1932. They finally voted, but rumors quickly spread that the vote would turn down the final offer. The ballots were on their way to a Marine Bank vault to be counted and on the way there, they vanished. Angry miners, believing that Lewis had stolen the ballots, broke off from the union and started their own organization, the Progressive Mine Workers of America. Violence followed and during a riot outside the Leland Hotel, a police detective was killed. War broke out between the two unions all over Central Illinois, including in both Springfield and Decatur. A number of men and women were arrested and injured in the fighting and several were even killed. Eventually, the violence stopped and a troubled peace was reached between the two unions. Although the coal industry has continued to decline over the years, the violence of 1932 has not been repeated.

The 1930s slowly rumbled past in Springfield and the economy continued to improve. The hard times of the early part of the decade made citizens eager to escape reality and be entertained. Movie theaters opened and so did local night clubs. Spots like the Blue Danube and the Lake Club became famous in downstate Illinois as popular gambling spots and places to catch big name acts like Guy Lombardo and Bob Hope.

Springfield entered World War II with a vengeance. Young men stampeded the recruiting offices after the bombing of Pearl Harbor. Meanwhile, women's groups and civic organizations organized drives for scrap metal and war bonds, netting over $11 million. Local manufacturers produced over $5 million in war supplies and the government opened the Sangamon Ordnance Plant near Illiopolis to make munitions. In conjunction with wartime rationing, public transportation became a way of life for many in Springfield. The city's aged streetcars had been replaced with city buses a few years before the war and served the community for many years to come.

With the end of the war came another era of peace and prosperity, which has continued on and off ever since. Although Springfield continues to grow and expand, it remains beleaguered by the troubled state of Illinois politics, mired in controversy, and always endeavoring for hope and change. Even so, it is hard to imagine that this is the same city today that started out as a wooden stake in John Kelly's friend and feared it would never grow because no riverboats could navigate to its shore.

As far back as the early 1830s, Illinois lawmakers had been working to get the state's capital moved away from Vandalia. As the Illinois population expanded in the northern parts of the state, it seemed prudent to relocate the center of the state's politics to a more central location. It was Abraham Lincoln and the "Long Nine" who maneuvered the capital to the small village in Sangamon County in 1837. The Illinois General Assembly passed a law that created a two-year transition period with the goal of moving the capital to Springfield.

Construction began for the new capitol building on Springfield's central square in 1837 and lasted for the next three years. Designed by local architect John Francis Rague, it was built using yellow Sugar Creek limestone and contained chambers for bother houses of the General Assembly, offices for the Governor of Illinois and other executive officials, and a chamber for the Illinois Supreme Court.

It was in this building that Abraham Lincoln served his final term as a state lawmaker and where he pleaded cases before the state supreme court. It was also here, in the Illinois House chamber, where he made his famous "House Divided" speech, announcing his candidacy for the U.S. Senate in 1858. It was in this same chamber, in May 1865, where his body lay in state prior to his burial in Oak Ridge Cemetery.

It was also in this building where political corruption in Illinois first took root. In our state, politics and crime seem to go hand in hand and nowhere is this more embarrassingly true than in the governor's office. In the past century, one out of five Illinois governors has been charged with a felony after committing some kind of malfeasance running the gamut from fraud to racketeering and embezzlement. Although we often like to think of political corruption as a product of modern times, Illinois's brand of corruption dates all of the way back to Lincoln's era in Springfield.

Trouble began with Illinois's tenth governor, Joel Matteson, a man of humble origins who was, by the time he finished his term in office, one of the wealthiest men in the state. Not content with the previous official governor's mansion, he had a new one constructed at a cost of $50,000. He had land, stores, banks, and a woolen mill, among other things. He also had a shocking secret: as governor, he had embezzled more than $200,000 in state funds.

His crimes were not revealed until two years after he left office. It seemed that, in 1839, the state of Illinois, largely bankrupt at the time, issued $338,554 of scrip in $50 and $100 notes to help fund the construction of the Illinois & Michigan Canal. Over the next few years, all but $316 of it was redeemed. The state's financial record-keeping was so sloppy, though, that not all of the scrip was canceled when it was redeemed, nor was a record kept of who redeemed it. Instead, most of it found its way back to the canal offices in Chicago, where it sat forgotten for the better part of the next 10 years.

Soon after taking office in 1853, Governor Matteson discovered the redeemed but never canceled piles of scrip and apparently decided that it would be safer in his custody than in the canal offices. He ordered a clerk to pack the canal records and scrip into a trunk and send it to the governor's office in Springfield. The trunk remained in his office for the next three years – literally a blank check that no one knew anything about. But Matteson could only live with the temptation for so long. In 1856, he started redeeming the scrip, trading it in for state bonds that he deposited into banks that he owned.

Unbelievably, Matteson almost got away with it. Three years after he left office, a shrewd state congressman learned of fraudulent scrip that was in circulation and looked into the matter. He discovered that Matteson had secretly redeemed almost $250,000 worth of scrip. An official investigation was started and Matteson's guilt became quickly apparent. Unable to come up with a clever story as to why he redeemed the scrip, he claimed that he had bought it in good faith without realizing that it was no good. He couldn't remember who he had bought it from; but it wasn't his fault. In a letter to the investigative committee, he stated that he had "unconsciously and innocently been made the instrument through which gross fraud upon the people has been attempted." Fearful of his reputation and wanting to avoid arrest, he offered to repay the state for the scrip, still claiming it had all been an honest mistake. But the state's Republicans weren't about to let him off so easily. They had already taken to calling his home, dubbed "Scrip Villa," a monument to corruption and greed and they wanted to see him fall.

But Matteson was slick and had friends in high places. His lawyers initially tried to shift blame to a former canal employee, a dead man named Joseph B. Well, who couldn't defend himself. When that didn't work, a jury was called to decide if Matteson should be indicted for larceny and made to stand trial, but rumors spread that the jury was stacked with Matteson cronies and supporters. In the end, he slipped out of the whole thing without a trial. He mortgaged his property and repaid the state $200,000 for money that he claimed he hadn't stolen.

Matteson may have avoided a trial and prison, but he couldn't escape the court of public opinion. He packed up his family and moved them to Europe for two years, hoping the scandal would blow over. Things did not improve much for him when he returned. The Civil War sent his business interests into a decline and his banks lost huge amounts of money. Eventually, he auctioned off his grand mansion for just $40,000, but it was purchased by his son-in-law, who allowed him to continue living there – until it all went up in smoke. On January 28, 1873, the mansion burned to the ground. A careless staff member left a fire unattended when he went home for supper and the mansion was soon engulfed in flames. Matteson, already in poor health after being thrown from a buggy a few weeks earlier, reportedly could not stand the shock of losing his home. He died three days later, on January 31, leaving a legacy of scandal, corruption, and lies in his wake.

And Joel Matteson would not be the only Illinois governor to lie. In fact, the state's eleventh governor should have never legally been governor at all. He perjured himself while taking the oath of office, claiming that he had not broken a law that would have prevented him from being governor.

Aside from being a liar, though, William H. Bissell was a pleasant and likable man. He had a sharp wit, wrote beautifully, and spoke powerfully for the cause of his party and country. During his life, he had many careers: doctor, lawyer, soldier, congressman, and governor. He performed them all well and yet, quite unintentionally, Bissell often found himself immersed in controversies and scandals that made him one of the most colorful figures to ever serve as governor of Illinois.

He came to Illinois from New York in the 1830s and opened a medical practice. He made many friends in Illinois and by 1840, had been elected to serve in the state legislature as a Democrat. His short stint in the statehouse gave him a taste for politics and the law, and so he abandoned medicine and became a lawyer. It should be noted that neither of these professions required much in the way of study or training in those days. Any sort of degree was largely considered optional.

In 1846, when war broke out with Mexico, Bissell joined the army and was soon elected colonel of the Second Illinois Regiment. He quickly found that military life was not as heroic as he had hoped and spent monotonous weeks marching through the hot, dusty desert and suffering from poor food, boredom, and homesickness. The only bright spots of army life to Bissell were the comradery of his fellow soldiers and the Mexican ladies – who would give him a souvenir that he would bring home later to Illinois. In February 1847, Bissell finally had his chance for glory in the Battle of Buena Vista, when the Second Kentucky, First Illinois, and Bissell's Second Illinois had the line during some of the bloodiest fighting of the war. Bissell returned home a hero, which paved the way for his eventual political victories.

The other thing that Bissell brought home with him would not trouble him for a few years, but his war hero reputation paid off right away. A year after his return, he was sent to Congress on a wave of popular acclaim. He arrived in Washington during a bitter conflict about slavery in the new territory that had been acquired from Mexico after the war. Bissell, in the House of Representatives, listened in disgust to southern congressmen who wanted slavery to be expanded into the western regions. He was especially irritated with a Virginian named James Sheldon, who claimed that a Mississippi regiment had been the one to save the day at the Battle of Buena Vista. Bissell became so incensed that he delivered a speech on February 21, 1850, that not only rebuked the southern states for their promotion of slavery but called out the Mississippi regiment by saying they had "not been within a mile and a half of the scene of action" at Buena Vista. Bissell received notes of congratulations and support from all over the country, but at least one letter threatened his life.

That letter came from a southern senator named Jefferson Davis, who had commanded the Mississippi regiment in the battle. He sent a note to Bissell demanding an explanation for his speech, and when he didn't like what he heard, he sent another letter that challenged him to a duel. Bissell accepted and chose the weapons: military muskets, loaded with buckshot. It was enough fire power to blow a man to pieces.

In the end, though, the duel didn't happen. Tempers cooled and Bissell modified his statement regarding the battle at Buena Vista, taking extra care to praise the gallantry of the Mississippi regiment. It is believed that President Zachary Taylor, Bissell's wartime commander and Jefferson Davis's father-in-law, intervened in the matter to prevent any bloodshed.

It turned out that the greatest threat to Bissell's health was not a dueling musket, but the syphilis that he contracted in Mexico. It first flared up in the winter of 1851, leaving him almost completely paralyzed from the waist down. The illness came and went over the next few years. In 1852, he was forced to do his campaigning for Congress while seated in a chair or carriage. His pelvic bone was slowly and painfully devoured by the disease and he used crutches for the rest of his life. Ill and in pain, he decided to leave politics in 1854, but changed his mind two years later, when he was persuaded to run for governor of Illinois under the banner of the newly formed Republican party. Bissell was opposed to slavery, was a war hero, and remained popular with the people. He was the perfect candidate – almost.

The only problem with Bissell's candidacy was, ironically, the reason he was so popular in the first place – the duel that he agreed to take part in with Jefferson Davis five years earlier. According to the 1848 Illinois Constitution, anyone who had ever given or accepted a challenge to a duel was barred from holding state office. If Bissell was elected, he would have to swear that he had never been involved in a duel. Obviously, this was not something he could honestly do, and the Democrats knew it. If Bissell took the oath of office, he would perjure himself. But the Republicans were not about to let a tiny problem like perjury stand in the way of a governor's seat. They claimed that since Bissell accepted the challenge to the duel in Washington, D.C., and not in Illinois, it was not subject to the Illinois Constitution. It was slippery, but it worked. Bissell won the election by more than 5,000 votes and took the oath of office in January. In his defense, friends later claimed that what Bissell still perceived as being "personally unethical" helped to drive him into an early grave. He died from pneumonia on March 18, 1860, at the age of 48. He was the first Illinois governor to die in office.

These Illinois governors, as well as many others, served in what is now called the Old Capitol building, which was replaced by a larger structure about four blocks away. After that, the state government turned the old capitol over to Sangamon County to be used as a county courthouse. It served in this capacity until 1966, but was altered several times over the years. In 1898, for instance, the entire structure was raised 11 feet, a third floor was added, and the interior was demolished and reconstructed to hold circuit court rooms and office space.

By the 1960s, Sangamon County needed more space than the historic building offered and work began on a new courthouse building. The county then returned the old capitol to the state of Illinois to serve as a place of public assembly and a museum of Lincoln history. But in order to restore and preserve the site, which had been altered during its time as a courthouse, workers completely dismantled it, stone by stone, and rebuilt it to look as it had in 1860 – the way that Lincoln had last seen it when he left Springfield for Washington. The state also excavated the plaza under and around the building to construct a large parking and office complex, which began serving as the headquarters of the Illinois Historic Preservation Agency.

The work was completed by 1970 and has since been used as a historic site and for ceremonial functions, like the 2007 announcement by then-Senator Barack Obama of his candidacy for President of the United States.

Although there have been a handful of stories about mysterious happenings at the Old State Capitol, there doesn't seem to be any that have occurred within the last several decades. The ethereal tales of phantom footsteps and mysterious figures all date from the years when the building was used as a courthouse. A former staff member once told me that doors in the building had a tendency to lock and unlock under their own power. On a number of occasions, he had found himself unable to get out of rooms that should have been easily accessible. He was convinced the doors had been unlocked just moments before. He never could explain this phenomenon. Combined with stories of disembodied voices and eerie figures that were present one moment and gone the next, he felt sure there was something otherworldly about the place.

But, as mentioned, all of those stories pre-dated the dismantling and subsequent rebuilding of the old capitol in the 1960s. It seems, after that, whatever eerie presence had been in the place found itself scrambled up, dislodged, and without a home, for no such stories seem to "haunt" the site today. It seems that when the bricks and stone of the building were scattered and displaced, the energy that resided within it simply disappeared. If the Old State Capitol was ever haunted, it no longer seems to be today.

But can the same be said of the current Capitol Building?

The current Illinois State Capitol Building in Springfield is actually the sixth structure to be used for the purpose of housing the executive and legislative branches of the state's government. The French Renaissance-style building was designed by Cochrane and Garnsey from Chicago and it took more than 20 years to complete. By the time it was completed in 1889, it had cost over $4 million to build.

The site of the Capitol had an unusual history. Originally known as Mather's Hill, it was home to a large mansion that had been built by businessman Thomas Mather. After the assassination of Abraham Lincoln in 1865, Springfield leaders decided to convert the mansion into a luxurious tomb for the fallen President – against the express wishes of Mary Lincoln, who wanted her husband buried in rural Oak Ridge Cemetery. Feeling that the secluded burial ground was not the proper resting place for Lincoln, the city ignored her orders and worked around the clock to prepare the tomb in downtown Springfield. When Mary found out about their scheme, she threated to have her husband buried in Washington or, worse, in Chicago. A new tomb was soon under construction at Oak Ridge and Mather's Hill became the site of Illinois' new capitol building.

It was a grand structure, towering in height even above the U.S. Capitol in Washington. Aside from modern buildings that serve as state capitols in Louisiana and Nebraska, it is the tallest capitol building in the country. It stands 361 feet high, with the dome making up 92 feet of that, and it is supported by solid bedrock, 25 feet below the surface of the earth. Constructed in the shape of a Latin cross, the capitol occupies nine acres of land. The dome is covered in zinc to provide a silvery façade that does not weather. The interior of it features a plaster frieze, which illustrates scenes from Illinois history, and stained glass windows.

The building has some oddities. When it was constructed, empty shafts were included for the future installation of elevators. The first elevators, installed in 1887, were operated by water and became the subject of constant ridicule by local newspaper editors, who deemed them embarrassing and inadequate for a building with the prestige of the Capitol. Electric elevators were later installed, but no one knows when. The first mention of them was in 1939, when the Legislature appropriated $30,000 for their repair.

In 2011, the Capitol underwent a $50 million renovation, which provided for an upgrade to the mechanical, electrical, and plumbing systems, as well as restoration of the interior, including the copper-clad doors, new lights, and maiden lamp posts for the grand staircase. The addition of the maiden statues is most interesting, since they were supposed to be installed in the building back in the 1870s as part of the original plan that was drawn up by architect Alfred Piquenard, who also designed the Iowa State Capitol. Illinois politicians of the era thought that the scantily clad women were too risqué, but the Iowans had no objection to them. Illinois had plain lamps installed at the base of the grand staircase and the maiden lamps, intended for Illinois, were delivered and installed in Des Moines, where they remain today. The light installed in Springfield in 2011 were replicas of the Iowa lamps.

Corruption also reared its ugly head in the new Capitol building. In recent times, Governor George Ryan served a lengthy stint in a federal prison. His successor, Governor Rod Blagojevich, also ended up in prison for trying to sell the Senate seat of newly elected President Barack Obama, among other things. As we have already seen, corruption in the Illinois governor's office is nothing new. There have been six Illinois governors charged with crimes during or after their time in office. Four were convicted, one got away with it, and another had some help in convincing the jury that he wasn't guilty.

Prior to George Ryan, the most recent governor to serve time was Dan Walker, the governor from 1973 to 1977. He was later involved in the Savings and Loan scandals and convicted of federal crimes related to fraudulent loans he made to himself from his own First American Savings & Loan Association of Oak Brook. He was sentenced to seven years in prison with five years of probation following his release.

In 1965, Governor William Stratton, who served from 1953 to 1961, was acquitted of tax evasion. His successor, though, was not so lucky. Otto Kerner, Jr. was governor from 1961 to 1968, and he was later a judge on the United States Court of Appeals for the Seventh Circuit. In 1973, he was convicted of 17 counts of bribery, conspiracy, perjury, and income-tax charges from his time as governor. He received 3 years in prison and a $50,000 fine. Ironically, he was prosecuted by future Illinois Governor Jim Thompson – a friend of and attorney for convicted Governor George Ryan.

Even though he was never convicted, perhaps the most notoriously corrupt governor was Len Small, who served from 1921 to 1929. He was indicted in office for corruption, and while he was acquitted, eight of the jurors in the trial later received state jobs. Among his defense lawyers was former Governor Joseph W. Fifer, who asserted, in pre-trial hearings, that the Illinois governorship had the divine right of kings!

Famously a friend of Chicago Mayor "Big Bill" Thompson (Al Capone's favorite mayor), Small was born in Kankakee County, Illinois, and was educated in the public schools. He attended Northern Indiana Normal School, taught school, and invested in real estate, eventually owning a farm, a bank, and Kankakee's daily newspaper. In 1883, Small married Ida Moore, and they had three children together.

Small began his political career in 1901, when he became a member of the Illinois Senate. He served in the Senate for the next four years and then became Illinois State Treasurer from 1905 to 1907, and served again from 1917 to 1919. In between, he was the Assistant U.S. Treasurer in charge of the sub treasury at Chicago between 1908 and 1912. In 1920, Small won the election for the governor's office and was re-elected in 1925. As Governor, Small pardoned 20 members of the Communist Labor Party convicted under the Illinois Sedition Act. He also pardoned or paroled over 1,000 convicted felons, including Edward "Spike" O'Donnell of the South Side O'Donnell Gang.

Another important pardon – repaying a favor to the Chicago Outfit – was the pardon of Harry Guzik (brother of John Torrio and Al Capone money man, Jake Guzik), who had been convicted of kidnapping young girls and forcing them into prostitution with a white slavery ring. This was a favor repaid after Small was indicted while in office for embezzling $600,000 and running a money-laundering scheme when he was state treasurer. The Outfit would get him out of trouble – but they would need a favor in return.

In 1921, John Torrio moved into Chicago Heights, where he opened the Moonlight Café, and two thriving roadhouses in Burnham, the Coney Island Café and the Barn. In Posen, he established the Roamer Inn, under the management of Harry Guzik, one of three brothers who had been long entrenched in the rackets, and his wife, Alma.

The Roamer Inn became a strong test for Torrio's political connections. The Guziks placed an advertisement for a housemaid and when a pretty, young farm girl applied, they stripped her naked, made her a prisoner, and had her broken in as a prostitute. After five months in captivity, she managed to get word to her family. By the time that her brothers rescued her, she was a mental and physical wreck. In court, her father told how the

Guziks had tried to bribe him not to testify. They were convicted and sentenced to hard time. While free on bail, pending an appeal to the Illinois Supreme Court, they came to Torrio for help. Torrio, in turn, approached Walter Stevens, one of the most respected gunmen in Chicago.

Stevens had been a lieutenant for Maurice "Mossy" Enright for many years and was considered a pioneer in labor union racketeering, slugging, bombing, and killing during the industrial strike problems of the early 1900s. He was the last survivor of the Enright gang after Mossy himself was killed as a favor to rival labor racketeer Big Tim Murphy in 1920. After Enright's death, Stevens joined up with the Torrio-Capone gang. He had many contacts, but perhaps his greatest was Illinois Governor Len Small. When Small was indicted, Stevens began working behind the scenes to make sure he wasn't convicted. Stevens had help from "Jew Ben" Newmark, a former investigator for the state's attorney as well as a thief and extortionist, and Michael "Umbrella Mike" Boyle, a business agent for Electrical Workers' Union No. 134. Boyle's nickname came from his practice of standing at a bar on certain days of the month with his umbrella partially open so that contractors who wanted to avoid union problems could drop cash into it.

As the Governor's trial progressed, the three men kept busy bribing and intimidating jurors. Small was acquitted and he did not forget any of the men who helped him. Eight of the men on his jury later received state jobs and Stevens and his cronies always had a "get out of jail free" card when they ran into trouble. All three men were later arrested -- Newmark and Boyle for jury tampering and Stevens for an old murder – and Small pardoned them.

After the Guziks got into trouble of their own, Stevens went back to Small and before the Supreme Court could hand down its decision in their case, the Governor pardoned them. Within three months, the Guziks were running a new brothel, the Marshfield Inn, just outside Chicago's southern limits.

The stage for how politics would always run in Illinois had already been set. Far too many of the governors that followed continued to play their parts in what is, without a doubt, the most corrupt state in America. It's unlikely that things will change anytime soon.

Perhaps the strangest stories of my own experience with the Capitol came during the administration of Governor George Ryan. It was not a story that I could tell for many years, but since several governors have come and gone since that time – and Governor Ryan has been in and out of prison – it's probably safe to recount what occurred in 2000, around the time when Ryan was first embroiled in the controversy over capital punishment in Illinois. At the time, I had already received scores of calls from people who wanted me to investigate their home or office because they believed it was haunted, but I never expected to receive such a call from staff members at the Governor's Office.

Like Len Small, George Ryan grew up in the Kankakee, Illinois, area. After serving in the military during the Korean War, he worked for his father's two drugstores and attended the Ferris State College of Pharmacy in Big Rapids, Michigan. Over time, he turned his father's two pharmacies into a successful family-run chain, making a fortune from lucrative government contracts selling prescription drugs to nursing homes. In 1954, Ryan was drafted back into the Army and served for 13 months in Korea, working in the base pharmacy. After his return, Ryan married his high school sweetheart, Lura Lynn Lowe, on June 10, 1956. The couple had five daughters, including a set of triplets, and one son, George, Jr.

Ryan began his political career on the Kankakee County Board from 1968 to 1973. He was then elected to the Illinois House of Representatives, where he served from 1973-1983, including two terms as Minority Leader and one term as Speaker. He spent the next 20 years in statewide office, as Lieutenant Governor under James R. Thompson, as Secretary of State from 1991-1999, and then as Governor from 1999-2003.

Ryan won the 1998 election by a narrow margin, beating challenger Glenn Poshard. One of Ryan's pet projects was an extensive repair of the Illinois Highway System called "Illinois FIRST," which stood for "Fund for Infrastructure, Roads, Schools, and Transit." It was essentially a fund for use in school and transportation projects and it spent billions working on Illinois roads and schools. Ryan also improved the state's technology infrastructure, served as the Chair of the Midwestern Governors Association, and drew criticism by becoming the first sitting U.S. governor to meet with Cuban President Fidel Castro.

But there was nothing in Ryan's term in office as controversial as the moratorium that he declared on the state's death penalty in 2000. He believed that the system was "flawed" and that it needed to be studied. At the time, Illinois had executed 12 people since the reinstatement of the death penalty in 1977, with one execution, that of "Ripper Crew" killer Andrew Kokoraleis, occurring early in Ryan's term. Ryan called for a commission to study the issue, noting that he still believed the death penalty was a proper response to heinous crimes, but that he wanted to be sure that innocent people were not put to death.

The issue had gained the attention of the public when an inmate named Anthony Porter, who had spent 15 years on death row, was within two days of being executed when his lawyers won a stay of execution on the grounds that he was mentally disabled. He was ultimately exonerated with the help of students at Northwestern University, who uncovered evidence to prove his innocence. In 1999, the charges against him were dropped and Porter was released. Soon after, another man confessed to the crime of which Porter had been wrongfully convicted.

On January 11, 2003, just two days before leaving office, Ryan commuted (to life terms) the sentences of everyone on Illinois' death row – a total of 167 convicts – due to his belief that the death penalty could not be administered fairly. He also pardoned four inmates who were part of the group known as the "Death Row 10," due to widely reported claims that the confessions in their cases had been obtained by police torture. Ryan won praise from death penalty opponents. He had already been praised by various groups and in 2005 was nominated for the Nobel Peace Prize.

But not everyone was happy by his last minute decision. Many members of the public, families of crime victims, and scores of politicians were opposed to the commutations, questioning his motives at a time when a federal corruption investigation was closing in on Ryan and his closest political allies. They suggested that Ryan was attempting to salvage his public image in hopes of avoiding prison himself.

By that time, Ryan was already embroiled in the "Operation Safe Road" scandal, which involved the illegal sale of government licenses, contracts, and leases by state employees during his prior service as Secretary of State. In the wake of numerous convictions of his former aides, he chose not to run for reelection in 2002. There were 79 former state officials, lobbyists, and others charged in the investigation, and at least 76 of them were convicted.

The scandal began more than a decade earlier during a federal investigation into a deadly accident in Wisconsin. Six children from the Willis family of Chicago, Illinois, were killed and their parents, Reverend Duane and Janet Willis, were severely burned in an auto crash. The investigation revealed a scheme inside of Ryan's Secretary of State's office in which unqualified truck drivers obtained licenses through bribes. Arrests and convictions soon followed. In March 2003, Scott Fawell, Ryan's former Chief of Staff and campaign manager, was convicted on federal charges of racketeering and fraud. Former deputy campaign manager Richard Juliano pleaded guilty to related charges and testified against Fawell at trial. Roger Stanley a former State Representative who was hired by Ryan, also testified against Fawell and pleaded guilty to corruption charges, admitting that he paid kickbacks to win state contracts, secretly mailed out vicious and false attacks on political opponents, and helped obtain "ghost payroll" jobs. And the list went on and on.

The investigation finally reached the former Governor and in December 2003, Ryan and lobbyist Lawrence Warner were named in a 22-count federal indictment. The charges included racketeering, bribery, extortion, money-laundering, and tax fraud. The indicted alleged that Ryan had steered state contracts to Warner and other friends, used campaign funds to pay relatives and personal expenses, and obstructed justice by attempting to end the state investigation into the license-for-bribes scandal. He was also charged with lying to investigators and accepting cash, gifts, and loans in return for official actions as governor.

The case went to trial in late 2005. Fawell, under pressure from prosecutors, testified against Ryan. He publicly expressed his disdain for the process, stating that he was only testifying against his former boss to spare his fiancée a lengthy prison term of her own. A lot of ugly allegations were made from the witness stand, including claims that Ryan's daughters, son-in-law, and housekeeper received illegal payments from the Ryan campaign fund. The prosecution took nearly four months to present their case and a parade of other witnesses followed Fawell on the stand.

On April 17, 2006, the jury found Ryan guilty on all counts. However, when ruling on post-trial motions, the judge dismissed two counts against Ryan for lack of proof. Needless to say, Ryan announced that he would appeal the verdict. Federal prosecutor Pat Fitzgerald noted, "Mr. Ryan steered contracts worth millions of dollars to friends and took payments and vacations in return. When he was a sitting governor, he lied to the FBI about this conduct and then he went out and did it again." He called Ryan's term in office "a low water mark for public service" – and that's saying a lot for Illinois.

In September, Ryan was sentenced to serve six-and-a-half years in prison, starting in January 2007, but an agreement was reached that allowed him to remain free pending the outcome of his appeal. His conviction was affirmed by the Court of Appeals of the Seventh Circuit in August 2007 and a review by the entire Seventh Circuit was denied in October. The Seventh Circuit then rejected Ryan's bid to remain free while he asked the U.S. Surpreme Court to hear his case. The opinion of the court called the evidence of Ryan's guilt "overwhelming."

Ryan's defense was provided pro bono by Winston & Strawn, a law firm managed by former Governor Jim Thompson. Ryan had served as Thompson's Lieutenant Governor from 1983 to 1991. After the U.S. Surpreme Court declined to hear Ryan's appeal, U.S. Senator Dick Durbin wrote a letter to President George W. Bush, asking him to commute Ryan's sentence to time served, citing Ryan's age and his wife's poor health. President Bush did not pardon Ryan and the disgraced former Governor reported to the Federal Prison Camp in Oxford, Wisconsin, on November 7, 2007. He was transferred on February 29, 2008, to a medium security facility in Terre Haute, Indiana, after Oxford changed its level of medical care and stopped housing inmates over 70 years old.

In 2010, Ryan put in a request for an early release, partly on the grounds that his wife had terminal cancer and had only been given six months to live, and partly because some of the charges of which he had been found guilty should be vacated in light of a Supreme Court ruling that was alleged to have affected the legitimacy of those convictions by the prosecution. On December 21, 2010, his request was denied.

On January 5, 2011, Ryan was taken from his prison cell in Indiana to a hospital in Kankakee so that he could visit his terminally-ill wife. He was also present when she passed away five months after that visit. Technically, he was still incarcerated at the time. On January 30, 2013, Ryan was released to a Salvation Army halfway house in Chicago and then allowed to be on home confinement in Kankakee for the remainder of his prison term. He was a free man on July 3, 2013, a day earlier than had been originally planned.

My own encounter with Governor Ryan – or rather his office, not the governor himself – came in 2000, around the time of the controversial moratorium that he placed on death sentences in the state. Not long before this, I had been featured on the cover of *Illinois Country Living* magazine, which was sent out to every rural electric customer in the state, which led to literally hundreds of calls from people who wanted to tell me about their ghost stories, or to ask that I come and check out the haunting in their home or business. One of those calls came from a staff member in the Governor's office in Springfield, who described some strange happenings that were taking place there.

According to the staff member, the office was being plagued by unexplained banging noises, lights that turned on and off, doors that slammed shut, and physical objects that flew off desks, were tossed against the wall, and disappeared, only to turn up again in bizarre places. He had no explanation for what was happening and wanted to know if I was aware of any reason why the Governor's office might be haunted. After a lot of discussion and agreements that nothing would be discussed publicly, I got the chance to visit the office after hours and set up equipment that we hoped would provide some clues about the reported activity. In the company of three staff members, I remained in the office most of the night, watching for any sign of the phenomena had been described to me. It was a long quiet night and nothing out of the ordinary was seen or heard. It's possible that a haunting of some sort was taking place, but I never saw any evidence of it during my visit.

The request for secrecy applied to me, but not to everyone involved. A few days later, Governor Ryan quipped to reporters that his office was "apparently haunted." The story appeared briefly in newspapers and then vanished altogether. As far as I know, that was the last time that the weird activity in the office was publicly discussed.

But that was not the end of the story. As time went on, the controversy around Ryan multiplied and, several years after he left the Governor's office, he was charged and convicted of various federal crimes. On September 6, 2006, he was sentenced to a term in federal prison. According to an eyewitness, who asked to remain anonymous, he was working in the same office that had been occupied by George Ryan's staff back in 2000, when accounts of ghostly happenings were first passed on to me. He was watching the former Governor's sentencing hearing on television and at the exact moment that his sentence was announced, a water pitcher and several glasses, which had been sitting on a nearby table, suddenly flew into the air. The objects were flung to the floor, spilling water and shattering two of the glasses. He was certain there was no one near the objects – he had seen them lift up and fly to the floor by their own power.

Was it possible that the "ghosts" who received suspicious paychecks were not the only spirits that plagued the Ryan administration?

2. HAUNTED HISTORY
Central Illinois' Haunted Landmarks, Businesses & Historic Sites

The tiny village of New Salem, located on the Sangamon River, came into existence just a short time before its most famous resident, Abraham Lincoln, settled there. It was barely a speck on the map at that time, dreamed up by two entrepreneurs who envisioned it as a thriving river community that it would never become. It remains a historic site today, a reminder of times long past, and some say, a place where the spirits of yesterday still linger.

Between 1825 and 1826, James Rutledge and his nephew, John Cameron, arrived in the region, and settled with their families along Concord Creek, a tributary of the Sangamon River. They had plans to build a mill along this small stream, but soon realized that it would not be able to produce the water volume necessary to power the mill. They began to search for a more promising location.

On July 19, 1828, Cameron purchased land along the Sangamon River and applied to the Illinois State Legislature for permission to build a dam across the river. The place was known as "Fish Trap Ford" and was the site where the road from Beardstown to Springfield, the only major road in the area, crossed the river. In anticipation of a favorable response from the Legislature, the two men moved their families to a bluff overlooking the mill site, and Rutledge soon converted his home into a tavern, providing food and lodging for travelers on the road.

Permission for the building of the dam was obtained in January 1829 and work began immediately. Wooden bins were built in the river and local farmers provided wagons and teams to haul what turned out to be thousands of wagon loads of rocks to fill the structures. When the dam was completed, a combination grist and saw mill was constructed on a platform over the river. It was a success from the start and drew customers from miles around. It was later recalled that it was not unusual to see more than 40 horses tethered to the trees on the hillside as their owners waited for their grain at the mill.

In the fall of 1829, Samuel Hill and John McNeil built a general store on the hill that was crossed by the Springfield Road. Around that same time, a tavern was built by William Clary above the mill and began dispensing alcohol to the thirsty customers who waited for their orders to be completed at the mill.

With the mill, tavern, and store already becoming a center of trade for the area, Rutledge and Cameron began to plan a town around them. On October 29, 1829, a town was platted and lots were drawn up with the name of the settlement as New Salem. The first lot was sold on Christmas Eve and New Salem began to take shape. On Christmas Day, an official post office was established in the Hill and McNeil store and Samuel Hill was named as postmaster.

The town grew rapidly over the next two years. Most prominent among the arriving settlers were Henry Onstott, a cooper who made barrels and wooden utensils, the Herndon brothers, and Dr. John Allen, a graduate of Dartmouth College. Each man left his mark on the small village, but none of them so much as the young man who arrived there in April 1831.

Abraham Lincoln's arrival in New Salem was anything but auspicious. Although accounts vary as to what actually happened, most agree that he was part of the crew of a flatboat that got hung up on the dam below

The reconstructed village of New Salem today is said to be home to several ghosts of the past.

the village. From the shore, the townsfolk watched as he and the other crew members struggled to save the boat from sinking. Lincoln was described as an "ungainly youth," but despite his appearance, his thinking was obviously quick. He ordered most of the cargo to be unloaded and taken to shore and then moved the rest of it to the stern of the boat. After wading to shore to borrow a wood drill, he opened a hole in the bottom of the craft and let out the water that had gathered in the bottom. When the vessel was free of water, he plugged the hole and the flatboat slipped effortlessly over the dam.

Lincoln did not stay around in New Salem for long. In July, though, he returned to the small community and began running a store for Denton Offutt, who had originally hired Lincoln to take his first flatboat to New Orleans. He made a lot of friends in the community and was highly regarded by everyone. He was a hard worker, joined the local debate society, and borrowed books from the local schoolmaster, Mentor Graham, to further his education. As people in the community got to know him better, they realized just how intelligent and well-spoken the tall young man was and they encouraged his dreams of a career in law and politics. They also watched as the rowdy, fun-loving frontiersman turned into a moody, deep-thinking intellectual with a tendency toward melancholy.

According to local New Salem legend, however, it was not the furthering of Lincoln's education that changed his personality – it was the death of a young woman that changed his life forever. There are those who believe that it was their ill-fated love affair that altered the course of Lincoln's life.

When Lincoln first met Ann Rutledge, the auburn-haired beauty was being courted by the storekeepers, Samuel Hill and John McNeil. It was McNeil who eventually won the girl's favor and soon they were engaged to be married. However, in 1832, McNeil sold his interest in the store to his partner and made plans to depart from New Salem for a time. Before he left, he made a startling confession to Ann --- his real name was not John McNeil, but John McNamar, and he had changed it before leaving home because at the time he believed his family would find him and financially burden him. Now that his future in Illinois was assured, he intended to return to New York, retrieve his family, and return to New Salem and Ann. Surprisingly, Ann accepted the story and sent McNamar away with a promise to write. He wrote a handful of letters but eventually his correspondence faltered and then stopped altogether.

After sufficient time had passed, Lincoln began courting Ann and a love affair quickly blossomed between the two of them. Lincoln was already making plans to open a law office and Ann intended to enroll in the Female Seminary in Jacksonville. After her graduation, with Lincoln firmly established as a lawyer, the two planned to be married. Tragically, though, those plans never came to fruition.

Before Lincoln could start his career as an attorney, he was sidetracked by friends, who persuaded him to try his hand at politics. He decided to make a run for the state legislature. Despite being involved with the disastrous plan to bring the *Talisman* steamboat to Springfield and being kept away from the campaign by the Black Hawk War, Lincoln arrived home just in time for the election. He lost, but tried again in 1834, drumming up votes at dances, barbecues, cock-fights, and wrestling matches, and this time, he won a seat in the Legislature. In November, at the age of 25, he left for the capitol in Vandalia wearing the first suit he had ever owned.

Soon after, his dreams of a life with Ann Rutledge came to a shattering end.

In early 1835, Ann, now understood to be engaged to Lincoln, received word from the long absent John McNamar. Her fiancé had apparently met with unavoidable delays, including his own serious illness and the death of his father and two brothers in New York. His letter to her stated that he was now returning to New Salem for their wedding. Ann was distraught by this "good news." She loved Lincoln and yet she was honor-bound to marry McNamar and saw no way out of the situation. She continued her preparation for college and as the summer wore on, she nearly completed her studies.

In August, Ann fell ill with a fever that worsened until she was confined to bed. It grew steadily worse until the doctor announced that there was little hope for her recovery. Although the doctor had ordered strict silence and had forbidden any visitors, Ann repeatedly called for Lincoln and he was eventually summoned to the Rutledge farm. Lincoln entered her sickroom and the door was closed behind him. What may have been said during that final meeting will never be known, but the family later recalled that when Lincoln left the house that day, he fell sobbing against a tree in the yard and stayed there for hours.

A day or so after Lincoln's visit, Ann slipped into unconsciousness and never awakened. Her death came quietly on August 25, 1835, and while the family listed the cause of death as "brain fever," others claimed that the young girl died of a broken heart.

It was said that Ann's death drove Lincoln to despair and that he became so distraught that his friends, fearing that he might take his own life, took his knife away from him and watched him constantly for weeks. Eventually, Lincoln recovered, but some say that he was never the same again. Ann's death stayed with Lincoln the rest of his life – and perhaps beyond it.

Lincoln served out his term in Vandalia, and in 1836, he was elected again and this time headed for Springfield, where he also practiced law. He had read all of the books required and in March 1837, passed the exam that made him an attorney. He borrowed a horse and bid goodbye to the dwindling town of New Salem. The citizens had lost all hope of the river bringing prosperity to the town and, three years after Lincoln departed, New Salem became an abandoned ghost town.

According to author John Winterbauer, the term "ghost town" has a variety of meanings when it is used in reference to New Salem. He has maintained for many years that if there is any place in Menard County that has ghosts; it is this small, reconstructed village. He has recounted many stories of ghostly lights that burn in windows at night, the eerie face of a woman that peers from the window of the cabin that once belonged to Samuel Hill, and even an unidentified ghost that is believed to haunt a cabin that once belonged to the Isaac Burner family.

While the identity of the ghost that haunts the Burner cabin remains a mystery, there is at least one ghost in New Salem who is quite recognizable. She is a spirit who seems to have a very good reason for lingering behind at the site of her former home. A small piece that appeared in the Springfield newspaper, *Sangamo Journal*, for January 25, 1833 tells a tragic story:

TERRIBLE ACCIDENT ---- We learn that on Wednesday last, while Mr. R. Herndon of New Salem was preparing his rifle for hunting excursion it went off, and the ball, striking his wife in the neck, separated one of the principal arteries, and in a few moments she was a corpse. It is hardly possible to conceive the anguish of the husband on this melancholy catastrophe. The community in which he lives deeply sympathize with him in this afflicting event.

The home where this horrific event occurred is located on the edge of reconstructed New Salem, an Illinois State Park and historic site. The cabin belonged to John Rowan Herndon and his wife, Elizabeth, the sister of village schoolmaster, Mentor Graham. She had married John in Kentucky in 1827, and in the spring of 1831, the couple moved to New Salem. Rowan, or "Row" as he was affectionately called, and his brother, James, opened a store in the village the following autumn, but the business was short-lived. By that summer, James had moved away and had sold his half of the business to William Berry. Row and Berry did not get along and Herndon later sold his interest in the store to Abraham Lincoln.

Herndon remained in New Salem until the tragic accident recounted in the newspaper gave him reason to leave. The incident occurred on the morning of January 18, when he was cleaning his gun. As it happened, Abraham Lincoln was at the nearby Rutledge Tavern that morning, helping to repair a broken bed. He needed a certain tool to finish the work and he sent 10-year-old Nancy Rutledge down to Herndon's house to borrow it. Nancy later recalled: "When I arrived there Mr. Herndon was loading his gun to go hunting, and in getting ready to go out, his gun accidentally discharged, and his wife, who was sitting near talking to me, was shot right through the neck, her hands fluttered for a moment; then I flew out of the house and hurried home and told Annie and Mr. Lincoln what had happened."

Elizabeth Herndon slumped over to the floor and died immediately in a pool of her own blood. Not long after, her husband moved away, unable to deal with the haunting rumors that her death might have been anything but accidental. New Salem cooper Henry Onstott recalled the incident many years later and said that local residents were divided on whether Herndon had killed his wife, or whether it had been simply an accident. But regardless, he said "he was fooling with a loaded gun and it went off and killed her."

No matter how Elizabeth died, the question remains as to whether or not she ever left New Salem. In recent years, sightings of a woman in an old-fashioned dress --- who promptly disappears --- around the old Herndon cabin have been many. During one afternoon visit, a man and his daughter were walking near the cabin and the little girl claimed to see a woman on the steps, who then vanished. The father never saw the figure but was so convinced by his daughter's story that he looked into the history of the house and discovered the dark tale of Elizabeth Herndon. He became convinced that she was the woman that his daughter spotted that day.

A summer volunteer told John Winterbauer that she saw the ghost of a woman at the far end of the village on two separate occasions over three years. The first time, the volunteer was alone and walking down the path from the second Berry-Lincoln Store when she saw a woman on the path in front of her. The ethereal figure took a few steps and then blinked out of sight. There was no mistaking the sighting of the woman – or the fact that she vanished. It was a bright and sunny afternoon and no one else was around.

The volunteer saw the woman again a short time later, but this time she was not alone. She and another volunteer were walking down the path together and it was again a bright and sunny day. As they were walking toward the Herndon house, her companion pointed to the porch and asked who was working there that day. She looked up and saw a woman on the porch of the cabin, in full pioneer costume, holding a broom. As the two volunteers drew closer, they realized that they did not recognize the woman as anyone on the staff and wondered who she might be. They decided to walk over and talk to her. Before they reached the cabin, the woman turned and vanished through the building's closed door. The volunteers tried both doors of the cabin but found them to be locked. They peered into the windows but could see no sign of the mysterious woman. Whoever she had been, she had simply vanished without a trace.

The wide variety of ghostly stories told about New Salem, from floating lights to spectral cold spots and phantom figures, leads many to believe that Elizabeth Herndon does not walk there alone. There is at least one other substantiated ghost that has been spotted here and John Winterbauer believes that he knows this specter's identity – a man with a close connection to the community named Jack Kelso.

Little is known about Kelso, other than that he was a man of many skills, but no fixed trade. He hunted the forests, fished the streams, and acted as a general handyman around the village. Kelso was well-liked by his neighbors and he was the man who introduced Abraham Lincoln to the works of Shakespeare and the poetry of Robert Burns. He would be remembered fondly in all of the accounts that mentioned him. Thomas Reep wrote of Kelso: "No one at New Salem lived better than he, nor was any family more forehanded. He led a happy and contented life."

By 1840, the village of New Salem had all but faded away. Kelso departed in 1841 for Jasper County, Missouri, near Joplin, and then moved again in 1850 to Atchison County, Missouri, where he eventually vanished from history. The last record of him that exists was in 1868, when he acknowledged a deed for some land that he sold.

John Winterbauer believes that Kelso may still roam the forests around New Salem because he loved the place so much. Even after the town was dying, he stayed behind, and it was not until the last house was shuttered and the last store closed that he reluctantly departed. But did he return after death?

Many believe so, including a former Menard County teacher, who used to jog through New Salem each day in the early morning hours. One morning, she was passing one of the cabins and spotted a man standing on the porch who was only there for a few moments before disappearing. The cabin that she passed is a unique structure in New Salem. It is a "dogtrot" cabin, which is essentially two cabins joined together by a shared porch. This cabin once belonged to Jack Kelso and his brother-in-law, Joshua Miller, who was the town blacksmith. The two men had married sisters and upon arriving in New Salem, they constructed their home so that the two women could be near one another. The families remained together the rest of their lives, moving to Missouri after New Salem was abandoned.

Another possible sighting of Jack Kelso was experienced by a man who worked at the park for many years. He claimed to have seen a man wandering about near the cabin, dressed in clothing from the 1830s. The man walked about the yard, seemingly contented, and then disappeared.

John collected another story of Jack Kelso from a retired Jacksonville couple, Jan and Rex, who camped at New Salem for a week one summer and liked to stroll through the village just before the park closed at dusk. On the fourth night they were there, they spotted a man in costume alongside the path. He was wearing dark pants, a long white shirt, boots, suspenders, and a strange, floppy-looking hat. He seemed completely at ease and there was nothing out of the ordinary about him, as many of the volunteers in the village were dressed in similar costumes.

"We got right up on him," Jan recalled, "and Rex nodded and said "good evening', then this man opened his mouth as if to answer but then he was gone. He didn't fade away or anything like that, he just wasn't there anymore."

John asked the couple if they could point out the location of this strange encounter on a map of the park. They both agreed that it had taken place just a short distance down the road from the blacksmith's shop --- only a few feet away from the Kelso-Miller dogtrot cabin.

Broken Spirits
History & Hauntings of Illinois' First Hospital for the Insane

If spirits are truly the personalities of those who once lived, then wouldn't these spirits reflect whatever turmoil might have plagued them in life? And if hauntings can sometimes be the effects of trauma being imprinted on the atmosphere of a place, then wouldn't places where terror and insanity were commonplace be especially prone to these hauntings? As an answer to both of these questions, we need point no further than to the crumbling remains of the former state hospitals that dot the landscape of Illinois.

The city of Jacksonville was home to the first state hospital for the insane in Illinois. In the final years of the hospital's operations, after the last patients had departed, staff members in the building started to report some odd occurrences. Could events of days gone by still be lingering here? What macabre history had occurred in these now ramshackle buildings? There are many tales to tell about this sad and forlorn place. It is a strange story that is filled with social reform, insanity, ghosts, and it even maintains a connection to a supernatural incident that is known all over America.

We tend to think of mental hospitals of the past as places of terror, hells of chaos and misery, squalor, abuse, and brutality. Most of us think of them now, shuttered and abandoned, and we experience a shiver of horror as we contemplate being confined in such a place. Before the middle nineteenth century, the mentally ill were hidden away from the rest of us, kept out of sight from the "decent folk" and often hidden in cold basements, locked in cages or chained to walls. Mental health care barely existed. In those days, anyone suffering from a mental disorder was simply locked away from society in an asylum. Many of these hospitals were filthy places of confinement where patients were often left in straitjackets, locked in restraint chairs, or even placed in crates or cages if they were especially disturbed. Many of them spent every day in shackles and chains and even the so-called "treatments" were barbaric.

Not surprisingly, such techniques brought little success and patients rarely improved. In those days before psychiatry and medication, most mental patients spent their entire lives locked up inside of an asylum. There was little preparation for them to return to life outside, because no one ever expected them to be freed. After years in the asylum, residents became "institutionalized," and no longer desired, or could no longer face, the outside world. They lived in the state hospitals for decades, died in them, and were buried on the grounds. Under such conditions, it was inevitable that the asylum population would grow and individual asylums, often large to begin with, came to resemble small towns. It was inevitable too, that with a large inmate population, and inadequate funding and staffing, that state hospitals fell short of their original ideals. By the latter years of the nineteenth century, they had fallen into states of squalor and negligence and were often run by inept, corrupt, or even sadistic bureaucrats – a problem that persisted into the twentieth century.

But most state hospitals did not start out to be places of squalor and fear. The first hospitals were often palatial buildings with high ceilings, lofty windows, and spacious grounds, providing abundant light, fresh air, exercise, and a varied diet. Most asylums were self-supporting and grew and raised their own food. Inmates would work in the fields and dairies, work being considered a form of therapy for them, as well as supporting the hospital. There were gigantic kitchens and laundries and they, like the gardens and livestock, provided work and therapy for the patients, as well as an opportunity to learn life skills. These were things that many, withdrawn into their illnesses, might never have acquired before. Community and companionship, too, were vital for patients who would be otherwise isolated in their own mental worlds, driven by their own obsessions or hallucinations. Thanks to this, even when things became so dismal in the 1950s, some of the good aspects of asylum life could still be found in them. There were often, even in the worst hospitals, pockets of human decency and kindness. By the start of the twentieth century, asylums were no longer places of isolation, but rather meant to be places of comfort and safety for the mentally ill.

And often they were, enjoying a sort of "golden age" between the latter part of the nineteenth century and into the years of the Great Depression. But things would change and conditions, in many hospitals, began to deteriorate, declining back to the days when mental illness was a stigma and when the insane were kept away from the "normal people."

The 1950s brought the advent of specific antipsychotic drugs, which seemed to promise, if not a "cure," at least an effective alleviation or suppression of psychotic symptoms. The availability of these drugs strengthened the idea that hospitalization need not be for life. If a short stay in a hospital could "break" a psychosis and be followed by patients returning to their own communities, where they could be maintained on medication and monitored as outpatients, then it was felt, the prognosis, the whole history of mental illness, might be transformed and the vast and hopeless populations of asylums drastically reduced.

During the 1960s, a number of new state hospitals were built with this idea in mind, dedicated to short-term admissions. Sadly, though, the new hospitals found themselves soon overwhelmed by the influx of patients from older hospitals that were now being closed down. Legal changes followed, now making it illegal for the patients to work. This meant that instead of doing useful activities in the laundry, or outdoors, they were now left sitting zombie-like in open wards, in front of now never-turned-off televisions. With many patients filled full of drugs, their complacency allowed them to be released, or "deinstitutionalized," to use one of the psychiatric catch-phrases of the day. And what started as a trickle of released patients in the 1960s became a flood in the 1980s, even though it was clear by then that it was creating as many problems as it solved. Every major city was filled with daily reminders of those problems in the form of untreated patients wandering the streets. There was no way to deal with the hundreds of thousands of inmates who had been turned away by the few state hospitals that remained. Most of the hospitals had, by then, been closed down by federal budget cuts that swept the nation.

By the 1990s, it was clear that the system had overreacted and that the wholesale closure of state hospitals had proceeded far too rapidly, with no alternatives in place. It was not closure that the hospitals needed, but fixing: a plan to deal with overcrowding, understaffing, negligence, and brutality. Simply treating the problems with drugs was not enough. The benign aspects of the asylum had been forgotten, and they had stopped offering the safe haven that the first state hospitals were meant to provide.

But by then, it was too late. The state hospitals had been shuttered and left to decay and soon became havens for the homeless, many of whom had once been inmates, for urban explorers, and thrill-seekers. It was not long before many of them gained a reputation for being haunted.

In the 1840s, Illinois did not have a system in place for the care of the state's mentally ill citizens, who were then either living with their families or kept in the local poor house. The catalyst for the creation of Illinois' first asylum – as well as asylums in other states – was schoolteacher-turned-reformer Dorothea Dix, who, beginning in the early 1840s, traveled across America lobbying states to build hospitals for the proper care of the "indigent insane." She knew just how bad things were. Her tours of America's asylums revealed that people with mental illness were often treated no better than criminals and were often kept in jails and cages. The insane asylums that did exist were a slightly better option, but offered no treatment.

Dix's humanitarian appeals were persuasive and they were well timed: expansionist America was eager to create large civic institutions that would serve as models to an enlightened society. Public schools, universities, prisons and asylums were all part of this agenda, though the high-minded rhetoric was not always matched by the less-than-altruistic motives of politicians. Regardless, Dix bullied and cajoled one state legislature after another until they bent to her will. In Illinois, she addressed the State Legislature in December 1846, asking for an institution to be founded to serve people with mental illnesses.

On March 1, 1847, the Legislature established the Illinois State Asylum and Hospital for the Insane with a nine-member board of trustees that was empowered to appoint a superintendent, purchase land within four miles of Jacksonville, and construct facilities. At the time, only two other states had state-operated facilities for the mentally ill. The hospital was created to shift the economic burden of the mentally ill onto the state, which paid all of the patients' expenses. However, patients (or their county of residence) remained responsible for transportation, clothing, and incidentals.

The original board hired James M. Higgins as the Superintendent and purchased 160 acres of land for $3,270 on the south side of Jacksonville, along what is now Morton Avenue. Construction began in 1848, and although Dorothea Dix expressed the wish that the Jacksonville State Hospital be opened by 1849, it actually took more than three years, thanks to construction problems and other delays.

Dix was the catalyst for the first wave of asylum building, but it was Thomas Story Kirkbride who provided the blueprint for their expansion. Kirkbride, who served as the superintendent of the Pennsylvania Hospital for the Insane in Philadelphia, drew on his own experience and travels in Europe to devise the model asylum. As a skilled administrator, he was obsessed with asylum design and management. He believed that a well-designed and beautifully landscaped hospital could heal mental illness. If the insane were placed in a peaceful, structured environment, he believed, they had a much better chance of returning to the outside world as an improved individual. His belief – and the design that he created – helped to spread the idea that lunacy could be cured in a hospital, not at home.

The asylum building was the cornerstone of Kirkbride's idea. It consisted of a central administration building flanked symmetrically by linked pavilions, each stepping back to create a "V, like a formation of birds in flight, or as some have called it, a "bat-wing design." The layout was designed by sex, illness, and social class. The most disturbed patients were housed in the outermost wards, while those more socially adjusted lived closer to the center, where the staff lived. The stepped arrangement of the wards made the hospital easier to manage, while at the same time, admitted an abundance of light with views of the outdoors. The location of the planned asylums – like the hospital in Jacksonville – was meant to be in the country, away from the city, offering privacy and land for farming and gardening. The land immediately around the asylum was used for pleasure, where the patients could take a relaxing stroll and admire picturesque views.

The "Kirkbride Plan" was an American invention and the state hospital brought this design to Jacksonville. For many local residents, especially those who had never been to a major city, the Kirkbride building on the state hospital grounds would be the largest building they would ever see. Building the asylum required enormous state expenditures and an army of workers who lived on-site during the construction. It was a technological marvel of the time, offering modern amenities such as fireproof construction, central heating, plumbing, and gaslight. But it was not a hospital in the modern sense of the word. On the outside, it exuded grandeur, but inside, it resembled a dormitory. Each pavilion in the structure was three stories high, with one ward per floor. The ward consisted of a long, wide hallway, lined by small bedrooms. Each ward also contained a dining room, a parlor or sitting room, bathrooms, storage closets and rooms for attendants. Patients spent most of their time in the hallways or common areas, not in the bedrooms, which were locked during the day and used only for sleeping.

The Illinois State Hospital in Jacksonville finally opened on November 3, 1851. Only two of the wards were ready for occupancy, but that day saw the first patient arrive at the asylum's doors. Sophronia McElhiney, of McLean County, was admitted with a disagnosis of "extreme jealousy." She remained at the hospital for the next 16 years.

The requirements that allowed people to be admitted to the hospital in those days would be totally unacceptable in the modern age. The "supposed exciting causes of insanity," as they were called at the time, ranged from "novel reading" to "abortion." According to the hospital's 11th biennial report, there were 623 patients admitted between 1866 and 1868. The "exciting causes" of four of those were "jealousy," seven were admitted for "overexertion" and 30 for religious excitement. Early treatment emphasized fresh air, activities, and exercise. More sophisticated treatment methods, including any kind of medication, were extremely limited. Many of the residents remained at the hospital for decades and new patients continued to be admitted on a regular basis.

In 1865, the Jacksonville hospital saw the admittance of a young woman named Mary Roff, from Watseka. Mary had been suffering from seizures and fits that sent her into what her family called "trances." These spells could last for minutes or hours. The only relief that she found was through blood-letting with leeches, but Mary became obsessed with cutting herself. After a particularly violent session, she nearly bled to death. Her family had no choice but to admit her to the asylum. She died mysteriously on July 5, 1865, from no apparent cause.

But that was not the end of Mary Roff's story.

In 1877, another young woman from Watseka named Lurancy Vennum began to suffer from the same type of fits and seizures that had afflicted Mary. In Lurancy's case, her spells included claims of speaking with angels and with dead family members. Like Mary, various doctors and religious men examined Lurancy and could do nothing to help her. They recommended that the Vennum family send Lurancy away to the asylum. But before this could happen, a man named Asa Roff called at the Vennum home. He explained to them that his own daughter, Mary, had been afflicted with the same condition that Lurancy was suffering from. He begged the Vennums not to send Lurancy to the asylum. He had mistakenly sent his own daughter away years before and she had later died. Despite her death, though, he was convinced that his daughter's spirit still existed. Little did he know, however, that it would soon become apparent to many that his daughter's spirit was now inside of the body of Lurancy Vennum.

This was the beginning of a series of strange and fantastic events that rocked the little town of Watseka and created a mystery that remains unsolved to this day.

Lurancy Vennum, born April 16, 1864, was the daughter of Thomas Jefferson Vennum, and his wife, Lurinda. Thomas Vennum had come to Illinois when he was a child and had been a farmer all of his life. He was well-liked in Watseka and was known as an ordinary, hard-working man. There was nothing out of the ordinary about the family until their troubles began in 1877.

Lurancy had never been a sickly girl, nor an especially imaginative one. For both reasons, her family was surprised when the strange events began. She had never been seriously ill and she had never made up stories

Lurancy Vennum (Left) & Mary Roff

or told fanciful tales about much of anything at all. However, in the early days of July, she began speaking of mysterious voices that came to her in the night. According to her story, they had roused her from her sleep. She stated: "There were persons in my room last night, and they called 'Rancy, Rancy…' and I felt their breath upon my face." She seemed to be frightened by what had occurred and was convinced that she had not dreamed it. Her parents had never known her to lie but, not believing in such things, they were not inclined to give credence to her story. They merely assumed that their daughter had experienced a very vivid nightmare, one so real that she believed that she was awake when it happened.

The following night, the same thing happened again. Lurancy was terrified and refused to stay in her room. She rose in the dead of night and nervously paced the parlor, too frightened to return to her second-floor bedroom. She told her mother that each time she tried to sleep, the presence would return, whispering her name. Finally, Lurinda took Lurancy back to her room and they lay down together on the bed. She wrapped her arms around her daughter and coaxed her back to sleep. The rest of the night passed without incident.

But on July 11, 1877, the possession truly began.

On that otherwise ordinary morning, Lurancy got out of bed feeling dizzy and nauseated. She complained to her mother about feeling sick but went about her household chores as usual. Around six o'clock that evening, after the day's heat had begun to fade, Lurinda asked Lurancy to help her start supper. Lurancy had been sewing a carpet that afternoon, and she put aside her things and rose to come into the kitchen. The moment she walked into the room, she said that she felt strange, and collapsed to the floor. She was so quiet that she seemed to be dead and every muscle in her body had gone rigid and cold.

She stayed in a deep, catatonic sleep for the next five hours but when she woke up, she said she felt fine. The following day, Lurancy again slipped into a trance-like sleep but this time was different. This time, as she lay perfectly still, she began to speak out loud, talking of visions and spirits and carrying on conversations with people that no one else could see. She told her family that she was in heaven and that she could see and hear spirits. She described them and called some of them by name. Among them was her brother, who she affectionately called "Bertie." He had died when Lurancy was only three years old.

In the days and weeks that followed, Lurancy's spells came more and more frequently, and they sometimes lasted for more than eight hours at a time. While she was in her trance state, she continued to speak about her visions, which were sometimes terrifying. She began to see more and more spirits, including those who had terrorized her at night in her bedroom. So many of them were unfamiliar and frightening to her and she would cry out while in the midst of her spells. At times, Lurancy reportedly spoke in other languages, or at least spouted nonsense words that no one could understand. She lapsed into lengthy trances that would sometimes last for hours each day. When she awoke, she would remember nothing of what had happened during the trance and was always ignorant of her weird ramblings.

On November 27, 1877, Lurancy began to complain of a violent pain in her stomach. The pain remained a dull, throbbing ache, but several times each day, it became excruciating. The sharp, stabbing pain would always come on quite suddenly, making Lurancy scream and moan in torment. She would fall to the floor, her teeth grinding in agony, as the pain ripped through her body.

These horrendous episodes went on for about two weeks, only coming to an end on December 11, when Lurancy slipped once more into one of the dreaded trances that her parents thought had gone away. She was seized by one of these spells and slowly sank to the floor, completely unconscious. Her body rigidly remained in the same position for the next several hours. When she awakened, the abdominal pains were gone.

Unfortunately, though, the spells had returned. For the next several weeks, the trances came over her and lasted for two hours, three hours, or even as long as eight hours. They occurred as many as twelve times each day, sending Lurancy into a place where she once again began to speak with the spirits that she saw there. She called them "angels" and held long eerie conversations with them, of which she would remember nothing when she finally regained consciousness.

Shortly after the trances had begun, Lurancy was placed under the care of Dr. L.N. Pittwood, who was one of the city's best-known medical practitioners. He could find nothing physically wrong with her. The family turned to a physician called Dr. Jewett for answers after the stomach pains and new spells, but he was also at a loss as to what was causing the illness. Many of the friends and family members of the Vennums believed that Lurancy had gone insane, and the family's minister, the Reverend B.M. Baker from the Methodist church, went as far as to contact the state asylum in Jacksonville to see if the girl could be admitted there. It was the general opinion among those whose counsel the Vennums valued, that the girl should be institutionalized.

Stories and rumors about Lurancy and her visions began to circulate in Watseka. People were talking about the weird happenings and the local newspaper printed stories about them. No one followed the case more closely than Asa Roff. During his own daughter's illness, she had also claimed to communicate with spirits and she fell into long, sometimes violent, trances. He became convinced that Lurancy Vennum was suffering with the same affliction that Mary had. In spite of this, Roff said nothing until the Vennum family had exhausted every known cure for Lurancy and it appeared that she was going to be sent away to the asylum. At this point, he became determined to try and help.

Asa Roff came to the Vennum home in January 1878. The family was naturally skeptical of the reason for his visit. Roff had little more than a casual acquaintance with Thomas Vennum, but he explained that he had become interested in Lurancy's case after hearing the rumors that were going around town. Lurancy claimed to have had contact with the spirits of the dead, the possibility of which, being a devout Spiritualist, he did not doubt in the slightest. However, his real interest was concerning her illness. His late daughter Mary had suffered from an identical condition and she had also given incontrovertible evidence of supernatural powers in the form of clairvoyance. In her time, Mary had also been regarded as insane, although now, years later, Roff was convinced that she had been of sound mind but had been the victim of a "spirit infestation." He believed that the same could be said of Lurancy and he begged the Vennums not to send her to an asylum.

He believed there was a way to help the girl and he convinced the Vennums to allow him to call in one more physician. If there was nothing that this man could do, then they could take whatever steps they believed were necessary to try and help Lurancy. With some reluctance, the Vennums agreed to his plea. Although they didn't know it at the time, their lives would never be the same again.

Roff returned to the Vennum house in the company of Dr. E. Winchester Stevens on January 31. Dr. Stevens was a physician from Janesville, Wisconsin, who, like Roff, was a devout Spiritualist. He was curious about the case, having visited Watseka a few times and had heard about it during the preceding fall. He wanted to offer whatever help he could to the beleaguered family. His interest had been piqued by the medical aspects of the case and by the possibility that Lurancy might be "spirit infested," as he had come to believe that his friend's daughter, Mary Roff, had been.

Stevens and Roff were considering the idea that Lurancy was a sort of vessel through which the dead were communicating. Roff only wished that he had seen the same evidence in his own daughter years before. He believed that if Mary had actually been insane, that she had been driven to madness by the bizarre gifts and abilities that she possessed. No one had been able to help Mary but he believed that Stevens could help Lurancy Vennum. He didn't want to see what had happened to Mary befall someone else's daughter, and so he had brought Dr. Stevens to Watseka in order for him to examine Lurancy.

When they arrived at the house that afternoon, Dr. Stevens found Lurancy sitting in the kitchen next to the stove. She sat in a chair with her feet curled up under her. Her chin was in her hands and her elbows rested on her knees. She was slumped over, staring at the stove as though entranced by something in the dancing flames. Mrs. Vennum spoke to her but she did not respond. She remained with her eyes fixed straight ahead, as if she was unaware of anyone else in the room. Dr. Stevens attempted to communicate with either Lurancy, or the spirit inside of her. At first, the girl refused to speak. Dr. Stevens made several attempts to communicate, and then stood up from his chair. When he did, Lurancy also stood up. Almost immediately, her hands fluttered in the air and her eyes rolled back into her head. Her body stiffened and she fell, crashing to the hard wooden floor. Her body was rigid and it appeared that she had gone into another of her mysterious trances.

Mr. Vennum and Mr. Roff managed to get Lurancy back into her chair and Dr. Stevens sat down in front of her again. He managed to pry her hands, which were stiffly held against her chest, away from her body and took them into his own. His voice lowered to a soft, even tone and he began to speak to her, stroking her hands and easing her out of the control of the spell. Soon, Lurancy's voice became her own and she began to speak to Dr. Stevens, maintaining that while her body was in the Vennum house, her consciousness was in heaven, where she was conversing with angels.

In this hypnotized condition, Lurancy answered the doctor's questions and spoke of her seemingly insane condition and the influences that were controlling her. She spoke of various spirits that had been controlling her body, forcing her to do and say horrible things. Stevens explained to her that she was able to control what spirits influenced her and then asked her that, if she was going to be controlled by spirits, wouldn't it be better to be controlled by a happier, more intelligent and rational being? Lurancy agreed that this would be preferable if she could do it.

Lurancy sat for several minutes in eerie silence. By this time, the winter sun had long since set and the Vennum kitchen was dimly lighted by the fire from the stove and one kerosene lamp that had been placed on the table. The lengthening shadows danced across the room as Lurancy waited, then let out a long sigh before she spoke again. She said that she had looked about, and had inquired of those around her, to find someone who would prevent the cruel and insane spirits on the other side from returning to annoy her and her family.

She said: "There are a great many spirits here who would be glad to come."

Lurancy waited for several more minutes and then explained that she had found one spirit who wanted to come with her. The spirit was a young woman who believed that she could help Lurancy in a way that no other spirit could.

Dr. Stevens asked her the name of the spirit and her whispered reply echoed in the kitchen. Lurancy spoke: "Her name is Mary Roff."

While the name of Mary Roff may have sent shivers down the spines of some of the adults who were present, the name meant nothing to Lurancy herself. She had never heard of the girl and could not have known what had happened to her years before. Even if we take into consideration that rumors may have circulated about the Roff family and their crazy daughter that they once had to lock up in an asylum and who had subsequently died, it's likely that Lurancy would not have been exposed to them. The Roff and Vennum families had never had any real contact with one another and Lurancy had been a very young child when Mary had died.

Asa Roff soon recovered from the surprise of hearing his daughter's name on Lurancy's lips. He quickly assured the girl that Mary had been a good and intelligent young woman and would certainly help her in any way that she could. He added that Mary had once suffered from an affliction much like the one that was now bothering Lurancy.

Silence again filled the kitchen as Lurancy's unconscious mind appeared to deliberate about Mary's presence. Finally, she agreed that Mary would take the place of the troubled and disturbed spirits who had initially possessed her body.

Lurancy remained in her trance for the rest of the evening and into the next day. During this time, she claimed to be Mary Roff. She was not a spirit inhabiting another girl's body; she insisted that she actually was Mary! She claimed that she had no idea where she was, was unable to recognize the Vennum house, which was a place where Mary Roff had never been. She wanted to go home, she said, which meant back to the Roff house.

Lurancy was so insistent about this that on the following morning, Friday, February 1, Thomas Vennum called at the office of Asa Roff and explained to him what was happening. He said that his daughter continued to claim that she was Mary and demanded that she be allowed to go home.

The Vennums had mixed feelings about these latest developments. They were happy to see that the rigid, corpse-like spells, excruciating pain, and weird trances had passed, but now they were faced with having a stranger in their home. She was very polite, mild, and docile, but she constantly begged the Vennums to let her go home. They tried to convince her, as did Mr. Roff, that she was already at home but the girl was having none of it. She would not be pacified. The Vennums were becoming more and more convinced that this girl was no longer their daughter.

The news of this amazing new development quickly spread, and when Mrs. Roff heard what had happened, she hurried to the Vennum house in the company of her married daughter, Minerva Alter. The two women hurried up the sidewalk of the Vennum house and saw Lurancy sitting by the window. When she saw them approaching, she cried out: "Here comes Ma and Nervie!" As they came into the house, she hugged and kissed the surprised women and wept for joy. It was said that no one had called Minerva by the nickname "Nervie" since Mary's death in 1865.

From this time on, Lurancy seemed even more homesick than before, frantically wanting to leave and go home with the Roffs. It now seemed entirely possible to everyone involved that Mary Roff had taken control of Lurancy. Even though the girl still looked like Lurancy Vennum, she knew everything about the Roff family and she treated them as her loved ones. To the Vennums, she was distantly polite, as though they were strangers. The Vennums were understandably shocked and unnerved by the turn of events. Their daughter had become someone completely unknown to them.

Finally, some friends of the family insisted that the Vennums allow the girl to go home with the Roffs for a time. The Vennums were reluctant to do so. They were still befuddled by what was going on and they felt that it would be an imposition to send their daughter to be cared for by strangers, no matter who she claimed to be. But after a few more days of the girl's weeping and begging to "go home," the Vennums decided to discuss the situation with the Roffs. It was a delicate problem but one that Mr. and Mrs. Roff agreed to take on. Braving the ridicule of people in town, and with no other motive but one of kindness, they opened their home to receive Lurancy.

On February 11, Lurancy --- or rather "Mary" --- was allowed to go to the Roff home. The Vennums agreed that this arrangement would be for the best, at least temporarily. They desperately hoped that Lurancy would regain her true identity. The Roffs, meanwhile, saw the possession as a "miracle," as though Mary had returned from the grave. They took Lurancy across town, and as they were riding in the buggy, they passed by the former Roff home, where they had been living when Mary died. The home now belonged to Minerva and her husband, Henry Alter. The girl demanded to know why they were not stopping, and the Roffs had to explain that they had moved several years before to a brick home on Fifth Street. The young woman's lack of knowledge about this move, as well as her identification of the old house, was further proof to the Roffs that Lurancy had been possessed by their dead daughter.

Lurancy's arrival in the Roff home, as Mary, was met with great excitement. She immediately began calling the Roffs "ma and pa" and recognized each member of the family. Even though Lurancy knew none of them herself, she greeted them, as Mary, with affection. One of them asked her how long she would stay and she replied: "The angels will let me stay until sometime in May."

For the next several months, Lurancy lived as Mary and seemed to have forgotten about her former life. As the days passed, Lurancy continued to show that she knew more about the Roff family, their possessions, and their habits than she could have possibly known if she had been merely faking. Many of the incidents that she referred to had taken place years before Lurancy had been born. Her physical condition began to improve while staying with the Roffs and she no longer suffered from the frightening attacks that had plagued her.

She appeared to be quite contented while living in the Roff home, and she recognized and called by name many of the neighbors and family friends known to Mary during her lifetime. In contrast, she claimed not to recognize any family members, friends, or associates of the Vennums. Even though the Vennums allowed their daughter to live with the Roff family, they visited her often. Lurancy, while living as Mary, soon learned to love these "strangers" as friends.

Her day-to-day life in the Roff home was anything but unusual. She was easygoing, affable, and hardworking, helping with the household chores, cooking and cleaning and going about the activities of any young girl of the time. She liked to read and sing, as Mary always had, and she loved sitting with her father and talking about anything that came to her mind. One day, she met an old friend and neighbor of the Roffs, who had been a widow with the surname Lord when Mary was a girl. Some years after Mary had died, the woman had married a Mr. Wagoner. This seemed to be unknown to the girl. When the two were reunited, Lurancy hugged her tightly and called her by the last name of her late husband. She did not seem to be able to comprehend that this family friend had remarried. And events like these continued. She met distant relatives and old friends and spoke of fond memories and connections that she had with them – trivial information that Lurancy could not have known. People were becoming convinced that Lurancy really was possessed by the spirit of Mary Roff.

But, of course, not everyone believed it. The Vennums' minister, Reverend Baker, after learning that Lurancy was staying with the Roffs, pleaded with the family once again to have the girl committed to the state asylum. He told them: "I think you will see the time when you will wish that you had sent her to the asylum." He said others in the congregation shared his opinion, and added: "I would sooner follow a girl of mine to the grave than have her go to the Roffs' and be made a Spiritualist."

Several of the doctors who had attempted to treat Lurancy started spreading scathing rumors about Dr. Stevens and dismissed the case as nothing more than catalepsy and "humbug." They believed that Lurancy was faking the whole thing and making fools of her parents and the Roff family. Of course, no one who voiced these opinions in Watseka had actually visited either family and had no in-depth knowledge of the situation. This ignorance did not stop the rumors from being spread, though, and the Roffs and Vennums were ridiculed by many in the community. For the most part, they ignored the laughter and the disdain, believing that something truly authentic and supernatural was taking place.

On May 7, Lurancy (as Mary) called Mrs. Roff to a private room and there, in tears, informed her that Lurancy Vennum would be coming back soon. She could feel the other girl's spirit returning and she had no idea whether or not Lurancy would be staying or not. If Mary was going to be released from the body, then she hoped that she would have time to see Allie, Minerva, and Henry so that she could tell them goodbye. The girl wept as she told these things to Mrs. Roff and it was almost as if, no matter how much she wanted to help Lurancy, Mary didn't want to let go of the earthly form that she had managed to obtain.

The young woman sat down in a chair and over the course of the next few minutes, a battle took place for control of her physical form. Her eyes slowly closed and her face shifted expressions several times before her eyes fluttered open again. The girl, confused, looked wildly about before exclaiming: "Where am I? I have never been here before!"

Lurancy Vennum had returned.

Mrs. Roff sat down next to the girl and held her hand, gently rubbing her arm. She tried to calm the girl: "You are at Mr. Roff's, brought here by Mary to cure your body."

Lurancy burst into tears. "I want to go home!"

Mrs. Roff soothed her and told her that someone would send for her parents. She then asked the girl if she felt any pain in her breast. (Lurancy, or Mary, had been complaining of the pain for a few days, continually holding her left breast and pressing on it with her fingers).

Lurancy looked puzzled for a moment and then seemed surprised when she spoke with some confusion: "No, but Mary did."

Lurancy remained with Mrs. Roff for only a few minutes and then a subtle change seemed to sweep over her body and her features. A quiet humming sound came from the girl's lips and then softly turned into song that had been a childhood favorite of Mary's. The dead girl had returned to the body of Lurancy Vennum.

Mary's return was marked by sadness. Everyone knew that, after the brief return of Lurancy, it was nearly time for her to leave. Over the next two weeks, a battle raged for the control of Lurancy's body. At one moment, Lurancy would announce that she had to leave and at the next she would cling to her father and cry at the idea of leaving him. She spent nearly every day going from one family member to another, hugging them and touching them at every opportunity. She became increasingly upset with each passing day, weeping at the thought of leaving her "real family."

As more time passed, Lurancy's control over her own body began to slowly return. Mary's spirit would sometimes recede for a time. Mary's identity was not lost, nor did Lurancy's personality return, but it was enough to provide evidence that she was slowly returning to her own body.

On the afternoon of Sunday, May 19, Lurancy was sitting in the parlor with Mr. Roff. Henry Vennum, Lurancy's brother, was seated in a chair in the hallway. Other members of the Roff family waited with him in the corridor. He had come to the house to visit his sister and Roff, based on recent experiences, felt that Lurancy's spirit was near. It soon turned out that he was correct in his assumptions. In a matter of moments, Mary departed and Lurancy took control of her body again. Henry was called in and when he stepped into the room, Lurancy wrapped her arms around his neck, kissed his cheek and burst into tears. She was so happy to see him that Henry started to cry, which caused everyone else in the household to weep.

Mr. Roff asked Lurancy if she would be able to stay with them until someone could go to the Vennum house and bring back her mother. Lurancy answered that she could not, but if her mother were brought over, she would come again and be able to talk with her. Her eyes seemed to waver for a moment and her body shook slightly --- Lurancy was gone. It was obvious to everyone gathered in the parlor that Mary had returned. However, Lurinda Vennum was brought to the Roff house within the hour and when she came into the parlor, Lurancy once again regained full control of her body. Mother and daughter embraced one another, kissed and wept until everyone assembled was crying in sympathy. Lurancy stayed for a few minutes and then, as mysteriously as she had gone, Mary Roff returned and Mrs. Vennum was a beloved stranger once more.

But it would not stay that way for much longer.

On the morning of May 21, Asa Roff wrote to Dr. Stevens that Mary was planning to leave Lurancy's body that very day. Word was sent to family members and friends so that they could say goodbye to her. After a time of farewells and kisses, the girl's eyes rolled back into her head and she was Lurancy again. She told Minerva and Mr. Roff that she felt as though she had been asleep for a very long time, yet knew that she had not. She asked Mr. Roff if he would take her home and he immediately agreed to do so.

Lurancy returned home to the Vennum house. She displayed none of the strange symptoms of her earlier illness and her parents were convinced that she had somehow been cured, thanks to the intervention of the spirit of Mary Roff. She soon became a healthy and happy young woman, suffering no ill effects from her strange experience. She had no memories of the possession, other than of those things that Mary allowed her to know. It was as if the months that she spent as Mary Roff had never happened at all.

In June 1878, Dr. Stevens returned to Watseka to renew his friendship with the Roff and Vennum families. He was especially curious as to whether or not any of Lurancy's spells or trances had returned and whether Mary Roff had actually managed to cure the girl of her affliction.

On Sunday, June 2, Stevens met with Lurancy and her parents at the house of a friend, who lived about two miles away from the Vennums. Lurancy was introduced to him by her father. She was sure that she had never met the man before and came across as a little shy, as one might expect from a young girl meeting a stranger for the first time. They spoke very little that day and Stevens left the meeting feeling both disappointed that he could learn nothing more from the girl and excited that she truly seemed to have been the victim of a possession. She remembered nothing of meeting the doctor during the time that she was living as Mary Roff.

The next day, June 3, brought him a great surprise. Without any notice to anyone as to where he was going that day, Dr. Stevens stopped unannounced at the home of a friend, a noted attorney in Watseka. As he was entering the gate, Lurancy Vennum walked up beside him and greeted him warmly. The doctor was surprised by her presence, especially as she had seemed so reluctant to talk with him the previous day. Lurancy said: "How do you do, Doctor? Mary Roff told me to come here and meet you. Somehow she makes me feel that you have been a very kind friend to me." Lurancy then went on to deliver a long message for the doctor that she claimed to have received from Mary.

Dr. Stevens later wrote that since the June 3 meeting, he had seen Lurancy many times and on every occasion, she was very friendly and forthcoming. Something about her demeanor had changed and he was convinced that it was because of the intervention of Mary Roff.

As weeks passed, everyone involved in the case watched very closely to see how Lurancy behaved. Would they see a return of the strange seizures and spells? Would they see the possession by Mary Roff return? We can only imagine the anxiety that must have filled the hearts of the Vennums, and even those of the Roffs, who had come to consider Lurancy almost a part of their own family.

The story of what became known as the "Watseka Wonder" changed forever the town of Watseka. Whether local residents believed in the veracity of the possession or not – and scores of them did believe it, based on the number of signed affidavits that remain in town archives today – they knew that something truly mysterious had taken place in the community. It is regarded today as the best-documented case of spirit possession in history.

Lurancy remained in touch with the Roff family for the rest of her life. Although she had no real memories of her time as Mary, she still felt a curious closeness to them that she could never explain. On January 1, 1882, Lurancy married George Binning, a farmer who lived about three miles west of Watseka. In 1884, they moved west to Rawlins County, Kansas, in the northwestern corner of the state.

The Roffs visited with Lurancy often, and saw her at least once each year after she moved to Kansas. Whenever she returned home to Watseka to see her parents, she always stayed with the Roffs for part of the time. During these visits, she would allow Mary to take control of her, just as she did when living with them in 1878.

Aside from this, Lurancy had little occasion to use the mediumistic skills that she had acquired. Her parents rarely spoke with her on the subject, fearing that it would cause a return of the "spells" that plagued her before she was possessed by Mary. Her husband had no interest in Spiritualism and this, combined with her household chores and care of her children, made her spirit possessions and talking with the dead things of the past.

Oddly, Lurancy told the Roffs that she was never sick a day in her life after Mary cured her in 1878.

Lurancy lived in Kansas until the death of her husband when he was in his 50s. After that, she moved to Oklahoma for a time and then eventually settled down in Long Beach, California, in 1910. She died there, at the age of 88, in 1952. She raised eleven children but it was said that none of them knew of her strange time as the "Watseka Wonder" until they were informed of it after her death by a cousin.

The Vennum family stayed on in Watseka for many years, but after the death of her husband, Lurinda Vennum moved to Kansas to live with Lurancy and her grandchildren. Both of the Vennums are buried in Oak Hill Cemetery in Watseka.

Dr. Stevens wrote a book about the case and lectured on the "Watseka Wonder" for eight years before dying in Chicago in 1886. He was convinced that what had occurred had been genuine and that Mary Roff had actually taken over the body of Lurancy Vennum for a time.

Asa and Dorothy Ann Roff received hundreds of letters, from believers and skeptics alike, after the story of the possession was printed in newspapers and appeared in magazines all over the country. In 1879, Roff was elected as justice of the peace in Watseka but resigned the position in June of that same year. Without much explanation, he moved to Garden City, Kansas, where his sons lived and where the family had invested considerable amounts of money. He invested in farmland but found that the climate was too dry for it to be profitable and moved to Emporia, Kansas, where he and his wife lived for a year. From Kansas, Roff moved to Council Bluffs, Iowa, for two years and then moved to Kansas City, where he lived for several more years.

In 1885, Roff moved back to Watseka and there he and his wife lived the rest of their lives. In the spring of 1889, he was elected police magistrate for a term of four years and once more served as justice of the peace. He and Dorothy Ann were both buried in Oak Hill Cemetery.

The story of the Watseka Wonder remains one of the strangest unsolved mysteries in the annals of American history. What really happened in this small Illinois town in 1878? Did the spirit of Mary Roff really possess the body of Lurancy Vennum? It seems almost impossible to believe, but the families of both young women, as well as hundreds of friends and supporters, certainly believed that it happened. One thing is certain --- something extraordinary happened in Watseka involving Lurancy Vennum, her family and the family of a dead girl named Mary Roff. Was it a true spirit possession, a case of mental illness, or the most elaborate and carefully constructed hoax of the 1870s?

The reader will have to decide what they choose to believe. As for my thoughts on this mysterious case? Well, I still don't know. I do believe that something amazing occurred in Watseka in the spring of 1878 and believe that it permanently affected not only the Vennum and Roff families, but also the entire town of Watseka itself.

Was Lurancy actually possessed by the spirit of Mary Roff? Logic tells us that it couldn't have happened, but this case certainly gives us pause. The story of the "Watseka Wonder" can make just about anyone wonder if we know as much about the unexplained as we think we do.

Like so many lofty ideals, the state hospitals often failed to live up to their expectations. Jacksonville's asylum was no exception. It soon became overcrowded by an influx of the poor, many of them immigrants, who did not respond well to "moral treatment," which was biased by class. The elderly and the chronically ill – two groups that would never get better – began filling up the wards. As the population of the place began to expand, the need for control prevailed, making the treatment more custodial than curative. The hospital was held accountable to the State Legislature for its expenditures and so the financial panics of 1873, 1893, and 1907, as well as periods of recession, took their toll, leading to budget cuts and staff shortages. Low wages, high turnover rates and inexperienced attendants led to patient abuse and corruption.

By the latter part of the 1850s, the hospital had outgrown the Old Main building, its only building, which had been built to accommodate 250 patients, but held many more. In 1858, the west wing was added to the main building. An east wing was added in 1867, as the hospital's population rose to 450. By 1876, the hospital had 1,200 residents and the need for another building was apparent. The Annex was built in 1886 and expanded in 1892. At three stories high and a quarter-mile long, it briefly held the distinction of being the longest continuous three-story building in the world.

When the Board of State Commissioners of Public Charities was abolished in 1909, the institute was reorganized and renamed Jacksonville State Hospital. In 1917, the Department of Public Welfare assumed responsibility for the hospital and retained control until the creation of the Illinois Department of Mental Health in 1961.

The hospital's population reached its peak in 1952 with 3,616 residents. Keeping the inmates busy was a priority. A broom shop, print shop, carpentry shop, greenhouse, and gazebos were all constructed for the patient's diversion. Patients worked for free, supplementing the work done by employees, and allowing the ever-shrinking budget of the hospital to stretch further. They grew crops, raised cattle, pigs and chickens, and made furniture and clothing. The hospital, with thousands of patients and staff, along with hundreds of acres of land, functioned more like a work farm than a medical facility.

Just caring for all those people's basic needs was a massive undertaking. The facility was almost like a city. There were 100 buildings on the campus, which had its own dairy farm, butcher, kitchen, fire station, bowling alley, and power plant. The complex even had its own medical hospital, known as the Acute Care Hospital and later as the Bowen Building. There was a morgue and an existing cemetery on Lincoln Avenue, where residents who died at the facility were buried.

After a peak in the middle 1950s, the patient population began to decline steadily after the introduction of psychotropic drugs, changes in commitment laws, and a shift in policy about community-based care. Medications that were effective in treating involuntary behavior became available at this time, leading to the discharge of many patients who otherwise would have remained institutionalized for the rest of their lives. A series of court decisions confirmed a constitutional right to treatment and establishing minimum standards of care. This ultimately resulted in the loss of patient labor and deprived the hospital of its important inmate work force. This delivered a fatal blow to the hospital's economic viability.

Thanks to this, population at the Jacksonville institution began to decline. By 1967, there were 1,699 residents, and in 1972, the population dropped to 591. It continued to drop during its remaining years in operation.

In the early 1970s, the state hospital wound down its agricultural and manufacturing programs. Shops closed, services were contracted to the private sector, and farms were sold off to help pay for mandated services. Buildings already in disrepair were left to deteriorate further, too expensive to renovate and bring up to code.

In 1970, the facility was renamed the Jacksonville Mental Health and Developmental Center, and later, the Jacksonville Developmental Center (JDC), to reflect its declining psychiatric population and its rising population of developmentally disabled residents. The facility closed its last unit for the mentally ill in 1976. Today, most people with mental illnesses are treated within their own communities. For those who are committed, their stays are usually numbered in days instead of months and years. Hospitalization is a last resort.

Much of the hospital's acreage was sold off or donated to other public agencies, including the 62 acres that were given to the city for Jacksonville's Community Park in 1982. In September 2011, Governor Pat Quinn announced a plan to close the facility in February 2012 due to budget issues. The last residents moved out in November 2012.

These days, there are only a scattering of buildings from the old hospital still in existence. Many buildings, including the Annex and the Old Main, have been demolished. While many are gone, others have been renovated and have been put back into limited use. The empty structures stand forlorn and abandoned, slowly crumbling on land that once was home to a thriving hospital.

They continue to stand, silent and dark – but are they empty?

The debris of decades still remain in many of them. As the buildings decayed, packed with vast amounts of old patient files that were left to gather mold and dust in dank forgotten basements and broken pieces of furniture that haven't been used in decades, we wonder about the patients that once lived and died within these walls. But what else has been left behind?

With decades of trauma being experienced within these walls by patients who faced both their own mental afflictions and forced treatments in search of a "cure," it's no surprise that the psychic "debris" of decades remains behind with the broken furniture and crumbling artifacts. Imprints of their disturbed thoughts and erratic emotions are eerily strong in the buildings where the insane were housed and strange disturbances are common. Hospitals have long been regarded as places were the spirits of the dead can linger. Are there lost and broken souls trapped in the abandoned halls of these crumbling buildings? Are they truly the personalities of those who once lived here? Or are they simply spooky ideas conjured up by staff members and visitors who venture into these forbidding places? The atmosphere of many of the buildings at JDC is more than enough to justify the reports of apparitions and ghostly encounters, but we'll leave the truth to such tales up to the reader to decide.

Those who have worked in the buildings that remain at the site, renovated and used for other businesses and agencies after being abandoned by the developmental center, have unnerving stories to tell of ghosts – phantom footsteps, tapping and knocking sounds, voices, and shadowy figures that seem to be solid and yet disappear without warning. Telephones rang and no one would be on the other end of the line. Or the line would be discovered connected to a room that had been locked up for years. One supervisor confessed that she would often get calls at home that came from the Winslow Building of the old hospital – mysterious calls that came between 1:00 and 3:00 a.m. There was no one in the building at the time. It was locked up tight all night and security guards patrolled the grounds. The calls were never explained. Even now, a number of years after the former hospital was abandoned, stories are told of phantom figures that are seen on the grounds, faces peering from windows, and lights in buildings that have been dark and empty since the center closed down.

Who still lingers in the remaining buildings of the old Jacksonville State Hospital? Spectral patients or lingering staff members from days gone by? We may never know, but we can certainly all agree that its past is filled with some of the strangest stories in the annals of Central Illinois and its ghosts.

Sounds in the Night
Ghosts of the Norbury Sanatorium

During the nineteenth century, the city of Jacksonville was known throughout the region as the "Athens of the West." The city was home to Illinois College, a women's seminary that eventually became MacMurray College, the state's first school for the hearing impaired, a school for the blind, and, as mentioned previously, Illinois' first state insane asylum.

In the midst of this center for learning and health, a number of private hospitals offered care to residents of the city. There were also two private hospitals for the mentally ill that opened in Jacksonville during this time, for those who could afford a better level of care than what most believed was being offered by the state.

Oak Lawn Retreat, which was also known as McFarland's Insane Retreat, was a private asylum for the mentally ill that was located on a 60-acre site that fronted Morton Avenue on the east side of the city. Unlike the state hospital, Oak Lawn was not hampered by strict budgets or oversight from the Illinois Legislature. Opened by Dr. Andrew McFarland in 1872, the hospital, which was modeled after a Scottish abbey, provided care and treatment that could not be offered in the state institution. For this reason, it attracted patients from all over the Midwest and from states as far away as Colorado, Wyoming, and Oklahoma, which was then Indian Territory. It had room for about 20 patients at a time, each of them from backgrounds that were as diverse as their ailments.

Dr. McFarland was the son of a Concord, Massachusetts, clergyman named Asa McFarland and his wife, Elizabeth Kneeland McFarland. Born in July 1817, he attended Dartmouth College and lectured at Jefferson Medical College in Philadelphia in 1843. He then practiced at Sandwich and Laconia, New Hampshire, and was appointed as the superintendent of the New Hampshire Asylum for the Insane in August 1845. He resigned in November 1852 and traveled to Europe, where he visited and worked in a number of insane asylums, hoping to bring back new ideas for the treatment of the mentally ill in America.

In 1854, he came west and became the third superintendent of the Illinois State Asylum for the Insane in Jacksonville. It was during this time that he met and attempted to ease the "insanity" of Elizabeth Packard, a woman who had been committed against her will because she argued with her husband's religious teachings. In 1867, Dr. McFarland would be one of the people that she filed suit against during a heavily-publicized trial. The trial and the investigation surrounding it earned McFarland a terrible reputation all over the country. Until that time, he had been known as an expert on the treatment of mental health and had consulted on cases across the country. Following the accusations by Mrs. Packard, he began to be seen, as the newspapers called it, "as a fiend in human form." According to his family, his health was shattered by the trial and he remained at the state hospital only a short time longer before resigning. In 1872, he opened his private asylum, Oak Lawn Retreat.

The hospital was a great success and Dr. McFarland finally seemed to be himself again. Unfortunately, an injury he suffered in September 1887 finally ruined his health for good. A fire broke out at the three-story hospital on September 21, and while all of the patients and staff got out of the building safely, McFarland was badly hurt when a piece of furniture that was tossed out of an upstairs window landed on his head. His skull was fractured and doctors feared that he would not survive. Somehow, though, he managed to pull through, but he was never the same again.

After stepping down from the day-to-day operations of the asylum, he turned the management of it over to his son, Dr. George McFarland, and his granddaughter, Dr. Annette McFarland, a graduate of the Rush Medical College in Chicago. Gradually, as his health declined, his personality changed, causing violent mood swings. In time, he became a resident at the hospital that he had started 20 years before.

By November 1891, McFarland's moods were so dangerous that he often had to be locked away. Toward the end of the month, though, he began to seem more like his old self and he was given the freedom of the building. On November 23, McFarland had dinner with his son and then excused himself so that he could to go and visit with one of the inmates with whom he had a special regard. Nothing more was seen of him until later that night, when his body was discovered hanging in the doorway of an empty room in the asylum. Dr. McFarland had twisted a bed sheet into a rope, tied it through a transom above the door, and then took his own life.

The newspapers stated that he was "wearied of existence," but he left no note behind or any indication that he planned to commit suicide. It was ironic that, after all of the people he had helped over the years, there was no one there to try and save him from his own mental demons.

Oak Lawn Retreat remained in operation for 20 more years, operated by McFarland's son and granddaughter. By the early 1900s, the focus of the hospital had changed from strictly a mental hospital to a sanatorium for those who were both wealthy and physically ill. According to advertisements in the early 1900s, they were specializing in the treatment of diseases that were generally considered to be incurable: Bright's disease, hardening of the arteries, Diabetes, high blood pressure, uremia, asthma, various forms of rheumatism, blood poisoning, pyorrhea, acute and chronic ulcers, stomach, heart and kidney diseases, eczema and hay fever. The hospital boasted of being "especially equipped with scientific hydrotherophy," which could apparently cure just about anything.

The fad of using mineral baths such as those at Oak Lawn lasted into the early 1910s and began to fade from popularity. In time, the hospital closed, only to see new life a few years later, when tuberculosis was sweeping the nation and new hospitals were opening for treatment of the disease on a weekly basis.

During the nineteenth and early twentieth centuries, America was ravaged by tuberculosis, or "consumption," as it was often called. This terrifying plague, for which no cure existed before antibiotics were discovered, claimed entire families and occasionally entire towns. After tuberculosis was determined to be contagious in the 1880s, campaigns were started to stop people from spitting in public places and the infected were "encouraged" to enter sanatoriums where they could be quarantined and treated.

Treatments for tuberculosis were sometimes as bad as the disease itself. Some of the experiments that were conducted in search of a cure seem barbaric by today's standards but others are now common practice. Patient's lungs were exposed to ultraviolet light to try and stop the spread of bacteria. This was done in "sun rooms," using artificial light in place of sunlight, or on outside porches and patios. Since fresh air was thought to also be a possible cure, patients were often placed in front of huge windows or on open porches, no matter what the season. Old photographs show patients lounging in chairs, taking in the fresh air, while literally covered with snow.

Other treatments were less pleasant --- and much bloodier. Balloons would be surgically implanted in the lungs and then filled with air to expand them. Another operation was developed in which muscles and ribs were removed from patients' chests to allow the lungs to expand and let in more oxygen. Needless to say, such operations had disastrous results, but were often used as a last resort. Most patients did not survive. Death tolls were high at most such hospitals across the country. It was not until the 1930s that cases of tuberculosis began to decline, thanks to the discovery of antibiotics, which could treat the illness.

In the early 1900s, Jacksonville was just as terrified of tuberculosis as other towns across the country. One of those leading the fight against the disease at this time was Dr. T.O. Hardesty, who helped organize the Morgan County Anti-Tuberculosis Society in 1905, the second such group in Illinois. A few years later, Hardesty established a clinic and began treating patients with tuberculosis. Hardesty lobbied the state of Illinois for help and the Legislature passed a bill authorizing county governments to levy a tax for the purpose of establishing and maintaining tuberculosis sanatoriums. The tax dollars helped Hardesty's organization buy the empty Oak Lawn Retreat in 1917. After the association remodeled the building, they renamed it Oaklawn and it began to serve as Morgan County's tuberculosis sanatorium.

Few drugs were used in the early years of the sanatorium. Sick patients would have their beds wheeled onto a porch on the south side of Oaklawn, where they would be exposed, even in cold weather, to fresh air and sunlight, which were thought to improve the patients' health. An average stay at Oaklawn was from 18 months to two years – if they survived that long. The main use for the hospital was to isolate those who had come down with the disease and to keep them away from those who were still healthy. Families were tragically divided with parents, and even children, forced into the sanatorium with little contact with their loved ones.

After antibiotics were developed, the patient count at Oaklawn began to decline. By the 1960s, Oaklawn was turning more to prevention and early diagnosis, as fewer patients were hospitalized at Oaklawn each year. In 1969, the clinic was moved to the Medical Center on West Walnut Street, and the old sanatorium was torn down in 1981.

The Norbury Sanatorium in the early 1900s

During the last years that the buildings stood in ruins on Country Club Road, just off Morton Avenue, rumors ran rampant that the former hospital was haunted. Stories were often told of strange sights and sounds and even a wandering apparition that might have been Dr. McFarland himself – or perhaps one of the scores of patients and inmates who called the place home over the years.

But the handful of ghost stories that were connected to Oak Lawn Retreat were nothing compared to those told about the second private hospital for the insane that opened in Jacksonville in 1901. The Norbury Sanatorium on South Diamond Street was founded by Dr. Frank Parsons Norbury, who had started his medical practice in Jacksonville in 1888. He was trained in Neurology and Psychiatry and later worked at both the state hospital and Oak Lawn Retreat before opening his own hospital to serve the needs of the mentally ill.

Dr. Norbury was born in Beardstown, Illinois, in August 1863, the youngest son of Charles Joseph Norbury and Elizabeth Peters Norbury. They had 13 children altogether, six sons and seven daughters. As a child, Frank attended public schools and graduated high school in Beardstown in 1881. Immediately after graduation, he became an office and field assistant to Captain R.A. Brown, U.S. Engineer Corps, engaged in improving the Illinois River. He served for five years, and during the winter, when work was stopped, he attended classes at Illinois College. He eventually took up the study of medicine, working for Captain Brown during the summer. In 1886, he entered the Medico-Chirurgical College in Philadelphia and then spent his senior year at Long Island College Hospital in Brooklyn, New York, from which he received his medical degree. Soon after, he took a position on the residence staff of the Pennsylvania Training School for Feebleminded Children, near Philadelphia. The institution, with over 800 inmates, gave Norbury the chance to train in clinical neurology, neuropathology, and mental illness in children. His training continued until he decided to return home to Illinois and accept an appointment on the residence staff of the Illinois State Hospital for the Insane. In addition to his private practice, he remained on staff at the state hospital for five years.

In October 1890, he married Mary Garm, one of his graduating classmates from Beardstown High School, and they made their home at the state hospital for three years. It was there that their son, Frank Garm, was born in January 1892.

In July 1893, Norbury resigned from state service to work full-time in private practice in Jacksonville. During this time, he helped to establish Our Savior's Hospital and was, for many years, an attending physician and a lecturer at the Training School for Nurses. In July 1893, he also began teaching and was a professor of mental and nervous diseases at the Keokuk Medical College. Later, in 1895, he moved to St. Louis and accepted an appointment to the chair of internal medicine at the St. Louis College of Physicians and Surgeons and also as professor of mental and nervous diseases at the Women's Medical College. It was during this time that he also became an editor for a medical journal, a position that he held for 10 years.

Dr. Norbury remained in St. Louis for only one year before coming back to Jacksonville. He returned to his private practice and he also took a physician's position at Oak Lawn Retreat and at the Illinois State School for the Blind. In addition, he continued teaching at Keokuk Medical College, took a teaching position at Illinois College, and a third position at Drake University in Des Moines, Iowa. Then, in 1901, having resigned from Oak Lawn Retreat, he established the Norbury Sanatorium on South Diamond Street.

The new sanatorium was Dr. Norbury's brainchild. He recognized the need for more defined and individual private care for mentally ill patients – the kind of care that they certainly couldn't get in the state facility and which was lacking at Oak Lawn in the years following the death of Dr. McFarland. Norbury felt that advancements were needed in the mental health field and by opening a private hospital that did not depend on state funds was the best way to keep step with, and contribute to, those advancements. He took on two partners to be his Board of Directors, his son, Dr. Frank G. Norbury and Dr. Albert H. Dollear, a student of Norbury's who graduated from the St. Louis University's Medical Department in 1904.

The hospital began modestly with only 15 patients at 806 South Diamond Street, a home that had been remodeled to meet the requirements of hospital service. As the hospital grew, eventually reaching a capacity of 100 patients, more buildings were added. The four buildings – three for patients and one for nurses – were dubbed Maplewood and were situated on 13 acres of ground on what was then the outskirts of the city.

As the sanatorium grew, it became necessary to add more doctors and staff, and Norbury himself never stopped traveling, teaching, and attending conferences that advanced his skills and techniques. He was very active in the social welfare work of the state and served as the president of the Illinois State Conference of Charities and Corrections for 12 years. Illinois Governor Charles S. Deneen also appointed him superintendent of the Kankakee State Hospital in 1909, and he served there two years. At the end of that time, the governor then asked him to serve as the medical member of the Board of Administration of Illinois. This forced him to move to Springfield and he appointed Dr. Dollear to take his place as administrator of the Norbury Sanatorium.

Dr. Norbury continued medical work on a state and national level until 1917, when he was sent overseas during World War I to study conditions there by the Surgeon General's Office of the Army. He served in various capacities with the military until returning to Springfield in May 1919. At this time, he was called upon to assist in organizing the care and treatment of mental cases in returning soldiers.

Although he was seldom not working in some capacity in the medical field, he eventually settled down in Springfield and in 1922, began limiting his work to consultations and the Sanatorium in Jacksonville. He passed away in 1939, having achieved more during his decades of service than most doctors could ever dream of. Three generations of Norbury doctors dedicated their lives to the people of Jacksonville. Frank Garm Norbury and his son, Frank Barnes Norbury, continued the tradition started by their father and grandfather. Together, they provided over 100 years of medical service to others.

As for the hospital created by Dr. Norbury, it lasted until 1967, when the Norbury and Dollear families finally closed it down. The hospital buildings on South Diamond Street still exist today. They were abandoned for a number of years, but in recent times have been converted into apartments. Although some of the buildings have been torn down to make way for other structures, a large part of the hospital, along with the nurse's building, remains intact. The lower floors of one side of the main building have been converted into apartments, combining two former patient's rooms and a section of hallway into a single unit. The other side of the main building, as well as the top floor, are still abandoned.

And that's where things get weird.

In 2015, I had the chance to see the abandoned portions of the old hospital with the owner of the building, Lisa, and my son, Orrin. We spent a couple of hours wandering the hallways and poking into the former patient's rooms, sifting through the debris that had been left behind when the hospital had closed down in 1967. There were bed frames, pieces of decaying furniture, piles of paperwork, and the remnants of scattered lives that were once lived at Norbury Sanatorium.

But the physical evidence of yesterday is not all that has been left behind. According to many of the people who have lived in the apartments that have been fashioned from the wing of the hospital, a presence remains behind there, too. It seems that not all of the patients and staff members of the asylum have truly left. The years of mental anguish that occurred within its walls have left an indelible mark behind.

Over the years, many of the residents have told stories of a haunting at the former hospital. Ghostly encounters have become commonplace. Tales are told of voices that have been heard – sometimes shouting and other times, in calming tones. There are knocking sounds, slamming doors, and footsteps pacing back and forth. But the most chilling part is that the majority of the sounds seem to come from the upper, abandoned floor. There are no apartments on that floor, the doors leading upstairs are either locked or, in some cases, have been walled over. There is no one on the upper floor of the sanatorium when these sounds are heard – no one living anyway.

Occasionally, the encounters with the spirits in the building become a little too close. Not all of the eerie happenings are confined to the top floor. Several tenants claimed to have witnessed a chilling shadow of a tall, slender figure creeping about the building. Another common occurrence is the sound of the wheelchair that has often been reported. The apartments were built so that the hallway on the main floor is cut into sections, alternating between being an entryway from the outside and a portion of the tenant's apartment. There is no straight hallway through most of the building on the lower floor. It's been cut into pieces by the renovations – but this doesn't seem to stop the phantom wheelchair. A number of tenants have reported the sound of the wheels on the tile floor, squeaking along through the building passing through the walls that were not there when the hospital was still in operation.

The Grave of A "Bookbinder"
History & Hauntings of Peoria State Hospital

A few miles outside of the city of Peoria, Illinois, on a bluff that overlooks the Illinois River, are the crumbling remains of the Bowen Building, the administration building of the Peoria State Hospital. It was a place that was built with the best of intentions and part of an asylum filled with hope when the first patients arrived in 1902. By the time that it closed its doors in 1973, though, it had become a relic of the past and a sad reminder of the unrealized dreams of many of the people who had founded it more than 70 years before.

Before 1907, the people of the Peoria area took great pride in what was then called the "Illinois Asylum for the Incurable Insane at Bartonville." Their feelings did not change when the name was altered to the "Illinois General Hospital for the Insane" or, finally, the "Peoria State Hospital" in 1909.

Early in its history, and throughout most of its years of operation, the hospital and adjacent grounds were almost park-like in appearance. This is a far different scene than what can be found there today. For many years, the few original buildings that remained after 1973 were decrepit and badly in need of repair. Those who visited the site were drawn to the large, looming structure, but always with a sense of unease. Today, the

The Peoria State Hospital in the early 1900s

Bowen Building is almost all that remains of the Peoria State Hospital. There are a few others, but they are mostly unrecognizable from what they once were. The cottages and outbuildings have been destroyed and the grounds of the asylum on the hilltop have been filled with new buildings, industrial-type businesses, and garages.

For the most part, people don't come here today looking for the grand place that thousands of mentally ill men and women once called home – they come because of the ghosts. For well over a century, the Peoria State Hospital has almost become synonymous with ghost stories. It wouldn't be until the 1970s when the general public would start to hear stories of the abandoned building being haunted. Since that time, countless tales of encounters with the spirit world have swirled about the old asylum. Prior to that, dating back to the very early days of the institution, the Peoria State Hospital was known to be home to a very famous spirit.

He was called the "Bookbinder" when he was alive and after all of these years, his grave can be found in the oldest cemetery that is located on the hospital's former grounds. He only made one appearance, but it was a sensational one that was witnessed by several hundred people, including the superintendent of the hospital himself.

But there is much more to the story of the Peoria State Hospital than just ghosts – and more to the ghost story that haunts it than most people probably realize.

The Peoria State Hospital (which was actually located in the small, nearby town of Bartonville but named for Peoria because it was the closest railroad station) got off to a rather inauspicious start. The original Kirkbride building that was built in 1896 had to be torn down just one year later after it was found to be collapsing into an abandoned coal mine. The asylum was started over from scratch and by that time, the Kirkbride Plan had started to fall out of favor and had been replaced by the "Cottage Plan," which involved a large administration building and a number of smaller buildings spread throughout the property. These cottages bore little resemblance to the harsh and foreboding look of the original building. When the first patients arrived in February 1902 (they would number 640 by April), they found a new, modern facility waiting for them – and a new way of thinking in regards to the treatment of mental health.

One doctor at the forefront of this new medicine was Dr. George A. Zeller, who was appointed as the first superintendent of the Peoria asylum in 1896, long before it had even been built. During the problems with construction, Dr. Zeller was serving with the military in the Philippines in the Spanish-American War. He did not return to Illinois until about eight months after the asylum opened, when he took over from Dr. H.B. Cariel, who had been acting superintendent in his absence. For Dr. Zeller, his arrival in Bartonville began his 36-year connection to the Peoria State Hospital.

Dr. Zeller's initial impression of the hospital was not a favorable one. He even expressed his dislike for the name, feeling that it hearkened back to mental illness treatment of the past. In time, he would see the name changed, but this was not what displeased him the most. He felt that this hospital had been created not to help the mentally ill people who were languishing in the poor houses across the state, as had been intended, but had been filled with problem inmates from other asylums. Of the 690 patients that he had when he started, Dr. Zeller found that not a single inmate had come from a poor house. He knew the horrors that were being experienced by those patients and wanted to do all that he could to help them. They would become the focus of some of his initial changes at the hospital.

Other changes were physical. While Dr. Zeller was away serving the military, the state had installed heavy iron gratings and bars on the windows and doors. He discovered this when he returned, along with the addition of rooms designed to be seclusion rooms, with heavy doors and peepholes so the staff could monitor those restrained inside. This had been common practice for many state hospitals of the era, but it was unacceptable to Dr. Zeller. He immediately started to implement drastic changes, starting with the removal of the bars and grates from the windows and doors of as many cottages as possible. At first, the bars were only removed from the dining rooms, and once success had been determined, then from doors and windows of other cottages. Dr. Zeller believed this would contribute to the bucolic, peaceful atmosphere that he was trying to maintain at the asylum, and he was right. By October 1905, the last of the bars and guards were removed from all of the buildings on the grounds.

Another of Dr. Zeller's programs involved the reduction and eventual banning of all forms of mechanical restraints. By June 1904, he wrote that all forms of straitjackets, chains, and shackles had fallen into disuse, except for rare cases with the most violent inmates. He believed that such restraints were more for the convenience of the attendants, rather than for the good of the patient.

Dr. Zeller also instituted an eight-hour work day for the staff at the hospital, which was revolutionary at the time. He believed that employees who were forced to work longer than eight hours were, in many cases, too exhausted to properly care for their charges. He worked hard to get this into the hospital's budget and still make sure that all of the cottages were properly staffed. He solved that problem by having the hospital do a systematic reclassification of all of the patients. Once this was accomplished, Dr. Zeller was usually able to reduce the number of attendants needed in some cottages. The excess attendants were now able to not only supplement the cottages that contained violent and destructive patients, but to schedule more time off for all of the attendants.

Once the news of Dr. Zeller's innovations started to emerge, a great deal of attention was focused on him and the hospital – not all of it favorable. Many believed that he had gone too far. They could not fathom how he could manage a facility with 1,800 patients without any sort of restraints, no cells, and no places of seclusion and confinement. They were even more puzzled by the lack of bars and grates on the doors and windows. In fact, many of the wards and cottages were unlocked day and night. Some of Dr. Zeller's detractors were so alarmed that they voiced their concerns to his superiors in the state capital. According to Dr. Zeller, they had reported, "that a reign of terror existed in our neighborhood and that our paroled patients were committing all sorts of depredations."

As a result, and unknown to Dr. Zeller and the staff, an investigator was sent to the hospital by the State Board. After spending three days visiting various homes and interviewing people who lived in the area, the investigator found that there was no basis for the complaints. In fact, quite the opposite was found. He found that the community supported not only Dr. Zeller, but his new open-door policies as well. Due to the investigation, the board encouraged Dr. Zeller to not only continue what he had been doing, but to expand on it however he wanted.

But Dr. Zeller knew his days at the asylum were numbered. He had been appointed as the asylum's superintendent in 1896 and his appointment, by his own admission, had been as the result of his political activities. In 1912, the general election saw the Republican Party's power and influence diminish both on a national and state level. As a result, Dr. Zeller was replaced as superintendent. He knew that no matter what he had accomplished at the hospital, politics would always get in the way. Dr. Zeller had been assured by many that his job was secure, but he knew otherwise, so he began lobbying for the position of state alienist. In those days, "alienist" was a term for a specialist in mental disease. He assumed the position on December 1, 1913, and was succeeded at Peoria State Hospital by Dr. Ralph T. Hinton.

The following year, Dr. Hinton began undoing many of the changes that Dr. Zeller had made over the last decade. His first order of business was to have the bars and restraints placed back on the wards and cottages. A zoo that Dr. Zeller had built for the patients using the metal bars that had once confined them in the buildings was shut down. Dr. Hinton remained as the superintendent until 1917, when he was replaced by Dr. Ralph Goodner.

It was during his tenure that the first staff member at the hospital died on the premises. She was a housekeeper named Anne M. Stuart, who had fallen ill while working. Soon after she was moved to her room, she slipped into a coma and died. Her death was never explained. And neither was the brutal beating of a patient in October 1903. Two attendants were accused of his murder, but they were never charged.

After his tenure as the state alienist, Dr. Zeller took over the position of superintendent at the state hospital in Alton, Illinois. He remained there for several years and then returned to Peoria State Hospital – although no one knew it right away. After hearing rumors of overall neglect and abuse at the asylum, he checked himself in as an inmate for three days, living on a different ward every night. He was so moved – and so sickened -- by his experience that he ordered all of the staff to serve an eight-hour shift as an inmate so they could see what the patients were forced to endure.

Once again, Dr. Zeller began implementing changes to the hospital. He reformed the nursing academy that had been allowed to fall apart during his absence, introduced new social services, and worked to bring the hospital back to its earlier standards. He was also active in social affairs in Peoria and bought the Jubilee College and grounds in 1933 and donated the grounds to the state of Illinois. His wife, Sophie, later donated the chapel. Dr. Zeller retired in 1935, and he and his wife continued to live in a home on the grounds of the Peoria State Hospital. He died on June 29, 1938, and his funeral was held at the hospital attended by friends, family, dignitaries, and former and current patients.

After the death of Dr. Zeller, the hospital remained in use for many years, adding buildings, patients, and care facilities for children and tuberculosis patients. But not all of the advances that occurred in the modern era were positive ones, no matter how they might have seemed at the time. In October 1938, the hospital took a big step away from the hydrotherapy, color, and music treatments that had been instituted by Dr. Zeller. It was in that month that the first Insulin Shock Therapies were introduced as "shock therapy." Lobotomies began being performed in the 1940s, and in September 1942, the first Electro Convulsive Therapy was introduced to treat epilepsy.

By the 1950s, the asylum's population had started to decline with the introduction of new drugs that could not only balance out the problems being experienced by many patients, but make them capable of leaving to live in the community again. In the 1960s, reform laws prevented patients from working at the institution, which led to increased budgets and patient idleness. The activities that had been given to these lost souls had given them a feeling of worth and usefulness, but that was now lost to them. They were left to wander about, likely wandering back and forth to the places where they had been working each day, only to be turned away from the tasks that made them feel useful.

By the 1960s, mental health treatment had changed from a pastoral community that cared for patients for decades to a quick turn-around, open-door treatment plan that fed the patients drugs and put them back out onto the street again. In 1965, the population of the Peoria State Hospital was at 2,300, and by the time it closed in 1973, there were only 280 remaining. Only five of the buildings were in use.

The final years of the hospital seem to have been a time of chaos and neglect. In 1967, a nurse was killed by one of the patients. He struck her in the head with a steel bar from a garbage can lid. In June 1972, patient Bernard Roe was struck in the head with a chair while standing in the line for lunch. He collapsed in the dining hall, did not receive treatment until the following day, and died a short time later. A few days later, another patient, Jerome Spence, was beaten to death by a fellow inmate. In August 1972, James Logan died from an untreated ear infection, which turned into spinal meningitis.

When the hospital finally closed down, it was in deplorable condition. A report from the Illinois Investigating Commission on December 18, 1973, told of the shocking condition of the buildings and the last remaining patients. The buildings were filthy and falling apart, crumbling into a state of decay and disrepair. The odor of urine and filth filled the air. Blood and excrement had been smeared on the walls. The patients wandered the halls, naked, or in torn and soiled clothing. Most of them were filthy and had open sores and untreated physical illnesses. The heavy use of narcotics kept them in a constant stupor – and, of course, under control. The last remaining patients were transferred to the Galesburg State Research Hospital.

The city of Bartonville acquired the hospital land, intending to turn it into an industrial park. All of the original buildings that formed the main part of the complex were left intact for a time, even though all of them were in various stages of decay, disrepair, and collapse. In time, most of them vanished altogether.

The end had come at last to what had once been one of the finest mental health facilities in the country.

The Tale of "A. Bookbinder"

The first patients arrived by train to the Peoria State Hospital on February 10, 1902, and by June 30, of that same year, there had already been 22 deaths among them. Such numbers would not change much through the asylum's history, largely due to the poor health conditions often faced by the patients who came from terrible circumstances to find a new home at the hospital. They were quite literally killed by their pasts.

The Peoria State Hospital was in operation for a period of 72 years – 1902-1973. It was over this relatively short span of time that 4,132 patients died and were interred on the hospital grounds. This did not include those who died and then were taken to be buried elsewhere. The early reports gave numbers as to how many deaths occurred each year, but the later reports did not offer such detailed statistics. This makes it impossible to know just how many patients actually died during those 72 years.

Dr. Zeller was well aware of the fact that deaths would occur at the Peoria State Hospital and that not all of the deceased would be claimed by family and friends. He later wrote, "I recognized that along with the problem of the living, the disposal of the dead was one that must also have its share of attention. We buried the bodies of the friendless and unclaimed, as the remains of the well-to-do were shipped at the expense of friends and relatives to such points as they designated."

Dr. Zeller supervised the creation of cemeteries, where the bodies of unknown and forgotten patients could be buried. The burial grounds would eventually spread into four separate cemeteries. From the very beginning, every attempt was made by Dr. Zeller to show proper respect for those unfortunates that were interred at Peoria State Hospital. Dr. Zeller's sense of propriety when dealing with the deceased came about partially as a result of his military service, which left a lasting impression on him. He also believed any disrespect for the dead would inevitably lead to a disregard and unconcern for the living. With this in mind, Dr. Zeller instituted a short burial service for the staff to perform at the grave of the dead. For the first few years, he personally presided over the services.

It would be Dr. Zeller's close connection with the burial of the dead at the asylum that would lead to the telling of the very first ghost story associated with the hospital. And this was no mere rumor or folk story, but a documented account of a supernatural event – told by Dr. Zeller himself in his autobiography.

Shortly after organizing the cemeteries for the hospital, Dr. Zeller also put together a burial corps to deal with the disposal of the bodies of patients who died. The corps always consisted of a staff member and several of the patients. While these men were still disturbed, all of them were competent enough to take part in the digging of graves. Of all of the gravediggers, the most unusual man, according to Dr. Zeller, was a fellow that he dubbed in his writings as "A. Bookbinder."

This man had been sent to the hospital from a county poorhouse. He had suffered a mental breakdown while working in a printing house in Chicago and his illness had left him incapable of coherent speech. The officer who had taken him into custody had noted in his report that the man had been employed as "a bookbinder." A court clerk inadvertently listed this as the man's name and he was sent to the hospital as "A. Bookbinder."

Dr. Zeller described the man as being strong and healthy, although completely uncommunicative. He was attached to the burial corps, and soon, attendants realized that "Old Book," as he was affectionately called, was especially suited to the work. Ordinarily, as the coffin was lowered at the end of the funeral, the gravedigger would stand back out of the way until the service ended. Nearly every patient at the hospital was unknown to the staff so services were performed out of respect for the deceased and not because of some personal attachment. Because of this, everyone was surprised during the first internment attended by Old Book when he removed his cap and began to weep loudly for the dead man.

"The first few times he did this," Dr. Zeller wrote, "his emotion became contagious and there were many moist eyes at the graveside but when at each succeeding burial, his feelings overcame him, it was realized that Old Book possessed a mania that manifested itself in uncontrollable grief."

It was soon learned that Old Book had no favorites among the dead. He would do the same thing at each service and as his grief reached its peak, he would go and lean against an old elm tree that stood in the center of the cemetery and there, he would sob loudly.

Time passed and eventually Old Book also passed away. Word spread among the employees and as Book was well liked, everyone decided they would attend his funeral. Dr. Zeller wrote that more than 100 uniformed nurses attended, along with male staff members and several hundred patients.

Dr. Zeller officiated at the service. Old Book's casket was placed on two cross beams above his empty grave and four men stood by to lower it into the ground at the end of the service. As the last hymn was sung, the men grabbed hold of the ropes. "The men stooped forward," Dr. Zeller wrote, "and with a powerful, muscular effort, prepared to lift the coffin, in order to permit the removal of the crossbeams and allow it to gently descend into the grave. At a given signal, they heaved away the ropes and the next instant, all four lay on their backs. For the coffin, instead of offering resistance, bounded into the air like an eggshell, as if it were empty!"

Needless to say, the spectators were a little shocked at this turn of events and the nurses were reported to have shrieked, half of them running away and the other half coming closer to the grave to see what was happening.

"In the midst of the commotion," Dr. Zeller continued, "a wailing voice was heard and every eye turned toward the Graveyard Elm from whence it emanated. Every man and woman stood transfixed, for there, just as had always been the case, stood Old Book, weeping and moaning with an earnestness that outrivaled anything he had ever shown before." Dr. Zeller was amazed at what he observed, but had no doubt that he was actually seeing it. "I, along with the other bystanders, stood transfixed at the sight of this apparition... it was broad daylight and there could be no deception."

After a few moments, the doctor summoned some men to remove the lid of the coffin, convinced that it must be empty and that Old Book could not be inside of it. The lid was lifted and as soon as it was, the wailing sound came to an end. Inside of the casket lay the body of Old Book, unquestionably dead. It was said that every eye in the cemetery looked upon the still corpse and then over to the elm tree in the center of the burial ground. The specter had vanished!

"It was awful, but it was real," Dr. Zeller concluded. "I saw it, 100 nurses saw it and 300 spectators saw it." But if it was anything other than the ghost of Old Book, Dr. Zeller had no idea what it could have been.

A few days after the funeral, the Graveyard Elm began to wither and die. In spite of efforts to save it, the tree declined over the next year and then died. Later, after the dead limbs had dropped, workmen tried to remove the rest of the tree, but stopped after the first cut of the ax caused the tree to emanate what was said to be "an agonized, despairing cry of pain." After that, Dr. Zeller suggested that the tree be burned, however, as soon as the flames started around the tree's base, the workers quickly put them out. They later told Dr. Zeller they had heard a sobbing and crying sound coming from it. "In the clouds of smoke that curved upward," the workman said, "he could plainly outline the features of our departed mourner."

Eventually, the tree fell down in a storm, taking with it the lingering memories of a mournful man known as "Old Book."

The tale of the "Bookbinder" has been told so many times over the years that it has – and rightfully so – taken on the status of legend. For many, it seems hard to believe that Dr. Zeller would have confessed to witnessing a ghost in the cemetery that day. Surely the story was merely a tall tale, embellished by the superintendent to make his autobiography more interesting. Zeller also wrote fiction, it's been claimed, based on life at the asylum. He must have invented the character of "Old Book" for pure entertainment. Right?

We shouldn't be too quick to dismiss the story because as has been proven time and again, almost every legend contains at least a kernel of truth. In this case, records show that the "Bookbinder" really did exist.

In 1974, a newspaper reporter decided to track down the story of the Bookbinder and discovered that there really had been a patient at the asylum who had been dubbed "Manual Bookbinder," which would have been a description of his duties at the bookbindery where he worked. Dr. Zeller did slightly alter his name in the story. Bookbinder was a native of Austria who had been admitted to the asylum in 1904. According to additional records, he died during an outbreak of pellagra in 1910.

Pellagra was a vitamin deficiency disease most frequently caused by a chronic lack of niacin in the diet. It's classically described by "the three Ds": diarrhea, dermatitis, and dementia but makes its physical presence known by red skin lesions (often on the hands), hair loss, insomnia, mental confusion, and aggression. During the 1909-1910 outbreak, Dr. Zeller estimated that at least 500 patients were afflicted with the disease and this resulted in the death of 150 of them.

There is no direct reference to this man being "Old Book" and the character was never mentioned in any of the asylum's annual reports. However, in the statistical tables of the "Sixth Biennial Report of the Commissioner, Superintendent, and Treasurer of the Illinois Asylum for the Incurable Insane at Peoria," on page 32, listed under the "Nativity of All Patients Present June 30, 1906," there are six male patients from Austria. The "Eighth Biennial Report" contains a report dealing with the outbreak of pellagra, noting that there were 38 male deaths from the disease. One could say that this substantiates at least some of the findings of the newsletter reporter.

The most reliable evidence that "Old Book" really did exist was found in a 1905 Supervisor's Journal. This ledger contains the clothing accounts of the patients at the hospital and on pages 2 and 24, there are entries that state that "Bookbinder, M." received six handkerchiefs with a total value of 12-cents.

Does this mean that there really was a "Bookbinder" at the Peoria State Hospital? Yes, it does. But it's up to the reader to decide if the story of his ghost actually occurred or if one of the most respected doctors in the history of Illinois' treatment of mental illness simply made up the story because he wanted to concoct a spooky tale. We'll likely never know for sure, but there is no question that the legend of "Old Book" will make sure that the Peoria Asylum is never forgotten.

The Ghost of Rhoda Derry

While the legend of "Old Book" is the most famous tale of the Peoria State Hospital, if his ghost still walks the grounds, it does not do so alone. One of the most unusual of the thousands of patients who called the asylum home over the years was a woman named Rhoda Derry. Her story – albeit likely containing more than a little mythology – is a heartbreaking one and, truth or largely fiction, the end results of it were plainly visible on her ruined face and broken body. She was the perfect example of why Dr. Zeller wanted to rescue so many of the insane from the evils of the poor houses across the state.

Rhoda Derry arrived at the asylum in 1904. At that time, the population at the hospital was still growing rapidly with more than 200 new patients being admitted every month. One night, a train car arriving from Quincy, Illinois, was late and did not reach the Peoria station until after 1:00 a.m. The exhausted hospital staff had been admitting patients since early that morning and set off to meet the latest group of arrivals. As the group was led from the car, one of the railroad men handed down a clothes basket, which was taken along with the new patients to the hospital. It was believed that the large basket contained the effects of the newly arrived patients, so the staff was surprised when the basket began to move and a strange, guttural voice was heard babbling from inside of it. As the nurses uncovered the cloth from the top of the basket, they came face-to-face with Rhoda Derry.

The legend of Rhoda Derry states that she was born in Adams County, Illinois, and was the daughter of a wealthy farmer. She was a strikingly handsome girl, and while in her teens, was wooed by the son of a neighboring land owner. The young man's family, however, was opposed to the match. In order to prevent the couple from marrying, the boy's mother visited Rhoda and threatened to bewitch her if she did not release her son from the engagement. The mother scared the girl so badly that she went insane, exhibiting all of the signs of being possessed by an evil spirit. One night, Rhoda came home and jumped on her bed, standing on her head, and spinning like a top. She declared that the devil was after her and she was never the same again. For a time, she was taken care of by relatives, but was eventually sent to the Adams County poor house – and there she remained for the next 43 years.

During her time at the poor house, Rhoda lost the ability to walk upright. As a result, she moved about by using her arms and balled fists to drag herself across the floor. Her body was contorted in such a way that her knees naturally rested against her chest. She refused to wear clothing and was often tied to her bed to prevent her from wandering the halls naked. She slept each night in a Utica bed, a crib-like bed with a top that could be fastened down to hold a person in place. The bed was kept lined with straw that was changed periodically since Rhoda usually soiled the bed. She was often subject to violent episodes and would beat herself and others within her reach. During one such spell, she had scratched out her eyes and was now blind. She ate with her hands and would shove into her mouth anything that she came into contact with. She was in such pitiable condition that her handlers at the poor house bundled her into a basket and placed her on the train to the Bartonville asylum, likely happy to be rid of her.

She was 66-years-old when she arrived at the hospital and she quickly became the object of sympathetic interest to the nursing staff, and they treated her with love and compassion. For the first time, she slept in a clean bed at night, was given edible food, and was cleaned and cared for. When the weather was nice, the nurses would place her on a mattress and place her on one of the open porches where she could get fresh air and feel the sunshine.

Rhoda only lived two more years but her last days were peaceful and filled with affection. Although likely so demented that she could barely understand what had happened to her, it seems likely that she could comprehend that her circumstances had changed and perhaps she felt at peace for the first time in more than four decades.

And perhaps this is why her spirit allegedly never left her last home. Soon after her death, there were stories that claimed Rhoda's spirit had remained behind at the beloved institution. The nurses would frequently claim to see her sitting on the sun porch, just as she had done during the last years of her life.

Asylum Hauntings at Bartonville

After the hospital closed down and the site was sold at auction in 1980, the doors were seemingly thrown open for every kind of trespasser, vandal, urban explorer, and ghost hunter imaginable. Many of these curiosity-seekers, drawn to the building because of its legends and ghosts, claimed to encounter some pretty frightening things in the old Bowen Building, which was added to the asylum campus in 1929 for administration offices and dormitory rooms.

So, is what's left of the old hospital really haunted? Scores of people who have visited the place certainly think so. The reader must agree that the place certainly has the potential for a haunting, even without the story of the Bookbinder and Rhoda Derry. The atmosphere of the place alone is more than enough to justify the reports of apparitions and strange energy. The impressions of the past would certainly be strong in a building where mentally ill people were housed and where "psychic disturbances" would be common. And then, of course, there are the spirits who simply don't want to depart. The hospital was the only home that many of the patients knew and, even after death, there was no reason for them to leave.

Even before the hospital closed its doors for the final time, rumors spread about disturbing sights and sounds inside of the asylum buildings. There were reports of strange lights, footsteps, eerie sounds, disembodied voices, and doors that opened and closed on their own. The stories continued after the hospital was abandoned and curiosity-seekers began making their journeys into the crumbling building. Some reported seeing shadows that flickered past doorways and darted around corners. They would walk into freezing blasts of cold air that seemed to come from nowhere, without explanation, and then fade away.

The first floor of the building was once used for administration offices, and there is said to be the ghost of a young woman in a white hospital gown who often appears at the north end of the hallway. She wears her hair in two long braids and she is believed to be the spirit of a former patient.

On the second floor were patient rooms, nurses' dormitory rooms, and communal areas. At the north end, more than 120 women lived and worked within the hospital. Sadly, many of these women had been sent to the hospital while pregnant, or became pregnant as a result of what was then termed a "hospital romance." At that time, insanity was considered to be a hereditary disease and few were willing to risk adopting the child of a woman who had been pronounced to be insane. The women were allowed to keep their child with them at the asylum until the age of four, at which time they became wards of the state. Many of the nurses who cared for these women later adopted the children and raised them on hospital grounds. This may explain accounts of the presence of children in the building. A number of accounts tell of hearing the sounds of small feet running through the hallways, often accompanied by singing or children's laughter. The asylum was home to many children over the years and it seems possible that some of their spirits simply never left.

The second floor also contained classrooms and work areas at the south end. In one of these classrooms, the apparition of a nurse is said to sometimes be spotted. She wears a long gown, crisp apron, and has her hair pulled back into a bun. The figure, dressed all in white, has been seen in the classroom and also peering out of the second-story windows at the south end of the building.

The nurses' ward was at the opposite end of the hallway. The small, dormitory-style rooms were each shared by two nurses at the school that had been established in Dr. Zeller's time. The sounds of doors opening and closing, as well as the giggling of young women, have often been reported in this area.

The third floor – which I found to be the most menacing while shooting with a documentary film crew at the Bowen Building in 2008 – was once the men's living quarters. There was a large metal gate installed in the 1960s to separate part of the hallway from a communal area. It has been reported that this gate can often be heard going up and down on its own, but the gate itself is never actually disturbed.

There were also medical treatment rooms on the third floor, some of which were used as late as the 1960s. It was in these rooms where many of the "treatments" took place, including shock therapy and, most disturbing to me personally, lobotomies. There have been many reports of people being touched and feeling hands gripping their arms and shoulders while in the treatment rooms. While I have visited the Bowen Building a number of times over the years, I have only been in the old treatment rooms one time – I've never gone back.

Even the attic of the building is alleged to be haunted. The massive room, with its high, exposed-beam ceiling, is in much the same shape as it was in Dr. Zeller's day. It was mainly used for storage of hospital supplies. The center part of the attic contains the original elevator that would have been in use during Dr. Zeller's tenure. Toward the end of his life, Dr. Zeller maintained an interest in every aspect of the hospital's operation and often went to the attic to inventory supplies and equipment. There are stories that say that the figure of Dr. Zeller can still be seen exiting the elevator and walking across the attic floor to a large dormer window, which looked out over the asylum grounds.

Whether the figure is actually Dr. Zeller's ghost or a residual impression of this piece of history, it is not the only presence in the attic. Another is said to be an orderly who worked at the hospital in the 1960s and who became despondent over the poor treatment of the patients during that declining period of the facility. One night, he took the elevator to the attic and ascended a metal staircase that led to the storage loft. He tied a rope to the overhead rafters and hanged himself. His body was not discovered until two days later. The stories say that his ghost remains behind, manifesting in the sounds of heavy boots that thud up the metal staircase. There are also claims that on moonlit nights, passersby can peer into the attic windows and see the body of the orderly hanging there, swaying on the end of the rope that strangled him.

At the far north end of the attic is another woman in white that lingers at the asylum. In life, her name was Anne Stuart and she was a housekeeper at the hospital until she died in 1933. There are many stories surrounding her death, including that she died after contracting an illness during her rounds. Another more lurid account claims that she was in love with a married doctor and following his rejection of her affection for him, she jumped from an attic window to the ground below. Since then, she has been seen looking out of the attic window and has been heard moving about and singing – apparently as she still goes about her cleaning duties after all these years. Several visitors to the hospital today have asked about the source of the singing that they have heard echoing on the upper floor and are chilled to discover they have heard the voice of a dead woman.

Beneath the building is the old hospital basement, which once marked the entry way to the tunnels that ran between many of the cottages on the property. Those who have spent any time in this area report the eerie feeling of being constantly watched and often don't stay underground for long. It's not uncommon for visitors to hear knocking sounds, footsteps, and men's voices in the darkness. Legend has it that in the 1970s, after the hospital was closed, two homeless men were trapped inside one of the tunnels beneath the building and died there. The stories say their spirits never left, which causes many visitors to walk quickly toward the stairs leading out of the basement when they hear the slightest strange noise.

When the hospital closed in 1973, there were 4,132 patients buried in the asylum's four cemeteries, most of them in unmarked graves in the two oldest burial grounds. Dr. Zeller developed a numbering system for the cemeteries and that system – as well as all of the names that went with each number – has never been publicly disclosed. For many years, the cemeteries have been a great source of controversy, mostly relating to the lack of care and maintenance that they have received. Gravestones have fallen and been lost, the grounds are often overgrown, and in the 1980s, a large portion of one cemetery began sliding down into a ravine. A huge section of it has been lost in the years since then.

There have been many sightings of mysterious figures in the cemeteries, which still remain on the hilltop, hidden among the trees and behind the buildings that have been constructed there over the years. One of the most-reported ghosts is that of "Old Book." It is said that if one goes to the cemetery where he was buried on a peaceful summer day (he can be found in Cemetery II and grave #713 is the grave site of Manual Bookbinder) his spirit will appear, crying and wailing, and mourning the loss of the patients who died, appearing just as he did before Dr. Zeller, the staff, and patients on that day many years ago.

Pollak Hospital

During its time in operation, the Peoria State Hospital not only treated mental illness, but a wide variety of physical maladies and ailments as well. Pollak Hospital was built on the grounds of the Peoria State Hospital in Bartonville in 1949 to serve the needs of patients at the state asylum that were suffering from tuberculosis, even though tuberculosis deaths on the grounds dates back to the earliest days of the asylum.

By 1906, it was the leading cause of death at the hospital, and during a single year, 64 patients succumbed to the disease. The high number of deaths convinced Dr. Zeller to try and control the spread of the illness by segregating the sick in tent colonies.

The first colony at the hospital was a large porch on one of the cottages that was enclosed by heavy canvas. The canvas could be rolled up during fair weather to allow patients to take in fresh air, one of the earliest treatments for consumption. The experiment was largely successful, so more tent colonies were added to the grounds. The tent colonies remained in use until Dr. Zeller left the hospital in 1913.

Tuberculosis, though, continued to be a problem. In 1937, patients and employees of the asylum were tested by Dr. Maxim Pollak, director of the Peoria County Tuberculosis Sanatorium, and it was discovered that more than half of all of them tested positive for tuberculosis.

In 1949, the Pollak Hospital and Infirmary Building was built to care for patients with tuberculosis. The northern wing was for female patients and the southern wing was for male patients. It was named in honor of Dr. Pollak, who carried out the exhaustive research at the asylum in the late 1930s. As medicines finally came along to treat the illness, fewer patients died but many still contracted the disease. By 1973, the Pollak Hospital was one of the last buildings on the grounds of the asylum that was still in use.

During the hospital's years of operation, hundreds died within its walls, and according to stories and eyewitness accounts, scores of their spirits stayed behind to walk the wards and hallways of the crumbling building. A number of the ghosts believed to linger at Pollak Hospital are children. Many witnesses have heard their voices and the patter of small feet as they pass by them in hallways and on staircases. As one guide who worked in the building in recent years pointed out, "Just because you heard a child laughing doesn't mean that there's actually anyone there."

Pollak Hospital took in not only the mentally ill from the asylum, but also tuberculosis patients from the surrounding area. For this reason, many of the tuberculosis victims who were treated – and died – at Pollak were children. For whatever reason, their pain and suffering kept them lingering behind. They seem to be especially attracted to visitors to the hospital who have children of their own. One of the guides suggested that perhaps "they are looking for their mommy and daddy."

I spent most of the night at the Pollak Hospital in April 2014 with a group of American Hauntings guests and my partner in crime, Lisa Taylor Horton. We were able to spend a lot of time exploring the old building, and aside from a few odd noises that weren't easy to explain, we hadn't experienced anything that we would call supernatural. After walking around for a while, exploring the historic old structure, we sat down in one of the rooms with some electronic equipment to see if we could pick up anything unusual with it. It was when we stopped looking for anything weird that the weird finally found us.

Lisa was unpacking some equipment from a case and suddenly looked up at me. Before I could ask her what was wrong, she said she was making sure of where I was sitting. There was no way, she realized, that I could have reached her from where I was. She explained that when she looked down, she felt a small hand pat her on top of the head. It was very gentle – as though a child had done it. I didn't have time to say anything before I realized that the hair on her head was moving, as if someone was stroking it. That was when Lisa called out that it had happened again! Startled, she looked all around but there was no one behind her. Except for the two of us, the room was empty.

Had she made contact with one of the young ghosts at Pollak Hospital? Perhaps so, for the guides had assured us that they tend to seek out parents. Perhaps this would be a good place to mention that Lisa's daughter, Lux, was just about six months old at the time. Maybe one of the lost spirits had found some little girl's mommy that night at Pollak Hospital.

Ashmore Estates
Ghosts of the Coles County Poor Farm

Resting quietly near the small town of Ashmore is the site of the former Coles County Poor Farm. The massive red brick building has a long history in the area, dating back to 1870, when it became the county's second poor farm. During that era, poor farms were county-operated residences where indigent, elderly, and disabled people were supported at the county's expense. They were common in America, starting in the middle part of the 19th century and declining in use after the Social Security Act took effect in 1935. By 1950, they were forgotten relics of yesterday.

Most were working farms that grew at least some of the produce and grain and raised the livestock that the inmates consumed. The residents were expected to provide labor to the extent that their health allowed, both in the fields and in providing housekeeping and care for the other inmates. Rules were strict and the accommodations were sparse. The poor farms were often a place of last resort for those who could no longer care for themselves and the inmates were too poor, too sick, or too old to make it on their own. The counties where they resided reluctantly took them in and offered just enough for them to survive – at least in most cases.

County poor farms were the last stop for many people and they died, unknown or at least forgotten, and were buried in pauper's graves. Not surprisingly, many of the old farms have left ghosts and spirits lingering behind.

The former poor farm outside Ashmore is no exception.

Poor farms were first created in Illinois around 1839. Twenty years earlier, when Illinois first became a state, one of the first acts of the Legislature had been to provide for care for the most vulnerable members of society. The act established the Overseers of the Poor, who arranged for the care of orphans and destitute adults. In exchange for labor and a small amount of money, the committee clothed, fed, and housed those in their care. In February 1839, an amendment was made to the earlier act that authorized county governments to establish almshouses and levy a tax for their support. Nearly every county in the state began maintaining an almshouse and a poor farm, creating a system that lasted for more than a century. The farms took in the infirm, the destitute, the orphaned, and the vagrant – all deemed by society of being unable to care for themselves. The farms were built with the best of intentions, but they rarely lived up to the dreams of the designers. The idea of the poor farm had been to provide a safety net for those who were suffering through desperate times. Many of the residents were older, some with physical and mental disabilities, and there was no other system in place to help them. The original plan had been a good one, but over time, it all began to fall apart. To many residents, the poor farms became places of horror.

By the early 1900s, investigations of poor farms across the state revealed bed bugs, unsanitary conditions, poor food, inadequate clothing and sleeping arrangements, and deteriorating buildings. Reports stated that bedrooms were bare and unfurnished, save for the resident's old trunks, a few old tables, and some straight-backed chairs. Paper and plaster was torn, broken, and falling, and some residents had to battle the rats for their dinner. Blankets were washed only twice each year.

There was also the stigma attached to the poor farm. According to a 1911 report of the Illinois State Charities Commission: "The deserving poor are loathe to apply for alms. They conceal their plight. Mortification accompanies honest misfortune. To be unable in the stress of economic severity to sustain one's self and family intensifies shame. The stings of poverty wound the heart long before they are felt in the flesh." To add insult to injury, in many counties, the names of the poor receiving relief were published in community newspapers.

In 1949, the Public Assistance Code of Illinois began to specifically ban poor farms from taking in children and "feeble-minded" women under the age of 45, which meant fewer people were being sent to the county poor farms. In 1967, a new version of the code put an end to poor farms altogether, forcing the few that remained in Illinois to close. By that time, most of the poor farms that still existed had been sold to private companies, or had been torn down years before.

Many of them, like the Coles County Poor Farm, would begin writing another chapter of their existence.

The first poor farm in Coles County was started in 1857 and was located in Charleston Township, near the small town of Loxa. The building located there, which was soon deemed inadequate, only housed about 27 residents. Organizers began searching for a new site and found one in 1869. Located 14 miles away, in Ashmore Township, the county purchased 260 acres alongside the Indianapolis & St. Louis Railroad. The first building on the property was a two-story wood and brick structure, built by H.B. Truman, and the first superintendent of the farm was Oliver D. Hawkins, who had come to Coles County from Kentucky. He became a prominent member of the local community and remained as superintendent at the farm for three years.

The farm never housed an abundance of residents. The population peaked at 41 people in 1870, and then gradually declined over its years of operations. According to county records, there were 35 residents in 1880, 23 in 1890, and only 18 by 1910. Many of the residents died at the farm. In 1879, superintendent Joshua Ricketts noted that there had been 32 deaths out of the roughly 250 residents who had stayed at the farm between 1870 and 1879. With no family to care for their remains, the dead were buried on the property and the county maintained a small cemetery somewhere north of the farm. A second pauper cemetery that was established a few years later still exists south of Route 16 and contains the graves of between 60 and 100 people.

On June 9, 1880, the Board of State Commissioners of Public Charities visited the Coles County farm and was generally satisfied with conditions. According to reports, "the inmates are well-fed and in good health. Of the three insane, who are now in this almshouse, only one has been committed by the verdict of the court." The commissioners were present for the residents' meals: "Breakfast: coffee, meat, biscuit, butter, molasses, rice, and hominy. Dinner: meat, bread, milk, beans, potatoes, and other vegetables. Supper: the same as breakfast, with the addition of fruit."

In 1902, the Board returned to the poor farm and had found that conditions had slightly changed. The inmates were still well fed, but obvious problems had started to appear. They wrote, "The heating is by stove and is sufficient. There is no regular system of ventilation, but plenty of fresh air is easily obtained. There is no plumbing... there is no fire protection." There were also concerns about the mentally ill at the farm: "There is no special provision for the insane. None are locked up or in restraint." As might be recalled from an earlier section, Dr. Zeller at the Peoria State Hospital had grave concerns about the treatment of mentally ill patients at the county poor farms in the state. The health of many of the poor farm inmates sent to the hospital was so broken, most never recovered.

Over the course of the next decade, conditions at the farm grew worse. In 1911, stories appeared in area newspapers after the farm was visited by the Auxiliary Committee of the State Board of Charities and released the discoveries made during their inspection. They condemned the almshouse for having "vermin infected walls," "rough floors," "small windows," and a continued lack of ventilation. It was noted that "flies swarmed everywhere" and "were especially noticeable on the poor food prepared for dinner." The committee felt so strongly about their disapproval of the facility that they remarked, "our pride and our humanity should make us determined to remove the disgrace of it from us."

The committee, so angered by what they saw, began receiving bids for a new building for the poor farm in January 1915. The Almshouse Committee, headed by John Goodyear, Ivory W. Merritt, Jr., E.N. Carter, W.R. Zimmerman, and William Knollenberg, approved a design by Danville architect L.F.W. Steube and awarded the construction contract to S.C. Sailor of Oakwood. In February 1916, however, Sailor backed out of the project and the construction was then turned over to J.W. Montgomery. He laid the cornerstone for the new "fireproof" building, which still stands today, on May 17, 1916.

Life on the farm rapidly began to improve. A full-time caretaker and his family took turns living in the almshouse and a white farmhouse that formerly sat on the property. While the county still provided most of the staples for the residents of the farm, the inmates raised much of their own food, tapping the maple trees for syrup and tending livestock. They milked the cows, raised chickens, tended gardens, and did their own butchering.

As the laws changed in Illinois in regards to caring for the indigent, the poor farms closed down and the almshouses were shuttered. Coles County retained the farmland around the property, but sold the building to a private company in 1959. Ashmore Estates, Inc. re-opened the building as a private psychiatric hospital, but it turned out to be a short-lived enterprise. After suffering from financial difficulties from the state, the hospital closed after only five years. In 1965, it opened again, but changed its focus from a private facility to a hospital that accepted overflow patients from state institutions.

In July 1976, new owners, Paul Swinford and Galen Martinie, purchased the hospital. Their original plan was to construct a new, one floor residency that would house up to 100 patients, but the state planning committee refused to approve the plan after considering it for six months. New plans were made and Swinford and Martinie invested over $200,000 for a modern addition to the old building. Construction began in 1977, but it was not completed until the early 1980s. Additional money was invested bringing the 1916 building up to code. In December 1981, Barbara Jean Clark became the director of the promising new facility.

Ashmore Estates operated for the next four years, but in February 1986, Paul Swinford entered into a limited partnership with Peoria-based Convalescent Management Associates, Inc. to help manage the institution's finances, but by then, it was too late. It had taken nearly a year for the departments of Public Aid and Public Health to issue the proper licenses and certificates for the facility and now Swinford was forced to file for permission from the Illinois Health Facility Planning Board to close the hospital. At that time, Ashmore Estates had lost more than $1.5 million. By the end of April 1986, the residents had been transferred to area homes and the institution closed its doors.

Ashmore Estates in recent years

Three years passed before anyone tried to re-open the building. In 1990, Paul Swinford, working with a Tennessee company called Corrections Corporation of America, attempted to develop Ashmore Estates as a mental health facility for male juvenile offenders. When the corporation appeared before the Ashmore Village Board, the request for a zoning permit was denied after a unanimous vote. The board cited concerns over fire safety, but there was also public resistance to the idea after some residents worried about what might happen if anyone of the inmates escaped.

Problems soon began to plague the abandoned building. On Halloween night 1995, a fire destroyed an outbuilding that was located across the lawn from the front entrance to the main building. The building had been used to teach motor skills to the developmentally disabled prior to the facility's closure in 1986.

With ownership of the building unclear (Paul Swinford has owned the building, but had released the deed to a real estate broker) and facing the possibility of being condemned, Ashmore Estates was put up for auction in 1998 because of delinquent taxes that went back two years. The building was purchased by Arthur Colclasure, a Sullivan resident, for $12,500. He dreamed of remodeling the place and living there, but constant vandalism ended his plans.

By that time, the building had been empty for years and was frequently visited by urban explorers, thrill-seekers, and vandals. Not surprisingly, it had gained a reputation for being haunted, as so many abandoned old buildings do. Ashmore Estates was only about 40 minutes from my parent's farm in Central Illinois and when I was growing up, I made several trips to the old building while hunting down the stories I heard about haunted places. During one visit in the late 1980s, some friends and I were exploring an upper floor and were startled by the sounds of breaking glass. We discovered that some vandals had unknowingly followed us to the site and were shattering some of the remaining windows. We scared them away, but I'm sure that they – or others like them – returned another night. After that, I never went back.

Ashmore Estates was abandoned until August 2006, when it was purchased by Scott Kelley. He began renovating the building as a haunted attraction and to finance the project, he offered flashlight tours of the interior. To discourage trespassers, he put up signs and then, when all else failed, came to live on the property.

His haunted attraction opened on October 13, 2006, and ran for several years as a great success. In the off-season, he opened the place up for paranormal investigations.

Bobbi Brooks, a tour guide for American Hauntings, once hosted an internet show about the haunted history of the paranormal. She visited Ashmore Estates for one of the shows, filmed an interview with the owner at the time, Scott Kelley, and then explored the old building. Bobbi later recalled, "While I was interviewing the owner, the place seemed very calm. After the interview he left us to do our investigation alone. As soon as he left, the tension in the building picked up. It was an extremely cold night so we were not planning on staying very long."

About 45 minutes after Kelley had left, Bobbi and a friend were doing an EVP session at one of the nurse's stations and she suddenly felt her hair pulled very hard from behind. She turned around to see who had done it, but there was no one there. "I was a little shaken," she said, "but I kept going. After a few minutes, I started thinking that maybe my hair had gotten caught on my jacket, and it hadn't been anything strange at all. So, I decided to text the theory and I asked, out loud, 'who pulled my hair?' As soon as I said it, it happened again." She distinctly felt the sharp tug of her hair and once again, there was no one behind her.

"We wrapped up shortly after that," Bobbi admitted.

And Bobbi was far from the only person to encounter the spirits. On October 30, 2009, meteorologist Kevin Orput was filming a segment for a local television station and had experienced Ashmore Estate's resident ghosts. He was sitting in a chair in the nurse's station on the second floor around 4:30 a.m. Suddenly, he found himself lying on the floor. He insisted that he was not asleep, but could recall nothing about the incident. Several people saw it happen and hurried to help him. Orput firmly believed that unseen hands pushed him out of his chair. His shoulder was injured in the fall and he claimed to feel "different" for several days afterward. He was a skeptic before he came to Ashmore Estates, but he left with a new appreciation for the supernatural.

In January 2013, bad luck struck at Ashmore Estates again. A terrible winter storm, with wind speeds between 80 and 100 miles an hour, badly damaged the building. The roof was blown off and the support gables were all but destroyed. Coles County Emergency Management Director Dan Ensign said that the building appeared to be damaged beyond repair. Scott Kelley's home, adjacent to the property, was untouched by the storm.

In April, Kelley sold the building at auction for $12,700 to Robert Burton and Ella Richards. The new owners quickly announced plans to repair the roof and other storm damage, and to add a concession, lobby, and restrooms at the site. They retained ownership for only one year. In May 2014, the property was sold to Robin Terry. The building was till in deplorable condition when Robin purchased it, but through his efforts, along with many volunteers, the building has been restored to how it was when the last patients left the building in 1986. Robin has no plans to open the place back up as a haunted attraction but he does continue to allow paranormal investigations of the building. A number of television shows have filmed at Ashmore Estates, including a 2011 episode of *Ghost Adventures.*

Tales of ghosts and hauntings have surrounded Ashmore Estates since the doors were closed 30 years ago, and while many of them can be regarded as nothing more than folklore, there is an element of truth to the many first-hand encounters that have taken place in the former hospital. Those who have visited the place, answering the offer to explore the confines of the building, have experienced mysterious voices, sounds and cries. They have witnessed shadows that have come to life and watched apparitions as they descended staircases, or entered otherwise empty rooms. The place is alive with the dead, but there are no demons who lurk within the walls. No matter what might be said on television or hinted at by unexperienced investigators, no one has ever experienced anything demonic at Ashmore Estates. Robin Terry is protective of the place and conjecture about demons is definitely unwanted.

No one can say for sure what spirits still wander the corridors of the building. Over the years that it was in operation, scores of the poor, the lonely, the broken, and the desperate called this place home. They endured their physical ailments, their suffering, and their shame, and managed the best life they could within the walls of the almshouse and on the poor farm that surrounded it. It seems many of those lost souls have returned to the only safe haven they ever knew and are content to remain at Ashmore Estates for as long as they are allowed to do so.

"The Million Dollar Courthouse" History and Hauntings in Carlinville

There is no question that Carlinville can proudly boast one of the most beautiful town squares in the state. Many of the nineteenth century buildings have been preserved and restored and are now home to shops, restaurants, antique stores, and art galleries. The wide streets circle a picturesque little park, and a gazebo in the center of it completes this Norman Rockwell-like view of small town America. Dominating the northeast side of the square stands a silent sentinel that looms above the streets and the passing automobiles. The stark white structure is known as the Loomis House, a once-grand hotel, and it's a place where time seems to stand still.

Just beyond the Loomis House, silhouetted against the sky, is the stately dome of the Macoupin County Courthouse, which will be forever linked to the hotel that stands just a block away. The Loomis House was named for its builder, Judge Thaddeus Loomis. There was a time when Loomis' name garnered great respect in Carlinville, but that was before the construction of the opulent courthouse mired him in scandal and forever sullied his reputation.

Is it any wonder that many believe that his ghost still walks in this little town?

Thaddeus Loomis was descended from Joseph Loomis, who had come to America from England in 1638 and was one of the original settlers of Windsor, Connecticut. The family prided itself on their education and became prominent in science, literature, and politics, and one family member became a professor at Yale University. Horace Loomis, Thaddeus' father, was born in Connecticut and later moved to New York where he married Julia Tuttles. The couple had three children, all boys, the oldest of which was Thaddeus, born in 1826.

In 1838, Horace Loomis packed up his family and moved west to Illinois, settling in Chesterfield Township. He became a successful farmer, raising livestock, and running a large dairy until his death in 1850.

After arriving in Illinois, Thaddeus, age 12, began a rigorous education. Studying through the winter months and helping his father on the farm the remainder of the year, he gained a reputation as an intellectual and something of a prodigy. At 19, he entered Illinois College in Jacksonville and attended for one year. The following year, he entered the law department at the University of Kentucky in Louisville, graduating in March 1849.

Returning home to Illinois, though, he soon found himself restless. Like so many other young men of the time, he was struck with "gold fever." Rich deposits had been discovered in California and Loomis struck out for California. Accompanied by eight other young men – one of which was future Illinois governor Richard J. Oglesby – he set out from St. Joseph, Missouri, for his westward trek. After an arduous 90-day journey, the wagons reached California and Loomis remained there, working as a prospector, for the next five years.

Loomis returned to Illinois in 1854, never gaining the fortune that he had hoped for in the California gold fields. On December 13, he married Sarah Dukels and purchased a farm near Carlinville. For the next six years, he lived much the same life as his father had. In addition to tending his farm, he contracted with the Chicago and Alton Railroad to cut timber to make ties for the rail line. He also purchased land around Carlinville and laid out an addition to the town known locally as "Loomis' Addition."

In 1861, the Democratic Party nominated Loomis to run for county judge, and in November, he was elected by a large majority. Loomis served as a judge for the next eight years. During his tenure, he was able to levy, collect, and pay off the county's debt of a staggering $200,000. But that accomplishment, unfortunately for

Loomis, would soon be overshadowed by the scandal wrought by his involvement with what would be called the "Million Dollar Courthouse."

The Illinois General Assembly created Macoupin County on January 17, 1829, its name derived from the Native American word "macoupiana," which meant "white potato." There was a type of white artichoke that grew along the creeks of the county.

Thomas Carlin, who was a state senator at the time and later become governor, worked hard to pass the bill that created the county. His efforts were later rewarded when the town of Carlinville was established in his honor. It was also chosen to be the seat of the new county. The first county courthouse was a small log building, which was soon obsolete. A second, larger courthouse was built on the square in 1830 and served the county for the next three decades.

By 1865, the county was in need of a larger courthouse, and it became understood that a vote for Judge Loomis, then up for re-election, was a vote for a new courthouse. Loomis carried the election and he immediately put his plans for the new building in effect.

Architect Elijah Meyers created a new design for the courthouse – as well as for the new jail that would be included in the project – and construction began in 1867. It was completed over the winter of 1869-1870 with Judge Loomis playing a major role in the work. As construction was taking place on the courthouse, Loomis also began building the hotel that he would name for himself on the nearby square.

Almost immediately, charges of corruption were leveled against Judge Loomis. One angry citizen wrote an open letter to several area newspapers, asking Loomis: "Who pays the courthouse contractors for the building of your house?"

Why were people so angry and suspicious about what was going on with the courthouse and Judge Loomis' hotel? It was undoubtedly due to the unbelievable cost overruns, construction delays, and missing funds connected to the courthouse project. Almost as soon as construction began, clouds of controversy began to swirl about the endeavor and, as one might expect, it involved money – lots of it. Immediately, a 50-cent levy on each $100 of property value was established and bonds were issued in the amount of $50,000 to pay for the project. By September 1867, with little more than the foundation underway, the new courthouse had already cost the taxpayers $13,000. By the time the cornerstone was laid in October, the costs were already exceeding the estimates that architect Meyers and Judge Lewis had provided for the entire project.

As January 1869 rolled around, the cost for the courthouse had risen to an astounding $449,604 and an additional $125,000 was still required to complete the roof and the building's magnificent dome. The county issued more bonds to meet the ballooning costs. When the building was finally completed in 1870 the bill was a whopping $1.3 million!

Taxpayers were enraged and accusations of corruption were hurled at a number of people, but mainly at Loomis and the County Clerk, George Huston Holliday.

Holliday was born in Harrisburg, Kentucky, on August 5, 1824, and came to Illinois with his family sometime between 1834 and 1836. George earned an early reputation as a scholar. He was fluent in Latin, Greek, Hebrew, and was a respected orator. In 1845, he graduated from McKendree College in Lebanon, Illinois, and returned home to Carlinville.

In April 1852, Holliday married Cinderella Chism, a Macoupin County native who was 10 years his junior. The marriage produced six children, four boys and two girls. As an outlet for his "keen intellect" and political interests, Holliday became the publisher of the *Carlinville Spectator*, a Democratic newspaper. The venture was short-lived, but, after selling his own paper, Holliday continued to write for several others in the area.

In 1868, he purchased the *Conservative*, another Democratic vehicle, which only ran from March to June of that year. During this time, Holliday was acquiring one of the largest private libraries in the state. His next position was a political one, serving as the County Surveyor. In 1850, he and John Shipman laid out the town

The Macoupin County Courthouse

of Shipman, Illinois. Additionally, Holliday served as a school commissioner during the 1855-57 term of the Illinois Legislature.

When County Clerk Enoch Wall died in office in 1858, Holliday was appointed to finish out his term. He was re-elected in 1860, and soon after, he became part of the so-called "Courthouse Crowd," and later invested in Loomis' hotel. Both situations, as it turned out for Holliday, were very bad decisions.

The staggering costs outraged local citizens, and in November 1869, three men formed an investigative panel to look into the exorbitant costs of the building project. Their submitted report laid blame squarely on the members of the building committee who had let spending run amok. Thaddeus Loomis, who was the first judge to preside in the new courthouse, George Holliday, and the rest of the old committee members resigned in disgrace as talk of illegal activity began to filter thru the citizenry.

Loomis seems to have taken the brunt of the abuse, likely because he never publicly answered all of the claims of corruption made against him. It was suspicious to many that his magnificent hotel should be constructed at the same time as the new courthouse. Fueling this suspicion was the fact that the building was also designed by E.E. Meyers and built from the same limestone as the courthouse. Although Meyers had received the commission for the fortress-like jail, across the street from the courthouse, in the initial contract, the hotel was part of an additional agreement between Loomis and the architect. The details of that agreement have never been discovered. Like much of the association between Meyers and Loomis, they remain a mystery.

For his part Loomis agreed that the limestone was, indeed, taken from the courthouse project, but he argued that the stone had been leftovers, and that he had obtained the material legally. Though many called for it, proof of this was never forthcoming from Loomis, Meyers, or anyone else involved. Eventually, Loomis was cleared of any wrong doing --mainly due to lack of substantial evidence --and life went on for the judge. His name had been tarnished, but he survived.

But what of the county clerk who had overseen the project's finances? George Holliday, just as the investigation was reaching its most heated period, skipped town in 1870, and was never seen again. Holliday's sudden disappearance convinced many of his guilt, but he was forgotten and no proof of his wrongdoing was ever confirmed. Many years later, in 1879, a man claiming to be Holliday arrived in Carlinville. He was immediately arrested and locked up for questioning. "Holliday" had been living in Washington state, he claimed, under the name S.W. Hall and working as an attorney. Holliday's wife denied the man was her missing husband and since no one else could identify him, the matter was dropped and the county paid to have the man sent back to Washington. It was later learned, though, that when Hall returned to Washington, he abruptly sold his law firm, settled his accounts, and fled the area. Could he have been George Holliday after all?

It took the residents of Macoupin County 40 years to pay off the debt left by Loomis and company for the grand courthouse. On September 7, 1904, the town of Carlinville held a great celebration when the last of the bonds was paid off. Today, the lavish building stands proudly in place, its past long over but not quite forgotten.

Over the years, stories have circulated

The Loomis House in Carlinville

about the courthouse's resident spirits. It's not uncommon for staff members, clerks, and visitors to encounter eerie phantoms from years gone by. Footsteps are heard in empty rooms and corridors, voices and whispers echo off the walls and floors when no one else is there, and apparitions are often spotted, crossing the hallways or lurking in the historic main courtroom.

During the American Hauntings tours that go through the building, we have had a number of guests who have had their own paranormal encounters. One of our guides even quit working for us because she became so frightened at the courthouse that she refused to go back inside after dark. One night, during a tour of the building, I actually witnessed one of the huge, metal courtroom doors slam shut on its own. There was no one near it at the time and if a draft had blown it shut, it would have had to have been one with hurricane-force winds – the doors weigh several hundred pounds and are not easy to open and close.

Over the nearly century and a half of its existence, dozens of horrific trials have been held at the courthouse. Could some of the lingering spirits be the ghosts of the killers and thieves who received their sentences here? Or could they be the specters of their victims, hoping for some kind of justice after death?

Some believe that at least two of the spirits are those of Judge Loomis and George Holliday, the two men who faced the greatest controversy after the building of the magnificent structure. Do they remain here, doomed to revisit their crimes for eternity?

But the courthouse may not be the only place where the spirit of Thaddeus Loomis lingers.

After his resignation, Loomis retreated to his new hotel and devoted his time to making it a showplace in Carlinville. When it opened in 1870, it boasted three floors with 50 guest rooms and a large dining area. Over the course of the next 11 years, the Loomis House played host to travelers from every walk of life, from traveling salesmen to actors, circus performers, politicians, railroad men, and a number of shady characters. A man named William Siemens was known to entertain patrons in the saloon on the hotel's ground floor while, according to rumor, another type of business was carried on upstairs. It was said that travelers and gentlemen from town could hire "fair ladies" employed by Siemens for more discreet entertainment in the rooms on the upper levels.

It was Siemens who led to the downfall of the Loomis House. In 1881, Siemens was convicted of violating Illinois liquor laws and the saloon was closed down. Profits began to shrink and Loomis was forced to surrender the hotel to the banking firm of Chestnut & DuBois, which held the mortgage on the property. But the bank firm was facing problems of its own. They had also been deeply involved in the controversy surrounding the courthouse and, eventually, the firm folded. The hotel was sold to William A. Robertson, a wealthy farmer and businessman who also happened to be the bank's largest creditor. Robinson was strictly anti-liquor and he vowed that the "devil drink" would never be served at the Loomis House again. A short time later, Robinson died and his family took over operations. Unfortunately for the travelers and locals who might want to have a drink at the Loomis House, they shared his views on alcohol.

The hotel was closed for six months, it's future in doubt, but then it re-opened – and no one came. The self-imposed ban on liquor kept the customers away and the building was finally put up for sale at public auction.

The winning bidder was a man named Simonson from Decatur. Simonson believed that the name of the hotel had an "unsavory reputation" and he changed its designation to the St. George Hotel. He spent a large amount of money remodeling and refitting the place with all of the latest luxuries. But he didn't hold the deed for long.

In 1909, Simonson sold the hotel to Theodore C. Loeur, a druggist, who opened a pharmacy on the ground floor. Today, much of the pharmacy fixtures remain intact and offer a wonderful look at what was then an ordinary store – that seems out of the ordinary today – in that bygone era.

In time, Loeur's nephew, Ralph Surmon, took over the pharmacy and became a longtime fixture on the square. Surmon sold the hotel to the Carlinville Elks Club in 1953, and they operated it for nearly two decades under the name of the Elk Hotel. Men who were down on their luck always had a place to stay in the now fading hotel, which was starting to fall into disrepair. The roof had started to leak, and over time, each hard rain sent torrents of water into the upper floors and inside the walls. The damage caused peeling paint and crumbling plaster on the top two floors.

In 1975, Alex and Fern Perardi purchased the old building from the Elks and changed the name back to the Loomis House. The saloon was re-opened as the St. George Room, which still operates today. But the hotel itself was too far gone to be opened again, so the Perardis closed off the top two floors and set about converting the second floor into a restaurant. The spacious dining room was a welcome addition to Carlinville's downtown business community at the time and it operated for nearly a decade.

The restaurant is long gone now, but it was during its time in operation that the tales of ghostly happenings first began to be reported at the Loomis House.

The staff in the restaurant were among the first to report an unnerving presence in the hotel. A waitress was working alone one night after the restaurant had closed. She was preparing the dining room for customers the next day. As she walked out of the kitchen and into the dining room, she was startled to see a man standing in the middle of the room. At first she thought that someone had stayed after hours and she started to tell him the kitchen was closed, but the man turned and started to walk away. Halfway across the dining room, he vanished! The waitress ran screaming from the building. She didn't stop working there, but she never worked alone in the Loomis House again.

The waitress could never give a clear description of the man, but a patron at the restaurant's bar was able to do so. He was drinking with friends one night and happened to glance toward the back of the room. He saw a man standing there, looking very out of place. He claimed the man was wearing a turn-of-the-century (early 1900s) style suit and had a thick, white beard. The man turned to point out the odd-looking fellow to his friends, but the old man just as quickly turned, and vanished into a brick wall! None of his friends had seen the man, but later, when he had the chance to identify the man from a photograph, he learned the identity of the ghost – he identified a photo of Judge Thaddeus Loomis.

And Loomis apparently does not haunt the place alone.

A woman was in the abandoned hotel section one evening and encountered a man standing alone in one of the rooms. He was tall, in his mid-40s, and was wearing a dark suit with a pocket watch chain across his vest. The woman said that the man looked at her and spoke. "Find me in an armoire," he said. A moment later, he vanished into a wall. At the time, the woman had no idea what the man could have meant. However, an old armoire was discovered on the second floor of the building and inside of it were three men standing in front of a dry goods store on the square. The photograph had been taken in the late nineteenth century and the men were identified as F.L.J. Breymann, Albert Muller, and William Grotefendt. The woman was sure that the man she had seen was F.L.J. Breymann. It was later learned that he was a local businessman who had run a men's clothing company adjacent to the Loomis House.

One of the most widely known hauntings of the Loomis House was the staircase that led from the sidewalk outside to the restaurant on the second floor. The marble staircase can be very imposing, especially if a visitor is aware of the ghostly reputation that it has. Legend has it that an older man, a transient, was staying at the Elks Hotel in the 1960s. One night, he took a fall on the staircase, tumbled down the marble steps, and broke his neck when he hit the bottom. He died at the foot of the marble staircase and ever since that time, visitors have reported an odd feeling on the stairs. Some say that they feel as though they are being watched. Others speak of eerie cold spots that cannot be explained, while others say that they have caught a glimpse of a shadowy figure lurking on those stairs. It is often seen from the corner of their eye, but it always quickly vanishes.

Other strange things have been reported in the former hotel, including in the basement. When the Loomis House first opened, a number of businesses rented spaces below street level. A flight of steps led patrons from the street down to the shops below and the pathway was lighted by glass panels that were embedded in the sidewalk overhead. One of the first businesses below the street was a barbershop that opened in 1870, operated by two men named Winn and Hinton. They were two of Carlinville's earliest African-American business owners and they enjoyed a long, successful run in the basement shop.

Another long-time tenant under the building was a bakery. It was said that, during the early morning hours, the smell of warm, fresh bread and hot, sweet rolls would waft up the stairs to the street, filling the air along the whole east side of the square with wonderful aromas. A year after it opened, though, a fire swept through the bakery. Fortunately, no one was injured in the blaze, but the damage was severe. Repairs were made, and the business was re-opened, but even today, charred ceiling beams remain as a reminder of the fire.

Memories of those former businesses make themselves known today in the basement. In addition to phantom smells of baking bread and the clatter of metal objects, footsteps, and eerie voices, witnesses claim to have encountered areas of terrible cold that they cannot explain. Two people who were once exploring the basement, discovered a liquor storage closet for the hotel's saloon. The door had a padlock, which was not latched, and as they walked toward it, the lock began to rattle violently, shaking back and forth. When they opened the door, they found no one inside.

The Loomis House – along with the Macoupin County Courthouse – are symbols of Carlinville from days gone by. They are places with long histories, colored by crime, corruption, and the inevitable passage of time. Many of the people who walked the hallways and corridors, and spend time in the offices and rooms, left little bits of themselves behind – a passing history that has returned as a haunting.

Hauntings of the Hockenhull Building

On January 15, 1966, seven people were killed when a fire raged through the apartments above Walgreen's drug on the east side of Jacksonville's downtown square. This was, by all known accounts, the greatest loss of life from fire in the city's history. Investigation later ruled that the fire had been an accident, started by a burning cigarette, but the eerie result was that it left a haunting in its wake – a chilling presence that still makes itself known in the building today.

Warga's (the name of the Walgreens store) in Jacksonville was still located on the downtown square in 1966. It had opened in 1935 and was a remnant of what had once been a thriving shopping district during the heyday of the smaller, family-owned businesses that once dominated commerce in every American city. Jacksonville was no exception. After World War II, a shift in where people shopped began to occur, but before that, you could buy everything from suits to dresses, furniture, tools and auto parts in downtown Jacksonville. Many locals purchased toiletries or had prescriptions filled at Walgreens, which was located in what was known as the Hockenhull Building.

John and Robert Hockenhull arrived in Jacksonville in 1839. Both men had been apothecaries in England and they opened a small drug store on the city square. They prospered and soon opened a dry goods store on East State Street. In 1866, Robert branched out further and with Raymond Kind and Edward Elliott, opened the Hockenhull, King, and Elliott Bank. By this time, Robert had purchased a home on Grove Street and had become a trustee for Illinois College and for the All-Female Academy, that later became known as MacMurray College. He was one of the most important men in the city and one of the wealthiest. In 1891, he expanded his holdings with the construction of the Hockenhull Building on the east side of the square. The towering stone building still looms above the sidewalk today, although any business that would have been known to Robert Hockenhull has long since vanished from Jacksonville.

During its heyday, the Hockenhull store was downtown Jacksonville's most prominent department store. It offered pretty much everything you could possibly need for a household of the 1890s: furniture, stoves, clothing, baby carriages, and the list went on and on. The building was in a large L-shape, with one entrance opening onto the square and the south entrance opening onto State Street. The annex offered largely goods that were used for the home or farm, like tools, farm

The Hockenhull Building in 1892

implements, and outdoor equipment. In time, both sides of the store closed down as shopping habits changed.

Before its recent revitalization, the square declined for decades, much like most downtown business districts across the country. As new businesses opened along Morton Avenue, a more centrally located business district for the city, downtown Jacksonville slowly began to die. Warga's was one of the few still-thriving businesses operating during the fading days of the old square. Warga's, like several other stores, had apartments over the shops, often cramped and dingy lofts that were as weary as the declining businesses below them. In the Hockenhull Building above Warga's, there were apartments on the second and third floors, as well as more apartments in the L-shaped annex that faced State Street -- apartments that became death traps on that cold winter's night in January 1966.

According to newspaper reports at the time, the scene at the fire was chaotic. Residents in the building frantically tried to escape the flames while firefighters were working to extinguish the blaze and save the tenants. One man, Robert Lee Brown, 18, who was sleeping with his family in one room of their four-room flat, was rescued by firefighters who used an aerial ladder truck to whisk five people from the upper part of the building within five minutes of their arrival on the scene. The only other member of the Brown family to escape death that night was one of Robert's younger siblings. The rest of them perished from asphyxiation from the smoke.

John Yeager, his wife and two children were trapped in their third floor apartment, but remaining calm, he managed to get them out of a rear window and to a roof below. Tragically, an elderly couple, Alice Leggett and Charles Souza, who lived just on the other side of the Yeagers' wall, were not so lucky.

Authorities believed that about a dozen people escaped from the apartments on the second and third floors, including Kathryn Wease, 19, and her two children, ages 13-months and 6-weeks. The janitor of the building, Virgil Duncan, managed to make it out with two unidentified tenants, who lived above Barney's gift shop. Those who died in the blaze were Leota Mae Brown, 46; her four children, Ray, 15; Donna, 14; Rickey, 10; and Jimmy, 2; along with Leggett and Souza.

Elsie Brannan, 76, was the first to realize that something was wrong in the building around 1:30 a.m. Unable to sleep, she repeatedly thought she smelled smoke, opened her door and saw the flames in the hallway. Although elderly, Elsie reached a window transom, some six feet off the floor, and managed to pull herself up over the door and through the narrow opening. She dropped to the floor in the dense smoke and made her way through a storeroom above the drug store, breaking a window to reach the roof. Several people who escaped from the fire later told reporters that they heard someone yelling "in back, and ringing what sounded like a bell or someone banging on pans."

Mrs. Brannan would later admit that she did what she could to rouse the other sleeping tenants. She then broke out a window at the rear of Birdsell's tailor shop, making her way through the darkness to a window above East State Street, which she promptly shattered. Waving a piece of cloth from the tailor shop, she was eventually spotted by a motorist driving past.

Gary Strubbe, who was driving around the square a few moments later, saw Clara Davis, her daughter, Kathryn Wease, and her two young children frantically screaming for help from an upper floor. He went immediately to the police department and sounded the alarm. Within minutes, the fire department was on the scene. When firefighters arrived, Clara and Kathryn were each holding a child out of the apartment windows and rescue workers at first thought they might throw them from the second floor. Mrs. Davis later explained that they were holding the infants outside of the window to keep them out of the dense smoke. Firefighters used the aerial ladder to save the women, children, and Robert Brown and then to work looking for other survivors.

Led by Assistant Fire Chief Alvin Smith, a crew equipped with oxygen masks groped their way through the smoke to the third floor. Meanwhile, other firefighters battled their way to the second floor, where they discovered the origin of the fire and quickly began trying to douse the flames that were roaring up the wall to the third floor. By this time, nearly 100 people had gathered in the square and many of the men assisted the firefighters in moving hose lines.

A cheer went up as survivors were brought to safety, but then a hush fell over the crowd when someone called out that there were still people trapped on the third floor. By this time, though, the crew led by Assistant Chief Smith had reached the victims and were carrying the bodies out onto a roof at the rear of the building. The departure of several ambulances without their emergency lights bore mute witness to the fact that some of the people trapped in the building had not escaped with their lives. "On Saturday morning," one news reporter wrote, "Jacksonville asked why and how?"

Fire Chief Dale Bond attempted to answer the questions. The fire, he stated, had started in the second-floor apartment, occupied by a woman named Alice McCausland. She had been found semi-conscious in a lower floor hallway between Warga's and Edward's jewelry store. When Police Officer John Irlam asked her at the scene how she escaped the fire, she reportedly told him, "There's no fire up there, I put it out."

According to Chief Bond, the fire spread from McCausland's bedroom up the wall. The intense heat shattered a transom window and spread up the hallway wall to the third floor. Damage to the building was estimated in excess of $50,000.

Later that month, at a coroner's inquest, Chief Bond testified that, during two separate interrogations, McCausland confessed that she had dropped a lighted cigarette in bed, which caught fire, starting the blaze. Bond stated, "She said 'I dropped a cigarette in bed, and when I found it, smoke was coming from the covers. Then I put it out.'" Bond then said that he asked her what she did next and she replied, "'went to bed.'"

During later questioning, the chief said that McCausland would not repeat her earlier confession and firmly told him that she made it a rule not to smoke in bed. According to Charles Runkel, the police chief at the time, no charges were ever filed against McCausland for the deaths of the seven people killed in the fire. Officially, the blaze was listed as accidental.

But accident or not, seven people, including four children, died that night in the rundown apartments above the drug store. According to scores of people who have experienced the haunting that lingers in the Hockenhull Building, those who perished in the fire do not rest in peace.

In the middle 1990s, life began to return to the downtown square. Old buildings saw new activity as coffee shops, art galleries, and small shops began seeking out the nostalgia of yesterday in the brick buildings and ornate structures from Jacksonville's past. The lower portion of the Hockenhull Building was opened as a pet store, later became an art gallery, and is now a thriving coffee shop. In recent times, the owners of the building have successfully turned a portion of the once fire-damaged structure into a loft apartment, but there are still portions of the building that remain abandoned and serve as jarring reminders of the building's tragic past. Evidence of the fire remained starkly visible, from burned floors and walls to even charred clothing that still hung in the closets.

And these physical reminders of the past are not all that can be found in the Hockenhull. Stories have long circulated about strange shadows, footsteps, laughter, and the eerie voices of children -- perhaps the same children who died in January 1966. The artists who were once on the first floor had their own experiences, speaking of cold chills, lights that turned on and off by themselves, office equipment that operated on its own, and the smell of cigarettes when no one was smoking in the building.

Loren Hamilton, who has led American Hauntings ghost hunts in the building, has had more than his share of strange experiences at the Hockenhull. Guests who have accompanied him for these outings have witnessed and recorded many strange things, from disembodied voices, unexplained knocks, unknown shadows, apparitions and more. I have personally heard some very strange recordings from those who have stayed the night in the building and have claimed to capture the voices of the dead with their devices.

A tenant who lives in a building next door, actually in the nook of the L-shape of the Hockenhull, related hearing the sounds of people talking, music, and shouting coming through the back wall of his loft – a wall that is the only barrier between him and the abandoned sections of the Hockenhull. After checking, it was discovered that the building next door was silent, empty, and awaiting renovation. No one lived there and no one was present at the time of the eerie noises.

To this day, the Hockenhull Building remains one of Jacksonville's most notoriously haunted sites. It is a place where the past truly comes back to life and where the dead are unafraid of making their presence known to the living.

A Piece of the Past
Hauntings at the Emporium

William Norvell, Jr., or Bill as his friends called him, knew his way around tools and equipment. For a good part of his 55 years, he worked as a psychiatric aide at the Jacksonville State Hospital, but his true passion was for gears and machinery and making things work. When not working at the hospital, he could almost always be found at the Emporium, Jacksonville's biggest department store, on East State Street, right off the square. Back in 1926, the Emporium had installed an elevator, the first store downtown to have one. People marveled at the chance to ride from one floor to the next in comfort, but now, 45 years later, the elevator needed almost constant repair. But Bill Norvell didn't mind. He loved tinkering with it and making sure that it ran just the way that his boss, Edward Goldstein, who he always called "Mr. G," wanted it to run.

On a crisp fall morning, October 13, 1969, Bill came to the Emporium after one of the managers called to tell him that the old elevator had stopped working again. He gathered his tools and left his home on South Fayette Street, which he shared with his wife, Loretta, until her death in 1964, and drove downtown. It was

143 | *Ghosts of the Prairie*

around 7:15 a.m. when Bill arrived at the store, well before opening time, and listened to yet another report of how strangely the elevator had been acting. It was a familiar story to the genial man, and with a smile, he climbed the stairs to the highest floor of the building, where the elevator's control box was located. The elevator's car had stopped about 10 feet below, stuck at the third floor.

Bill worked his way through the tangle of gears, pulleys and cables and peered down into the darkness of the elevator shaft. He could plainly see the top of the car below. Bending down, he opened his tool box and reached for a screwdriver. A metal panel would have to be removed before he could get to the electrical wires and see what might be wrong with the controls. But as Bill reached down for that screwdriver -- something happened. We'll never know for sure what it was, but he lost his balance and for just a split second, his body was suspended in the air at the top of the shaft.

And then he fell.

Plummeting downward, Bill Norvell fell only 10 feet to the top of the car. It wasn't far, but it was far enough. His body slammed onto the top of the metal car and impacted with the gears and brackets that held the cables in place and allowed the car to smoothly travel between floors, when it worked correctly, that is. Bill was probably killed instantly, but we'll never know that for sure either. Nearly two hours passed before anyone thought to check on him and when a fellow employee saw his body crumpled on the top of the elevator car, he immediately called for an ambulance. When firefighters arrived on the scene, they managed to lift Bill's broken body out of the elevator shaft. He was rushed to a local hospital, but it was far too late for him. He was gone.

Over the years, as stories of ghostly activity at the old Emporium building have spread through Jacksonville, it's the legend of the man that fell down the elevator shaft that is always recalled. Few remember his name or even that he was a real person. Most assume that it's nothing but a "ghost story" about a mythical repairman that never existed at all. But Bill Norvell was a real person and he really did die after falling to his death in the Emporium's elevator shaft.

And it's even possible that his ghost still haunts this building. But we believe that if he does, he does not walk here alone.

The building that is known to most Jacksonville residents as the "Emporium" started on East State Street, just off the downtown square, in 1899 as Johnson & Sons, which sold furniture, stoves, furnaces, and home furnishing goods. The store was owned by W.H. Johnson and did a thriving business for several years, until Johnson passed away. It was sold to Edwin Galbraith in 1907, who started Galbraith Furniture. The new store was managed by the owner's son, Oliver, who lived in the third floor apartment above the store. The Galbraiths remained in business until 1915, when H.S. Greenstone bought the building and started the Emporium, a women's "ready to wear" clothing store.

The store did very well for several years, but after the passing of Greenstone's wife, Esther, the owner's health began to fail and the business began to suffer. After spending a number of weeks in the hospital in Springfield, Greenstone began looking for a buyer for the business. He found a buyer with Edward Goldstein, whose family owned several retail stores in Central Illinois. Goldstein was familiar with Jacksonville and liked the town, and after receiving a good deal from Greenstone, decided to invest in the Emporium – sight unseen. The contracts were signed in a Springfield hotel lobby in December 1919, and Goldstein drove over to Jacksonville to see his new store for the first time. He would later say, "It wasn't too encouraging," but he planned to make the best of it. Little did he know that the time at the Emporium would become his whole life and that he would spend the next 50 years turning it into the finest department store in the city.

Edward Goldstein, who would affectionately become known as "Mr. G" to his friends and associates, was born in Eastern Europe, the son of Moses and Edith Goldstein, and he came to the United States at the age of four. He had two sisters, Gertrude and Elizabeth, and four brothers, J.W., Harry, Herman and Benjamin. Over the years, the family had operated a number of retail stores and businesses, but Goldstein would leave his greatest mark on Jacksonville with the Emporium.

When the newspapers announced the sale of the store, Goldstein had nothing but praise for the city, which he had visited frequently, and spoke of how much he liked the people. He had big plans for his new store. He told the *Jacksonville Daily Journal*, "I am expecting to offer the women of Jacksonville fine service in ready to wear garments and I am sure they are going to find the Emporium a store where garments correct in style and dependable in quality can be purchased at prices lower than they have heretofore known about."

And the Emporium wasn't going to be just any store. Goldstein planned to make a place that would be talked about by everyone in the city. For starters, it would be the first store in town to offer shopping in air-conditioned comfort. But there were no air-conditioning units available in town and no craftsmen who could install them anyway. Goldstein purchased three systems from buildings that had been torn down in New York and, doing all of the work himself, rigged them together to make one huge unit – much larger than the building even needed. Then he installed the whole thing himself. His jerry-rigged air-conditioning unit continued working until the building was remodeled in 1964, when it was replaced by a modern system. Each time it broke down, Mr. G simply dug out his toolbox and went to work. It wasn't long before the cooling unit would be humming again.

In 1926, Goldstein purchased the three-story building from the Greenstone estate. The business had done so well that he wanted to expand out of the first floor and occupy the entire building. This started an extended period of remodeling, and when it was over, the Emporium had gone from simply a ladies' dress store to a full-fledged department store, which carried clothing for the entire family, furniture, and a shoe department. Later on, the Emporium would serve as the starting place for other businesses that were owned by Goldstein, including Mr. Eddies, Walker Furniture, and a number of commercial properties that were leased to other businesses. By the 1940s, the Emporium was the largest department store in Jacksonville and the busiest.

During his years in business, Goldstein never married. He said, "I've never stopped working long enough to get married." Although a bachelor, he donated both time and money to children's charities, including the YMCA, to which he donated $100,000 during the summer before his death. He was also a leader in the Chamber of Commerce, Jacksonville Industrial Corporation, Intown Merchant's Association, and the initial program to secure an electric plant for the city. He supported many other charitable organizations, like the Salvation Army and the United Fund.

The long hours that he worked and time that he put into the Emporium likely kept him from ever establishing a permanent residence in town. When he first arrived in Jacksonville, he lived at the Colonial Inn and later at the Pacific Hotel for a few years. In the middle 1930s, he lived in an apartment just a few blocks from the store, on State Street, and then moved into the apartment on the top floor of the Emporium in 1941. He stayed there until he became too ill to live alone, moving into the apartment of long-time employee and friend, Louise Cowdin, on East Court Street in 1969.

On October 30, 1969, Mr. G passed away at Norris Hospital. He had been sick for some time and had been a patient at the hospital for several months. His body was taken to the Williamson Funeral Home and a private service and burial was conducted by Rabbi Meyer Abramowitz. He was buried in Diamond Grove Cemetery.

Goldstein's death left the Emporium without its driving force. His close friend, Louise Cowdin, took over the running of the store after his death, but things were never the same. Even so, the Emporium lasted until 1981, when Louise retired and the Emporium closed for good. The building remained vacant for the next two years – but was it really empty? In a time span of only three weeks, two men connected to the store had died – one tragically in an accident and the other so closely connected to the store that he had spent a lifetime building it into Jacksonville's most successful retail store. What kind of lingering presence had these two men left behind?

In 1983, long after most other downtown businesses had either closed up or had moved out to Morton Avenue, leaving the square a sort-of ghost town, Kruwag's Emporium Mall opened in the old Emporium building on East State Street. Operated by Harold Wagner, Jr. and Michael Kruthaupt, they specialized in one of the most popular furniture items of the day – waterbeds. The store thrived, offering furniture at a discount price, and not surprisingly, getting out of the waterbed business after a few years. They remained in the building until 2001, when the business closed.

For the next five years, the Emporium was abandoned once again. Leaky ceilings, winter months with no heat, and summer months with nothing to keep out the dampness took their toll on the old place. The Emporium had turned into a ghost of itself. In early 2006, though, Joe Thomas bought the building with the idea of turning it into a center for troubled youth. He purchased it for a very low price, but quickly found that the deteriorating building would cost much more to repair than he could possibly afford. Even after he rented out the upstairs apartments – Mr. G's old place had been converted into three units – he found that the revenue they generated was not enough to pay for the building's upkeep. Later that fall, he put the building up for sale.

In 2008, the Emporium was converted into a tavern that bears the same name as Edward Goldstein's department store – the Emporium. The clothing racks and shoe departments are long gone now. Pool tables fill the first floor area where the furniture department was once located. The elevator shaft where Bill Norvell fell to his death has been removed – but not all of the remnants of yesterday have vanished.

According to first-hand accounts, spirits of the past still remain.

The first ghost stories about the Emporium building began making the rounds in the 1990s, when it was being used as a furniture store. Staff members spoke of the uncomfortable feeling of being watched and of hearing footsteps in hallways and rooms where no visible person was present. During an interview, one former staff member claimed that she had been touched on the shoulder by an unseen hand. When she turned to see who was trying to get her attention, there was no one there. She quit working at the store that same day.

The stories continued during the time when the apartments on the third floor were being rented out. Tenants complained of hearing footsteps on the stairs and in the hallways. One told of lights that turned on and off by themselves, with no explanation. Oddly, this same occurrence took place during a paranormal investigation of the building in 2006. As ghost hunters moved from floor to floor, they discovered that the lights on the first floor kept turning themselves back on again after they were sure they had been turned out.

Loren Hamilton, who led the group that night, also told of a loud bumping sound that he heard coming from behind the elevator doors on the building's third floor. It was, he explained, like the sound of someone knocking, trying to get out. Of course, this was at the exact spot where Bill Norvell had fallen to his death in 1969 – a fact that Loren did not know at the time. The building's legend claimed that a repairman had fallen down the elevator shaft and died in the basement, after falling three stories. It was not until Lisa and I started doing research into the building's history that we discovered that Bill had actually only fallen about 10 feet and died on top of the elevator car, which was stuck on the third floor at the time. Coincidence? Perhaps, but it seems pretty unlikely based on all of the other stories that have been told.

During the time when the building was being remodeled into the Emporium tavern, the new owners and workers complained about objects that would disappear, move around and reappear while the construction work was being done. Tools vanished, showing up later in strange places where no one had left them, and they often came in certain mornings to find that recently hung drywall was lying on the floor. On one occasion, a "force" was said to have held back a worker's arm as he was trying to nail some woodwork onto the wall – as if someone didn't want the place to be changed.

Are there really ghosts that haunt the old Emporium building? Those who have encountered them certainly think so. Could one of them be Bill Norvell, who fell to his death in the elevator shaft? And if so, is he the only spirit here that doesn't rest? Could Edward Goldstein, who spent most of his life at this building and poured his heart and soul into it, have also remained behind? It certainly seems possible, especially when considering this:

One of the tenants who rented an apartment in the Emporium building in 2006 told a chilling story of waking up in the middle of the night to see a thin man with glasses standing at the end of his bed. Startled into a sitting position, the tenant watched the man suddenly disappear. He would never think too much of the encounter, telling me a couple of years later that he assumed that it had just been a dream. But I never forgot the story, especially when Lisa and I were researching the place and ran across the first photograph that we'd ever seen of Edward Goldstein -- a thin man who wore glasses his entire life. Could this be the apparition the tenant saw in his apartment that night?

Truthfully, I'd like to think so. If, when someone dies, they have the choice to move on to another place or stay behind in this world, it seems possible – perhaps even likely-- that Mr. G would remain in the one place where he was the happiest during his life. He literally created the Emporium. He designed it, crafted the ideas, lived upstairs, and even built and installed the air-conditioning unit with his own hands. He never had a wife because he was already married in a way to his store.

But if his ghost does not still reside in the building that he loved, there is no question that he left an indelible mark on the place and on the city of Jacksonville itself.

Clipped Wings
The Hauntings of Chanute Air Force Base

Although its runways are silent, its streets are empty, and its buildings are now decaying and covered in graffiti, the former Chanute Air Force Base was operational for the majority of the twentieth century, from 1917 to 1993. During those 75 years and though two World Wars, it functioned as a technical training center for the Air Force. At the time of its closure, it was the country's third-oldest active base.

Time has marched on and the last two decades have not been kind to the old air base. When it closed down in 1993, it had a devastating effect on the community. One newspaper echoed the feelings of the nearby town of Rantoul with

"Traumatic. Devastating. Eerie. As if a family member had died." The town had relied on the base for its economic prosperity and its closure devastated the town. Literally half the population vanished, home values plummeted, and jobs disappeared. Now, more than 20 years later, Rantoul is still recovering and the demise of the air base still looms over the town like a dark shadow.

And while some parts of the former base have started to be used for other purposes, large portions of it remain just as it was left in 1993 – now forlorn, barren, and forgotten. It is in these places, the stories say, that the ghosts of the past still linger.

Chanute Field had its beginnings during the bloody years of World War I. The United States had been the birthplace of powered flight and yet the Army Signal Corps had never tried to adopt it for military use. Even as America entered the war to fight with its Allies in England and France, it did little to build its air strength. British and French pilots were doggedly fighting against German aviators, and yet, the United States possessed only one fully manned and equipped fighter unit, the 1st Aero Squadron, made up of only 250 aircraft. In comparison, France began the war with 1,500 planes.

Hurrying to meet demand, Congress appropriated $640 million to build up the Air Service. The War Department immediately opened ground schools at eight colleges and established 27 flying fields where pilots could be trained. The town of Rantoul was selected as the site of one such flying field. It boasted a level site, a proximity to the Illinois Central Railroad, and a ground school at the nearby University of Illinois. The field would get its water and electricity from the village of Rantoul.

The contract to build the field was given to English Brothers Construction in Champaign on May 22, 1917, with the expectation that work would be complete within 60 days. Building material was hauled to the site and construction began on June 4. At the peak of construction, there were 2,000 men, 200 teams of horses, three steam shovels, and multiple steam tractors, all working on the field at the same time. Payroll reached over $96,000 each week. The project became an economic boom for Rantoul, with money and men flowing into the village at a rapid rate. Visitors also flocked to town to see the construction, most of them witnessing a spectacle like nothing they had ever seen before.

The new air field was named in honor of Octave Chanute, a pioneer aeronautical engineer and experimenter who had been a friend and advisor to the Wright Brothers. The biplane glider that he invented became a prototype for the airplanes that followed.

In late June, Chanute Field's first commander, Captain Charles C. Bennett, arrived in Rantoul and on July 4, the first airplanes arrived. A few weeks later, Major James L. Dunsworth took command of the field and ordered flight training to begin. Soon, Curtiss JN-4 "Jenny" trainers were flying from dawn to dusk. The air field was completed on July 22, and on August 20, the field was closed to visitors as they had become a distraction to the pilot training school.

By November 1918, Chanute Field had trained several thousand pilots, but with the end of the war, pilot training ended. In December, the last Aero Squadrons were demobilized and the plans were sent out to other airfields. The base became a storage depot for aircraft engines and paint, with a skeleton staff of about 30 men.

Chanute was not the only field to be largely shuttered. At the end of the war, the Army Air Service, along with the rest of the Army, faced critical reductions. Thousands of officers and enlisted men were released, leaving only 10,000 personnel to fly and repair the planes and engines left over from the war. Hundreds of small flying fields across the country were closed down and Chanute was scheduled to be one of them, until it was saved by Congress in 1920. At the time, the field was in poor condition. It had been built rapidly because of the pressing need for pilot training during the war and within a few years, it had fallen into a state of disrepair.

But in January 1921, the Air Service Mechanic's School was transferred to Chanute from Kelly Field in Texas, along with the Air Corps Training School. In 1922, the photograph school at Langley Field in Virginia and the communications school from Fort Sill in Oklahoma were also moved to Chanute. They were consolidated to form the Air Corps Technical School in 1926. During this time, nine steel hangars were built on the south edge of the original 1917 airfield. A tenth hangar was added in 1923. Chanute Field now provided all of the technical training for the U.S. Army.

In 1938, work began to completely rebuild Chanute Field. Since most of the base was of wooden construction, the threat of fire became one of the field's greatest enemies in the 1930s. After several fires, the Army Air Corps named Chanute as one of four bases to be rebuilt. In late summer 1938, work began on two massive hangars. By the following year, the headquarters building, hospital, warehouses, barracks, officer quarters, fire station, and a massive water tower were finished. The construction budget climbed to $13.8 million, with most of it being funded by President Roosevelt's Works Progress Administration (WPA). Two additional hangars, theaters, barracks and family housing units, a gymnasium, and a network of concrete runways were also added. The additional projects were completed in 1941 – just months before the Japanese bombed Pearl Harbor.

When the United States entered World War II in December 1941, men from all over the region came to Chanute Field to enlist in the U.S. Army Air Corps. Chanute Field was forced to immediate transition from peace to war following Japan's surprise attack. The technical mission remained the same, however, a massive influx of new recruits led to a critical housing shortage. The new barracks that had just been built proved insufficient to accommodate the new personnel. Many of the soldiers had to be temporarily housed in large tents, camping out on the lawns until gigantic White Hall was completed. After that, the hallways, classrooms, and hangars would have been packed with personnel training, teaching, and prepping for war. During the war, the mess halls at Chanute served over 75,000 meals per day. The candidates for pilot training nearly overloaded the school, reaching a peak of 25,000 in January 1943. The Women's Army Air Corps School was established at Chanute in 1944.

Chanute Field also had the important designation of activating the first all-black fighter squadron in American history. Formed without pilots with the purpose of training the officer corps and ground support personnel, the 99th Pursuit Squadron was formed at Chanute. Over 250 enlisted men were trained in aircraft ground support trades such as airplane mechanics, supply clerks, armorers, and weather forecasters. This small number of men became the core for other African-American squadrons forming at Tuskegee Field in Alabama – the famed Tuskegee Airmen.

It was also during the war that the economic impact of the airfield would affect another Central Illinois community in much the same way the base's closure would affect Rantoul almost 50 years later. On January 7, 1942, local officials in Bloomington were said to have been shocked to learn that commanders at Chanute had declared their town "off limits" to its personnel. The reason for the ban? Because too many of the airmen at Chanute were patronizing Bloomington's red light district when visiting the city and bringing back cases of venereal disease to the base.

Like many cities at the time, Bloomington had a segregated vice district and its "disorderly houses" were grouped along the 500 block of South Wright Street, the 300 block of East Moulton Street, and a stretch of Elm Street to the immediate south. This area was bulldozed in the late 1960s as part of the city's urban renewal efforts, and was replaced by the Wood Hill public housing development, but during World War II, the impact of the Army's ban led to the first attempt to close the brothels in the community. The Mayor's office called the military order "the climax of a long story of community humiliation." The ban was also a blow to the local economy, since visiting airmen flooded the central business district to patronize legitimate businesses such as department stores, restaurants, and movie theaters, too.

Despite mayoral promises and the best efforts of reformers, Bloomington's red light district quickly returned to what it was before. It remained into the 1950s and even led to a scandal involving the forced retirement of a police chief over the shakedown of prostitutes. It took a bulldozer to finally bring it to an end for good in 1967.

At the end of the war, Chanute Field became a primary separation center for the armed forces, processing about 100 men each day, from the military back to civilian life.

In 1948, Chanute Field became Chanute Air Force Base with the establishment of the U.S. Air Force as a separate military service. At the time, Chanute was also dealing with a major technological shift with the introduction of jet engines and the knowledge needed to service them. One of the first generalized courses was airplane and engine mechanics and jet propulsion, which began in September 1948.

Chanute would continue to be in the forefront as an Air Force training center in the decades to come. During the Korean War, the base was in charge of inducting about 20,000 men into the service. In 1960, Air Force Command made Chanute its center for the foreign language training program and in the middle 1960s, the base became the prime training center for the LGM-30 Minuteman, one of the most important missile programs in history. The Minuteman ICBM became a key missile deterrent against the Soviet Union for America and her western allies. Beginning in the late 1960s, Chanute also trained thousands of allied airmen from Asia and the Middle East. During the 1970s, Chanute provided training for thousands of USAF airmen for service in Vietnam. In 1977, the base became the prime training center for the Air-Launched Cruise Missile and was also later involved in the Ground-Launched and MX missile programs. In 1978, after introduction of newly-designed engines for the F-15 and F-16 aircraft, new Chanute training courses emerged to keep abreast of the changing equipment students would encounter in the field. In 1982, the 928th Tactical Airlift Group proposed the establishment of drop and landing zones at Chanute. The zones would be used to conduct short-field landings and air drops to help C-130 pilots and navigators maintain proficiency.

Chanute served as a major training facility for Air Force aircraft maintenance officers, Air Force, Navy and Marine Corps meteorology personnel (officer and enlisted), and enlisted technical training for Air Force fire fighters, aircraft maintenance, flight simulator maintenance, fuel system maintenance and ICBM missile maintenance. It also contained training ICBM Launch Facility "silos" for the Minuteman ICBM maintenance personnel. Additionally, Chanute was the site for training USAF firefighters, life support specialists, welders, airframe repair and most of vehicle maintenance technical schools.

Chanute's importance to the Air Force during its years of operations is almost impossible to describe, which explains the shock that must have been felt by area residents in 1988 when it was learned that the Department of Defense recommended that the base be closed to save money. The end of the Cold War with the fall of the Soviet Union prompted the government to downsize the armed forces. Chanute Air Force Base was one of the many casualties of this decision. The base was officially closed on September 30, 1993.

Since that time, parts of the base have been converted to civilian and other alternative uses. Many of the Air Force base's buildings have found new life as restaurants, retirement homes, an aerospace museum, a data center, and a few light manufacturing facilities. The golf course, once only available to service members and their guests, is now privately owned and open to the public. The housing on base, once comprising homes for airmen with families, is now occupied by civilians. The airfield and its hangars have been converted into an aviation center and there is even a 6-month boot camp program, Lincoln's Challenge Academy, for troubled youths on the former base.

Abandoned White Hall at the former Chanute Air Base

But things are not so bright for other portions of the old base. Many of the buildings still remain unoccupied and are slowly decaying in their abandonment. The widespread use of asbestos and the discovery of toxic chemical dumps have caused some parts of the base to be condemned. In other sections, the buildings continued to deteriorate, covered with graffiti and subjected to late-night forays by urban explorers and their less-friendly counterparts, the vandals.

Although the public is allowed to wander the grounds of the former base, trespassing in the buildings is forbidden. The area is heavily patrolled by the local police. Of course, this does not keep everyone out of the buildings. Until it became the target of the wrecking ball in the spring of 2016, White Hall, the massive building that dominated the base, was a prime attraction for those fascinated with abandoned sites. The 500,000-square-foot building, equivalent in size to 11 football fields, was the largest military center in America before the Pentagon was constructed in 1941. White Hall was a self-contained troop barracks for more than 2,000 men. Its amenities included a barber shop, post office, communications office, mess hall, bakery, library, and study halls. In recent years, it stood abandoned, filled with the debris and refuse of the past – and, some say, with ghosts.

Stories abound when it comes to White Hall, and the rest of the abandoned base. Trespassers have reported hearing footsteps in otherwise empty buildings, disembodied voices, music playing, and metallic hammering, as if someone is repairing one of the many aircraft engines that were used for training at the base in days gone by. Others claim to have seen the ghosts. There are reports of men in uniform who have been seen through broken windows, airmen who have been seen walking through the buildings, and eerie accounts of shadowy figures who stare out across the now empty airfields.

One report from 2001 is especially unnerving. On September 13, a police K-9 unit responded to a trespassing call at White Hall around 10:00 p.m. The officer took his partner, Dutch, an experienced canine with hundreds of drug arrests, into the building and Dutch began to pursue what was assumed to be the trespasser. Off his lease, he chased the suspect onto the roof, where he suddenly leapt off the building and fell to his death. Who, or what, was Dutch chasing? There was no one else on the roof with him.

By the time this book is in your hands, White Hall will be gone. The hazardous conditions of the building finally spurred plans to demolish it. The strange tales of ghosts and the unexplained that surround the building will soon be nothing more than memories. What will happen to the spirits that are believed to linger behind at White Hall? Will they continue to haunt the vacant site, continue their bleak existence at some other part of the base, or pass on from this world to the next?

The Sinking of Columbia
Tragedy and Terror on the Illinois River

On the night of July 5, 1918, a passenger steamboat called *Columbia*, returning from a moonlight excursion, collapsed and sank in the middle of the Illinois River. Of the nearly 500 passengers on board that night, 87 of them lost their lives in the dark, churning currents of the river. It became known as the worst maritime accident in the history of the Illinois River, although it is mostly forgotten today – except for the dire accounts of the survivors and the lingering spirits of those who died beneath the water.

The Illinois River snakes through the very heart of the state. Formed by the convergence of the Des Plaines and Kankakee Rivers, it eventually empties itself into the Mississippi River, miles after touching the towns, farms, and settlements of Central Illinois. Its history is long and it has played an important role in the state's history, the Native Americans who paddled its waters to the barges that later transported goods downriver to

New Orleans. Early traders used canoes and flat boats to carry pelts and trade goods between St. Louis and Canada, and its importance had been recognized as far back as 1673, when Louis Joliet wrote that a canal was needed to connect the Chicago River and Lake Michigan with the waters of the Illinois. His prediction would come true with the completion of the Illinois and Michigan Canal in 1848.

The first steamboat was launched on the Illinois River in 1819 or 1820, and others soon joined it. Shipping companies soon appeared at various spots along the river, offering steamships, packet boats, and towboats to transport household goods, food, supplies, clothing, grain, and livestock to the towns that also sprang up on the river banks. The early steamboat boilers burned wood, and each boat used as much as a cord of wood every 24 hours, for each ton of weight that it hauled. To support this consumption, the river banks filled with wood yards, eager to sell fuel for the ships.

From around 1820 to the middle 1850s, when the railroads arrived in the region, the Illinois River was the primary means of conveying people and merchandise across the state. By the 1830s, there were hundreds of them operating along the river, with 17 packet lines in service by the 1840s, with owners competing to control the waterway. The most famous of the steamboat dynasties was that of David M. Swain, who built packet and excursion boats on the Illinois from 1880 to 1930. Many of the steamboats were dubbed "floating palaces," offering mahogany bars, brass fixtures, crystal chandeliers, luxurious carpets, and upscale amenities that were designed to offer comfort to those who could afford it.

Between 1850 and 1860, steamboat excursions reached the height of their popularity. In those days, a guest could book a two-week trip along the river for about $6 per person. The fascination with river travel faded during the Civil War but returned in the years that followed, continuing to thrive into the early twentieth century. By that time, most excursion boats on the Illinois River offered daytime and evening cruises with food, drink, and dancing. A steamboat would arrive at a river town like Beardstown or Peoria and play cheerful music from its calliope to let the locals know that it had arrived. Hundreds flocked to the riverfront to board the popular excursion boats of the time, like *East St. Louis, Julia Belle Swain, Idlewood*, and *Columbia*. The boats could carry as many as 600 to 1,200 people on a trip and the riverboat captains and crews enjoying a booming and profitable trade.

In 1918, *Columbia* was owned and operated by the Herman F. Mehl Excursion Company. Captain Herman F. Mehl, the primary stockholder, had command of the boat, which had been built in 1898. It had three decks of chairs with a pilothouse on top, and had been licensed to carry 1,000 passengers at a time. That year, *Columbia* began the summer season with trips from Peoria to Pekin. There were also a series of 40-mile Saturday trips up the river that offered "moonlight dancing excursions." Entire families often boarded the riverboat for the evening tours.

On the night of July 5, the South Side Social Club of Pekin scheduled a dance on *Columbia*. The Peoria, Pekin & Western Railroad was also hosting a family night for its employees on the boat. The cost of the cruise was 50-cents for men and 25-cents for women. Captain Mehl, and his pilot, Tom Williams, were both veterans of the river and were looking forward to an excursion. The crowd on board was in high spirits and were in the mood to be easily entertained.

The steamship left Pekin, headed for Peoria's Al Fresco Park, a popular amusement park that had opened on the banks of the Illinois River. It boasted a Ferris Wheel and concession stands. On the way, about 100 people were picked up at Kingston Mines, and the rest of the crowd came largely from Pekin. There were 563 tickets sold and the majority came from Pekin, Peoria, Kingston Mines, Green Valley, Petersburg, and Bloomington. They crowded the decks of *Columbia* for the festivities, which were promoted by 20 crew members and a three-man orchestra. The ship also had a full cargo hold of coal that had been loaded earlier that evening.

The boat left Pekin for the round-trip excursion at 8:40 p.m. The one-hour-and-thirty-five-minute cruise to Al Fresco Park was uneventful. The guests on board enjoyed beer, soda, candy, peanuts, and popcorn, offered by the onboard concession stands and café, and people danced to the band or walked on the promenade deck.

The dance floor on the lower deck stayed open, and many passengers swayed to the music for the remainder of the night. The rest stood on deck or leaned on the railings, watching the silent river glide past in the darkness. The steamboat set off for the return trip to Pekin at just after 11:00 p.m.

The pilot, Tom Williams, entered a narrow river bend above the village of Wesley City (present-day Creve Couer), easing through a light fog that hung over the river. Heavy rains the weekend before had caused the river to rise about one foot. The river at this point had some treacherous curves, and the current forced *Columbia* over the western bank. The boat was moving at full speed when it glanced off a submerged stump near the shoreline. It pulled sideways and trees along the bank scraped along the white paint on the sides of the ship, breaking several windows on the starboard side and tearing off some wooden railing. Captain Mehl, thinking they had hit a sandbar brought the ship to a halt. Tom Williams then signaled the engine room and ordered the crew to reverse the engines. *Columbia* pulled away from the shore and moved slowly out into the open river. At this point, the boat was only 200 yards from shore.

Suddenly, the steamship started to tip and water began flooding into the lower level. Captain Mehl descended to the lower deck to look for possible damage and immediately realized that *Columbia* was sinking. He called out for the pilot to get them to shore as quickly as possible. Williams headed full steam for the shore, but it was too late.

The initial impact with the tree stump was jarring, knocking passengers to the deck and upsetting tables and chairs. Few on board realized the danger they were in, and there were calls from the dance floor for the orchestra to keep playing. For a few moments, the ship was still in the water. Some of the passengers warily examined the damage, and many began to head for the railing to see the cause of the impact. A moment later, though, the electrical system went out, plunging the boat into pitch darkness. There was a sudden panic to get to the deck. The exits from below became jammed with bodies. Parents tried to locate their children. Others searched for their loved ones. The dance floor suddenly split along the center, and as water rushed in, those still standing on it slid across the floor and into the dark water. Passengers began pushing, shoving, and climbing over another to try and get to the observation deck above. Captain Mehl shouted down to the crowd, ordering them to stay calm, but it was no use. The panic-stricken crowd now fought desperately to escape the boat. Men, women, and children were pummeled by feet and fists. Glass windows were broken and doors were shattered by those trying to escape from interior rooms.

The hidden stump had ripped a hole through the steel on the bottom of the hull that was 11-feet-long and two-feet-wide. When Captain Mehl issued the order to back away from the stump – an order later criticized by investigators – the hole in the bottom of the boat widened further and water flooded the lower compartment. The result was sudden and dramatic. As the river rushed in, it quickly unbalanced the boat. The extra 100 tons of coal in the cargo hold further weighed down *Columbia* and there was a deafening crash as the boat simply collapsed. Within a few moments, the ship sank down into 25 feet of water.

As had happened aboard *Eastland*, a steamer that sank in even less water in the Chicago River just three years before, passengers were pulled down with the boat, trapped in the lower levels or pinned under wreckage. There were 87 people who drowned on *Columbia,* that night, unable to escape the roaring water. At least eight of them were killed by falling debris. Watches recovered from the bodies of two women were found stopped at 12:05 a.m. on July 6, pinpointing the exact time of the sinking.

News spread quickly of the disaster. Rescuers rushed to the scene, trying to pull the still-panicked survivors away from the tangled wreckage. They were pulled from the water and dragged onto the nearby shore. There were no lights on the scene. Darkness hung over the gruesome scene and it became a place of chaos as screams, cries, moans, and wailing echoed from unseen victims. The rescuers groped with their hands into the murky wreckage, and took turns diving under the water. They pulled at jumbles of arms, legs, and feet, lifting bodies from the debris. Some were alive; many more were dead.

The wreckage of Columbia in the Illinois River

The dance floor had cracked in the center and dropped down into the hull, trapping the bodies of the dead in the deep canyon created in the middle of the deck. Once it had collapsed, there was no way to reach the upper exits. Those lucky enough to survive managed to climb through the upper skylight windows to the top deck.

The bodies recovered from the dark, muddy, sunken hull that night were mainly women and children. The few lanterns that arrived on the scene revealed terrifying sights. One woman was pulled from the wreckage with her hands still holding tightly to a baby carriage. The corpse of an infant was inside. The bodies were placed into baskets, with identifying tags for those who could be identified. They were covered with white sheets and sent downstream on barges bound for Pekin. When the death barges arrived, they were greeted by hysterical family members, roused in the early morning hours, looking for word of their loved ones. The mourners shouted questions at the survivors and eagerly waited for word from the rescuers about who was alive and who was dead.

After they were unloaded in Pekin, the dead were transported to a temporary morgue in the Empire Building on Court Street. The ambulances could not handle the number of bodies, so delivery trucks and express wagons were put into service. Once at the morgue, the bodies were examined and laid out in rows under white sheets so that they could be identified by family members. Every undertaker within 25 miles of the city was pressed into service to care for the dead. Militia members patrolled the morgue to keep out the curiosity-seekers, and women from the Red Cross arrived to administer to the relatives of the deceased, many of whom were hysterical and fainting at the scene.

When the fog lifted off the river the next morning, a grim tableau could be observed from shore. The tangled wreckage of *Columbia* thrust jaggedly from the water. Life preservers, woodwork, hats, clothing, and handbags floated around the ship. The boat's exit sign, which cheerfully asked for those disembarking to "call again" could be seen hanging crookedly above the companionway. Along the shore, hundreds of discarded life preservers lay in the mud.

The dismal vessel had quickly drawn a crowd. Automobiles filled with the morbid and the curious lined the banks on both sides of the river. Small boats schooled around the scene of the tragedy. Some of them were filled with volunteers and rescuers, while others held those who tried to pull souvenirs from the water. Divers were sent down into the wreckage on Saturday morning, as workmen tore away the top decks. Parts of the hull ended up being left in the water as a memorial to the departed and a warning to those who passed on the river. The eventual fate of many parts of *Columbia*, including the paddle wheel, remain unknown. One section that was removed from the murky bottom proved to be an ironic one – it was a piece of wood with the ship's motto: "Safety First."

The funerals of *Columbia's* dead took place every day over the next two weeks. Recreational activities came to a stop in Peoria, Pekin, and the surrounding towns and small communities. As more of the dead were laid to rest, people became angrier. They were looking for someone to blame. The easiest targets were the owner and crew. Rumors spread about drunken pilots and poor construction of the boat. Militia soldiers were moved into East Peoria when people began calling for the lynching of Captain Mehl and Tom Williams. However, after an official investigation, it was stated that "no evidence of unseaworthiness has been found... and the life-saving equipment was found to be in good condition and available." Investigators concluded that the cause of the sinking and loss of life was due solely to improper seamanship. Both Captain Mehl and Tom Williams lost their riverboat licenses. Mehl was fined $800 and was ordered to relinquish the remaining hull of *Columbia*.

In the wake of the horror, people grieved and survivors recounted their brushes with death in local newspapers and, likely, from the nearest barstool in many cases. Entire families were lost together in the wreck. It became the worst riverboat disaster in the history of the Illinois River and the tragedy brought an end to the excursion steamboat business in the area. Today, there are few outside of the immediate area who know of this terrible accident, but among those who do, the legend of it lives on – with tales of ghosts.

With so much terror and so many gruesome deaths associated with the *Columbia* tragedy, it comes as no surprise that stories of ghosts surround the doomed ship. One of the many stories was that of a phantom ship that was seen near where *Columbia* sank. These stories date back almost to the time of the disaster and rumor had it that the ship could be seen on foggy nights, just like the night when the accident occurred. Those who claimed to see it said that they often heard the faint sound of a calliope playing, just before the boat vanished from sight. Others claimed to see a ghostly green light that would sometimes show up in the river where the boat went down. Legend had it that the light was the spirit of one of the doomed passenger, still searching for a way out of the depths. Or that it was a grieving relative, searching for the body of a loved one that was never found. Whatever the case, it was said that when the green light was seen, the living should immediately leave the area. If they did not, the spirits of the dead would attempt to pull them down into the river with them.

Perhaps just as eerie are the stories of ghostly sounds that were linked to the disaster. In addition to the eerie calliope music that was reported when the phantom steamboat was spotted, many tales of hauntings along the river involved only unexplained sounds. Stories were told of an orchestra playing dance music, floating out across the water, even though no boat could be seen on the river. More frightening were stories of screams and shouts of terror that echoed in the darkness. Occasionally, splashing in the water could be heard, and yet, in every case, there was no one in the water. Were these echoes of 1918, playing over and over again as the tragedy repeated itself like an old recording?

And the Illinois River was not the only haunted site linked to the *Columbia* disaster. The Empire Building, located at 337 Court Street in Pekin, was also reportedly haunted for many years. The building (vacant at the time of this writing) became the source of a number of legends, likely linked to its use as a temporary morgue after the sinking of the steamboat. The bodies were laid out there in rows, waiting to be identified by the surviving family members. For a few of them, there was simply no one left to mourn. The family of Clyde Witcher of 109 Fayette Street had all gone on the excursion cruise together. Clyde, his wife, and their two children, died together on *Columbia*.

It seems that those who did mourn left an impression behind on the old building. Reports were made of women in mourning dresses, weeping, and men in old-fashioned clothing who simply vanished. These ethereal figures were often silent, but occasionally the sounds of cries, gasps, and weeping were reported.

It seems that the *Columbia* tragedy, no matter how hard history has tried to forget it, continues to make us remember it, nearly a century after it took place.

The Library Curse
The Strange Tale of "Old Lady Gray"

The old Peoria Public Library

Every town has its ghost stories, strange happenings, and mysterious events. For more than a century now, whenever anyone discusses the supernatural in Peoria, talk always turns to the city's public library and the haunting curse that has long plagued the property. For many readers, ghosts and spirits seem within the realm of possibility, but their imagination is stretched to the limit when asked to believe in the validity of a curse. If you are such a reader, keep your skepticism in check for just a bit longer – you may soon become a believer.

Andrew and Mary Gray first came to Peoria in the 1830s. The Irish immigrants bought a parcel of land, built a two-story house at 105 North Monroe Street, and settled into the growing community. Andrew was a commissioner and forwarder, assisting newly arrived visitors in the shipment and placement of their household goods, and soon earned great respect for his hard work and industrious nature. Mary gained her own reputation, as well. She was an avid gardener and lovingly cared for the ground around her home. Those who passed by often pointed and stared in awe at the patches of flowers, shrubs, and greenery that grew lushly around the house.

Late in the 1830s, Mary's brother died in a neighboring state and her teenage nephew came to live with the couple. According to accounts of the time, he was a troubled and lazy young man. He refused to get a job and spent his days drinking and socializing with the local toughs who loitered on the riverfront. Stories claimed he was "without morals" and was in constant trouble with the law, largely due to drinking and fighting. He was a source of constant grief and disappointment for Mary Gray.

Around the same time that Mary's nephew came to Peoria, a young attorney named David Davis also moved into the community. He opened a one-man law firm and his first client was the ne'er-do-well nephew of Mary Gray. Davis quickly became a force to be reckoned with, building his reputation by repeatedly defeating the town attorney as he tried to prosecute the nephew for his exploits. Eventually, Davis became concerned about the debt that the Grays were incurring for his services and he decided to use the mortgage on the Gray's property to secure his attorney fees.

On November 10, 1847, the Grays entered into a trust deed to David Davis for Lot 7, Block 27, in the original town plat of Peoria. When the mortgage on the property came due, Davis asked for his attorney fees.

The Grays refused to pay, arguing that they had never signed the mortgage paper. Davis filed a lawsuit against them and during the trial, the Grays angrily denied signing the papers, even though Mr. Gray's signature was plainly visible on the note. Davis introduced the notarized document at trial and easily won the suit.

By this time, Mary Gray had reached her limit with her nephew. She threw him out of their house and he began wandering the streets of Peoria, cursing the family to anyone who would listen. He vanished and his body was later found floating in the Illinois River. The Grays were removed from their home and forced to find a new place to live. Local legend claims that, in her despair and anger, "Old Lady Gray" called on God to bear witness to the injustice that had been visited upon her family. She cursed the ground of her former home on Monroe Street with "thorns and thistles, ill luck, sickness and death to every owner and occupant."

David Davis was now the owner of the cursed property. The soil that had been so rich and fertile under the care of Mary Gray was now choked with weeds. The flowers died and the bushes and shrubs withered away. The house was abandoned and was soon overrun by rats. Locals not only feared the curse on the house, but stories also claimed that the ghost of Mary Gray's nephew haunted the place. Those who passed by at night claimed that they glimpsed him at the front door, crying and pleading for his aunt's forgiveness. No one would accept money to care for the house or to maintain the grounds and the once stately home became a ramshackle eyesore.

Mary's curse, it was said, extended beyond the house and yard. David Davis's law firm suffered after his triumph over the Grays. The couple had been well-liked in the community and most people pitied their misfortunes. Shortly after he obtained his judgment over the Grays, Davis moved to Bloomington and never returned. He never even took possession of the cursed land.

The Gray house remained abandoned and one winter night, it inexplicably caught fire and burned to the ground. The townspeople gathered to try and put out the blaze, but they arrived too late. The stories claim that, as the house burned, some of them saw the figure of Mary Gray, writhing in the flames and laughing with delight over the house's destruction. Shortly after the fire, the land was sold to pay off the property taxes. It then sat empty for years, overgrown with choking weeds, and people often crossed the street instead of walking directly past it. It was as if they believed that the curse might affect them if they dared to walk too close to it.

Time passed and the legends faded. A new rooming house was later built on the site and one of the tenants was former Illinois Governor Thomas Ford and his wife, Frances. It was the worst possible place that Ford could have chosen to live – especially since he was already living under a separate curse.

Ford had been born in Uniontown, Pennsylvania, in 1800. He was the first governor to grow up in Illinois. His widowed mother took him and his siblings west in hopes of crossing the Mississippi River in 1804 to buy cheap land. When she reached St. Louis, she was told about the recent Louisiana Purchase and informed that land to the west was no longer cheap. She settled in Illinois instead.

Ford served as a state's attorney, then was elected as a state court judge in 1836. He advanced politically to become Illinois's governor from 1842 to 1846. He was a controversial political figure. His career was hampered by rumors that he took "stimulants," although no definitive evidence of drug abuse exists. He refused to repudiate state bonds issued by the previous administration for a failed internal improvement system and for construction of the Illinois and Michigan Canal. He also paid off the state debt by raising taxes, but became infamous for his role in the death of Mormon leader Joseph Smith.

Ford hated Mormons and he wrote extensively about his dealings with them. He called Joseph Smith "the most successful imposter in modern times" and did little to impede the anti-Mormon factions in Western Illinois. As the conflict in the Nauvoo area grew heated, with hundreds driven from their homes and mobs forming in the streets, Ford encouraged Smith and his brother, Hyrum, to go to the county seat in Carthage and faced criminal charges for the destruction of the *Nauvoo Expositor* newspaper. Once there, the Smiths were charged with treason, and Ford abandoned them to be guarded by the Carthage Greys, an anti-Mormon militia group that helped murder them on June 27, 1844.

Ford denied responsibility for the murders, however, two men later gave affidavits that suggested Ford knew of the plot against the Smiths, and approved of it. The Mormons, who soon fled Illinois for Utah, were convinced that Ford planned the death of their prophet. They allegedly placed a curse on Governor Ford and his family.

In 1846, Ford left office and returned to Peoria to live. He was in debt, aged beyond his years, and was now living in a house that had been built on cursed land. Those who watched one misfortune after another befall the family came to believe that at least one of the curses was wreaking havoc on them. The Fords' three daughters all died of consumption. Frances Ford died from cancer on October 12, 1850. Governor Ford followed his wife to the grave just three weeks later, a broken and forgotten man. In 1872, the Fords' son, Tom, was mistaken for a cattle rustler and he was killed. His brother, Swell, sought to avenge his brother's death and killed several of the men responsible. He was also shot to death a short time later.

The house where Ford had lived was again abandoned. By now, the stories of Old Lady Gray's Curse had been revived and locals were convinced the house was haunted. No one dared live there. Everyone feared the curse. In time, it was demolished and part of the land was purchased by a downstate grocer, who gave it to one of his father's former slaves, Tom Lindsay. After the Civil War, Lindsay built a small house on the exact same piece of land where the Gray home had once stood. Three months after it was completed, the house was struck by lightning and burned to the ground. After the fire, Lindsay was informed of the curse by some of his neighbors. Although he had a healthy respect for the supernatural, he needed a place to live so he built a new house on the land that he owned.

One of his friends, who had his own beliefs in the supernatural, gave Lindsay a gift for his new home – a mummified rabbit's foot, which was meant to bring good luck. He buried the rabbit's foot under the front door of the new house. And he didn't stop there. He also obtained horseshoes to be hung in every room of the house. Apparently these precautions paid off for he was able to live on Monroe Street for the next 25 years, without incident.

After Tom Lindsay died, the land was purchased by a local businessman who built an ornate home on the site for his new wife. He did not fare as well as Lindsay had – his bride died within the year and tragic stories of the curse once again began to spread throughout Peoria.

The remaining part of the Gray property was purchased by a local banker, who built his own home on the land. He was soon married and the happy couple was blessed by the arrival of a baby boy. Their happiness was short-lived. The young mother died soon after the baby was born and days later, her infant son followed her to the grave. The banker stayed on in the house. Eventually, he recovered from his grief and remarried. His new wife also gave birth to a son but this child also died. The young woman lost her sanity and spent the rest of her days in an asylum.

The next occupant of the old Gray property opened one of the mansions as a rooming house. His daughter drowned in Lake Peoria and his son was killed after a fall from a hot-air balloon. For a time, the house was occupied by a company that made women's hats, but they didn't stay there for long. They spent a great part of their time, they claimed, trying to locate the source of a strange and sickening odor that hung in the air. It became so foul, and drove away so many customers, that they finally moved out.

Then, in 1894, the land was sold again and a new library building was erected on the site one year later. And, the curse of Old Lady Gray continued.

The first library services in Peoria started in October 1855. Reverend J.R. McFarland and a group of friends gathered together a collection of books and began loaning them out. A second library was started a month later by another group and they consolidated their efforts in 1856 as the Peoria City Library. They moved to a building on South Main Street and this remained the city's library for the next 10 years.

In 1880, the city voted to establish a large free library that would be supported by local taxes. The Peoria Public Library was established in a rented building at the corner of Adams and Fulton Streets, but it would not remain there permanently. The library's directors closed the deal for a new site on June 28, 1894 – a section of land that had originally belonged to Andrew and Mary Gray. A handsome, three-story brick building was completed in 1895.

Library board member Erastus S. Willcox was appointed as head librarian and when the new library opened to the public, he gave a moving public address about the importance of education and expansion of library services. Willcox was a scholar and educator and was responsible for selecting a number of books that became the pride of the library's collection. He was a conservative, staid figure, who always wore formal attire in public, insisted that gentlemen remove their hats inside of the building, and frequently scolded vagrants or children who loitered in the halls or in the stairways.

Willcox was the next victim of the curse. While walking to the library on the afternoon of March 30, 1915, he was struck by a streetcar at the intersection of Main Street and Glen Oak Avenue. According to witness accounts, Willcox had stepped out into Main Street and was struck. The streetcar had sounded its bell, but Willcox apparently didn't hear it. The motorman managed to avoid hitting him directly, but the fender of the car knocked him down and he sprawled unconscious on the pavement. Willcox was taken to Proctor Hospital with a deep gash in the back of his head. He died a few hours later.

The curse had, many believed, claimed another victim – and Erastus Willcox would not be the last. Tragedy struck subsequent librarians. Willcox's successor, S. Patterson Prouse, attended a meeting of the library board on December 21, 1921. He showed no signs of illness during the afternoon meeting, taking part in a spirited discussion regarding library bonds. However, just as the meeting was coming to an end, he was walking to the door and collapsed onto the floor. Dr. A.J. Foerter was summoned from his office across the street from the library and while he did everything that he could, he was unable to revive him. He later said that he believed Prouse was dead before his body hit the floor.

After the untimely death of Prouse, the board searched for a new librarian to take charge, reorganize the library, and deal with the growing number of volumes. They hired Dr. Edwin Wiley in May 1922, and he immediately went to work. Up until that time, the public had been required to request books that were brought to them from secure stacks. Dr. Wiley implemented the "open shelf" system, where the books were kept on shelves that were accessible for library patrons. Dr. Wiley soon became a prominent figure in Peoria's social circles and he became known for his charitable work, like the Bedside Book Program, which delivered library volumes to hospital patients and invalids.

But good works could not save him from the curse. Dr. Wiley died from poisoning on October 20, 1924. His wife told police officials that she awoke early that morning and heard her husband groaning in bed. When she checked on him, he told her that he had swallowed a fatal dose of arsenic, obtained from a collection of chemicals that belonged to their son, who was a student at Bradley Polytechnic Institute. Mrs. Wiley immediately called the family doctor, who rushed over to the house to find Wiley writhing in pain, He was taken to the hospital, where his stomach was pumped, but it was already too late. He remained conscious for part of the time, but refused to say why he had taken the arsenic. Wiley died later that day. It was later discovered that the doctor had a history of mental illness and a year prior to his suicide, he had taken an overdose of sedatives and nearly died. He was admitted to a sanitarium for several months, but recovered and resumed his duties.

It should come as no surprise that some locals attributed his madness and death to the Gray Curse. And there were other oddities that occurred at the library. In 1907, a school superintendent blew up a safe at the library to cover his embezzlement of school funds. At the time, the school district's offices were in the library. The library also became embroiled in a blackmail plot that followed the death of George McNear, Jr. (which will be recounted later in the book). His widow was told that the name of his killer would be revealed if she placed $1,000 in a special drawer on the library's third floor. Police arrested two men, father and son, William Anthony

Gibson and William John Gibson, who retrieved the envelope. They had no clues as to the murder and claimed their appearance at the library was a coincidence. A jury didn't believe them and both men went to prison.

But is the long list of deaths and tragedies really proof that the property is cursed? While many believe so, it can also be said that the stories associated with Mary Gray and the curse are simply local legend. In fact, much of the history associated with the Gray family has been lost, or at least mixed up, over the passage of time.

The current Peoria Public Library branch on Main Street opened in March 1968. The story of the curse is still part of the fabric of the library's history, despite the years that have passed and the many renovations that have taken place over the years. However, it seems that a curse is not all that haunts this branch of the library – the building is also said to be home to a number of ghosts.

Among the lingering spirits is the specter of Erastus Willcox, the doomed librarian who was struck by the streetcar. Visitors and staff members have reported seeing a man in early-1900's clothing walking down hallways or prowling about in the stacks.

There may be other ghosts, too. Staff members who have been in the basement claim that they have been startled by icy cold spots, or strange cool breezes that seem to come from nowhere. Books are heard falling off the shelves and crashing to the floor, even though no books have actually been disturbed. Doors open and close, lights turn on and off, and sometimes voices are heard in empty basement rooms. When the sounds are investigated, no one – among the living, at least – is found.

Who wanders the library? The victims of the legendary curse? Ill-fated librarians and property owners? Or perhaps a former staff member or two who after finding the library to be a wonderful place in life, chose to return to their beloved books after death.

The Mystery of Vishnu Springs

Hidden away in a secluded valley along the Lamoine River in McDonough County is a secret place -- a place long forgotten by the outside world. It was once considered a magical valley by those who came there seeking peace, serenity, and the healing waters of the local springs. Today, it is an abandoned village of which no homes, streets, or residents remain. There is now only a ramshackle three-story hotel, abandoned for decades, to serve as evidence of greater things in days gone by.

But while Illinois history has forgotten Vishnu Springs --- Vishnu Springs refuses to forget the history that took place in the hidden valley.

That history lingers behind as a ghostly echo of the past.

The shady valley that would someday be home to Vishnu Springs, surrounded by rocky bluffs filled with caves, proved to be an attraction to the early pioneers of the region. They used the quiet spot as a place to picnic and hold parties, and, in 1884, one gathering was said to have drawn as many as 1,500 people from the surrounding area. It was not long after this that many residents of the nearby town of Colchester began to realize that the water in the valley was different than the drinking water that could be found elsewhere. According to old accounts, the water from the springs in the valley had a peculiar salt content, an appealing taste, and contained seven medicinal properties that were "restorative and curative" to the body. People began making the trek from nearby towns and farms to sample the water, hauling away bottles and jugs of liquid from the springs. Claims were made that doctors sent their patients to the springs on crutches and they walked away without them.

In the middle 1880s, as many as 1,500 to 2,000 people at one time gathered in the valley to eat, drink, hold religious camp meetings, and consume the cold, curative waters. In an era when effective medicines were rare, the strange-tasting water offered hope to a great many people. The owners of the land and the springs claimed that the water would "cure of benefit all kinds of debility, neuralgia, rheumatism, palpitation of the heart, dyspepsia, kidney trouble, worms" and even "female troubles, dislocated limbs, broken backs, deafness, blindness and laziness." The claims were easy to accept. A simple trip to the springs would introduce skeptics to people from all walks of life who said they had been cured of their afflictions. The sick and the pitiful bought a gallon of the water for 25-cents and carried it home with them.

The owners of the springs were not shysters, taking advantage of the gullible. They were also swept away by the magical charm of the valley. They called the place "Vishnu" after one of the owners, Darius Hicks, read about the 1861 discovery of Angkor, an abandoned city that had been perfectly preserved for 300 years by vegetation growing out of the Krishna River. Vishnu was a Hindu deity whose earthly incarnation was the river that had covered Angkor.

After a Holiness Camp Meeting that was held at Vishnu in 1889 managed to draw nearly 3,000 people to the valley, Hicks decided that the valley should be developed into an actual community. The land was surveyed, lots were drawn up, and they were sold for $30 each. Within days, all of them had been purchased. People were eager to be a part of the new town.

Darius Hicks had a great vision for Vishnu. He was the man who shaped the community and the first to see the opportunity that the town could offer. Sadly, though, it would never meet his expectations. By the 1920s, the once thriving village would be virtually abandoned. But the community would survive longer than Hicks himself, whose personal problems would drive him to self-destruction.

Hicks was born on May 5, 1850, in Hire Township of McDonough County, Illinois. He was one of three surviving children of pioneers Ebenezer and Mary Hicks. His oldest brother died in the Civil War and a younger sister succumbed to a childhood illness. The Hicks were a wealthy and successful family. They owned more than 4,000 acres of land in McDonough County and were known for breeding fine cattle. But despite the family's wealth, Ebenezer Hicks did not allow money to ruin his sons. They attended school until the age of 16, when Darius and his brother, Franklin, were each placed in charge of 1,000 acres of family land. They were expected to develop it for the sake of the entire family.

It was on one of these sections of land that Darius became acquainted with the rich mineral springs that would become Vishnu. He was toiling in the fields one hot summer day and wandered into the shady valley for a drink of water. He later described how he immediately fell under the spell of the place. Inspired by the article he read, he dubbed it "Vishnu," and later started marketing and selling the water from the springs.

Hicks soon learned a valuable lesson about Vishnu – that he could not have the magical valley and his farmland, too. When 3,000 people came to Vishnu for the Camp Holiness meeting, they trampled down and entire field of corn and frightened a prize bull so badly that he disappeared. A herd of his cows, startled by the scores of church faithful in their meadow, wandered into a field of young wheat and decimated it. Hicks had a choice. He could farm the land or he could develop it. He could not do both. In 1889, he gave up farming and decided to build his town.

Since Vishnu was meant to be a health resort, Hicks needed a hotel. He went into partnership with John and Milton Mourning and by May 1889, construction had been started on a building near the spring. Hicks named it the Capitol Hotel and it rose to a height of three stories. It was completed in September at a cost of $2,500.

Over the summer, Hicks continued to publicize the spring and the new town. Lots were quickly snatched up and by October, Vishnu had its first full-time resident. His name was Andrew Ruddle and he constructed a small house near the hotel. That winter, David Reece opened the town's first store.

By the following spring, Vishnu had two more stores, a restaurant, a livery stable and blacksmith, and a photo gallery. Hicks organized the "Vishnu Transfer Line" that made trips from Colchester to the new resort. For the cost of 75-cents, a passenger could be transported to Vishnu, have dinner, and then be driven back to

The Capitol Hotel at one of the many gatherings that took place at Vishnu during the heyday of the town.

town. For an additional fee, a passenger could be driven to the resort in a carriage or canopied buckboard, instead of the spring wagon that was normally used.

Although local newspapers reported that Vishnu was an idyllic "boomtown," there was an undercurrent of trouble at the springs. Hicks evidently did not get along well with his developer, Charles K. Way, and there was talk of dividing the community into two parts. Way eventually developed land southeast of the hotel. Also, the resort became known for the sale and consumption of illegal alcohol (Colchester and the county were both "dry" at that time). The drinking on the grounds of the resort led to occasional fighting. In the fall of 1890, Andrew Ruddle stabbed restaurant owner John Mourning, and while the wound was not fatal, Ruddle was arrested anyway.

Meanwhile, despite the drinking and the fighting, Hicks continued to develop the resort as a place of peace and healing. A new organ was installed in the hotel parlor and the building boasted a number of other improvements, like running water and an elevator that took guests to the third floor ball room. Amusements were added for the resort travelers, including a carousel that was powered by actual horses. The lawn around the hotel was filled with swings, hammocks, a croquet grounds, a picnic area, and a large pond that was dubbed "Lake Vishnu" and stocked with goldfish. A small stream flowed away from the lake and vanished into the mouth of a large, unexplored cave. Hicks also built a racetrack and established a park, both of which were not in the valley but on a nearby hill. A set of 108 wooden steps had been constructed to reach the part of the town located on the hill. He also promoted and arranged for cultural activities like dances, band concerts, and holiday celebrations. He organized a literary society and opened a schoolhouse for the children who had settled in Vishnu with their parents. In 1896, it gained a post office and Hicks eventually moved from his nearby farm and settled in town as the postmaster.

Although all of this sounds as though the town was rapidly growing, in truth, it wasn't. Most of Hicks's efforts were being spent on a small number of full-time residents and on the travelers who came to take in the waters. There were never more than about 30 homes in the valley and the hotel closed in the cold weather months, which meant that no one was coming to take in the waters. For this reason, the village never really gained an economic base, even as a popular resort, for there was no railroad connection to it and it was far from any sizable town of the era.

While Hicks struggled to create a viable community at Vishnu, he had much bigger problems in his personal life. In 1889, Hicks had married for a second time to Hattie Rush of Missouri, one of the many pilgrims who had traveled to Vishnu in search of healing waters She had also been married before and had children of her own, including a 12-year-old daughter named Maud. Hattie suffered from a variety of health issues, including Bright's disease. She also had heart trouble, which led to her death in 1896 at age 40.

After Hattie's death, Hicks committed what many considered an unforgivable act, which scandalized the community for years to come -- he married his step-daughter. Maud became the third Mrs. Hicks in September 1897 in a private, civil ceremony at the McDonough County courthouse. She was only 20-years-old at the time. Although the marriage was not actually incestuous, it was regarded as improper and Hicks was shunned by the more conservative members of the community. Maud later gave birth to a son in 1898, followed by a daughter, but died in childbirth just five years later.

This was one of two events that marked the beginning of the end for Vishnu.

The first event occurred one warm summer day in 1903. The resort had opened for the season and the carousel was filled with children. They were carefully supervised by the owner, who watched over things and kept the horses moving so that the gears on the machine would turn. It is unclear just what happened, but somehow, the owner's shirt sleeve became tangled in the gears of the carousel and he was pulled into them. The children's cries of delight and laughter turned to screams of terror as the man was crushed to death. The carousel came to a stop and it never ran again.

Later that same year, Maud and a baby girl died during the delivery. To this day, it is said that this tragic event can still be experienced at the abandoned Capitol Hotel. Visitors have claimed to hear the sounds of a baby crying and a women weeping within its decaying walls, as if the terror Maud experienced left a horrific memory inside the place and it can never be erased.

Stories of a haunting aside, there is no question that Maud's death shockingly changed Darius Hicks. He certainly never dreamed that his wife, 27 years younger than he was, would precede him to the grave. On the day following Maud's funeral, he took his young son and he turned his back on Vishnu. He never returned to the village he created, but his problems were not yet over.

After leaving Vishnu, Hicks bought a farm a short distance north, near Blandinsville, and took up residence there. He soon hired a housekeeper named Nellie Darrah, a widow, who was needed to help care for Hicks' two young children. In the years that followed, Nellie became a mother figure to the children and became romantically involved with Hicks. By the winter of 1908, Nellie became pregnant and confronted Hicks, demanding that he marry her. He refused and she in her grief, sought out an abortion. The procedure did not go well and she had to be hospitalized. While she was in the hospital, Nellie sent a letter to Hicks and threatened to publicize their entire affair.

Hicks never replied to her threat. Instead, he took a .32-caliber rifle from his closet, wrote a letter that explained the entire situation, and shot himself in the head. He was dead at age 58.

The suicide of Darius Hicks was the final nail in the coffin for the struggling town of Vishnu. He had moved away from the town, but had remained involved in village business and with the hotel. He had literally created the place and there was no one who was as invested, both financially and personally, in Vishnu. Hicks's death sent the community into a decline from which it never recovered.

The hotel and the town, now treated with indifference by the owners, began to attract gamblers, thieves, and criminals. On one occasion, a huge quantity of counterfeit half-dollars, which looked like the real thing but were made from pewter, were seized by the authorities at the hotel. The counterfeiter had been passing them during poker games at the hotel, and eventually, someone had gone to the sheriff. There were other stories of lawbreakers captured at Vishnu, too, and legends that some of their loot was hidden in the caves around the valley. If there is any element of truth to such stories, the money still remains lost today.

Dr. Isaac Luce, who had settled in the village during its time of greatest prosperity, tried to develop the land that he owned on the north side of the village, but he was unsuccessful. His efforts were followed by another property owner named Campbell, who also tried in vain to keep people from moving away from Vishnu, but he also failed. More and more of the homes and businesses began to be abandoned.

Eventually, the property was sold and left to decay. By the 1920s, Vishnu was nothing more than a scattering of empty buildings, abandoned, and largely forgotten in the secluded and overgrown valley. Vandals stole valuable hotel furnishings and broke out the windows of the buildings and the old hotel. Other visitors found their way to the valley and left their names behind at the hotel. The earliest signatures scrawled on the walls were those of Marie Feris and Lil Baker, who came to the Capitol in 1893, when it was still in business. The owners encouraged the graffiti in those days, but the marks and scrawls that can be found today have lost the charm and the innocence of the signatures of the past.

By the 1930s, the houses were mostly gone, swallowed by the forest or simply fallen down. The hotel was now little more than a shell and the property owner, a local banker, lost everything during the Depression. Vishnu seemed destined to be forgotten.

In 1935, though, a restoration effort was started by Ira Post. He bought the hotel and 220 acres around it. He restored the building and hired Lon Cale as the caretaker. They opened the former resort as a picnic and recreational area, which had a limited amount of success. Even though Vishnu would never be a community again, Post and his family did live at the hotel for weeks during the summer, supervising the cleaning up of the valley. As with Darius Hicks, the magic of the little valley had worked its charm on Ira Post and he longed to bring people back to Vishnu again. But it was not meant to be. Post died in 1951, and while the hotel was occasionally rented in the years that followed, the valley again became unkempt and overgrown. Post's children had all moved away, the caretaker was no longer needed, and the property was abandoned once more.

In April 1968, Alfred White and Albert Simmons talked Ira Post's niece into letting them try to revitalize the place once again. Their plan was to open the hotel and offer food and country music to the public. The venture soon folded and Vishnu was empty once more.

In the early 1970s, Vishnu Springs saw life again as a sort of commune for a group of Western Illinois University graduates and their friends. They turned the hotel into their home and sacrificed their professional careers to live with nature. Earning enough money to pay the rent and the expensive winter heating bills, the group gardened and raised livestock to make ends meet, occasionally hosting music festivals that featured groups with names such as "Morning, Morning" and "Catfish & Crystal." Eventually, they too were gone and Vishnu was once again deserted.

As the years have passed, the old hotel has continued to deteriorate and today it is little more than a crumbling shadow of its former self. Despite the interest of local societies and historic groups, the valley remained private property until the death of the last member of the Post family. The status of the land was in limbo for years, but it was eventually purchased by Western Illinois University. There is hope that it will be opened again to the public in the future, but at the time of this writing, it remains closed to visitors.

The fact that Vishnu is a forbidden place seems to add to the mystery of it. Thanks to its isolation and unusual past, there are legends about the place that date back many years. As the town fell into ruin, those who ventured into Vishnu came away with strange and perplexing tales. The accounts spoke of a woman in black who roamed through the abandoned streets. Who this woman may have been is unknown, but she was said to vanish without a trace when approached. Visitors also told of sounds from Vishnu's past, echoing into the present. There were the sounds of voices, laughter, and music -- as if glory days of Vishnu were still being lived out.

Some were the sounds of everyday life. One visitor told me of being inside of the hotel and hearing the sound of someone pounding on metal outside. It would not be until I showed him an old map of Vishnu that he realized the sounds were coming from the direction of the old livery barn and blacksmith shop. No trace of this building remains today and no hammers and anvils can be found among the ruins of Vishnu.

Is Vishnu a haunted place? Perhaps not in the traditional sense, because, aside from the legendary woman in black, there are no ghostly apparitions that have been found wandering through the valley. Nevertheless, how do we explain the eerie sounds that have been reported by several generations of visitors to this quiet place? Can they be anything but echoes of a time gone by? I do believe that Vishnu is haunted – haunted by the memories of what once existed in the valley where it has been forgotten.

Today, Vishnu remains closed to outsiders and perhaps this is for the best. Vandals have wreaked havoc on the old Capitol Hotel, a sad fate that befalls many old buildings that are abandoned to the mercy of trespassers. The state of Illinois declared that the hotel was not old enough, or important enough, to be considered significant and for this reason, was beyond their protection. Thankfully, though, the isolated location of the valley manages to keep the worst of the destruction away.

Should Vishnu ever be opened to visitors again, it requires more than two miles of walking through dense forest to find it. But if the reader is ever lucky enough to see the place, reaching that little valley is like stepping back in time. Little remains now except for the old hotel --- the carousel, the restaurants, and the 108 steps are long gone now --- but if you look closely, you are bound to stumble across other pieces of the past. Remnants of gardens and patches of flowers remain among the undergrowth, along with forgotten souvenirs of the town that was once nestled under the trees. The stream still trickles into Darius Hicks's lake and a stroll along the water may still reveal a goldfish or two, descendants of those left here more than a century ago.

But be careful how you step in Vishnu and leave nothing of what you bring with you behind. It is up to those who consider themselves caretakers of the past to preserve what the state of Illinois will not. Years ago, Ira Post's niece and daughter erected a sign at the entrance to Vishnu and while the sign is gone now, the sentiment behind it remains. It would be good of us to remember this – for if our history is gone, our ghosts will also be lost.

The sign read in part: "Vishnu Springs was preserved as planned by Ira Post. The spring water of the wonderful world of nature is left to enjoy. The springs should be left as nature provided it. Take care of it all and then all will be benefited in the years to come. Ira Post died in 1951. The wishes expressed here were his. Help us to see that his wishes are carried out."

3. HAUNTED GRAVEYARDS
Where the Dead Don't Rest in Peace in Central Illinois

After President Abraham Lincoln was assassinated in April 1865, his body traveled west from Washington, spending several weeks visiting towns and cities along a circuitous route. His funeral service in Springfield did not take place until May 4, and it followed a parade route from the former Lincoln home to Oak Ridge Cemetery, on the far edge of the city. But it would be many years before Lincoln was allowed to rest in peace. His tomb has long been a place of mystery, intrigue, speculation, bizarre history, and some say, a haunting.

Oak Ridge Cemetery was a rural burial ground on the outskirts of Springfield in 1865. The site was so rustic that many national and city leaders did not feel that it was the proper place to bury a fallen leader of the stature of Lincoln. Before his death, though, Lincoln had expressed the wish to be buried in a quiet, country cemetery someday and Mary Lincoln did her best to honor his wishes.

The remote wooded graveyard had been started around 1860. Made up of mostly unbroken forest, there was little done to improve it until after Lincoln was laid to rest there. After that, roads were added, along with iron gates, and a caretaker's residence.

After the funeral, Lincoln was taken to the temporary receiving vault in the cemetery and placed there with his sons, Willie, who had died during the presidency, and Eddie, who had died many years before. Willie's body had accompanied his father's from Washington, while Eddie's had been exhumed and brought over from another cemetery. A short time later, a temporary vault was built for Lincoln and on December 21, he was placed inside. Six of Lincoln's friends wanted to be sure the body was safe, so a plumber's assistant named Leon P. Hopkins made an opening in the lead box for them to peer inside. All appeared to be well and Lincoln and his sons were allowed a temporary rest. Hopkins stated in a newspaper story at the time, "I was the last man to look upon the face of Abraham Lincoln." Of course, he had no idea at the time just how many others would look upon the President's face in the years to come.

Construction on a permanent tomb for Lincoln lasted more than five years and on September 19, 1871, the caskets of Lincoln and his sons were removed from the hillside crypt and taken to the catacomb of the new tomb. The plumber, Leon P. Hopkins, opened the coffin once more and the same six friends peered again at the President's face. There were several crypts waiting for Lincoln and his sons, although one of them had already been filled. Tad Lincoln had died in Chicago a short time before and his body had already been placed in the nearly finished monument.

During the move, it was noticed that Lincoln's mahogany coffin was beginning to deteriorate, so his friends brought in a new iron casket. Lincoln had been encased in an inner coffin of lead and this was transferred over to the new container. The dead president was laid to rest again, for another three years, while the workmen toiled away outside.

On October 9, 1874, Lincoln was moved again. This time, his body was placed inside a marble sarcophagus, which had been placed in the center of the semi-circular catacomb. A few days later, the monument was finally dedicated. The citizens of Springfield seemed content with the final resting place of their beloved Abraham Lincoln and the tomb became a place of almost religious significance to many.

But then a strange event was put into motion. It was something that no one ever could have predicted, and unlike anything that had taken place before in American history. A plot was hatched to steal Lincoln's body and hold it for ransom. This bizarre plan became one of the strangest tales in the annals of Illinois crime and is undoubtedly the source of the mysterious legends connected with Lincoln's tomb.

The story began with the arrest of Benjamin Boyd, a petty criminal who had, by 1875, established himself as one of the most skilled engravers of counterfeit currency plates in the country. Boyd had been doggedly pursued by Captain Patrick D. Tyrell of the Chicago office of the U.S. Secret Service for eight months before he was finally captured in Fulton, Illinois, on October 20. Following his trial, Boyd was sentenced to a term of 10 years at the Joliet Penitentiary.

Shortly after Boyd's arrest, the details of the Lincoln "kidnapping" plot began to be concocted in Lincoln, Illinois. The city was a staging point for a successful gang of counterfeiters run by James "Big Jim" Kneally. The place was an ideal refuge for Kneally's "shovers," pleasant-looking fellows who traveled around the country and passed, or "shoved," bogus money to merchants. It's been said that, around this time, at least half of the currency being used in Logan County was counterfeit. Following Boyd's arrest, in the spring of 1876, business took a downturn for the Kneally Gang. With their master engraver in prison, the gang's supply of money was dwindling fast. Things were looking desperate when Kneally seized on a gruesome plan. He would have his men kidnap a famous person and, for a ransom, negotiate the release of Benjamin Boyd from Joliet prison. Kneally found the perfect candidate for his kidnapping victim: Abraham Lincoln, or at least his famous corpse.

Kneally placed Thomas J. Sharp in charge of assembling the gang and leading the operation. Sharp was the editor of the local *Sharp's Daily Statesman* newspaper and a valued member of the counterfeiting gang. Meanwhile, Kneally returned to St. Louis, where he owned a legitimate livery business. He wanted to be far away from the events as they unfolded and have an airtight alibi. In June, the plan was hashed out at Robert Splain's saloon in Lincoln. Five of the gang members were sent to Springfield to open a saloon that could be used as a base of operations.

This new place was soon established as a tavern and dance hall on Jefferson Street, the site of Springfield's infamous Levee District, a lawless section of town where all manner of vice flourished. Splain worked as the bartender while the rest of the gang loitered there as customers. They made frequent visits to the Lincoln Tomb at Oak Ridge, where they found the custodian, John C. Power, more than happy to answer questions about the building. On one occasion, he innocently let slip that there was no guard at the tomb during the night. This clinched the last details of the plan, which involved stealing the body and spiriting it away out of town. It would be buried about two miles north of the city, under a Sangamon River bridge, and then the men would scatter and wait for Kneally to negotiate the ransom. They chose the night of July 3, 1876 to carry out their plan.

The Springfield saloon was up and running by the middle of June, leaving the men with several weeks in which they had nothing to do but sit around the tavern, drink, and wait. One night, one of the men got very drunk and spilled the details of the plan to a prostitute, who worked at a nearby sporting house. He told her to look for a little extra excitement in the city on Independence Day. He and his companions planned to be stealing Lincoln's body while the rest of the city was celebrating the holiday. The story was too good to keep quiet about and the woman passed it along to several other people, including the city's Chief of Police, Abner Wilkinson, although no record exists how these two knew one another. The story spread rapidly and Kneally's men disappeared.

Kneally didn't give up on the plan, however. He simply went looking for more competent help. He moved his base of operations to a tavern called the Hub at 294 West Madison in Chicago. Kneally's man there, Terence Mullen, operated a secret headquarters for the gang in the back room of the tavern. One of Kneally's operatives, Jack Hughes, came into the Hub in August and learned that a big job was in the works. Kneally wanted to steal Lincoln's corpse as soon as possible. Hughes and Mullen had no desire to do this by themselves, so they brought another man into the mix. His name was Jim Morrissey and he had a reputation for being one of the most skilled grave robbers in Chicago. They decided he would be perfect for the job. Unknown to the gang, "Morrissey" was actually a Secret Service operative named Lewis Swegles. He had a minor criminal background and had served time for horse stealing. When released, he went to work as an undercover agent for Captain Patrick Tyrell. When he heard what was happening with the counterfeit gang, he posed as a grave robber.

In 1876, grave robbery was still a national horror and would remain that way for some years to come. Illinois, like most other states, had no laws against the stealing of bodies. It did, however, have a statute that prevented selling the bodies that were taken. Needless to say, this put medical schools into dire need. They often had to depend on "ghouls," or grave robbers, to provide fresh corpses for their anatomy classes. These "ghouls" had become the terror of communities, and friends and relatives of bereaved families sometimes patrolled graveyards for several nights after a funeral, with shotguns in hand.

Swegles, pretending to be "Jim Morrissey," came into the Hub and discussed the methods of grave robbery with the other two men. The three of them quickly devised a plan. They would approach the Lincoln monument under the cover of night and pry open the marble sarcophagus. They would then place the casket in a wagon and drive northward to the Indiana sand dunes. This area was remote enough to provide a suitable hiding place for however long was needed. Swegles, being the most experienced of the group, agreed to everything about the plan except for the number of men needed. He believed the actual theft would be harder than they thought and wanted to bring in a famous criminal friend of his to help them. The man's name was Billy Brown and he could handle the wagon while the others pillaged the tomb. The other two men readily agreed.

On November 5, Mullens and Hughes met with Swegles for a final conference. They agreed the perfect night for the robbery would be the night of the upcoming presidential election. The city would be packed with people, but they would all be in downtown Springfield, waiting near the telegraph and political offices for news. Oak Ridge Cemetery, over two miles away and out in the woods, would be deserted and the men could work for hours and not be disturbed. It would also be a perfect night to carry the body away, as the roads would be crowded with wagons and people returning home from election celebrations. One more wagon would not be noticed.

The men agreed and decided to leave for Springfield on the next evening train. Swegles promised to have Billy Brown meet them at the train, but felt it was best if he didn't sit with them. He thought that four men might attract too much attention. Hughes and Mullen conceded that this was a good idea, but wanted to at least get a look at Brown. Swegles instructed them to stay in their seats and he would have Brown walk past them to the rear car. As the train was pulling away from the station the next night, a man passed by the two of them and casually nodded his head in their direction. This was the mysterious fourth man. Brown walked past them and disappeared into the back coach. Hughes and Mullen agreed that he looked fit for the job. While they were discussing his merits, Billy Brown was hanging onto the back steps of the train and waiting for it to slow down at a crossing on the outskirts of Chicago. At that point, he slipped off the train and headed back into the city. "Billy Brown" was actually Agent Nealy of the United States Secret Service.

As Nealy was slipping off the train, more agents were taking his place. On the same train on which Swegles and the conspirators were steaming toward Springfield, Captain Tyrell and a half-dozen operatives were riding just one coach ahead of them. They were also joined on the train by a contingent of Pinkerton detectives, who had been hired by Robert Lincoln after he got word of the plot to steal his father's body. The detectives were led by Elmer Washburne, one of Robert Lincoln's law partners. A plan was formed between Washburne and Tyrell. Swegles would accompany the grave robbers to Springfield and while assisting in the robbery, would signal the detectives, who would be hiding in another part of the monument. They would then capture Mullen and Hughes in the act.

When they arrived in Springfield, Tyrell contacted John Todd Stuart, Robert's cousin and the head of the new Lincoln National Monument Association, which cared for the tomb. He advised Stuart of the plan and together, they contacted the custodian of the site. The detectives would hide in the museum side of the monument with the custodian. This area was called Memorial Hall and it was located on the opposite side of the structure from the catacomb. They would wait there for the signal from Swegles and then they would rush forward and capture the robbers.

The first Pinkerton agent arrived just after nightfall. He carried with him a note for John Power, the custodian, which instructed him to put out the lights and wait for the others to arrive. The two men crouched in the darkness until the other men came inside. Tyrell and his men explored the place with their flashlights. Behind the Memorial Hall was a damp, dark labyrinth that wound through the foundations of the monument to a rear wall of the catacomb, where Lincoln was entombed. Against this wall, in the blackness, Tyrell stationed a detective to wait and listen for sounds of the grave robbers. Tyrell then returned to the Museum Room to wait with the others. Their wait ended just as darkness fell outside.

A lantern flashed outside the door and sounds could be heard as the grave robbers worked at the lock. Almost immediately, Mullen broke the saw blade that he was using on the lock, so they settled in while he resorted to the long and tedious task of filing the lock away. After some time, Mullen finally removed the lock and opened the door to the burial chamber. Before them, in the dim light, he and Hughes saw the marble sarcophagus of President Lincoln. Now, all they had to do was to remove the lid and carry away the coffin, which turned out to be much harder than they had anticipated. The stone was too heavy to move, so using an ax, they broke open the top, then moved the lid aside, and looked into it. Swegles was given the lantern and was stationed nearby to illuminate the work area. Left with no other option, he complied, although he was supposed to light a match at the door to alert the Secret Service agents that it was time to act. Meanwhile, Mullen and Hughes lifted out the heavy casket. Once this was completed, Mullen told Swegles to go and have the wagon moved around. He had assured Mullen and Hughes that Billy Brown had it waiting in a ravine below the hill.

Swegles raced around to the Memorial Hall, gave the signal to the detectives, and then ran outside. Tyrell whispered to his men and, with drawn revolvers, they rushed out and around the monument to the catacomb. When they arrived, they found the lid to the sarcophagus was moved aside and Lincoln's casket was on the floor --- but the grave robbers were gone!

The detectives scattered outside to search the place. Tyrell ran outside and around the base of the monument, where he saw two men near one of the statues. He whipped up his pistol and fired at them. A shot answered and they fought it out in a hail of gunfire, dodging around the monument. Suddenly, one of the men at whom he was shooting called out Tyrell's name --- he was firing at his own agents!

Mullen and Hughes had casually walked away from the tomb to await the return of Swegles, Brown, and the wagon. They never suspected the whole thing had been a trap. They had only wanted to get some air and moved into the shadows where they wouldn't be seen in case someone wandered by. After a few minutes, they saw movement at the door to the tomb and had started back, thinking that Swegles had returned. They heard the pistol shots and saw a number of men around the monument. They took off running past the ravine and vanished into the night. Assuming that Swegles had been captured, they fled back to Chicago, only to be elated when they found him waiting for them at the Hub tavern. He had returned with the horses, he told them, but found the gang gone. He had come back to Chicago, not knowing what else to do, to await word of what had happened. Thrilled with their good fortune, the would-be grave robbers spent the night in drunken celebration.

The story of the attempted grave robbery appeared in the newspaper following the presidential election, but it was greeted with stunned disbelief. In fact, only one paper, the *Chicago Tribune*, would even print the story because every other newspaper in the state was sure that it was not true. To the general public, the story had to be false and most believed that it had been hoaxed for some bizarre political agenda. Most people would not believe that the Secret Service and Pinkerton agents would be stupid enough to have gathered all in one room where they could see and hear nothing, and then wait for the criminals to act. The Democrats in Congress charged that the Republicans had faked the whole thing so that it would look like the Democrats had violated the grave of a Republican hero and in this way, sway the results of the election. To put it bluntly, no one believed that Lincoln's grave had been, or ever could be, robbed!

The doubters became believers on November 18, when Mullen and Hughes were captured. The newspapers printed the story the following day and America realized the story that had appeared a short time before had actually been true. Disbelief turned into horror. Letters poured into the papers, laying the guilt at the feet of everyone from the Democrats, to southern sympathizers, to the mysterious John Wilkes Booth Fund.

The people of Illinois were especially outraged and punishment for the two men would have been severe --- if the law had allowed it. After their arrest, the conspirators were placed under heavy guard in the Springfield jail, and on November 20, a special grand jury was convened in Springfield and returned a bill against Mullen and Hughes for attempted larceny and conspiring to commit an unlawful act. There was nothing else they could be charged with. Grave robbery was not a crime in Illinois and the prosecution, bolstered by Chicago lawyers dispatched by Robert Lincoln, could find no grounds to charge them with anything other than the minor crimes of larceny and conspiracy. Ironically, the charge was not even for conspiring to steal President Lincoln's body. It was actually for planning to steal his coffin, which was the property of the Lincoln National Monument Association.

The public was aghast at the idea that these men would get off so lightly, even though the grand jury had returned a quick indictment. Continuances and changes of venue dragged the case along to May 1877, when it finally came to trial. The jury was asked by the prosecution to sentence the men to the maximum term allowed, which was five years in prison. On the first ballot, two jurors wanted the maximum; two of them wanted a two-year sentence; four others asked for varying sentences; and four others even voted for acquittal. After a few more ballots, Mullen and Hughes were incarcerated for a one-year stay in Joliet.

And Abraham Lincoln was once more left to rest peacefully in his grave, at least for a while.

It was not long before the story of the Lincoln grave robbery became a hotly denied rumor, or at best, a fading legend. The custodians of the site simply decided that it was something they did not wish to talk about. Of course, as the story began to be denied, the people who had some recollection of the tale created their own truth in myths and conspiracies. The problem in this case, however, was that many of these "conspiracies" happened to be grounded in the truth.

Thousands of people came to see the Lincoln burial site and many of them were not afraid to ask about the stories that were being spread about the tomb. From 1876 to 1878, custodian John C. Power gave rather evasive answers to anyone who prodded him for details about the grave robbery. He was terrified of one question in particular and it seemed to be the one most often asked: was he sure that Lincoln's body had been returned safely to the sarcophagus after the grave robbers took it out?

Power was terrified of that question for one reason, because at that time, Lincoln's grave was empty!

On the morning of November 1876, when John T. Stuart of the Lincoln National Monument Association learned what had occurred in the tomb with the would-be robbers, he rushed out to the site. He was not able to rest after the incident, fearing that the grave robbers, who had not been caught at that time, would return and finish their ghoulish handiwork. So, he made a decision. He contacted the custodian and told him that they must take the body from the crypt and hide it elsewhere in the building. Together, they decided the best place to store it would be in the cavern of passages which lay between the Memorial Hall and the catacomb.

That afternoon, Adam Johnson, a Springfield marble-worker, took some of his men and they lifted Lincoln's casket from the sarcophagus. They covered it over with a blanket and then cemented the lid back into place. Later that night, Johnson, Power, and three members of the Memorial Association stole out to the monument and carried the 500-pound coffin around the base of the obelisk, through Memorial Hall, and into the dark labyrinth. They placed the coffin near some boards that had been left behind in the construction. The following day, Johnson built a new outer coffin while Power set to work digging a grave below the dirt floor. It was slow work, because it had to be done between visitors to the site, and he also had a problem with water seeping into the hole. Finally, he gave up and simply covered the coffin with the leftover boards and wood.

For the next two years, Lincoln lay beneath a pile of debris in the labyrinth, while visitors from all over the world wept and mourned over the sarcophagus at the other end of the monument. More and more of these visitors asked questions about the theft, questions full of suspicion, as if they knew something they really had no way of knowing.

In the summer and fall of 1877, the legend took another turn. Workmen arrived at the monument to erect the naval and infantry groups of statuary on the corners of the upper deck. Their work would take them into the labyrinth, where Power feared they would discover the coffin. The scandal would be incredible, so Power made a quick decision. He called the workmen together and swearing them to secrecy, showed them the coffin. They promised to keep the secret, but within days everyone in Springfield seemed to know that Lincoln's body was not where it was supposed to be. Soon, the story was spreading all over the country.

Power was now in a panic. The body had to be more securely hidden and in order to do that, he needed more help. Power contacted two of his friends, Major Gustavas Dana and General Jasper Reece, and explained the situation. These men brought three others, Edward Johnson, Joseph Lindley, and James McNeill, to meet with Power.

On the night of November 18, the six men began digging a grave for Lincoln at the far end of the labyrinth. Cramped and cold, and stifled by stale air, they gave up around midnight with the coffin just barely covered and traces of their activity very evident. Power promised to finish the work the next day. These six men, sobered by the responsibility that faced them, decided to form a brotherhood to guard the secret of the tomb. They brought in three younger men, Noble Wiggins, Horace Chapin and Clinton Conkling, to help in the task. They called themselves the Lincoln Guard of Honor and had badges made for their lapels.

After the funeral of Mary Lincoln, John T. Stuart told the Guard of Honor that Robert Lincoln wanted to have his mother's body hidden away with his father's. So, late on the night of July 21, the men slipped into the monument and moved Mary's double-leaded casket, burying it in the labyrinth next to Lincoln's.

Visitors to the tomb increased as the years went by, all of them paying their respects to the two empty crypts. Years later, Power would complain that questions about Lincoln's empty grave were asked of him nearly every day. Finally, in 1886, the Lincoln National Monument Association decided that it was time to provide a new tomb for Lincoln in the catacomb. A new and stronger crypt of brick and mortar was designed and made ready.

The press was kept outside as the Guard of Honor, and others who shared the secret of the tomb, brought the Lincoln caskets out of the labyrinth. In all, 18 people who had known Lincoln in life filed past the casket, looking into a square hole that had been cut into the lead coffin. Strangely, Lincoln had changed very little. His face was darker after 22 years but they were still the same sad features these people had always known. The last man to identify the corpse was Leon P. Hopkins, the same man who had closed the casket years before. He soldered the square back over the hole, thinking once again that he would be the last person to ever look upon the face of Abraham Lincoln.

The Guard of Honor lifted Lincoln's casket and placed it next to Mary's smaller one. The two of them were taken into the catacomb and lowered into the new brick and mortar vault. Here, they would sleep for all time.

"All time" lasted for about 13 more years. In 1899, Illinois legislators decided the monument was to be torn down and a new one built from the foundations. It seemed that the present structure was settling unevenly, cracking around the "eternal" vault of the President.

There was once again the question of what to do with the bodies of the Lincoln family. The Guard of Honor (who were still around) came up with a clever plan. During the 15 months needed for construction, the Lincolns would be secretly buried in a multiple grave a few feet away from the foundations of the tomb. As the old structure was torn down, tons of stone and dirt would be heaped onto the gravesite, both to disguise and protect it. When the new monument was finished, the grave would be uncovered again.

When the new building was completed, the bodies were exhumed once more. In the top section of the grave were the coffins belonging to the Lincoln sons and to a grandson, also named Abraham. The former President and Mary were buried on the bottom level and so safely hidden that one side of the temporary vault had to be battered away to reach them.

Lincoln's coffin was the last to be moved and it was close to sunset when a steam engine finally hoisted it up out of the ground. The protective outer box was removed and six construction workers lifted the coffin onto their shoulders and took it into the catacomb. The other members of the family had been placed in their crypts and Lincoln's casket was placed into a white marble sarcophagus.

The group dispersed after switching on the new electric burglar alarm. This device connected the monument to the caretaker's house, which was a few hundred feet away. As up-to-date as this device was, it still did not satisfy the fears of Robert Lincoln, who was sure that his father's body would be snatched again if care were not taken. He stayed in constant contact with the Guard of Honor, who were still working to ensure the safety of the Lincoln remains, and made a trip to Springfield every month or so after the new monument was completed. Something just wasn't right. Even though the alarm worked perfectly, he could not give up the idea that the robbery might be repeated.

He journeyed to Springfield and brought with him his own set of security plans. He met with officials and gave them explicit directions on what he wanted done. The construction company was to break a hole in the tile floor of the monument and place his father's casket at a depth of 10 feet. The coffin would then be encased in a cage of steel bars and the hole would be filled with concrete, making the President's final resting place into a solid block of stone.

On September 26, 1901, a group assembled to make the final arrangements for Lincoln's last burial. A discussion quickly turned into a heated debate. The question that concerned them was whether or not Lincoln's coffin should be opened and the body viewed one last time. Most felt this would be a wise precaution, especially in light of the continuing stories about Lincoln not being in the tomb. The men of the Guard of Honor were all for laying the tales to rest at last, but Robert was decidedly against opening the casket again, feeling that there was no need to further invade his father's privacy. In the end, practicality won out and Leon P. Hopkins was sent for to chisel out an opening in the lead coffin. The casket was placed on two sawhorses in the still-unfinished Memorial Hall. The room was described as hot and poorly lighted, as newspapers had been pasted over the windows to keep out the stares of the curious.

A piece of the coffin was cut out and lifted away. According to diaries, a "strong and reeking odor" filled the room, but the group pressed close to the opening anyway. The face of the President was covered with a fine powder made from white chalk. It had been applied in 1865 before the last burial service. Lincoln's features were said to be completely recognizable. The casket's headrest had fallen away and his head was thrown back slightly, revealing his still perfectly trimmed beard. His small black tie and dark hair were still as they were in life, although his eyebrows had vanished. The broadcloth suit that he had worn to his second inauguration was covered with small patches of yellow mold and the American flag that was clutched in his lifeless hands was now in tatters.

There was no question, according to those present, that this was Abraham Lincoln and that he was placed in the underground vault. The casket was sealed back up again by Leon Hopkins, making his claim of years ago true. Hopkins was the last person to look upon the face of Lincoln.

The casket was then lowered down into the cage of steel and two tons of cement was poured over it, forever encasing the President's body in stone.

That should have been the end of it, but as with all lingering mysteries, a few questions still remain. The strangest are perhaps these: does the body of Abraham Lincoln really lie beneath the concrete in the catacomb? Or was the last visit from Robert Lincoln part of some elaborate ruse to throw off any further attempts to steal the President's body? And did, as some rumors have suggested, Robert arrange with the Guard of Honor to have his father's body hidden in a different location entirely?

Most historians would agree that Lincoln's body is safely encased in the concrete of the crypt, but let's look at this with a conspiratorial eye for a moment. Whose word do we have for the fact that Lincoln's body is where it is said to be? We only have the statement of Lincoln's son, Robert, his friends, and of course, the Guard of Honor. But weren't these the same individuals who allowed visitors to the monument to grieve before an empty sarcophagus, while the President's body was actually hidden in the labyrinth, beneath a few inches of dirt? It's interesting to consider, but it's likely that we will never know, one way or another.

And what of the stories that claim that Lincoln's ghost still walks the tomb?

Many have reported that he, or some other spirit, does not rest in peace at the tomb. Many tourists, staff members, volunteers, and historians have had some unsettling experiences that aren't easily laughed away. Usually these encounters have been reported as the sound of ceaseless pacing, tapping footsteps on the tile floors, whispers and quiet voices, and the sounds of someone crying or weeping in the corridors.

Is it Abraham Lincoln? Most likely, it's not. In fact, it's unlikely that the tomb is even "haunted" in the traditional sense of what we think of when we consider a place to be haunted by ghosts. If there are strange things occurring at the tomb (and based on the hundreds of mysterious reports and encounters, there seems to be), it's most likely that they are "echoes" of events from the past that are still making themselves known today. Are the weeping sounds simply "memories" of the millions of grief-stricken people who have visited this site? Are the voices, banging sounds and the restless tapping a "residue" of the dark events that occurred with the grave robbery in 1876?

Many paranormal researchers, especially those well versed in the history of President Lincoln, believe this to be the case. Residual hauntings like those reported at the Lincoln tomb are not ghosts in the truest sense of the word. They are actually memories or events that have somehow become impressed upon the atmosphere of a location. These events then replay themselves like a recording when conditions are right. The haunting at Lincoln's tomb may be just this kind of manifestation. There have been literally millions of people who have passed through this monument between 1871 and the present, including friends of the Lincolns and mourning admirers of the President. If we also factor in the drama of the opening and re-opening of the grave and the wide range of emotion that has been expressed on this stone structure, then conditions are certainly ripe for something unusual to happen. The attempted grave robbery in 1876 likely left a greater impression behind than any other event in the tomb's history. The fear and excitement of that emotionally charged evening may have etched itself on the atmosphere of this place in the same way that Leon Hopkins' chisel carved its way into the lead of Lincoln's casket.

So, does the ghost of Abraham Lincoln haunt his burial site? Probably not, nor does any other "spirit" likely linger in the tomb. What does linger behind is the residual energy of more than a century and a half of grief and pain experienced by millions of mourners, the tragedy of the grave robbery, and the paranoia of the men who were sworn to protect the President's remains at all costs.

"Camp Misery" History and Hauntings of Camp Butler National Cemetery

Scattered throughout America are the burial places of fallen American heroes. These vast graveyards, with their rows of identical stones, tell the story of our nation's wars. Far from the battlefields of war, just outside Riverton, Illinois, is Camp Butler National Cemetery, a place where the dead from the Civil War, Spanish-American War, World War I, World War II, Korea, Vietnam, and the Middle East have been buried to find their eternal rest.

But just as the rows of stones at the cemetery tell a story, so do the dead. According to those who have experienced the supernatural among these gravestones, the dead at Camp Butler still speak.

Camp Butler had its beginnings at the start of the Civil War. The announcement that the country had been plunged into the Civil War stunned the people of Central Illinois. On Sunday, April 12, 1861, rumors swept through the area that Confederate troops had fired upon Fort Sumter. News arrived the following day that substantiated the rumors and it was realized that the trouble that had been brewing in America over slavery had finally erupted into war. President Abraham Lincoln called for 50,000 volunteers to fight and plans began to be made for camps where troops could be trained. The War Department sent General William T. Sherman, who would soon distinguish himself in war, to Springfield to meet with Governor Richard Yates to decide on a location in Sangamon County for a training camp. Since Sherman and Yates were unfamiliar with the county, they took Secretary of State Oziah M. Hatch and State Treasurer William Butler with them to show them the land. They chose an area northeast of Springfield, near Riverton, with suitable high ground for camping and a level ground for training exercises. Once the parcel of land was secured, the camp was established on August 2, 1861, and named in honor of William Butler.

Within days, the first recruits began to arrive at the camp and by the end of the first month, more than 5,000 fresh recruits were gathered for their one-month training period. By August, the camp housed over 20,000 men. During their training, soldiers often had to use wooden sticks in place of rifles due to weapon shortages. Over the course of the war, nearly 200,000 troops passed through the camp.

In January 1862, Colonel Pitcairn Morrison took over command of Camp Butler, and less than a month later, with the Union's victory at Fort Donelson, Tennessee, about 2,500 Confederate soldiers were shipped to Camp Butler. The mustering-in point and training camp had now become a prison. No one was prepared for the change. The camp's stockade was not secure and escapes were common. But worse were the rampant deaths and the disease.

Soon after the prisoners began to arrive, they started dying. In less than a month, 148 prisoners were buried in a newly developed Confederate cemetery at the camp. The huge influx of prisoners created an immediate need for more medicine. On March 1, camp surgeon Dr. Thomas Madison Reece sent the Medical

Camp Butler in 1861

Purveyor's Office in Chicago a request for nearly every type of medicine available to hospitals. Among other things, he asked for ether, 192 bottles of alcohol, belladonna extract, sulfate of magnesium, opium, and potassium iodide. According to the *Illinois State Register*, "The sickness among the prisoners has almost assumed the features of an epidemic."

The conditions at the camp added to the problem. Men came down with dysentery, typhus, and pneumonia and a severe, lingering winter made things worse. The newspaper account added, "Sharp winds, cold rains for the 2 weeks past have produced colds, coughs and sore throats innumerable." The hospital was filled to capacity and a day with four or five deaths was not uncommon. Fatalities became such a problem that Colonel Morrison – who also contracted severe pneumonia – became worried about the cost of coffins and ordered a camp carpenter to start building them so that they could save money.

As winter turned to spring, the change in weather brought more disease and death. Prisoners sickened and died from measles, chronic diarrhea, strange fevers, and erysipelas, a highly contagious and often fatal skin infection. When the camp was inspected by the U.S. Army in May 1862, the inspection committee was not pleased. The report noted that the stench was "horrid and sickening." The medicine supply was lacking and the camp's six hospitals were "in a miserable sanitary condition." The floors were filthy, the sick were crowded in wooden bunks, with some on the floor on blankets. A camp clean-up was ordered and while the number of fatalities dropped, the cases of typhoid, pneumonia, and erysipelas continued to rage out of control.

By mid-June 1862, 336 soldiers and prisoners were hospitalized, the largest number during Dr. Reece's tenure at the camp. Obviously, he needed more medicine, so he sent another request to the Purveyor's Office. This time, government bureaucracy got in the way of saving lives. On July 30, he finally got an answer to his call for help – the request, the office responded, "should have been in duplicate." The purveyor would not fill his order until it was sent again in the proper manner, which caused an even greater delay for the sick and dying at Camp Butler. How many men died as a result? We will never know, but in July 1862, a portion of Camp Butler was selected as one of the countries original national cemeteries, designated by President Lincoln.

Overcrowding remained a problem at Camp Butler throughout its existence. The recruitment of soldiers was still high in 1862, and Governor Yates was forced to open temporary camps to handle the arrival of more soldiers. Hundreds of prisoners also arrived, from battles at Murfreesboro and Arkansas Point. The barracks were holding twice as many soldiers as they had been built to handle and the prisoner's compound was overflowing. Contagious diseases like measles and smallpox – over 700 prisoners died during a smallpox epidemic in the summer of 1862 – broke out at a "fearful rate." At one point, more than 500 men were sick and more hospitals had to be built to accommodate them. Little relief came before May 1863, when just over 1,800 Confederate prisoners were taken from the camp and returned to Virginia in an exchange.

The camp continued to serve as a training center and mustering-out facility until the end of the war. It's most distinguished service occurred in May 1865, when soldiers from the camp were assigned to serve as the honor guard for the funeral of President Lincoln in Springfield. They were also assigned to guard the receiving vault that held the remains of Lincoln and his sons at Oak Ridge Cemetery.

Camp Butler was officially closed as a military training camp in June 1866, but its role as a national cemetery endures. Today there are 1,642 Civil War graves in the cemetery – 714 Union soldiers and 866 Confederates. The grave markers of each can be distinguished by their shapes. The Union headstones are rounded on the top and the Confederate stones are pointed. It is said that the Confederate stones are pointed to keep the devil from sitting on top of their tombstone.

The cemetery also holds the remains of fallen soldiers from every war that has followed in American history, and yet it is the Civil War that predominantly continues to play out at Camp Butler. Between the horrific conditions of the prison camp and the everyday life of the training camp, it is this period that seems to have left its greatest mark. Sights and sounds are often reported by those who visit the cemetery, or who live nearby. Apparitions have been seen among the rows of stones and on some nights, local residents report the smell of gunpowder, or campfires, lingering in the air. Others say they have been overwhelmed by the stench of illness and disease while walking through the cemetery. There are also those who have visited the cemetery and have reported the spectral figure of a man in a Union military uniform standing among the graves. During one instance, several people saw just such a figure standing near a tree, about 40 yards away. When they looked away and turned back, the man was gone. The rest of the cemetery was empty and there was nowhere that he could have gone. He simply vanished.

And the cemetery itself is not the only place where the turbulent events of the Civil War left an impression. Near Camp Butler is the town of Riverton, where Civil War troops departed by train after they completed their training. Perhaps the emotions experienced by these young men, on their way to the fields of war, from which they might never return, left an indelible mark at Riverton's railroad depot. Over the years, locals have spoken of seeing the apparitions of men in uniform near the old depot. Some claim to hear the sound of heavy boots on wooden boards, or smell the phantom scent of cigarette smoke in the air, even when no one nearby is smoking.

The Dead Beneath Their Feet
Decatur's Common Burial Grounds

The small city of Decatur, Illinois, has long been regarded as one of the most haunted towns in the Midwest. With a long history of violence and death, there is little wonder as to why so many spirits have been left behind, but the hauntings in Decatur may have a source that goes back to when the first settlers arrived in the area. The city's haunted history may have actually gotten its start because of forgotten burial grounds.

Many believe that old cemeteries, including those of the Native Americans, are the reason why the city has become so well known for its ghosts and hauntings over the years. The downtown area of Decatur rests on land where a number of American Indian burial sites are located. Centuries ago, the land around Decatur belonged to tribes within the Illinwek Confederation. During this time, a number of these tribes settled in the area, although none of them lived within the boundaries of the future city limits. When the first settlers arrived, they would find this land abandoned by the Native Americans. They had used it for their burial grounds. Today, several of the city's reportedly haunted buildings rest on land that were once burial locations.

In addition to the Indian burial sites, sketchy records still exist to say that there were once a number of private and family cemeteries scattered throughout old Decatur. In the early days of the city's history, there were no regulations about how burials of the dead were to be handled. Most people buried the dead in small plots, or even out in the backyard of their home. When these graves were marked at all, it was usually with crude wooden planks that deteriorated after a season or two.

There are records that state that small cemeteries were scattered throughout what is now downtown Decatur. Some of them were relocated, others were simply built over, their occupants forgotten. The tiny graveyards faded from memory in a generation or two and will likely never be discovered again. However, the same cannot be said for Decatur's first official cemetery – it has continued to return to "haunt" the city over and over again during the course of the last century and a half.

Decatur's first real cemetery was actually made up of two separate graveyards that were located so close together that they were generally referred to by the name of the larger one, the Common Burial Grounds. The other burial ground, King's Cemetery, was located next to the other, along West Wood Street. Contemporary accounts stated that it was hard to tell where one graveyard ended and the other began. The cemeteries were located on land that was far outside of the boundaries of Decatur when they were originally planned. Today, that area is marked by the corners of Oakland Avenue, West Main Street, and West Wood Street. They comprised several acres of ground and extended east as far as Haworth Avenue.

The property was part of a farm that belonged to Amos Robinson, who had settled in Decatur around 1832. When the city began searching for a site to use as a burial ground, Robinson donated the land that became the Common Burial Grounds. When he died in 1836, he was buried in an orchard that still existed within the cemetery grounds. The graveyard was continually used over the course of the next three decades and began to become crowded. There were few rules about burials because it was free and open to anyone who wanted to use it. The grave sites were, unfortunately, poorly marked, which caused the boundaries of the cemetery to spread out in all directions. In 1865, John E. King, who had property next to the Robinson farm, donated another section of land for burials and it was dubbed King's Cemetery. This land ran along Haworth Avenue and extended down West Wood Street to Oakland.

The cemeteries remained in use for the next 20 years, but eventually, they began to stand in the way of progress on the west side of the city. When originally platted, the graveyards were outside of the city limits, on the open prairie, but as Decatur grew, this was no longer the case. In addition, they were overcrowded and poorly kept, which provided all the excuse the city needed to close them down in 1885. The land was sold to the city, for the extension of streets to the west, and to private developers who wanted to sell plots to be used for new homes and businesses. Once the sales had gone through, workmen were called in to remove the bodies to Greenwood Cemetery.

However, these unlucky workmen faced a problem. No one had any idea just how many people had been buried in the two cemeteries over the years, thanks to unmarked graves, poor records, and lost grave markers and stones. The city pushed the move ahead and the workmen were advised to do the best they could with what information they had to work with. Construction was started a few months later and the old cemeteries were all but forgotten. But they wouldn't stay that way for long.

In 1895, while work crews were excavating the extension of West Main Street, they discovered dozens of lost skeletons, the remains of caskets, and buried tombstones. This was the first gruesome find, but it would not be the last. Sheridan Tuttle, a Decatur paving contractor, uncovered dozens of skeletons when he was excavating and bricking West Wood Street. Rudolph Klein, one of Tuttle's employees, later recalled a long stretch of street where dozens of bodies were turned up.

New home construction in the area unearthed skulls, bones, and pieces of coffins. As basements and foundations were dug, sewer pipes laid, and sidewalks put in place, it became common for workmen to turn up wayward skeletons. Newspaper reports from the middle 1930s told of a man working in his backyard who found four skulls and three long bones in the spot where he planned to put a vegetable patch. This convinced him to find another location. The discovery of bones throughout the neighborhood became such a sensation that young boys organized "digging parties" as more remains surfaced each week. There was no clue as to how many bodies had been accidentally left behind, but the gruesome discoveries continued for years – and sometimes still occur today.

In 2002, new construction took place along West Wood Street. A new parking lot was excavated for the structure and as work was being carried out, bulldozers began churning up literally hundreds of skulls, bones, and assorted human remains. The construction was halted until an archaeologist from the state of Illinois could be called in to verify that the remains were part of the old Common Burial Grounds. They were covered again but the parking lot excavation could not be continued. A visit to this site today shows a very strangely shaped parking lot, marking where the bodies of Decatur's dead still remain beneath the ground.

With all of the disturbed cemeteries and remains in this part of the city, is it any wonder that it has become known as one of the most haunted parts of Decatur? There are a number of businesses on the site of the old Common Burial Grounds that claim to have resident ghosts, including two drinking and eating establishments where apparitions have been seen and objects have been known to move about on their own. However, the most famous haunted restaurant in this area was torn down a few years ago.

Decatur's landmark restaurant, the Blue Mill, started out in the 1920s as a hangout for Millikin University students, offering music, sodas, burgers, and all the shrimp you could eat for $1. Interestingly, the first mention of ghosts in connection with the Common Burial Grounds appeared in newspapers in 1927. The story made reference to ghostly happenings at a small place that was popular with Millikin students on West Wood Street. The name of the place was never mentioned, but there were several references to the soda fountain and to students listening to "rollicking jazz music," which made it likely that the story was referring to the Blue Mill. No details were given of the ghostly events, but the story did cite the most likely cause as being the old cemetery.

The cramped little place expanded in 1935 and turned into the restaurant that became known as one of Decatur's finest dining establishments. During the renovations, the basement of the Blue Mill was lowered and broken wooden boxes that contained complete skeletons were found beneath the dirt floor. Rumor had it that the bodies were never moved, merely paved over, and the dead were left to rest in peace – but did they? According to staff members who once worked at the Blue Mill, ghostly events frequently occurred in the basement of the building. Many of them were afraid to go down there alone and spoke of things that moved about on their own, banging and rattling sounds, and lights that turned off under their own power, plunging the basement into complete darkness. The Blue Mill was torn down a number of years ago, bringing an end to an era and to the haunting that long plagued the building.

Businesses in this corner of the city are not the only places where ghosts can be found. Scores of homes in the surrounding blocks also have their phantom residents. Stories have circulated – and have been passed on to me first-hand – about eerie events along West Main and West Wood Streets. Homeowners and tenants tell of lights that turn on and off, doors that open and close, spectral footsteps, disembodied voices and whispers, toilets that flush by themselves, water faucets that mysteriously turn on, and apparitions that wander about.

One family told me of a phantom little girl that was often seen in the downstairs hallway of the house. She was usually seen chasing a little red ball and then would disappear into a wall. Another family spoke of a man who appeared in their backyard, only visible from the knees up. The man always vanished whenever he was approached. A young woman who moved into a house on West Main Street in 2007 was startled one night about two weeks after moving in when she saw a young man in a plaid shirt come down her staircase, walk across the living room, and disappear into the kitchen. She followed in a panic but found the kitchen empty and her back door locked. There was no place that the man could have gone, but he simply wasn't there anymore! Since that time, he has continued to walk through the house about every other month or so. Who this man might be remains a mystery, but it's likely that he is just another forgotten occupant of one of Decatur's forgotten graveyards.

Where the Dead Walk
The Haunted History of Decatur's Greenwood Cemetery

The beginnings of Greenwood Cemetery are a mystery.

No records exist to say who was the first to bury their dead in what became the graveyard. It's the oldest cemetery established by the white settlers to the city that is still in existence today, but the Native Americans were already using the grounds when they arrived. As mentioned previously, the Indians in the region chose many sites throughout what is now downtown Decatur as their burial grounds. One of those sites was the southern portion of current Greenwood Cemetery. There are many unmarked graves and impressions on the hills at the south end that suggest a number of burials that have taken place and have been unrecorded.

When the first settlers arrived, they began making their homes near the Sangamon River, which is just south of the cemetery. Life was hard in those days and anything from weather to illnesses could wipe out an entire family with ease. There were no real burial customs in those days, no undertakers, and no embalming. Funeral services consisted of nothing more than a few prayers and bible passages over an open hole in the ground. The corpses were placed in these holes without benefit of coffins and were normally just wrapped in a winding sheet. And while some of these burials took place literally in the back yards of the log cabins scattered throughout the area, many of the settlers searched for a communal place to bury the dead. This led them to begin burying in places that the Native Americans had also used, namely what would be Greenwood Cemetery.

Burial records did not exist in this time, so we are now forced to speculate on the number and the exact location of these burials. There are many unmarked graves in the cemetery and it is also known that the settlers often used wooden planks and perishable materials to mark their burial sites. These items would have long since been lost to the elements, leaving both the locations and the occupants of the graves unknown.

It would not be until the 1830s that the burial ground would turn into a full-fledged cemetery. About the time that the Common Burial Grounds were being established on the west side of the cemetery, settlers who lived on the south side began burying their dead at what would be called "Greenwood."

Around 1840, a few records began to appear that chronicled burials in Greenwood Cemetery. The first recorded burial was of a man named "Samuel B. DeWees" and the second was that of a "Dr. Burrell," both of which died in 1840. William Pratt, who also died in 1840, has the oldest remaining tombstone in the cemetery.

On March 3, 1857, Greenwood Cemetery Association was organized and the cemetery was incorporated into the city of Decatur. One of the main stockholders in the association was a prominent local businessman named Henry Prather. He would ultimately be responsible for the design of the main cemetery gates and for

Decatur's Greenwood Cemetery

much of the design and layout of the cemetery itself. Things were still fairly primitive in those days, though, and the association had little outlook for the future of the cemetery. Burial plots were sold for $10 each and the idea that an entire work force would someday be needed to tend the grounds never occurred to them – a problem that would plague Greenwood in the years to come.

By 1900, Greenwood Cemetery was widely accepted as the most fashionable place in the city to be buried. It was the place where even the most common could spend eternity next to the elite of Decatur society. In 1908, the Greenwood Cemetery constructed a large mausoleum for public burial. Years later, the mausoleum would deteriorate into such poor condition that it would be torn down. Questions would arise as to the actual ownership of the building and many of the bodies interred inside would be relocated. Originally, though, the mausoleum was a beautiful building and was complimented by the 13 other mausoleums that were constructed throughout the cemetery during this period. All of the private tombs were built from granite, save for the Miller mausoleum, which is an underground vault.

Greenwood was regarded as a showplace for funerary art with all of its mausoleums and the ornate statuary that was used on many of the gravesites. This attracted many visitors to the grounds and it became a popular attraction for local people on Sunday afternoons. The park-like setting, rolling hills, and towering oak trees made the cemetery a frequent spot for picnic lunches and casual strolls. There was no stigma attached to the fact that this was a burial ground and the peaceful atmosphere of the place caused any initial misgivings to vanish.

The cemetery was in pristine condition and was managed with a crew of about eight men. There were three miles of water pipe installed with spigots at various intervals to send water through the property. The roads and driveways were smoothed and covered with red shale rock, providing easy access to points throughout the cemetery. They also offered a quiet place to walk in the cool of the summer evenings. Greenwood Cemetery had become known as the "Beautiful City of the Dead," but it would not hold onto that designation for much longer.

In the middle 1920s, things began to change for Greenwood Cemetery. The change began with a startling announcement that was made by the association in charge of the management and the upkeep of the cemetery. In short, the association was completely out of money. The cemetery had been losing as much as $1,800 per year trying to pay the staff to maintain the grounds. In 1926, they had reduced the crew of the cemetery to just two men, who admittedly were unable to give the grounds the attention needed. The only logical solution was to allow the burial ground to revert back to nature and salvage what they could from the disastrous financial situation. It wasn't long before a large portion of the cemetery began to be overrun by tall grass, rampant weeds and brush, fallen branches, and tipped and broken gravestones. In 1938, it was reported that the entire cemetery had been mowed only one time that summer.

It was during these dark times in the history of Greenwood when the stories and legends that still "haunt" the place today were first told. The desolate conditions in the older parts of the graveyard gave birth to stories of ghosts, strange happenings, grave robbery, and worse. These intangible tales were only solidified by tales of marauding gangs and outright lawlessness in the area around the cemetery and at least one unsolved murder that occurred within the bounds of the graveyard itself. How many of these weird tales were true and how many were legends?

Many of them certainly had a basis in fact. A flood had wiped out a portion of the cemetery in the early part of the century and the bodies that had been dislocated were moved to other parts of Greenwood. But were the strange balls of light seen around the original corner of the cemetery the spirits of the dead searching for their new burial places? And there were dozens of other tales that were told. Greenwood Cemetery was quickly becoming a place to be avoided, a spooky novelty on the side of town that was better known for crime and disreputable neighborhoods than for peaceful burial grounds.

The 1940s are a lost portion of Greenwood Cemetery history. The tales of wandering spirits and glowing apparitions continued to thrive while decay and decline came ever closer to bringing about the graveyard's final destruction. As 1950 rolled around, the place once called the "Beautiful City of the Dead" was no more. Greenwood Cemetery was in ruins.

The roads, which had once been smooth pathways of shale, were now partially covered cinder tracks that were so deeply rutted that most of them were no longer passable. The huge oak trees, which had always added a great beauty to the cemetery, were now the graveyard's greatest curse. The falls of leaves, which had not been raked in years, were knee deep in places. They choked the grass and drifted across roadways and covered grave markers. Branches that had fallen from the trees littered the ground, which were overgrown and tangled with weeds and brush.

Water, time, and vandals had wreaked havoc on Greenwood's tombstones and markers. Years of rain, harsh weather, and wind had caused many of the stones to sag at odd angles and a lack of care caused many of them to become permanently lost. Others lay broken and damaged beyond repair, having given up the fight against the elements.

The old public mausoleum was pronounced unsafe by two city inspectors but nothing was done about the dangerous condition of it. They simply chained the doors closed and added a padlock, but curiosity-seekers and neighborhood children still managed to slip inside. Later, court proceedings would be undertaken to determine just who owned the building and to settle the question of removal and proper consent to move the more than one hundred bodies that remained inside. The mausoleum remained standing until 1967, further mired in the quicksand that had become Greenwood Cemetery.

In 1957, after decades of decline, Greenwood Cemetery was finally saved from total destruction. A vote at the annual Decatur town meeting declared that ownership and operation of the graveyard would revert to the city. The financial state of the nearly defunct cemetery association had never improved and this was a last chance effort to revive the property. The operation of the cemetery would now be paid for out of the township budget and the association would finally be laid to rest.

Of course, major problems faced the city when it had to address what could be done to restore the cemetery for proper use. A private firm that was engaged to inspect the grounds estimated that it would cost more than $100,000 to restore the cemetery. Needless to say, this kind of money was not available, but public support did seem to be behind the restoration of the graveyard. What could not be paid for was volunteered and a number of organizations donated time and labor to help save an important part of the city's history.

A day was set up in April 1958, and over two hundred volunteers arrived to clean, repair, rake and burn the cemetery. The Wagner Memorial Co. furnished trucks and drivers to haul away sticks, branches and debris. Other volunteers ranged from the VFW to the Boy Scouts and the Marine Corp League and VFW Post 99 served lunch.

The restoration was largely a success and despite a few setbacks, Greenwood has managed to prosper over the years. The cemetery has continued to make improvements and changes, including expanding for more burial space, but it continues to face some of the same problems of the past with the funds simply not being available to save the failing sections of the graveyard. The old historic markers continue to deteriorate and time continues to take its toll on these bits of memory from days gone by.

We can only hope that Greenwood's connections to the past will not be lost and that concerned citizens will still be there, as they were in 1958, to help save the last vestiges of the Decatur that used to be.

Secrets, Suicides, Crimes & Murder in Greenwood Cemetery

There have been nearly as many legends and strange stories told about Greenwood Cemetery over the years, as there have been tales about ghosts, phantoms, and specters. The history of the graveyard is riddled with unsolved mysteries and even the very beginnings of the cemetery are an enigma. And so are many of the events that have occurred in the years that followed.

In the section that follows, I have collected the weird legends, stories and secrets that surround Greenwood Cemetery. These stories are not the product of the supernatural, but are certainly the stuff of the strange and the unexplained. In some cases, the reader will find more questions than answers and realize there is much about Greenwood Cemetery that we will never know.

The Greenwood Tunnels

The tunnels that are said to run beneath Greenwood Cemetery have long been one of the graveyard's most intriguing mysteries. The accounts say that the tunnels and shafts plunge deep into the hills of the graveyard and have caused tragic accidents and graves to collapse over the years.

Many of Decatur's older residents consider it common knowledge that the central and southern parts of the city are honeycombed by mazes of abandoned mine shafts. In the past century, several coal companies operated in Decatur and combined, they sank hundreds of shafts beneath the city. In addition, other tunnels have long been rumored to run beneath the cemetery, accessible through basements of some of the city's oldest buildings.

It has also been said that one of these tunnels (not a mine shaft) actually leads into the cemetery and that the tunnel opens inside of the Miller Mausoleum, located a short distance from the graveyard gates. The mausoleum is the only underground vault that still exists inside of the cemetery. Its door was long ago bricked over and sealed shut, so it remains a mystery as to what exactly is inside. There is one thing about the vault that is curious, however. On the back side of the crypt is a steep rise where the structure was built into the hillside. On the top of this hill, right behind the crypt's stone facade, is a metal pipe that disappears into the ground. If everyone inside of this vault is dead (and we certainly assume this to be the case) and there is no link to the outside— why does the vault need a ventilation shaft? Rumors have circulated for many years that this was a purposely-built tunnel that actually extended to an old church located downtown. It was said that access to the tunnel could be found in the basement of the church behind a large door that was always kept locked. Could the stories be right? Did a tunnel actually enter this tomb at one time? Not surprisingly, this remains a mystery.

Past cemetery caretakers have also confirmed the tunnels under the cemetery and one location on the far west side of Greenwood once offered access to them through a brick cistern. It still exists today, but was sealed shut with a metal plate about 20 years ago. Leading away from the cistern is a long mound that travels east, below the cemetery. Inspection of this mound shows that a lining of bricks is hidden under the ground, bricks used to shore up the sides of the tunnel underneath. What was the tunnel built for? No one seems to know.

Over time, it's been said that these tunnels have been responsible for accidental collapses that have taken place inside of the cemetery. Cemetery records tell of one family vault that collapsed into a hole caused by a tunnel. The official version of the story was that the crypt was "unsafe" but handwritten notes maintain that the real story of what happened to the crypt was far stranger. The Bullard family crypt was a badly deteriorated tomb that once existed in Greenwood Cemetery. One morning, it was found to have collapsed in upon itself during the night. When a work crew investigated, they found that the interior floor of the crypt had caved into a tunnel that ran beneath the graveyard. Several of the bodies interred inside were reportedly never found. After receiving permission from family members in California, the interior of the tomb was filled with concrete and then covered over with dirt. It still remains there, hidden beneath the earth, in an unknown location within the borders of the cemetery.

In addition, there is another story that has been passed along about two gravediggers who stopped for a lunch break one afternoon after lowering a casket into the ground. They took their time with their meal under a nearby shade tree and then returned to work. When they walked back to the grave, they found that the casket had disappeared into an open hole at one end of the site. The hole had to be shored up with wood before the grave could be filled. The family members of the person in the missing casket were reportedly never notified.

Suicide in Greenwood Cemetery

Tragically, there are records of two separate suicides and a single murder that have occurred within the confines of Greenwood Cemetery over the years. One can only wonder how these tragic events have added to the mysterious sightings of apparitions in the cemetery in the decades since they occurred.

The first suicide occurred on October 24, 1901, when a man named John H. Johnston shot himself at the grave of his infant son. Johnston was a well-known man in the city and worked as a salesman at a dry goods store that was owned by his brother, C.T. Johnston. He was a quiet, unassuming man and was deeply in love with his wife of several years. A son had been born to the couple in 1900, but the child had died during the summer of 1901. Friends later said that the baby's death had preyed on his mind and had caused him to be despondent. C.T. Johnston stated that he could think of no other reason why his brother would have taken his own life.

On October 23, Johnston, who lived at 959 North Main Street, told his wife that he would not be coming home that night. Apparently, little thought was given to this, which suggested that the death of the child likely had an adverse effect on the marriage, as well as on Mrs. Johnston's mental health. No one knows where Johnston went during that night, but at 9:15 a.m. on Thursday morning, October 24, he walked into a pawn shop on Prairie Street that was owned by D. Young. He asked Young, with whom he was acquainted, if he could look at some revolvers. He told him that he was going into the country and wanted to do some target shooting. Young showed him a $3 weapon and Johnston asked for something cheaper, finally settling for a Harrington & Richards revolver that was $2. According to the law, he gave his name, signed a license, and left the shop with a box of cartridges. Young later reported that his friend manifested no nervousness and was very polite and friendly, just as he had always been.

Johnston left the pawn shop and walked to Greenwood Cemetery. Just 20 minutes later, he fired a bullet from the revolver into his head.

W.M. Deakin, a laborer at the cemetery, testified at the inquest that was held into Johnston's death that he had arrived at the cemetery office at 10:00 a.m. and with Charles Braden, another worker, went toward the cemetery gate. Braden, who also testified, said that they saw a man lying on the ground and thought that they should go and rouse him from his sleep. Before they reached the body, though, they saw that the man was not asleep, he had been shot. The body was face downward in a small pool of blood and a revolver was resting just inches from his outstretched fingers. The man was breathing, but was unconscious. Without touching anything, Braden hurried to the office and telephoned the police. They soon arrived in a patrol wagon and several physicians hurried to the cemetery. Johnston was first taken to Dawson's undertaking establishment, but then was moved to St. Mary's Hospital when it appeared that he might survive. Tragically, he took his last breath at 4:45 p.m. and died.

When questioned, Charles Braden said that he had seen Johnston enter the cemetery that morning, but there was nothing about him to cause concern. Perhaps 20 minutes later, he saw him talking to a man near the grave of his child. Braden did not know who the man was. A short time later, Deakin arrived with a load of sod and asked for directions in unloading it. Braden went into the office and when he came out, he forgot all about Johnston – until he saw him on the ground with the revolver a few minutes later.

The man that Johnston had been talking with turned out to be Charles Maywood, a marble worker who was laboring in the cemetery when he saw Johnston. Maywood stopped to talk with him. He was acquainted with Johnston, who had once been a marble worker himself. They chatted casually for a few minutes and Johnston mentioned to him that he had come to visit his child's grave. During the conversation, Johnston smoked a cigar or cigarette, but Maywood said that he didn't smell any liquor on him and he gave no indication that he had been drinking. Maywood said that he had walked about 200 yards away from the spot when he heard a pistol shot. At first, he paid no attention to it, but then decided to investigate. He reached Johnston's body just moments after Deakin and Braden arrived.

A coroner's inquest later ruled that Johnston had taken his own life in a fit of depression, caused by his grief over his son's death. It was a terrible ending to what had once been a good life, horribly marred by despair.

A second suicide occurred in Greenwood Cemetery on July 2, 1906. A well-liked bartender and saloon owner named Jacob Knox drank carbolic acid at the grave of his first wife, who had died 15 years before. All that his friends could offer in explanation was that, even though he had remarried, he had never gotten over his deep affections for the woman that he called the love of his life.

Knox had lived in Decatur for many years and had tended bar in a number of establishments in the city, making many friends and acquaintances. He was a neat man who wore a gray mustache, dressed well, and was regarded as very pleasant. He had a little dog that followed him everywhere and the two were known as inseparable companions. Until a short time before his death, Knox had tended bar at Casper Bolay's place on Lincoln Square and then he had purchased his own saloon on Franklin Street. He planned to apply for a license during the next meeting of the city council and there was no reason to believe that he would be turned down.

Knox's sadness was not caused by any financial or business difficulties. He was, by all accounts, a fairly prosperous man and everyone assumed that he was happily married. He had been widowed 15 years before and while Knox always spoke of his late wife with fondness, no one knew the extent of his feelings for her until just weeks before he took his own life. According to friends, he had begun to have problems at home and the trouble with his second wife seemed to stir up memories of the "domestic bliss" that he had enjoyed in years past. Knox fell into a somber mood, but no one ever imagined that he would commit suicide.

On the afternoon of July 2, Knox walked through the gates of Greenwood Cemetery. Hiram Carr, and several other workmen in the graveyard, noticed him enter at about 1:00 p.m. All of the workers were busy and paid little attention to him. Carr only noted that there was nothing peculiar about him. He was walking on the roadway, as anyone else would do, and stopped once or twice to wipe the perspiration from his head because it was a hot day. In a few minutes, Knox passed out of sight, walking toward the southwest side of the cemetery.

At some point after 2:00 p.m., the workmen, as they went from one part of the cemetery to another, came across the still form of Jacob Knox. He was lying on his back and at first, the men just thought that he was asleep and called out to him. There was no response and so they went over to him and realized that he was probably dead. One of the workmen ran to the office to notify the cemetery officials, who called the police.

Knox was lying on a grave that belonged to W.W. Conrad, close to his wife's plot. His wife's grave was covered with weeds and brush, so it was assumed that he had gotten as close to where she was buried as he could and then took his own life with poison. Next to his body was found a small glass, which was still wet with the foul drink, and nearby was a two-ounce bottle that was half-filled with carbolic acid. Knox had apparently filled the glass before corking the bottle and tossing it aside. He drank the contents and fell over onto his back. Doctors surmised that he had died almost instantly.

We can only hope that his wife was waiting for him on the other side.

Murder in Greenwood Cemetery

Greenwood Cemetery is obviously not an average graveyard. There are few cemeteries that can claim not only suicides within its borders, but an unsolved murder, as well. And it's likely that there are even fewer cemeteries that can claim that the ghost of that murder victim still roams the burial grounds.

The murder of cemetery worker Melbourn Savage stunned the city in the spring of 1930. Savage was a caretaker employed at Greenwood Cemetery at the time he was murdered in the graveyard. There have been many questions raised in the years since about the unsavory aspects of Savage's character and whether or not they led to his death. No matter what happened, though, his killer was never caught – and some say Savage's spirit does not rest in peace.

Savage's murder was directly connected to a "hobo jungle" that had taken shape just outside of the cemetery grounds. This was an encampment where transients and small-time criminals slept and stayed. The railroad tracks passed close to this area and it was convenient for the hoboes to hop a freight train from one town to the next. The police would be quick to point out after the murder that many of these men were of questionable character and often were on the run from the law. It's likely that Savage's killer was one of these drifters but no one can say for sure and to make matters more puzzling, Savage's own criminal ties could have also marked him for death.

On the morning of May 22, 1930, Savage went down to a hobo camp that had appeared overnight in the southeast corner of the cemetery. This was a common occurrence, as the proximity of the railroad line often forced the caretakers to have to run drifters out of the graveyard. Men who found the shacks and shanties in the already established camp to be full would often spread out their bedrolls among the cemetery grave stones. The caretakers were then forced to run the hoboes out the next morning. Unfortunately, Savage ended up with four bullets in the back for his trouble and he died a few hours later without regaining consciousness.

His body was found by Dave Waybright, another caretaker, who had heard the sound of shots being fired and came to see what was going on. He discovered Savage's body some distance from the temporary hobo camp, on the edge of one of the cemetery's gravel roads. He assumed Savage was already dead, so he ran to the office of the cemetery superintendent to summon the police. A couple named Mr. and Mrs. John Duffey were arriving at the cemetery at the same time and they also heard the shots.

Although covered in blood and with bullets through both his brain and his abdomen, Savage was still alive. John Duffey, who followed the sound of the gunfire, found that Savage was still breathing and he moved him under a shade tree to make him more comfortable. His wife ran to find cemetery superintendent Charles Braden and he summoned a Moran & Sons ambulance to take Savage to St. Mary's Hospital. He died later that morning without regaining consciousness.

Melvin Savage Killed By Unknown Hobo

Greenwood Cemetery Employe Had Gone To Camp To See Who Was There.

Melvin Savage, thirty-six years old, employed at Greenwood cemetery, was shot to death by an unidentified hobo about 9:30 o'clock Thursday morning at the hobo camp at the southeast corner of Greenwood cemetery. The murderer escaped.

Hobo Victim and Girl Friend

Melvin Savage   Sadie Lewis

Savage had gone to a hobo camp to see who was there with a view to asking the police to drive the hoboes away.

Mr. Savage was shot four or five times. He died in St. Mary's hospital at 11:15 o'clock without regaining consciousness.

Two of the bullets entered the back of his head, one through the center of his abdomen, one entered his chest under the right arm and there on in, he following in the car of Harry H. Seltz, the photographer.

NO PATROL WAGON.

He had sent in a call for the patrol wagon, but was told there was not an

While there were no witnesses to the actual murder, there were a number of conflicting accounts of what happened just after it. According to Dave Waybright, who had heard the shots and first found the body, he had seen a man with a bundle under his arm running toward the Illinois Central Railroad tracks shortly after the shots were fired. He told police investigators that he was sure this had been a vagrant from the hobo camp who was angry with Savage for running him off. The man retaliated by shooting Savage in the back and then he had run away.

Strangely, though, ambulance driver Roy Hudson told police officers that he had seen a different man as he was leaving the cemetery. This man was no vagrant and was very well dressed, although he also had a bundle under his arm. He was hurrying away from the scene in the opposite direction from the railroad tracks and was outside of the cemetery gates. He had hailed a southbound Essex car and had climbed inside. Investigators later found the car, which was driven by a young woman, but found no weapon inside. The young man she had picked up was questioned but the police were forced to let him go. With nothing else to go on, the police rounded up nine or ten hoboes for questioning. The working theory was that Savage had been murdered by one of the men he had been rousting from the cemetery. Soon, however, the list of suspects grew.

Investigators began looking into Savage's past and began to find that he was not as well-liked, or as reputable, as they first believed. He had been divorced in St. Louis three months prior to his death and his ex-wife had filed charges against him for beating her. In addition, the police also found that Savage was possibly linked to organized crime in the St. Louis area. A number of letters found in the room of a boarding house that he rented on South Main Street were posted from St. Louis and his landlady said that whenever he was asked about them, or his family, he always evaded the questions. It was also said that the caretaker often had more money than his salary would allow and that this spending cash may have come from valuables stolen at the cemetery. Savage was suspected of opening caskets before they were placed in the ground and helping himself to the contents. First-hand testimony and sketchy evidence suggested that a south side of the city gang was robbing graves at Greenwood. Savage allegedly claimed, on more than one occasion, that he worked with this gang and that he sold jewelry and gold teeth to his criminal contacts in St. Louis.

Savage's personal life was not much better. In addition to the wife that he had divorced in February, he was also seeing a local girl at the time of this death. Her name was Sadie Lewis and she was only 16-years-old. Savage, who was 36 at the time of his death, had told Sadie that he was 10 years younger and had talked her mother into letting him date her.

And it didn't stop there. Rumors in the neighborhood where he lived said that Savage had also been involved with a number of married women and that one of their husbands had found out about the affair. Greenwood superintendent Charles Braden recalled that Savage had been badly beaten the winter before. He told his employer that he had been "ganged up" on by a group of men. Whether this had something to do with his extramarital affairs, or the mysterious source of his extra cash, is unknown.

The suspect list was long and tangled and the police were forced to hope that someone would come forward with information about the mysterious killer. A $300 reward was offered but it was never claimed. Savage's killer simply vanished into thin air. Two months later, an inquest ruled that Melbourn Savage had been killed by "person or persons unknown." No mention was made of further suspects and even though the case remained open, no further leads were discovered.

Who killed Mel Savage? Was it someone that he knew, like a cheated partner in crime or a jealous husband? And how did the killer disappear so easily after the murder? Did he hop a passing freight train or drive away in a car with a young woman?

These questions remain unanswered, as does the question of whether or not Mel Savage now rests in peace. Stories have circulated for years that Savage's ghost is sometimes seen along a roadway in the western part of the cemetery, the same area where he was murdered. There have been a number of accounts, including some recent ones, of witnesses who have seen a pale, darting man running through the trees and then falling down near one of the cemetery roads. The witnesses didn't know it, but this was the same place where Mel Savage's body was found in 1930. The fact that those who have reported this have done so independently, without knowledge of one another, and without details of the crime, lends real credibility to the sightings. In every instance, the fallen man vanishes when the witness goes to see if he needs help.

Ghosts of Greenwood Cemetery

In addition to the lingering spirit of Melbourn Savage, Greenwood Cemetery boasts an inordinate number of ghosts. In fact, there seems to have been nearly as many legends and strange stories told about Greenwood as there have been people buried there. They are the stories of the supernatural, of ghosts, phantoms, and things that go bump in the night and what follows is a sampling of eerie tales from this very haunted graveyard.

The story of Greenwood's most famous resident ghost, who is known as the "Greenwood Bride" began around 1930 and concerned a young couple that was engaged to be married. The young man was a reckless fellow, who was greatly disapproved of by his future bride's family. In those days, during the waning years of Prohibition, many men did whatever they could to make their fortune. In this young man's case, he sold illegal whiskey. This was not an uncommon profession in those times, and while everyone did not frown upon bootlegging, it could still be dangerous.

One summer night, the couple decided not to wait any longer to get married and made plans to elope. They would meet just after midnight, as soon as the young man could deliver one last shipment of whiskey and have enough money for their wedding trip. Unfortunately, he was delivering the bottles of whiskey when he was murdered. The killers, rival businessmen, dumped his body into the Sangamon River, where two fishermen found it the next morning.

The young woman had gone to the arranged meeting place the night before and she had waited until daybreak for her lover. She was worried when she returned home and devastated when she later learned that he had been killed. She became crazed with grief and her parents were forced to summon the family doctor, who gave her a sedative and managed to calm her down. She disappeared later that night and she was found the next day, floating face down in the river, near where her lover's body had been pulled ashore. She had taken her own life near the place where her fiancée's life had been lost, perhaps hoping to find him in eternity.

Her grieving parents searched through her closet in hopes of finding a suitable dress in which their daughter could be buried in and found the wedding gown that she planned to take with her when she eloped. They blamed themselves for the tragedy, believing that if they had given their blessing to the union, the young man's life might have been saved— and their daughter would still be alive. As some small measure of atonement, they buried their daughter in the bridal gown that she was never able to wear.

A funeral was held and her body was laid to rest on a hill in Greenwood Cemetery. It has been said however, that she does not rest here in peace. As time has passed, dozens of credible witnesses have reported encountering the "Greenwood Bride" on that hill in the cemetery. They claim the ghost of a woman in a glowing bridal gown has been seen weaving among the tombstones. She walks here with her head down and with a scrap of cloth gripped tightly in her hand. Occasionally, she raises it to her face, as if wiping away tears.

Could this sad young woman still be searching for the spirit of her murdered lover? No record remains as to where this man was laid to rest, so no one knows where his spirit may walk. Perhaps he is out there somewhere, still looking for the young woman that he was supposed to marry many years ago.

The phenomenon of the "phantom funeral" is one that is unique to cemeteries. The stories of single mourners, or even entire funeral parties with automobiles, are more commonly reported than people might think. These tales are scattered throughout the country and even appear in Greenwood Cemetery.

One witness, Ann Cummings, was in the cemetery one afternoon visiting her father's grave. She was carrying flowers and walking up a small hill when she saw a woman in a long, black dress standing near a tree. The woman was holding a small bundle of yellow flowers. Ann turned away for a moment, and when she looked back, the lady in black had vanished. She looked around to see where she had gone, but there was simply no one there.

Not all of the phantom mourners in Greenwood have been individuals. Some of the stories have told of entire funeral parties that have vanished without a trace. A former employee of the cemetery told me about a time when he was working one summer afternoon with some other men. They took a break from mowing the grass when a funeral party arrived in the area where they were working. They walked away for about five minutes but when they came back, the funeral party had vanished. No funeral had been scheduled to take place that day.

Another man was visiting the cemetery one day and came over a hill to find a funeral was taking place. He waited for a few minutes out of sight and when he climbed the hill again, the party was gone. He could find no sign of the mourners or an open grave. He first believed that he had been mistaken about the location, until he explored further. He then realized that the mourners had been gathered around the tombstone of a woman who had died on that day – but nearly 60 years before.

Another former staff member was raking leaves one fall afternoon and spotted a funeral that was taking place. Not remembering that any were scheduled for that day, he took a closer look and noticed that the hearse and the other cars parked nearby were from the 1940s. Intrigued by the idea of someone using vintage automobiles for a funeral, he later asked another crew member which funeral home in town was arranging old cars for their services. His friend looked at him rather strangely, so he explained what he had seen. Together, they checked the calendar and learned that no funerals had taken place that afternoon. Further investigation revealed that no graves had been opened in that area of the cemetery.

One of the cemetery's most enduring legends is the story of the "ghost lights" that appear on the south side of the burial grounds. These small globes of light have been reported here for many decades and are still reported today. There is no logical explanation for what they are, or why they appear here, but the lore of the cemetery tells a strange and tragic story.

The legend tells of a flood that occurred around 1905, which wiped out a portion of the cemetery. The Sangamon River, located just south of the cemetery, had been dammed in the late 1800s and was often prone to floods. During one particularly wet spring, the river overflowed its banks and washed into the lower sections of the cemetery. Tombstones were knocked over and the surging water even managed to wash graves away and to force buried caskets to the surface. Many of them went careening downstream on the swollen river.

Once the water receded, it took many days to find the battered remains of the coffins that had been washed down the river and many were never found at all. For some time after, farmers and fishermen were startled to find caskets, and even corpses, washing up on riverbanks some miles away. Many of the remains could not be identified and so they were buried again in unmarked and common graves. These new graves were placed on higher ground, up on the southern hills of Greenwood. Since that time, the mysterious lights have appeared on these hills. The stories say that the lights are the spirits of those whose bodies washed away in the flood. Their wandering ghosts are now doomed to search forever for the place where their remains are now buried.

Dozens of trustworthy witnesses have claimed to see the spook lights on the hill, moving in and out among the old, weathered stones. The mystery of the lights has managed to elude all those who have attempted to solve it. Many have tried to pass them off as reflections from cars passing over the lake, although many sightings occurred before Lake Decatur even existed. In those days, a covered bridge over the Sangamon River took travelers along the old county highway and there were few, if any, motor cars that used it.

Whether the cause is natural or supernatural, the lights can still be seen along the edge of the graveyard today. Want to see them for yourself? Seek out the south hills of Greenwood some night by finding the parking lot that is located south of the cemetery fence. You have to have a lot of patience, and may even have to make more than one trip, but eventually, you will probably be lucky enough to see the ghost lights.

Located in the heart of Greenwood Cemetery is a low, flat area where the old public mausoleum was once located. This site rests at the bottom of a steep hill and grass and earth now cover the foundation. However, if a visitor to the cemetery looks closely, he can still see the stone outlines of the building. There are many secrets about this place – stories of odd sights and sounds that threaten to chill the blood. They are mostly forgotten now, as is the old mausoleum itself, but some believe that the ghosts still remain.

The Greenwood Mausoleum was built in 1908 and for years held the bodies of several hundred of Decatur's former citizens. The structure was a long, narrow building that was fitted with crypts in both interior walls. A long, open hallway ran down the center and opened on both ends. Overhead, glass skylights provided dim lighting. Each corner of the building was fitted with a tall, fortress-like tower. The only security provided for the building was a set of

The old Greenwood Cemetery Mausoleum

iron gates located at each end of the center corridor. They were locked at night with a steel padlock, which may have kept the grave robbers out, but certainly didn't stop the weird tales from being told about the place.

The tomb deteriorated rapidly, whether because of poor construction or harsh weather, no one really knows. It did, however, begin to crumble and lean. The overhead skylights began to leak and it became common to find puddles of water on the floor after a hard rain. The mausoleum became a place where neighborhood children would go only on a dare and people started to tell tales of unexplainable shadows and strange noises inside. It was often said that visitors could hear the ominous sounds of whispering and disembodied voices echoing off of the stone interior walls. The most commonly repeated stories recalled the sounds of screaming that bellowed out from both ends of the empty building.

Soon, the mausoleum fell into disuse and interments in the crypt dropped off rapidly. By the early 1950s, they had ended completely and the tomb became a forsaken place. The cemetery itself had fallen into abandonment and disrepair by this time and the old crypt had followed suit.

In 1957, Greenwood Cemetery came into the hands of the township and plans were made to restore the graveyard. One of the first items on the improvement list was the destruction of the mausoleum, which had been declared unsafe by city inspectors. Once these plans were made, caretakers had to begin the long and time consuming process of trying to locate family members of the people interred in the mausoleum. Permission was needed from these family members to rebury their loved ones in other locations in the cemetery. This search would take nearly 10 years and by the time it was finished, there would remain more than a dozen bodies left unclaimed.

The crypts inside of the building had been broken open over the past decade, leaving gaping holes in the walls. By the middle 1960s, the last of the bodies were removed and the mausoleum was left with nothing inside but empty crypts and floors covered with stone and plaster. The area around the mausoleum was barricaded and no one was allowed near it while the last of the unclaimed bodies were being taken out. These remains were moved directly across the road from the mausoleum site and placed in a common grave. The bodies were placed there in random order and no one ever attempted to try and discover the identities of the various remains. The grave can be found today, directly east of the old mausoleum site. The building itself was finally torn down in 1967.

Many believe that the spirits of those who were moved from their resting places still linger in this area today. While the empty building was still standing, witnesses reported the cries of people coming from inside of it, even though the tomb was clearly empty. Strange energy and sensations were also reported around the site of the common grave across the road. In more recent times, the empty lot where the mausoleum once stood is still the site of weird cries, wailing sounds and eerie temperature drops of more than thirty degrees or more. It seems that the disturbances of the past are still occurring today.

Located on the edge of the forest that makes up Greenwood's northwest corner is an old burial plot that sits upon a small hill. It is the plot of a family named "Barrackman" and if you approach this piece of land from the east, walking along the cemetery's narrow roads, you will find a set of stone steps that lead to the top of a grassy hill. There are four, rounded stones there, marking the burial sites of the family.

Greenwood's "Barrackman Staircase

Little is known about the Barrackmans, other than that four members of this family are buried in Greenwood. No records have been found about who they were, when they may have lived here, or even about what they may have accomplished in life. We simply know their names -- father, mother, son, and his wife, as they are inscribed on the identical tombstones. As mentioned, two of the stones bear the names of the Barrackman women and one of them just might be the woman who haunts the burial plot.

According to accounts, collected over the years from dozens of people who never knew one another, a visitor who remains in the cemetery as the sun is going down may be treated to an eerie, breathtaking sight. The strange vision occurs at the staircase, just as dusk falls on the graveyard. As the sun begins to dip behind the trees to the west, a semi-transparent woman in a long dress appears on the stone steps. She sits there on the staircase with her head bowed and appears to be weeping, although she has never been heard to make a sound. Those who have the chance to see her, never see her for long. She always inexplicably vanishes as the sun dips below the horizon. She has never been seen in the daylight hours and never after dark – only just at sunset.

Who is this lonely woman and why does she haunt the staircase and the Barrackman graves? There are some who suggest she may have been a member of the family buried here, but what could have brought her back to her burial site? I tend to favor the idea that she may have been another person entirely, who found peace on this staircase and came to the place during her lifetime to weep for someone who died and was buried nearby.

Most likely, we will never know for sure just who she is or what brings her to that place, although she is still seen today. Perhaps one day she will break her silence and speak to some unsuspecting passerby, who just manages to get a glimpse of her before she fades away into the night.

Perhaps the most famous legend of Greenwood Cemetery is linked to a memorial section in the southwest corner that was created to honor Decatur's Civil War dead. The memorial was created in 1908, two years after the U.S. government passed an Army appropriation bill that provided for the marking of the graves of the Confederate dead that were buried in the north. The memorial that was created coincided with a tragic event that occurred in Greenwood Cemetery – an event that left a number of lingering ghosts.

Events began during the years of the war, when a great many trains passed through Decatur. Lines that belonged to the Illinois Central Railroad ran deep into the south and many of them passed through Decatur. Many of the northbound trains carried Federal troops, as well as Confederate prisoners who were on their way to Camp Douglas, outside Chicago. Many of the soldiers were sick, often near death, and men of both armies occasionally died while en route. When this occurred, the dead men were taken from the trains and buried in Greenwood Cemetery, which was very close to the railroad tracks, in often shallow, unmarked graves. Many of these soldiers, especially the Confederate ones, were unknown victims of gunshot and disease and many were past the point of revealing their identity. These men will never be known and their families never discovered what became of them after they departed for the battlefields of war. Those men are now silent corpses scattered about the confines of Greenwood Cemetery.

Under most circumstances, such burials were infrequent events but in the summer of 1863, a prison train that was packed with Confederate soldiers suffering from yellow fever arrived in Decatur. The Union officers in charge of the train had attempted to separate the Confederates who had died in transit, but to no avail. Many of the other men were close to death from the infectious disease and it was hard to tell which men were alive and which were not.

Several soldiers were dispatched and a group of men and wagons were brought to the train. The bodies were removed from the train and taken to Greenwood Cemetery. They were unloaded there and the corpses were stacked in piles at the base of a hill in the southwest corner of the graveyard. This location was possibly the least desirable spot in the cemetery. The hill was so steep that many of the gravediggers had trouble keeping their balance. It was the last place where anyone would want to be buried, so it would likely never be used for anything better than for the diseased corpses of enemy soldiers.

Shallow graves were hastily dug and the bodies of the prisoners were tossed inside. It has been said that without a doctor present, no one could have known just how many of the soldiers had actually died from yellow fever and how many of them were only near death – and were accidentally buried alive. Some believe that this is the reason why this is the most haunted area of Greenwood Cemetery.

But this may not be the only reason. Many years later, in 1905, spring rains and flooding caused the side of the hill where the unmarked graves were located to collapse. As the hillside peeled away, it carried trees, mud, stones, and skeletal remains into a small valley at the bottom of the incline. To make matters worse, it was not only the Confederate dead that were disturbed but so were the remains of Union men who had been laid to rest in a military memorial section that had been established at the top of the hill. In the end, the remains were buried again and the hill was constructed into terraces to prevent another mudslide in the future. All of the bodies were placed together and, thanks to the appropriations money offered by Congress, the graves of those men who could not be identified were marked with stones bearing the legend of "Unknown US Soldier."

Since the time of the mudslide, that portion of the cemetery has been considered to be haunted. Is it haunted by the eerie disturbance of the forgotten remains, or by the angry spirits of men who were buried alive? Some people believe that it may be both, as reports from the past century have revealed unexplainable tales and strange apparitions lingering around this hill. Visitors who go there, many of them knowing nothing about the bizarre history of this place, have told of hearing voices, strange sounds, footsteps in the grass, whispers, cries of torment, and some even claim to have been touched or pushed by unseen hands.

There are also the reports of the soldiers themselves returning from the other side of the grave. Accounts have been revealed over the years that tell of visitors to the cemetery actually seeing men in uniform walking among the tombstones --- men that are strangely transparent.

The most stunning tale was reported a few years ago and was told to me first-hand. It happened that a young man was walking along the road in the back corner of the cemetery. He saw a man standing on the top of the hill, who beckoned to him. The boy walked up to him and was surprised to see that he was wearing tattered gray clothing, which was very dirty and spotted with what looked like blood. The man looked at the boy oddly and he wore an expression of confusion on his face.

"Can you help me?" the man asked softly of the boy. "I don't know where I am..... And I want to go home."

Before the boy could answer, the man simply vanished.

The Chesterville Witch's Grave

The story of the so-called "witch" that is buried in a grave in Chesterville, Illinois, is one that has plagued me for many years. I first wrote about this legendary spot back in 2004, and since that time, my account has been re-published and copied dozens and dozens of times. In hopes of expanding on this history behind this strange tale, I have searched through records, archives, and old newspapers, and yet no real evidence of the witch can be found. And yet, somehow, this mysterious story got started among the local people of Chesterville, a place that still doesn't exist on most maps of the state. What is now a small collection of houses, stands just west of Arcola, which is the heart of Illinois Amish country. Most of the area residents are of the Amish and Mennonite faiths, religious sects that shun the use of electricity and modern conveniences.

And it is among the people of these faiths that our story of the witch begins.

Her name is no longer recalled; her identity is unknown. But she was said to be one of them – a young Amish woman who was far too spirited, liberal, and out-spoken to truly blend into the tradition-bound community. At the time, the Amish were experiencing an internal struggle. Having come to Illinois in the middle nineteenth century, there was a deep divide that existed as to the progression of the Amish faith in this new place – were they to remain faithful to tradition, or accept the social and industrial advancements that had started to develop in other communities.

Whatever the beliefs this young woman dared to voice, or whatever powers she was said to have, it certainly raised the ire of the church

The grave of the "Chesterville Witch"

elders, and in turn, the rest of the faithful in the Amish community. Ultimately, her behavior saw her branded as a "witch," but she was given the opportunity to repent. She refused and her continued challenges to the faith earned her banishment from Chesterville. Rumors surrounded her banishment, claiming that she practiced witchcraft, that she was a servant of the devil, and worse. Soon after, she disappeared.

But this was not the end of her story. Soon after she was shunned by the community, her lifeless body was discovered in a farmer's field. Regardless of what may have happened to her, the authorities ruled that her death was a natural one. Her body was placed on display and people from all over the countryside came to see the "witch's body." Many of them, filled with fear, wanted to be sure she was dead. Others were just as terrified that she might return to life.

She was buried in the Chesterville Cemetery and a tree was planted on her grave so that her spirit would be trapped within its roots and branches and she could not take her revenge on the community that mistreated her. Today, her grave can still be found in the cemetery, which is just outside of town and across an old, one-lane bridge. The tree remains intact, towering over the old iron fence that surrounds the grave. It was allegedly placed around the gravesite so that no one could go near the tree. It is still widely believed that if the tree is damaged or cut down, her spirit will be released to wreak havoc. Since her burial, the spirit of the witch has purportedly appeared to passersby and to cemetery visitors. Thanks to the tree, though, she has been confined to the area around her grave.

As mentioned already, the source of this strange story remains unknown. I cannot tell you if it is a true tale, or merely a legend. I have no idea who this young woman may have been, or what she could have done to earn her the harsh treatment that she received. Was she really a witch, or simply someone who dared to question the community's faith, aggravating a situation that was already a sensitive one?

We may never know the answer to that – unless, of course, something happens to the tree.

The Lady in White
The Lingering Spirit of Springdale Cemetery

Peoria's historic Springdale Cemetery was established in 1851 and, tragically, has not always been considered a place of rest. The graveyard saw periods of decline, neglect, and vandalism, but has managed to endure as beautiful and fascinating city of the dead, made up of acres of tombstones, mausoleums, and rolling hills.

It is also a place of mystery.

There are many tales of ghosts and spirits that have emerged from the confines of Springdale Cemetery. Among them are the wandering Civil War phantoms that have been seen around Soldier's Hill, and the young girl in the nineteenth century dress that pops up from behind tombstones and playfully frightens visitors, only to disappear. Her childish laughter is sometimes heard echoing among the grave markers. And not all of the ghosts of the cemetery are human. The old city pet cemetery was once located at the site of the caretaker's cottage. It was later moved, but at least one canine spirit has remained. Some have claimed to see a spectral German Shepherd who prowls the grounds at night, protecting the cemetery from intruders.

But there is no ghost of Springdale Cemetery that is as infamous as that of the "Lady in White," the tragic figure Mildred Hallmark, whose body was found in the cemetery after she was brutally murdered in 1935. Her ghost is now linked to one of the most sensational murders in the city's history and seems forever doomed to wander the grounds of Springdale Cemetery.

The site of Springdale Cemetery was chosen as a burial ground in 1851. The land, about two miles from the city's business district, was located on a bluff, overlooking the Illinois River and Lower Peoria Lake. Local money was raised for purchasing the grounds and the cemetery was organized three years later by the Springdale Cemetery Association. In 1855, it was incorporated by Thomas Baldwin, William A. Hall, and Hervey Lightner, making it the second-oldest cemetery in Illinois.

When the cemetery opened, the main road on the south ran toward the city, and a shady dirt road led to the entrance. A streetcar trolley ran up Perry Street to the cemetery. By the 1870s, the streetcars were used to pull caskets and funeral parties out to the end of the tracks because the dirt road had turned to mud, preventing carriages from getting through. When it started, Springdale was made up of 200 acres, which were surrounded by a wooden fence. Within two decades, there had been more than 7,000 burials in the cemetery.

In the nineteenth century, a plot could be purchased for a price between 30-cents and 50-cents per square foot. The cemetery grounds originally included a temporary receiving vault that was built into the bluff below Soldier's Hill. Bodies could be stored in the vault for up to 20 days in order to allow families the time needed to make funeral arrangements. In the winter months, bodies were kept in the vault until the ground thawed in the spring.

Even from the earliest days, the cemetery went through periods of neglect. The graveyard became overgrown and choked with weeds, and vandals stole and knocked over gravestones. There were also accusations of mismanagement and embezzlement by past trustees. Eventually, a historic preservation foundation was organized by concerned citizens to save the cemetery. Today, funds are kept available for the maintenance of the land and graves, and visitors can now tour over 230 acres of park-like grounds, shaded by towering oak trees. It is a place where the past truly comes alive and one can walk among the graves that hold the remains of city founders, leaders, and local dignitaries.

And it's also possible, if the tales are to be believed, that one can also come face-to-face with Springdale's resident spirit, the Lady in White.

Mildred Hallmark, age 19, a recent graduate of the Academy of Our Lady Catholic school in June 1935. The pretty, auburn-haired girl was born on April 19, 1916, the daughter of John and Esther Hallmark. The family had moved to Peoria in 1928. At the time of her murder, Mildred was working as a waitress at Bishop's Cafeteria in an area of town that boasted bars, theaters, and restaurants that ran the length of Main Street and beyond.

On the night of June 16, Mildred left the cafeteria after her shift ended at 8:30 p.m. She left with a fellow employee, John McGinnis. They were out on their first date together. McGinnis was a student at Bradley Polytechnic Institute and worked part-time at Bishop's as a busboy. The couple had plans to see the film *The People's Enemy* at the Rialto Theater at 9:00 p.m. McGinnis later testified that Mildred tried to telephone her parents about her plans but could not get an answer.

It was a wet, rainy night and the couple hurried up Jefferson Street to get to the theater. After the film ended, Mildred again tried to call her parents and let them know where she was, but could not reach them. The couple left the theater at 11:00 p.m. and tried to catch a country club streetcar at the corner of Main and Jefferson Streets. They missed this car and boarded a different streetcar at the corner of Main and Perry Streets at 11:15 p.m. The couple then got out at Knoxville and Pennsylvania Avenues. McGinnis caught a streetcar back downtown, leaving Mildred to wait for a Peoria Heights streetcar that would take her home.

He waved as he climbed onto the car and departed. It was the last time he would ever see Mildred alive.

At some point between 11:30 p.m. and 2:00 a.m. the next morning, Mildred was kidnapped, savagely raped, and murdered. Her nude body was thrown into a ditch at Springdale Cemetery. The white lace dress that she had been wearing was ripped to shreds and was twisted up beneath her body. Her white sandals were lying in the dirty sand of the ditch and a soggy paper bag was found next to her. It contained white yarn, knitting needles, and a partially finished sweater that she had been working on. She was lying on top of her purse, and a diamond ring was still on her finger, making it obvious that her death had nothing to do with robbery.

The ditch where her body was found was along Valley Road – only four blocks from her home.

News quickly spread about the discovery of Mildred's body. Panic swept the area, and women were cautioned to travel in groups and not accept rides from strangers. The entire city mourned the loss of the young girl and "Peoria's Greatest Manhunt," as the newspaper called it, began. Detectives began questioning suspects, including sideshow workers from a traveling carnival, and known "abnormals" and "morons" in the area. The police were ordered to arrest anyone picking up young women waiting for streetcars, or urging them to accept a ride. Reports came in about an escaped convict from Detroit and a reward of $250 was raised for anyone who helped bring Mildred's killer to justice. Governor Henry Horner even contributed another $100 to the reward fund from his own pocket.

As the tension mounted, a number of young women came forward with stories of rape and assault committed by the same man – 25-year-old Gerald T. Thompson. The stories and tips led to the arrest of the young, athletic, and good-looking man. He was a popular, well-liked employee at the Caterpillar tractor plant in East Peoria. He worked there with John Hallmark, Mildred's father, and had even contributed to the flower fund for the girl's funeral. He seemed an unlikely killer, but investigators couldn't ignore the evidence that was piling up against him.

Thompson was arrested on June 21, and fearing a lynch mob, the authorities moved him to the McLean County Jail in Bloomington. He confessed to the murder on June 23. He told police that he had committed a large number of assaults and that Springdale Cemetery was his favorite place to rape women. He usually picked up married women, he said, because they put up more of a fight and that excited him. He kept a list of his attacks in a small black book. He was able to keep the women from reporting him through blackmail. After he raped them, he forced them to stand naked in front of the headlights of his car and then he took photographs of them. If they threatened to report him to the police, he promised to expose them to their husbands and claim they had been willing adulterers. The threats were surprisingly effective, and Thompson got away with it for years. The photographs were later discovered in his home.

The previous year, Thompson had confessed some of his crimes to a friend, Sam Sprinkle. Sprinkle had worked with Thompson at Bemis Bag Company in Morton and had known him for four years. Sprinkle later testified at the trial that Thompson told him that he was going to try and assault at least 52 women in 1934, one each week. Late in November, Thompson claimed that he already had 54. Even though Thompson showed Sprinkle nude photographs of himself and naked women on three occasions, Sprinkle said that he did not believe Thompson had actually raped anyone. He testified at trial that he believed Thompson was insane.

Soon after his confession, Thompson tried to deny everything he said. He claimed that he was not given any food after his arrest and that the police had promised to go easy on him if he confessed. They had also threatened to turn him over to a lynch mob, he said. However, Thompson submitted to questioning with a lie detector from the Northwestern University crime detection laboratory and again made a full confession. This time, he admitted that he had not been beaten or abused and that he was confessing of his own free will.

And he had a depraved and sadistic story to tell.

On the night of June 16, 1935, Thompson had picked up his girlfriend, Lola Hughes, and took her to the movies. After dropping her off at home, he cruised the streets, looking for new victims to add to the list in his black book. At 11:20, he turned onto Knoxville Avenue and followed the streetcar tracks to Knoxville and Pennsylvania Avenues. Standing on the corner, Thompson saw Mildred in her white dress, patiently waiting for the next streetcar to arrive. He decided to try and pick her up. He slowed down in his 1934 Willys Sedan and leaned over to roll down the passenger side window. The door couldn't be opened from inside – Thompson had removed the inside door handle so that once his victim was inside, she would be trapped. He smiled over at Mildred. He was a young man, attractive, and clean cut. Mildred would have no reason to see him as a threat, and would likely not have been alarmed when he offered her a ride. He asked her how far she had to go and Mildred replied that she had to go out to Maywood Avenue, a few miles away. At first, Mildred declined his offer for a ride, but she knew that it was getting late and if she was not home soon, her parents would worry. She looked for the streetcar, which was nowhere in sight, and then agreed to accept the offer of a ride. She climbed into the passenger side of the car and they drove off down Knoxville Avenue.

Thompson kept up an easy banter with Mildred as he drove. He was used to making his victims feel at ease. Mildred was soon chatting with him, and started to relax. But that feeling did not last long. She became concerned when Thompson turned north on Prospect Avenue, rather than south toward her home on Maywood. Thompson continued to drive and ask Mildred questions, but she became more and more uneasy. She finally asked him straight out to take her home, and he acted as though he planned to do so. He turned around and headed back south on Prospect toward Maywood.

Then, he turned into the entrance to Springdale Cemetery.

Did Mildred now feel as though she was in real danger? It's hard to say. She was only four blocks from home and she was innocent enough to believe that Thompson didn't intend to hurt her. She told him that she couldn't stay out any longer; she needed to go home. But Thompson drove deeper into the cemetery. The only light was the glare of his headlights on the wet, hanging trees, the soaked grass, and the shining tombstones. Finally, Mildred must have known she was in trouble. She pleaded with Thompson to take her home, but he ignored her, kept driving, and then crossed a bridge and stopped next to a pond. He ordered Mildred to get into the backseat of the car. She argued with him, demanding to be taken home, until Thompson threatened to beat her. Finally, she slid across the front seat and got out on the driver's side. Thompson tried to push her into the back seat, but Mildred resisted. They fought and when she started to scream, he tried to choke her but Mildred bit his left thumb and scratched the back of his head. Finally, he raised a fist and punched her in the jaw, knocking her unconscious.

At this point, Thompson wrestled her limp body into the back seat, tore off her clothes, and raped her. After he was finished, he got out of the car to smoke a cigarette. Mildred was still laying across the back seat when he returned to the car. He tried to rouse her, but she didn't move. When he couldn't find her heartbeat, he decided to get rid of Mildred's body.

Although Thompson would later claim that he had no intention of harming Mildred, he did say that after he raped her he decided to strip the body completely so that she could not be easily identified by her clothing. He ripped her clothes to shreds, tossed aside her shoes, stockings, and other belongings, and then made a plan to go to the bridge and dump her body into the Illinois River. He never made it that far. He drove to the cemetery's main entrance and decided to leave her in the ditch. He stopped the car, rolled her body over the shallow embankment, and watched her fall into the water below. Thompson later said that he really had no idea if Mildred was dead when he dumped her there or not. He never bothered to check again. He took one last look at her body, sprawled on the sandy gravel, got in his car and drove away. He returned to his grandparent's home, where he lived, and went to bed.

The following morning, Thompson acted as if it was any other day. He went about his usual activities, worked on his car, and then reported for his third shift job at Caterpillar. When he arrived at work, he pretended to be surprised when he heard about the rape and murder of his co-worker's daughter. He donated to the flower fund for the funeral and even went as far as to sign a petition, vowing to avenge the young woman's death.

Thompson's murder trial began just six days after Mildred was murdered, on June 22, 1935. The trial was at the courthouse in Peoria. A crowd began forming at the front door hours before it began. In addition to the usual courtroom seats, benches were provided to fit the maximum number of people into the courtroom. Along with the spectators were the reporters, jostling for a look at the killer. They came from all over Illinois, from Chicago, and even *Life* magazine sent a reporter and photographer to cover the trial. A workroom had been set up for the reporters in the courthouse, which had six direct telegraph lines, four telephones, and one radio microphone. Messengers were even hired to take copy from the press benches to the wire room.

After Thompson's confession, he had been secretly taken to a jail cell in Decatur to await trial. On June 21, he had been smuggled back into town. There were still many people calling for him to be lynched. The location of Thompson's cell in Peoria had an ironic view – it looked out over Bishop's Cafeteria, where Mildred had worked.

The trial began with jury selection. Each side tried to find jurors most sympathetic to their cause. Jury selection lasted until 3:00 p.m. While it was taking place, Thompson sat at the defense table with his chin in his hand, picking at his lips or his neck, with the other hand draped over the back of the chair in which he was slumped. He did not look interested in what was going on, although, occasionally, he would whisper to his attorney.

With the jury seated, the parade of witnesses began. The Deputy Coroner described the state of Mildred's body and noted that she was identified by the library card in her purse. He also testified that Mildred had died because her neck was broken when she was struck in the face. Ruby Hallmark, Mildred's sister, testified about what she had been wearing on the night of her murder. She also described the knitting wool that she had carried with her that night. When Mildred's clothing was admitted into evidence, it had a shocking effect on the audience in the courtroom. Many who were dozing in the hot, humid courtroom craned their necks to get a glimpse of the ragged clothing that told the story of Mildred's final hours.

In his defense, Thompson's court-appointed attorney, Ren Thurman, gave a 10-minute opening statement that declared that he would show that his client was sexually insane. He claimed that Thompson's father was also sexually unnatural and his son had inherited this trait. He also pointed out that Thompson's brother had recently been sent to jail for indecent liberties with a young boy. The attorney made references to "tainted ancestry" and "tainted offspring."

The case was continued the next morning. There was a mad scramble for seats in the courtroom and a stampede of women pulled the hinges off the courthouse doors. Several people were knocked down and trampled, but no one was seriously injured.

The defense called its first witness, Dr. Peter James, who was the physician for Thompson's mother, Florence Whiteside. She was, the attorney stated, crucial to the defense's claims of sexual insanity. However, Mrs. Whiteside had a nervous breakdown when Thompson was arrested, and Dr. James testified that it would endanger her life to be present in court. She remained in the hospital for the duration of the trial. The defense then called Jessie Hughes, the mother of Thompson's girlfriend, Lola. Mrs. Hughes kept a folded newspaper in front of her face while testifying, too ashamed to be seen. She testified that she had known Thompson for five years and he had always been a perfect gentleman. He did not smoke, drink liquor, or use profanity in her presence. The only other witnesses called by the defense said the same thing – that Thompson was well-mannered and didn't drink. There was no one who could bolster the defense's claims that he was insane.

The jury deliberated a very short time and quickly returned with their verdict – guilty of first-degree murder.

Thompson was taken to Joliet Penitentiary on August 17. His execution was set for two months later. There was an appeal for a new trial, but it was denied. Thompson's lawyer sought clemency from the governor, but there was no response. The case went to the Illinois Surpreme Court on October 3, 1935, but the death sentence was upheld. The argument that Thompson had committed manslaughter in the heat of the moment was rejected by jury, trial judge, appeals courts, and even Governor Horner.

Thompson's execution was scheduled for October 15. He had fried chicken for his last meal, followed by black walnut ice cream for dessert. At 10:00 p.m., he was prepared for the electric chair. There were 200 spectators waiting to witness his final breath. It was so crowded that those in the front were ordered to get on their knees so that the people in the back could see. Mildred's father, John Hallmark, was forced to stand on a chair to watch.

At 12:15 a.m., Warden Joseph E. Ragen raised his hand and the first jolt of electricity coursed through Thompson's body. In two minutes, Thompson was dead. The tragedy of Mildred Hallmark's murder was finally over – but the story of the "Lady in White" was just beginning.

Ever since Mildred Hallmark's death, there have been reported sightings of a woman in white who roams the grounds of Springdale Cemetery. This ethereal figure is often seen in the vicinity of the Lightner monument, which is close to the spot where Mildred's body was found. She drifts across the grounds, giving off an unearthly light, and then she vanishes.

The woman in the white dress never speaks, but those who are familiar with the terrible murder that took place in the cemetery are convinced of her identity. Her presence alone is enough to remind us of her short life, and violent death, and the fact that she still walks the earth tells a cruel story of a young woman whose existence ended much too soon.

4. THE SHOW MUST GO ON
Haunted Music, Movie, and Entertainment Venues of Central Illinois

Located along the original alignment of Route 66 through Central Illinois was the legendary Coliseum Ballroom. The ballroom's long and often mysterious past has been linked to big band history, bootlegging, gangsters, murder, and more, and it was one of the great old landmarks of the region for many years. The ballroom stopped being a dancehall a few decades before the fatal fire that destroyed it in 2011, but it still managed to attract people from all over the region who came looking for a little history – and for its resident ghosts.

The Coliseum stood for more than eight decades in the small town of Benld, a once- prosperous mining community that was known as a melting pot of nationalities who came to south-central Illinois to work in the coal mines. Situated in the middle of three mines, Benld furnished residences, churches, schools, and more to the immigrants who settled the area. They came from many countries, including Austria, Bohemia, Croatia, England, France, Germany, Greece, Ireland, Italy, Lithuania, Russia, Scotland, Slovakia, and Sweden.

The history of the area began in the late 1800s with the arrival of the Dorsey family, who settled the Cahokia Township of Macoupin County. In the early 1900s, the Superior Coal Company, a subsidiary of the Chicago & Northwestern Railroad, bought 40,000 acres of coal and mineral rights from the Dorsey family and began to sink mines to furnish coal for their locomotives.

In 1903, the town of Benld was established, taking its name from its founder, Ben L. Dorsey. Legend has it that the name was actually a mistake. The story goes that a sign once existed outside of town that had Dorsey's full name on it. A storm came along and tore off the end of it, leaving the letters "Ben L. D." By default, this became the name of the town.

Benld was laid out in the middle of the three mines and soon began to grow. The original town was platted so that North Sixth and Seventh Streets would be the hub of the community, with growth spreading in every direction. At the western edge of town, a station was built and tracks were laid by the Illinois Traction System for their trolley. The Chicago & Northwestern Railroad also laid their tracks to the west of town, creating a surge of business toward Central Avenue, where a rail yard and a roundhouse were developed, creating additional employment for the area. In 1916, a fourth mine, the No. 4, was sunk west of Benld and more people came to the area. By the early 1920s, the population of the town had grown to over 5,000. Benld boasted a racetrack, a football field, where a professional football team played, and a city band that consisted of coal miners who played every Sunday, their only day off. Benld also had barbershops, blacksmith shops, dairies, a feed store, hardware and grocery stores, laundries, a hemp factory, a soda factory, a lumber yard, a bowling alley, a theater, taverns, and numerous other establishments during its heyday.

One unusual incident in Benld's history occurred on September 19, 1938, when a local resident named Edward McCain was surprised to find that his garage and automobile had been damaged by a falling meteorite. The meteorite, which was about four inches in diameter, fell from space and penetrated the roof of the garage. It ripped through the top of the car, through the car's upholstered seat, and the floor of the car before coming

The Coliseum Ballroom in Benld

to rest on the garage floor. The "Benld Meteorite," as it came to be known, is now on display at the Field Museum of Natural History in Chicago.

But it wasn't a meteorite that gave Benld its lasting infamy; it was liquor. During the years of Prohibition, the town of Benld was home to more than 40 taverns, which operated wide-open, even though it was against the law to sell alcohol anywhere in America. In Benld, alcohol wasn't just sold, it was also manufactured. In a wooded area east of town and along Cahokia Creek, was a place known locally as "Mine No. 5." Of course, it was not a coal mine at all but a large, well-funded, alcohol distillery with three 50-foot smokestacks and the capability to produce hundreds of gallons of whiskey each week. The distillery was one of the largest illegal operations of its kind in the United States at the time and it was owned either by gangsters from St. Louis, Springfield, or by Al Capone himself, depending on the stories you hear. There are some pretty solid recollections of Capone actually visiting Benld later in the 1920s, so it's possible that the distillery was connected to his Chicago operations in some way.

Illegal liquor operations in Benld would also give birth to what remains as the town's greatest historic landmark, the Coliseum Ballroom. The large brick ballroom, with a main floor that could hold up to 800 dancers, was opened on December 24, 1924. It had been built for the grand sum of just over $50,000, an exorbitant amount for the time period. The Coliseum was constructed and operated by Dominic Tarro, a local businessman, but rumors spread that the funding for the project had come from unsavory pockets, namely, those of gangsters who planned to use the ballroom as a hideout for syndicate gunmen and as a way station for liquor runners between Chicago and St. Louis.

And as it turned out, the rumors apparently had some basis in truth. In January 1930, Tarro was one of many people indicted by a U.S. Department of Justice investigation into bootlegging in Central Illinois. Indictments were returned against the Corn Products Co. and the Fleischmann Yeast Co. for supplying materials for making liquor. In addition, 17 bootleggers were charged with conspiring to violate the Volstead Act, which enforced Prohibition as law. This was the first time that the government criminally charged the companies that made the supplies used in illicit distilling, but investigators believed they could make a case against them. Prohibition agent James Eaton was able to track more than 200 carloads of corn sugar that were sent from a St. Louis plant of the Corn Products Co. to bootleggers in Benld. He also believed that the Fleischmann Yeast Co. had sold products to distillers in Benld, a town where, prior to Prohibition, there was little legitimate market for their product.

The alleged go-between for the bootleggers and the suppliers was Dominic Tarro, owner of the Coliseum Ballroom, and according to the indictments, the purchasing agent for the raw materials and a distributor for the illegal finished product. On January 30, Tarro posted a $30,000 bond and was freed from custody. Rumors began to circulate that Tarro planned to offer testimony about the Benld operations in exchange for immunity and, a few days later, he disappeared.

On February 5, Tarro's automobile was found near Mason City. He left home that morning in Benld and was on his way to see his attorney, but he never arrived. The car was discovered later that same day. It had been riddled with bullets and left on the side of the road. Tarro was nowhere to be found, and while his lawyer publicly stated that he feared his client had been murdered, the prosecutor in the case surmised that he was hiding out because someone had heard that he planned to be a government witness. He was sure that Dominic Tarro would turn up soon, alive and well.

Tarro did turn up, on May 2, but he was neither well, nor alive. His body was found in the Sangamon River and was positively identified by his cousin, Fazzio. His arms and feet had been tied together with wire, a strand of which had been looped around his neck to draw his head down almost to his knees. He had been badly beaten and the clothing stripped from his body before he was thrown in the river. The corpse was badly decomposed and the coroner surmised that the body had been in the water since the day that Tarro had disappeared.

Dominic Tarro had learned the hard way that it didn't pay to turn informant against the mob.

Following his murder, Tarro's wife, Marie, took over management of the ballroom, and in the years that followed, the Coliseum gained legendary status for the big name groups that were booked to play there. The ballroom drew top talent of all types, dating from the 1930s all the way into the 1970s.

Some of the bands and acts that played at the Coliseum included Sammy Kaye, Tommy Dorsey, Count Basie, Lawrence Welk, Duke Ellington, Lionel Hampton, and Guy Lombardo, who treated patrons to what became one of his signature tunes, "Auld Lang Syne." Years later, former customers would remember this song as a special favorite from the heyday of the Coliseum.

After the Big Band era, the Coliseum wholeheartedly embraced rock-n-roll. Performers that came during the 1950s, 1960s, and 1970s included Ray Charles, Ike and Tina Turner, Fats Domino, Chuck Berry, Chubby Checker, the Everly Brothers, Jerry Lee Lewis, Bill Haley and the Comets, Fleetwood Mac, Ted Nugent, Bob Seger, and many others. People came from all over the region, even the state, to see the acts that Marie, and later her daughter, Joyce, booked into the Coliseum. The ballroom had the largest dance floor in the state of Illinois, outside of Chicago, and could seat hundreds on the main floor and the balcony.

The place enjoyed great success for many years, especially after Joyce Tarro took over operations after her mother's death in 1955. She was a tough, hard-headed businesswoman who, her friends always said, would never back down from a fight. She had a habit of carrying around the ballroom's weekend receipts with her, which could amount to several thousand dollars, a fact that was commonly known in the small town of Benld. But what was also well-known was the fact that Joyce also carried a gun, and she was not afraid to use it. Unfortunately, the gun was not enough to save her life in February 1976.

On February 16, a huge party was held at the Coliseum to celebrate St. Valentine's Day. It was packed for the event with over 800 people in attendance. Bartenders at all five of the ballroom's bars were kept busy throughout the evening. With admission prices set at $2.50 per person, and thousands of dollars made from the free-flowing drinks, Joyce had a very good night. When she got home, though, she surprised two robbers who had broken into her house and was shot five times. Joyce returned fire but died moments later. The killers, a long-time criminal and his girlfriend, were later captured by the police. After a trial, each received sentences of 50 to 150 years on the murder charges, plus 25 to 75 years for the armed robbery, and an additional 10 years for theft.

It was a fitting end to a bloody chapter in the history of Benld and the Coliseum Ballroom. This second violent death brought down the curtain on the Tarro era at the Coliseum.

Many feared that, after Joyce Tarro's death, the ballroom would be closed for good. In her will, Tarro had left the Coliseum to Bonnie Anderson, a former Benld resident who had gone on to become a singer and entertainer in Ft. Lauderdale, Florida. The ballroom was operated for a short time by Tarro's cousin, Bud Tarro, who owned a grocery store in town, but his tenancy was short-lived. After the Coliseum was closed for two months, Anderson began leasing it to Patty Ferraro, a close friend of Joyce's, and Hiram Franzoi, the owner of a construction company. Sadly, their occupancy of the ballroom would also not last for long. Ferraro had vivid memories of the night that Tarro was killed and she remained at the ballroom for as long as she could. She said, "It's not the same place with her gone, and the atmosphere to me, is different. The ballroom business isn't the ballroom business without Joyce."

As the years passed, times turned tough for the ballroom. New owners attempted to revitalize the place a time or two with music acts and even as a roller rink, but it never again enjoyed the success of its earlier days. However, it was during these days of decline that employees began to report strange incidents in the building. Eerie footsteps were often heard and shadowy figures were sometimes reported in dark corners. One former employee, George Luttman, who worked there from 1977 to 1981, told me that he often came in to clean in the mornings and on several occasions he saw people in formal clothes who looked as if they were ready to swing to the sounds of Tommy Dorsey or one of the other big bands of the era. When approached, the figures always vanished.

The Coliseum fell into years of abandonment and further decline, but then, in the late 1990s, it was re-opened as an antique mall and a roadside attraction on Route 66. The new owners bought the building in October and had a lot of work to do before they could make their planned opening in February. Almost immediately, they later reported, a woman was spotted upstairs who should not have been there. The figure had short dark hair and was there one moment and then gone the next. No one had any idea who she might be, but she was seen in the building many times after that.

Customers, visitors, and even antique dealers who came in to stock their booths reported a litany of odd happenings. A local carpenter, who helped renovate the building, saw a man ascend a back stairway that the owners had blocked for safety reasons. When the carpenter went up the rickety stairs to investigate, he found that the opening of the stairs was inaccessible. There was no way that anyone could have climbed up the staircase.

Dealers and customers experienced cold spots among the booths and in hallways and told of a misty woman who was often seen near a former bar area. In spite of the fact that the owners paid to have the place re-wired, lights frequently turned on and off without explanation. Others told of feeling a presence as the hair on the backs of their necks stood on end. They also talked of a breeze that moved past them as if someone had just walked by. In every case, no one visible was near.

Eventually, the owners closed the Coliseum, likely discouraged by the lack of traffic that ventured off the interstate, and moved their operations a few miles south to a former school building in Livingston. The Coliseum was closed, dark, and empty for several years, but then re-opened again, first as an antique mall and then as a venue for live music once again. It seemed that things were finally starting to happen again at the legendary ballroom, but then disaster struck. On July 31, 2011, a fire broke out during a music show and the Coliseum was gutted by flames. The building was beyond repair, marking the end of a small piece of Central Illinois' haunted history.

Last Dance at the Lake Club
The Haunting of Rudy Cranor

Firefighters were called to a scene near Lake Springfield one early Sunday morning in August 1992. When they arrived, they found a dilapidated, old building that had been closed for years completely engulfed in flames. The fire, which later turned out to have been deliberately set, destroyed a place once called the Lake Club, a grand restaurant and nightclub that had gone out of business in the 1960s.

Other businesses had come and gone in the building since the demise of the club, but most people recalled the 1940s and 1950s as the golden age of the Lake Club. It was that era that older residents of Springfield and Central Illinois recalled when they talked of the big bands that came to town, the all-night dancing, the swanky bar, the live radio shows, and, of course, the secret casino in the back room.

It would be the 1970s, however, when the old club made national news. It had a different name then, but the place was the same. It was this era when the first stories began to be told of the club's resident ghost – a tragic nightclub employee who simply couldn't leave.

The Lake Club in Springfield had opened as a nightclub in 1940, but the building on Fox Bridge Road had seen many incarnations in the years prior to that, including as several restaurants and even a skating rink called the Joy Inn. In 1940, two dance promoters named Harold Henderson and Hugo Giovagnoli renovated the place and opened it for business.

The club soon became one of the hottest night spots in Central Illinois, drawing customers from all over the area. It boasted a raised dance floor, which was surrounded by a railing, curved walls, and a slick, big city atmosphere that made patrons feel as though a New York club had been transported to the shores of Lake Springfield. The owners concentrated on bringing big name entertainment to the club and they succeeded. Among the many top performers were Bob Hope, Ella Fitzgerald, Guy Lombardo, Pearl Bailey, Spike Jones, Nelson Eddy, Woody Herman, Mickey Rooney, and many others. The constant stream of entertainers and big bands brought capacity crowds to the club every weekend.

The Lake Club thrived for more than two decades, becoming known not only for its swinging entertainment, but for its first-rate gambling, as well. Wealthy customers and the society elite of Springfield and Central Illinois frequented the club for the musical guests and for the billiard tables, craps and gaming tables, slot machines, and high-stakes card games. This part of the club operated in secret in a back part of the building, known only to high-rollers and special customers. However, in December 1958, the golden days of the Lake Club came to an end. The partners had survived many setbacks over the years, from lawsuits to foreclosures, but the club

The Lake Club, just outside of Springfield

would not survive the two undercover detectives who gained access to the gambling rooms that Christmas season.

The club was immediately shut down, although the restaurant and dance hall were allowed to operate. This was not enough to save the business. Things began to falter in the wake of the raid and the club finally closed down in the 1960s. Hugo Giovagnoli refused to give up on the Lake Club, though, and opened it up again in the 1970s with other parties managing different projects in the building. During this time in the club's history, it was managed by Bill Carmean and Tom Blasko as a rock club. In 1980, it was leased by Pat Tavine, who also operated it as a rock club until 1988, when it closed down for good. Sadly, the Lake Club was destroyed by fire in 1992.

It was in August 1979 that the Lake Club, known then as the Sober Duck Rock and Disco Club, gained national notoriety. It was at this time when the ghost of Albert "Rudy" Cranor was finally put to rest.

According to the many patrons and staff members who had experiences there, the haunting of the Lake Club first began in 1974. At the time, the club was in the midst of a revival in interest and the business was under the ownership of Tom Blasko and Bill Carmean, two Springfield men who were booking rock acts into the club. Odd sounds began to be heard in the building, as well as a feeling of being watched in some of the rooms. A piano played by itself. Lights turned on and off, doors opened and closed, and things moved about by themselves. By 1976, the haunting had intensified and things began happening more often, and in front of more witnesses.

Bill Carmean was the first of the club's staff to guess the identity of the ghost who was plaguing the establishment. He recalled that a former employee had committed suicide in the building several years before. On a lark, he started calling the ghost by this man's name --- "Rudy."

Albert "Rudy" Cranor had worked at the Lake Club during its heyday of the 1950s. He was always described as being well-liked and popular with the entertainers and the customers. He was also a very large man, well over 250 pounds, and he had snow-white hair. He was remembered as one of the club's most memorable characters.

After the club fell on hard times following the gambling raid, Rudy also started experiencing some personal difficulties. He was a very private person, so no one really knew what was going on, but they did notice that he began to drink heavily while on the job. He also seemed to be more tired than usual and dark circles had begun to appear under his eyes. One night, he got so sick that he had to be rushed to the hospital. He returned to the club after a two-week stay in the hospital, but he was never the same again.

On June 27, 1968, Rudy committed suicide with a high-powered rifle in one of the back rooms at the club. No one was ever sure why Rudy had killed himself, but regardless, he wouldn't stay gone for long. In a few short years, he would return to haunt his beloved club.

The strange events at the club continued in the form of weird antics and pranks, apparently carried out by the ghost of Rudy Cranor. A frightening event took place in the summer of 1979 when a waitress at the club claimed to see the floating head of a man with white hair who warned that one of the owners of the club was going to die. The waitress fled the room in hysterics and Tom Blasko stated that when he went to investigate, he found that the room was ice cold. Blasko and Carmean were unnerved by the ghost's warning. The two men waited for something terrible to happen and then, two weeks after the incident, Harold Henderson, one of the original owners of the club, died at the age of 69. He was still the owner of the building itself and was an owner that Rudy would have known during his lifetime.

Blasko was shaken by the incident and after two weeks of living in fear, decided to try and get rid of the ghost. He contacted his parish priest, but the man declined to get involved. He suggested that Blasko pray for Rudy on his own and Tom spent the next six months carrying a rosary around the club with him. But it didn't help --- Rudy was still there.

Finally, in August 1979, Blasko attended a high school class reunion and ran into one of his former classmates, Reverend Gary Dilley, a priest who now lived in Texas. Tom mentioned the problems at the club to Father Dilley and the priest was intrigued. After some discussion, he agreed to come out to the club and take a look around. After arriving at the club, Father Dilley also sensed something out of the ordinary there. He was convinced that something was going on, but he declined to do an "exorcism" of the club. To do that, the case would require a thorough investigation and permission from the local bishop, which he doubted he would get. Instead, he decided to bless the place and pray for the soul of Rudy Cranor, hoping this would perhaps put the lingering spirit to rest. He contacted two other priests and they blessed the building with holy water and prayed in each of the rooms. Eventually, they entered the room in which Rudy had committed suicide and prayed that his spirit be at rest.

So, was that the end of the haunting? Apparently, it was. The same people who considered the club to be haunted became sure that Rudy had departed. The day of the religious ceremony was the last day when anyone was aware of Rudy's presence in the building. It seemed that the prayers and blessings had helped the bartender find his way to the other side. It certainly seems possible that Rudy may have chosen to stay behind in a place where he had many attachments in life. Perhaps the intervention of the priests was all that he needed to be convinced to move on.

Rudy had finally found some peace.

A Ghost Named Joe
The Haunting of the Springfield Theatre Center

There is an old adage that claims that "every good theater has a ghost," but unlike the grand old palaces that will follow in this chapter, the Springfield Theatre Center always seemed to be an odd place to find a lingering spirit. There was no glittering marquee on the front of the building, no grand lobby, no palatial auditorium that was filled with hundreds of seats. It was an unassuming building that was easy to miss with its plain front façade on Lawrence Street and its ordinary concrete block construction. It looked more like a modern movie house than a performance center for community theater. In spite of all this, the Theatre Center also had something that many of those grand old theaters had – it had a resident ghost.

Joe Neville

The Springfield Theatre Guild got its start in 1947 and, thanks to community support, easily raised the funds needed to construct its new theater in 1951. The doors opened on Lawrence Street on November 6, with all 482 seats filled for a sold-out performance of *Born Yesterday.* And that was just the beginning of a long run of notable performances and well-known plays. The cast and crew earned rave reviews for almost 50 years at the Theatre Center, but all during that time, they were plagued by a secret.

Beginning in the middle 1950s, strange and inexplicable events occurred in the building. Footsteps were heard and lights turned on and off. Objects and props disappeared, only to turn up somewhere else. Doors opened and closed, without assistance from human hands. Set pieces moved about and sometimes fell over, even when no one was near them. Heavy objects were hurled at unsuspecting crew members. And, of course, there was the smell – the pungent aroma of Noxzema facial cream that permeates the air on occasion, even though the recognizably-scented cream had been banned in the building for years.

The Springfield Theatre had a ghost, and he was no mysterious presence. They knew exactly who he was. Those who worked and performed in the building could say right away that his name was Joe Neville. He had been with the theater group since its very beginning.

Neville had been part of the early days of the Theatre Guild, before they had a building to call their own. He was a rather strange and eccentric man – even for an actor – and other members of the group had a hard time getting along with him. According to interviews that I conducted with members of the Theatre Guild who worked with him, Neville had a massive ego. He was arrogant, demanding, but yet was a talented actor so everyone made an effort to look past his surly attitude. Neville also had a questionable past. Rumor had it that he had done some acting and directing in England, but under another name. After his death, his will was read and he apparently left a lot of property in England to various people. The problem was that Neville didn't actually own any of the land. He was a strange and very unpopular man. His death was taken so lightly by other Theatre Guild actors that the lead role he was slated to play in an upcoming production was simply given to another actor on the night before it was scheduled to open. The show really must go on.

In the late 1990s, I interviewed Tom Shrewsbury, a long-time Theatre Guild member who had performed with Joe Neville in the early days of the group. He also went on to have a number of encounters with Neville's ghost. Shrewsbury told me, "If there was anyone who was going to come back as a ghost, it would be Joe. I knew Joe from many, many years ago, back in the 1950's. We were doing a show called *Mr. Barry's Etchings* and Joe played the lead. One night after dress rehearsal, Joe went home and committed suicide. There was apparently an audit of the books at that place where he worked. A lot of money had been misappropriated and it looked as though Joe would be caught the next day."

Many of those involved with the theater believed that Neville's suicide was the reason he returned to haunt the theater. He couldn't bear the humiliation of the charges that were going to be brought against him, and yet he still had unfinished business with the play. He may have felt that the work audit cheated him out of the chance to play the lead role in the performance, and in many more that would have undoubtedly followed. The theater was probably the only place where this bitter, jaded man was happy and so his spirit had no desire to leave it. His need for attention, in life and in death, was evident.

As the years passed, staff members and performers became used to the weird happenings. One of the great superstitions of the building was that a disbelief in Neville's ghost could act as a trigger, causing the strange things to take place. One actor told me on my first visit to the building, "Whether you believe in him or not, you don't say out loud that you don't believe in him.... because then things happen."

The actor described an unusual occurrence that took place one evening when he and another man were building a set for an upcoming show. The friend who was working with him was skeptical about Neville's existence and made a point of stating this while onstage. The actor told me, "the power saw he was using started up by itself and as soon as it did, some sheets of plywood fell over and a ladder that was standing nearby fell over on its own. The saw started to rev up again, and right then my friend shouted 'I believe, I believe!'"

But skepticism was not the only thing that made Neville act out. Occasionally, he would make an appearance for no reason at all. One of the most repeated occurrences at the theater involved the front counter, located in the building's small lobby. Many people, including guests with no knowledge of the theater's haunted history, noticed that the door to the counter would swing open and closed on its own. The cast and crew of the Theatre Guild were quick to recount evidence of Neville's presence, telling tales of props and objects that would fall from rafters, or fly across the stage, and hit people. They told of actors being pushed off the stage, a filmy white shape that was seen on an overhead catwalk, and a shadowy figure that was seen seated in the back of the auditorium during a rehearsal. When an actor pointed it out, the shape vanished.

Colleen McLaughlin, who was an actor with the theater, had a number of ghostly experiences that she blamed on Neville. She noticed that things often disappeared and re-appeared around the theater. One night, during the run of a show, she had to make some very quick costume changes during a particular song. She ran backstage, changed, and then went back on again. She had to repeat this a few moments later, so she returned to change her costume again – and got a surprise. "Everything was missing, " she told me. "It turns out they [her costume] were behind a stairwell, all folded up neatly. No one used that stairwell during the production, and we have no idea how the clothes got there. They had been next to the piano when I came on and off stage. No one saw them disappear... and no one could have taken them."

Other actors experienced similar incidents, including Rebecca Sykes, who was the theater manager when I first visited the Theatre Center. One night, during a show, the clothing she was supposed to change into had also disappeared. It was later found strewn up and down a ladder in the back, a place where no one had gone during the show.

And the actors were not the only ones troubled by Neville. The crew members who built the sets and arranged the props also had their share of ghostly encounters. One night, a stage crew volunteer was alone in the theater, painting a set for an upcoming show. He used a roll of tape to mark off areas where set pieces would be placed. He finished with one section and laid the tape aside. A few moments later, he reached for the tape roll, but it was gone. Thinking that he must have used the last of it, he decided to call it quits for the night.

He closed up his paint cans and moved them up to the front of the stage. He went behind the curtain and was about the shut down the stage lights when he spotted his missing tape roll. It was propped up next to the last can of paint he had moved to the edge of the stage. He knew for a fact that it had not been there just seconds before. He left the theater in a hurry that night.

The first time that I visited the Theatre Center was in the early part of 1997. I had the chance to spend several hours at the place, interviewing actors and staff members about their encounters with Neville's ghost. I spoke with a couple of dozen people who all expressed their respect, and a sort of fondness, for the ghost that haunted the place. I would have had to say that more people seemed to like Neville after he was dead than ever did when he was alive.

Before the interview, though, I was able to wander about the building on my own. I had already received the guided tour and this was my chance to look around and get a real feel for the place. It was larger than it looked from outside, especially the basement, which had a lot of rooms for storage, bathrooms, a furnace room, and several small dressing rooms. I also walked across the stage and through the auditorium. I had no idea what I was looking for, but I hoped to find something.

I was not disappointed.

When I left the stage, I went down the back staircase and back to the basement. There was a dressing room at the bottom of the steps. This dressing room had been mostly used in the early days of the theater. A newer addition had been built years later and the dressing rooms were moved upstairs. The old dressing room at the bottom of the stairs was mostly just used for storage and was usually only occupied by Joe Neville – although I didn't know that at the time.

As I walked into the room, I suddenly smelled something very heavy. I identified it immediately as the overwhelming smell of Noxzema. To be honest, I thought nothing of the odor. This was a theater, after all, and Noxzema was undoubtedly for makeup removal after the shows. I shrugged the whole thing off and went to meet the crew and cast for my interviews.

My surprise wouldn't come until later. I was speaking with Rebecca Sykes and she told me that one indication they had of Neville's ghost being present was the smell of Noxzema in the air. Because of this, superstitious actors had banned the use of the cream from the theater years before. So, whatever I had smelled in that room had not been the lingering odor of an actor who had removed his or her make-up.

"They say that Joe had this horrible rash on his legs that never seemed to heal," Rebecca explained when I asked how the smell had been linked to the ghost. "He used to slather layers of Noxzema on them. I guess that everywhere he went, you used to be able to smell it around him."

I would have loved to laugh the whole encounter in the dressing room off to nothing more than my overactive imagination, but that would be impossible to do since I had no idea of the tell-tale "smell" until after I actually caught a whiff of it. That seemed to rule out the idea that it was just my imagination. To this day, I believe I came face to face with Joe Neville.

Eventually, the curtain closed at the theater on Lawrence Street. For years, the seats were empty and the doors were locked. No one walked the boards of the empty stage. A few years after my encounter with Joe Neville, the Theater Center closed its doors and the organization moved to the Hoagland Theater of the Arts, a modern building with three separate auditoriums.

The old building remained dark and one had to wonder what became of the ghost of Joe Neville. Did he still wander the empty rooms, abandoned stage, and deserted dressing rooms of the old theater building, wondering if anyone would ever return? Or had he followed Theatre Guild members to the new building, where he tried to unnerve them as they performed the shows? The veteran cast and crew members certainly kept his story alive, re-telling the stories of Neville's ghost and the devious pranks that he liked to play. In this way, their memories kept the spirit of Joe Neville alive and present in a modern place while the old building silently decayed a few blocks away.

Was Joe gone for good? It's hard to say and the new owners of the Lawrence Street building aren't talking. In 2011, Scott Richardson bought the old theater and after some extensive remodeling, opened it up as the Legacy Theatre, and is now using it to bring entertainment to the city of Springfield again.

But what about Joe? It seems the ghost of the past is not anything that the current staff wants to focus on. Although audience members often ask about hauntings in the building, no one offers up stories of the supernatural. Scott Richardson doesn't allow ghost hunting at the theater and he sums up his thoughts on the issue of ghosts with the same thing that he tells everyone: "We have many friends here, both physical and non. Everyone who comes with love is welcome to stay. We mean that literally. Joe is here, but there are so many others from the past who've dedicated time to making this place be what it is. They all deserve our love and respect."

So, is Joe Neville still around? It seems that he is, but what he might be up to these days remains a mystery.

"Absolutely Fireproof" *The Haunted History of the Lincoln Theater*

The Lincoln Theater, located on North Main Street in downtown Decatur, is one of only two of the city's grand theaters that remain in existence today. It opened in 1916 with a large seating capacity and a sprawling stage. It was a labyrinth, and remains so today, with its mezzanine, high balcony, basements, and sub-cellars. The theater holds many secrets, and according to some, many ghosts. In fact, there are so many ghosts at the Lincoln Theater that it's hard to imagine that they could have all come from the history of the building. And it's very possible that they didn't. I believe the majority of ghosts at the Lincoln were present before the theater was even built.

The Lincoln Theater was not the first building to be located at the North Main Street site. There were two different hotels that occupied the site over the years and the names of these establishments changed many times. In April 1915, though, it was called the Decatur & Arcade Hotel. On the night of April 15, a fire broke out in the hotel's boiler room when some oily rags ignited. The blaze quickly began spreading through the building. Grover Phillips, the hotel's night clerk, was in the office when the fire started and when he realized that the hotel was in danger, he took the elevator to the top floor and began working his way down, alerting the guests, often battering open doors when no one answered his knocks. He was still knocking on doors when firefighters forced him to leave the building, which was filling with smoke.

Most of the guests that made it out into the street were in their night clothes and had left all of their belongings and money behind. Clothing, shoes, and hats were scattered in piles throughout Lincoln Square and most of the guests were given shelter in nearby stores, or at the St. Nicholas Hotel. The newspapers claimed that more than 1,000 people came downtown to see the fire and many of them were generous enough to offer food, shelter, clothing, and money to those who had fallen victim to the blaze.

The fire quickly spread through the building. At first, the firefighters were able to contain it in the basements, but soon, the flames could be seen through the front doors. The firemen began dragging hose into the building, but, in a matter of minutes, the blaze was inside of the walls and was climbing floor by floor to the roof of the hotel.

Hotel manager Howard Hanthorn was still inside when the fire reached the first floor. He managed to get eight guests out of their rooms and was rousing a visiting baseball team when he heard screams coming from down the hall. After getting the baseball team to safety, he and another man ran back inside to try and find the person who had been screaming, but the flames drove them back. Whoever it was, they perished in the fire.

As the blaze swept through the hotel, Fire Chief DeVore realized the hotel was lost. He directed his men to try and save some of the other buildings nearby, including the Bachman Bros. & Martin Co. furniture store, the YMCA, the First Presbyterian Church, and the Odd Fellows Building. All were damaged, but survived the fire. When the north wall of the hotel collapsed, it struck the Bachman warehouse with a tremendous crash and a loud explosion. The furniture store was saved from heavier losses thanks to a heavy firewall and a new sprinkler system.

Of the 70 guests that were checked into the hotel that night, most survived. Two bodies were discovered in the ruins on April 23, those of William E. Graham, an engineer for the Decatur Bridge Co. and C.S. Guild, a traveling salesman from Lockport, New York. At least a dozen others were never found at all. Their remains were believed to be completely destroyed in the fire, reduced only to ashes.

The fire was extinguished hours after it began and Decatur's downtown was saved. Chief DeVore later stated that if it had not been raining before the fire started, it was possible that the entire west side of the downtown district, including many homes, could have been lost.

The hotel was never rebuilt, but in 1916, the Lincoln Theater was erected on the site. With fires being so prevalent in Decatur's past – and being built on the site of another building destroyed by fire – the designers of the Lincoln Theater were determined to make the place "absolutely fireproof" by housing the theater's boilers in a separate building from the theater itself and placing a thick firewall between them. The walls of the theater were constructed to be more than two-feet thick and the interior was designed so that the walls, floors, railings, ceilings, fixtures, and even the curtains, were said to be impossible to burn. The designers boasted that the entire block could burn, but the theater would be left standing. It was a claim that would later be tested.

The public got its first look at the new theater in October 1916, when John W. Dooley held a Christian Science lecture in the auditorium. However, the formal grand opening took place at the end of the month, on October 27, 1916. The Lincoln opened to "standing room only" crowds, dressed in black tie and formal wear, and eager to see the new, glorious theater about which they had heard so much. The first program to be presented was the George M. Cohan stage comedy, "Hit the Trail Holliday," starring Frank Otto. In addition to the show, speeches were given that night by Mayor Dan Dineen and by owner Clarence Wait, who bragged about the "fireproof" status of the theater and its solid and safe fire escapes. The audience loved the show and raved about the spectacular design of the theater, from the private seating boxes, to the massive ivory-colored columns, to the 1,346 seats, all of which offered a splendid view of the stage and wonderful acoustics. New to Decatur was the mezzanine section of the theater, which ran just below the balcony and offered seats that were only slightly above the level of the stage.

In those early years, the main emphasis at the Lincoln was on stage shows and vaudeville acts. The community also put the theater into use and it hosted many small, local productions as well as the Decatur High School commencement exercises each spring. Many famous stars of the vaudeville era appeared on the Lincoln's stage, including Harry Houdini, Lionel and Ethel Barrymore, John Phillip Sousa, Geraldine Farrar, Al Jolson, Ed Wynn, Anna Palova, Jeanette MacDonald, Chico Marx, Louis Armstrong, and many others. Audiences also thrilled to such attractions as a sparring exhibition by World Heavyweight Boxing champion Jack Dempsey after his famous fight with Georges Carpentier.

In February 1926, the theater hired a 12-member orchestra to provide music for all stage productions and silent films. Films were frequently shown but vaudeville still remained the most popular attraction the theater had to offer. The orchestra's leader brought a young, unknown comedian named Bob Hope to the Lincoln in 1926 to show Decatur how to dance the "Charleston." Hope was just starting his career in those days and he returned often during the 1920s to appear in vaudeville shows and comedy productions as a master of ceremonies.

Decatur's Lincoln Theater during its heyday

Moving pictures continued to increase in popularity in the city and Decatur was demanding more and more films to take the place of stage shows. Only major attractions were needed to fill in between the films, so the theater booked live emcees to host the movies months in advance. This filled the need for live actors and celebrities and still managed to bring the moving picture crowd into the theater. Every movie became a major attraction with the orchestra playing overtures to accompany the action on the screen. A pianist, and later an organist, was hired to provide lighter music for the serials, newsreel footage, and the comedy films.

In April 1928, the first "talkies" came to Decatur and played at the Empress Theater. The Lincoln began showing them 14 months later at the close of the vaudeville season. This heralded the end of vaudeville days at the Lincoln, and perhaps in the entire city. Sound equipment was installed in the theater for films, making silent movies obsolete, and bandleader Billy Gail and his orchestra were promptly dismissed. From that time on, two films were shown each week with one running from Sunday through Tuesday, and the other from Wednesday to Saturday. The first talking films shown were *Nothing but the Truth* starring Richard Dix and a musical called *Desert Song*.

That same year, the Lincoln was purchased by the Great States chain of theaters, which also purchased the Empress and the Bijou. The building itself remained the property of Clarence Wait until his death in 1936. Ownership of the theater was then passed to his brothers, Arthur and Fao Wait.

Although movies had largely replaced live entertainment at the Lincoln, there were still special performances booked there on a regular basis. It was during one of these performances that the "fireproof" claims of the theater were first tested.

In September 1942, one of the great magicians of the century, Harry Blackstone, was performing at the theater. Blackstone had performed at the Lincoln a number of times and always drew huge crowds. On this afternoon, the auditorium was filled with about 1,000 school children and word reached the staff that a fire had broken out at the Rambo drugstore, located next door to the theater.

Alerted to the danger, Blackstone remained calm and jokingly told the audience that for his next trick, he was going to make them all disappear from the theater in five minutes. He then directed them to leave, row by row, out of the alley doors and out of the fire escapes in the balcony. He promised the children that they were assisting him in a marvelous new illusion, which he would explain to them outside. After he had successfully cleared the theater and learned that the danger was past, Blackstone is said to have sobbed with relief from the stress of his heroic evacuation of the theater. Years later, in 1960, while a guest on the television program "This is Your Life," he stated this had been the "greatest trick of his career."

The fire lasted for four hours and completely gutted the drug store and Cook Jewelers, which shared the space. The fire was so intense that the floor of the building collapsed into the basement. It also heavily damaged an adjoining flower shop and beauty parlor, but no damage was reported to the Lincoln. Apparently, it really was "fireproof" after all.

These claims were tested again in 1960 when another fire did major damage to buildings south of the theater. The section of the building that was located above the theater lobby was destroyed, which explains why this section can be seen in older photographs but is not present today. The Lincoln itself, which was showing the film *The Bramble Bush* at the time, was only slightly damaged. The "fireproof" claims have not been tested since and the building has remained architecturally sound after a century in existence.

The theater operated steadily for many years and was sold again in 1974 to Plitt Theaters Inc., which bought out the entire Great States chain. The Lincoln Theater only remained in the chain until December of that year, when management was passed to the Kerasotes chain, based in Springfield, Illinois. They leased the building on a month-to-month basis and in December 1980, were informed by William Wait that their lease would not be extended past the end of the year. After 64 years as a vaudeville and movie house, the Lincoln closed its doors on December 12, 1980, ending with the Don Knotts film, *The Private Eyes*.

The theater opened again briefly in 1981, offering musical performances by live acts such as Muddy Waters, Black Oak Arkansas, Ernest Tubb, Steppenwolf, Pure Prairie League, Ozark Mountain Daredevils, B.B. King, Alabama, and a number of others. Unfortunately, the theater's bookings were not successful enough to keep the Lincoln open full-time, and for the next several years, the theater was only sporadically opened for live music and special events. By 1990, the building had deteriorated badly and was suffering from neglect. It had been abandoned by everything except for the bats and pigeons that had taken up residence in the auditorium.

Soon after, a restoration group began trying to bring back some life into the old place. Years of fund raisers, donations, special events, and finally large state grants managed to sink thousands of dollars and countless hours of work into the theater, but even after more than 20 years, it still has a long way to go before it can be considered restored. Board members have come and gone over the past two decades, but recent efforts appear to be paying off. The restoration of the theater is far from complete, but this has not stopped many local and national acts from performing there. Often, during these performances and events, visitors and guests have not only enjoyed the show, but have also encountered things in the theater that can only be described as otherworldly.

Stories have circulated about a haunting at the Lincoln Theater since at least the 1930s. Reports from witnesses during those early days of film, combined with all of those who have encountered the unexplained in the theater since that time, lead many to believe that a multitude of spirits may linger in the Lincoln.

Over the years, dozens of witnesses have reported hearing strange sounds and footsteps in the otherwise empty theater, and these are noises that cannot be explained away as simply the building's acoustics. They have also reported whispers, voices, laughter, and even applause. The apparition of a woman in a dress from the early 1900s has been seen in the balcony and other ghosts have been reported on the mezzanine, on the stage, and lurking in the auditorium.

In addition to seeing ghosts, people have felt them, as well. Many have experienced inexplicable cold chills in the building and others claim to have been touched by unseen hands. Often, those seated in the auditorium have experienced having their clothing tugged, their hair pulled, taps on the shoulder, caresses on the back of the neck, and some have even reported the annoying sensation of someone kicking the back of their seat. When they have turned around to ask the person behind them to stop, they discover there is no one there. Others state that they have felt someone walk past them, only to turn and see no one there. Some even report seeing seats in the auditorium actually raise and lower without assistance from human hands, as if an unseen audience was watching the performance on the stage.

Other unexplained incidents have occurred around what may be the most actively haunted spot in the theater. It is a metal, spiral staircase that is located in a back corner of the stage. Many witnesses claim to have had unearthly encounters on and around the staircase. For example, in 1994, an entertainer who was performing in a traveling production reported that she saw a man lurking on this staircase. She was in the back corner changing her costume when she heard a voice whispering to her. When she looked up, she saw a shadowy figure on the steps. She was unable to describe the figure, but she was convinced that it was a man. She complained about the presence to a nearby theater staff member, but when they checked the staircase, they found it empty. The man was gone but there was nowhere for him to go; the staircase leads up to a small utility room, high above the stage, and there is no other exit. Strangely, the actress had no idea about the stories of the Lincoln being haunted.

I can personally vouch for at least one encounter on this intimidating staircase, and to this day, I have no explanation for what occurred, other than to say that I was followed up the stairs by one of the theater's resident ghosts.

I was in the theater one evening in October 1995 with a reporter and a cameraman from a local television station. They had contacted me about haunted places in Central Illinois for a news special and one of the places that I took them to was the Lincoln Theater.

After an interview about the hauntings, I decided to join the cameraman for a trip up the spiral staircase. He took his camera along, hoping to film the theater's stage from this vantage point. It was a good thing that he brought it, because without it, we would have had no other source of light with which to see. We rounded the staircase and then reached the top. We looked around the confined space for a few moments and then we stood talking. What happened next was the strange part.

Nothing seemed out of the ordinary at first. We had climbed the spiral staircase and left the reporter down on the stage by herself. We weren't surprised when we heard the sound of her footsteps as she followed us up the stairs. Her hard-soled shoes made a distinctive sound as they echoed on the metal steps. Realizing that we had the only portable light on the camera, and the staircase was quite dark, the cameraman leaned over the railing with his camera so that the reporter would have some light on the stairs. Just as he did this, from out on the stage, we heard the sound of the reporter's voice calling to us. We looked and saw her standing in the middle of the stage, dozens of feet from the base of the steps and much too far away to have been climbing the staircase just moments before.

We suddenly realized the footsteps on the staircase had not belonged to the reporter. So, who was climbing the staircase? We didn't know but when the sounds finally stopped, the once-skeptical cameraman rushed past me and hurried out of the theater, obviously shaken by what had occurred. He later confessed, "I never believed in ghosts, but the Lincoln Theater made me a believer."

And he hasn't been the only one. Dozens of staff members, visitors and hardened skeptics have come to this place, or have spent the night within the Lincoln's walls, only to discover that odd things do happen there – things that often cannot be explained.

In 2005, during the height of the restoration effort, we brought a group into the theater during one of our Haunted Decatur Tours. At the time, the massive proscenium arch, which frames the opening between the stage and the auditorium, was being painted and portions of the ceiling were being repaired. This meant that the auditorium was closed because it was completely filled with wood and metal scaffolding. Using the corridor along the wall that traveled along the edge of the auditorium floor, we used the side door to the stage and brought the group of about 40 people onto the stage itself. The electricity was turned off in the theater while the work was being done, so we stood there in the darkness, peering out toward the rows of seats. It was very dark in the auditorium and little could be seen aside from a dim light near the doors at the back of the building and shadows made by the scaffolding.

Using the darkness to set the mood, I recounted the history of the theater and then told some of the ghost stories and spoke about some of the reported encounters in the building. While I was talking, I noticed that some of the group members had started to stir. They were whispering to each other and walking up to the edge of the stage to try and peer out into the dark auditorium. Finally, one of them stopped me and explained that they could hear someone walking around out among the scaffolding. We froze and listened carefully, and they were right – the clear sound of footsteps could be heard walking around in the dark. Knowing that the front door was locked and there was no one else in the building, I pointed a flashlight in the direction of the sounds. There was no one there. The auditorium was empty. And yet, the entire group definitely heard someone walking toward us.

And there have been plenty of other times when tour attendees have gotten more than they bargained for at the Lincoln Theater. There have been other nights when sounds have occurred that no one could explain. There have been several sightings of figures in the balcony, or at the back of the auditorium, that have not been explained. For a period of time around 2010, when a number of different people – unconnected, who did not know one another, and who were in the theater at different times – were hit in the head by coins that seemed to drop from nowhere. The random coins just seemed to fall out of the air when no one was around who could have dropped them. These mysterious happenings eventually stopped, but they have never been explained either.

Who are all of the ghosts who walk in the Lincoln Theater? The answer to that is not a simple one. I believe that in addition to the ghosts that are simply a part of the theater's past, like former stagehands, actors, and staff members who just never departed, the spirits of those killed in the hotel fire still linger within the walls. The theater now stands directly on the site of the former hotel and I have often speculated that the ghosts of those who perished in the flames could have passed into the new building and taken up residence there. This might explain the inordinate number of specters that can be found in this place.

But whoever they are, the current staff has made it clear that they are welcome to stay.

Flickering Images
Hauntings of the Avon Theater

Decatur's Avon Theater officially opened in November 1916. The Avon was a unique place in that it was a large, grand theater, on the scale of the Lincoln, but yet it had been constructed for showing moving pictures only. There would be some live entertainment and music later on, with hosts appearing for the parade of films to follow, but this theater seemed like a folly to many. They thought it could never succeed, believing that moving pictures were a passing fad that would never last. But over the years, the American film industry has defied the odds and endured. Fortunately, even after a number of near disasters, the same can be said for the Avon.

Some of those connected to the theater believe that it's more than just luck that keeps the Avon Theater in business. They believe that it has something to do with the resident ghost, as well. This enduring spirit was around during the days of the theater's greatest successes and those who have encountered him can assure anyone that he still hasn't left.

In the spring of 1916, entrepreneur Joseph Allman announced plans for a brand new theater in Decatur. It would be unlike any other in that it would be the city's first "movie palace," dedicated only to

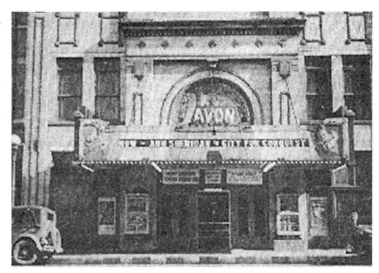

The Avon Theater in the early days of film

showing films. There were already a number of moving picture houses in the city, but most were cramped storefronts that operated on a shoestring. The Avon Theater – as it was dubbed after a city-wide contest was held to chooses its name – would have main floor and balcony seating for over 1,000 people, private boxes on either side of the screen, original artwork, and a grand design only found in the big cities of the era. Allman even convinced a friend, a student of Lorado Taft, to furnish statuary to be installed in niches in the theater. They would be joined by illuminated lion's heads, which would be mounted to the ends of each row of seats. Their glowing eyes would guide patrons in the darkness. Outside of the theater, Allman installed twin, seven-foot-tall statues to posts at the north and south ends of the building. A third statue, a woman reclining in the nude and holding a wreath, was placed above the whitewashed back wall of the theater, which served as the screen. Parallel with this figure, circling the auditorium, were bas-reliefs of women's heads.

The artwork and the decor were not the only things that make this theater special. The new film projectors were the best models available and an orchestra was scheduled to appear on a regular basis to provide musical accompaniment for the films. In addition, the theater was also equipped with a giant pipe organ that was electrically controlled. It was located in three different parts of the building so that it would be acoustically correct for the entire audience.

The theater opened on November 28, 1916. The first film was *Fall of a Nation*, based on a book by Thomas W. Dixon and it was shown to a standing-room only audience, packed into every available seat. In the months that followed, the Avon hosted dozens of well-received films, musical performances, and even fashion shows, presented by local dry goods stores. Occasionally, the theater would also host the stars of some of the films that were shown, especially those from the Essanay Studios in Chicago.

By early 1917, Allman had hired a manager for the theater, J.A. Carrier, and had stepped away from most of the daily responsibilities of the business. To the general public, things were going quite well with the Avon, but behind the scenes, the theater was a financial disaster. The cost of construction had nearly bankrupted Allman and he was soon forced to seek opportunities in addition to his beloved movie house. Even the best films, the music shows, and the personal appearances couldn't save the Avon and in August 1917, it was closed.

Later that same month, it was announced that an "outside firm" had leased the Avon from Allman. The former owner would still retain control over the building, but the business would be leased and operated by someone else. The new company announced that the Avon would remain dark until a "general overhauling" could be given to the place.

During this brief period, there was a lot taking place out of the public eye. The "outside firm" that was taking over the Avon was Carrier Amusement Co., which was owned by C.E. Carrier, brother of the Avon's manager. What actual business arrangements were involved remains mysterious to this day, and it has been suggested that some underhanded dealings may have taken place in regard to Allman. All that is known about the building's owner is that after Carrier Amusement Co. took over the theater, Allman retired quietly to his farm in Monticello. He was never involved with Decatur entertainment again. The official word was that the Carrier Amusement Co. made it a practice to take over theaters that were in financial trouble and then to make those theaters attractive to investors again.

Carrier's company, which was based in Chicago and also operated five other theaters in Illinois, wasted no time in moving into the Avon. They announced a number of plans for the near future, including some additional remodeling. The interior was redecorated and the paintings were removed. They also installed the first real lobby in the theater and lined a portion of the walls with marble and painted the rest in old rose with cream trimming. They also removed the center doors and replaced them with a box office that would allow tickets to be purchased from the street or from two side windows in the lobby. This box office would remain in place until 1972.

The Carrier brothers also announced that they would be making some changes to the theater's programming as well. Like most of the other venues in Decatur at that time, they would begin offering vaudeville shows in addition to films. The new policy would present two "quality" acts of vaudeville in addition to the films. The performances would be changed two times each week, on Sundays and Thursdays, and the films would be changed four times.

In March 1918, the Carrier brothers erected a new stage for the Avon and added small dressing rooms on either side. They hoped to lure larger vaudeville acts to the theater by removing the old stage (which was only 10 feet deep) and putting in a much larger one. It was constructed from brick, concrete and steel and cost around $1,600.

But the Carriers would not remain in charge of the theater for long. Although they would continue their lease, the management of the Avon was taken over by R.J. La Voise, who had previously been the Carriers' house manager. His immediate boss, J.A. Carrier, had gone into the Army and was preparing to leave for Europe. In April 1918, he officially took over the theater's reins. He remained in that position through the war and in the troubling period that followed: the time of the Spanish Influenza epidemic. The epidemic led to the closure of the theater for a time – along with all other public places in the city – and saw many deaths in the city.

In March 1919, J.A. Carrier returned from Europe and announced that he would be selling the lease to the Avon Theater to a theatrical company that consisted of theater manager R.J. La Voise and a number of others. The lease, the equipment, and the goodwill of the theater were transferred to the new corporation and while the names of the new owners were not being released, the newspaper assured its readers that the company would "mean much to the city theatrically as it is prominent in the motion picture theater business." A month or so later, Carrier announced that he was leaving Decatur and was taking over the management of the Pershing Theater, located on the west side of St. Louis. The company that took over the Avon was the Mid-West Theater Corporation and for the next several years, it operated the Avon without incident, continuing on with the business plan first instituted by the Carrier brothers. Programs at the Avon continued to be divided between films and vaudeville entertainment.

In April 1924, Mid-West merged with Balaban & Katz, which already owned five of Chicago's largest theaters (the Chicago, the Tivoli, the Riviera, the Roosevelt and the Central Park), and this gave the company controlling interest in 50 theaters in the Midwest, including the Avon. They planned a number of changes for the theater and closed the Avon for more than two months for "elaborate improvements." When it re-opened, everything with the theater had changed.

Despite the extensive plans made by Balaban & Katz, a small item appeared in the *Decatur Herald* newspaper on July 22, 1924. Apparently, Balaban & Katz had begun to have second thoughts about the viability of the Avon. Rumors were flying that W.N. VanBatre, the owner of the company, had traveled to Decatur to meet in secret with the managers of the Empress Theater, Gust and Christian Constan. It was said that the brothers were possibly interested in the theater and that negotiations were pending. On July 21, Gust Constan left for Chicago and it was reported that the deal had been finalized. When asked by the newspaper, however, Christian would not verify this. He only stated that he himself had not signed the necessary papers.

The following day, the rumors turned into fact. Balaban & Katz had abandoned their plans for the Avon Theater and had turned over the operation to the Constan brothers and their cousin, George Stevens of Chicago. The brothers had previously operated the Butterfly Confectionary, at 211 North Water Street, and had been part owners of the Empress Confectionary, across the street from the Avon Theater. They announced that the theater would be opened again in mid-August and from that point on there would be no more vaudeville performances. The Avon was strictly a movie house again.

The Constanopoulos brothers were Greek immigrants who became familiar fixtures in the Decatur entertainment business. During a more than 40-year span, they would manage and operate the Avon Theater, Rogers, Varsity, Castle Theater in Bloomington, and Times Theater in Danville. The four brothers, who shortened their surname to Constan, were Angelo, Gust, Christian and Theodore. They became very involved with the Avon (especially Gust) and truly moved the theater forward into the modern era. Their tenancy in the theater lasted the longest and had the greatest effect on what the theater has become today.

 Angelo Constan was born in 1895 in Tripolis, Greece, and came to the America in 1922, joining two of his other brothers in Decatur. At that time, Gust and Christ were already operating their soda and candy shops and he went to work in the family business. Sadly, Angelo died at the age of only forty-seven in 1942.

Theodore Constan was born in Tripolis in 1900 and was the youngest of the seven children of George and Anastasia Constanopoulos. He came to America in July 1925 and joined his brothers in the theater business. As with all of the brothers, he became active with the local Greek Orthodox Church and was also involved with the American Hellenic Educational Progressive Association and served as a delegate to its national conventions. In 1945, he married Argero Tsevelekos and together they had five children. After he retired from business, Theodore moved to Denver, Colorado, and in 1992, he passed away at the age of 91.

Christian George Constan was also born in Tripolis and he came to Decatur in 1915. He was the first to join his brother Gust in business, and together they operated soda shops before getting involved with the Empress, the Avon, and the other theaters. Christ and Theodore were the last two Constan brothers in the entertainment business when they both retired in 1966. Christ remained in Decatur until his death at the age of 87 in 1978.

Of all of the brothers, the most actively involved in Decatur theater (especially with the Avon) was Gust. Born in January 1891 in Tripolis, he was the oldest of the brothers and he came to American in 1912. In 1913, he moved to Decatur and opened the Butterfly and the Chocolate Shop confectionaries. In 1924, he was instrumental in getting the family involved in the lease, and later the purchase, of the Avon Theater. He would remain active at the Avon (and with the Rogers and Varsity theaters) until his death in 1965.

The Avon opened again on Saturday, August 16, 1924. For the next nine years, the theater prospered into the "talking films" era and the Constan brothers enjoyed much success in the city. In 1935, the theater closed again, but only for renovations as the financial troubles of the past seemed to be over. This period of remodeling marked the first major changes that had been done to the building since the Carrier brothers had taken over years before.

During the renovations, the balcony of the theater was completely rebuilt for the price of $2,500. In addition, offices were added on the second floor, directly above the lobby. Across the hall from the new offices, and behind the new balcony, was the location of the men's restroom. It had always been a small, cramped space but was slightly enlarged and remodeled during this period. Later on, a men's room would be added downstairs.

Another major change was also made to the projectionist's booth in 1935 with a door finally being added. Before this, the projectionist had to go up onto the roof of the theater, open a trap door, and then climb down a ladder into the booth. This was done to keep the patrons of the theater safe in the event of a fire. During the silent era, movies were made using volatile nitrate film and under certain conditions, it could combust into flames. By not having a door on the projectionist's booth, the theater hoped to protect the audience should such a fire break out. The projectionist, I suppose, was considered expendable.

That same year, Gust Constan returned to Greece and while he was there, he married Vicky Platopoulou. She returned with him to Decatur. The Constan brothers still had two sisters and a brother in Athens.

The next several years in Avon history were largely uneventful, save for the outbreak of World War II and the death of Angelo Constan in 1942. The next set of changes for the theater came about in 1953, when the Avon was again renovated to keep up with the changing times. In addition to an expansion of the concession stand, a new screen was installed for showing wide-screen and 3-D films. And while 3-D movies, turned out to be a short-lived fad, the wider screen was an innovation that put the Avon ahead of other theaters in the city. The new screen was 12-feet high and 24-four-feet wide, which was eight feet wider than the previous screen. In order to install it, the old private seating boxes that were located in the front of the theater finally had to be removed. The new screen weighed over 300 pounds and was coated with a silver-tone finish that would not absorb the light. The screen was also perforated so that sound from the system behind it could reach the audience. The owners stated that the new wide screen "gives some illusion of depth and a great feeling of audience participation."

In 1965, after a three-month illness, Gust Constan passed away. Funeral services were held next door to the theater at the Moran Funeral Home and Gust was laid to rest in Fairlawn Cemetery. The Avon, Rogers, and the family's theaters in Bloomington and Danville were closed on the day of the funeral. It was truly an end of an era for the Avon Theater.

A few months later, on April 15, 1966, a 42-year period in Decatur entertainment came to an end with the announcement that Christ, Theodore, and Gust's widow, Vicky, were leasing out the Avon and their other theaters to the Kerasotes theater chain, based in Springfield, Illinois. With this acquisition, the chain boasted 53 theaters in Illinois. The small, family-operated business had come to an end and the Avon had been absorbed into another company. It was now just another theater, and it would remain that way for the next two decades.

The lease became effective at the date of signing and with that, the Constan family ended their connection with the operations of the Avon. However, they continued to own the building until 1989, when it was purchased by the late Bob Lewis. Over the course of the next two decades, though, the Constan family would enjoy a relationship with the Kerasotes chain that has often been described as "unfriendly," to say the least.

The next major renovations at the Avon took place in 1972. It was time, the owners decided, to update the theater's look and bring it into the modern era. Gone were the days of the old-time movie palace and audiences were demanding a slick, modern look for theaters. With that thought in mind, the old fixtures were torn out, the walls were paneled over, new carpet was laid, new seats were installed, and the lobby was given a gaudy, 1970s look that dated the décor in ways that the owners could not have imagined. The addition of the new seats also reduced the capacity of the theater from 900 (what it had been after the Carrier brothers installed the new stage) to around 700. The old center-door box office was removed and a new one was installed in its current location.

For the next several years, the Avon continued to enjoy success in downtown Decatur, and then in August 1980, the death knell sounded for all of the old theaters in town. Some of them were not aware of it yet, but the heyday of Decatur's movie houses was finally coming to an end. It was announced that six movie theaters were being built at the new Hickory Point Mall in nearby Forsyth. The new multiplex was a joint venture of Kerasotes Brothers, which would book the movies, and American Multi-Cinema Inc. of Kansas City, which would operate the business. Placing a number of screens into a single building was a fairly new idea at the time and such theaters were popping up all over America, following closely behind the proliferation of shopping malls.

Business was already beginning to suffer for the downtown theaters. The Lincoln stayed open until December 31, 1980, when it was closed down at the end of the Kerasotes lease. The Rogers was closed in 1984, even though its lease actually ran until 1986. It was cheaper, according to the Kerasotes chain, to simply close the place and continue paying the rent than it was to operate it. As for the Avon Theater, said president George Kerasotes, "We have a lease that goes for five and one-half years. We're obligated by our lease to keep it open. Either keep it open or keep paying the rent."

The theater struggled to stay in business over the next several years, and in 1985, the theater converted to showing second-run movies and changed its name to the Avon Cinema. By this time, the Kerasotes chain had been split apart and George Kerasotes owned the Avon. In April 1986, it turned out that second-run movies just wouldn't pay the bills anymore. The Avon was closed down, just a few days after the lease with the Constan family expired. This date would mark the last time that the Avon was part of a theater chain.

Over the course of the next 13 years, the theater alternated between being closed and being home to one failed business plan after another. It operated as a county music opry, a second-run movie theater, and even as a "dollar theater," but nothing worked until 1999 when Skip Huston re-opened the Avon as a full-fledged movie theater again. It has since become one of the largest attractions in downtown Decatur and still operates with three screens today. And, as mentioned, much of the success of the Avon has been attributed to an otherworldly source.

I have no problem with saying that I believe the Avon Theater to be one of the most haunted places in the city of Decatur. In addition to all of the first- and second-hand accounts that I have collected from the place over the years, I have experienced things there myself that have defied all rational attempts to explain them away.

The tales of restless ghosts at the Avon go back to the early 1990s, when I was working on my first book about local ghosts. I advertised widely that I was looking for ghost stories and reportedly haunted spots. The Avon had opened again in 1993 and I was contacted by some of the staff members who worked there. I was able to record a lot of information about the alleged haunting during my visit. The theater manager, and the rest of the staff, reported that things had started to turn up missing in the building, both small items and large. They also told of hearing footsteps in the hallways and offices and felt as if they were being watched.

That night, as I took a walking tour of the place, I found the sensations in some of the areas in the theater were very unsettling. One of the most frightening locations was a hallway that is located upstairs above the theater's lobby. This hallway had been added to the theater during the renovations in 1935 and the theater's offices, and a small bathroom, opened off this corridor. The feeling that I had while walking down this corridor was very disconcerting, and while I certainly don't claim to be psychic, it was a strange experience. I would soon learn that the theater staff felt the same way and largely avoided the place whenever possible. There had been many occasions when the sound of footsteps had echoed in the corridor and those who looked to see who was there found it empty. This corridor would be where more than one person would encounter a ghost.

Unfortunately, the Avon closed again a short time after my visit and I wondered if I would be able to get inside again. Rumor had it that the theater might be torn down. Later that year, though, I was able to return. Skip Huston, who now operates the theater, was part of a group interested in buying it in 1995. The plan was to turn the place into a movie-themed nightclub that would serve food and drinks, along with films and live entertainment. The project never came about, but I was able to spend quite a bit of time there doing research and prowling about the place. During this brief period, a number of strange encounters took place and several incidents happened that were not easily explained.

I experienced one such incident first-hand. I was in the upstairs hallway one day, taking photographs, and had just passed the first office on the left side of the hall when I felt something take hold of the tail of my shirt. It distinctly felt as though a hand had sharply tugged on it but (always the skeptic) I quickly turned around to see if I had somehow snagged it on something or if someone was playing a joke on me. Not only was no one there, but I was nowhere near a door frame or anything else that I could have caught the shirt on. Needless to say, I didn't spend very much more time in the hallway that afternoon.

But of all the things that happened that spring, it has become known for one very bizarre event. It was during this period that Skip came face-to-face with the theater's resident ghost.

During the process of evaluating the building for the nightclub project, Skip came down to the theater one rainy afternoon in the spring of 1995. On this day, his trip to the Avon had a double purpose. He was not only looking over the building, but was also borrowing some marquee letters for use at an upcoming show at the Lincoln Theater. Even though it was a "dark and stormy" afternoon and he knew the theater was probably haunted, he had no problem with going there by himself. He grabbed a flashlight and a couple of garbage bags to hold the letters and proceeded to the theater.

Skip made his way through the theater to the "letter room," which is located off the previously mentioned hallway on the upstairs level of the building. The room is a small office where all of the plastic letters for the theater marquee are stored. After he entered the dimly lit room, he used his flashlight to begin looking for letters and checking them off the sheet he carried with him.

A few minutes after he started working, he distinctly heard a noise behind him in the hallway. He turned around, but saw no one there. A few minutes later, he heard it again. Were those footsteps? He looked out into the corridor again, but it was just as dark and empty as it had been before. Skip shook his head and went back to work, hurriedly filling one of the plastic bags with letters. Again, he heard another strange noise and reflexively turned around. This time, he found that he was not alone.

"A man stood in the doorway to the room," Skip recalled. "My first thought was that someone else was in the theater, perhaps a homeless person hiding out there. He was of medium height and slender build. His age appeared to be in his late fifties or early sixties. His hair was close-cropped gray and black. He was not transparent or wraith-like. He appeared solid. His face was nondescript and he stared into the room, not looking at me, just staring. I started to speak to him and then he slowly turned and started down the hallway. Recovered from my surprise, I darted to the doorway to say something but all that I saw was an empty hall. I grabbed the finished bag of letters and left the theater as fast as my legs would carry me!"

A few years later, the theater finally re-opened. As with any sort of major restoration, a lot of time, money, and hard work was involved. The Avon had deteriorated badly during the time it was closed down and initially it looked as though opening the place would be impossible. There were simply too many things wrong with the old building and every time that one thing got fixed, something else would break down. In addition, Skip had skeptics to deal with among his partners and his staff. They constantly badgered him about the theater's so-called ghosts and poked fun at his belief that the building was haunted. "They started out as skeptics," he laughed later on, "but they're all believers now!"

As the restoration and repair work began to shake loose the dust and grime of the building, it awakened other things as well. It was not long before everyone on the crew, including those who had been the most skeptical about the haunting, began to report eerie incidents that they couldn't explain away. Nearly everyone talked of hearing phantom voices in empty rooms and in the deserted auditorium. They also complained of disembodied footsteps and inexplicable cold chills that simply should not exist. Most easily convinced were those who spent the entire night either working or sleeping in the building. They were soon coming to Skip and apologizing for doubting him.

Later, as customers began to arrive at the re-opened theater, they reported their own encounters. Many people spoke of feeling as though they were being watched and of pressure of hands on their backs and arms when no one was present. None of the incidents were particularly frightening. It was more like the resident specter was simply trying to make his presence known.

In the early part of 2005, I was working out of an office at the Avon. One chilly afternoon in March, I was in one of the offices above the lobby, talking to a friend on the telephone. As we were chatting, I happened to glance up and see someone walk past the door of the room, which was open just a few inches. I couldn't see who this person was, or anything about him, just the form of someone walking quickly past.

Assuming that it was another staff member who happened to be in the theater that day, I put down the telephone and got up to speak to him. I left my friend on hold and told her that I would be right back. I quickly opened the door and leaned out to see who was there but saw no movement expect for the door of the room next to the office. It was softly clicking shut and I guessed that whoever it was had gone into the room. I had gotten up too quickly for them to have gone anywhere else and the door that led downstairs to the lobby was shut tight. I walked down the corridor a few steps and opened the door of the next room to say hello. But the room was empty.

I suddenly realized that whoever had been walking down the hallway was not among the living. I hurried back into the office, picked up the telephone again, and told my friend what had happened. She gasped. "What are you going to do?"

I answered that question as I was in the process of doing it. "I'm closing the door to the office," I replied. "That way, if any more ghosts walk by, I won't see them."

Since the theater re-opened in 1999, the hauntings at the Avon have continued. Weird encounters often occur with staff members and customers alike, but there is little that is frightening about them. I believe that each one signals the continuing presence of Gust Constan, who simply wants us to know that he is still there, watching over the place, hopefully, content with the way that things are going. For the first time in nearly 40 years, the Avon is a family business again, just like it was in the days of the Constan brothers. It's not hard to imagine that Gust would be pleased.

The "Lady in the Lobby" and Friends Hauntings of the Times Theater

Located on East State Street in downtown Jacksonville is the former Times Theater. It operated for many years as one of the city's premiere movie spots, before going out of business when changes in the film industry made it too costly to equip the theater with all new technology. After a period of abandonment, the building has gained a second life as a fitness center but remnants of the theater days still remain – as lingering spirits.

The Times Theater opened for business on Christmas Day 1940. For many, it was like receiving a brand new brick and mortar Christmas present. Adults paid a quarter and children a dime to get into a packed house to see Joan Bennett in *The Housekeeper's Daughter* and Jackie Coogan in *Streets of New York*.

Kenneth Childs, from Streator, spent more than $40,000 to build the Times, which originally had seats for 680 people in the auditorium. In May 1941, less than five months after it had opened, Childs announced that he had arranged for the Times to be operated by Fox Midwest Theaters, which already operated the Illinois Theatre in town. The Times was closed a short time later so that air conditioning could be installed, but it soon re-opened to big crowds.

At that time, Jacksonville had three movie theaters – the Illinois, the Times, and the Majestic, the latter two both on East State Street. George Hunter, manager of the Illinois, said in 1941: "The Times will present mainly first-run attractions at popular prices. The Majestic will operate as a popular-priced family theater, playing the pick of outstanding second-run features. The new policy will give Jacksonville a wide range of attractions to choose from, as well as an admission price to please every type of patron."

In 1953, Fox sold the Times to El Fran Theater Corp., which was owned by Ben Montee and Howard Busey, both local Jacksonville men. The partners named the business after their wives – Eleanor Montee and Frances Busey. Both men had a great love for the theater business and Busey remained involved with the Times for many years, even after it was put up for sale in 1960. After the Times was sold to Frisina Theaters, he worked for the new company, dividing his time between managing the Times and the 67 Drive-In Theatre, which he, Ed Bonacorsi, and Elmore Suter built in 1949. He was a member of the Church of Our Savior, Knights of Columbus and the Elks Club. Like his partner, he also served in World War II. Howard Busey passed away in 1980.

His partner, Ben Montee, also loved the Times. A well-known local businessman and very active in the Lutheran Church, he began working for Fox Theaters in Southern Illinois after World War II. He eventually came to Jacksonville and decided to settle in town. In addition to co-owning the Times with Busey, he also founded Cater-Vend, a Jacksonville vending machine business. After the Times was sold in 1960, he bought the Jacksonville Coca-Cola bottling plant, retiring in 1981. He served as president of the Passavant Hospital Board, director of the Elliott State Bank, president of the Jacksonville Chamber of Commerce, and was a lifelong member of the Elks Lodge. Montee was also a generous supporter of Illinois and MacMurray Colleges. He died in 1992, outliving his partner by 12 years.

The most dramatic incident to occur at the Times Theater took place on September 20, 1953. A fire broke out behind the screen during an evening showing of *South Sea Woman*, starring Burt Lancaster and Virginia Mayo. It sent 600 people fleeing from the theater. Phillip Busey, Howard's son, recalled that night very well nearly 50 years later. "When the fire started, my father was at the Times," he said. "I was with my mother, probably at the drive-in. I remember riding in the car with my mother up South Main and we could see that there was a fire in downtown Jacksonville. After the fire was out, but before the fire department left, we were allowed to go just inside the doors. The lobby, concession area, offices, and projection booth survived. The damage was to the auditorium." The interior of the theater had sustained major damage, due to a combination of fire, water, and smoke. While the Times was repaired, Busey and Montee leased the Majestic, which had closed down the year before.

Frisina Theaters gave the Times a major makeover in 1972, installing a new soundproof ceiling, screen, projection equipment, and curtain controls. Eventually, they sold the theater, and it was taken over by Mid America Theatres, which declared bankruptcy in 1982. They were closing theaters all over the region and were forced to cancel their plans to build a new twin drive-in at the site of Howard Busey's old 67 Drive-In outside of town. The Times sat empty until the following year, when it was taken over by Kerasotes Theatres of Springfield. They remodeled the building and re-opened the Times as a twin theater.

In July 2008, the Times and Illinois Theatres were purchased by Great Dreams Theatres, a partnership between Dr. Peter Karras, of Springfield, and Joe Avampato, of Delavan, Wisconsin. After the change in ownership, both theaters underwent a series of renovations. But changes in the theater industry in the early 2010s forced movie houses all over America to make an expensive switch to digital projection equipment. Only the Illinois Theatre survived this costly – and mandatory – overhaul. The Times closed down in January 2011. But even though the building sat silent and dark, based on the eerie stories that have circulated about the theater for many years, one has to wonder if it was ever truly empty.

When a visitor walks into the front doors of the theater, they immediately notice the long stretch of mirror that adorns the back wall of the lobby. Numerous employees of the theater described the same woman who appeared in that mirror – the "lady in the lobby." She was always described as a young woman, wearing late 1800's dress, and with her light brown hair pulled back in an intricate bun on top of her head. During the years that the theater was in operation, she was commonly reported by many different employees, many of whom did not know one another and had no idea – prior to seeing the ghost – that the theater was believed to be haunted.

In one account, a new employee was asked to clean the mirror while the manager went upstairs to take care of the nightly paperwork. The employee obliged, but while cleaning the mirror, he saw a young woman with an old-time dress and a bun in her hair, standing right behind him. The figure took three steps and disappeared right before the young man's eyes. Struck with terror, the young man scrambled up the stairs to the manager's office. After several minutes of collecting his thoughts and catching his breath, he described the incident to his manager. Although the manager was not surprised, having heard of this occurring many times before, she agreed to stay with the new employee in the lobby while he finished his work.

Another similar event took place when a new employee had a run in with the lady in the lobby for the first time. He was so petrified that he left the building without locking the doors and never returned for his second night on the job.

Although he did not run away, another staff member, saw his job a little differently after some encouragement from the lady in the lobby. The manager had been noticing that this employee was often cutting corners and leaving tasks unfinished. While alone in the lobby one afternoon, the manager, speaking out loud to herself, decided that she needed to talk with the young man and persuade him to straighten up. That night, after "cleaning" the auditoriums and lobby, the man entered the stairwell to turn off all of the lights before going home. As he quickly glanced over his shoulder to confirm the lights were all out, he immediately noticed a large amount of popcorn had been thrown all over the lobby floor. Knowing he was the only living person in the building at the time, he took the hint as he cleaned up the mess. After this event, the man was much more thorough about how he cleaned things up.

Most employees never felt any fear or malevolent sensations from the lady in the lobby. In fact, one manager felt she was quite protective. She recalled one night when she felt unusually unsafe in the building. She was overcome with anxiety and felt as though the spirit wanted her to leave, and quickly! She decided that she could come back in the morning and complete the work she had left unfinished. That night, soon after the manager locked up the building to go home, a burglar broke into the theater. The manager was convinced that a spirit within the building was concerned for her safety and had warned her to leave.

Who is this "lady in the lobby?" Some believe that she could have connections to the Rialto Theater that once stood on the same plot of land that the Times Theater now occupies. Perhaps she is there to see a show, or maybe an actress waiting for her curtain call. Very little is known about the Rialto Theatre, other than that it was a vaudeville house that was destroyed by fire, and the identity of the young woman remains a mystery.

The lobby is not the only area of the building with ghostly activity. The upper floor of the Times Theater has had its fair share of paranormal happenings, as well. There have been multiple reports of spectral entities that haunt the projection booths. In the first booth, there has been a calming spirit reported. One former employee recalled the overwhelming sensation of calm she would sometimes experience in the first projection booth, as well as a memorable time when a spirit whispered in her ear. Right outside of Booth 1, a manager recalled clearly hearing voices on the stairwell, as if a full conversation was taking place through the wall that connected the Times Theater to the golf store that was once next door. The manager was so convinced of what she heard that she entered the building next door on the following day to determine what was on the other side of that wall. She found nothing. No staircase. No electrical equipment. Nothing that could explain her experience. As if that wasn't enough, the manager was teased and tormented by the sounds of stomping footsteps coming up the stairs while she worked in the office. Turning in anticipation to see which employee was coming up to the office, she found that it was no one, or at least no one that she could see.

The second projection booth on the west side of the building was home to a particularly active prankster. This spirit, presumed by theatre staff over the years to be a small boy, was notorious for moving objects about the room or making them disappear altogether, not to be found for hours, or even days. This spirit also caused problems during the staff screenings at the theater. In the days of actual film reels, a projectionist had a lot of work to do before a movie could be shown to the public. Since each film arrived at the theater in multiple reels, the projectionist had to piece them together into one large continuous strip of film. To insure the continuity and the quality, the theater employees would screen the film in advance, usually on Thursday nights, since most new movies opened on Friday. Night after night, though, the prankster ghost in the projection booth interrupted the screenings, causing the film to inexplicably stop working or causing the projectors to turn off. The ghost had wreaked so much havoc that one of the desperate staff members finally came up with the idea of putting toys in the projection booth for the ghost to play with. The staff hoped that the teddy bear, toy cars, and wooden blocks would keep the spirit happy so that he would leave the equipment alone. To their relief, it actually worked.

After sitting empty until late August 2014, new owners, Josh and McKea Jones took over the Times Theater and transformed the building into a space focusing on physical fitness and nutrition. They installed workout equipment, obstacle courses, and a play area for kids and changed the name to Krush Time. It doesn't look much like a theater inside anymore, but the ghosts don't seem to mind. They are just as active now as they ever were – perhaps even more so!

Since moving into the space, the new owners have experienced voices calling out down the long hallway to the second auditorium, mysterious footsteps, lights that turn on and off, doors that open and close, and even an up-close-and-personal encounter with the childish ghost of the projection booth.

With the theater having been abandoned for several years when Josh and McKea took over, they found that they had a lot of cleaning to do. The theater looked as though the former staff had just walked away one day and left everything where it had been. They started cleaning up four years of dirt and grime and Josh was working in the second projection booth one day, cleaning up the junk that had been left behind, including (oddly, he thought) some children's toys. As Josh was gathering things up and throwing it away, he suddenly saw something flash in front of his eyes. A piece of flat metal landed on the floor right in front of him. He knew there was certainly no way that he had flipped the metal into the air. He turned around and looked behind him and saw the outline in the dust on the floor, where the piece of metal had been lying. How had it moved like that?

Then Josh remembered the stories of ghosts in the building. There was something, he thought, about the toys in the projection booth. A short time later, he found out the story, and even though the room is no longer a projection booth, the toys have been put back in place. John and McKea aren't taking any chances!

A Spirit that Behind Hauntings of the Marvel Theatre

Just a block and a half away from the downtown square in Carlinville is the Marvel Theatre, which was a popular stop on the highway when Route 66 passed through town. The 800-seat theater, built by Frank and

Frieda Paul, opened its doors in August 1920, and it not only brought movies and live theater to the area, but acrobats, comedians, and even live animal shows. There was a little something for everyone at the Marvel Theatre.

Although some would say that the star attraction at the Marvel was Frieda Paul herself, a gifted piano player and entertainer who had gotten a taste for Hollywood stardom during a brief time that she lived in California. Frieda loved being the center of attention at the theater – and some believe that she still does.

The Marvel Theater in Carlinville

When the Marvel opened in 1920, Frank and Frieda wanted it to be a movie theater and a playhouse all rolled into one. It cost $40,000 to build and another $10,000 was spent on an elaborate pipe organ so that music could always accompany the films. Frank was an established and successful businessman in Carlinville and he would have done anything to make his wife happy.

There is no question that Frieda was the most glamorous woman in the town's history. She grew up in Morrisonville, Illinois, entertaining at dances and parties. She was not your average farm girl of the early 1900s. Frieda had been well-schooled in theater and music and in 1914, had gone west to Hollywood. She worked in a Los Angeles theater, where she played piano as a musical accompaniment to silent films, a skill that she brought back to Illinois when she and Frank opened the theater. Combining their experience and skills, they made a success of the Marvel and Frieda always had a place to shine. She soon became known for her passion for the theater and became one of the first prominent businesswomen in Carlinville. She took the lead in the theater's business and was not easily discouraged by business setbacks.

In 1925, three armed bandits followed Frieda and Frank home from the theater one winter night, bound and gagged them, and stole jewelry and cash valued at over $1,200 before fleeing the scene. Frank was able to get free and untie his wife and their son, but the police never found the robbers.

Then, during the early morning hours of December 18, 1926, another tragedy occurred when police officers discovered the Marvel engulfed in flames. Although the fire department worked valiantly to save the theater, it was a total loss. Many suspected arson. Someone had tried to set fire to the theater a few years before, but nothing could be proven.

Frieda was determined to keep the theater alive and assured the public that the Marvel would be rebuilt. On the same morning that the Marvel burned, Frieda leased the closed-down Grand Theatre building and even arranged a show for that same night.

The Marvel re-opened on January 19, 1928, with continuous shows between 3:30 and 11:00 p.m. The new theater was decorated in blue and gold with cut glass chandeliers, plate glass mirrors, and silk draperies. The new projection booth, built at the back of the balcony, was said to be fireproof. Frieda continued to charm the patrons, whether selling tickets or accompanying the films on the organ. A short time later, the need for Frieda's musical talents largely came to an end when the Marvel became the first theater in the area to offer talking pictures. The first show was Al Jolson's, *The Jazz Singer*.

Frank Paul passed away in 1937. In the 1960s, Frieda retired and their son, Norman Paul, and his wife, Delphine, became the operators of the Marvel. Frieda died in 1976. A year later, the Marvel was split into a twin theater, dividing the balcony from the main floor. When Norman passed away in 2011, and Delphine in 2014, a second generation of theater owners was gone.

After Delphine passed away, the Marvel was closed down and it remained empty for the next year and a half. The doors were locked, the curtains were closed, and the screen was dark. The theater was silent, but it was far from abandoned.

It wasn't long before the Marvel was re-opened by Eisentraut Theaters and is currently back in business. We can only assume that this change in fortunes was met with happiness by the spirit that has remained at the theater for many years.

According to former staff members, the ghost of a woman has been seen, watching over the activity that takes place at the theater. She keeps a watchful eye over things, pleased or displeased with what she sees taking place. It's believed that this lingering spirit is that of Freida Paul, who remains behind at the place where she was the happiest in life. You see, not all ghosts remain behind because of tragedy and horrible events.

Some of them stay behind because they simply don't want to leave.

"Will it Play in Peoria?" *Hauntings of the Madison Theater*

During the vaudeville era, a popular phrase that circulated among show business people was, "Will it play in Peoria?" because the Illinois town was seen as a barometer of public interest. If it could play in Peoria, it was said, it was just about guaranteed to be successful. If it didn't work out in Peoria, the production was either rewritten or canceled. Over time, the phrase was picked up by music promoters and politicians and began to be used all over the country.

Vaudeville left its mark in other ways on Peoria, too. There were a number of grand theaters in the city by the time that talking pictures became popular in the late 1920s. The magnificent architecture of the theaters was designed to amaze the audiences who came to see the shows and watch the movies. A number of them didn't survive into the modern era, but the Madison Theater not only withstood the test of time, it thrived. And while there are a few theaters in Peoria that boast resident ghosts, there are none as haunted as the Madison.

The Madison Theater opened at 502 Main Street in downtown Peoria on October 16, 1920. In those days, vaudeville was still the most popular entertainment of the day, but moving pictures were growing in popularity. Like many other theaters, the Madison offered a limited amount of live entertainment, but devoted most of its show times to movies. It was, as noted in a newspaper article of the time, a "shrine to the silent art." Talking pictures wouldn't come along for another eight years, but lines were always long for the films that played at the Madison. When it opened, with the film *Humoresque*, the theater had a maximum occupancy of 2,000. Ticket prices were 30-cents for matinees and 40-cents for evening shows.

The Madison was designed by Peoria architect, Frederick J. Klein. The front of the theater was in an Italian Renaissance design with domed ceilings in the lobby. A triple-arched window loomed above the marquee. The main floor was made up of an outer lobby with a ticket booth on Main Street. It was decorated in a palate of muted gold, cream, and white. There were two balconies, with a stage and orchestra pit at the opposite end of the auditorium. The ceiling of the auditorium consisted of concentric circles, surrounded by a covered cornice. Under the orchestra pit were six dressing rooms, an instrument room, musician room, and organist room.

In the early days, the Madison featured a 20-piece orchestra to provide musical accompaniment for the films. However, when the "talkies" came along, and the orchestra was no longer necessary, a pipe organ was installed and the orchestra platform was removed. In 1936, the outer and inner lobbies were remodeled with decorative downlights and the art deco décor was tempered by a more modern style.

A vintage photograph of the Madison Theater

To go along with the movies, the Madison also played host to many of the famous vaudeville stars and film actors of the 1920s and 1930s. The theater was known for its family-friendly fare and attracted a wide audience. During the 1940s and 1950s, it hosted free Christmas shows and business continued to boom until the early 1980s, a difficult time for downtown theaters across the country. By then, shopping malls were sprouting up across America and the slick, multiplex theaters on the outskirts of town offered a bigger draw to audiences, especially to younger movie-goers, who were also the biggest crowd at the malls.

Years later, the Madison underwent a revival, was restored, and opened again for live shows and musical events. It remains a thriving destination spot in downtown Peoria today and a great place to see a variety of different kinds of performances.

It's also said to be a great place to experience a ghost.

The Madison is reportedly home to three different ghosts. The spirit who haunts the basement is said to be the ghost of a child who was allegedly murdered in the theater in the 1950s. The stories say that he was lured away from his parents during a show and killed by a predator in the theater's basement. While there is no record of this event actually taking place, witnesses have encountered the little boy on numerous occasions and over time, this story has taken on a life of its own. The spectral boy is seen wearing brown pants and a white shirt and his laughter has been reported by staff members. He has also been spotted in the main auditorium, where workers have reported hearing small footsteps pattering up and down the rows. One staff member stated that he was cleaning the auditorium one day and felt a wave of cold air rush past him, followed moments later by the disembodied laughter of a child.

There is also believed to be the ghost of an actor who also haunts the auditorium. He is usually encountered around the main stage, although legend has it that he was murdered in the alley next to the theater after a performance one night. It is said that his spirit has never left the building. His footsteps can be heard pacing back and forth across the empty stage when no one else is in the theater, and his presence is often realized by the overpowering smell of an old-fashioned men's cologne. For the most part, this spirit attracts little attention – which is hard to believe from an actor – but did become more active during the renovations that accompanied the re-opening of the theater. Possibly upset by the work that was being done on the stage, the ghost was blamed for tools moving about, items disappearing, power shutting down, lights turning on and off unexpectedly, and more.

The Madison's last ghost is that of a former staff member. He reportedly haunts the foyer area that is located outside of the auditorium. In the days when he worked at the theater, he was an usher, helping patrons get to their seats when the auditorium lights were down and it was difficult to see. Today, the flashlight that he once used to assist the guests can still be seen, gliding up and down the aisles when the auditorium lights are lowered, and then vanishing into the darkness.

Ghosts of the Great River Road Opry
With Lisa Taylor Horton

Located south of Winchester are the ramshackle and overgrown ruins of what was once one of the most popular country music venues in Central Illinois, the Great River Road Opry. For years, Charles and Jeanie Craver hosted musical acts and scores of fans at this secluded hideaway. Every weekend, the surrounding bluffs, field, and forests echoed with the sounds of music, laughter, and applause. Sadly, the opry closed a few years ago and has since been slowly torn down. The last remaining pieces of its history are vanishing into the Illinois prairie, swallowed by the woods, and collapsing into a tangle of wood, concrete, and steel. The walls are gone, the roof has fallen, and the Great River Road Opry is no more.

When it vanishes completely, it will take with it a rollicking era of entertainment – and stories of a myriad of ghosts. There is little question that the old Opry was one of the most haunted places in the state.

The Great River Road Opry actually began as an airplane hangar, located on the grounds of Scott Air Force Base, outside of Belleville, Illinois. After World War II, many of the buildings on the base were sold as surplus and this particular hangar was disassembled and moved to Winchester, where it was used as a seed corn company facility. The name changed a few times over the years, but the operation that used it the longest was Columbiana Seed Company. Hard times closed the company in the late 1980s, but not before one of the employees allegedly hanged himself in the building. Unfortunately, no records of this death exist, thanks to a courthouse fire in Winchester. The story of the suicide is often told by locals, though, and many blame this occurrence for at least one of the spirits that lingered at the building.

The building was empty for over a decade before Charles and Jeannie Craver turned it into a music venue. Connie Bugg, a well-known country singer in West Central Illinois, explained that her husband worked for the Craver family and comes from a long line of musicians. His brother was interested in the old seed corn building because he was convinced that it would make a good place for country shows. Charles and Jeannie agreed and they went to work on the renovations. It turned out to be a huge task. The large building needed a stage, dressing rooms, concessions area, a ticket booth, and more. Plus, they had to remove the corn conveyor belt that ran the entire length of the building. With the help of friends, though, the work was completed and the opry was opened for business.

And soon, the staff, musicians, and patrons were having encounters with the ghosts.

The Great River Road Opry — seed company turned country music venue

In truth, the strange occurrences began while the renovations were still going on. Connie's brother-in-law, Everett, often felt as though he was being watched while he was working, and he later told her that his tools often vanished and turned up again in odd places. One day, Everett and a friend, Bob, were working together and Everett stopped to look over his plans for the stage. He was having some trouble figuring out the construction, but Bob spoke up and told him the best way to do it. When Everett turned around to thank him, though, he discovered that Bob wasn't there — he was on the other side of the building and he hadn't said a word!

Another time, Everett was back behind the stage, fumbling around in the dark because he was still trying to finish wiring the lights. He muttered, "I can't see a thing back here." He said that, as soon as he spoke, a hand grasped his shoulder and pushed him out toward the auditorium.

After the opry opened, the weirdness continued. Connie still recalls her first encounter in the building. She was at the opry with her daughter, cleaning the stage and preparing for the next show, when both of them heard someone call out "hey!" from the back of the room. Connie looked up and saw that the room was empty. They were alone — and quickly left. The incident terrified Connie's daughter so much that she never again went into the opry alone.

More strange events followed and more and more people began to witness the supernatural happenings. If there had been a seed corn company employee who committed suicide in the building, and remained behind as a ghost, then he wasn't alone. The music and happy atmosphere of the place apparently served to attract spirits to the place. Noises were frequently heard, including voices, footsteps, laughter, and whispers.

Apparitions were sometimes seen, including the ghost of a local musician named "Jim," who had been thrilled by the opening of the opry. He enthusiastically led much of the work to convert the place from a seed corn company to a music venue, but sadly, he passed away before the opry opened. Since that time, he has been both seen and heard. Del Dawdy, a friend who was very involved with the opry when it was open, has heard recordings that were later obtained in the building and swears that at least one of the voices on the tape – recorded years after his death – is Jim.

My partner, Lisa, has spent a lot more time at the old opry building that I ever have. Her first experience there occurred after the music venue had closed its doors, but in contrast, I have never visited the building except when it was already nearly in ruins.

Lisa wrote about her experiences:

My first time at the Great River Road Opry would prove to be one of my earliest and most exciting experiences to take place during an EVP session. There was a small crowd of investigators that night, and after a couple hours of investigating, we rallied together to share our many experiences thus far. People described many shadow figures in the distance, one light touch on someone's arm and another through someone's hair, and many admitted they thought they heard someone whispering behind them but turned to find no one. I would, in the years to follow, discover that claims such as these would be "business as usual" for the spirits that linger in this location, but never again would I experience something as blatant as what happened next.

The group decided to combine efforts and limit contamination by joining together on the stage for an EVP session. Two seasoned opry investigators, Loren Hamilton and Del Dawdy, opted to sit among the many chairs in the audience to keep watch in our direction. Between the casual conversation and the bouts of silence, no paranormal happenings took place for several minutes. Suddenly, heavy boot steps rattled the building and our nerves. The sounds were coming from the wooden wheel chair ramp at the front entrance behind the ticket booth. The thunderous steps took their time descending the ramp and then silence fell upon the group once more. Moments passed before someone found the nerve to say "Who's was that?" and "What in the world!" Before we could regain composure, loud crashes and banging came from the shadows of the kitchen. Not just one, but many, causing us to believe that everything in the room must have been pushed to the floor, but by whom? Loren and Del took off from their seats to investigate the cause of the racket only to find nothing, and no one. Everything in the kitchen was in its place, covered by the dust of many lonely months. This experience was enough to make the two first-time ghost hunters in our group reconsider their new hobby. I've never seen them again. But I'm sure they, too, are still talking about that night at the Opry.

Since that night, I have returned to the Opry many times. I recall spending a great deal of time one night seated on a moldy couch behind the stage. With our digital recorders powered on and K-2 meters scattered about, my partner, Misty Taylor, and I spent over an hour communicating with an enduring spirit. Since the dilapidated building had been stripped of its copper wires, leaving it powerless, and with our cell phones locked up in the car, we knew there would be no contamination. The direct responses to our line of questioning through the EMF detectors was mesmerizing. According to the responses, we very well may have been communicating with the man who took his own life in the building long ago.

But I do not believe this man was the only spirit to reside within the walls of the Opry. Oftentimes during an investigation, men and women alike would claim to hear whispers throughout the building – the voice of a woman—and she doesn't sound too happy. We have never found out who or why there might be the spirit of a woman lingering about the property, but perhaps she was just searching for a listening ear. Unfortunately for me, I must need to have my hearing checked. Anytime I have heard the voice, I have never been able to make out the words, even when captured on the digital recorder. Perhaps her grouchy words were never meant for me, at least that's what I hope.

A couple of years after Lisa's first experiences at the Great River Road Opry, I had the chance to see the place for myself. We scheduled a late-night investigation one summer evening and I was curious to see the place that I had been hearing about for so long. By then, the opry had been closed for several years and the building was in a pretty poor state of repairs. Remnants of the old days still remained in some parts of the building and, as I would find out, so did some of the ghosts.

As the night went on, our group of investigators roamed the building, recording and documenting the premises and the atmosphere, hoping, of course, that something would happen. It was a quiet night, at least at the start, although there had been several reports of shadowy figures that were seen on the south end of the building, near where the kitchen had once been. We decided that we would gather at the north end of the opry and set up equipment to monitor anything that happened on the south side. Things remained quiet and Lisa mentioned that, during past ghost hunts, she had often asked our friend Connie Bugg to sing some country songs and "stir things up," so to speak. If the spirits that lingered in the opry were those from the building's past, we thought it might be possible that some of them had come there in life to enjoy the entertainment. However, Connie wasn't with us that night (and I certainly wasn't going to sing – since that definitely would have scared away the living and the dead) so I thought I would try and play some music from my phone. I had an application that searches out millions of songs and I decided to look up some Patsy Cline. What country music fan – dead or not – wouldn't want to listen to Patsy?

But I wasn't prepared for this plan in advance and had not downloaded the music to my phone ahead of time. Trying to use the cellular phone service in this remote location, my phone tried in vain to connect to the music service. I even tried to go outside, hoping that by leaving the metal building that I might get better service. I eventually connected, but couldn't get the music to play. After a few minutes, I gave up, went back inside, and told Lisa that I couldn't get the music experiment to work after all.

The building returned to a heavy silence. About a dozen people were scattered around the dark room. Everyone had electronic equipment with them, including recorders and a variety of devices to monitor temperature changes and changes in the room's electromagnetic fields. Whether or not, those devices can actually seek out spirits remains a matter of debate, but many feel that they can at least keep track of any changes in magnetic energy that occurs in a room. In all honesty, I've always been a little skeptical about whether or not those devices can do what so many people claim – but I can promise you, *something* happened that night.

As we were standing there in the darkness, there was suddenly the sound of music that filled the air. Keys began to tinkle on a piano, followed by a soft rhythm guitar, and then came the sound of one of the most beautiful voices ever recorded – it was Patsy Cline singing her gigantic hit, *Crazy.* Somehow, my phone had finally decided to connect to the music service and started to play from the pocket of my jeans.

But this wasn't the weird part.

As soon as that voice echoed out in the building, *every* single electronic device that had been set up in the room suddenly lit up at the same time. Every. Single. Device. Red, yellow, green, and blue lights began flickering and flashing. White motion sensor warning lights began to blink. It all happened at the same time, as soon as that classic country song began to play. The strange reaction continued for the next two minutes, forty seconds – the length of the song – and then they all went dark again. And I know what you might be thinking. My phone didn't set off the devices. I wasn't anywhere near them. I was standing at least 25 feet from the closest monitor, by myself on the east side of the long room. Whatever happened that night, I'll never stop believing that it was the music that made it happen.

Maybe for one brief moment, the Great River Road Opry became the place that the spirits remembered one last time.

In recent years, the opry building, long closed and abandoned, has been partially demolished. Over time, it will be removed altogether and erased from the landscape, but not from our memory. It will always be one of my favorite spots. I just hope that whatever ghosts remained there will finally find some peace once the place they loved so much is gone for good.

5. SCHOOL SPIRITS
Haunted Schools and Colleges of Central Illinois

There are few spirits in Central Illinois that have achieved the notoriety of the ghost who haunts the women's dormitory known as Pemberton Hall at Eastern Illinois University in Charleston. The building has a long and rich history, filled with tradition, and tales of a lingering ghost.

Who is this phantom? Is she, as some believe, the spirit of a dorm director whose life ended in an insane asylum? Or is she a slain student, whose murder was never documented, and who has never left the dorm where she once lived? Or have the legends of Pemberton Hall so overshadowed the true haunting of the building that the spirit's identity will remain forever unknown?

Pemberton Hall at Eastern Illinois University was the first college building in Illinois to provide housing for young women on campus. In 1901, the university's president, Livingston C. Lord, went before the Illinois State Appropriations Committee and asked for $60,000 to build a women's dormitory for the school. The committee promptly denied the funding. However, one senator, Stanton C. Pemberton, took the idea seriously and began to lobby on behalf of the idea. Finally, in 1907, Lord and Pemberton prevailed and obtained the money for construction. On January 4, 1909, the completed hall, named for Senator Pemberton, was officially opened. It houses up to 100 women and Miss Estelle Gross became the first headmistress. She only served in that position for one year before being succeeded by the most infamous name in the building's history, Mary Elizabeth Hawkins.

Mary Hawkins was born in Moat, a small town in Northern England, almost on the border with Scotland. She came to America in 1901 at the age of 24. Not much is known about her life in the United States, until 1910, when she assumed the position of dorm director at Pemberton Hall. She was not a beloved figure by the young women under her charge. She once wrote, "As head of Pemberton Hall, they are under my control entirely." She imposed strict rules on the residents, which included a 7:30 p.m. curfew and a 10:30 p.m. bedtime. Class and church services were the only places that the women were allowed to go unchaperoned. However, they were free to go home on weekends and allowed to entertain guests on Saturday and Sunday evenings until 10:00 p.m.

Mary continued to serve the school for the next several years, but in early 1917, her mental health began to deteriorate. She left her position at Pemberton Hall in March of that year and as her condition worsened, she spent two weeks at the M.A. Montgomery Memorial Sanitarium in Charleston in September 1918. According to doctors, she was "depressed and irrational," accompanied by hallucinations, insomnia, and memory loss. They believed that she was suffering from "overwork and over worry." She died on the night of October 29, 1918, at the Kankakee State Mental Hospital. Hospital orderlies discovered her body the next morning. Mary's death certificate listed the cause of death as "general paralysis of the insane." She was buried in Charleston's Mound Cemetery and two years after her death, the university hung a bronze tablet that commemorated her service to the school.

Life at Pemberton Hall continued on without Mary Hawkins. As time passed, it's likely that she would have largely been forgotten, barely remembered as a name on a memorial plaque that still hangs near the entrance. But, at some point, the story of Mary Hawkins became part of the legend of Pemberton Hall. It's unknown today

Pemberton Hall on the Eastern Illinois University campus

how folklore and history merged to create the tale of the residence hall's ghost, but she has been a very real part of the fabric of the place.

For nearly a century, the ghost of Mary Hawkins has haunted Pemberton Hall. Or has she? That seems to be one of the many problems with the story, which has been told and re-told so many times, in so many different ways, that some versions of the tale can't decide if the spectral Mary is a young woman who knocks on doors, hides objects, or wanders up and down the fourth floor halls dressed in a gown, or a benevolent housemother who makes sure the doors are locked at night and the girls are all tucked into bed. Or, as I suggested in some of my earlier books, that there are two ghosts in the building – one of a young woman who died and the other of Mary Hawkins, who returned from the other side to watch over the girls at Pemberton Hall as she did in life.

The ghost's first appearance in print was in October 1976. Karen Knupp explained that the strange events in Pemberton Hall had been going on for "years and years" and the stories had been passed along to incoming freshmen every fall.

There are many (and by that, I mean dozens) of variations of rhe story of how Mary Hawkins's ghost ended up haunting Pemberton Hall, but here's one that I have recounted in the past:

As with every chilling tale, it began with a series of terrifying events. In this case, they took place on a cold winter's night in 1918. It was bitterly cold that night and one of the residents of Pemberton Hall went upstairs to the music room on fourth floor of the building to play the piano. It was very late, but the young woman had been unable to sleep. She hoped that some soft music might ease her mind and help her to relax.

The story goes that a janitor who worked on campus somehow managed to gain access to the women's hall that night. He may have been watching the young women there for some time and may have even slipped into the building on previous occasions. It isn't hard to imagine a deviant sneaking into the rooms, perhaps watching the girls sleep and perhaps imagining the events that would later come. Regardless of what he may have done in the past, on this night, he found one of the girls isolated and alone in the upstairs music room. She was far away from the other girls and with the wind howling outside, no one would hear her scream.

The janitor cautiously made his way through the dark building to the upper floor. As he entered the music room, he found his victim with her back turned to the open doorway, lost in her thoughts and in the simple melody that she played on the piano. Before she realized what was happening, the man was upon her. He grabbed her savagely and beat her with his fists. Then, tearing and pulling, he tore away her nightgown and attacked her, raping her, and leaving her for dead. Soon after, he made his escape and vanished into the cold winter's night.

The young woman, however, was not dead. She managed to drag herself to the stairs, leaving a bloody trail in her wake, and crawled down the steps. Dragging her bloodied body along the hallway, she feebly scratched at the doors, trying to awaken someone to help her. Finally, she made it to the door of the dorm director and managed to rouse her from her sleep. When the director came to the door, she found the young woman in a pool of blood, her body bruised, torn and now lifeless.

As the years passed, residents of Pemberton Hall heard and saw this horrific event from the past, repeating itself in the building. They heard the dragging sounds near the stairs to the upper floor, and the sounds of scratching on doors and walls. Even more disconcerting were the bloody footprints that would appear in the corridor, only to vanish moments later. They believed that the ghost of the murdered young woman returned to haunt Pemberton Hall. But if she did return, as the stories claimed, she did not walk the building alone.

The director who discovered the murdered girl was Mary Hawkins. She never recovered from the shock of the night and the murder had a devastating effect on Mary's life. She became haunted by the death of the young woman and students spoke of seeing her pacing the hallways at all hours of the night, unable to sleep, and tormented by horrible visions and guilt. Finally, unable to cope with her depression, and the nightmares that accompanied it, Mary was institutionalized and later committed suicide.

Shortly after her death, the residents of Pemberton Hall started to report some strange occurrences in the building – spooky events that continue to this day. They believed the incidents could be explained as the ghost of Mary Hawkins, still making her rounds and checking in on the young women who lived in the building. Perhaps her spirit was unable to rest after losing one of the women in her care and she roamed the hall after death, watching out for them, and protecting them from harm. The spirit would glide through the rooms, lock and unlock doors, turn off radios and lights, and generally keep track of the things that went on in the hall.

By the 1990s, events were taking place at Pemberton Hall that convinced even the most skeptical of residents that the place was truly haunted. On many occasions, there were first-hand reports of late-night door knocking and inexplicable sounds in the halls. When doors were opened to see who might be there, the corridor was always found to be empty. On other occasions, residents claimed to find clothing had been removed from their locked rooms at night and then had been thrown haphazardly up and down the halls.

For years, that was the story that I told about Mary Hawkins and the ghost of Pemberton Hall. My initial interest in the story had introduced me to Amy Van Lear, a resident of the hall in the middle 1990s. Through Amy, I met several dozen other Pemberton residents who all had their stories of the ghost to tell. They were experiencing very real paranormal events in the building – even if many of the details of the legend turned out not to be true.

For one thing, there is no record of any murder taking place in Pemberton Hall. Because Mary left the school in 1917, most of the legends have the story taking place around that time. It was never reported in the newspaper, the stories say, because the college wanted to cover up the story, but in truth, rationing during World War I forced the newspaper to only publish occasional issues.

The details of the incident, including how and why the girl was killed, where the murder happened, and even who killed her, have changed many times over the years. Some stories are unable to decide if Mary Hawkins was murdered, or one of the students was. It was suggested that the homicidal janitor's wife had recently died and his grief caused him to commit the murder. Some say that Mary had been having an affair with a married professor and that she was killed to cover up the adultery. One writer claimed that Mary was murdered by her brother, John Hawkins, a man who actually did kill his sister in Coles County in 1917. However, Mary had no relatives living in this country. She also, as historical record tells us, died in an insane asylum in October 1918. She was not murdered, nor did she commit suicide.

If there was no one murdered in the building, and Mary Hawkins did not commit suicide because of her grief over the death of one of the students in her care, then who haunts Pemberton Hall? The legends may not have much truth to them, but former and current residents of the building can assure you that supernatural events have happened – and continue to happen – in the building.

The legends have been passed along for "years and years," but when did they actually begin? The ghost stories may have first appeared in print in 1976, but I have been able to collect interviews with former residents that date back to the fall of 1952. According to a woman who lived in the dorm at that time, girls were being awakened at all hours of the night by banging on the doors and knocks that seemed to be coming from inside of the walls. No cause was ever determined for the string of bizarre incidents. Most assumed that it was the resident ghost, trying to make her presence known.

In the 1960s and early 1970s, residents reported hearing the sounds of whispers in the building, especially on the fourth floor, and there were a number of reports of an apparition on the stairway. The figure appeared very briefly and then vanished. In the 1976 account by Karen Knupp, she recalled the problems that the resident advisors had with the furniture in one of the lounges. It seemed that all of the furniture in this room was often found to be overturned or, at the very least, rearranged. It often happened during the overnight hours, but not always. One morning, an RA walked into the room and discovered that all of the furniture had been moved around – chairs were turned backwards, the couch moved out of the corner, a table was blocking the door – and she assumed that someone had been playing a prank on her. She went to get some help to straighten up the room and when she and another resident came back, they found that everything had been restored to order. After that, the RA just always left the room in whatever state she found it and, somehow, it would always be cleaned up again. The students on the floor all denied knowing how this continued to take place.

In 1984, the *Decatur Herald & Review* published an account by Patty O'Neill, who had lived in Pemberton Hall for three years. She had been up very late studying one night in the spring of 1981. She was in one of the lounges and eventually returned to her room to go to bed. Her roommate was already asleep when she came in and rather than slam the door closed to lock it, she decided to just pull it closed and leave it unlocked for the night. This was a common occurrence because the old door was slightly wider than the frame and the only way to secure it was to pull it very hard into place. Besides, the residents all knew one another and no one thought there was anything wrong with leaving doors unlocked at night.

Patty climbed into bed and drifted off to sleep. She had not been sleeping long before she was startled awake. She wasn't sure what had awakened her at first, but then she realized that the room was freezing. She reached out for a blanket, but then stopped suddenly. She saw a woman in a long white nightgown standing at the end of her bed. The woman stood there for a few seconds, and then she turned and walked toward the door. Patty noted in her story, "She opened the door and started to leave and then she turned, with one hand on the door, and looked back at me for several seconds. She then left, closing the door behind her."

And Patty's room was not the only one visited by this nocturnal specter. As the apparition had left the room, she had locked the door behind her. Strangely, a number of other residents, who distinctly remembered leaving their doors open, also found them to be mysteriously locked the next morning. Patty surmised that the spirit had been checking on them and had been worried about their safety. Needless to say, the implication was that it was the ghost of Mary Hawkins.

According to Michelle Mueller in the *Daily Eastern News*, another chilling event occurred in 1984. A resident at Pemberton Hall discovered small, black footprints on the floor of her room. The prints appeared to be from someone who had tip-toed across the room. They led from the door to the closet, and then back out of the room again. Was it a prank? No one knows, but the prints proved to be impossible to remove.

In the 1990s, Pemberton Hall remained an actively haunted place. According to accounts, doors locked and unlocked, furniture moved by itself, and lights and radios behaved erratically. Could this be attributed to an old building, or a ghost? Some of the encounters were just too eerie to dismiss as failing electrical work, or the settling of an aging building. Amy Van Lear, who lived at Pemberton Hall for three years, spoke of her strange encounters and introduced me to a number of other residents who also believed they had encountered the resident ghost.

Amy never came face-to-face with the ghost, but she did have several disconcerting experiences. One recurring incident involved the lights on the fourth floor of the building, where the music room was located. The room itself – where legend has it that the young woman was murdered – was locked for many years and never used. This made it difficult to explain the faint sounds of piano music that were sometimes reported coming from the room. In the middle 1990s, the fourth floor was off-limits to residents and yet many of them reported seeing the windows on that floor open and close and seeing lights turn on and off. There was never a logical explanation for why this occurred. When several of the residents investigated after a night of seeing lights moving about on the floor, they found the door to the music room was locked. Peering in through the glass window in the door, they saw years of dust on the floor – undisturbed. If someone living had been in the room, they would have left footprints behind.

Amy also told me of another incident that occurred after she and a number of other students left a communal shower room. When they closed the door behind them, they were sure that all of the curtains to the individual shower stalls had been closed. When they walked out into the hallway, they heard a loud sound like something large sliding across the floor of the empty room they'd just left. They ran back in to find that all of the shower curtains were now open and a heavy wooden chair had somehow traveled all of the way across the room on its own. It was now sitting directly in front of the room. No one had entered, or left, the room since Amy and the others had walked out.

As the years have passed, the story of Pemberton Hall and its resident ghost lives on at Eastern Illinois University. The jumbled legends of Mary Hawkins and the murdered young student are still told and tales still circulate about the sounds of a piano playing in the fourth floor music room. The question remains as to the identity of the ghost who haunts this building – but there is no question to most students that someone does. The spirit has been here for "years and years" and seems to be content to linger for a few decades more.

"One of the Most Haunted Colleges in the Midwest"
Ghosts of Millikin University

Millikin University in Decatur began on the open prairie west of the city as the dream of a local man who wanted to bring higher education to the masses. James Millikin, for whom the college would be named, founded the college because when he was growing up in rural Pennsylvania, few of his friends had the money to attend

A vintage panoramic photo of Millikin University in the early 1900s

a university. He hoped to change this for the people of Central Illinois, and give them a college that all could afford to attend. He carved out a piece of land that had been used as a training ground for soldiers during the Civil War and started construction on the first building on campus in 1902. A year later, the new university was dedicated and it remains one of the most respected schools in the Midwest today and – without a doubt – one of the most haunted.

James Millikin was born in Clarkstown, Pennsylvania, on August 2, 1827. Growing up, he attended the local school at Ten Mile Creek and was later enrolled at Washington College in Washington, Pennsylvania. During that time, Millikin later spoke of being moved by the struggles of some of the other boys to obtain funds to attend the college. He vowed that, if he ever made his fortune, he would create a school that all classes of people could attend.

Millikin's family wanted him to become a doctor, but he always had a head for business. This, along with a thirst for adventure, drew him to the western states. In 1849, he drove his first flock of sheep across western Pennsylvania, Ohio, and Indiana, where the animals were sold for a healthy profit. The next spring, he drove cattle to Illinois and made even more money. At the age of 22, he started his first business, importing livestock, grazing them on rented land in Illinois, and then selling them at market. He was dubbed the "first Cattle King of the Prairie State."

In 1856, Millikin settled in Decatur. He brought with him a sizable fortune and planned to start a business. At the time, Decatur had a booming economy, thanks to the arrival of the railroads, and Millikin began investing in real estate. He bought several large parcels of land, including one on which he would later build a grand home.

On January 1, 1857, Millikin married Anna M. Aston, a native of Washington, Pennsylvania. She had moved west with her family and her father, a minister and evangelist, had become the pastor of the Cumberland Presbyterian Church in 1855. Anna was a graduate of the Washington Female Seminary and she was teaching school in the community when she met Millikin. The couple remained married for 52 years, until Millikin's death in 1909, but never had children of their own.

Millikin was soon entrenched in local business and politics. He was a close friend of Abraham Lincoln and firmly backed him as a Republican candidate for president in 1860. Millikin also served as a Macon County supervisor for several years, but never ran for office himself. Instead, he decided to open a bank. He knew nothing about banking, but was encouraged to try it after the failure of the Railroad Bank in town. Millikin's bank was soon recognized as both safe and stable and it remained in business for well over a century, before being bought out by a large institution.

The more wealth that he accumulated, the more Millikin donated to charitable causes. During his lifetime, it was estimated that he gave away more than $500,000 of his fortune and a trust fund that he created still benefits the community. Perhaps the greatest gift that he gave to Decatur, though, was Millikin University, which fulfilled his own ambitions from his college days.

In April 1901, Millikin received a charter to begin a new university in Decatur. He was prepared to supply the land and a large portion of the funds needed to start the construction of the school. He only asked that local business leaders and the governing bodies of the Presbyterian Church match his own donation. The new college was to be an offshoot of Lincoln College in Lincoln, Illinois, which was also under the auspices of the church. Millikin believed that this would eliminate much of the paperwork and provide some tax benefits. The money was quickly matched by the city and soon plans for the "Decatur College and Industrial School" were under way.

The arrangement with Lincoln College lasted until 1953 and the tenuous and ill-defined connection with the Presbyterian Church eventually faded away. Millikin always planned to offer an education at the school that would be "secular, but moral" and this lack of adherence to religious teachings gradually ended the association.

The university's first president, Dr. Albert Reynolds Taylor, was hired that same year and he first had temporary offices at the Millikin Bank. In the early years of the college, Dr. Taylor would serve as president, dean, registrar, business manager, teaching chair in philosophy, pedagogy, and education, and often taught several classes each week. His annual salary was $5,000.

In September, Dr. Taylor outlined nine "schools" for the new university, including Engineering, Commerce and Finance, Fine Arts, Domestic Sciences, Horticulture and Landscaping, Economics and Sociology, Pedagogy, Library Training, and Liberal Arts and Sciences. He also traveled east to determine an architectural style for the campus and chose a modified Elizabethan style with rough-faced brown and red brick and terra cotta ornamentation. The buildings would be fitted with bay and circular windows and would have red tile roofs. A brickyard to the west of the campus would provide the materials.

In late September, the Patton & Miller architectural firm from Chicago was hired and they traveled to Decatur to examine the site. The portion of the campus that had once been Oakland Park was quite a bit lower in elevation than the frontage along West Main Street, so the university paid to have the street lowered in accordance with the designer's directions. However, the site of the school itself – which was then a cow pasture -- posed its own problems in that a portion of it was under water. The architects had their work cut out for them.

During the construction of the first university buildings, a spur of railway track was run from the main line of the Wabash line and along William Street to a convenient unloading point at the back of the campus. It was removed when the Women's Hall was built in 1907.

Unfortunately, construction got off to a rocky start. The original work was set to begin in the spring of 1902, with hopes that the college would open in September of that year. Thanks to numerous delays, mostly caused by a shortage of materials and bad construction, the opening had to be put off for an entire year. In fact, when the cornerstone was laid with full Masonic rites in June 1902, the walls had only been built as high as the first floor.

The biggest problem was the lake in the middle of the campus. Not only was it an issue for the construction, but it also meant that the university would have difficulty if there was ever a need for expansion. So, in October 1902, when the Millikin Power House and the Machinery Hall were started, the lake was drained through a nearby park. The grounds were now empty, save for a small stream. Then in 1911, when the gymnasium was erected, the stream was forced underground, although it still remains beneath the campus today.

Millikin University was officially dedicated on the afternoon of June 4, 1903. At just past 3:00 p.m., President Theodore Roosevelt stepped from the rear platform of a Wabash train that had stopped near the southeast edge of the new campus. At the time, Roosevelt was at the height of his popularity and Decatur was near the end of a 65-day, 14,000-mile western trip. He had graciously agreed to speak at the dedication ceremony for the new college. James Millikin, Dr. Taylor, and a number of other prominent Decatur citizens, greeted Roosevelt. He was led directly to a platform and there, he spoke at some length, praising Millikin for his generous gift to the city. Following the speech, the President was taken by carriage to the Wabash station, where he spoke to another large crowd. He left Decatur at 4:35 p.m. and returned to Washington just two days later.

The celebration for the new college continued on into the evening. A picnic and a fireworks display were held at the Decatur Trotting Association Park. The party included a collection of specially designed fireworks pieces that were made in the shape of President Roosevelt, the late President McKinley, and even the new university. Trains crowded with people from other communities flooded into the city for the event.

On September 15, 1903, the school opened with the Assembly Hall decked out in the blue and white colors of Stephen Decatur's naval flagship during the Barbary Wars. They were to become the chosen colors for the new college. Despite a current of enthusiasm at the university, James Millikin himself was very nervous. He remarked that he hoped enrollment at the school might reach 500 in a few years. He even suggested that it might be wise to close off the Engineering Hall for the first year. He simply did not believe they would need the space.

Millikin was seated in the rear of the faculty box during the opening exercises and Dr. Taylor, following his address, asked that all of those assembled who expected to enroll to please stand. The sound of applause seemed to shake the building as 562 enrolling students stood up. Millikin faced the audience and bowed, unable to keep from crying. His greatest expectations for the new college had already been fulfilled.

In 1909, James Millikin passed away. Funeral services were held at the college's Assembly Hall and a horse-drawn carriage bore his remains to a temporary vault in Greenwood Cemetery until the Millikin-Aston family tomb could be completed. A long line of solemn students led the procession to the gravesite. Although he virtually created the university, most of the students only knew him as a kind and quiet man, who mingled with the crowd during university events rather than take his place at the podium. And although nearly every one of the mourners could recall speaking personally to the man, James Millikin was never known to speak a public word at his own university.

In the years before Millikin's death, he took a very personal interest in the operations of the university. He and Dr. Taylor worked closely together to establish what they believed to be a suitable curriculum for the school. Neither man took the dominant position and enjoyed a close relationship built on personal regard and a similar philosophical outlook. Both men had initial misgivings about organized sports and Greek letter organizations on campus but both were allowed to flourish by 1905. Later, literary groups, glee clubs, and other activities became popular on campus.

But there was trouble coming in the years ahead and with Dr. Taylor's retirement in 1913, the "era of good feeling" at Millikin was over. The seeds of discord were first sown at the time of James Millikin's death. Anxiety was felt among members of the faculty when it was learned that his estate would go to serve "educational and charitable" purposes that would be decided by the Board of Trustees, which had been formed in 1901. Most assumed that the university alone would benefit from the will, but they were wrong, causing a number of financial problems to be dealt with by the board.

Soon, financial problems were forgotten in light of the management issues that began to plague the college. Thanks to conflicts with both the boards of Millikin University and Lincoln College, two different university presidents left office rather quickly. This forced Dr. Taylor to step out of retirement to fill in on two separate occasions. In 1924, the college suffered with no president at all. The board dismissed professors William Casey and William Selvage without any sort of warning, prompting a strong reaction from the students. Professor Casey was very popular (and an alumnus of the school) and so students voted to hold a "walkout" in May. Dr. Taylor was called upon to calm the heated tempers on campus and to act as president until a successor could be chosen later that month. Dr. Taylor passed away in August 1929, still serving his beloved school at the end.

The problems with the Presbyterian Church also came to a head at about this same time. Although they donated generously to the college during the endowment campaign of 1925, they soon faded out of the picture. In spite of this, daily chapel services were held in the Assembly Hall (later re-named the Albert Taylor Theater in 1939) until 1970. Attendance at these services was mandatory.

The saving grace for Millikin University came with the increased support of the college's alumni groups. They managed to successfully ease the school through many changes over the years, including the 1924 "student strike" and the declining enrollment of the World War II years.

During the latter period, more changes came to the college. World War II saw a number of barracks added to the campus, which were used to house returning soldiers and their families. Two complexes, dubbed "Trailer City" and "Campus City," were located on the north side of the campus and the barracks lasted until 1962. Just before the end of the war was a period that marked the lowest enrollment in Millikin history with a total student population of only 303 students. Out of that number, only 54 of the students were men.

As time has passed, Millikin University has continued to flourish. With almost each passing day, a new building is completed or some expansion or renovation is begun. In recent times, the college has added housing dorms, new halls, campus apartments, and even a massive sports complex. Its borders continue to grow and spread and one can only wonder where the boundaries of the university will someday end. Not since the early days of the school has the college grown and developed at such a pace.

And that leads many to wonder – with all of the ghosts that are rumored to be haunting the campus, could James Millikin and Dr. Taylor still be around to watch over things and usher Millikin University into the future?

There are many tales of ghosts and hauntings at Millikin University from haunted dorms to university buildings and sorority houses. One such spirit-infested place is said to be the Orville B. Gorin Library, which was built in 1931. The stories of a ghost in this building date back many years, and all of the tales are associated with a small room in the basement of the building. According to accounts, a maintenance worker was killed there by accident and, apparently, his ghost has never left. Strange smells are said to permeate this room without explanation, lights flicker and turn on and off by themselves, and staff members claim they are sometimes overwhelmed by the uncomfortable feeling of another presence in the room with them. Of course, this only happens when they are alone.

They have also reported the sounds of shuffling feet and paper being thrown around. One staff member, who was locking the building one late afternoon to leave for the day, claimed to hear the sound of muffled hammering coming from inside of the room. It was as if someone were trapped inside and desperately wanted out. However, the employee knew that she was in the building alone. Instead of venturing back into the basement, she locked the library door and went home.

The basement room also holds the entrance to an old elevator. It's no longer in use by the living occupants of the building, but the resident ghost sometimes operates it, making it inexplicably move up and down. "I was in the building by myself at 1:00 a.m. and was working upstairs," reported an assistant registrar named Karen Klein in 2003. "I could feel the vibrations of the elevator and I could hear it, and I thought housekeeping was coming up into the museum to vacuum, so I didn't pay much attention to it. But when I left my office, there was no one up there. So then I called to see if they had housekeepers or security going through the building and they didn't. I called the physical plant the next day to see if they'd been there. But no... I'm not a believer in ghosts, but this is an occurrence for which I can find no explanation."

There are also rumors of a woman in black who haunts the Music Building and a poltergeist who disrupts electrical devices and opens and closes doors at Blackburn Hall. Several of the Greek houses on campus also boast resident ghosts, including the Kappa Sigma house, which is allegedly haunted by the ghost of a young man who died there back when it was used as a rooming house. Millikin's Alumni House, which was once a Greek house and prior to that, a private residence, has a ghost named "Louise." She was once a maid for the family who lived in the mansion. The ghost was seen so many times over the years that Millikin students began calling the front foyer of the house "Louise's Lounge," a nickname that stuck.

Perhaps the most famous haunted Greek House at Millikin University is the Delta Delta Delta sorority house, which is located just west of the campus. Literally dozens of residents of the house have had encounters with the resident phantom and the sightings go back through several generations of students. Most of the witnesses, being completely unconnected to each other, have had strikingly eerie stories to tell. Besides seeing the ghost, many of them also spoke of hearing her and feeling her presence. It seems that chilling whispers are sometimes heard in the upper dormers and residents have told stories of walking into patches of extremely cold air, which dissipates moments later.

When they have spotted the ghost, she is normally seen on an upper floor of the house. She is described as a young woman who is faded, or very pale in color. Her clothing appears to be homespun, and "from pioneer days," as one witness described her. Her skin is transparent and she is sometimes hard to see, as if she is a reflection in a pool of murky water. Some have described her as off-white or gray in color. The apparition has been reported for many years, appearing both in the daytime and at night.

Whoever this ghost may be, she likely has no connection to the sorority or the house itself, which was built around 1909. The apparition's homespun clothing seems to suggest that she comes from a much earlier era. Research suggests that she may have been an occupant of the cemetery that was once located on the site where the house now stands. In 1874, a small family graveyard vanished from maps of this part of the city. The John Miller Cemetery was not re-discovered until 1909, when construction was being done on the home that eventually became the sorority house. The 13 bodies found in the burial plot were moved to another cemetery and it's possible that the disturbance of this woman's grave may have caused her ghost to remain behind in the building.

Another haunted site is the university's old gymnasium, which was added to the campus in 1911. Prior to its construction, there had only been a small gymnasium located beneath the Assembly Hall in the Schilling Building. There was a small basketball court that was set up on the upper floor of the Mueller Building, but it was strictly for general exercise and not for organized play. Regulations of the university stated that female students were not allowed to cross the campus dressed in gym clothing.

When construction was started on the gym, the designers still had to contend with some of the problems of the past. One major issue was the small stream that still ran across the back part of the campus. The students had dubbed it the "River Sticks" and it was all that remained of the lake that had been drained. The creek, fed by a natural spring, was forced underground so that the gym could be completed.

The gymnasium was used for many years, even serving as the location of Illinois State High School Association championship basketball games, but was eventually replaced by the Griswold Physical Education Center. Today, only a weight room and a dance studio are left to remind us that the building was once the sports center for the college. Since the departure of most sports activities, the upstairs portion of the gym, with its high ceilings and elevated running track, has been abandoned. It has been used by the theater department for many years as an area for both prop storage and as space to build sets for upcoming performances. It is in this part of the building where ghostly sounds from the past echo into the present.

Countless students claim to have had strange encounters in the building and most of these encounters seem to be echoes of events from the past being heard in the present day. These events, strangely enough, are repeating in the form of sounds. Visitors, staff members, and students who come to the upstairs portion of the building tell of hearing voices, laughter, cheers, applause, whistles blowing, and even the sound of a basketball bouncing across the floor when no one else is present.

In 1994, a former Millikin security guard heard the sound someone running around the gym's third floor running track. The gymnasium was completely dark and this was during the holiday season, when most of the campus was deserted and all of the buildings were supposed to be locked. He climbed the stairs to see who was running in the dark and looked around with his flashlight. He quickly discovered that no one was there and, in addition, realized that the track was completely blocked with stored props and set pieces. There was no way that anyone could be running around the track, and yet, he distinctly heard the sound of the running feet. Unnerved, he scrambled for the lights and flipped them on and the sound abruptly stopped. A search of the building revealed that no living person was present. The security guard never returned to the old gym by himself during the rest of his tenure at Millikin University.

These strange events have continued to occur at the old gym over the years, and many believe that the building acts like a battery, storing up sounds from the past that have somehow been imprinted on the atmosphere of the place. Today, they repeat themselves over and over again, just like a recording would, offering a glimpse of sights and sounds from yesterday.

As mentioned in a previous chapter, it seems that "every good theater has a ghost," and the Albert Taylor Theater on Millikin's campus is no exception. The "Rail Girl," as she has come to be known, takes her name from the fact that she normally appears along a rail in the upper part of the theater. However, she often makes her presence known in other ways – and nearly every Millikin theater student can recount at least one story about the spirit's handiwork or the problems she has caused in the theater during one show or another.

The theater was originally the school's auditorium and it can be found inside of Schilling Hall, the main building on the Millikin campus. The former Assembly Hall was the place where men like Dr. Albert Reynolds Taylor, James Millikin, and others met and addressed both the students and the people of Decatur from the stage. When the theater was originally built, a private seating box was designed for Mr. and Mrs. Millikin on the east side of the auditorium and another was reserved for the college's president on the west side. The boxes were eventually removed during renovations in 1952-53. The hall was named for Dr. Taylor in 1939.

No one knows for sure when the story of the ghost who haunts this theater got started, but it seems to have been around for a number of years. Almost every theater student on campus has heard of the "Rail Girl" or has a first or second-hand story about something that she has done. Many Millikin theater alumni also have stories to tell.

The legend states that the little girl who haunts the place will do anything to get the attention of the actors and stage crew. The most famous tradition of the theater is the long-standing ritual of leaving three pieces of candy for the ghost prior to any performance. This is said to insure the approval of the ghost and to make certain that she does nothing to ruin the show. In the past, those who have scoffed at the tradition have suffered for it with botched performances, lighting problems, sound equipment failures, rigging and prop damage, and even actual injuries. Anything that could possibly disrupt the show can and does happen under these circumstances.

A theater student who attended the university in the early 1990s claimed that she expressed her disbelief in the ghost and suffered a fall down a flight of stairs that caused her to miss a performance. She later swore that small hands had grabbed her ankles and tripped her – even though no one was on the stairs with her. She became a believer in the "Rail Girl" after that.

Nate Claus, a theater student during the 2000-2001 school year, was an assistant stage manager for a show and told of a director who refused to let anyone leave the candy for the ghost because she didn't believe in her. During a rehearsal, a fog machine that was being used for the play somehow switched itself on and began filling the auditorium with artificial fog. Nate swore that he had just checked the machine a few minutes earlier and it had been turned off. To make matters worse, when Nate was told about the problem, he ran down the stairs and fell, scraping his wrist against the wall. It later became badly infected. "After that night, I brought an entire bag of candy to the ghost every night," he said. "My shows in there have been running smoothly ever since."

One evening, a group of actors was on the stage during a performance and the "Rail Girl" decided to wreak havoc with some of the props. One of the props was an old rotary dial telephone that was placed on a table near the center of the stage. During a particular scene, one of the actors was supposed to go to the telephone, lift the receiver, and then make a call, during which he was supposed to be addressing another character to his right. He would then hang up the phone, turn around, say his lines and then pick up the receiver again. Everything with the scene went fine until the actor turned around to pick up the telephone for the second time. He reached for it, but grabbed nothing but air – the telephone had somehow vanished. Luckily, he was able to adlib his lines and after a moment of two or fumbling around, the show continued with the audience completely unaware of what had happened. After the performance was over, the actor told his friends and fellow actors what had occurred. Several of them scoffed at his report. One of them had been on stage at the time and while he had noticed the telephone was gone, had seen nothing out of the ordinary take place. Trying to convince them of what had happened, the actor led them back onto the stage and amazingly, the telephone was right back where it was supposed to be. When questioned, the props people claimed to have no knowledge of its odd disappearance.

While something strange seems to be going on at the Albert Taylor Theater, the question remains as to whether or not the "Rail Girl" is real. Many have suggested that she is merely a figment of the imagination, a clever legend that was invented by the theater students to explain away their own superstitions. Perhaps this is the case, but then again, perhaps not.

In 1998, I met a former Millikin theater student who came to believe that the "Rail Girl" was quite real. She told me of a night when she was in the theater alone and rehearsing for an upcoming show. It was very late when the back door of the theater swung open and a little girl stuck her head into the auditorium and looked around. She looked to be about eight years old and was wearing a white dress with a pink sash around it. She stood there for a moment and then went back out the door. The student, wondering what a little girl was doing inside of the campus building at such a late hour, went to the door and looked out. She looked in every direction but the corridor was completely empty. Only a few seconds had passed, but the mysterious little girl was nowhere to be found.

In 2000, another student was working in the balcony control room, when, during the middle of a show, she heard a knock at the door. Assuming that it was some sort of emergency, she opened the door and found a small girl in a white, old-fashioned dress standing outside. When she asked, "Can I help you?" the girl answered, "No." She then ran away – and vanished.

So, does ghost of the Albert Taylor Theater really exist? There are many who are skeptical, but there are a number of Millikin theater students, both past and present, who can say, with certain conviction, that this particular phantom is more real than most of us would care to imagine.

Aston Hall is the oldest building on campus devoted to women's housing. It was originally called simply the "Women's Hall" and that name was later changed in honor of Reverend Samuel Aston, the father of the wife of James Millikin, Anna Aston Millikin. The hall was completed in September 1907, but is barely recognizable from older photographs as two separate additions have been built onto the structure in a line running south. Before the hall opened, Mrs. Millikin presented Dr. Albert Taylor with a list of suggested rules for female behavior in the hall, based on her own collegiate experiences years before. Dr. Taylor had to gently remind her that practices from her seminary days were a bit outdated for a university in the modern 1900s.

The Women's Hall was a greatly admired piece of architecture on the Millikin campus and it was described in an excerpt from a 1908 yearbook as: "The Women's Hall is five stories high, including the basement and the attic floors. The basement accommodates the splendid dining room, the kitchen, storage, and other necessary adjuncts. The first floor provides the handsome parlors and Dean's rooms and eight student's rooms. The second and third floors have a dozen student's rooms each. The attic floor has eight rooms for students and the necessary help. At the opposite ends of each corridor on the three main floors is a cozy alcove with a writing table and accessories.... the living room is tastefully furnished; the mantle being especially worthy of mention because of its simplicity and neatness."

Originally, the Women's Hall was also the location of the university dining hall, where lunch cost the students seven cents. While much of the aspects of the past, like seven-cent lunches and maid services, have vanished from Aston, one thing about the old hall remains the same— the resident ghost.

This building boasts the oldest reported spirit on the Millikin campus. The stories of this phantom have been around for a long time and rumor has it that the third floor of the hall was actually closed down for a time in 1937 because of frequent sightings of the ghost.

The ghost of Aston Hall is believed to be that of a young Mattoon woman named Bernice Richardson, who committed suicide in her third-floor dorm room on Tuesday, February 1, 1937. Prior to this, Bernice had been a happy young woman and was regarded as one of the most popular girls in Aston Hall. She had come to Millikin in the fall of 1936, excited and perhaps overwhelmed by the idea of college life. At first, she excelled in her classes but as the distraction of parties, campus activities, and life on her own began to catch up with her, her grades began to suffer and by the second semester, she was doing poorly in several courses. She became depressed and on one occasion, even joked with her roommate, Marian Schebits, that she would take poison if her grades didn't improve.

On February 1, however, Bernice got some good news. She had received a bid from one of the sororities on campus and was invited to attend a rushing party that weekend. Her roommate later reported that she was in good spirits when she left the dorm room to attend a meeting with Dr. Fenner about some of her classes. At the meeting, Bernice learned that her grades had not improved and, in fact, had gotten worse. She was now failing two of her courses, which would prevent her from attending the sorority party to which she had been invited. This was apparently more than Bernice could stand and she was in a horrible state when she returned to Aston Hall.

At a few minutes after 11:00 a.m., Bernice drank a bottle of carbolic acid and lapsed into unconsciousness. At 11:45 a.m., two friends, Eva Spelbring and Phyllis Foeser, knocked on the door of her room and when there was no answer, opened the door, and went inside. They found Bernice sprawled out on the floor and when they were unable to wake her, feared that she might have suffered from heart failure. The bottle of poison had rolled under her bed and was not found until later. However, Eva and Phyllis did find a note card on Bernice's desk and a pencil was clutched in her hand. The coroner's inquest later determined that she probably intended to write a message but either changed her mind, or was unable to do so because of the poison. The girls summoned a doctor as soon as they discovered Bernice's body, but by the time he arrived, he stated that she was beyond medical help.

Bernice died a few minutes later – but it's said that she has never left Aston Hall.

Over the years, her solid-looking form has become famous for her journeys through the Aston Hall dorm rooms on the third floor. The accounts say that she often appears out of the wall of one room and crosses the room to the opposite wall. She then vanishes into the wall and enters the next room, passing from one room to the next as if the walls did not even exist. In addition, residents of the third floor also speak of items that move about, disappear, and appear at will. They often hear knocking and rapping sounds coming from inside of the walls. Lights turn on and off, doors open and close, and ghostly footsteps are often heard pacing the halls at night.

Aston Hall remains not only the first, but one of the most haunted, places on the Millikin campus. Bernice's story continues today and students still encounter her on occasion. In the spring of 2008, a young woman told me that she had spotted a flash of a white dress as a girl disappeared around a corner. She looked after her, but whoever it was, she had vanished.

Why does she remain here? Is Bernice hoping to hang onto the college life that she loved so much, or is she trapped here because her life was cut short at such a young age? Or could it be because she still hopes to communicate whatever it was that she planned to write on the card that was found in her room? Was there some message that she wanted to pass on, or was the note meant to be merely the last despondent thoughts of a tragic young woman? Until her ghost decides to speak, it's unlikely that we will ever know.

"Athens of the West"
Hauntings of Illinois College
With Lisa Taylor Horton

There are few colleges in Illinois – I'd even go as far as to say the entire Midwest – than can boast the kind of haunted history that has been connected with Illinois College in Jacksonville. As one of the oldest colleges in the state, it's roots go all of the way back to the very founding of the town and the school has been connected to some of the most important events in Illinois, from the days of the Abolitionist movement, the Underground Railroad, and the Civil War.

Is it any wonder that it's home to so many ghosts?

It was education that provided the foundation for the city of Jacksonville. The frontier town was not even five years old when it gained its first institution and arguably, it's greatest one. Illinois College was founded in 1829 by Reverend John M. Ellis, a Presbyterian minister who felt a "seminary of learning" was needed in the new rugged state of Illinois. His plans came to the attention of a group of students at Yale University in New England and seven of them – the fabled "Yale Band" – came west to help establish the college. It became one of the first institutes of higher learning in Illinois, and it became nationally known in the years prior to the Civil War. Illinois College was one of only two colleges to be marked in "Mitchell's Geography" in 1839. Harvard University was the other.

Even the first graduates of Illinois College made a mark in history. The first two men to graduate were Richard Yates, who became the Civil War governor of Illinois and later a U.S. Senator, and Jonathan Edward Spilman, the man who composed the now-familiar music to Robert Burns' immortal poem, "Flow Gently, Sweet Afton." Both men received their baccalaureate degree from Illinois College in 1835.

Nine students met for the first class at Illinois College on January 4, 1830. Julian Sturtevant, the school's first instructor and the second president, reported, "We had come there that morning to open a fountain for future generations to drink at." Shortly after, Edward Beecher left the Park Street Church in Boston to serve the new college as its first president. He created a strong college and retained close intellectual ties with New England. His brother, Henry Ward Beecher, preached and lectured at Illinois College, and his sister, Harriet Beecher Stowe, who wrote the controversial book *Uncle Tom's Cabin*, was an occasional visitor. Another brother, Thomas, graduated from Illinois College in 1843. Ralph Waldo Emerson, Mark Twain, Horace Greeley, and Wendell Phillips were among the college's visitors and lecturers in the early years.

In 1843 and 1845, two of the college's seven literary societies were formed. Possibly unique in the Midwest today, these societies have continued in their roles as centers for debate and criticism. Abraham Lincoln was one of many speakers appearing on the campus under the sponsorship of a literary society.

In the years leading up to the Civil War, Illinois College became heavily involved with America's abolitionist movement. Thanks to the family of President Beecher, it seems nearly impossible for the college to have avoided the entanglement. Illinois College is still widely regarded as having been a station on the Underground Railroad, and rumors abound that slaves were hidden at the Smith and Fayerweather houses on campus, as well as at Beecher Hall. Over time, the school gained a reputation as an "abolitionist college" and its name was spoken with contempt by pro-slavery activists. And the students were often just as involved as Edward Beecher was in protesting against slavery. Many of them lost the respect of their families. An irate southern father once complained that the college was turning his son into an "abolitionist pup" and disowned him. Other students even ran into trouble with the law.

But the leaders of Illinois College were torn between a cause they believed in and getting the young college mired in a heated political debate. Julian Sturtevant, the college's second president, hated slavery but never enough to satisfy the die-hard abolitionists. He once wrote, "I went too far against slavery to win the favor of its advocates, and not far enough to gain the approbation of its assailants."

In 1837, Professor Sturtevant counseled Elijah Lovejoy, the abolitionist editor from Alton, against purchasing another printing press after a mob had destroyed his previous ones. He said that it would result in disaster. Lovejoy was killed just a few days later, trying to prevent a mob from destroying his new press. Edward Beecher, who was president at the time, was with Lovejoy on the night before he was killed. He had just reluctantly agreed to chair an anti-slavery convention, still worrying about the effect on the school. He needn't have worried. Lovejoy's murder further inflamed the passions of the students and professors at Illinois College, leading to its first brush with the slavery laws of the era.

A year later, when armed Jacksonville men kidnapped a slave, Bob Logan, and placed him on a steamboat heading south, the protests increased. Logan had claimed his freedom four years earlier after his master brought him to Illinois. Logan's sister, Emily, managed to escape and successfully sued for her freedom in Sangamon County court in 1840. The leader of the kidnappers, who were relatives of the people who hid the Logans, was acquitted at trial, further angering the anti-slavery protesters at Illinois College.

In 1843, a student named Samuel Willard was arrested for harboring a fugitive slave and attempting to escort her to freedom. He and his father, Julius, learned of the young woman's plight when a former slave the Willards helped free came to their door one night and begged them to help the other woman, Judy Green. She was owned by a Louisiana woman who was visiting friends in Illinois. The laws weren't clear at that time about the status of slaves when they were brought into free states. Abolitionists said they were free the moment they stepped into places like Illinois, but pro-slavery advocates, obviously, disagreed.

Julius Willard took the slave and headed to Greenfield, where friends would then escort Miss Green to safety. But a group of armed men, organized by the family of the slave's owner, began searching for her. They began raiding homes in the black section of the town until someone informed on the Willards.

Both of the Willards were arrested and thrown in jail, and they later took their case to the Illinois Supreme Court, where they lost. Julius Willard was fined $20, plus court costs, and Samuel was fined $1. Unfortunately, Judy Green was later captured and returned to Louisiana.

The actions of the Willards and the court case, though, served as a call to arms for the anti-slavery proponents. However, it also raised the anger of a lot of Jacksonville people who wanted the college and other anti-slavery activists to stay out of the south's business. At worst, there was talk of tarring and feathering the Willards as retribution. There were 36 citizens that signed a petition condemning the fact that a visitor to Jacksonville had had her "property" taken away from her. These 36 citizens were members of the newly-formed Anti-Negro Stealing Society, and they wrote in their petition, "An outrage has been committed upon the property of a widow lady visiting our town." But the pro-slavery outbursts were short-lived – and there's no record that the Anti-Negro Stealing Society ever held another meeting.

Beecher Hall at Illinois College

Nervous members of the Illinois College Board of Trustees toyed with the idea of expelling Samuel Willard, who was a senior that year. However, every faculty member came to the young man's support and he was allowed to stay. He graduated from the Illinois Medical College in 1848 and later became a surgeon during the Civil War. After being seriously wounded in the fighting, he retired from medicine and became the superintendent of schools in Springfield and later taught in Chicago. He died in 1913 at the age of 91.

In the years following the Civil War, graduates contributed with distinction to the national scene. Among these was William Jennings Bryan, who, within 15 years after graduating, was the Democratic candidate for the U.S. presidency in the race with William McKinley. He continued with a prominent role in politics even after being defeated in the election.

Illinois College, continuing its founders' progressive way of thinking, began accepting women in 1903. There have been many prominent graduates of the school over the years, both men and women, and it has maintained an outstanding program of scholarship.

Hauntings at Illinois College

The long history of Illinois College includes its connections to the supernatural. Like many other historic spots in Illinois, the events of the past have certainly left their mark on the college. These events come back to "haunt" students and faculty members today, and there are many who have encountered the ghosts of yesterday face to face.

One place where strange events have been reported is in Beecher Hall, which was built in 1829. This two-level building is now used as a meeting hall for two of the school's literary societies, Sigma Pi and Phi Alpha. The Sigs meet on the upper floor and the Phis meet in the lower part of the building. The majority of the encounters here seem to involve the groups who frequent the upper floor. The most commonly reported events are ghostly footsteps that can be distinctly heard in one room, always coming from another. If a curious witness follows the sound, the footsteps will suddenly be heard in the other room instead.

In 1843, Illinois College opened its very own medical school. For the next 5 years, Beecher Hall would house a very important, yet secretive space for the students of the Medical Department. It was in the attic where cadavers were stored and dissected in the name of science. Some believe that this may explain the ghostly activity. Campus legend has it that the students and faculty repeatedly denied the existence of the bodies that were secreted away in the building. Blinded by their dedication to acquiring and practicing new medical knowledge, they stole corpses from local hospitals and cemeteries, and introduced the practice of "body snatching" to Illinois College. In 1844, a mob of enraged townspeople formed outside of Beecher accusing the group of stealing the corpse of Governor Joseph Duncan! Of course, this claim was denied like all the rest, but this pioneer medical institution was closed with few explanations given in 1848.

Other legends claim that the ghost who haunts the building is that of Williams Jennings Bryan, who has returned to his old school. He was a member of Sigma Pi and was often in the building during his years at Illinois College. There are others who say that it might be Abraham Lincoln's ghost instead. He was an honorary Phi Alpha and while he did not attend the school, he spoke at Beecher Hall on occasion. In addition, William Berry (Lincoln's partner at new Salem), William H. Herndon (his law partner), and Ann Rutledge's brother, David, all attended Illinois College.

Another allegedly haunted spot on campus is the David A. Smith House, built in 1854. Today, the structure is home to three of the women's literary societies, the Gamma Deltas, the Chi Betas and Sigma Phi Epsilon. There is a parlor for all to enjoy, but in addition, the Delts use a room on the main floor while the Betas and the Sig Phips have rooms on the second floor. The attic is used by all of the groups, and there is also a dining room, a kitchen, and an apartment at the back of the house.

There are several versions of the historic legend concerning the ghost in this house, but all of them claim that she is the daughter of the original owner and that her name was Effie Smith. The story goes that Effie was being courted by a young man from town and they became engaged. When he proposed to her, he gave her a diamond ring and she was said to have scratched the stone against her bedroom window to see if it was real. When she realized that it was, she etched her signature into the glass where it remained for many years afterward. The window has recently been removed and this small and unusual piece of history has been lost.

Then, the story begins to take different paths. In one version, David Smith disapproved of his daughter's fiancée. Fearful of her father's wrath, the young man hid himself in a small room that was only accessible from the attic. For some reason, he nailed himself in and later died there. According to students who have been in the attic, the nails are still visible there today on the inside of the door. It is said that when Effie learned of her lover's cruel fate, she threw herself from an upstairs window and died in the fall.

In the second version of the story, Effie's young man went off to fight in the Civil War. Every day, Effie climbed up to the attic and sat in a rocking chair by the window, watching for him to return. When she learned that he had been killed in battle, she committed suicide by jumping out of the attic window. Yet another variation of the legend has Effie being jilted by her lover, at which point she committed suicide. Regardless of what happened, the story claims that she has since returned to haunt the house.

A rocking chair believed to be Effie's is still in the attic and the stories say that if you move it away from the window (where it sits facing out), then leave the attic and return later, the chair will have returned to its original position. This window is located in a storage area for the Chi Beta society and every year, they test the chair and discover that the story is true – or so the story goes. One young woman walked into the room one day and the door suddenly slammed closed behind her. It is also not uncommon for cold air to suddenly fill this room, even though for years, the windows were painted shut. It was said that an icy cold wind would often come from the window that had Effie's name etched on the glass.

The history of this long-told legend was further unfolded in 2014 when a freshman at Illinois College was assigned a project involving the use of the extensive archives on campus. She decided to learn more about Miss Smith and was shocked to find out that she most certainly did not die after hurling herself out of her window. She discovered that Effie lived out her life in Southern Illinois until her death in 1907.

If the troubled spirit in Smith House was not the lingering energy of Effie Smith, then who could it be? Thanks to this student's efforts in uncovering Effie's life story, she discovered that Effie had a sister named Emma. Emma was diagnosed and treated for a "nervous disorder" at the Illinois State Asylum and Hospital for the Insane located in Jacksonville. Under curious circumstances, Emma died in the Smith home in 1887 at the age of 36. While many presumptions could be concocted surrounding Emma's death, few students would deny the frequent evidence of the persistent spirit residing within the familiar walls of the David A. Smith House.

Another reportedly ghostly location is Whipple Hall, which was constructed in 1882. The spectral occupant of this place is known only as the "Gray Ghost." The building, which was once a preparatory school, has been updated and renovated many times over the years. The upper part once served as the meeting hall for the Alpha Phi Omega society (the Eta Sigma chapter), a national service fraternity, as well as the location of the security office. The lower part housed the meeting hall of the Pi Pi Rho Literary Society. More recently, though, it has been renovated to house Congressman Paul Findley's Congressional Office, and the Communication and Rhetorical Studies department.

Perhaps the most astounding encounter of the Gray Ghost occurred to a girl who was leaving a Pi Pi Rho gathering one night and had to retrieve something from the Alpha Phi Omega hall. She said she had started climbing the curved staircase and as she reached the middle of the curve of the stairs, she looked up to the top landing and saw a man standing there. He was dressed all in gray and she quickly realized that he was not a security officer. As she peered into the shadows, she also realized something else -- he had no face! She began screaming and ran back down the staircase and out of the building. Due to the noise of the festivities, no one heard her screams and the revelers wouldn't learn of the strange experience until later.

Since the renovations to Whipple Hall, the Gray Ghost has been a more frequent disturbance. A professor whose office is located on the upper floor of Whipple has admitted his occasional fear when hearing approaching footsteps outside of his workspace. Every time he has craned his neck to take a hesitant peek, he sees no one. There have been several times office doors have been opened, and later closed, by an unseen entity. This professor, after a few years of "getting the creeps," decided to reach out to the ghost in order to come to an agreement. He explained that the space belonged to the ghost and that he was simply borrowing it for a while. He asked the ghost to respectfully stop being so creepy.

A room that is located on the third floor of Illinois College's Ellis Hall is also rumored to be infested with ghosts. According to reports, no one lives there if they don't absolutely have to. Rumor has it that a girl hanged herself in the room's closet around 1986 after failing to get a bid from a literary society. It is said that doors open and close on their own, appliances and radios turn on and off and that windows have a habit of going up and down under their own power. Or at least that's one version of the story....

Other students and alumni of Illinois College claim that the girl who haunts Room 303 was a young woman named Gail who died of natural causes in the room. Apparently, her parents were aware that she was terminally ill when she went to school, but since attending college had always been her dream, they allowed her to go anyway. She died while living in Ellis Hall and a small plaque was mounted on the door of the room in her memory, but has since been removed. It is said that her ghost is a mischievous one, opening doors and hiding things. Legend has it that if third floor residents lose anything, they will call out to Gail and ask her to return it. The missing item is usually found a short time later.

A former student at the college who lived for two years in Ellis Hall, wrote to tell me of her experiences while living below the "haunted room." She said that she often heard knocking sounds coming from the other side of the wall, even though there was nothing there. It was the outer wall of the building and there were no trees nearby.

Sturtevant Hall

Gail is only one of the deaths that took place on "the Hilltop." Fayerweather House, a residence hall for women, has its fair share of startling occurrences. It has been said that windows and doors open and shut on their own and that lights turn on and off without explanation. Stories say that a girl hanged herself in the house, committing suicide in the closet of Room 5, which is located on the stairway landing between the first and second floors of the house. "Susie," as she has been called, is noisy and can often be heard walking around the house, opening doors in the middle of the night and scratching on walls.

Many legends claimed that the attic of the Fayerweather house was converted into dorm rooms that were never used. The stories claimed that the rooms were closed when too many strange things started to happen to the students who lived there. This was not the case, but the rooms were indeed haunted. Several students that we interviewed told of doors slamming, lights turning on and off, and objects that purportedly moved about on their own.

Another haunted site is Sturtevant Hall, one of the most famous spots on campus. Sturtevant was the third building on the Illinois College campus and is said to be the structure that truly gave the school its identity. Beecher Hall was the first college building on campus (and in the state of Illinois) and while it gave the college its life, it's the top of the main tower at Sturtevant that is pictured in the campus logo, and it gave the school credibility. Beecher Hall had been criticized for being plain and awkward and so President Julian Sturtevant wanted to provide the campus with a "suitable, commodious, elegant building." The Romanesque Revival-style building, prominent in public buildings from about 1840 through 1900, has two asymmetrical towers, one square and one round. It is a grand building and when fundraising slowed, it delayed its completion until 1857. When it opened, it was known simply as "The College Building" but in 1888, two years after President Sturtevant's death, it was named in his honor.

The building came about as the result of a disaster. A four-story dormitory once stood on this site and it was destroyed by fire on December 30, 1852. Apparently, Jacksonville had a new fire engine that winter, but no one knew how to use it and the building was destroyed. President Sturtevant disliked dormitories. He felt that the young men of Illinois College would be better served by boarding with upstanding, local families. So, even though it replaced a four-story dormitory, Sturtevant Hall did not have a single bedroom inside of it. The plans instead called for a chapel, library, lecture rooms, five classrooms, and the college's science rooms.

In 1920, the building caught fire, destroying the roof and most of the interior. The inside was rebuilt, the science labs updated, and the chapel moved to Jones Memorial Hall. In 1965, the building was remodeled and the science labs were moved to the Crispin Science Building. Sturtevant became a building for classes and faculty offices. In 1993, it was renovated again, adding air-conditioning, an elevator, new light fixtures, windows, and restrooms.

At one time, the building housed the Pi Pi Rho Literary Society, and for years, members maintained that the toilets in the place often flushed by themselves. This may have been the first ghostly stories told about Sturtevant Hall, but they would not be the last. Recent stories say that a ghostly young man in a Civil War uniform is sometimes seen here. In addition, it is said to be nearly impossible to find someone who is willing to spend the night in the north tower of the building due to strange noises that haunt the place. For decades, a rite of passage for many of the literary societies on campus was for a new member to attempt to sleep – or at least stay all night – in the tower. Few have ever succeeded.

Crampton Hall, which was built in 1873, is also believed to be home to a ghost. The residence was built to house 69 men, and it was named in honor of Rufus C. Crampton, a former professor and president of the college. According to the story, there was a male student who left a party one night and was later found hanged in his closet. Rumors still state that he was hanged in a way that he could not have done it himself. His former room is believed to be haunted.

And apparently closets in Crampton Hall are as mysterious as the stories that revolve around them. One student told me of three of the residents who were waiting for a fourth friend to get ready so that they could all go somewhere together. Finally, they tired of waiting and went to check on him, only to find that he was hanging upside down in the closet, stark naked, and so frightened that he was almost incoherent. The student had lived in Crampton Hall for one semester -- and would never live there again. One night, he said he fell asleep with his lights on only to be awakened by a noise. When he looked up, he saw a man standing there looking at him. The man quickly turned and vanished into the closet. After the eerie closet incident, he sought out new housing for the rest of his year at Illinois College.

Another resident haunt can be found in the McGaw performing arts building. It has been reported that you will never find anyone who is willing to be alone in the auditorium at night. The place is allegedly haunted by the ghost of a man dressed in clothing from the 1940s. People on the stage are said to glimpse him out of the corners of their eyes. Many who have been seated in the auditorium claim that they have been touched, pinched, and caressed by invisible hands. One student stated that he felt someone pass behind him, even feeling the fabric of their clothing as they passed, but when he looked to see who it was, there was no one there.

Rammelkamp Chapel allegedly has a haunted basement. Some of the students tell stories of classroom doors that open suddenly and then slam shut, sometimes in the middle of lectures. The classrooms are located on both sides of a long hall. By looking out the door, it is possible to see into the classroom across the hall. One day, during a class, a student reportedly became quite upset when she looked across the hall and spotted a woman in white in the adjoining classroom. This would not have been so strange if the woman had not vanished in front of her eyes.

As the years go by, the ghostly tales of Illinois College continue to grow, many of them taking on a new life of their own as they shift and change with the arrival of new students every autumn. What tales will manifest at the college in the years to come?

Pam & the "Blue Lady"
The Burning History & Hauntings of MacMurray College

Lisa and I were standing in the dark one night, just after Halloween, crowded into a dorm room in MacMurray College's Rutledge Hall, waiting for something to happen. It had been an uneventful night so far. For several years, we had been coming to Rutledge Hall to take part in an evening of ghost hunting with some of the students and residence advisors that lived there during the school year. Strange things had happened in years past, but this year had been quiet – until we got to "Pam's" room.

According to Rutledge lore, Pam had been a student at MacMurray in the early 1970s and had passed away in her suite, which contained two sleeping rooms with a bathroom between them. Ever since that time, her ghost was said to haunt the room. Students who had been unlucky enough to end up there had eerie stories to tell of unexplainable sounds, voices, moving objects, and on many occasions, the apparition of Pam herself, walking from one room to the next and disappearing in and out of the bathroom.

On this particular night, we had divided the students into groups and we had taken one group (which included two young women who lived in the room at the time) to Pam's room. They each had weird stories to tell, including many hair-raising incidents that had occurred during the few months that they had been living in the suite that semester. Some of them – like the night one of the young women woke up and saw a woman draped in shadow appear from the doorway to the bathroom – were enough to make them leave the room and stay elsewhere for a night.

While the stories certainly set the stage for something spooky to happen, nothing did – at least at first.

For our night of ghost hunting with the students, we always bring along as many electrical gadgets as possible. Some are worthwhile, some are not, but all are interesting. One such gadget was a device that measured the level of electromagnetic energy in a room (some researchers believe that ghosts can change or manipulate this type of radiation in a location. Can they? Jury's still out on that one) and it also measured the ambient temperature too. Nearly everyone who has an interest in ghosts has read about "cold spots" and it's believed that this is a significant sign that a spirit is present. And while perhaps that's not scientific, researchers have believed this for over 150 years, which seems to give it some credibility.

So, after moving from one room of the suite to the bathroom – and crowding six people into the tiny bathroom where Pam died– and then onto the second bedroom, we all sat down to wait in the dark for that "something" to occur. We placed several gadgets and recording devices around the room, hoping to capture whatever might take place, including the device that measured the electromagnetic fields and the temperature in the room, which, by the way, was a balmy 76 degrees on November 2.

The early days at MacMurray College

We didn't have long to wait. It started off with asking questions to whatever spirit might be present (presumably Pam) and waiting a few seconds to see if a spectral reply might turn up on the recorder when it was played back. We didn't hear anything and all of the devices stayed dark. A couple of additional devices to measure the room's energy had been placed on a nearby table, not far from the device that has already been described. The rather one-sided conversation that we were having with thin air trailed off after a few minutes and we began talking about past ghost hunting nights at Rutledge Hall and some of the odd things that had occurred. Lisa mentioned that after the previous year's outing, strange things also began happening in her home. She blamed them on Pam...

Almost as soon as she mentioned Pam's name, one of the young women present hissed, "Did you hear that?" We hadn't, but she later said that it sounded like a woman crying. But we didn't get a chance to think about it. Almost immediately, the lights on all of the measuring devices flared to life. None of them had been touched. No one passed near them. They hadn't been moved in any way. And yet, not only did all of the lights go on, signaling a sudden change in the room's atmosphere, but the digital temperature read-out on the main device inexplicably dropped almost 20 degrees!

Pam, it seemed, had come to visit.

The story of MacMurray College stretches all of the way back to the days of the Illinois frontier, when any higher education offered for women was extremely hard to find. In those days, nearly all education was promoted by religious groups and so the schools for women that did exist had largely been founded so that ministers and educated laymen could find more suitable wives.

During the 1830s and 1840s, the largest Protestant denomination in the state was the Methodist Church. It had established McKendree College in 1829, as well as several elementary and secondary schools. In keeping with the general theme of educating young women to make better wives, the Illinois Conference of the Methodist Church voted to establish a female academy in Jacksonville on September 23, 1846. The school was to be called the Illinois Conference Female Academy, and on October 10, 1846, the first meeting of its Board of Trustees was held at a nearby Methodist church.

Nine men, all of whom would be regarded for their generosity and organization, made up the new Board. Five of them were clergymen and the other four were laymen. The two men who were best-known among them were Peter Akers, a Methodist minister and the chairman of the education committee of the Illinois Conference who was most responsible for the school's establishment, and Peter Cartwright, the famous Methodist circuit rider and the Board's first president.

At the meeting, the Board instructed its new prudential committee to secure a lot and make plans for constructing a building. The committee found five acres available on East State Street and they purchased it for the bargain price of $500. The Board immediately began raising funds for a building, but their efforts fell far short of their goal. Undeterred, though, they decided to start the school in a rented space. The next plan was to find a president for the school, and after a long and difficult search, they decided on a 29-year-old Methodist minister from Springfield named James F. Jaquess. The school opened on October 1, 1848, and classes were held in the basement of the church with most of the students being housed with Methodist families throughout Jacksonville.

Jaquess served as the school's first president for seven years. Under his leadership, the Academy expanded to a size that was unusual for colleges for women in those days (282 enrollments in 1855 alone) and retained a good faculty despite many financial setbacks. In the opinion of many, he also raised the academic level of the school to equal that of the men's colleges of the time. It was an amazing accomplishment and an uphill battle. In 1851, the academy's name was changed to Illinois Conference Female College to reflect its advanced status. This made it one of only two women's colleges in the western United States.

In the midst of these exciting events, the actual school building was being constructed. The cornerstone had been laid in 1849, and it was finally completed in the winter of 1852. The brick structure was four stories tall, with an observatory on top. Combining Georgian architecture with a classical style that was more common in the southern states, its most striking feature was the four massive Corinthian columns that decorated the front. The building encompassed all functions of the school – classrooms, library, chapel, dining hall, and living space for teachers, students, and the president's family. It soon became recognized as "one of the best college buildings in the west." In 1855, a five-story wing was added to the west side to accommodate dormitory space for an increasing enrollment. The school's reputation was attracting students from all over the region – but that wasn't the only reason for the influx of new students.

The college seemed to be constantly in debt. Money had to be borrowed to complete the building, and fund-raising efforts by various agents had been disappointing from the start. It was at this time that President Jaquess came up with the idea of "perpetual scholarships" to reduce the debt. Scholarships were sold for $100 each, and the holder had the right to keep one person at a time in school, with the scholarship paying the tuition fees. This right could be passed on to an heir, then another, perpetually. Ten-year scholarships were sold for $25. Scholarships were sold to Methodist clergymen for half price, but they were the only ones to receive the discount. The result of the perpetual and ten-year scholarships was a dramatic increase in attendance, thus requiring a new wing to be added on to the original building, but also brought the college to the brink of bankruptcy.

By 1855, the debt was more than $28,000 and by 1857, had increased to $40,000. The perpetual scholarship plan brought in money in the short term, but then it was gone and there was no room for new students or more scholarships to be sold. Things were so bad at times that President Jaquess had to go out and solicit not only funds for the school, but fuel for the furnaces and food for the students. He wrote, "Things are in a desperate condition." By 1855, he had not been paid a full salary in quite some time and when he resigned that same year, he and his wife only received one-third of the salary that was due them.

Unfortunately, Jaquess' administration began a recurring pattern for the college of continued growth and academic excellence, but tough times when it came to finances.

The years before and immediately after the Civil War were dark days for the college – and for most colleges and academies in the north and south. It was a time when men and boys went away to fight the war, emptying nearly every school, and when young women were expected to go and take care of things at home while the men were away. Nearly every college, seminary, and academy for women closed down during the war and the era of Reconstruction.

Dr. Charles Adams was the president of the Illinois Conference Female College during this time and made a heroic effort to keep things running. He would eventually be highly praised for his administration, even though he had to deal with a difficult time in history, and he had also inherited the college's overwhelming debt and all of the problems that accompanied it. Interest charges alone were $4,000 per year and pressure from creditors grew worse with each passing month.

In 1860, the Illinois Conference met in Jacksonville. With the country on the brink of a civil war and the financial future of the college uncertain, the Conference was considering the idea of closing the school and selling off the property to pay its outstanding debts. It turned out to be a simple woman from Carlinville who changed the mind of the Board. Her name was Ann Dumville and she was a poor and uneducated housekeeper who had nevertheless managed to send two of her three daughters to the college. In those days, women did not hold any leadership positions in the Methodist Church. They rarely attended the annual conference and, if they did, they never spoke. However, this woman, described as "saintly" and who "gave what little she had to the church and charity," dared to speak up when it was suggested that the college be closed. Her speech was brief, but wonderfully effective, and it stirred the hearts of everyone in attendance.

This crisis was narrowly averted, with the college still heavily in debt, but a new crisis occurred the following year when a fire destroyed the west wing of the building. The blaze occurred in November 1861, and while no one was hurt, the loss was about $40,000 and, of course, the college had no insurance.

To save the college from bankruptcy, an arrangement was made with the creditors in which certain trustees would purchase the college and all of the assets at a sheriff's sale, and they in turn would assume all of the debt. It was a risky, yet generous move on the part of the school's supporters. Under a new financial agent, Colin D. James, a tremendous fund-raising effort was started and money was contributed by the trustees, ministers of the Illinois Conference, Jacksonville businessmen, and even farmers in the surrounding area. Future college president Dr. W.F. Short sold his horse and buggy and his only cow to meet the payments of his promised contribution. Mrs. Dumville donated her $100 life savings. Peter Cartwright donated the equivalent of four years' salary from the church. The Board (which now had 29 trustees) contributed 90 percent of the funds that were raised.

The subscribers in this great effort became known as the "Founders of 1862" or the "Second Founders." They had literally saved the college from ruin. By October 1862, the Board was able to report to the Illinois Conference that the school was free from debt.

In January 1863, the college was incorporated with a new charter and a new name: Illinois Female College. In addition to being free from debt, the school was also free of all obligation to honor the perpetual scholarships that had raised short time cash, but proved to be a financial hardship for the school. However, at the first meeting of the new Board, a vote was taken to allow for their partial use. This decision reduced the income from tuition for many years (some were used as late as 1910), but the Board felt bound to honor the scholarships purchased in some manner. The Board also voted to begin the task of rebuilding the west wing, which was completed in 1864, three years after the fire.

Life at the college was not one of leisure. Behind the main buildings were the barns, stables, and outhouses. Horses, pigs and cows were kept where Rutledge Hall is located today. The horses were used for recruitment trips to visit prospective students and for plowing the large garden. The garden was used to both feed the students and also to raise money from the sale of produce to the community. During his presidency, Jaquess made soap for the college and President Adams chopped wood for heat and personally hauled it to the various floors of the building using a hand-operated elevator. He also owned a horticulture business on the side and sold a variety of trees.

The students also worked hard, at their studies and household chores. There were strict rules of conduct and a strict daily schedule, rising early in the morning and remaining in continual motion from classroom to study hall to dining room to dorm room for "lights out." They would start over again the following day. The curriculum included science (physical geography, geology, astronomy, physics, chemistry, botany, zoology, and physiology), social science (ancient and modern history, American history, ancient and modern geography, political science and economy), mathematics (geometry, algebra, trigonometry, and conic sections), rhetoric (grammar, composition and literature) and philosophy and religion (ethics, logic, psychology and evidences of Christianity). Latin was required and French, German and Greek were also offered, along with training in harmony, musical composition, piano and voice, art, domestic economy, and gymnastics. This was a true college, not a finishing school that taught sewing and manners to young ladies. Those lucky enough to attend the Illinois Female College received a true education.

The new era that the college enjoyed after the war was shattered by two more fires – and they would not be the last. The first occurred on February 28, 1870, when a blaze destroyed the main building. It was thought that the fire was caused by a defective chimney flue. The building was insured this time, but the contents were not. The undamaged west wing was large enough to house the displaced students and classes had to be moved to nearby buildings. Costs for the new construction wiped out the school's bank accounts and it was forced to borrow again.

A new building replaced the burned one in January 1871. Built on the same foundation, it was three stories tall, with three towers and a mansard roof. Lit by gas and heated by steam, it contained parlors, a chapel, classrooms, offices, dorm rooms, and an apartment for the president and his family. One feature added was the gymnasium in the basement. Best of all, it was built to be fireproof – a claim that it failed to prove when it burned again on November 18, 1872. This time, the fire was thought to have started in the "dust shaft," extending from the basement to the tower, which was constructed to make the removal of refuse from sweeping more convenient. A burning match, or friction caused by a mouse, was blamed for the blaze. The dust shaft acted as a chimney and spread the fire over the entire building.

After three destructive fires, there had to have been some of those involved with the college who wondered if the school was truly meant to be. With three fires in 26 years, plus the prospect of going into debt once again, a mass meeting was called to discuss the future of the school. In spite of the doubts, though, board members and supporters refused to give up. Peter Akers, then 82 years old, was among the leaders insisting that the school had to go on. President William H. DeMotte, still grieving over the death of his wife just a few months before, cheered on the others. He had no intention of closing the college, even temporarily.

Offers of support flooded in, including from Chaddock College in Quincy, which offered the use of its buildings. But once again, the college returned to a nearby church basement and a collection of empty rooms around the neighborhood. Students who could not be placed in the west wing were given rooms in town. Benefit concerts were held to raise funds and donations poured in. The loss of the main building was valued at $40,000. Insurance coverage was for $35,000, but since some of the materials could be re-used, not all of it was needed. The new main building, the third built by the college (called Main Hall by generations of alumni), was constructed using the same plans as the last that burned and was ready for use in December 1873.

Over a period of 25 years between 1868 and 1893, the college was forced to survive on the income that came in from tuition, fees, and board. Various plans to raise an endowment were tried, but the results were poor. And what money was raised was nearly always borrowed back by the school to pay for fire damage, supplies, and various shortfalls. The Board even attempted to speculate in railroad land out west, with the college earning a commission on sales, but there is no record of any profit being made. The college had been free from debt, but the money troubles were far from over. The school continued to struggle for years to come.

Always searching for ways to broaden the appeal of the school. An Academy of Music and Art was founded in 1875, with the right granted by the state legislature to give diplomas for completion of the required course work. The first diplomas were granted in 1879, with the college being the first in the state to do so. From that point on, music and art became increasingly more important to the college and the Academy of Art was judged as an equal to the finest conservatories in the country. The Art Department also drew a large number of students and in 1888, a Department of Elocution was added. The program of lectures and concerts at Strawn's Opera House was another attraction for students. Among the lecturers featured were Ralph Waldo Emerson, Henry Ward Beecher, Susan B. Anthony, Frederick Douglass, Oscar Wilde, and Mark Twain.

A turning point came for the college in 1893. It was in this year that Dr. Joseph R. Harker became president of the school, and under his administration, closer relations were established between the college and the former students of the school. An Alumni Association had been started in 1893. Dr. Harker, pushing the school into the modern age, convinced the Board to change the name to the Illinois Women's College in 1899. Continuing with his grand plans, he achieved another goal for the school, raising it to four-year college status, which allowed it to grant bachelor's degrees. This was completed in 1907 and within two years, the first Bachelor of Arts degrees were awarded.

The changes led to greater opportunities for fund-raising and the chance to construct more buildings on campus. As enrollment increased, more classroom and dormitory space was needed. In the fall of 1909, a five-story building was constructed to fill both those needs. Connected to the main hall by corridors, it was named Harker Hall by an act of the Board of Trustees in recognition of the president's tireless service.

The last structure built during Dr. Harker's presidency was the gymnasium, which was built in 1917. It did not receive the name Harker Gymnasium until 1936. On the main floor were the basketball court and the stage for dramatic productions. The basement contained a swimming pool and a bowling alley.

Among President Harker's many talents was his ability to interest prominent businessmen in the college. The greater the businessman, he knew, the deeper the pockets. Two of the donors to the college were Andrew Carnegie and Dr. C.E. Welch, head of the grape juice corporation. The most important, though, was James E. MacMurray, president of the Acme Steel Corporation in Chicago and a one-time Illinois Senator. An active member of the Methodist Church, he had sent his daughter, Miriam, to Illinois Women's College. President Harker encouraged his interest in the school by upgrading to a four-year institution. In 1916, MacMurray became a member of the Board of Trustees and, in 1921, became president of the Board. By the time Dr. Harker retired in 1925, Senator MacMurray had donated about $45,000 to the college.

Under the subsequent president, Clarence P. McClelland, MacMurray's interest in the school stayed strong. MacMurray Science Hall was built in 1928 with $125,000 matching funds from the senator and an equal amount raised by alumni and supporters of the college.

Tragedy returned to the college on February 22, 1929. It was on that evening that the school's fourth – and first deadly – fire occurred. At a Washington's Birthday party in the gymnasium, a photographer was taking pictures of the party-goers in their costumes. The powder from an exploding flashbulb apparently ignited a curtain on the stage. The flames spread quickly, causing an intense wave of heat to sweep across the balcony. Although the fire caused little damage to the building, three people were killed and 15 students and faculty members were seriously injured by the flames and in accidents while trying to escape the building. Among the dead were a student who was killed when she jumped from an upper floor to escape the flames and two staff members, including the college's librarian, who were burned to death. Mrs. McClelland, wife of the college's president, was hospitalized for a month from a complicated leg fracture caused by her fall from a window to the pavement below.

The college was closed for two weeks after the fire. The gym was eventually repaired, but the impact of the tragedy lingered much longer – and it became the scene of some of the college's first ghost stories. Accounts soon circulated of hearing footsteps in the empty gym, voices and even the screams of those who died in the fire. As time passed, though, the stories began to fade, as if the remnants of horror that had been imprinted on the place slowly dissipated as months and years went by.

As enrollment at the college continued to grow, more living and dining space was needed. As a gift to the college, Senator MacMurray financed the construction of Jane Hall (named after his wife) and McClelland Dining Hall, both completed in the spring of 1930. Soon after, President McClelland proposed a name change for the school to MacMurray College for Women. It received the unanimous approval of the Board of Trustees.

Even with the generosity of Senator MacMurray, the early 1930s were a difficult time for the school. This was during the lowest years of the Great Depression and few could afford to feed their families, let alone contribute to the college. Building plans and even desperately needed repairs were postponed. The salary budget was reduced and yet the college began sinking into debt. The school began using the endowment and annuity funds for operating expenses and that income decreased also. But, once again, James MacMurray came to the college's rescue. Between 1934 and 1939, he provided either full or partial funding to pay off the deficit, refurbish Main and Harker Halls, build Ann Rutledge Hall in 1937, and add two wings to Jane Hall in 1939. In 1938 and 1941, he made gifts to the college's endowment that totaled over $3 million. In 1940, the college purchased Liberty Hall and converted it into the Little Theatre.

James MacMurray died in 1942, still president of the Board of Trustees at the time of his death. Under President McClelland's administration, he donated more than $4 million to the college. In 1947, Kathryn Hall was built and named for his widow (Jane had died in 1937), marking the last major gift that he made to the school. More than anyone, James MacMurray changed the face of the campus and made it possible for the college to reach and exceed its goals of expansion. It seems only right that it continues to bear his name today.

During the 1940s, the academic quality of the college was raised yet again. In 1942, a graduate school was started. Master's Degrees were granted in psychology, physical education, and special education. The program earned national recognition and continued through 1961.

More changes soon arrived at MacMurray College. The late 1930s and early 1940s were years of more relaxed rules for dormitory hours, required chapel, smoking, and "weekend permission." Playing bridge was the most popular informal pastime. This period was also noted for the development of the women's initiation ceremony, which has become known as the "Green Ribbon."

The 1940s were occupied with activities in support of American efforts in World War II, but by the latter part of the decade, the campus had returned to normal and student life came to be characterized by such events as presentation of the senior song, senior cut day, the Lantern Drill, and the highlight of the year, the Faculty Show, which was sort of a combination of follies and a talent show.

But it was during the presidency of Dr. Louis W. Norris that an unsettling trend began to be realized in America. Due to a lower birth rate during the Depression, students were now entering colleges in fewer numbers. Fewer yet were entering schools that were designed for women – or men – only. Public high schools had been coeducational for decades, but most colleges had not. All-female colleges around the country were experiencing enrollment and retention problems and MacMurray was no exception. Young women were enrolling in sufficient numbers, but few of them stayed for the entire four years. Most were busy getting married and starting a family in the wake of World War II.

On October 9, 1955, on a motion made by Milburn Peter Akers, the great-grandson of founder Peter Akers, the Board voted to establish the MacMurray College for Men as a coordinate college to the existing school. Other coordinating colleges existed at the time, but MacMurray was the first in the Midwest. The college would not be completely co-educational, as it is today, until 1969. From 1957, when the first class of men were enrolled, until 1969, there were two MacMurray Colleges, one for men and one for women. The men had the same professors, but for the first two years, had separate classes. Initially, there were two separate student newspapers, two student governments and even two yearbooks. Separate housing and dining halls were also needed. The men and women did eat together on Thursday and Sunday evenings, however, formal attire was required. The men's campus grew as far from the women as possible. Their dorms were even given a "contemporary" design to make them look different than the women's. Over time, men's sports were added, including soccer, basketball, baseball, track, golf, wrestling, and finally, football in 1984.

By the time the first men's class graduated in 1961, men and women were working together in music, drama, and at the campus radio station. The 1961 yearbook was the first to be jointly issued. The Hub, a popular student meeting place located in the basement of Rutledge Hall, soon became inadequate and was moved to the new Campus Center in 1965. In 1967, men and women shared a dining hall. In time, as a natural course of events and by the student's choice, coordinate education was finally dropped and, in 1969, the trustees officially declared MacMurray to be a coeducational college.

Following the turbulent 1960s and 1970s, the 1980s ushered in a period of relative calm on college campuses across the country, including at MacMurray. For many students, their attention became focused on career preparation and graduate school placement, and new programs were started to meet these needs. Academic emphasis returned to the liberal arts in the form of a new general education program, otherwise known as MacMurray's Core Curriculum, the "Ideas in Perspective" sequence. The general education program included studies in humanities, religion, history, and literature.

MacMurray College today is among a select group of American colleges that has been in existence for nearly 170 years – and given its often troubled history, that's a remarkable achievement. Time and again, the college has proven itself to be a survivor, adapting to meet the changes of time, turning trials into triumph through hard work, sacrifice and sometimes, amazing luck. There is no question that MacMurray has had an often exciting, tragic, and colorful history – and its one in which ghosts and hauntings have long been a part.

There is no question that MacMurray College has had its brushes with strangeness over the years. One of them involved a psychic prediction of a murder that was going to take place at the college, made by none other than famous psychic Jeane Dixon, who supposedly predicted the election and assassination of John F. Kennedy in 1960, among other things. Of course, she also predicted that World War III would start in 1958 and that the Russians would put the first man on the moon.

Regardless, Dixon predicted that a ghastly murder would take place in a small, Midwestern town with two colleges and a state hospital. The horrific axe murder would occur on a rainy day in April and on the steps of a dormitory with pillars that faced to the east. Many became convinced that this was MacMurray College, even though a university in Missouri also fit the description. The year the murder was supposed to take place? 1978 – So we can rest assured that we're safe on this one.

Another erroneous legend, although probably the most famous, is the story of the infamous "Blue Lady" of MacMurray College. The tale dates back to the late 1800s and involves a young student who attended a dance (or some other social gathering) one night and was supposed to meet her lover there. Unfortunately, he never showed and she returned to her dorm room in Rutledge Hall very upset and depressed. The Blue Lady – who would be so named because of the color of the gown she wore to impress her date that night – walked into her room to find her lover and her roommate together. She was so enraged that she murdered both of them and then flung herself from the window of the room, which was located high on an upper floor of the building. To this day, the Blue Lady lurks in a haunted room in Rutledge Hall and she stalks the campus with a black rose in her hand. If she approaches a young man and hands him the rose, he is soon to die.

It's an eerie story – but one rife with problems. In the late 1800s, the college was still an all-female school and it's unlikely that any co-ed dances would have taken place or that a young man could have easily have been smuggled into one of the dorm rooms. In addition, there is no record of any murders or a suicide taking place on the campus at that time. The biggest problem, though?

Rutledge Hall

Even though there is a room in Rutledge Hall that has been dubbed the "Blue Lady Room," which is said to be haunted by her spirit, the building wasn't actually constructed until 1937, long after the story is said to have taken place. So, while the tale of the "Blue Lady" is a great story, it's unfortunately that – just a story. But that does not mean that Rutledge Hall is not haunted. And it also does not mean that a tough-to-track-down story can't have some basis in fact.

The haunted history in the Blue Lady's room is, however, very real. So real, in fact, that the college recognizes the room as haunted and has not assigned any student to live there for many years. Students who live in dorm rooms nearby have heard noises inside the room, much like if someone were living in the room. Voices and footsteps, the sound of items be shuffled around, even the sound of a telephone ringing when there is no telephone inside the room. One student even recalled hearing a typewriter at work when walking passed the room. He put his ear to the door, and sure enough the sound was coming from inside.

Even during our investigations, we have had our fair share of occurrences in the Blue Lady's room. During one late night investigation, the voice of a woman came through the only walkie-talkie that was not yet powered down and very clearly asked "Can you hear me?" Another time, when asked to make a knocking sound, the spirit responded with two very loud and clear knocks on the chest of drawers positioned under the room's one window.

But one experience we will never forget was one of the most frustrating. We had arrived on campus for the annual investigation of Rutledge Hall with the students. The one room the students were dying to investigate was, of course, the Blue Lady's room. The room is normally locked and the students, except for the Resident Director, do not have access to this part of the third floor. When we arrived to the Blue Lady's room, the RD could not get the door to open. It seemed to be stuck. Campus security came by to give it a try, but could not get the door to budge. It was unlocked, but would not open. Something was keeping it closed but we could not see what it was. Finally, the security officer was granted permission to enter the dorm room next door to gain entry through the adjoining bathroom, using the master key that was only in the possession of campus security. Upon entering the room, it was clear why the door would not open. An additional safety latch attached to the back of the door had been secured preventing the door from opening even when the knob was unlocked. Since this added security measure can only be manually locked and unlocked from inside the room, who locked it?

Perhaps the spirit within was not welcoming guests that night.

Although the legend of the Blue Lady has been passed down through the generations, her room is not the most active space in Rutledge Hall. The story of Pam may not be famous and while we have had a lot of trouble tracking down the real "Pam" of the story, there is definitely something going on in the suite of rooms where she allegedly once lived that cannot be easily explained. As noted in the introduction to this section about MacMurray College, Pam was said to have lived in Rutledge in the early 1970s. As the story goes, Pam, who was very involved in campus activities, was absent at choir practice that night. Since this was so unusual for Pam, a friend decided to stop by to check in on her. When she arrived, she discovered Pam's lifeless body lying on the floor of the bathroom.

Her friends remember her as being joyful, funny, and a bit of a prankster. Recent residents of Rutledge Hall would agree. Some of the students find Pam's spirit to be fun loving, while others are quite disturbed by her antics. Some of her favorite tricks include turning on the water in the students' restrooms and taking items and replacing them in other parts of the room or building. For quite some time, Pam fixated on a large rubber exercise ball that belonged to one of the students who lived in her former room. This exercise ball would be moved to different locations in the building, once being found in the shower, in the hall, in the dorm rooms of other students, and even once it was found in the Blue Lady's room. Students report these kinds of happenings almost daily, and while Pam makes her presence known throughout the building, the most active location is the suite in which she took her final breaths.

A number of strange events have occurred with those who have lived in this suite of rooms, but we've been there to witness many of them ourselves. During one of the annual student investigations, one of the team members who was with us wanted to try placing another trigger object in the room – this is an object that will hopefully entice the spirit to interact with it. She asked one of the young women living in the room to choose one small object to place on the desk and then ask Pam to move the object while they were out of the room. The student opened a desk drawer and pulled out a packet of mustard that she had brought back from the dining hall and placed it on the corner of the desk. After asking Pam to show herself by participating in their experiment, the two left the room, locking the door behind them. When the whole group returned about an hour later, the young woman screamed with excitement and fear. The mustard packet that she placed on the corner of the desk had been left undisturbed, but the desk drawer was open and a dozen mustard packets had been strewn across the floor.

In the fall of 2013, we returned to MacMurray and Rutledge Hall for another outing with the students in search of the resident ghosts. We chased down the legends, checked out the "Blue Lady's" room, and settled down in Pam's room to see if she might be around. As described earlier, Lisa and I were both convinced that she was. No matter how many questions might remain about the validity of using scientific and electrical devices to search for ghosts, we can't offer a reasonable explanation for how the temperature dropped so suddenly in the bedroom, or why the lights and alarms on all of those meters went off at the same time, signaling a drastic change in the magnetic atmosphere of the room. We're sure that a hardened skeptic might be able to come up with something, but would it be any more believable than the possibility that it was a ghost? We don't think so.

Once the reaction of those devices are combined with literally years of eyewitness testimony about strange experiences in the rooms, then it's hard to dismiss at least the chance that it's truly haunted. We believe it's better than a mere chance that a ghost makes her presence known there but, of course, the truth of such things remains for the reader to decide.

But if "Pam" – or whoever the spirit might be – truly does linger in her former dorm room, why does she stay? A tragic life ended too soon? Some sort of unfinished business that she still needs to complete? No one can say, at least so far. Perhaps one day, we'll find out. We hope that we'll be around when she decides to let us know.

Restless Spirits at the University of Illinois

Ghost stories of the University of Illinois in Champaign-Urbana have always been of an elusive sort. It has been suggested that perhaps because it is primarily an engineering school, that students at this school are simply not suited for ghosts. They say that these unimaginative scientists have no interest in the spirit world, but I have never been convinced of these claims. Regardless of the type of university it is, I have yet to find a college that does not have at least a ghost story or two.

The University of Illinois is no exception.

The University of Illinois had its beginnings in 1862. It was established as one of 37 public land-grant institutions in the Morrill Land-Grant Colleges Act, signed by Abraham Lincoln. The Act granted each state a portion of land on which to found a major public state university, which would teach agriculture, mechanical arts, and military training, without excluding other scientific and classical studies.

In 1867, Illinois established a university that would offer higher education for working people. After a contentious battle between several cities, Urbana was selected as the site for the new school in 1867. The university opened for classes on March 2, 1868, with two faculty members and 77 students. That same year, the College of Agriculture, Consumer, and Environmental Sciences and the College of Fine and Applied Arts were established. The College of Engineering followed in 1868. From the beginning, there was a great debate over whether the school should be focused on science and mechanics, or on liberal arts, and it raged for years until it finally forced the resignation of the university's first president, John Milton Gregory.

A library was started in 1868 with just over 1,000 volumes, but grew steadily to become one of the largest in the nation. In 1870, the Mumford House was constructed as a model farmhouse for the school's experimental farm. It is the oldest building on campus today. Main University Hall was built in 1871, and stands where the Union presently stands today. That same year also saw the start of the university's student-run newspaper, the *Daily Illini*. Harker Hall was built in 1877 and was known as the Chemical Laboratory. It was later named in honor of Oliver A. Harker, who served as the dean of the university's law school from 1903 to 1916.

When the school began, it was known as the Illinois Industrial University, but in 1885, the name was officially changed to the University of Illinois. The new name better reflected the agricultural, mechanical, and liberal arts curriculum of the university. It was also done to avoid confusion with schools for delinquents. This remained the official name for 50 years, until it was changed again to the University of Illinois at Urbana-Champaign in 1935.

In 1882, the College of Medicine was established. Two years later, the university's first Native American student, Carlos Montezuma, who was also known as Wassai, graduated with a medical degree. He was the first Native American to earn a degree in medicine from any university in the United States.

In the late 1880s, enrollment, courses, and departments increased. The addition of new agricultural, engineering, and information science stations brought national attention to the school. Soon after, the university added the College of Applied Sciences and the College of Law. Around this time, Altgeld Hall was designed by architecture department students Nathan Rocker and James McLaren Wright. The university also ran into bad luck with another administrator. President Selim H. Peabody struggled to keep money flowing into the school by selling off the university's land. His methods came under attack by students and the school's new alumni groups, and he was forced out of office by the Board of Trustees in 1891.

In 1904, Edmund J. James became the university's president and during his tenure, the university added a College of Education, College of Liberal Arts and Sciences, and the College of Business. He also established ties with China through the Chinese Minister to the United States. James and Wu Ting-Fang created a direct connection between China and the Urbana campus, with James establishing the first office for foreign students in the United States. Between 1911 and 1920, the University of Illinois was educating a third of all the Chinese students in the United States.

After James, David Kinley served as president from 1920 to 1930. During this era, the university became known as one of the strongest fraternity and sorority campuses in the country. The College of Media was also established during this period.

President Harry Woodburn Chase followed in 1930 to 1933 and saw the establishment of the School of Social Work. President Arthur Hill Daniels served from 1933 to 1934. The Great Depression slowed new construction and expansion of the university and the school struggled under Arthur C. Willard's term, which ran until 1946. After World War II, however, the university experienced rapid growth. It was a "boom time" across America, including on university campuses. Thanks to the G.I. Bill, many returning soldiers were able to attend college and the schools rushed to keep up with the wave of new enrollments. Campus population doubled and the university's academic standing soared. This prompted the creation of the University of Illinois Willard Airport, which began service in 1954. This period was also marked by large growth in the Graduate College and increased federal support of scientific and technological research.

In the 1960s and 1970s, the University of Illinois experienced the turmoil that was common on many American campuses of the era. It began with protests over the war in Vietnam and then saw the founding of a number of progressive movements for women, African-American students, and others. The 1970s also saw the first questions about the political correctness of the school's mascot, Chief Illiniwek. Critical writings and protests began to emerge about the university's use of a "hostile or abusive" image as its mascot. The debate went on for years with groups complaining that the use of the Native American figure was inappropriate and promoted ethnic stereotypes. Chief Illiniwek was finally retired in 2007.

Over the last century and a half, the university has expanded far beyond its roots as a single building on the Illinois prairie. The campus, which has grown to more than 785 acres, includes not only the old buildings of the 1800s, but high-tech, ultra-modern buildings of the modern age. While still home to agricultural students, more than 41,000 students of every field of study call the campus home each year. The University is a world leader in research, teaching, and academic excellence and ranks among the top 50 schools in the country for research and development dollars spent in science and engineering.

And it may also, many claim, to be home to a number of restless ghosts.

There are a handful of haunted spots on campus, but the most notorious location seems to be the English Building. Constructed in 1905 in a New Colonial Style, it served as a women's dorm until 1937. During those years, the building had a swimming pool that was later converted into an atrium. According to legend, a young female student committed suicide by drowning herself in the pool, distraught over bad grades or an unwanted pregnancy, depending on the version of the story that is told.

It's a great story. And while the building may be haunted, it's not for the reason that so many stories claim. The main problem is that the English Building was never a dormitory. Unlike the history of the building's ghost, the history of the actual building can be traced through blueprints and documents. After it opened in 1905, it was called the Women's Building. After World War II, it was renamed Bevier Hall for about a decade before becoming the English Building in the 1950s. It has housed the Department of English ever since.

In the building's early days, it housed women's activities on campus. The women in charge of students – not yet called the Dean of Women – had offices there, and female students had rooms where they could meet friends, study, and relax. The building housed the academic work in domestic science.

Just because the building was never a dorm does not make it any less colorful, though. In the October 17, 1905, edition of the student newspaper, the building's dedication ceremony included 400 female students dressed in white, marching from University Hall to the gymnasium, where President James said that the new building signified the university's commitment to "co-education; second, that the fathers and mothers of Illinois want the best possible care taken of their daughters, and third; that physical culture is as necessary for the girls as for the young men." It should be noted that the new Women's Building included a gymnasium and a pool – which does add some credibility to the ghost story – as well as sewing rooms, a kitchen, and other amenities to teach women the art of household science.

The English Building at the University of Illinois

Later, the building's club rooms made it a major social center for meetings and formal events. There was also a two-bedroom home management apartment on the third floor, where students learned the details of household science, but that's the closest that it ever came to being a dormitory.

Does this mean that a student never died in the building? No, and for that reason, the story continues to thrive. But would she rest easier if her story had a basis in truth? Perhaps, because if the accounts are true, she certainly does not rest in peace.

According to student interviews in the campus newspaper, the janitors in the building have dubbed the female ghost "Clarabell" and will often call out to her when they want the phenomena that is associated with her to stop. Over the years, she has been blamed for flickering lights, slamming doors, cold spots, and has appeared as the filmy apparition of a girl in a 1930s-era dress. Much of the activity takes place around the former rhetoric room, which later was turned into offices for graduate teaching assistants. It's believed that she has some sort of attachment to this part of the building.

She still wanders the hallways of the building today, but students never see her at night. The English Building is one of the only buildings on campus that remains locked overnight. Most other buildings on the Quad allow key card access after-hours, but not the English Building. Perhaps "Clarabell" likes to spend her nights alone.

Next door to the English Building is the Lincoln Building, home to the College of Liberal Arts and Sciences. It is reportedly home to a ghost that roams the third floor. She has only been spotted peering out the windows that look out over Wright Street. She is always seen long after the building has closed for the night. Those who have witnessed her nocturnal survey of campus say that her face bears a very sad expression. For this reason, the stories say that she is the ghost of a long-dead teaching assistant or a young student who jumped to her death from the top floor. Needless to say, no one knows for sure.

Another reportedly haunted spot is the central foyer of the Psychology Building. A number of years ago, a memorable event took place here when a student became irrational and threatened to kill himself by jumping off one of the railings on an upper floor, overlooking the foyer. He survived the incident, but died a few years later. The stories say that after his death, he did return to haunt the place and has been lurking in the foyer ever since. The ghostly presence has resulted in people experiencing unexplained cold spots, a whispering voice that comes from nowhere, and the sound of footsteps pacing in nearly empty hallways.

A University of Illinois alumni named Steven Herrington contacted me about some strange experiences he had at the Natural Resources Building while working there as a graduate student from 1997 to 1999. Part of his research assistantship was to work in the ground floor Ichthyology collection, curating specimens. Because of his class schedule, he often worked there alone during the late night hours. On a few occasions, the building's elevator would engage and would come down from an upper floor to the floor where Steve was working. Upon reaching the ground floor, the doors would open and no one would be in the elevator. This happened on several occasions and Steve later learned that it also happened to a friend of his, who also worked in the building under the same circumstances.

Steve explained: "What made this creepy is that, to my knowledge, it never happened in the daytime and I knew that I was the only one in the building when this occurred because the doors were always locked after work hours. I could see the parking lot outside was empty and on one occasion, I checked the hallways and rooms on the floor to see if anyone else was there. It's possible that this may have been something mechanical, but if it was, it should have occurred in the daytime, too. I watched for it to happen and this is what made me question it. It was a minor occurrence that probably doesn't qualify as a 'ghost story' but it truly creeped me out when it happened."

The Ghosts of Simpkins Hall & Others
Hauntings at Western Illinois University

There are few buildings on Illinois college campuses that are said to be as haunted as Simpkins Hall at Western Illinois University. It is a place, students and staff members claim, of many spirits, although few seem to be able to agree on just how many, or the identity of the restless dead. Perhaps the answers lie in the history of the building, or the university itself, which began in the early days of the last century. Or perhaps we will never know who slams the doors, jingles the keys, paces the hallways, clacks on the old typewriter, and rattles the nerves of those who have had encounters with the specters in this place.

And perhaps we are better off not knowing.

Off the beaten path of busy Illinois interstates and away from big cities is the small town of Macomb, which is home to Western Illinois University. The school began as a teacher's college in 1899, called the Western Illinois State Normal School, and its classes were confined to a single building known as "Old Main." It would later become Sherman Hall, but not until 1957, when it was named for Lawrence Sherman, a local lawyer, judge, and lieutenant governor.

In 1902, the university added a training school to the Main building so that students could get teaching experience in the classroom. Local children were enrolled there and were taught by students at the college. By the start of classes that first season, there were 103 students enrolled and it quickly gained a reputation for producing well-trained, educated teachers. The students who attended the experimental school thrived, too. All of the students, including the girls, participated in basketball, baseball, and track. The establishment of female sports was seen as another innovative and advanced educational concept for the college, which changed its name to Western Illinois State Teacher's College in 1921.

By the latter part of the decade, it had become nationally-known as a top teacher's college and as student enrollment increased, Old Main became increasingly overcrowded. Plans began to be made to expand the school and construct a new building just west of Old Main. Construction was delayed for almost 10 years, though, thanks to the Great Depression.

Finally, in 1937, the school received a federal grant through the Works Progress Administration, part of President Roosevelt's New Deal, for a new

Simpkins Hall

training school. The new structure, later named Simpkins Hall after Dr. Rupert Simpkins, was completed and opened in 1938. The training school became a self-contained educational unit. The ground floor housed kindergarten and first grade classes, along with a lunchroom, gymnasium, and infirmary. The next floor was used for administration offices, as well as second through fifth grades. The sixth through eighth grade classes occupied the next floor, and high school classes were on the top floor. The building accommodated up to 300 students.

In the 1960s, the teaching college became Western Illinois University and the training school was converted to house the Department of English and Journalism. The children who once learned from aspiring teachers were replaced by scores of incoming university students, who found many reminders of the building's past occupants. There were rows of small desks, lockers, chalkboards, and coat hooks that were hung no higher than waist level. It looked as though the children had simply packed up one day and disappeared.

Is it any wonder that the first reported ghosts of Simpkins Hall were believed to be children from the past?

The ghostly tales of Simpkins Hall are rooted in the very fabric of the university. They have been told and re-told since the teacher's college was replaced by Western Illinois University, and professors and students alike have been debating the reality of the haunting stories for more than 50 years now. Few can agree on the origin of the tales, the number of ghosts that are present in the building, and who they might be. Some say the ghosts in the building are two little girls who drowned in Lake Ruth, a pond directly south of Simpkins Hall, and now wander the building, singing, laughing, and running up and down the stairs.

Others claim the resident ghost is a young boy, who drowned in the pond. Sarah Cash, writing for the student newspaper, *Western Courier*, learned from a former student that the boy was attending a school picnic and drowned in the lake in the late 1930s. He was unconscious when he was pulled from the lake, and for some unknown reason, he was taken to the fourth floor of Simpkins Hall. The story claims that he died in the former Training School Library, which is now the Writing Center.

Another lingering spirit is said to be the ghost of a former student – or employee, depending on the storyteller – who has been dubbed "Harold." He is said to be responsible for the numerous strange noises that plague the building's third and fourth floors. Harold seems to be a specter of recent origins, earning his nickname in the 1980s. His was first reported by a former teaching assistant named C.K. Bryant, who worked into the early morning hours one night and decided to lay down and take a short nap in the Writing Center. She had just closed her eyes when she heard the hammering sound of someone pounding on the keys of an old manual typewriter. She got up to investigate, and the sound stopped. As soon as she lay back down, it started again and irritated, she yelled out, "Harold, knock it off!" She did not hear the sounds again that night. Bryant had no idea why she called the poltergeist Harold, but the name stuck.

She would not be the last to encounter Harold. One night, another teaching assistant was working late and returned to her desk after getting a drink from the vending machine to find a strange message on her word processor's screen. The words on the paper she had been writing had been replaced with a series of random characters and a single coherent word – "hi." The Writing Center had been locked while she was at the vending machine with the only other students in the entire building. Since then, stories have continued to circulate about the building's "typing ghost."

Students with an interest in ghosts have been fascinated with Simpkins Hall since the days immediately after its conversion into use by Western Illinois University. In the 1970s, a group of would-be ghost hunters set up cameras on the same floor as the Writing Center for an overnight vigil. There had already been a number of alleged encounters with ghosts in that area of the building so they decided to set up cameras at each end of the hallway and then leave, securing the building for the night. No one was allowed to enter until morning, when the group and the building's custodian returned. The cameras were still recording and the group sat down to watch hours of dimly lit, empty hallways. They saw nothing on the film – but it was what they heard that startled them! At one point, the cameras fixed on the empty hallway blurred for a moment and this was followed by the unmistakable sound of a young girl giggling. After that, the film returned to silence and nothing else was heard. Even so, the group deemed the night a success.

Since that time, there have been many other investigation groups in the building, as well as students, professors, and staff members. The stories of the ghosts continue to be told. For every time that someone claims to have encountered the "typing ghost," someone else can tell a story of their own about a young woman who sobs in the first floor restroom, or the boy that follows people down empty hallways. There are numerous tales that have been told, and apparently, there will be many more ghost stories of Simpkins Hall to come.

Simpkins Hall is not the only building said to be haunted at Western Illinois University. Bayliss Hall is plagued by two different stories of suicide. In the first, a freshman girl became pregnant while away at college and managed to hide the pregnancy from her friends, classmates, and parents. She ended up delivering the baby herself in her dorm room and afraid of what her parents would do if they found out, tossed the baby and the evidence of the delivery down the garbage chute. She then hung herself in the closet of her room. In the second story, a young woman suffering from depression was abandoned by her roommate for the weekend. In her loneliness, she hung herself in the closet.

Both stories – said to have vaguely occurred in the 1980s – had similar consequences. In the first room, students have reported the sounds of the young woman and her baby crying in the darkness. In the second dorm room, strange noises and electrical disturbances frequently take place.

In Tanner Hall, the ghost of a young man who accidentally died after he fell to his death in an elevator shaft from the twelfth floor. The legends say that he still roams the hallways and will open the elevator doors whenever someone calls out, "Hold the elevator!"

The ghost of a young woman who committed suicide after a fight with her boyfriend is said to haunt her former dorm room in Washington Hall. The stories say that the telephone in the room would frequently ring, but no one would be on the line.

Or so such stories go.

Unlike the historically-based ghost stories told in Simpkins Hall, the majority of tales told about these college dorms deal with anxiety-provoking issues. Incidents involving suicidal students and mothers discarding their newborn babies into the trash are far too real. Occurrences of young women murdering babies in college dorms don't happen often, but these kinds of stories remind students of this terrible reality. The tale of the roommate's suicide serves as a warning as to why we should take care of each other. Does this make them any less real? Are such stories merely legends that have been told over and over again to serve as object lessons that are never explicitly spelled out?

Or is there something more to them? Suicides and tragic deaths do take place so we cannot dismiss every college ghost story that we hear. There are those who maintain that all such campus tales are simply the product of overactive imaginations that are working overtime in those who are away from home for the first time. Students, they say, are far too susceptible to the trappings of the supernatural. But what about stories that have been told not just by students, but by professors, staff members, maintenance workers, and, in some cases, people who claim to not believe in ghosts at all?

Perhaps the stories are simply a mixture of fact and fancy. Few of us who have collected such stories over time can deny that we have chuckled a little when we find yet another report of a spectral coed who was murdered (or committed suicide) years before and now haunts her old dorm room. In most cases, a quick check of the local newspaper files will reveal that no coed was ever murdered at the school. So, how do we explain the mysterious happenings in the dorm room where the girl allegedly died?

In other words, is there another story hidden somewhere in the history of the place to explain why it is haunted? These college haunts are a perfect example of "ghostlore," the practice that society has devised to try and explain eerie events by attaching a legend to them. In many cases, stories of a "lady in white," a "headless railroad brakeman," or a "murdered coed" have been invented to try and add understanding to sightings of ghostly white mists, mysterious glowing lights, and knocking sounds that come from the closet. Without these chilling stories, the weird locations might never be explained. To put it simply, people just have a need to try and explain things. They crave a reason for everything, supernatural or not.

If a place is haunted for some inexplicable reason, human nature begs us to create a reason. In a dorm room, it's easy to grab hold of what might be the scariest thing that can happen to a college student – suicide, murder, accidental death, or for some, an unplanned pregnancy.

So, the next time you hear a story of young women who report phantom weeping in the night, or the sounds of a baby crying in the corridor, don't be too quick to dismiss it. There may be more to the strange tale than first meets the eye.

Spirits of Bradley University

The history of Bradley University in Peoria is unique among the colleges and universities of Central Illinois. It began through the generosity of a woman who had a desire to offer a greater education to others than she had been able to achieve for herself and the wealth to make that dream a reality. Wanting nothing more than to help others, and to forget her own grief after the death of her husband and all of her children, she carved a university out of the Illinois prairie, an institution that endures today. All she asked in return was that flowers be placed on her grave in Springdale Cemetery after she died.

Bradley University may have had an unusual start, but like so many other Illinois schools, it also has its share of ghosts.

Bradley University would not exist today without Lydia Moss Bradley, who was born in Indiana on July 30, 1816. She was the youngest child of Zeally Moss, a farmer who had served as a quartermaster during the American Revolution and as a Baptist minister in Virginia after the war. Moss and his wife, Jenny, moved to Indiana in 1815, where Lydia attended school in the kitchen of a neighbor woman. Her only real education was in caring for a home, spinning, weaving, cooking, making butter, and butchering and preserving meat.

When each of his children turned 18, Zeally Moss gave them a farm of 200 acres. Lydia, and her married sister, Nancy Chambers, shared a farm between them. Lydia invested her money in real estate at a young age and bought an additional 40 acres of land. She later sold it and made a good profit. Part of this money, after earning interest for years, was used to purchase the land for Bradley University.

When Lydia's father died, he named her as the sole heir to his estate. Her siblings were very angry about it and Lydia never forgot the acrimony that it caused. She later said that she believed that the death of all of her children was because of a curse that had been wished on her by her brothers and sisters.

In May 1837, Lydia married Tobias Smith Bradley in Vevay, Indiana. He had worked as a clerk at a local store before going into business for himself. As a wedding present, Lydia received $1,000 in gold from her paternal grandfather, Gregory Glascock. The couple lived in Indiana for a time but eventually moved west to Peoria in 1847.

When they arrived in Illinois with their four-year-old daughter, Clarissa, Peoria was a growing town. Lydia's brother, William, had moved to Peoria in the 1830s and went into the shipping business. In addition to his boats on the Illinois River, he was also involved in real estate, farming, mining, and distilling. William made Tobias the captain of one of his steamboats and he was soon thriving as a trader. Lydia continued her real estate speculation and made a fortune in the local market.

Their business interests were doing well, but their home life was filled with tragedy. Their daughter, Rebecca, had died in Indiana, and on December 3, 1847, their son, Tobias, Jr., followed his sister to the grave. Then, just 16 days later, on December 19, Clarissa also died. Another daughter, Mary, was born in June 1851, and died 10 months later. A son, named William, lived only two years before dying in August 1855. Lydia and Tobias bought a large plot in Springdale Cemetery and their five children were buried with a beautiful view that overlooked the river. Only their daughter, Laura, remained, and the couple fixed their hopes for a legacy on this young woman.

In 1858, the Bradleys built a large brick mansion on Moss Avenue, the wealthiest section of Peoria. They fit well into this neighborhood of real estate tycoons and whiskey millionaires. The house would remain Lydia's home until her death. Tobias, along with Lydia's brother William, invested in a distillery, in railroads, sawmills, and real estate, and saw their investments grow with each passing year. Tobias also operated the Peoria Pottery Company, which became one of the largest manufacturers of pottery in the country.

In the midst of their wealth and success, tragedy struck again. Their daughter Laura, now 15-years-old, died on February 7, 1864. Lydia, who had dreamed of becoming a grandmother, was inconsolable by Laura's death. She later donated land to the city with the provision that a park would be named in Laura's honor. The park is still in existence today and is made up of land that was once part of the original Bradley farm.

Lydia never really recovered from Laura's death and developed an interest in the Spiritualist movement, which was now sweeping the country in the wake of the Civil War. The Spiritualists believed that the dead could – and frequently did – communicate with the living, which brought peace to all of those who lost loved ones in the war. The movement also brought relief to Lydia, who participated in many séances where she allegedly spoke with Laura's spirit. She continued to set a place for Laura at the family dinner table until her own death in 1908.

After losing their last child, Lydia and Tobias sought relief from their grief by further expanding their business ventures and by developing the community. They were instrumental in the start of the Peoria Public Library, donating money and urging their wealthy friends to donate, as well.

But death was not yet finished with the Bradley family.

On May 1, 1867, Tobias was traveling in his carriage from Groveland to Peoria. He was later found kneeling by the side of the road with blood all over his face and hands. A doctor was called and he was taken home, where he lapsed into a coma and died on May 4 without ever speaking a word. His carriage was later examined, and it was determined that an axle had broken and Tobias had fallen into the road. When he fell, he was fatally kicked in the head by the horse, which was still attached to the carriage. He had been killed by a freak accident at the age of only 56.

Lydia was now a widow with over 700 acres of land and numerous business ventures. Lonely and heartbroken, she began searching for some direction in which to turn her energies. She began traveling, seeking out ideas for charity work and ways that her wealth could help others. She visited the Rose Polytechnic Institute in Terre Haute, Indiana, and the Chicago Manual Training School, and the Lewis Institute in Chicago. Lydia herself had a very limited education, but her strong work ethic and keen business skills had helped her to succeed. Now, she wanted to help others do the same. She decided to focus her philanthropy on providing a quality, affordable education for students who were eager to learn.

On November 13, 1896, the charter for the Bradley Polytechnic Institute was incorporated for the purpose of maintaining a school for young men and women who wanted to pursue an education in the arts, music, science, mathematics, ancient languages, ethics, engineering, and literature. The school eventually evolved from the original academy to a four-year college that offered a graduate program.

On April 10, 1897, ground was broken for Bradley Hall and classes began on October 4, before the building was even completed. Textbooks were provided free of charge to the original class of 105 students. The fee to attend the academy was $20 per quarter, or $60 for the year. Scholarships were available to students who could not afford the tuition but were deemed academically deserving.

Founders Day was set for October 8, 1897. The event was greeted with excitement by everyone in the community. Lydia had chosen red and white for the school's colors and she tied all of the keys to the school together with red and white ribbons. Dressed in her customary black mourning gown, she presented the keys to the president of the Board of Trustees, O.J. Bailey. After the ceremony, Lydia opened her home for a reception, which included an elaborate buffet and an orchestra.

As Bradley grew and prospered, it began to expand. The students and faculty formed a number of clubs and organizations, like the drama club, art club, and others. The school's first baseball team was started in 1898. A football team was organized in 1899, and basketball was added in 1904. The first issue of the school newspaper was issued on February 1, 1898.

Lydia remained actively involved in the academy as long as her health allowed. She also managed her various business interests and continued her charity work. Since 1900, though, she had been battling cystitis, which led to periods of terrible pain. On December 27, 1907, her family physician, Dr. A.L. Corcoran, was called to her home. Lydia's age, combined with exhaustion and constant pain, kept her in her bed for the remainder of her days. She developed lung inflammation and influenza in early January and Lydia knew she was dying. Despite the pain, she refused opiates, preferring to keep her mind clear. She called in her attorney and gave him directions as to how she wanted her estate to be administered. Lydia slipped into a coma and did not wake up. She died on January 16, 1908 at the age of 92.

Until the very end, Lydia remained a skilled businesswoman. She was careful and left nothing to chance. In May 1899, she had executed a warranty deed to the Bradley Polytechnic Institute and conveyed her entire estate to the school, keeping only her business profits until the time of her death. In 1906, she had drafted plans for her own funeral. They were carried out on January 18 with a wake at her home from 10:00 a.m. to noon, with a watch provided by an honor guard of students. Her coffin was draped with red and white carnations, four inches deep, with the letters BPI spelled out on top. The bell at city hall chimed 92 times, once for every year of her life. A burial followed in the family plot at Springdale Cemetery. It was a bright, sunny morning, just the way she would have liked it. Her grave was stacked with mounds of flowers from businesses, friends, students, teachers, and people who knew her from all over the state.

Lydia's own children died before they could continue her legacy, but her dreams continued on with the advancement of the academy into Bradley University, a full-fledged, four-year institute of higher learning. A graduate program furthers the work started by Lydia in developing academic minds of continuing generations.

And Lydia herself has not been forgotten. A statue of her greets visitors to Bradley Hall on campus. And after all of these years, Bradley University still honors the clause in Lydia's will that asked for fresh flowers to be laid on the graves of her family at Springdale Cemetery on Christmas Eve and on the "usual annual Decoration Day."

In the years that followed Lydia's death, Bradley Polytechnic Institute continued to thrive. With the start of World War I, the school helped to train a number of soldiers at Camp Bradley, an army school for mechanics. The academy that Lydia had founded came to an end at the close of the 1921-1922 school year. Soon after, Bradley became a four-year college that was embraced by the people of Peoria. In 1925, local citizens and businesses contributed the majority of a $750,000 endowment. Bradley held a series of public education lectures that became very popular and the university hosted a radio program that ran from 1925 to 1938. A new library, funded by local endowments, was built in 1948.

Athletics, which had long been important at Bradley, contributed to some of the hardships faced by the school. In the summer of 1951, at least three Bradley basketball players were accused of taking money for "shaving points" in games during the 1950-1951 season. There were indictments in New York, and charges of impropriety were leveled against President David Owens. In the scandal that followed, three players pled guilty to conspiracy charges and were given suspended sentences. In December 1952, Bradley was voted out of the Missouri Valley Conference. President Owens resigned on January 1, 1953. Bradley weathered the storm and remained a fully accredited university. The basketball team eventually restored its image, and a bid was accepted to again play in the National Invitational Tournament in New York in 1957.

By the end of the 1950s, Bradley had 23 educational buildings, 156 instructors, and over 4,300 students and was offering more academic, athletic, and social opportunities than at any time in its history. The school did suffer another setback in 1963 when Bradley Hall was destroyed by fire. The blaze began in a basement room under the chapel and gutted almost the entire building. To this day, the cause of the fire remains a mystery. Soon after, however, the school's president, Dr. Van Arsdale, received a telegram from Louis B. Neumiller, former president of the Caterpillar Tractor Company, who pledged $75,000 for the rebuilding of historic Bradley Hall.

In the years that followed, enrollment at the school steadily increased. Like most other colleges across the nation, Bradley made it through the turbulent years of the 1960s and 1970s and saw many additional changes in the latter part of the twentieth century. It continues to serve Peoria, and the state of Illinois, today and offers a quality education to thousands of students every year.

But, of course, that's only part of the what makes Bradley University such an interesting place. It has a unique history, unlike any of the other schools in the region, but like so many of them, it also has it share of chilling tales of ghosts.

It should come as no surprise that after Lydia Bradley's death, there were many reports of her presence lingering behind at her home on Moss Avenue. During the later years of her life, her keen interest in Spiritualism became known to friends and neighbors as she attempted to communicate with her daughter, Laura. A nephew of Lydia's, who lived with her while attending Bradley Polytechnic Institute, stayed on at the house after her

Bradley Polytechnic Institute

death. He frequently heard the sounds of Lydia's cane descending the main staircase of the house, as he had so often when she was alive. It was often accompanied by the strong smell of roses, which was Lydia's favorite flower.

He wasn't the only person to encounter her. Visitors to the home reported seeing her apparition walking in her rose garden, still wearing the black mourning dress that she always wore after the death of her daughter and husband.

It seems that a woman like Lydia, so attached to her life of business and charitable works, had a difficult time leaving it all behind to cross over to the other side.

One of the more haunted locations on the Bradley campus is the Hartmann Center, which was originally built as the Hewitt Gymnasium in 1908. It was completed in the fall of 1909 and was regarded as the finest facility of its kind in Illinois, and the third largest in the state. It had bowling alleys, billiard tables, a swimming pool, and an indoor track above the main floor. There was plenty of seating for basketball games, and sporting events were held in the gym until 1925. The Hartmann Center was renovated in the 1970s, changing it from a gymnasium to a theater and art gallery. The name was then changed to honor H.W. and Mary Hartmann, who contributed $500,000 for the renovations. Today, the center is home to the Meyer-Jacobs Theater, Hartmann Center Gallery, and offices for the Department of Theatre Arts.

It is also, if the stories are to be believed, home to at least three ghosts.

One of the resident phantoms is, according to legend, the spirit of a little boy who drowned in the old gymnasium's pool, which was once located in the basement. Those who have encountered him say that he can be heard sobbing beneath the floorboards of the orchestra pit, which now hides the location of the former pool. Some even claim that they have heard the sounds of his scratching against the wood as he tried to get out of the water.

Another spirit of the center has been dubbed the "Lady in White." She is said to be a former opera singer who now roams the backstage area of the Meyer-Jacobs Theater. Actors and crew members believe her to be a protective presence, watching over productions to make sure that nothing goes wrong. Some of the actresses have reported feeling a cold, strong hand, stroking their hair in a calming manner before they go on stage. One particular incident from the 1980s is often recalled when actors are questioned about the ghost. They tell of the night when high-heeled footprints mysteriously appeared in sawdust that had been spread behind the theater curtains as evidence that the Lady in White truly exists.

The center's third ghost is the "Brown Man," who was once a regular patron of the theater. No one knew his name, but he attended every show, always wearing the same brown suit. During shows, he always sat in the back of the theater and kept an eye out for anyone who might be talking or sleeping during the performance. He was never shy about reprimanding those who he felt took away from his enjoyment of the show. After his death, the Brown Man continued to show up for performances. Staff members often spotted him in the same spot where he always sat, night after night. He was never seen entering the theater, but was always in his seat just after the curtain went up. Stories are sometimes told about theater patrons who dare to talk during a performance, only to hear a sharp whisper telling them to be quiet. When they look to see who is scolding them, the seats behind them are always empty.

The Brown Man is still trying to enjoy the show.

Constance Hall was Bradley's first female dormitory. Built in 1930, it was named in memory of Jennie Constance, who was head of the English Department from 1919 to 1928. In the summer of 1928, Jennie was studying for her doctorate degree at Northwestern University in Chicago and while walking back to her apartment from the library, she was beaten and robbed. She died later that year from her injuries. To commemorate her service to Bradley, various women's clubs in Peoria raised the money to build a dormitory in her honor. The building was completed in June 1931, and by 1936, there were 21 young women living at the dormitory.

Constance Hall is reportedly haunted today by the ghost of Olive White, a dean at Bradley during the 1950s. She was known for being efficient and strict and always enforced curfews and kept a close eye on the young ladies in the dormitory. Her spirit is still on duty today, the stories say, and her heels can be heard clicking up and down the corridors late at night. Many have heard the footsteps, but are unable to account for the sounds.

In 1961, the hall was converted to the university music building, but Olive has never left. She remains behind as a protective presence, or at least a strict one, still looking out for any sort of bad behavior that she might be able to correct.

Sisson House on campus was built in 1915. The dormitory was originally called Laura Cottage, named after Lydia's late daughter, and it was mainly used for housing the wives of servicemen who were stationed at Camp Bradley during World War I. In 1931, the name was changed to the Greenhouse, and the building was used as a freshmen men's dormitory. In 1946, the name was changed again, this time to honor Edward Sisson, the first director of the Bradley Polytechnic Institute.

A few years later, in 1949, the hall was remodeled and became a women's dormitory. In the 1980s, it was converted into administrative offices. Soon after this renovation, a student named Roberta Jones hung herself during spring break in the women's restroom on the third floor. The college was nearly deserted during the break and her body was not discovered until students returned 12 days later. She was reportedly still hanging in a shower stall.

Roberta Jones has never left Sisson Hall.

To this day, there are frequent reports of the sound of running water in that third floor bathroom. When anyone goes to look and see where the sound is coming from, they find that no water has been left on. Stories also claim that a foul and mysterious odor is often found to be emanating from the bathroom. It is, the witnesses say, the smell of decomposing flesh.

The Harper / Wyckoff Dormitory has a stranger history than any other building on campus. It was never intended to be used by the school. It was actually built by Lydia Bradley in 1885 as the Bradley Home for Aged

Women, but in 1948, became part of the university when it was turned into a men's dormitory and named Wyckoff Hall, in honor of Dr. Charles T. Wyckoff, a member of the university's first faculty. A wing was added, Harper Hall, later on, and by 1951, the dormitory was able to house 441 male students.

The dorm is said to be haunted by the ghost of a young music student named John who died in Laura Bradley Park in 1987. According to legend, John had been drinking heavily on the day of his death to celebrate the end of final exams. At some point, already quite drunk, he decided to walk down Farmington Road for more drinking at one of the local bars. Apparently, while crossing a bridge in the park, he tripped and fell over the railing, fatally hitting his head on the rocks below.

John then returned to his former dormitory in death. His room was on the seventh floor, and often the elevator will take visitors to that floor, no matter which elevator button they press. There are also reports of stumbling footsteps in the seventh floor hallway later at night, which many believe is the presence of John trying to make his way back to the safety of his dorm room – a final walk that he was never able to make in life.

Leaving "Rachel" Behind
Springfield High School & the Hutchinson Cemetery

Like so many other towns in Central Illinois, Springfield was carved out of the wild prairie and turned into a tough and tumble frontier town. The streets of the city were muddy and nearly impassable, long after the state's capitol had been brought to town. Wild pigs roamed the downtown neighborhoods, making a nuisance of themselves.

And, as it was with so many other western towns of the middle nineteenth century, little thought was given as to the best place to bury the dead. Small burial grounds dotted the landscape of what would become downtown Springfield. All of them have vanished over the years and memories of those tiny graveyards have faded over time – all except for one of them. Located just a few blocks away from the Capitol Building was Hutchinson Cemetery, a family plot that became Springfield's formal burial ground. Even though the cemetery was closed in 1876, its story has not faded into the distant past.

And neither has at least one of its occupants.

John Hutchinson was a cabinetmaker and undertaker in Springfield in the 1840s. The two professions normally went hand-in-hand in those days. In 1843, Hutchinson started a small family plot on land that he owned on the west side of the city's downtown district. There was already a small city cemetery just one block over, but for unknown reasons, Hutchinson's burial ground became Springfield's formal cemetery. As many as 700 internments followed, spreading out to cover six acres of land. Among those laid to rest in the cemetery were many of Springfield's most respected citizens of the era, including land developer Pascal O. Enoes, Reverend Charles Dresser, and merchant Robert Irwin. Among the notable was Eddie Lincoln, the three-year-old son of Abraham and Mary Lincoln, who was buried in Hutchinson Cemetery in 1850. He would be moved to rest beside his father in the Oak Ridge Cemetery tomb in 1865.

The cemetery was also the final resting place for an unsettling number of Springfield children during the middle nineteenth century. Living conditions on the prairie would be harsh in those days, even in the settlements like Springfield. Children were usually the most susceptible to bad weather, poor hygiene, and the myriad of illnesses and epidemics that plagued the early settlers.

Hutchinson's Cemetery continued to receive burials through the Civil War years, but in 1874, a city ordinance closed the graveyard. As the city had continued to grow, the cemetery found itself in the path of

A vintage view of Springfield High School

progress. Plans began to be made to exhume the bodies that had been buried there and move them to Oak Ridge Cemetery, which was far beyond the city limits on the north side. Offers had been made to surviving family members to exchange their burial plots in Hutchinson for those of equal number at Oak Ridge. However, many of the bodies went unclaimed, which was the start of the problems.

As workmen began opening graves in Hutchinson's Cemetery, they found the burial records were poorly kept. Remains were discovered in places where burials had supposedly never taken place and some of the old graves had been lost when their markers had deteriorated over time. Indigent and unknown grave plots had never been marked at all. With at least 700 bodies that needed to be moved in a short amount of time, the workmen simply did the best that they could. In the end, it became a poorly-kept secret that not all of the bodies from Hutchinson's Cemetery had been moved.

A number of the dead – some say that it was as many as 100 – were left behind.

With the cemetery officially closed, the city developed the land into Forest Park. It remained a recreational and picnic area for the next 40 years, but in 1915, it was chosen as the site for Springfield's new high school.

Springfield High School opened on September 4, 1857, in a small building on Market Street (now Capitol Avenue) downtown. It was located there for only one year before it was moved to the Academy Building on South Fifth Street, until 1864. The following year, a $65,000 building was constructed for the high school at Fourth and Madison Streets. After a huge influx of new students in the latter part of the 1800s, Central High School was built in 1897, but was already overcrowded in just a few years.

In 1915, plans were made to build a new school in Forest Park. The school was designed in the Beaux-Arts Style, with impressive architectural features and four mosaics on the exterior walls that were completed by Henry Chapman Mercer, a major proponent of the Arts and Crafts Movement in America. When it opened in 1917, it was considered the most modern public school facility in the state.

For years, the school operated without incident, but it was only a matter of time before the old cemetery that it had been built upon would return to "haunt" the new structure. In 1983, an elevator shaft was dug into the foundation of the school. Workers were using a backhoe to dig out the shaft and as the bucket came up out of the ground, they noticed what appeared to be a large rock partially covered with dirt. As they brushed the soil away, they realized that it was not a rock – it was a tombstone. The stone had been badly worn by time, but it did have some legible words. Across the top were the words, "Our Daughter," and on one side, it read, "Cut Down, But Not Destroyed." It was surmised that the stone had once marked the grave of a young girl, who had died from some illness or accident.

After the grave was disturbed, the haunting began.

Soon after the tombstone was uncovered, witnesses began reporting the ghost of a young girl in old-fashioned clothing wandering the building. At first, she was often seen in the basement and in the utility tunnels beneath the school, but soon she was spotted in other parts of the building, as well. Those who didn't see her would sometimes hear her laughter, or hear the sounds of footsteps following them in empty hallways. Before the discovery in the elevator shaft, nothing out of the ordinary had been taking place in the school, but now many were convinced that the place was haunted. And it was not just students who claimed to see the girl. More often, she was spotted by maintenance workers, custodians, and teachers, who were often in the building in the evening, when no one else was around. She became such a fixture at the school that she was nick-named "Rachel," although what her true name may have been will never be known.

Some of the encounters with Rachel have become a part of Springfield High School lore. One day, two plumbers were working in a utility tunnel under the school, repairing a leak, when one of them turned around and saw a little girl in a flowered dress standing a few feet away. Startled at first and then confused as to why one of the students would be down in the tunnel, he scolded her and told her that she needed to go back upstairs to class. Oddly, she looked to only be about 10-years-old; too young for high school. Without a word, the girl turned around and walked out of the tunnel. The workman followed her for a short distance and watched her turn a corner, right past where his partner was working. The first workmen followed the girl around the corner, but found only the other plumber in the tunnel. He asked him where the girl had gone, but he had no idea what his partner was talking about – he hadn't seen any little girl.

An electrician was also working in the utility tunnels one afternoon when Rachel made an appearance. No one knows the details of the encounter, because he refused to talk about them. He pushed his way through a hallway filled with students and teachers who were in between classes and walked out the front door. He never returned to complete the work.

One evening a teacher was working later on a club project and was returning to her classroom from the restroom. As she walked down the dimly lit hall, she saw a light-colored figure glide across the entryway at the end of the corridor. Others had reported the sound of disembodied footsteps in the halls and classrooms, but this teacher heard nothing. There was no way, she knew, that anyone could have walked across the corridor without his or her shoes echoing on the tiles, but that person had. She called out, but there was no answer – and no one else in the school.

In addition to the eerie footsteps, teachers and students have reported the audible sound of someone taking harsh breaths, strange whispers, sudden cold spots, and brushes of chilly wind that come from nowhere.

One of the most active locations in the school seems to be the book room, where textbooks are stored, sorted, and handed out. Cold spots are frequently experienced there. The door to the room often slams closed on its own, and occasionally, a presence in the seemingly empty room becomes so strong that teachers will often leave. Usually, though, the encounters are more playful than frightening. One former teacher recalled placing a stack of textbooks on the table, turning to pick up another stack, and finding that the first stack had been moved and split into two smaller stacks of books.

Since Rachel's tombstone was found when the elevator shaft was being excavated, many have linked the activity in the building to the present-day elevator. Whenever it malfunctions, the prank-playing specter is blamed. On many occasions, people have approached the elevator and before they can press the call button, the doors have opened. Often the elevator will stop at a floor and the doors will open, but no one is there. Passengers are sometimes to taken to different floors than the ones for which the button was pushed. Custodians in the building have gotten so used to the elevator operating on its own that they hardly notice anymore. One electrician who worked frequently in the school became so unnerved by the elevator's strange behavior that he would often place just his toolbox inside, press the button for the floor that he wanted, and then turn around and take the stairs to where he needed to go.

6. DEAD MEN DO TELL TALES
Central Illinois Hauntings that Crime Left Behind

As any chronicler of crime stories can tell you, it is not uncommon to find that terrible crimes often inspire ghost stories. In any traditional account of a haunting, the reason that a ghost remains behind is because of some sort of unfinished business, often because his or her life was cut short, leaving too many tasks unfinished. There is no question that the worst way that a life can be cut short is because of murder.

One of the strangest tales of murder in Central Illinois history occurred on the Menard County prairie in 1826 and involved a killer named Nathaniel Van Noy. The events of his life and death created an eerie legend involving bloody murder, postmortem experiments, and a lingering ghost.

My friend, John Winterbauer, when speaking of the life and crimes of Nathaniel Van Noy put it best when he explained that the lives of the early pioneers in Central Illinois were sometimes disturbed by events of such magnitude that they were, from that point on, used to mark time. The murder of Elizabeth "Peggy" Van Noy was just such an event. For many years afterward, residents would recall events such as births and deaths by starting with the phrase, "two years before Van Noy was hanged…" or something very similar. The events that surrounded Peggy Van Noy's murder were so strange and so shocking that those living in the region at the time never forgot them.

Nathaniel Van Noy and his wife, Peggy, came to Illinois around 1820 and began homesteading a small tract of land that came to be known as the Van Noy Settlement. The area was about five miles west of present-day Athens, in Menard County. The property was made up of forest and carved-out farmland, and was traversed by the road that went from Springfield to Beardstown. This was the main artery of travel through the area. Thanks to the amount of traffic that could be found on the road on any given day, it was a prime location for Van Noy's blacksmith shop, which he constructed on the north side of the thoroughfare. The shop catered to locals and travelers alike and was soon doing a brisk business. Across the road from the shop, he constructed a large, comfortable cabin for himself and his wife.

The Van Noys' existence seemed peaceful and happy, aside from the fact that Nathaniel spent little time at home with his wife. Although he had established a good trade, he began closing down the shop without warning and departing on lengthy trips. The blacksmith would be gone for long periods of time and when he returned, he always had plenty of money, even though his business was sometimes closed for weeks at a time.

Van Noy's frequent closures did not seem to bother his neighbors very much and he still managed to get work done whenever he happened to be home. However, on August 27, 1826, a local man and his young daughter came to the shop and found the place to be deserted. They walked across the road to the Van Noy cabin to see when the blacksmith might be returning and knocked on the door. There was no answer from inside, so the neighbor peered in – only to be shocked by a horrible sight. Peggy Van Noy was lying on the floor of the cabin in a large pool of blood. He pushed open the door and searched frantically for Nathaniel, worried that the couple had been murdered by passing travelers on the Springfield road. A quick search revealed that the blacksmith was not in the house.

The man sent his daughter back through the forest to summon help and a number of local men soon arrived to await the return of Van Noy. At first, they were concerned that he would be grief-stricken by his wife's death, but while they waited, they made a shocking discovery that cast suspicion on Van Noy as having a hand in his wife's death. Hours passed as they waited at the cabin and at some time during the vigil, the men discovered the secret of Van Noy's wealth and the reason behind his many extended absences. Hidden on the property were all of the implements needed for a sophisticated counterfeiting operation. It would later be revealed that Van Noy would make up a batch of phony currency and then would travel to distant towns to "push" it on unknowing storeowners and businesses. Counterfeiting was one of the most lucrative criminal enterprises in Illinois at the time, and Nathaniel Van Noy would turn out to be one of the most prominent operatives in the region.

Van Noy finally returned home late that night. When he arrived, he was immediately seized by the waiting men. He was visibly agitated and claimed that he had spent the day stalking a deer that he had wounded while hunting. When questioned about his wife's death, he claimed that he was innocent and tried to shift the blame to a group of Native Americans who lived nearby. The men were not convinced and they turned Van Noy over to Sheriff John Taylor.

Judge John Sawyer immediately called a special session of the Sangamon County Circuit Court and a grand jury was sworn in to hear the case. Despite very little evidence of Van Noy's guilt, the jury decided that things looked bad enough that the blacksmith should be tried for his wife's murder. The trial began the following day, August 28. There is no record of testimony given at the trial, but whatever was said and done, the jury was convinced and took only one day to find him guilty. Van Noy was sentenced to be hanged for his crime, and he was removed to the Sangamon County Jail to await his execution.

There would be little to make this story unusual – it seemed a simple case of murder – if not for the visitor that Van Noy received while he was incarcerated at the County Jail. A Springfield doctor named Addison Philleo came to see Van Noy one day in his cell and the two of them made a strange, unsettling bargain. Dr. Philleo believed that he had created a device that, if applied to a corpse just after death, could reanimate the body. The doctor was convinced that this device would work and, apparently, convinced Van Noy of it, as well. He literally sold his body to Dr. Philleo with the belief that he would be brought back to life shortly after he was hanged.

On November 20, the day of Van Noy's execution, a crowd formed around the County Jail. Large numbers of men, women, and children arrived in Springfield from the surrounding communities and gathered at a spot just north of the present-day state capitol building to witness the hanging. A rumble went through the crowd when Van Noy appeared. He was driven to the execution site in a wagon, which stopped beneath two posts. A noose was tightened around his neck, and then the horses were whipped. They jerked forward, pulling the wagon out from beneath his dangling feet. Van Noy slowly strangled to death, his body twitching and shaking for several minutes until he finally became still.

Van Noy's body was left hanging for five hours before being cut down. Apparently, Sheriff Taylor had heard about the dead man's deal with Dr. Philleo and was determined not to allow him access to the fresh corpse – just in case his reanimation device actually worked. Dr. Philleo, his experiment ruined, began to conduct an autopsy on the corpse right on the spot. The onlookers were so disturbed and disgusted by the proceedings that law officers forced him to move to a nearby building to finish his work.

We will never know if Dr. Philleo's device would have worked or not, but he did earn a place in Illinois history after the gruesome events of the Van Noy execution. In 1832, he moved north to Galena and began publishing a newspaper called the *Galenian*. At the time, it was the only newspaper in the state, north of

Springfield. During the Black Hawk War, Dr. Philleo was attached to the command of Major Henry Dodge as a war correspondent. As the only newspaperman with the army, his columns were published all over the country – even though they were usually wildly inaccurate. Philleo frequently referred to Major Dodge as "General Dodge," creating the impression that Dodge was in command of the troops, even though General James D. Henry was actually in charge. The reports were never corrected and for years after, official reports asserted that Dodge, not Henry, was in command of the army during the Black Hawk War.

A single deed connected to the fighting can be attributed to Philleo during the war. One day, a scouting party came upon two Indians who attempted to flee. One of the Indians was immediately killed and a short time later, Dr. Philleo came upon the body and scalped it. For many years, he displayed the scalp as evidence of his bravery. He died in January 1841 in Tampa, Florida.

Nathaniel Van Noy was hanged on November 20, 1826, but his strange story did not end there. One of the last statements that he made claimed that he had buried a large quantity of gold beneath a tree that stood near his cabin on the Springfield road. Many neighbors and treasure hunters searched for the gold but, to this day, it has never been found.

Soon, though, even the lure of treasure was not enough to get people to trespass on Van Noy's former land. It became a place to be feared by travelers on the roadway and by settlers who lived nearby. A number of memoirs penned by area pioneers recalled how horses were always spooked when they passed by the Van Noy cabin, perhaps disturbed by the ghost that lurked there. The house remained standing until the 1850s, some say long after, and it was always regarded as a haunted place – and to some, it still is. Even after the house was torn down, stories circulated that the spirit of Peggy Van Noy wandered the fields where the Van Noy Settlement was once located.

One story was told by a traveler who journeyed past the house late one night. He was startled to hear the sound of a woman's bloodcurdling screams coming from inside. The man, who was not aware of the house's violent past, hurried into the building to see if someone needed help. After a few minutes of searching and calling out to anyone who might be inside, he realized that the cabin was abandoned. When he reached the Hall Tavern in Athens, he told his story and several locals who were gathered there recounted the tale of Peggy Van Noy's murder.

Other travelers reported the spectral form of a woman, believed to be Peggy Van Noy, floating through the woods. Stories of this female phantom – and at least one other ghost -- continued for many years. One such tale involved an Athens man named Alexander Hale, who, along with two friends, went out to the Van Noy farm one night, looking for the gold that was allegedly buried on the property. They searched the property as thoroughly as darkness and lantern light would allow but, after several hours, gave up without finding anything.

As they prepared to leave, one of the young men pointed out an unusual glow that was coming from deeper in the woods. Believing that it might be the lantern light of a rival treasure hunting party, they decided to sneak up on them and try and scare them away. They crept quietly through the trees, getting closer and closer to the strange light. Suddenly, one of the men hurried ahead, jumped out from behind a tree and came face-to-face with the eerie glow. He stumbled into a clearing and saw a man glaring at him. The translucent figure was not holding a lantern – the glow was actually emanating from the figure itself. The specter raised a threatening hand and the treasure hunter immediately turned and ran, colliding with his companions, who were several steps behind. Sensing his panic, they allowed themselves to be pulled along with him as he ran headlong toward the road.

The young man's companions, not having seen the ghost, were skeptical of their friend's story. He breathlessly recounted what he had seen while standing in the roadway near the house. Intrigued, Hale and the third man wanted to go back and take another look but their frightened friend was adamantly opposed to the idea. Finally, they relented and accompanied their shaken confederate back to Athens.

The next day, Hale and the other man returned to the Van Noy property to collect the tools that had been left behind the night before. They also wandered into the woods to look for any sign of the mysterious "glowing man" that their friend had so colorfully described. Finding no sign of any ghost, they returned home and no further mention was ever made between them of the haunted farm or the missing treasure.

Oddly enough, though, the following year, Alexander Hale, in partnership with John Overstreet, constructed a large, brick flour mill in Athens at a cost of nearly $11,000. This was no small amount of money in 1856 and no record has ever been produced as to where the funds for the project actually came from. Of course, there was a lot of speculation at the time (as there is today) about the source of the money, but it's unlikely that we will ever know.

Professional Baseball's First Execution
The Tragic Case of Charles "Pacer" Smith

No matter how it might seem to us today, when we expect more from our so-called "heroes" than we usually get, the idea of professional athletes getting mixed up with the law is nothing new. In fact, incidents of violent crimes go back almost to the beginning of professional sports. During the latter part of the nineteenth century, four major league baseball players committed murder. Edgar McNabb and Marty Bergen killed themselves before they could be brought to trial, and Charlie Sweeney spent several years in San Quentin Prison.

But on November 29, 1895, former professional pitcher Charles "Pacer" Smith was hanged for the murder of his daughter and sister-in-law – a bloody act that shocked the Central Illinois town of Decatur. It was a terrible event that left a black mark on the city's history – and left behind two separate hauntings in its wake.

Charles N. Smith was born in Pendleton, Indiana, on August 4, 1853. He was the fourth of 10 children of John and Rebecca Smith. John Smith was a shoemaker who joined the Union Army shortly after the start of the Civil War. In late 1864, he was thrown from his horse and reportedly spent six months in a hospital. He never completely recovered from the injury; the *Decatur Daily Review* described him as "practically a cripple." Family members described Charles as a very bright boy with a penchant for sports, although he never played professionally until he was 23. The game of baseball was just beginning to be popular during his early manhood and he naturally drifted into that profession. He had earned a good reputation as a pitcher and was offered and accepted a position with the Cincinnati Red Stockings.

Smith started his professional career in the mid-1870s. Although he was the property of the Cincinnati major league team, he never appeared in a regular season major league contest. His playing time was apparently confined to exhibition games (which were frequent during those seasons) and action with area independent teams. Even so, Smith's play in Cincinnati was enough to get him noticed and he spent the next few seasons in cities that would later have major league or strong minor league teams. He played for the Baltimore Blues in 1878 and 1879, and Nashville in 1880. He then returned to Indiana, spending 1881 with Terre Haute and the next two seasons with Indianapolis, both of the Northwestern League. Not retained when Indianapolis got major league baseball in 1884, Smith stayed in the area with the Noblesville team that year. In 1885, he played for clubs in Jacksonville, Florida, and in Greencastle and Evansville, Indiana.

During the early 1880s, John and Rebecca Smith separated, though they apparently remained married. Rebecca Smith and three of her children moved west to Illinois. Settling first in Danville and Mattoon, they eventually moved to the Decatur area. For a time, Charles lived with a married sister in Indianapolis, but in 1886, he was recruited by a local team in Decatur, where his mother now lived.

When Smith was urged to come to Decatur in the late 1880s, the city's once-outstanding professional team, the Yellow Hammers, was foundering at the bottom of its division. A few years before, Smith had earned the nickname of "Pacer," thanks to his infamous fastball style. He was lured to Decatur in hopes that he could revive the ailing team, and it worked, at least for a time. During the 1887 season, Smith brought new life to the dreadful team. He turned around their losing streak and in so doing, became quite popular around town, especially with the ladies. He was a smooth talker, a flashy dresser, widely traveled, and famous for his large handlebar mustache. Smith loved to have a good time and he loved to drink. When he wasn't on the baseball field, he was on a stool in a local tavern or in bed with one of his female admirers.

Smith's womanizing ways apparently came to an end in 1888, though, when he married one of his fans, a young woman named Maggie Buchert. He claimed that he wanted to settle down as a husband, but on the heels of wedded bliss came bad news. The Yellow Hammers disbanded after the summer season and Smith was left without a job. He began searching for work and he spent more and more of his time in the local taverns. Over the next few years, he managed to pick up work as a pitcher for clubs all over Illinois, including in Champaign, Bloomington, Ottawa, and Shreveport. He made several attempts to get back into the larger leagues, but his once lightning fast pitching had slowed down and his heavy drinking was starting to become common knowledge.

In 1890, Smith's wife, Maggie, became pregnant and gave birth to a baby girl named Louise. Soon after, Smith realized that married life was not to his liking and his drinking became even worse. He spent little time at home, choosing to frequent the saloons when he was not traveling out of town to play baseball. By 1893, he was considered completely unreliable by the more reputable clubs and he was forced to play baseball in Pana, Illinois, where he also served as a town policeman. After the end of the season, he was fired from both jobs and returned to look for work in Decatur. The once nationally-known baseball player was soon working as a cook at the Hoffman House, and other seedy taverns, setting out free lunches for drinking men. It was a long fall from the fame that he once enjoyed as a professional baseball player.

Smith's drinking and his increasing bitterness destroyed his marriage. Maggie finally decided to leave him and, with her daughter, moved back into her father's home on East Lawrence Street. She told Smith that he was welcome to come and see Louise anytime that he liked and, while he never contributed any sort of support for his wife and daughter, he did visit on a fairly regular basis. The rest of his life continued to deteriorate. His drinking grew steadily worse and, eventually, it would be alcohol that would ruin him for good.

On Saturday, September 28, 1895, Smith spent the entire day drinking in a downtown saloon. He was a regular customer, so he had little trouble convincing the bartender to loan him his revolver. He left the tavern and went to the home of his father-in-law, Frank Buchert, where Maggie, Louise, and Maggie's sister, Edna, also lived. When he arrived there, he asked for his daughter, but Louise was not there at the time. Edna offered to go and look for her and she went off down the street, leaving Smith waiting on the front porch. Louise, who was six years old at the time, was playing with friends in a neighbor's yard, but Edna brought her back home to see her father. Witnesses later testified that Smith never gave any inclination that he was upset about anything – or that he planned to kill anyone.

The house where the Bucherts lived was a one-story structure with a high basement. When Edna returned with the child, they sat down on the steps together. Smith was standing nearby and Maggie had also come outside to visit. She was standing on the steps a few feet away. One moment Smith was smiling and then, suddenly and without any warning, he removed the borrowed revolver from his coat and fired at his daughter. The shot struck Louise in the neck and she made a loud, choking cry as she pitched forward and rolled down the stairs to land at her father's feet. Maggie and Edna, utterly terrified, screamed and scrambled up the stairs and away from the gun. Smith fired a second shot at Maggie and it narrowly missed her, lodging in the ceiling of the front porch. She began to scream for help, rushing away from the house and in the direction of Jacobs' Butcher Shop, where her father worked, a half-block away.

The exact manner of Edna Buchert's murder will never be known as Smith was the only witness and he never spoke of it. The only thing that can be stated for certain is that Smith turned his gun on her and fired one time. She was struck near the back door of the house and she ran around to the east side of the house and fell dead on the front walk. Her father found her there, covered in blood, a short time later.

Maggie narrowly escaped the violence. She burst through the door of the butcher shop, screaming, "Charlie has shot Louise!" Frank Buchert immediately ran to his house, where he discovered Edna on the sidewalk. Buchert dropped to his knees and pulled Edna to him in a grief-stricken embrace. He called her name several times but it was too late, the young woman was already dead. Buchert looked up and saw Charles Smith standing just a short distance away. He was coldly gazing at the scene, the smoking revolver still in his hand. Buchert pleaded with Smith to tell him why he would have done such a terrible thing. Smith gave him an angry reply, "You be a little careful, or I'll give you your own dose of lead."

Buchert laid Edna's body carefully on the ground and, his hands crimson with his daughter's blood, ran to the fallen body of his granddaughter. Louise was unconscious, but still alive, although she was bleeding badly. He picked her up and carried her into the house, gently placing her on a bed. By this time, neighbors had started to gather and one of the men carried Edna's body into the house and placed her on a lounge in the living room.

With one last glance at the Buchert house, "Pacer" Smith walked calmly and slowly down the street in the direction of the butcher shop, possibly looking for his wife. Luckily, he never found her.

A telephone call was made to the police headquarters from the Jacobs' store and details were passed along about the crime, along with the identity of the murderer. Chief Mason and Officer Howard Williams jumped into a buggy and headed toward the Buchert home. Deputy Sheriff Frank Taylor and Officer Cross also started searching for the killer. At Clay Street, they ran into Mr. Jacobs, Frank Buchert's employer, who had been following Smith from a distance. He told the officers that he had started walking north. Moments later, they saw Smith heading into a nearby alley and both men jumped from the buggy and ran toward him, just in time to see him disappear into a yard. Both men drew their revolvers, expecting a fight, as they advanced on him.

As the officers rounded the corner of a house, though, they were surprised to see Smith walking toward them. He held the revolver in his right hand and when Cross grabbed hold of him, he released it. He offered no resistance, and when Cross asked him why he had done it, his only reply was "he had had lots of trouble and he had finally put an end to it all."

Chief Mason and Officer Williams arrived a few moments later and helped take Smith into custody. He was taken to the jail and, within 30 minutes after the murder, the killer was behind bars. Smith was charged with Edna Buchert's killing. He was charged with a second murder on Monday morning, when Louise died from her wound.

Word quickly spread throughout Decatur about the brutal murders – and about the famous killer. The excitement was intense and lynching was freely spoken of on the streets and in the taverns and saloons. Even police officers were upset and angry over the crime. Officer Brockway, who was described as "one of the oldest and most reliable men on the police force," rushed at Smith when he was first brought to the jail and tried to attack him with his billy-club. Other officers restrained him, but they did so reluctantly. Brockway was the uncle of Maggie and Edna Buchert and only the cooler heads of the other officers kept him from killing Smith with his bare hands.

Shortly after Smith was locked up, he was interrogated by Sheriff I.P. Nicholson. On Saturday night, he refused to talk. His replies to questions that were asked by Nicholson were disjointed and strange. Nicholson asked, "What was the matter with you today, Pacer?"

"What have I done? I don't know what you mean," Smith replied.

Nicholson was incensed. "Don't attempt that. You haven't got sense enough to play crazy. You had better 'fess up and tell the whole story, and it will go better for you," he said.

But Smith just shook his head and refused to explain the reasons behind what he had done. "I have had lots of trouble but it's all over now. I'm sick now but will tell you all about it tomorrow," he said.

The newspapers reported that Smith became sick that night and his "entire faculties seemed to collapse." The police feared that he was being seized by delirium from alcohol (everyone was aware of his heavy drinking), but the next morning, he seemed to rally and his health improved. In spite of this, he never kept his promise to Sheriff Nicholson and refused to explain why he had shot Louise and Edna. In fact, his only regret over the course of the next few days was that he had been unable to kill his wife.

On Monday, following the death of Louise, a grand jury indicted Smith for both murders. That afternoon, he was taken into court and arraigned for trial. Attorneys Bunn and Park were appointed to defend him, but they asked to be excused and I.A. Buckingham was appointed in their place. On Wednesday, Smith was brought into court, where he entered a guilty plea for the murder of Louise. However, he stated that he was not guilty for Edna's murder, apparently believing that since he meant to kill his wife, not his sister-in-law, he was less accountable for the brutal crime.

On Monday, October 8, Smith was brought back into court to have his sentence pronounced. After hearing evidence from a number of witnesses, Judge Vail asked Smith's attorney if he had a statement that he wanted to make on behalf of his client. Buckingham and Smith held a whispered conversation for a few moments and then Smith stood and asked to speak. He spoke quietly in a calm voice that was almost impossible to hear. His voice faltered several times as he made his statement.

"I borrowed the gun and went down there to kill the lady and the child – my wife. I understood that if I plead guilty that I would be hung and I am willing to do it, but would like to have it put off until the 16th of February. I am willing to face anybody and everybody," he said.

Smith then took his seat again and wiped the perspiration that had beaded on his forehead with a black silk handkerchief. The judge asked Buckingham if he had anything that he wanted to add and the attorney stated that he didn't.

Judge Vail then spoke. "When a man pleads guilty to murder in the first degree as is charged in this indictment, he places himself at the discretion of the court to be sentenced, to be hanged or to be confined in the penitentiary for life or for a term not less than 14 years. I can see that a man can be so injured, or so abused that his wrongs may so weigh upon him until he imagines that he is in a way justified in murder. But it is not apparent that there was any ill feeling in this family. I cannot imagine how any man could have any ill feeling or hold any hatred that would cause him to willfully take the life of a mere child. In my judgment, this is a case where justice demands the extreme penalty of the law, but it is not an easy task. The law is the highest exponent that teaches the duty of one citizen to another and no man has the right to take the law into his own hands. Now, if Mr. Smith has anything to say in extenuating him from this crime, then I want to hear it."

Smith only shook his head. He never spoke about why he had committed the murders.

The judge then ordered Smith to stand as he passed sentence. "It is the sentence of this court that you be taken back to the Macon County jail, and there be securely confined, until the twenty-ninth day of November, when you shall be taken out and hanged by the neck until dead," he said.

During the pronouncement of the sentence, Smith stared silently at the judge. He stood completely still, a blank expression on his face. It was not until the judge was finished that color came back into his face. He slumped in what seemed to be relief, bowed his head and whispered, "Thank you."

The silence of courtroom was shattered by the piercing tones of a woman's voice. A murmur of approval rippled through the courtroom as Maggie Smith cried out, "Thank God, he has got his just dues. My baby, oh, my baby!" Many of those in attendance that day later stated that they would never forget her words, or the crushing grief that could be heard in her voice.

Maggie then burst into tears and was comforted by several friends. Frank Buchert, who was next to her, sprang from his seat and turning to the crowd said, "That is all I want; the law will give him what he deserves."

Smith was hustled out of the courtroom and the crowd parted as he walked out between Sheriff Nicholson and Deputy Holmes. As he passed a group of his friends from the taverns, he made the motion of putting a rope around his neck and pretended to pull it tight. He laughed, "The twenty-ninth of November, boys."

When he was outside, he told the sheriff that he was perfectly happy with the sentence and only feared that he would be given a life sentence in the penitentiary instead. He never explained why he had asked for the hanging to be delayed until February.

Smith was removed from his common cell at the jail that afternoon and taken to a solitary cell in the upstairs portion of the building. The following afternoon, he was visited by Father Charles Brady, the assistant pastor of St. Patrick's Church. The young priest spoke to Smith at length about his spiritual welfare. Father Brady returned several times over the course of the next few days and, a week later, Smith was baptized into the Roman Catholic Church. Smith seemed to feel a great deal better after the service and the newspapers reported, "Despite what may be said to the contrary, Smith ever after his baptism seemed to feel better and bore up under the ordeal of awaiting his last day with remarkable fortitude."

Smith remained incarcerated in his solitary cell until about two weeks before his execution; he was placed on "death watch," which meant that he was constantly under guard. Deputy Sam Stabler performed the duty during the daytime and Tom Richardson stayed with Smith at night. Smith grew especially fond of Stabler and often spoke of him to reporters. Shortly before his death, he told one newspaper reporter, "The sheriff has been just as kind to me as I could wish. Anything I want, I get. A man could not treat a guest better than Sheriff Nicholson does me. Sam Stabler is all right, too. He is the same old fellow every day and we get along all right."

Thursday, November 28, was Smith's last Thanksgiving. He was in good spirits, visited with his priest and his family, and ate a hearty dinner of turkey with oyster dressing, gravy, sweet and Irish potatoes, a piece of pie, and a large glass of milk. His father, mother, brothers, and several sisters stayed with him in his cell for several hours, but when his mother started to leave, she collapsed with grief and had to be escorted out by the officers on duty.

Around 3:00 p.m., Smith's brother, J.E. Smith, went to the Buchert home and tried to convince Maggie and Frank Buchert to come to the jail and see Smith one last time. Both of them refused. Father Brady stayed with Smith throughout the remainder of the day and promised to return the next morning with Father Higgins of Taylorville to give Smith communion one last time.

Smith rose early on the morning of November 29. He ate breakfast and then took a short nap in his cell. He told reporters that he did this so that he would feel better about his ordeal at noon. One of the reporters asked him if he had heard about a reprieve that had recently been granted to another prisoner and Smith said that he had, noting that the man's death sentence had been commuted after he became a Christian and was baptized. Smith had written a letter to the man and he claimed this had been the key to the prisoner's religious conversion. When Smith was asked what he would say to a reprieve for himself, he snapped his fingers and said, "I don't care that much. I am all ready to go."

Just before noon, Sheriff Nicholson came to Smith's cell and read aloud his death warrant. Father Brady and Father Higgins stood nearby and Smith listened calmly. The sheriff led the procession to the jail yard, where a scaffold stood. Hundreds of people from Decatur came to see the gallows on Thursday afternoon, streaming in and out of the yard to see the "infernal device" that would claim Smith's life. On the day of the execution, only about 300 ticket-holders were allowed to witness the hanging.

As the procession climbed the stairs, reporters noted that Smith was "pale but determined." The two priests prayed with him a final time and then the hood and the noose were slipped over his head. Under the platform, three doctors waited to pronounce Smith dead. A few moments later, Smith plunged to his doom. It was the last public hanging in Macon County's history.

It was obvious to everyone who knew him in his final days that "Pacer" Smith wanted to die for the crimes that he had committed. He would never speak of what led him to commit the brutal crime of shooting his own child and trying to murder his wife and killing his sister-in-law instead. Whatever drove him to it, he seemed to believe that death was the only thing that would ease his conscience and assuage his guilt.

But was death enough? According to the legend of Charles "Pacer" Smith, it was not.

After the body was cut down, and Smith was pronounced dead, he was taken to the Martin Funeral Home and then delivered to his mother's house for the wake. Services were held at St. Patrick's Church and Smith was buried in an unmarked grave in Calvary Cemetery. The pallbearers for the service were former team members of Smith's from his days with the Yellow Hammers.

Ever since his burial, the legend states that Smith's ghost has been seen walking in Cavalry Cemetery, dressed in a baseball uniform from his days of glory. It has been said that he refuses to rest in peace, still tormented, even in death, by the horrible deeds that he committed in life.

The scene of Smith's crimes has also been reportedly haunted over the years. According to tenants in the house on East Lawrence Street, the ghostly echoes of a woman's screams were heard for decades, followed by the pounding of footsteps on the porch, as if Edna Buchert was still running for her life, fleeing from her crazed and murderous brother-in-law.

The "Hanging Tree" of Greene County

The story of the "hanging tree," and the phantom that haunts it, has been told in Greene County for more than a century. The strange tale of murder and the macabre was recounted for misbehaving children as a bedtime story and involved a traveling body that was used to frighten wrongdoers as it hung from a post at the railroad station. It remains today as one of Central Illinois' strangest tales of crime and a lingering ghost.

Dr. Charles MacCauliffe was the only physician in the small town of Wrights in 1879. While a respected and generally well-liked man, his sterling personality traits did not save him from death at the end of a rope after he committed murder one night. MacCauliffe and his brother-in-law, a local man named James Heavener, were drinking one evening in the town's only saloon and, at some point, got into a heated argument. Obviously fueled by too many drinks, the fight became so intense that Dr. MacCauliffe went behind the bar, grabbed a shotgun that the owner kept there and fired both barrels into Heavener's chest. His brother-in-law was instantly killed, and when he saw what he had done, the doctor panicked, threw the shotgun on the floor and ran from the saloon. He left Heavener on the floor in a growing pool of his own blood.

As MacCauliffe ran, a group of men who witnessed the murder chased after him. They quickly found the doctor hiding in a neighborhood barn, took him into custody and delivered him to the town constable. Wrights was not large enough to have its own jail, so after some discussion, the constable and several of the men decided to take Dr. MacCauliffe to nearby Carrollton. They loaded him onto a wagon and started out into the night.

Not far from town, the wagon rolled past a large oak tree that was located at the edge of Hickory Grove Cemetery and as the men looked up into the tangle of branches, they decided that they would hang the doctor right then and there. With the full approval of the constable, they tied a rope around MacCauliffe's neck and stood him up in the back of the wagon. Ignoring his pleas for mercy, one of the men slapped the horse on the hindquarters and it jerked forward, pulling the wagon out

Dr. MacCauliffe's forgotten grave

from under the struggling doctor's feet. He hung there, his feet kicking and his body twitching, as he slowly strangled to death.

Later on, the constable and some of the other men in the lynching party told people that a mob of men had surprised them, took the doctor away, and hanged him from the cemetery oak tree. Of course, most folks knew this was not the case because, after the hanging, all of the men involved had gone home to bed. If the doctor really had been taken away from them, they would have scoured the countryside for his abductors. Even though no one believed their story, no arrests were ever attempted for the doctor's murder.

Most of the local people found out about the lynching the next morning. A group of children were walking along the road near the cemetery and saw MacCauliffe's body still hanging there, gently twisting in the breeze. They became frightened and ran home to tell their parents. Several adults went back to the cemetery and cut down the corpse. There was a lot of discussion about what to do with the body. At some point, it was loaded on a wagon and taken to the railroad station in town. With the rope still knotted about his neck, the corpse was hoisted up on a pole and left on display as a warning to passersby about what happens to lawbreakers in Wrights.

The body became quite an attraction and people traveled from nearby towns to get a look at it. The late Vera Harr, a resident of Carrollton, recalled, "My mother was born that year and grandma wasn't allowed to see the body for fear that the baby would be marked for life."

Finally, after several days, the corpse was cut down and buried in an unmarked grave in the southeast corner of Hickory Grove Cemetery. The doctor was laid to rest with no ceremony whatsoever and no one was present at his burial, save for the two men who dug the grave. However, a local farmer, John W. Flowers, decided that MacCauliffe's grave should be marked.

From the nearby woods, Flowers dug up a small cedar tree and planted it next to the doctor's grave. He also used some cement and creek sand and created a small, stone monument. He took the metal nameplate from the door of the doctor's office in Wrights, and imbedded it in the wet cement. The plate read simply "Doctor MacCauliffe." Below it, he scratched out the words "Died 1879." The plate is still readable today but the lettering that was cut into the stone has faded over time. The ghostly lettering can only be seen if a visitor looks closely and perhaps brushes their hand across the stone.

Later, a marker was also placed on the old "hanging tree," telling the story of the murder and the lynching that occurred. Unfortunately, the tree blew down in a storm a few years ago, providing an ending to at least one part of the eerie story.

For decades, legends told in Greene County advised against walking the road beneath the "hanging tree" at night. It was said that on certain nights, the ghostly figure of Dr. MacCauliffe could still be seen hanging from the twisting branches overhead. As he swayed in the wind, his body rotated until watchers could see his face. If his eyes opened, the legend stated, then you were bound to die within the next year.

It was a warning of death that most superstitious local residents went out of their way to avoid.

The Murder of Joe Ricketts
Haunted History of the Wabash Railroad Station

One of the most sensational Central Illinois murders of the early 1900s was the brutal slaying of a young Decatur man named Joe Ricketts in 1905. The well-liked young man was an employee of the Pacific Freight Company and he was beaten to death right outside of the Wabash Railroad station. More than a century later, his murder remains unsolved.

Could this be the reason why his ghost still haunts the train station to this day?

The Wabash Station in Decatur was dedicated on June 18, 1901, with a crowd of several hundred people in attendance. The ornate brick and stone building had been constructed to replace the Union Station that the company had once shared with the Illinois Central Railroad. On the day of the dedication, more than 600 people arrived by excursion train and large numbers of local people turned out by way of street car, carriage, and on foot. Entertainment was provided by the Goodman Band and in the afternoon, speakers addressed the crowd from a second-floor balcony on the south side of the station. Only mid-day thunderstorms managed to put a damper on the celebratory event.

The station had been designed by architect Theodor Link, who also designed the Union Station in St. Louis and many other buildings. It was constructed of yellow brick with terra cotta trim and fitted with a number of classical details. A large tower was located in the center of the building and two large, uneven wings extended to either side, following the line of the Wabash tracks. A freight and baggage depot was located on the west end of the station.

The main portion of the station's interior had tile floors, marble wainscoting, and frescoed walls and ceilings. It was in the main lobby that railroad patrons found the ticket office, waiting room, rest rooms, news stand, lunch room, and the watch inspection office, where those employees who were required to carry standard watches reported with them for mandatory monthly inspections. On the second floor were the 14 Wabash division offices that served such officials and staff as the division superintendent, the chief dispatcher and his five assistants, telegraph manager, general roadmaster, trainmaster, resident engineer, and fuel inspector. The dispatcher's office, on the northwest side of the station with a bay window that offered a considerable view of the tracks, east to west, was considered one of the finest in the country. In those days, there were 22 Wabash

The Wabash Railroad Station in Decatur around the time that Joe Ricketts was killed. He worked in the freight building shown at the far left of the photo.

passenger trains and 11 regular freight trains leaving Decatur every day. It was one of the great transportation hubs of Central Illinois.

A little over two months later, though, the Wabash station became the scene of one of the most shocking murders in the history of the city. A young man named Joe Ricketts, who was only 21-years-old, was brutally clubbed to death on the west side of the station, right next to the freight depot. Local newspapers called the incident "the most foul and cold-blooded murder that has ever occurred in Decatur." The question that everyone wanted an answer to was why anyone would want to kill a man who was friends with nearly everyone in the city.

Joe Ricketts was born and raised in Decatur, the son of J.H. Ricketts, a respected carpenter. As a young boy, he went to work for Ehrhart's grocery store at the corner of Green and Union Streets and soon became a familiar face to everyone in the neighborhood. He began work there delivering goods to nearby customers with a basket and a little wagon. As he got older, his responsibilities increased and he became the head deliveryman for the grocer. His duties took him to all parts of the city and he became known personally to hundreds of families throughout Decatur. He was a beloved character, known for his good nature, pleasant smile, and cheerfulness. He went above and beyond what was required of him for his job and people remembered him for it.

After working for Ehrhart's for several years, he worked for the Conrad grocery until it closed, and then worked for a time for his father at his construction business. In July 1905, Ricketts took a position working nights for the Pacific Express Company at the Wabash Station. Joe stayed the entire night at the station, taking care of the express office during the early morning hours. He reportedly enjoyed the job very much and his supervisor, Pete Roby, had nothing but good things to say about him.

The admiration that everyone seemed to have for Joe Ricketts was what made his death so puzzling. Joe was killed on the west side of the station, in between the main building and the Pacific Express Company building. His body was discovered by W.A. Owens, who was walking between some freight cars and the station around 9:30 p.m. He called to two men who were working in the Wabash yards and they approached the body with a lantern, fearing that someone had been hurt. When they realized the man was dead, they gave the alarm to the station master, who notified the police. When police officers arrived, they discovered that the dead man was Joe Ricketts.

Ricketts' body was lying in a pool of blood, just a few feet away from the railroad tracks. Two clubs, both bloody at one end, were found near the body, and it was plain that the young man's head had been pounded with several solid blows. There was no evidence of a struggle and it did not appear that he had been robbed. When officers examined his body, they found that his skull had been crushed, splintering the bone and exposing the brains beneath. His forehead had been smashed in, covering his face and clothing with blood. His hands were stretched out straight and he was flat on his back. As he fell, his heels dug up a little place on the ground, and it looked as though the first blow that struck him had knocked him down where he stood. Joe's cap was lying about two feet away from his body. There was nothing about his hands to suggest that he ever got a chance to defend himself.

Joe had been missing for about an hour and a half. Peter Roby had first gone looking for him about 8:00 p.m., shortly after he was seen talking to a customer, A.L. Onstott, in the south door of the express office. He had been laughing and cheerfully performing his duties. He went to his death just a short time later, within easy shouting distance of his friends and co-workers and the scores of passengers who came and went on the trains throughout the evening.

Lights were used to illuminate the dark and isolated area where Joe's body was found. At first, it seemed strange that a man whose duties were in the express office would have been in such an isolated spot. Peter Roby had an explanation, however. He said that since there was no bathroom in the express office, he and Joe often ducked outside at night and relieved themselves in the dark corner. He believed that Ricketts must have been surprised while coming or going from the area. Deputy Sheriff Hendricks had another idea. He thought that Joe might have come across thieves who were pilfering melons from a nearby freight car and when he startled them, they beat him to keep him quiet.

As word began to spread about the murder – and the popular victim – a large crowd hurried to the scene, making it difficult for the police officers to search for clues. The body was left in place until word was sent to the coroner, but Dr. Buxton was out of the city, forcing Justice Keeler to come and act as coroner. The body was eventually taken to Hawkins & Davis' undertaking parlor, where an inquest was held the following afternoon.

In the meantime, at the Wabash Station, the police continued their search of the grounds. Several dependable men from the crowd were recruited to assist them in their efforts. When nothing besides the two bloody clubs was found, officers began scouring the city for anyone who had information about the murder. Messages were sent to surrounding cities, ordering that all strangers be taken into custody and held for questioning. By 2:00 a.m., eight men had been arrested in Decatur and another man had been taken into custody in Taylorville. All of the men were eventually released, since no evidence could be found against any of them.

On August 29, the mysterious murder became even more puzzling. A witness had come forward to say that he had seen three people in the vicinity of the spot where Ricketts' body had been found, likely within a few minutes of the murder. Marlon Spencer, a local laborer, had been on his way to his brother-in-law's house at about 9:00 p.m. on the night of the murder. Spencer lived on Wabash Avenue and left his house, walking east until he came to Morgan Street. He turned south along the railroad tracks and at the crossing, cut across to head toward the depot. Spencer was about halfway across the yards when he heard the sound of a man clearing his throat. He turned his head and saw a man standing against the signal house at the southwest corner of the crossing. There was a bright light at the crossing and Spencer said that he would have no trouble recognizing the man if he ever saw him again. The man was leaning against the signal house and was dressed in a dark suit and a black, soft hat. He was slim and had a light-colored, heavy mustache. The man was holding what Spencer thought was a shovel in his hands. He later realized that it could have been a club or a stick. The man was not looking in his direction. Instead, he was staring rather intently toward the east.

Spencer was walking in the direction that the man was looking, but did not believe the man saw him there because he was focused so strongly on something in the distance. At this point, a line of boxcars prevented Spencer from seeing the freight office, but as he got closer, he heard the distinct voice of a woman speak from the shadows. "I'm going this way," she said. Spencer looked up and saw a woman walking with another person in the darkness. He could not tell if the woman's companion was a man or another woman, nor could he describe the woman, other than to say that she was wearing some kind of dark-colored dress.

Spencer thought nothing of the incident at the time and he never saw Ricketts' body, which was probably already lying in the darkness. He walked on to the station and went inside. When he did, he looked at the clock and noted that it was 9:10 p.m. He only remembered the time because it was getting late and he was expected at his brother-in-law's house. Spencer went home by another route and because of that, knew nothing about the murder until the following day. Realizing that he might have a clue for the police, he went downtown and reported what he had seen. Sadly, the information led nowhere and if the man, the woman, or the unknown companion had any connection to the murder, they were never found.

Joe Ricketts was buried on August 30 in Greenwood Cemetery. His funeral was the largest ever held at the First Christian Church and was filled with express company employees, railroad men, and scores of people who knew and loved Joe from his days of service as a grocery deliveryman.

By early September, the case was already growing cold. The police had been over every clue several times and had questioned hundreds of people about the case. They were nearly overcome with theories and ideas from well-meaning citizens, but none of them led to the killers. Officers diligently followed up on everything that came along, but as more days passed, it became less likely that anything useful would be found. In time, investigators moved on to other cases and Joe Ricketts' murder became less and less of a priority.

As with every unsolved case, it remains open today, but it's unlikely that any new information will ever emerge about a murder that's now more than a century old. It seems almost certain that the identity of Joe Ricketts' killers will forever remain a mystery.

Time moved on and the story of Joe Ricketts was mostly forgotten. By the 1960s, the Wabash Railroad had merged with Norfolk & Western. The Decatur shops closed down and by the 1980s, there was no passenger service leaving town at all. The Wabash station was already a shadow of its former self by that time. The majestic tower had long since been removed and the wear and tear of decades had turned the old station into an eyesore. For many years, it sat abandoned and empty alongside of railroad tracks that were used less and less as time went by. Plans began to be made to tear down the crumbling building and most believed that its days were numbered.

In 2002, however, new life was breathed into the Wabash station when it was purchased, renovated, and turned into an antique mall. As the dust and decay of the years of abandonment were blown away, stories began to circulate about the ghost stories that once were told about the station.

One of them dated back to the early 1940s, when the station was still a hub of activity and passengers came and went all day and into the night. It was during many nighttime shifts that staff members and railroad workers encountered an eerie woman in white who was seen sitting on a bench in the station.

A legend began to be told about this woman. The young lady, the story went, had been married to a man who joined the service during World War I. After many months of fighting, she received a letter from him stating that he was coming home. Eagerly, she went down to the Wabash station on the scheduled date of his arrival to meet the train, but he never arrived. Several days went by and then she received word that he had been killed in a bus accident on his way to the train station. Out of her mind with grief, she committed suicide.

As the years passed, those who worked, and even passed through, the Wabash station reported the sight of a lovely young woman, still waiting expectantly on a bench in the station. Staff members often spoke of sightings of the young woman in a white dress. She appeared on a waiting bench, looking frantic and worried, but never stayed around for long. She would either fade away or would be there one second and simply gone the next. The sightings continued into the 1950s and then she began to be reported less and less until the accounts stopped altogether.

But was that woman in white the only ghost that haunted the old Wabash station? The new owners didn't think so. They began experiencing eerie events just before it reopened as an antique store. One winter evening, they reported seeing a white apparition near the former departure door. It was not a solid-looking shape, but very loose and filmy. It quickly vanished, but there was no mistaking what they had seen. And soon, they would not be the only ones seeing things.

Staff members and antique dealers alike began to talk about a voice that was heard in the quiet building, footsteps on the tile floors, and objects that would move from place to place overnight, when the station was locked up and empty. One employee said that she had turned off the lights in the men's restroom one evening before she left, but when she came back in the morning, they had been switched off again. On another day, she saw an antique scale swinging back and forth on its own. No one was near it and there was no movement of air that could have caused it to start swinging.

One afternoon, a staff member came down from the second floor and asked the owners if they thought there might be ghosts in the building. He said that he felt someone walk up beside him, assuming that it was a customer. When he turned to speak to them, he said that he saw a vague figure literally float around the corner away from him and disappear.

Another worker also saw the resident phantom. One day she spotted a man that she described as looking "sepia-toned" as he walked into an area of the upstairs that had once been a closet for storing statements and forms. The man never came out of the room. When she checked, she found it empty.

On another occasion, a customer saw a young man in what she described as "old-fashioned clothing, a shirt and pants with suspenders," walk out of the doorway on the west end of the station. There had once been a door there that led outside to the freight office – and it had been just outside of that door where Joe Ricketts was killed.

Could the spectral man who had been seen many times inside of the Wabash station be the spirit of Joe Ricketts, unable to rest because his murder was never solved? It certainly seems possible. While there were a number of other murders in that part of Decatur – the city's largest vice district was once located near the train stations – none of them were as closely connected to the station as the Ricketts murder. And none of them took place literally right outside of the station's back door.

Those who have seen this apparition always describe him as "pleasant-looking" or "with a smile on his face." He doesn't seem to be troubled by a desire to correct the wrongs that were done to him in life. He appears content in his afterlife, even if it means that he will continue to haunt the Wabash station for as long as it stands.

In my opinion, this makes it even more likely that the ghost is that of Joe Ricketts, a kind, well-liked young man who took the job at the express office because it was something that he loved to do. Perhaps Joe stayed behind in this world by choice, not looking for revenge because of his unsolved murder, but because he could continue to do the job that he loved for all time.

The First Murderess

The first woman ever convicted of murder in the Central Illinois town of Decatur was Josephine Cooper, who was convicted after her trial in 1921. According to accounts, a man named James Parker had moved into the Cooper home on East King Street in 1920. At the time, he was renting a room from Josephine, but the two soon became lovers. It was widely announced that they planned to be married but something soured those plans. It is believed that Josephine fell in love with someone else, a man named J.W. Gordon, and that she found Parker to be a little harder to get rid of than she had first thought.

In fact, he continued to linger behind at the Cooper house almost a century after his death.

We will never know what drove Josephine Cooper to murder. It's possible that she had homicidal tendencies all along, although there is no record that she ever committed an illegal act in her first 37 years on earth. But somewhere along the line, she realized that murder was an easy way to get rid of her husband, her uncle, and at least two of the men who rented rooms in her house.

Not long after Josephine and James Parker became lovers, he made the fatal mistake of signing over a $1,000 life insurance policy to Josephine. She had already tired of him by this time, but apparently that insurance policy was the motive that she needed to commit murder. Several letters were later discovered that she had written to her other lover, J.W. Gordon, asking him to supply her with poison. While it was never proven that Gordon actually got it for her, she eventually obtained it from somewhere.

James Parker soon became seriously ill. He deteriorated quickly and died just two days after showing signs of some mysterious ailment. His body was discovered in the Cooper home and the police immediately suspected foul play. Josephine was a very clumsy killer, as Parker's corpse became the fourth body to be found in her home in just a few years.

The first had been that of Charles Blake, another boarder, who had died in 1913. Her husband, Oliver Cooper, had died mysteriously in 1917 and, three years later, Josephine's uncle, Albert McDaniel, died suddenly as well. After Parker's body had been discovered, the coroner refused to sign a death certificate until a formal inquest could be held. A preliminary report from the unlucky man's autopsy showed that his internal organs contained arsenic in lethal quantities.

Josephine's lover, J.W. Gordon became the leading suspect in Parker's murder and the police quickly placed him under arrest. Under questioning, he admitted that he had received letters from Cooper asking for poison, but he denied giving it to her. He also confessed that he had been a rival with Parker for the woman's affections but that he had never harmed the other man. He believed that it had been Cooper who had killed him – and detectives agreed. Gordon was later set free due to lack of any evidence against him.

Cooper was arrested and put on trial in March 1921, and the testimony that was heard in the courtroom proved to be a strange and often convoluted tale of murder, insanity, and horror.

State's Attorney C.F. Evans made the opening statements in the case, outlining the events as they had occurred. He told the courtroom that in 1920, Josephine Cooper had been operating a boarding house in her home on East King Street. James Parker was a boarder there and the two became lovers, up until the time that Gordon entered her life. According to later testimony from Jennie Godwin, who did Josephine's washing, Cooper and Gordon went to Chicago for a few days in early 1921 and stayed at the Fort Dearborn Hotel as husband

and wife. Jennie had received a postcard from Cooper while they were away. The two remained lovers beyond the time of Parker's death, and although Gordon was married and living with his wife, he often posed as a widower and told people that the woman he lived with was his stepmother.

During the time that Parker was living with Cooper, Gordon joined the Supreme Tribe of Ben-Hur, a national fraternal organization that was later re-formed into Ben-Hur Life Insurance. He took out an insurance policy and told the examining physician that he was a widower and had the policy made out to his brother. Josephine Cooper joined the same lodge and then later on, Parker joined, as well. He had his policy made payable to Cooper and, initially, her policy was payable to Parker. She later changed it so that, in the event of her death, Gordon would collect instead. She never made Parker aware of the changes.

As Cooper tired of Parker's affections, the state's attorney revealed that she made other attempts to get rid of him. She often told friends and neighbors that he was cruel to her and beat her. She tried to concoct a plan with another, part-time boarder, Haven Whitehouse, to have a fake telegram sent from Parker's mother in Oklahoma, asking him to come home. Whitehouse declined to be involved and when she asked Cooper why she wanted to make Parker leave, she was told that Gordon treated her right and she liked him better.

Another witness who took the stand against Josephine was Amanda Ely, who lived across the street from the boarding house. She stated that she had seen Gordon at Cooper's house many times and that she was also a witness when Cooper asked Haven Whitehouse about sending the false telegram. This event occurred about one week before James Parker became ill. A few days later, Josephine was complaining to her neighbor and told her that she wanted to quit keeping a boarding house and go back to work, but Parker wouldn't let her. But, she added, "I and a friend of mine have a plan to get rid of Parker." Three or four days later, Parker became so sick that he was unable to get out of his bed.

Around this same time, Cooper wrote several letters to Gordon, who was living and working in the nearby town of Blue Mound, and asked him for "something to put in Parker's coffee." She also wrote that she wanted Parker to die away from home so that no one would suspect that she had anything to do with his death. Although Josephine didn't know it, her lover was unfaithful to her. In addition to being married, he was also keeping company with a Blue Mound woman named Addie Farrow, who believed that he was a widower. Gordon actually showed one of Josephine's letters to her and after learning of Parker's death, Farrow had gone to the police with her suspicions.

When Gordon was arrested, he first denied receiving the letters, but then took police officers to his garage, where he had hidden them, and turned them over. However, he was adamant about the fact that he had not given Cooper the poison that she asked for. Eventually, investigators came to believe him.

The prosecution maintained that after Parker became sick, Dr. W.A. Dixon was called and suggested that Parker be taken to a hospital, but Cooper objected. He also said that, following Parker's death, she had not only collected on his life insurance policy, but also managed to get the pay that was due to him from the Wabash Railroad where he worked. When arrested, she had Parker's watch and $58 in cash, a portion of which was sent to his mother in Oklahoma. When questioned by the police, she admitted that only $8 of the money belonged to her and the rest of it had been Parker's.

Evans added that when Parker's life insurance policy had been taken out, that he had only paid the first premium. Subsequent payments had been made by both Cooper and J.W. Gordon.

Finally, he noted, an examination of Parker's remains revealed that a fatal quantity of arsenic had been ingested into his system. His vital organs had been saturated with it and the deadly poison had taken his life. The arsenic had been given to him, Evans told the jury, by Josephine Cooper.

Attorney J. R. Fitzgerald made the opening statements and conducted a defense on Cooper's behalf. He claimed that she had played no part in getting James Parker to take out a life insurance policy naming her as the beneficiary. The two of them were engaged to be married and had planned their wedding for the first of the year. It was Parker who wanted that fact to be kept a secret, which is why none of her friends or neighbors knew anything about it. They had planned to take a wedding trip to the Southwest and even after Parker had become sick, Cooper was so certain he would recover that she bought him new shirts and underwear to take on their honeymoon.

Fitzgerald questioned the autopsy report that named arsenic as the cause of Parker's death. He had suffered a bad attack of the flu and sustained an injury at work a short time before he became fatally ill. Parker did not believe in doctors, but did take a considerable quantity of medicine, which may have contributed to his death. To make matters worse, he had also been engaged in making home-brewed beer and "white mule," a hard, colorless whiskey, and consumed great quantities of it. He spent much of his time, Cooper had claimed, in a drunken state, which made it difficult for him to work and take care of chores around the house.

After Parker became sicker, Cooper had called Dr. Dixon, who she claimed believed Parker's sickness was caused by too much "white mule." On the third day that Parker was unable to get out of bed, Cooper claimed that she wanted to take him to the hospital, but he refused to go. Finally, she contacted physicians at the Wabash Hospital, who insisted that he be brought in immediately. But it was too late, she said, and he died. She insisted that she had been trying to get medical care for him the entire time that he was sick, but she said Parker told her that his illness was brought on by drinking too much and eating too much candy from the Wabash freight house. She had been trying to help Parker, her attorney insisted, so why would she have killed him?

Fitzgerald admitted that Josephine had done some foolish things in her relationship with Parker, but added that Parker had done some foolish things himself. Cooper, however, had an excuse – she had the mind of a 13-year-old girl, he said. Just a few years before, she had been an inmate at an insane asylum as the result of an injury that she had sustained. This is why she went along with Parker's idea to write the letters to Gordon about slipping the man some poison. The letters were all Parker's idea, Fitzgerald insisted. He had actually dictated them himself. He had always liked Gordon, although he didn't know he was having an affair with his fiancée, and the "poison letters" had merely been a joke.

Spectators at the trial noted that the jury did not look convinced by this account.

Dr. R.C. Young, an intern at the Wabash Hospital, was the first witness called by the state. He testified that he was called to the Cooper home and when he arrived, Parker's feet were cold and clammy, his heartbeat was erratic, and his breathing was shallow and forced. He administered one-thirtieth of a grain of strychnine as a stimulant, but it had no effect. Parker died less than 15 minutes later. The next day, his vital organs were removed and given to the sheriff to be sent to Chicago for analysis.

Dr. Ludwig Hekoven, professor of pathology at the Rush Medical College in Chicago stated that he found irritation in the organs that appeared to be caused by poison. His examination revealed no sign of any illnesses that might have contributed to Parker's death.

Dr. W.A. Dixon testified that he was called twice to see Parker, once on Wednesday and once on Friday, the day the man died. He said that Parker had been vomiting and complained of burning sensations throughout his chest and abdomen. Dixon said that he didn't know what had caused the vomiting and pain, but admitted that it could have been caused by arsenic. He left some tablets to be dissolved in water and given to Parker when his stomach could retain any substance. They were supposed to stimulate the lining of his stomach. He also gave Parker a small amount of morphine to help for his pain.

Dixon called on Parker again on Friday and that morning, Cooper told him that she had given Parker some ice cream. Dixon told her not to give him anything else until his stomach had recovered from the irritation. That morning, Parker's feet were cold, his pulse weak, and his temperature below normal. He said he told Cooper that Parker's condition was critical and that he should be taken to the hospital, but Cooper refused.

Dixon admitted that he was concerned about the situation. He knew that Cooper had been sent to an insane asylum several years before and he was worried that she was not thinking clearly. He said that when he had first seen Parker, that he had not considered poison to be the cause of his illness, but a bad reaction to "white mule." However, when asked, Parker denied drinking anything that day and said that the only thing he had eaten had been some tomatoes.

The state continued its parade of witnesses, calling Jennie Godwin, Haven Whitehouse, Amanda Ely, and even J.W. Gordon, who insisted that while he had been involved with Josephine, he had not encouraged her to send the letters asking for poison and he certainly never intended to comply with her requests.

The trial was over a few days later and the jury only took three hours to return a guilty verdict. Cooper was sentenced to 14 years in prison, but investigators were never able to connect her to the earlier deaths that took place in her home.

Josephine Cooper served 11 years of her sentence and was released early for good behavior in 1933. She moved to Bloomington soon after but was hardly settled before she was being questioned by police for having written threatening letters to an Indianapolis man named Abe Rosenthal. In her letters, she demanded that he send her $500. Cooper was arrested in Decatur and taken to Springfield to answer to the charges, since using the mail for criminal purposes was a federal offense. She pled guilty and she was released on probation.

Josephine Cooper died at the age of 77 in 1954. Official versions of her death remain unclear as to whether she jumped, or was pushed, from the window of the second-story apartment where she was living. The incident occurred during the early morning hours and she died later that day from her injuries. She was never able to explain what had happened to her.

Cooper's death closed a page in history but left some unanswered questions behind. In addition to being Decatur's first murderess, was she also Decatur's first serial killer as well? Did she actually kill four people instead of just one? And, perhaps strangest of all, is the house where she once lived haunted by the ghost of one of her victims?

In the early 1990s, a Decatur man and his brother purchased the house where Josephine Cooper had once lived on East King Street for their elderly uncle. Shortly after moving in, he began to complain about strange noises in the house, doors slamming closed, and footsteps going up and down the stairs at all hours of the day and night. Believing that their uncle might be getting senile, they humored him at first. When his complaints continued, though, one of the brothers and his wife decided to stay the night in the house and see if there was any truth to his story.

Late that night, the man was awakened by strange sounds coming from one of the other bedrooms. Worried that something was wrong with his uncle, he hurried to the older man's room and looked inside. He was surprised to find him sleeping peacefully, -- especially when the weird groaning noises began to be heard again. He searched all over the house and could find no rational explanation for them. He described them later as sounding as though someone was in pain. The next morning, his wife admitted that she had heard the noises also, and added that, around 5:00 a.m., she also heard footsteps on the stairs. She thought at first it was her husband, but he was sleeping next to her at the time.

The weird events continued over the course of the uncle's occupancy of the house. He always maintained that the house was haunted. When he died a few years later, his two nephews spent many hours at the house making repairs, painting, and getting it ready to be sold. They often heard the phantom footsteps during this time, as well as the painful groaning sounds that came from a back bedroom.

It was during this time that I first heard about the haunting. Coincidentally, I had been writing about the house for an entirely different reason – chronicling its connection to Illinois crime and Decatur's first murderess. To discover that the house was haunted in the wake of the murders that had occurred there did not come as a big of a shock as it probably should have been.

Who haunted the old house on King Street? Most likely, it's one of Josephine Cooper's unlucky victims, men whose lives were cut short at her hand. The most likely suspect is James Parker and perhaps it is the pain that he endured in a back bedroom that still reverberates as the groans of a dying man.

Dead men do tell tales sometimes, and James Parker's tale is one of betrayal, agony, and murder.

Murder of the Railroad Boss
The Unsolved Mystery of George McNear, Jr. & His Lingering Ghost

The story of Peoria railroad tycoon George P. McNear, Jr. is one of the most tangled tales in the annals of Illinois crime. It is a dark tale of railroads, strike breakers, violence, money, and death, and it can only be told against the backdrop of union violence that plunged the Midwest into chaos during the late 1930s and early 1940s. McNear became a notorious opponent to the labor forces that wanted to unionize his railroad and the bitterness and strife eventually led, most believe, to his murder.

Decades later, the murder of McNear, which occurred just steps away from his home in the city's wealthiest neighborhood, remains unsolved. His killers were never brought to justice, which is why so many people are convinced that his spirit does not rest in peace.

The story of George McNear, Jr. will always be inexorably linked to the history of the Toledo, Peoria & Western Railway. The railroad dates back all of the way to 1837, when money was appropriated to build a rail line from Peoria to Warsaw, Illinois, on the Mississippi River. Eventually, the idea was abandoned, but on February 12, 1849, the state legislature granted a charter to the Peoria & Oquawka Railroad to build a line from Peoria to Oquawka, which is west of Monmouth and also on the river. An eastern extension to the Indiana state line became the eastern division of the Toledo, Peoria & Western Railway. The line operated out of Keokuk, Iowa, to Peoria, and then on to Effner, Indiana, just over the eastern border of the state. It was a total distance of 239 miles and moved hundreds of thousands of shipments back and forth across Illinois every year.

George P. McNear, Jr. bought the Toledo, Peoria & Western Railway on June 12, 1926, when he was only 32-years-old. Rumor had it that he had walked the entire 239-mile line prior to bidding on it at auction. McNear had graduated from Cornell University with a degree in engineering in 1913. He had served in France during World War I with the U.S. Army engineers. McNear bought the railroad for $1.3 million at a foreclosure sale. He had certified checks for $65,000, only a fraction of the cost of the sale, but had confidence that he could make the line profitable again. At that time, the railroad had been losing as much as $20,000 each month. By McNear's fourth month as owner, it had already started to show a profit.

In 1940, McNear faced the first attempt by labor group organizers to unionize the railroad. Allegations began to be made that trainmasters were threatening employees to resist the union. A federal investigation followed and McNear was arrested in January 1941. He was charged with attempting by threat and coercion to keep his employees from organizing, in violation of the Railway Labor Act. Two of his officials were arrested with him: H.H. Best, a superintendent, and trainmaster Bruce Gifford. The charges stated that the intimidation of employees had started in the summer of 1940.

From there, things got worse. When McNear refused to arbitrate a wage dispute between the Brotherhood of Railroad Trainmen and the Brotherhood of Locomotive Firemen and Enginemen, and then threatened to implement substandard wages and working conditions, both unions went on strike on December 28. 1941. The strikers contended that a new contract proposed by McNear would abolish seniority in job assignments and lower wages. McNear claimed this wasn't true. He stated that the contract that the unions wanted would raise the average wage more than 26-percent. He refused to go along with it. The workers appealed to President Franklin D. Roosevelt, requesting that the government take over the Toledo, Peoria & Western Railway in the interest of expediting the shipping of war materials.

On December 7, 1941, McNear locked out nearly all of the employees who had called for the strike. He hired thugs from Chicago to intimidate the strikers, with violence being a viable option in dealing with the problem. The confrontation between the hired thugs and the strikers turned bloody when bullets were exchanged.

George P. McNear, Jr.

On January 15, 1942, lawyers for the railroad requested an injunction against strike violence. McNear testified that he had attempted to protect his company against property damage from the strike and had been forced to hire additional guards because his requests for protection from local law enforcement had been denied. He had needed protection for the trains, but had ordered the guards not to use their weapons. They had been forced into violence by the strikers, he said. The U.S. District Court issues an injunction against the unions to prevent any further acts of violence and to keep them from interfering with interstate commerce.

McNear had won this round in the courts, and he continued to refuse any kind of federal arbitration to settle the strike. On March 14, 1942, he rejected a request for arbitration that came directly from President Roosevelt. He wanted the National War Labor Board to arbitrate the strike. When McNear refused, President Roosevelt seized the railroad by executive order on March 22. He appointed J.W. Barringer, Associate Director of the Office of Defense, Transportation Railroad Division, as the line's "federal manager." With the seizure of the railroad, the workers officially declared the strike at an end. Barringer had instructions to reinstate nearly all of the 104 strikers under wages and conditions that were in place prior to the start of the strike.

Even after his railroad had been seized by the government, McNear continued to refuse arbitration. He used the excuse that the unions were attempting to prevent the trial of a man named Paul Brokaw who, along with two other union members, conspired to blow up one of the railroad's bridges with dynamite. Until the trial was allowed to continue, McNear would not bargain with the union.

On April 23, 1942, McNear won another round in court when he and the two railroad officials were acquitted of federal charges that they had tried to prevent railroad employees from joining unions. Then, on January 17, 1944, the government seizure of the railroad was reversed by federal court. A federal judge found the government in violation of the law and ordered the railroad to be returned to McNear.

On October 1, 1945, President Harry S. Truman returned the railroad to private control, again under the management of McNear. Needless to say, the union had strong objections to this turn of events. Union President D.B. Robertson urged Truman to revoke the order until McNear would agree to bargain with the unions. McNear issued a statement that he was making voluntary increases to worker's wages, which would increase pay for all levels of employees, but he would not negotiate. He also noted that not all of the railroad's employees had been represented by the unions at the time of the March 22 seizure, and might not want that representation now either.

Union officials went ahead and made plans for a strike prior to the October 1 transfer. They had no intention of going back to work for McNear if he continued to refuse to negotiate with them. It was clear that there would be a confrontation on the day of the transfer, and many feared that it would end in violence and bloodshed.

On September 27, a few days before the transfer, McNear announced that, in view of strike threats and rumors of violence, that an embargo on all traffic would go into effect starting October 1. McNear claimed that there could not be a strike, as there was no employment relationship between the workers and the railroad, since the people involved were the employees of the federal government, not the Toledo, Peoria & Western Railroad. The unions ignored him and continued plans for a strike.

On October 1, large numbers of union men gathered, preventing railroad employees from gaining access to the offices, yards, and facilities. McNear claimed these were illegal acts because there was no strike. The union people were not his employees. McNear offered to hire back some of the workers that were on the "government payroll." After looking over the list, though, he said that he reserved the right not to hire 25 workers who he claimed had performed terrorist acts against the railroad. None of the union people crossed the line and asked to be re-hired.

Over the course of the next few months, tensions remained high. On Christmas Day 1945, gunshots were exchanged between union strikers and McNear's guards, but no one was injured. But that would soon change with the bloody events of February 6, 1946.

To this day, no one really knows what happened. There are conflicting accounts and in all of the confusion, a number of different stories were told. What is known is that a train was running that day from Effner, Indiana, to Peoria. The train was being protected by over a dozen of McNear's armed gunmen. It was being followed by a number of strikers, who were in their automobiles. After that, the story becomes a little blurry.

One version of the day's events stated that the Toledo, Peoria & Western train attempted to run through the picket lines as the strikers tried to forcibly stop the train, which resulted in a gun battle. Another version of the events said that the train had stopped at a grain elevator in Gridley to switch tracks. As four of the armed guards got off the train to throw the switch, strikers began hurling rocks at them. The four guards then opened fire on the strikers, killing Irwin Paschon of Peoria and Arthur Browne from East Peoria. Three other men -- Amos Vinson, Russell Esslinger, and Howard Williamson – were wounded. Williamson later testified that he believed the first shot that was fired that day, which struck his leg, was fired by accident by one of the strikers. When that gunshot rang out, though, the guards, believing they were under attack, opened fire on the strikers. Although the striking workers later claimed they had no guns, Gridley residents testified that they had seen the strikers with guns both before and after the shooting.

All four guards were charged with murder, but a McLean County circuit court jury acquitted the men of all charges on March 24, 1946. Even though they had been vindicated at trial, they were fired by McNear.

The legal battles continued. On December 6, 1946, a federal court injunction ordered 13 unions to stop interfering with railroad operations, and on January 10, 1947, federal Judge J. Leroy Adair ordered a stop to union interference with the transfer of freight cars.

According to McNear, this did not stop the violence, nor the problems with the cars. He appealed to federal and local law enforcement for assistance, claiming that his men were being shot at in the East Peoria yards and freight trains coming to be derailed. When he was unable to get help, he appeared before a congressional committee to complain that the FBI was refusing to step in and put a halt to the violence that union members were perpetrating against the railroad.

For McNear, personally, things were about to get worse.

As labor problems continued with the railroad, McNear tried to find solace in his home life. He owned a farm outside of town, but his pride and joy was the luxurious mansion that he lived in at 202 Moss Avenue, the heart of Peoria's best neighborhood. The house had once belonged to Tobias and Lydia Moss Bradley, the founder of Bradley University. Late in the evenings, McNear took long walks around the neighborhood, perhaps brooding about the day's events or worrying over the continuing problems with the railroad unions.

On the chilly night of March 10, 1947, McNear attended a Bradley basketball game at the National Guard Armory, located at Hancock and Adams Streets. After leaving the game, he began walking home, taking Main Street to High Street, and then on to Sheridan Street toward Moss Avenue.

Earlier that evening, the power had gone off in portions of the city, due to problems with an electric transformer. McNear's wife had been attending an Amateur Music Club concert at the time and with it cut short, she arrived home a little earlier than usual. McNear's car was in the garage when she got there and she assumed that her husband had gone for one of his late-night walks. She went to bed as soon as she arrived home.

McNear had gone for a walk, as she suspected, but he never returned from this one. He was only a block away from home when a shotgun was fired at him two times around 10:40 p.m. He was hit in the head and upper body and, while rushed to St. Francis Hospital, he died on the operating table at 11:05 p.m. He was unable to tell the police who had shot him.

In the wake of the shooting, investigators puzzled over what happened after McNear was hit. They believed that he tried to make it to his home at 202 Moss Avenue. He staggered from the corner of Sheridan and Moss and crawled to the Leisy residence at 100 Moss Avenue, more than 100 feet from the crime scene. There was evidence found around a nearby tree – a footprint, gloves, wadding paper, and six shotgun shells – that seemed to prove that the killer had hidden for some time, waiting for McNear to walk by. If someone had been watching him for a few nights, looking for a pattern to his movements, they would have quickly realized that he made a habit of taking a stroll around the neighborhood each evening.

McNear was buried in his family's mausoleum in Springdale Cemetery, but his body was later shipped to Petaluma, California, where his father lived. In honor of the man who had almost singlehandedly rescued the railroad from bankruptcy in the 1920s, and literally gave his life for it, the Toledo, Peoria & Western Railway shut down for a day. Railroad officials offered a $25,000 reward for the capture and conviction of the killer. An additional $16,155 was raised by local businesses and private individuals, but none of the reward money was ever claimed.

The police continued to investigate. Dr. Robert Sutton, a neighbor at 107 Moss Avenue, told detectives that he had heard the sound of a gunshot around the suspected time of the murder. An unidentified automobile was seen turning on High Street and driving away at a high rate of speed. Another car, a 1936 Ford, running without headlights, was seen by another eyewitness turning onto State Street. Investigators believed that McNear's killer may have been waiting for the moment when the railroad owner was alone and unarmed so that he could strike.

On March 22, almost two weeks later, a young boy found a box of Remington shotgun shells behind a billboard at the corner of Knoxville Avenue and Lake Street. The shells were the same size as the ones used in the gun that killed McNear – and the same size shell that had been used by the guards who fired on the strikers at Gridley. There were two shells missing from the box. No murder weapon was ever found, despite an exhaustive search of the sewer grates and backyards in the neighborhood.

The police arrested 14 of the strikers that had been at Gridley, but learned little. By this time, the story was national news and reporters from all over the country had descended on Peoria to write about the murder of the man who defied both the unions and President Roosevelt.

The FBI started its own investigation of the case, claiming federal jurisdiction due to McNear's dealings with the courts and the congressional committees. No mention was made of the fact that McNear had asked the FBI for help and had been refused. Within a few days, the FBI released a list of the leading suspects in the case. Included among them were Howard Williamson, one of the men wounded at Gridley, and his uncle, Charles Davis, who was also at Gridley that day. Both men were members of the railroad union and both of them, along with Davis's wife, Lucille, were questioned repeatedly about the murder. Charles and Lucille Davis refused to agree to a lie detector test. Williamson agreed to take one, but it was never administered for some reason.

A year and a half later, the case stalled out. The FBI and local police still believed that Williamson and Davis were the best suspects in the murder, but they could never prove it. Many believe that a lack of cooperation between the Peoria police and the FBI was what ultimately bungled the investigation. Neither man was ever charged for the killing. Williamson quit the railroad shortly after the strike was finally resolved. Davis died in 1965.

The murder of George McNear, Jr. was never solved, which makes for a compelling reason for the ghostly sightings that still take place today about the spot where he died. Even today, McNear's murder still generates rumors and speculation. The FBI file about the case is more than 3,000 pages long, although it is heavily redacted. What it does contain is information about Charles Davis, one of the main suspects. Apparently, he had left his home around 7:00 p.m. on the night of the murder and picked up his nephew, Howard Williamson. Davis was known for keeping a shotgun in his vehicle. According to the pair, they had traveled around Peoria that night, looking for a poker game. Several witnesses reported seeing them in the car that night, but there was nothing to link them directly to the murder scene. Did they kill George McNear on March 10, 1947? Perhaps, but no one could ever arrest them for it.

Nearly 70 years later, the crime remains unsolved, as does the mystery of the figure that has been seen near the spot where McNear was shot. Residents of the area began reporting the apparition as far back as the 1950s, lingering around the place where the fatal shots were fired. The figure continues on down the street, and then vanishes without warning. Local legend also states that the sound of shotgun blast can be heard on the anniversary of his death.

It's not hard today to trace the route that McNear took that night. The street remains the same, although some of the landmarks have changed. The mansion at 200 Moss Avenue is now gone, but the surrounding area still looks like it did that night in 1947. If you should ever stand on that street corner, have a passing thought for a man who was both beloved and hated during his lifetime and who can be pitied in death because, after all of these years, it's unlikely that he has ever found peace.

Murder & Mystery at Airtight Bridge

Spanning the muddy and churning waters of the Embarras River on the east side of Central Illinois is the rusted, creaking expanse known as Airtight Bridge. It has been considered a place of superstitious horror by locals for many years, although that's more likely because of its reputation as a drinking spot for teenagers and Eastern Illinois University students than for anything connected to the supernatural. But this did not stop the ghostly tales from being told. Visitors to the remote spot told of eerie cries and mysterious, mournful weeping, even though these tales seemed to have no connection to the history of the bridge.

But all of that changed in 1980. It was in October of that year when a grisly discovery was made at Airtight Bridge that would create a terrifying history of unsolved murder, horror, and connections to one of the most notorious serial killers in modern American history.

If Airtight Bridge wasn't haunted before that October, it certainly had a reason to be in the years that followed.

The old steel bridge, that earned such infamy in later years, was built in 1914 along the only road between the town of Ashmore and the unincorporated towns of Bushton and Rardin. Designed by Claude L. James and built by the Decatur Bridge Co., locals claimed that it earned the name "Airtight" because of the unnatural stillness that travelers experienced as they crossed it, but according to the Coles County Historical Society, the

Airtight Bridge

name came about because of the way that the air settled in the wooded valley where the road was located. Regardless, the bridge crossed the Embarras River in such a remote spot that few people ever journeyed there by accident.

Thanks to its secluded location, it became a popular drinking spot and a hangout for the Illinois chapter of the Sons of Silence Motorcycle Club, an outlaw biker organization that was founded in Colorado in 1966. The bridge's unsavory reputation continued in 1977 when the body of a drug overdose victim named Andy Lanman was found nearby. But the gruesome event that occurred in 1980 was bad enough to even send the Sons of Silence in search of a new place to drink beer and party.

On October 19, the nude body of a young woman was found floating in the Embarras River, just a few yards downstream from Airtight Bridge. The body was missing its head, hands, and feet (which caused the investigation to be dubbed the "Airtight Torso Case") and was the last in a series of murders of young women in Coles County that went back nearly a decade. It turned out that the Airtight case was unrelated to the others but, like the earlier crimes, remains unsolved today.

The body was discovered on a late Sunday morning by William and Tim Brown, brothers who lived near Urbana, Illinois, and were on a deer hunting trip. They took the road to Airtight Bridge at around 11:00 a.m. and as they crossed the metal span, they noticed something strange in the shallow water below. They quickly pulled over to the side of the road and encountered a local farmer named Victor Hargis, who was on his way to help his son dig a well. The brothers pointed out what appeared to be the partially decomposed remains of a woman, and Hargis and William Brown climbed down to the river's edge to take a closer look.

Hargis passed away in 2004 but his son, Victor, Jr., later recalled his father's reaction to the discovery. He stated in an interview: "You could hardly tell it was a woman because the head was gone. It's hard to believe someone would do something like that."

Hargis immediately returned to his truck and drove home to call the Coles County Sheriff's Department. Chief Deputy Darrell Cox, who was at pistol practice at the time, received the call and was the first law enforcement officer on the scene. It took him nearly 20 minutes to drive the back roads from Charleston, but he was very familiar with the area around Airtight Bridge, since it was part of his regular patrol. Years later, Cox, who went on to become the county sheriff, vividly remembered what he saw that day: "I could tell when

I got there that it was missing its head and feet. I remember when I first saw it standing on the bridge; it didn't look like a person."

Other officers soon arrived and the bridge was cordoned off as a crime scene. It wasn't long before word spread of the dismembered body and newspaper and television reporters rushed to the secluded spot. Such horrific crimes rarely occurred in the rural area and thanks to this, the case became a sensation, grabbing headlines for many days to come.

Investigators worked late into the night, scouring the bridge and the surrounding area for clues. Divers were sent into the river and officers tramped through the woods, but the missing body parts – which the coroner stated had been severed cleanly – were never found. Coles County Coroner Dick Lynch described the woman as being in her 20's and added that she had dark auburn hair, was "rather flat-chested," and was "not in the habit of shaving." She was approximately 5 feet, 9 inches tall, weighing around 130 pounds. Although he deduced that she had been murdered elsewhere and her body dumped at the bridge, he was unable to determine a cause of death. Sheriff Chuck Lister agreed with his findings, stating that he believed the woman had been murdered and dismembered and then taken to Airtight Bridge, where the body had been rolled down the bridge embankment to the water.

The remains were sent to Springfield to be examined by pathologist Dr. Grant Johnson at Memorial Hospital, but he was unable to find anything conclusive because of the advanced decomposition of the body and the fact that the vital extremities were missing. However, he did note that the woman had an uncommon A-Positive blood type, which would make it more likely to identify her if any family members came forward to list her as missing. Unfortunately, the torso was not marked by any major scars, tattoos, or birthmarks that might offer any clue to her identity. He was also unable to come up with a cause of death for the victim, or even a definite time of death. No one had seen the remains in the river prior to the morning of their discovery, but Dr. Johnson believed that she had been killed at least 48 hours before she was found. He did believe that she had been murdered, and believed the body had been stored somewhere before it was dumped in the river. With her hands missing, it was impossible to tell if she had struggled before she was killed. There were no drugs, poison, or alcohol in her system and no evidence of rape or violence. But it did appear that she had been pregnant at one time and had likely given birth. Somewhere, investigators grimly realized, was a child who was missing his or her mother.

The victim's rare blood type was a major clue in a case that was woefully lacking in solid leads. Unfortunately, a check of missing persons reports led nowhere and the investigation grew cold. On October 23, the sheriff's department called off the search at Airtight Bridge. Both police investigators and news reporters continued to delve into the case, running down every possible clue and checking into every theory, no matter how thin. Nothing turned up and the story eventually vanished from the headlines. Almost a year after the remains were discovered, the unidentified young woman was laid to rest in Mound Cemetery in Charleston. Her grave was marked only with the words "Jane Doe."

The case was largely forgotten for the next several years. Then, in the middle 1980s, interest was revived when a convict named Henry Lee Lucas confessed to the murder. Since his death in 2001, Lucas has earned a reputation as either one of the most prolific serial killers in history – or one of the greatest frauds. According to Lucas, between 1975 and his arrest in 1983, Lucas and an accomplice named Otis Toole roamed the country, murdering at least 11 people before being arrested in Texas. But while in prison, Lucas's list of victims began to grow, eventually reaching a list of between 350 and 600 murders. Investigators from all over the country brought him their cold cases and Lucas claimed to have committed one after another. A task force was set up to investigate his claims and has since been criticized for sloppy police work, accepting Lucas' claims at face value and helping him to perpetrate what many believe was a long-running hoax. Although initially sentenced to die, his sentence was commuted to life in prison by then Texas Governor George W. Bush. Lucas later died in prison from natural causes in 2001. Whether or not he committed all – or perhaps any – of the murders he confessed to remains a mystery. Most researchers believe his claims were wildly exaggerated, but that he certainly killed more than the 11 people that he was sent to prison for.

One of the many murders that Lucas confessed to was the Airtight Bridge case. Almost as soon as he took credit for it, the Coles County Sheriff's Department eagerly announced the news. Sheriff Lister announced at a press conference that the Airtight killer had been found and that an indictment would be forthcoming. According to Lucas, he was unable to remember his victim's name, but he did remember the bridge. He had picked up the woman in East Texas and brought her to Missouri, he said, where he had killed and dismembered her. He had left her torso at Airtight Bridge but had dumped the other parts of the body at other locations, which were searched by the Illinois State Police. No trace of the woman's head or limbs was ever found. The grand jury refused to return an indictment in the case that Sheriff Lister brought them, and it fell apart completely when Lucas recanted and claimed that he had not committed the murder.

The Airtight Case went cold again. It would not be until 1992 that a real break occurred. On November 20, the sheriff's department finally announced the name of the Airtight victim – Diana Marie Small, a resident of Bradley, Illinois. She had disappeared from her home a short time before her body was discovered over 100 miles away in Coles County. Detective Art Beier of Coles County and Detective Steven Coy of Bradley had been able to piece together the clues and reveal what had happened to Diana. She had never turned up in missing persons reports because she was never reported missing. Her husband told the police that he wasn't worried because she had left home before. No other relatives knew that she was missing either. Diana's mother and sister had joined a fundamentalist Christian sect and moved west, where they fell out of touch with Diana and her husband. More than 10 years later, her sister, Virginia, left the church and tried to get in touch with her estranged family. That was when she realized that Diana was missing, and soon after, filed a missing person report. Detective Beier saw the report on a national listing, recognized the description of the Airtight victim, and contacted the Bradley police. A DNA match confirmed that Diana had finally been found.

Tragically, her murder has never been solved. Coroner's reports in 1980 were correct when they stated that Diana had given birth. She had a daughter, Vanessa, who was only two-years-old when her mother disappeared. She had no idea what had happened to Diana for many years since her father refused to talk about it. Diana's case was re-opened in 1995, but her former husband refused to talk to detectives. Since that time, the case has gone cold once more.

In October 2008, the anonymous stone that marked Diana's grave was replaced by one that was etched with her name, bringing one part of this mysterious case to an end. However, most feel that it will never be completely over until the tragic young woman's killer is finally found.

The identity of the murderer remains a nagging question in this story – but it's not the only one. Does the spirit of Diana Small still linger at Airtight Bridge? Some claim that she does, but others say that the bridge was haunted long before she was slain. So, if the ghost that walks the old steel bridge is not Diana, then whose restless spirit remains there?

Perhaps there is more history to Airtight Bridge than any of us know.

Last Stop at the Parkway Tavern
The Ghost of Illinois Outlaw Bernie Shelton

In a state like Illinois, which was often controlled by guns and violence, there were few men as fearsome as the Shelton brothers. During Prohibition, they had run bootleg liquor across Southern Illinois and battled it out with the Ku Klux Klan, which would do anything to stop the bootleggers because they were "mostly Catholics and foreigners." With their ally, gangster Charlie Birger, they succeeded in wiping out the Klan in the southern part of the state, but then, with no one left to fight, Birger and the Sheltons turned on each other for control of the lucrative liquor market. By the late 1920s, after a series of gang shootings, bombings, and murders, Birger went to the gallows in Benton, Illinois, and the Sheltons were framed for a mail robbery that would have sent them to federal prison if the case against them hadn't fallen apart.

For a few years after Birger was executed, the Shelton brothers – Carl, Earl, and Bernie – used East St. Louis as the headquarters for the liquor, gambling, and prostitution empire that they had built. They were already known as men that no one wanted to cross, but an honest sheriff decided to run them out of town. Unfortunately, all he succeeded in doing was trading one set of gangsters for another and soon, the mob moved in and turned the city into a major gambling spot for the next three decades.

The Sheltons moved north to Peoria, a place they found to be more hospitable to the vices that they offered. It wasn't long before they established their organization as the biggest illegal racket in downstate Illinois.

The Sheltons became Peoria legends, both lauded and feared, but eventually they would also be wiped out, just as the Klan organizers and Charlie Birger had been wiped out before them. But at least one of the brothers would need quite a number of years before he realized that he was no longer the powerful gangster that he had once been.

It was at that point that he finally realized that he was dead.

When the Sheltons came to Peoria, they found a city that welcomed them with open arms. Vice was thriving in the city in the 1930s. One writer noted that Peoria was the "sleaziest, the orneriest, the rottenest and rip-snortingest town this side of... well, this side of Chicago and that side of St. Louis. Its sins are legend." It was a placed that offered a safe haven for gamblers and prostitutes and a good number of the residents took advantage of the city's tolerance for gambling dens and brothels. When Carl Shelton established the brothers' operations in town, illegal wagering was welcomed, especially by politicians and cops, who saw it as a great way to make a little extra money. Not surprisingly, the Sheltons soon became immune to prosecution.

Carl Shelton might never have achieved the notoriety that he did in Peoria if other outside gangsters had not already bungled their moves to take over operations in the area. There were several botched kidnap attempts on local gambling operators that terrified not only the would-be victims, but the politicians that protected them, as well. One failed attempt occurred in 1930. The victim was Clyde Garrison, the operator of the Windsor Club on Fulton Street, one of the biggest gaming houses in the Midwest. His wife was killed during the attempt and he needed no convincing that bringing in the Sheltons to protect the still- locally controlled gambling interests was the right thing to do.

Prior to the 1940s, Shelton worked for Garrison, protecting his interests and those of other local gamblers from outsiders, but not upstaging Garrison's role as the head of Peoria operations. The alliance between them was lucrative for both sides, but things started to sour amid the gambling upswing in the area at the start of World War II. No one knows what caused the falling-out, but most believe that Carl Shelton began taking a role in the political side of things, which had always been Garrison's side of the deal. He resisted Shelton's efforts for a time, but not for long. Realizing that he lacked the muscle to take on the Sheltons, Garrison got out of gambling and went into the wholesale liquor business.

After that, Carl had the field to himself, and from 1941 to 1945, the Sheltons' operations prospered like never before. Thanks to the dangerous reputation that the brothers enjoyed, they managed to maintain order among the unsavory elements in Peoria in the early 1940s. This was much to the delight of the city's political leaders, especially Mayor Edward Nelson Woodruff, who was perhaps the most corrupt Illinois mayor after "Big Bill" Thompson, Al Capone's man in Chicago.

Carl established a business network that combined his aboveboard activities with the illicit ones. The network required the enlistment of a number of different individuals to oversee things. For example, the Shelton

The Shelton Brothers (Left to Right: Carl, Earl & Bernie) moved to East St. Louis after the gang war with Charlie Birger and then moved the bulk of their operations to the Peoria area. From there, they controlled a large portion of downstate Illinois, battling hostile moves from gangsters in both St. Louis & Chicago.

Amusement Co., which was a legitimate operation, was run by Sheltons' trusted man, Jack Ashby. The amusement company handled jukeboxes and other legal coin-operated devices, while also delivering slot machines to the back rooms of bars and taverns throughout the area.

The Sheltons were making more money than ever before, but it would take an incident that was completely unrelated to their criminal operation to shake Carl Shelton so badly that he never forgot it. On November 16, 1943, while driving downstate, Carl struck and killed a nine-year-old girl named Violet Varner on State Route 121, near Decatur. Carl, who was driving the car with Bernie in the passenger seat, said that the child ran into the road and he was unable to avoid hitting her. After the impact, the car rolled over once and then landed back on its wheels. Carl never spoke about the incident. He was not blamed for the accident, but he paid for all of the little girl's funeral bills. The incident stayed with him for the rest of his life.

The Sheltons' hold on Peoria ended after the 1945 elections. A new mayor, Carl O. Triebel, came into office and became known as a reformer, even though he never ran on that platform. With his new persona in place, though, he decided to start cracking down on gambling, prostitution, and anything else that stained the reputation of the city. Just before he took office, Triebel held a meeting with Carl Shelton and informed him of his plans. When Shelton realized that Triebel meant business, he shrugged and simply said, "Well, I guess that'll give me more time to farm."

Triebel, who also owned farmland, sat with Shelton for almost 30 minutes, talking about agriculture. Then, they shook hands and Carl left his office, never to see the new mayor again. He had been in this situation before. When Sheriff Jerome Munie had ordered the Sheltons out of St. Clair County, where East St. Louis was located, Shelton had argued, but then agreed to his demands. With Triebel, there was no arguing and, as the Peoria mayor must have been relieved to find, no ill will toward Triebel by Shelton. By this time in his life, Carl really did want to retire to his farming and oil interests in Wayne County.

In the city of Peoria, pressure from Triebel forced gambling underground, but this was not the case in surrounding Peoria County. Carl Shelton may have abandoned his interests in the area, but Bernie served notice that he planned to take over what his brother left behind. The changeover was easily handled for Bernie because the rough brawler with the terrible temper struck fear in the hearts of friends and foes alike. He secured a free hand for the rackets through financial arrangements with certain county officials and moved the Shelton headquarters from downtown Peoria to the Parkway Tavern, an unimposing bar on Farmington Road, just outside the city limits.

With Bernie now in command, some assumed that Carl was out of the Shelton gang. Others were not so sure because he still lived part time in Peoria and met with Bernie on many occasions at the Parkway Tavern. He was, at the least, an advisor to the vice network that he had created. In addition, south of Peoria, Carl, and not Bernie, remained in charge of the numerous gambling operations, large and small, that were scattered throughout rural parts of Central Illinois. Regardless, with Carl stepping back from his highly visible role in Peoria, other gangsters began eyeing the Sheltons' territory. After years of a hands-off policy toward the Sheltons, the Chicago Outfit finally decided to curb the independence that had been given to them. The Outfit instructed their St. Louis emissaries to offer the Sheltons a deal that would bring them peacefully into the Syndicate. If that didn't work, the Outfit had other methods at their disposal – methods that became necessary when the Sheltons refused to deal.

Following World War II, the Outfit, with connections to the national Syndicate created by Meyer Lansky and Charles "Lucky" Luciano in New York, had expanded its underworld dealings across the country. After taking over operations in St. Louis, the Outfit inherited the services of a number of gangsters who had formerly worked with the Sheltons. Two of the most prominent were "Blackie" Armes and Frank "Buster" Wortman.

The defection of Armes and Wortman occurred in the early 1940s after the end of each of the men's prison stays for assaulting federal agents during a raid on a still in Collinsville in 1933. When the two were inmates at Alcatraz, the Outfit managed to make things more bearable for them on the inside, which earned their loyalty. In addition, when the two were released from prison, they claimed that Carl Shelton did nothing for them. Wortman soon went on to build an empire for himself in Southwestern Illinois, but Armes didn't live long enough to make any money. He was gunned down in a nightclub in Herrin in late 1944.

Word soon circulated that either Carl or Bernie was worth $10,000 to anyone who brought them to Chicago alive. But no one could get close to the Sheltons, who refused all contact with both St. Louis and Chicago gangsters. Soon, the reward was changed. It was still $10,000, but it was now for either of the Sheltons – dead or alive. Spurred by the reward, a gang of Chicago gunmen set a trap to ambush Carl and Bernie at the Parkway Tavern. Carl got wind of the plans, however, and several carloads of Shelton gunmen showed up at the bar instead of the brothers.

The Outfit gunmen returned to Chicago, but they -- or someone else with murderous intentions toward the Sheltons – returned to Peoria. In 1946, a number of Shelton associates were slaughtered. Frank Kraemer, a slot machine operator and tavern owner, was shot to death by an unknown gunman in February. Seven months later, the body of Joel Nyberg, who worked as muscle for the Sheltons, was found shot to death on a local golf course. A month after that, Phillip Stumpf, another slot machine operator, was gunned down while driving home from a bar on Big Hollow Road. With each murder, the level of protection afforded the Sheltons grew smaller, and when the killing went unanswered, many came to believe that the Sheltons were unable to defend their friends. More defections followed, but the Sheltons continued their operations, still defying the St. Louis and Chicago gangsters.

As gambling became even more widespread in Illinois after the election of sympathetic governor Dwight Green, Outfit racketeers became increasingly frustrated over the continued presence of the Sheltons in Central Illinois. Even after killing several of their allies, the Sheltons refused to give in. Nothing, it seemed, could eliminate the Sheltons' influence as long as Carl was alive. Attempts to kill him in Peoria, or take him out somewhere else had failed, but his enemies knew that his luck couldn't hold out forever.

After Carl began spending more time in Wayne County, he seemed harder to kill. But all was not well for Shelton at home. His farm prospered and his Basin Oil Well Service Company in Fairfield was doing well. He seemed to be on his way to becoming a successful, legitimate businessman and many in the area accorded him great respect. His only problems seemed to come from some of his neighbors in the Pond Creek area. One squabble followed another, mostly between Carl and members of the Harris-Vaughn clan, led by "Black Charlie" Harris, a former Shelton associate. Like Wortman and Armes, Harris served time in Leavenworth and when he got out, he came to believe the Sheltons owed him more than just their continued friendship and a little business every once in a while. He also became convinced that Carl had swindled him out of some Wayne County farmland. His long-time affection toward the Sheltons had turned to hatred. Harris became the protector of anyone with a grudge toward Carl or Earl, who also lived in Fairfield. The whole thing might have been dismissed as nothing more than a local feud, if not for the presence of Harris, who was a killer and well acquainted with the territory and habits of the Sheltons.

The assassination of Carl Shelton was foreshadowed by two events that occurred in 1947. Either of the events, or perhaps both of them, may have led to Carl's death, although we will never know for sure since his murder remains unsolved.

The first event was the murder of Ray Doughtery, a former Shelton gunman who had aligned himself with Roy Armes, the brother of the murdered "Blackie" Armes, a lieutenant of Frank Wortman. Doughtery's body was found blasted full of holes on the shore of Crab Orchard Lake, near Carbondale. The local coroner linked the unsolved murder to "trouble between gangs," but many suspected that the killing was the first step in a planned resurgence by the Sheltons. Rumors were running wild that the Sheltons were strengthening their hold in rural parts of Illinois and contemplating a comeback in the East St. Louis area. If true, then the murder of Ray Doughtery was seen as a warning sign of the Sheltons' intent. To the Outfit, this meant that Carl Shelton had to be taken out if new gang warfare was to be avoided.

The second event, brought on by Carl Shelton himself, involved the beating of Charlie Harris' nephew. This was part of the ongoing Pond Creek feud and resulted from the theft of some of Sheltons' blooded Black Angus cattle. In searching for the culprits, an angry Carl Shelton caught up with the young man and beat him badly. Then, later that same day, Harris' nephew was shot and seriously wounded by unknown assailants outside Fairfield. Harris was outraged by these events.

On the morning of October 23, 1947, Carl went out to the farm to take care of some things. He drove up Pond Creek Road in a military surplus Jeep with two of his men following behind in a truck. When the vehicles reached a small bridge that had to be crossed to get to Carl's property, a volley of gunfire exploded from the surrounding woods. Carl toppled out of the Jeep and hit the ground. The other men scrambled out of the truck and scurried for cover in a ditch. The two men survived, but Carl Shelton was dead --- shot 25 times.

Two hours passed before the men could notify police and return to the scene of the attack. They were accompanied by the Wayne County Sheriff, Hal Bradshaw, Lieutenant Ben Blades of the Illinois State Police, and Earl Shelton. Carl's body was found in a ditch by the bridge on the east side of the road. His feet were about a foot from the top of the ditch and his head and face were down in the bottom. The lawmen suggested that the body be left in that position until photographs could be taken, but Earl protested, saying that he didn't want his brother left lying like that.

When the body was moved, a gun was discovered underneath it. Earl identified it as Carl's revolver. Opening the weapon, Lieutenant Blades saw that five of the six shells had been fired. The officers searched the ground and found numerous empty cartridges and shells, many of which were a government type that was used in machine guns. Whoever the killers had been, whether Outfit gunmen or relatives of Charlie Harris, they had wanted to make sure that Carl Shelton was dead.

While new gang warfare seemed inevitable after Carl's murder, no trouble materialized during the funeral, which was the largest event that Fairfield had ever seen. The numerous law officers who were present ended up doing little more than directing traffic. It was hard to ignore the fact that the Sheltons and their men were wearing guns under their suit coats, but Earl did everything that he could to ease the tension that gripped the area. He stated publicly that his family's only reaction to the murder would be for law enforcement to "take its usual course." Many found this hard to believe, especially since the general consensus was that Charlie Harris was somehow involved in the assassination. Harris was later arrested for the murder (he fled for a time because he claimed to fear reprisal from the Sheltons,) but a grand jury was unable to indict him for the crime. Many reporters believed Harris was not involved. Their theory was that the crime had been carried out by gunmen connected to the Chicago Outfit, or by its allies in St. Louis. True to gangland tradition, the identities of the actual shooters remain a mystery.

There were many who suspected that the death of Carl Shelton would mean the end of the brothers' operations. As it turned out, though, the immediate reaction to Carl's death was mild by underworld standards. In the weeks that followed the murder, some Shelton associates closed down their gambling houses. Others handed over control of their operations to the Outfit, which was ecstatic about the demise of Carl Shelton. "Buster" Wortman, a man who may not have been an innocent bystander to Carl's murder, began to expand beyond the St. Clair and Madison County areas now that Carl Shelton was out of the way.

One part of the Shelton operations not affected by Carl's death was in Peoria, where Bernie was still running the family's gaming enterprises in the same way that he had been. He made it widely known that he was in firm control of the area and actually planned to expand the operation farther south across a wider area of Central Illinois. Needless to say, this caused a ripple of unrest among the Chicago and St. Louis gangsters, who had taken it for granted that the Sheltons would crumble after the death of Carl. They approached Bernie with offers of peace, but he rebuffed their advances. The Outfit's response was predictable. Bernie had been a marked man before Carl's death and the reward that had been offered for his life was still very much available. The Outfit wanted someone to collect it.

Throughout the early months of 1948, Bernie showed no signs of backing down. He continued his operations, kept up his payoffs to those who offered political protection, and made sure that he stayed very visible to those who might have some idea of moving in on his business. However, it was a tavern brawl that almost tripped him up. Bar fights were old, bad habits of Bernie Shelton's. He was lucky to have escaped prison time in the late 1930s after beating and shooting a man named Frank Zimmerman during a fight in a Cahokia bar. The fight at the Parkway Tavern on Memorial Day 1948 would turn out to be much more serious.

The fight reportedly started when Richard Murphy, a Navy veteran from Peoria, began mouthing off about the ejection of a drunken patron from the bar. A fistfight started in the parking lot, resulting in Murphy being pummeled by Bernie and a couple of his men. One account from witnesses claimed that they pistol-whipped the man. During the fight, A.L. Hunt, the proprietor of a popular drive-in that was located across Farmington Road from the tavern, came over to try and break things up. Hunt, who was no friend of Shelton's, claimed that Bernie shoved a pistol into his back and marched him back across the road with dire warnings about minding his own business. As a result of the brawl, a Peoria County grand jury returned indictments against Bernie and the other two men for assault with intent to kill, a felony.

The bar fight might have been dismissed by most as a minor altercation, but not by the man who led the grand jury investigation, Roy P. Hull, the state's attorney for Peoria County. In the Illinois primary elections of that year, Hull had been defeated in his bid for nomination for re-election to his post in the upcoming November election. One of those who helped to oppose Hull had been Bernie Shelton, which did not sit well with Hull. As a result, the indictment would plague Shelton for the rest of his life.

But Bernie wouldn't be around to worry about it for long.

The first attempt on his life was to have occurred while he was on his way to Muscatine, Iowa, to sell some horses. Two cars filled with gunmen had waited for him along a highway near Galesburg, but Bernie never showed. By chance, he took another route to Muscatine and thwarted the plan.

The scene outside of the Parkway Tavern after the shooting of Bernie Shelton in July 1948.

The next attempt to kill him was planned for July 26. Bernie left his home at 10:00 a.m. on that hot Monday morning and drove to the Parkway Tavern to meet with a bartender named Alex Ronitis. Shelton wanted the bartender to follow him to a Peoria auto agency, where he planned to leave his car for some work. Ronitis would then return Shelton to the tavern.

Shelton spent about 45 minutes handling some paperwork in his private office and then he and Ronitis started to walk out together. However, Ronitis stepped back into the bar to get a pack of cigarettes, leaving Shelton to walk alone to his sedan in the parking lot. Bernie was unaware, as he approached the car, that he was in clear view of a man who was hiding in the brush at the bottom of a wooded hill behind the Parkway. The man had a .351 caliber Winchester automatic rifle in his hands and he fired a single shot. The bullet slammed into Bernie's chest and he fell forward, slumped against his car. Witnesses later stated that they saw a well-dressed man run from the brush and jump into a green Chevrolet, which drove quickly away.

Ronitis was about to open the tavern door and come outside when he heard the rifle shot. After hesitating for a few seconds, he opened the door and saw Bernie kneeling next to his car. Ronitis started to move toward him, but Shelton waved him back. He held the door open as Bernie stumbled across the parking lot and into the tavern. He heaved himself onto a barstool and told Ronitis and another bartender, Edward Connor, "I've been shot from the woods." He was bleeding badly from a chest wound.

Connor called for an ambulance and when it arrived, Bernie insisted on walking to it. He collapsed onto a stretcher in the back of the ambulance and was driven to St. Francis Hospital. When he arrived in the emergency room, he asked an attendant to remove his shoes and his trousers, predicting that he was going to die.

And he did, just a few minutes later.

As with the killing of Carl Shelton, Bernie's murder was never solved. The assassin had discarded his rifle while making his escape and a cartridge from the fatal bullet was found lying in the grass. The rifle was subjected to fingerprint and ballistics tests, but they offered no information.

The death of Bernie Shelton brought an end to the era of the mob in Peoria. It also led to the end of the Shelton gang itself, or what was left of it, in Illinois. Talk was heard about some of the Sheltons' most trusted men continuing the operations but it never amounted to anything. Tragically, Bernie was not the last of the brothers to die. Roy, the eldest, was killed in June 1950, while driving a tractor on Earl's farm. Although he had a criminal record, he had never been associated with Carl, Earl, and Bernie.

After Bernie's death, Earl, the last of the feared Shelton boys, was reluctant to venture too far away from Fairfield. As it turned out, though, trouble came looking for him.

On the night of May 24, 1949, Earl was wounded by one of three bullets fired through a window of the Sheltons' Farmers Club, located on the courthouse square in Fairfield. The window at the rear of the second floor gambling den was the only one in the establishment not painted black. To see into the interior of the club, the unknown gunman had climbed a ladder to the roof of a car dealership next to the club. From there, he had a clear view of Earl's back as he sat playing cards. Earl had laid down his cards and was talking to some friends when three shots shattered the window. One of the bullets struck him in the back. The gunman hurried down the ladder and disappeared.

Earl was rushed to Deaconess Hospital in Evansville, Indiana, but, even though he had lost a lot of blood, he was not in danger of dying. An operation failed to find the bullet but Earl recovered. As he did so, many in Wayne County prepared for more violence. Suspects in the attack ranged from Chicago-St. Louis gangsters to Charlie Harris, who was perhaps still looking for a chance to even the score with the Sheltons.

The next attack against the remaining Sheltons occurred during the early morning hours of September 9, 1949. Residents along Elm Street were startled awake by the roar of gunfire coming from the home of "Little Earl" Shelton, a nephew who had been serving as a bodyguard for his Uncle Earl. Little Earl was just arriving home in his Buick when the shots rang out. Although hit, he threw himself on the floor of his car, which probably saved his life. As his attackers sped away, he managed to draw his gun from a shoulder holster and fire several shots in their direction. He would later claim that the fleeing sedan had belonged to Charlie Harris. Once again, Harris was charged with the crime, but the charges were later dismissed due to lack of evidence.

Once the attackers had fled, Little Earl managed to crawl out of his car, where his wife, Eleanor, found him bleeding next to the curb. She rushed him to the hospital in Evansville and doctors found that he had been hit eight times, mostly in the lower parts of his body. The Fairfield police said that Earl's car had been struck 21 times, likely by machine gun fire. Miraculously, Earl survived the assault. He had served with valor in an Army armored division during World War II and had been wounded in the invasion of Sicily. However, those wounds didn't compare to the ones that he suffered on the streets of his hometown.

The year 1950 became a time of open season on the last Sheltons. Roy was killed and Earl was hit in the right arm, but not seriously wounded, when he and Little Earl were driving in the Pond Creek area, inspecting some oil drilling operations. Two weeks later, Little Earl was grazed when a shotgun and a rifle opened up on him in front of a garage a few miles west of Fairfield. He and a friend, Dellos Wylie, managed to make it out of the car and into the garage. The gunmen, hidden in some brush across the road, continued to fire at them. Wylie tried to escape from the building and was cut down with several bullets in his back, leaving him badly wounded.

After Roy's funeral, Sheriff Bradshaw, along with others in the community, suggested that the remaining Sheltons consider leaving the area. But Big Earl and Little Earl refused to consider the idea, vowing not to be driven out. Their resolve was weakened a short time later when a homemade bomb wrecked Earl's home. He and his wife, Earline, were lucky to survive the attack. The Sheltons were in bed when someone tossed a can filled with nitroglycerine through their front window. They were awakened by the sound of breaking glass and while Earline telephoned the sheriff, Earl went out into the front room. Moments later, there was a deafening blast and Earl was thrown back into the bedroom. The resulting fire swept through the house and the Sheltons barely managed to make it to safety.

The loss of his home was enough to convince Earl that it was time to leave. A month and a half later, in January 1951, he and Earline, along with Little Earl and his family, left Illinois for good. They moved to Florida and settled in the Jacksonville area, which had been a favorite spot for the Sheltons during their bootlegging days.

Another notorious chapter in Illinois's criminal history had come to an end – or had it?

While the lives and crimes of the Shelton brothers became a part of the legends and lore of Illinois history, the story of Bernie Shelton became another part of Illinois lore altogether. There are many who insist that, while his life ended violently in July 1948, he simply refused to depart from this world. The criminal empire of the Sheltons came to an end, but Bernie did not end with it.

In August 1998, Bernie Shelton's name made the front pages of the local newspaper again when the owners of the Parkway Tavern publicly admitted that they believed his ghost was haunting his former headquarters. The bar's owner, Diane Kallister, was convinced that Shelton's ghost haunted the place. She told of a number of incidents involving opening and closing doors, lights turning on and off, and objects moving around. She was sure all of it could be linked to Shelton's lingering spirit.

She contacted Peoria newspaper writer DeWayne Bartels, who had recently penned a series of articles for the *Peoria Times-Observer* about the days of gangsters, and Shelton rule, in Peoria. Bartels was intrigued by her accounts of flying jars of hot sauce, slamming restroom doors, and staff members who felt they were being watched, so he contacted a Pekin man named Rob Conover, who had a reputation for contacting spirits. Conover was a former private investigator and U.S. Marine who had been featured in area newspapers on many occasions, along with appearances on television shows about the paranormal. Bartels had been skeptical about hauntings until he had gone along with Conover on a past excursion to a spirit-infested building. What he saw convinced him that Conover was the real thing, and that the place was genuinely haunted. He thought Conover would be the perfect person to come along and help track down the ghost of Bernie Shelton. The two agreed to check the place out on Friday night, August 13.

Bartels' editor, Rick Wade, noted, "I have found Bartels to be one of the most honest men and journalists I know. He would never pass fiction off as fact." These words will become very important as you read the pages that follow.

Conover arrived at the tavern shortly after midnight. A large part of the reputation that he enjoyed had not come from merely investigating ghosts, but from actually confronting them. He had a sensitivity that allowed him to see and hear things that others could not. These gifts allowed him to help spirits move from this world to the next. For more than 11 years, he had been helping spirits "pass on to face God's judgment" and up until that night, he had never failed.

His arrival at the Parkway Tavern gave him a sense that a spirit was present. Although he was not sure just yet that it was the presence of Bernie Shelton, he knew that something was there. He told DeWayne Bartels that he felt that something was going to happen that night.

A short time later, they made preparations for the night to follow. Bartels followed Conover into the kitchen, a place where, a few days before, Diane Kallister had seen an empty beer case fly to the top of an ice cooler in an adjoining room. They went into the storeroom, next to the kitchen, and even Bartels seemed to notice a change in the energy of the room. He was also sure that the temperature had started to fall.

The lights were turned down low and the group, which included Conover, Bartels, Diane Kallister, and Conover's assistant, sat down around a table. Conover began to speak, directly addressing the spirit that he believed was that of Bernie Shelton. He hoped to provoke a reaction, and it worked. Bartels' camera, which had been turned off, immediately snapped to life and the lens popped out. The air around the table became very cool. Conover suggested that Bernie was becoming very confused and thought perhaps it would be better if they went to the kitchen.

The group looked back toward the storeroom and Bartels later described seeing a dim blue light filter through the doorway. The strange haze hovered at the end of the kitchen. Conover stuck his hand up into the haze and Bartels followed his lead. "It was cool, much cooler than the rest of the very warm room," he later wrote. Bartels placed his camera on a kitchen counter and without warning, it again whirred to life and the lens extended. In seconds, it retracted and clicked off.

A few minutes later, the group returned to the table in the storeroom. Conover again began to try and communicate with the spirit. Soon, he was having a conversation that seemed one-sided to Bartels because he could see and hear nothing out of the ordinary. Conover told the others that Bernie was still angry about the way that he had died. Sweat was running down his face and then Conover turned and made a startling announcement. "I see him. He has on a brown jacket, brown pants, and a white shirt with no tie and white t-shirt," he said.

Bartels later admitted that he was fighting the urge to run in the opposite direction when Conover beckoned him to follow him to the storeroom. Apparently, Bernie had retreated toward the back door. They found the storeroom and the kitchen to be silent and empty. No cold chills, no haze, nothing. Bernie had vanished, at least for the moment. They returned back into the bar area and Conover suddenly stopped, throwing a warning arm against Bartels' chest. Bernie had slipped up behind them and Rob had actually spotted his spectral image in the mirror behind the bar.

Conover again began to speak to Bernie Shelton. Bartels reported a loud, popping sound that occurred a few moments later. He couldn't tell where it came from but he recalled that it seemed to surround them. A feeling of tension remained in the air, filling the silence. Then, footsteps were heard in the game room. No one in the group had left the bar area. Conover spent the next several minutes speaking aloud to the spirit but nothing else occurred. Bartels recounted that another loud pop sounded from under the table next to where he was sitting, but nothing else followed. Bernie was gone --- but he had not left the building. For the first time in 11 years, Conover had failed. Bernie Shelton was not going to pass over. The Parkway Tavern was still his, even decades after his death.

Unwilling to give up, Conover and Bartels returned to the tavern three nights later, on August 16. That evening, the two men joined Diane Kallister and her friend, Tracy Ford. The place had closed early and the parking lot was deserted when they arrived. Conover had come up with a new plan for the evening's assault on Bernie. The four participants would split up into pairs and stay in contact with one another using two-way radios. Conover and another person would go into the kitchen and storeroom, while the other group would remain near the tavern's door.

Diane Kallister accompanied Conover into the kitchen and Bartels and Tracy Ford sat down at a table near the other radio monitor. Soon, they heard Conover's voice coming through it, cautiously trying to coax Bernie Shelton into another conversation. For nearly a half-hour, nothing happened.

Restless, Bartels decided to stroll over near the game room, where he sensed a cold, electrical presence that seemed to come from nowhere. He called to Tracy, but she couldn't feel it. However, a short time later she began to complain of feeling very warm, even though they were sitting almost directly under a cold air vent. Unnerved, she went into the kitchen to be with Kallister. Bartels could hear Ford's voice over the monitor telling her friend that she was sweating and felt as though she had a fever. He heard Kallister's voice a moment later, stating that it was incredibly cold in the kitchen.

She later said that the cold seemed to seep into her bones. She urged Bernie to make an appearance and moments later, the same blue light that had been seen three nights before appeared inside the door to the storeroom. Conover also saw it, although while Bartels looked in from the other room, he was unable to see anything. The moment passed and Conover suggested that they take a break.

A little while later, Conover returned to the storeroom with Kallister and Ford and Bartels returned to the table in the bar. When a loud noise suddenly came over the monitor, Conover called for Bartels to bring a camera. The reporter hurriedly snapped off two quick shots. They turned on the light to see what had made the startling noise. Just inside of the entrance to the storeroom was a yellow bucket with wheels. A mop had been jammed inside it and it had been moved in such a way that it now blocked the entrance to the room. It had not been that way earlier in the evening.

Between breaks, the battle of wills continued for hours. No matter how Conover prodded him, Shelton refused to leave the tavern. Hours passed until finally, after encouraging him to look for a bright light, Conover convinced the spirit to pass on. He was exhausted when he finally left the kitchen. He told Bartels, "He was a battle. He's the biggest battle that I ever had."

Bernie Shelton had finally moved on, although in the wake of the strange tale that later appeared in Bartels' newspaper, there were many who asked if he was ever really there at all. Some of the long-time customers of the Parkway Tavern laughed about the idea of a ghost. One skeptic said that he'd been hearing that Bernie Shelton haunted the bar for years, but he was not buying what he considered a tall tale. He told Bartels, "When you're dead, you're dead."

But was this really the case when it came to Bernie Shelton? Many would argue about it, especially the four people who were in the tavern that night in August 1998. They experienced something extraordinary that night and no amount of skepticism on the part of non-believers was going to convince them that the events were not real. Bernie Shelton, they knew, had been lingering in the Parkway Tavern for more than 50 years. After that night, he was gone, giving the infamous gangster the chance to finally rest in peace – whether he deserved it or not.

7. THIS HOUSE IS HAUNTED
Spirited Dwellings of Central Illinois

Located at the corner of Eighth and Jackson Streets in downtown Springfield is the only home that Abraham Lincoln ever owned. In 1844, Lincoln felt that he was making enough money in his law practice to finally purchase a house for his family. The Lincolns' oldest son, Robert, had already been born by this time and Lincoln, Mary, and the new baby all needed the space. Years later, when Lincoln departed Springfield, bound for the White House, he bid a fond farewell to the home. He placed the house in the hands of Lucian A. Tilton and his wife, who maintained the house through the Civil War Years and during the chaotic "carnival of death" that followed the President's assassination.

Over the years, the house has gained a reputation for being haunted. Some have claimed that the well-traveled ghost of Abraham Lincoln still lingers here, while others claim that it's Mary's ghost who refuses to leave the home where the family knew both happiness and sorry. The National Park Service, which manages Lincoln's home today, will assure you that there are no ghosts here at all, even though numerous accounts say otherwise. If there are indeed spirits in this house, I truly don't believe they are those of the Lincoln family at all. I think the soul that remains in this house probably saw more anguish in this place than the Lincoln family ever did.

When Abraham Lincoln purchased the one-and-a-half story cottage at Eighth and Jackson, he picked a house that he could afford that was near to his law office in downtown Springfield. The house, built in the Greek Revival-style, was only five years old at the time. It had been built by Reverend Charles Dresser in 1839. When the Lincolns moved in, the house had just three rooms on the first floor and sleeping lofts upstairs. As the fortunes of the family increased, additions were made to the house. A bedroom was added to the first floor that later became a back parlor. Outside of the house, a brick wall was constructed and a fence was added along Jackson Street. The large kitchen was split into a formal dining room and kitchen, which Mary's sisters believed had ruined the kitchen. But Mary believed that her sons would not learn good manners by eating their meals in a kitchen.

On February 1, 1850, Eddie Lincoln died in the house. Edward Baker Lincoln was Abraham and Mary's second son, named after Lincoln's friend, Edward Dickinson Baker. Little is known about Eddie, other than he was beloved by his parents and older brother, Robert. He was described as a tender-hearted, kind, and loving child. He died just one month before his fourth birthday. Although census records noted that he died from "chronic consumption," many historians believed that he actually suffered from a type of thyroid cancer. In those days, "consumption" became the cause of death for anyone who died from a wasting disease. His parents were devastated, as they would be more than a dozen years later when their son, Willie, died in the White House. Eddie was buried in Hutchinson's Cemetery, but he was reunited in death with his father at Oak Ridge Cemetery in 1865, when Lincoln's body was brought to Springfield.

In 1856, the Lincolns added a full second story to the house, with three bedrooms and a master "his and hers" bedroom suite. Robert Lincoln had his own room for a few years before leaving for prep school and college. When he left, his younger brothers, Willie and Tad, moved from the trundle bed in their mother's room to Robert's old room. This gave Mary more room for sewing, dressing in private, and solitude for enduring the frequent headaches she had. Lincoln used his room as a second office, writing correspondence and doing legal

The Lincoln Home in Springfield

and political work at his desk. Lincoln often worked until well past midnight, writing letters and speeches. In the second room, he did not disturb Mary's rest.

After Lincoln was nominated for the presidency in May 1860, the house was overrun with reporters, well-wishers, friends, campaigners, and curiosity-seekers, all wanting some of Lincoln's time. The house was surrounded by well-wishers when Lincoln departed for Washington and said goodbye to his friends – and the family home – one last time.

Today, the house has been restored as closely as possible to how it looked during the Lincoln years. It was not an easy task to accomplish. In the summer of 1860, *Frank Leslie's Illustrated Newspaper* sent a reporter and artist to sketch the public rooms of the Lincoln home, never realizing how valuables those illustrations would be. Although most of the Lincolns' original furnishings do not survive, the newspaper drawings from that summer gave historical researchers the information to closely match the appearance of those rooms. A set of stereo-cards from 1865 were also used to confirm the types of furniture that the Lincolns had, as well as the wallpaper, carpeting, and drapes.

The home was owned by the state of Illinois for a number of years, but is now operated by the National Park Service, which frowns on the idea that the house is regarded as a "haunted" site. They have always maintained that there are no ghosts in the house, however, many of the witnesses who have come forward over the years to talk about strange happenings in Lincoln's former home are former employees and tour guides.

A number of years ago, the *Springfield State Journal-Register* interviewed some staff members of the house. Some were former workers, while others were working there at the time. One then current member was a woman named Shirlee Laughlin, who was a custodian at the Lincoln home. She claimed that her superiors were very unhappy with what they called her "vivid imagination." Was she delusional, making things up, or were there truly odd happenings taking place in the house?

In her interview, she claimed that she had experienced the ghosts in the house on many occasions. She didn't see them, she said, she saw the things that they did. Among the things she witnessed were toys and furniture that moved around to different rooms in the house, seemingly on their own; candles that lit and burned down without assistance; a rocking chair that began rocking on its own. Laughlin added: "At times, that rocking chair rocks and you can feel the wind rushing down the hall, even though the windows are shut tight."

She also told of an occurrence that took place while she was rearranging furniture in Mary Lincoln's former bedroom. Besides being a custodian, she was also well-versed in historic home restoration and would often attempt to recreate the layout of the household furniture as it looked when the Lincoln's lived in the house. She was in the bedroom alone one afternoon when someone tapped her on the shoulder. She looked around the room, but there was no one there. She decided to leave the furniture the way she had found it. Another time, she was searching for a key that had vanished from a wooden chest in Mary's bedroom. The staff searched everywhere for it and then it just showed up one day with a piece of pink ribbon tied to it. No explanation was ever discovered for where the key had been or for who had tied the ribbon to it.

Years after Laughlin's interview, a couple of unnamed staff members at the house disputed all of her stories, claiming that they had taken advantage of her belief in ghosts by setting up elaborate pranks around the house. They moved things around and, according to their story, even tied a string to the rocking chair and caused it to rock when she was present. Was this true? Or was it simply an attempt to dispel the rumors of ghosts that surround the house?

We may never know, but even if it was true, what about the other witnesses to strange activity? One former guide stated that she was on duty at the front door one afternoon and heard the sounds of music being played on a piano that used to be in the parlor. She went to stop whoever had touched it, but found there was no one in the room, or anywhere nearby. Another staff member recalled several occasions when odd sensations, as well as the touch of unseen hands, made her hurry to finish her closing duties on some evenings. One park ranger, who went on the record anonymously, said that she was in the front parlor by herself one day and saw something happen that she couldn't explain. There was a display in the room of items that were commonly found in households of the period, including some children's toys. She saw a movement out of the corner of her eye and realized that she was watching a small toy rolling across the floor on its own. She didn't stay in the room very long.

Staff members are not the only ones to have odd encounters. A number of tourists have also noticed things that are a bit out of the ordinary at the Lincoln home. They claim to have heard low voices in empty rooms, the rustle of what sounds like a period dress passing by them in the hallway, and to have experienced cold spots, the soft brush of a hand, and have seen the rocking chair moving gently back and forth.

For many years, stories have circulated about the apparition of a woman who has been seen in various places inside of the house. A tourist, an attorney from Virginia, even wrote a letter to the staff after he returned home to tell of his encounter with the woman. He claimed that she had been standing in the parlor of the house, but as he got close to her, she vanished. He wrote that he believed the woman was Mary Lincoln.

But was it really Mary? Those who believe that the spirit of a woman remains behind in this house feel that the ghost is actually not a member of the Lincoln family, but rather a later occupant of the house, Lucretia Jane Tilton, the wife of Great Western Railway president, Lucian A. Tilton.

When the Lincoln family left for Washington, the house was rented to Mr. and Mrs. Tilton. They purchased most of the Lincolns' furniture, so the house was largely unchanged after they left, except for an addition to the kitchen. But the Tiltons were never left in peace during their time in the house. While the Lincolns were in Washington, Mrs. Tilton was constantly plagued by visitors. She estimated that at least 65,000 people had visited the home and asked to take a tour of it, ringing the bell and knocking at the door at all hours of the day and night.

Mrs. Tilton was rather apprehensive about what might happen after President Lincoln was assassinated in 1865 and his body was returned to Springfield. But she was a kind-hearted woman and had already resolved herself to the fact that she was going to allow people to take grass from the yard, flowers from her garden or leaves from the trees. She had no idea what was coming --- by the end of the funeral services, she had to ask for military protection for the house. Her lawn and gardens had been stripped, paint had been scraped off the clapboards, and bricks had been carried away from the retaining wall as souvenirs.

The Tiltons left Springfield and the Lincoln home in 1869 and moved to Chicago. After that, it remained a rental property for several years. After Mary's death in 1882, Robert, who lived in Vermont, had grown tired of being an absentee landlord and fighting with a tenant who had turned the first floor into a paying museum. He deeded the house to the state of Illinois for $1, only asking that it be kept in good repair and "free of access" so that anyone could visit his father's home. The state conducted an extensive renovation of the house in the early 1950s, and then, 20 years later, turned things over to the National Park Service, who operates it as a historic site today. Access to the house is still free, just as Robert Lincoln wanted it to be, and hundreds of thousands of visitors tour the home each year.

And some of them, along with staff members of the Lincoln home, leave with a little more to their experience than they were prepared for – some of them leave after an encounter with the resident ghost.

Lucretia Tilton may have moved out of the house in 1869, but many believe that she never left it. They feel that the spectral woman that so many have encountered, cleaning and straightening the house, is the beleaguered Mrs. Tilton, still worried over the many disruptions that continually marked her short tenancy in the only home that Abraham Lincoln ever owned.

Bones from the Past
A Haunting at the Culver House

In a previous chapter in this book, we explored the idea that at least a portion of the haunting reputation that has been earned by the city of Decatur over the years comes from the fact that much of the downtown area was built on Native American burial grounds. For evidence of how the disturbance of a burial ground can affect the atmosphere of a place, we offer up the John Culver house, located on the city's west side.

It is a place of tragedy, death, horror, ghosts, and some believe, a lingering curse.

For many years, the Culver house was in ruins, a crumbling condition that was far from the praise that it once earned as one of the finest houses in the city. For more than two decades, the ramshackle place was boarded up and closed to trespassers. Its days of glory were long past, but the legends remained. The house was a place of tragedy and despair, and in more recent times, murder and death. Did the history of the house leave a dark shadow on the property, or was it the land itself? According to building records and newspaper reports, the original site of the house was excavated on the site of a Native American burial ground. Newspaper stories from the early 1880s, a far less politically correct time, note that workers actually removed bones and relics from the site and dumped them in a rubbish pile down the street. Of course, they had no idea at the time about the damage they had done – or what the repercussions would be for the future.

The land was originally purchased by Colonel Josiah Clokey in 1881, and he started construction on a house on the property. For unknown reasons, the construction continued on and off for the next two decades. It was during this time that the foundation was dug, exposing Native American remains, and work on the first floor was started. As the house was being built, the Clokey family was living in an estate across town that was known as "The Pines," which was regarded as one of the finest houses in the city. Clokey was an attorney in the city, one of the partners in the Clokey & Mills law firm, one of the members of the board of directors of the Decatur National Bank, and a real estate developer. While he was successful in business, Clokey suffered the tragic loss of two of his children while the property was being developed.

He was also the witness to a bizarre happening in the city that, while may have not had anything to do with the property, was certainly very strange. On May 18, 1896, a terrible spring storm deluged the city with rain and hail, caused several terrific lightning strikes, including one that set a house on fire, and caused thousands of fish to fall from the sky on Decatur. In the midst of a fall of hail, scores of "wall-eyed pickerel" began falling from the sky. Colonel Clokey was taking shelter in the doorway of the H. Mueller Gun Company when he saw something hit the ground that was larger than a hailstone. He stepped into the street and picked

The Culver House

up a small fish that was about two inches long. It was still alive when he picked it up, as were all of the others that rained from the sky that day. The newspapers of 1898 proposed that they had been swept up from some distant river by a whirlwind and dropped on the streets of Decatur during the storm.

In 1901, after being largely abandoned for 20 years, the land and the house that Clokey had never finished was sold to John Culver, who completed the construction and turned the mansion, with its looming towers and mansard roofline, into one of the finest in the area.

John Culver was born in Christian County, southwest of Decatur, in December 1858. He received only a grade school education and went to work at age 15. He later became a stone mason with his brother, James, in Springfield, and in 1899, came to Decatur to start his own monument and gravestone business. He also helped to bring electricity to Decatur and several surrounding towns as one of the organizers and operators of the Municipal Electric Light Company. But it was in 1901 that he truly began to amass his wealth. That year, he and James were awarded with the contract to rebuild Abraham Lincoln's monument and tomb in Springfield's Oak Ridge Cemetery. He now wanted a home that befit his social status and he began searching for a lot on the city's west side, which was then home to Decatur's elite. He found the uncompleted project that had been abandoned by Clokey years before and purchased it.

The house became a grand mansion. It was originally constructed of red brick with stone trim and boasted a turret on the west front side and a wide, rounded tower on the east side. The interior of the house had large rooms, built into odd sizes to match the particular interests of each room. The first two floors of the house were living quarters, while the third floor was used as a ballroom and had a stained glass skylight. The house also had a massive library with built-in bookcases and large French windows that looked out over the street. The house was also constructed so that every room on the first floor had its own fireplace. However, something occurred just a few months after the Culver family moved in that caused the fireplace in the formal dining room to be removed.

Many believe that this was the first time that the weirdness of the land exposed itself to the Culver family – but it would not be the last.

According to historical records, the Culvers were seated in the dining room for the evening meal when "something" came down the chimney of the house and entered the dining room. Some have dismissed this unnamed "something" as simply a bird, but legends suggest that it was far stranger than that. In fact, it was so strange that John Culver immediately ordered workmen to tear the fireplace out and brick over the opening. We will never know what this frightening "something" might have been, but it seems that it must have been more terrifying than a bird to have provoked such a drastic response.

The Culvers remained in the house until 1943. In July, John Culver passed away at the age of 84. His daughter, Elizabeth, who had married David S. Shellabarger, from another prominent Decatur family, in 1916, inherited the house, but they never used it. The mansion was left empty for the next seven years, although strangely, neighbors often reported seeing lights in the windows of the house, even though no one was living there at the time. A few people who were strolling by the house in the evening claimed to see a man peering out the windows of the library, which had once been John Culver's favorite room.

In 1950, the house was sold and divided into apartments and it seemed that each new decade brought another tragedy to the house. Two suicides occurred in the house, one in 1958 and one in 1966, and then in May 1979, a third floor apartment caught fire and caused over $90,000 in smoke and water damage to the mansion. The cause of the fire was said to be a faulty extension cord.

In 1988, though, a tenant of the building, Patsy Rosich, was brutally murdered by her boyfriend. Her assailant, Maseo Richmond, was convicted of first-degree murder and sentenced to fifty years in prison. One year after this horrific event, the house was found to be unfit for human habitation and was boarded up. It remained closed, slowly crumbling, for the next two decades.

Finally, after all of those years of abandonment, the house was purchased and a restoration effort was started that resulted in repairing the structure of the house, front porch, and many of the rooms on the first floor. But then, just over two years after the work was begun, the renovations fell silent once more and the house now remains – as of this writing – in a state of limbo. Is it doomed to never be restored to its original glory? Only time will tell.

Many questions remain about the Culver house. Is it haunted in the traditional manner? Or is it simply affected by the land on which it stands?   Some believe that ghosts haunt this old place, perhaps those of John Culver, Native American spirits, or perhaps the victims of suicides and murder in the past. Others believe that the mansion is better described as "haunted by history," a place that is tainted, maybe even cursed, by the land on which it was constructed. Does such a taint ever go away? Once again, only time will provide the answer to that.

The Tragedy of Towanda Meadows

Every one of us who has traveled along the interstate north of Bloomington, Illinois, has seen the house, nestled eerily in the cornfields just off in the distance, and every one of us with an interest in old houses and haunted history has wondered about it. The brick Italianate mansion seems out of place on the Illinois prairie, looking mournfully toward a highway and a railroad line that seems to have passed it by, leaving it stranded in the distant past. It has been crumbling there for many years – lost, abandoned, seemingly forgotten, and some say, haunted by tragedies of yesterday. It is a house of unrealized dreams, great fortune and premature death, strangely suited to the shadowy corners of Central Illinois.

The grand house, which came to be known as Towanda Meadows, was built in 1874-1875 by William R. Duncan, a pioneer farmer and stock-raiser who came to Illinois in 1863. When he erected the mansion, it was said that he purposely set out to make it so impressive that it would be noticed by travelers between St. Louis and Chicago. He attained his objective, building an Italianate mansion with six fireplaces, a winding staircase with hard-carved walnut spindles, and walls that were more than a foot thick. But he was destined to only enjoy the house for a short time. Not long after it was completed, death and tragedy came calling.

Duncan had been born in December 1818 in Clark County, Kentucky. Raised by wealthy parents in the slave state of Kentucky, William became rich himself after his father's death in 1836. Under the terms of his father's will, the family's slaves were set free, which convinced William to remain loyal to the Union when the Civil War began to rage years later. Eventually, the political division in his home state over slavery caused him to move north to Illinois.

William had a brother, Thomas, and two sisters, Elizabeth and Sally. In their father's will, Sally was described as being unable to care for herself, suggesting that she was mentally ill. If so, it was a condition that would return to haunt the family in 1882, when William's second son, James, was declared insane by a McLean County, Illinois, court and sent to the Jacksonville State Hospital.

William married his first wife, Nancy Redmon, in 1835 when both of them were only 17-years-old. She died young in 1848, and William married a second time in 1849. His second wife was a widow, Mary Chorn Quisenberry, and they would have four children, Nannie, Henry, James, and Mary Elizabeth.

In late October 1863, William sold off a large portion of his short-horn cattle herd and moved his family to Illinois. They traveled by train and ended up in Towanda, likely renting a home owned by Nathan Sunderland on property that Duncan eventually purchased in December 1865. But the start of the family's happy life in Illinois was shattered by the death of Mary Duncan on February 23, 1864. William was devastated by the loss of another beloved wife and the children were heartbroken, especially Mary Elizabeth, who was only three-years-old at the time.

Late in 1864, William, now only 45 and widowed twice, traveled back to Kentucky and married his third wife, Sarah Ann Bean, age 29. Sarah was wealthy in her own right and the two of them signed a pre-nuptial agreement of sorts, giving her control over her own money, which was unusual at the time.

The newlyweds returned to Illinois and William began building his cattle business and amassing a fortune. He brought a number of experienced cattlemen with him from Kentucky, including a number of free black men, who had worked for his family for years. In 1866, he became a member of the Advisory Committee of the McLean County Agricultural Society and was appointed to audit the treasurer's books. In some of the minutes of the society meetings, Duncan is referred to as introducing and cultivating some of the finest breeds of foreign cattle to the area. He had formed an alliance with a number of other forward-thinking farmers in the region, who advocated the improvement of crops and livestock through selective breeding and other "scientific means."

Tragedy visited the Duncan family again on June 16, 1868, when Henry, age 12, drowned in a pond on the family's property. He was buried next to his mother in a small home plot, although the bodies were later moved to Evergreen Cemetery in Bloomington. During his son's funeral, a grieving William had the grave of his second wife, Mary, opened up so that he could say goodbye to her one last time.

A few years later, construction was started on Duncan's three-story mansion, Towanda Meadows. The house was unlike anything that had been seen in the area before, and locals came from far and wide to watch the construction take place and to marvel at the unusual elements of the house. William welcomed them with open arms, which bolstered his reputation as a kind and generous man. Most regarded him as one of the esteemed residents of the county, and he was in great demand as a speaker for the State Agricultural Society and at the meeting of the National Agricultural Society, which was held in Cincinnati in September 1875.

Towanda Meadows was completed in 1875 but, sadly, William lived in the house for less than a year before he died in October 1876 at the age of only 57. At the time of his death, he was returning home from the State Fair, which was held in Ottawa, Illinois, that fall. He had been depressed for some time, following the death of his last remaining sister, Elizabeth, who had died in Clinton a short time before. Many blamed his melancholy for the fact that he was unable to shake off a severe cold that he contracted at the fair. After becoming ill in Ottawa, he was put to bed at the home of his friend Abner Strawn and remained there for several days. Feeling better, he departed for Towanda, but only made it as far as Normal before he collapsed. He was taken to the home of relatives and died with his third wife, Sarah, by his side.

Duncan never saw his beloved Towanda Meadows again, but he was buried on the property next to Mary and Henry until Sarah had their remains exhumed and moved to Evergreen Cemetery.

Sarah remained at the farm for a time with eight children, five of her own and three of William and Mary's. They had little time to mourn as drama, tragedy, and death continued to plague the family. Soon after the death of her father, Nannie, William's oldest daughter with wife Mary, filed a lawsuit on behalf of herself and her siblings against Sarah and her children. She was seeking a portion of her father's substantial estate and the courts divided the land into parcels. Nannie later became a schoolteacher and married Franklin Barnes, a successful farmer, in 1878. They had a daughter, Lucy, who was born in 1880.

Like other members of her family, Nannie was doomed to an early grave. In 1884, her health began to fail (although it's not listed in the records, she likely suffered from tuberculosis) and Franklin, very concerned about his wife, sold his farm and moved his wife and daughter to Pomona, California. He hoped that the mild climate might make her better. Unfortunately, California didn't turn out to be beneficial for Nannie. She continued to decline and as she neared death, she told her husband that she wanted to return to Illinois to live out her final days. She passed away while they were on their way home and she was buried in Evergreen Cemetery.

Tragedy struck the family again in 1896 when Nannie's daughter, Lucy, also died from consumption in her father's Bloomington home. Lucy died on the day before her 16th birthday. Her father, Franklin, later moved to Towanda and served as the town's postmaster for a number of years. He remarried and died in November 1905.

William and Mary's third child, James, was only 18 when his father died in 1876. Nelson Jones was appointed by the court as his guardian and James lived each winter in Texas, where he raised horses and brought them back to Illinois for sale. In September 1878, James, age 21, married Flora Dillon of Bloomington and his guardianship by his father's friend, Nelson Jones, was settled. In February 1880, James and Flora had a son, Levi William, and moved into a home next door to his sister Nannie and her husband, Franklin. James worked hard to improve the farm and was soon worth quite a bit of money. He began importing horses from overseas and establishing himself as a successful dealer. A second son, Floyd, was born in November 1882.

But tragedy touched James and his family, as well. In 1883, James, Flora, Flora's sister, Ida Dillon Harding, and other members of the Dillon family, traveled to France for both business and pleasure. James planned to arrange the purchase of a number of horses and to see the sights with his family. As they were preparing to make their way back across the Atlantic, Ida became seriously ill and was unable to depart for the return trip. James and Flora and another couple made the trip so they could care for the horses, but three others remained behind with Ida, who died a few days later.

This was the start of a terrible time for James and his family. In three years, James went from a prominent businessman to a severely depressed and mentally-ill young man. His malady struck in his late 20s and was likely an onset of bipolar disorder, for which no diagnosis existed at the time. On July 7, 1886, Flora's father, Levi Dillon, filed a petition with the court indicating that James, then age 28, was insane and asked the authorities to investigate the allegation. A warrant was issued for his arrest and James was taken to the Illinois State Hospital for the Insane in Jacksonville. He was judged unfit to manage his personal estate of more than $20,000, and while Levi was first appointed to be his conservator, he was later removed and a new one was appointed. There was a lot of controversy about what happened to James' money while he was in and out of the insane asylum, but accusations were made against Levi Dillon, and when James was eventually released from the hospital, his remaining property was restored. James and Flora divorced in December 1891. Their older son was raised by James, and Floyd was cared for by Flora. What happened to James after his release from the hospital and subsequent divorce is largely unknown. In 1891, he appeared in public records working at a livery stable in Bloomington and soon after, vanished from history.

Mary Elizabeth was William and Mary's youngest child and she was in Kentucky when her father died. She had been living there with her uncle, James Chorn, and his family. In 1881, she was in Illinois visiting friends and family when she met Ellis Dillon, Flora's brother. The two fell in love and despite being two years older than Ellis, Mary Elizabeth married him in December 1883.

The couple later moved to Wisconsin and Ellis enrolled at the University of Madison for training to become an electrical engineer. They had four children, Carl, Lula, Helen, and Dorotha and, apparently, lived a happy life for many years. Then, in September 1918, Mary was granted a divorce from her husband on the grounds of cruel and inhuman treatment. According to her testimony, she and Ellis had lived together in the same house for five years but never ate together or slept together and Ellis refused to speak to her. She was unable to cite a cause for this treatment. Ellis was ordered to pay her $50 per month in alimony while she remained unmarried. Ellis later moved to Montana, but what became of Mary Elizabeth is a mystery.

After William's death, Sarah and her five children with William, Asa, William, Eli, Harrison, and John, remained at Towanda Meadows for a short time before returning to Kentucky. Sarah eventually died of pneumonia in February 1922 at the age of 86. She never remarried.

In 1882, Sarah sold Towanda Meadows and her remaining 100 acres to F.M. Jones, who later sold it to D.W. Kraft of Normal. At the time of his death, it was inherited by his daughter, Helen. Over the years, the old mansion had gone through a succession of owners, and during the twentieth century, tenants occupied the grand old home. The fireplaces were bricked up, the second and third story windows shuttered, and it was left to decline in the wind and weather of the Illinois prairie.

It was the tenants who lived in the house who told strange tales of ghosts and lingering memories. Many of them spoke of footsteps on the stairs and in the hallways, whispers, sounds of a woman weeping, and knocking at the front door during the wee hours of the night. Every one of these weird happenings can be directly tied to the mansion's tragic past with a woman crying for a lost child and the fateful knock that summoned Sarah to the bedside of her dying husband. History has left an impression on this creaking old place and seems to be replaying itself over and over again.

One former resident of the house once related his own encounter with a spectral woman on the second floor. He was only a boy at the time but clearly remembered exploring the upper floors of the house when he was living there with his family. In one of the closed-off bedrooms, he clearly saw a woman standing and gazing out of the window. When he sharply inhaled at the sight, the woman quickly turned around and then vanished in front of his eyes. He never forgot the incident, but who the woman might have been is unknown. Despite the efforts of local researchers, no Duncan family photographs have ever turned up.

Do phantoms still linger at Towanda Meadows? No one can say for sure. For years, it has been in the hands of absentee landlords and the unforgiving elements, but efforts to restore it may someday succeed and life may be breathed back into the glorious home of William Duncan once again.

A House Where the Past is Present

Looking out over the downtown square of Carrollton, Illinois, is the Greene County Historical and Genealogical Society. There is no mere office building, however. The place that the Society calls home, the Lee-Baker-Hodges House, is one of the great mansions of the region and a location with a storied past that played an integral part in much of the history of Carrollton and Greene County. It once briefly served as the county courthouse, was owned by one of Abraham Lincoln's best friends, was used as a doctor's office, and now houses a collection of relics and artifacts owned by the pioneers of Greene County.

It is a place where history comes alive for the visitor – sometimes literally.

The town of Carrollton was founded in 1821, although it wasn't filed for the record until four years later. The initial town site was started on land that belonged to Thomas Carlin, one of the first settlers in the area. Carlin was born near Shelbyville, Kentucky, in 1786. In 1803, his family moved to Missouri, where his father died, leaving Carlin to care for his mother and siblings. They later moved across the river to Illinois and Carlin served as a ranger, fighting against the Native Americans that were supported by the British during the War of 1812. After the war, he and his brothers, James and William, started a ferry across the Mississippi River, and became very successful. He served as a captain in the Illinois militia during the Black Hawk War. In the spring of 1819, he came to the Carrollton area with his mother and step-father and built a home about a half-mile south of what is now the town square. A career in politics followed and in 1838, he was elected as the sixth governor of Illinois. The Macoupin County town of Carlinville was eventually named in his honor.

Before Carlin made it to the Illinois capitol, he was one of the founders of Carrollton. County commissioners, appointed by the Illinois General Assembly, had been searching for the site of the Greene County seat and chose Carlin's land as the best location. Isaac Pruitt, who lived nearby, initially approached Carlin about the plan and he agreed. On February 20, 1821, they met at a spot that is now the east side of the square and John Allen paced 50 yards to the west, drove a stake, and said," Here let the courthouse be built." The town was laid out and named in honor of a local doctor, Charles Carroll.

At this point, there were no houses located at the site of the new town, so Carlin offered Jacob Fry a lot in Carrollton if he would build a house on it. Fry came to town, cut the timbers, split the boards and put up a house, which stood for the next 57 years. For many years, it formed part of the St. James Hotel.

Before Fry had finished his construction, he stopped to help Thomas Rattan build a cabin, located on the northwest corner of the square. On May 1, 1821, Rattan was granted a license for the first tavern in Carrollton.

On June 13, 1821, the first courthouse was planned. County Commissioners William and Thomas Finley appropriated the sum of $380 for the construction. In September, Thomas Rattan was given a contract to build the courthouse chimney. He purchased 6,000 bricks for $55. The building was completed on June 1, 1822, and was located just to the east of the log hewn jail.

While the courthouse was being constructed, the need arose for a place to hold trials and legal cases, so officials approached John Skidmore about using a room in the home that he had recently constructed. His home was also the first store in town and he turned over one of the rooms to the court for $4 each month.

One of the other tenants in Skidmore's home was a young man named Samuel Lee, who, at various times, served as the Greene County clerk and recorder, circuit clerk, and justice of the peace. In 1824, Lee married Skidmore's 16-year-old sister-in-law, Mary Ann Faust, and he purchased the property from his friend three years later. As his fortunes improved, Lee began expanding the small home that Skidmore had built, with plans to turn it into a grand mansion. Sadly, Lee died in September 1829, before the house could be completed.

According to the history of Carrollton, Illinois, it was "known afterward as the haunted house."

In Lee's will, he directed that the house be completed for his wife and used as her home. The construction was finished by Moses Stevens, who built the second county courthouse across the street from the home in 1832.

The Federal-style Lee mansion was home to the widowed Mary Ann and her two young children, Frank and Maria. Several months later, though, the young woman began to be courted by Edward Baker, a tall, blue-eyed 19-year-old who had worked as a deputy county clerk for her late husband. Baker and Mary Ann were married in April 1831. The Bakers lived in the house for four years before moving to Springfield. Baker, an attorney, saw more business opportunities in the growing community. Soon after arriving, Lee met another young lawyer, Abraham Lincoln, and they became close friends.

Lincoln and Baker rose to prominence together in the Whig Party, in large part because they were both excellent speakers and always in demand at election time. Lincoln was so fond of Baker that he and his wife,

A vintage photograph of the Lee-Baker-Hodges Mansion in Carrollton

Mary, named their second son after him. Baker went on to serve in the Illinois House of Representatives and the United States House and Senate. In 1861, Baker even introduced his old Springfield friend before he delivered his inaugural address in Washington.

In 1860, the Baker family had moved west to the new state of Oregon, which elected Baker to the Senate. At the start of the Civil War, he organized the California Regiment and was commissioned its Colonel. Baker was killed on October 21, 1861, during the battle of Ball's Bluff, Virginia, making Mary Ann a widow once again.

The Bakers had sold the Carrollton "Brick Mansion House," as it was described in the deed, in 1836 to Dr. Orange Heaton for $4,000. In March 1850, Dr. Heaton sold it to Charles Drury Hodges. Like Baker, Hodges was a politician. He served in the Illinois House in the early 1850s, was elected a county judge and then served in the U.S. House. After the Civil War, Hodges was a circuit judge and a state senator.

The Carrollton mansion was changed substantially during Hodges's ownership. In 1854, he added a second floor to the east end of the house, incorporating it into a two-story Italianate style wing. The additions included a wide front porch, decorative cornice brackets, different windows, and an iron fence around the yard. It became a showplace of the period and was called the finest house in town.

Hodges died in 1884 and his wife passed away in 1899. The year after her death, her son, Beverly C. Hodges, converted the house into the Hodges Office Building. He then ended the family's 70-year ownership of the house when he sold it to Dr. N.D. Vedder in 1921, who converted it into his offices.

For the next six decades, the Lee-Baker-Hodges mansion was home to a variety of businesses and professional offices, including lawyers, dentists, physicians, and insurance agents. In 1974, the deteriorating old house was bought by Carrollton attorney William Vogt. In 1980, the home was listed on the National Register of Historic Places and its lease was transferred to the Greene County Historical and Genealogical Society two years later.

The non profit agency uses it as their headquarters today and works tirelessly to preserve the house, while offering a place for historical research and a collection of artifacts from the house's past and from the town of Carrollton. It is a place, as mentioned, where history can be experienced in the present day and it seems that occupants of the building have long been experiencing the past as lingering spirits.

As far back as the 1830s, the people of Carrollton regarded the house as being haunted. It fit all of the criteria of a traditionally haunted house, where the ghost of Samuel Lee might have stayed behind. He was a young man who died in his prime, leaving behind a wife and children and an unfinished house that he wanted to turn into the finest home in the community. Stories of his ghost became legendary in town, even making their way into conservative historical accounts of Carrollton.

In the present day, both staff members at the house and visitors have reported ghostly experiences. Strange sounds are heard, along with voices, knocks, footsteps, and creaking floors when no one is present. Doors open and close, lights turn on and off, and objects disappear without explanation. Ghost hunters who have stayed in the house with our American Hauntings overnights have reported unexplained voices on recordings, eerie cold spots, and once, the reflection of a woman in old-fashioned clothing who was photographed in a mirror.

But can all of the haunting experiences be explained as past occupants of the house that have never left? It's possible – perhaps even likely – that many of the strange events that have been reported are because of spirits that have been brought into the house and have no connection to it at all.

As part of the museum display, each room of the mansion has been given a theme, including a bank from the early 1900s, a Victorian-era bedroom, a sewing room, and many others. Each room of the house is filled with artifacts from the era. Some of them are from the house, but most have been collected from people in Carrollton and the surrounding county. Did ghosts come with these items?

There are a variety of reasons why buildings become haunted, but in some cases, hauntings are caused by the objects that are brought into them. These former possessions, owned and cherished by people from the past, can sometimes have spirits that are attached to them. By moving the items in question to a location, it's possible to bring along unseen energies which then begin to manifest in that new spot.

Is this what caused the Lee-Baker-Hodges house to become haunted? Or was it already home to ghosts who lived, loved, and died in the house so many years ago? If you have the chance to experience this house for yourself, perhaps you can be the one who finds the evidence to answer those questions. Until then, we are just left to ponder another mystery of the other side.

History in Stone
Hauntings at the James Eldred House

Hidden in remote, secluded spots in the wildest regions of Central Illinois are often the most haunted places that a traveler will encounter. The James Eldred House is just such a place. Along a twisting roadway that curves along the looming bluffs of the Illinois River Valley is a stone house that dates back to the days of one of the first families to settle in the region. It is a place that was nearly forgotten by time and the once-grand house that was left to the elements to decay, crumble, and collapse.

Rescued by historians and the hard work of volunteers, the Eldred House has not only been recovered from ruin, it has returned to life. It now pays tribute to its builders and its occupants from the past, but it also celebrates the spirits that still linger in the house and on the property. The Eldred House is a historic site that was truly saved by the ghosts that haunt the place and by the people like the readers of this book, who care so much about the past that we will go to great lengths to preserve it.

The Eldred family came to America from England and two brothers, Robert and William, settled in the Plymouth colony. They began making a name for themselves in America as Robert settled in the town of Yarmouth, Massachusetts, and married Elizabeth Nickerson. William married Anne Lumpkin and settled on a farm adjoining Anne's parents in the town of Dennis. William became a constable and a surveyor of highways, which was a post of great importance in those days. Anne died in 1676 and William passed away three years later.

One of their children, Samuel, later achieved fame as an Indian fighter before marrying Keziah Taylor and raising a family in Yarmouth. After his death in 1705, his children were assigned the task of distributing public lands. One of Samuel's sons, Jehosaphat, was born in 1683. He married Thankful Rider in 1709 and died in Falmouth in 1765. His son, also named Jehosaphat, was born in Falmouth in 1716 and married Elizabeth Swift in 1747. They moved to the town of Warren in Connecticut, where they purchased land and raised a family. In 1777, he was appointed to oversee the needs of American soldiers and their families during the Revolutionary War. He died in 1801.

Born in Connecticut in 1796, Ward Eldred was the first of the family to have an interest in the Illinois Territory. In 1818, he and his cousin, Swift, traveled by foot to Illinois from their home in the Mohawk Valley area of New York. In the months before statehood, they surveyed the land that would someday become Greene County before returning home. The Eldreds believed that Illinois would make a wonderful new home for their families but waited for assurances that it would not enter the union as a slave state before they committed to moving west. Their decision was made after Swift Eldred received a letter from an Illinois friend, George Churchill, who informed him that Illinois' state constitutional convention had "decided against slavery in general," although the presence of previously owned slaves had not been decided. Churchill was optimistic about the prospects of Illinois being a "free state."

In January 1819, Ward married the first of his four wives and returned to West Central Illinois with his brother, Elon, and a herd of sheep that the two had driven from Ohio. In March 1820, his father, Jehosaphat (the third to bear the name), and a group of 12 other relatives, journeyed from New York to Illinois, settling west of what would become Carrollton to await the creation of a new county on recently surveyed land.

In early 1821, the Illinois Legislature created seven new counties, dividing one of the largest, Madison County, to create Greene County. Lands were to be sold in lots of no less than 80 acres and for no less than $100. Before the sale of public lands took place, recent settlers in the region made an agreement that they would not bid against one another, but rather would divide the lands based on who had arrived first in the county. Unfortunately, it did not work out quite that way. Jehosaphat Eldred and Robert Hobson each claimed to be the first to arrive in the region and each believed that he had the right to choose the best piece of land. The two men failed to come to an agreement before the sale and the result was a bidding contest.

The Eldreds arrived on the day of the sale with an abundance of money. It was said that their saddlebags were so filled with gold and silver that it took two men to carry them into the land office. Jehosaphat won the land he wanted for $150, but he was so unhappy with the price that he told Hobson that he was going to bid against him for any piece of land that he wanted to buy, driving up the value so that he would have to pay the same outrageous price. Friends intervened and Jehosaphat agreed that if Hobson paid him $50, he would stay out of the bidding.

The Eldreds left that day with five 80-acre plots of land in the Carrollton Township, some of which remains in the Eldred family today. Ward Eldred's family made their initial homestead in one of those sections, where his son, James John Eldred, was born in 1828.

Meanwhile, Jehosaphat's wife, Polly, died in October 1822. She was buried on the farm, but the location of her grave has been lost to history. After Polly's death, Jehosaphat moved north to Galena, Illinois, and opened a lead mining operation. He also established a livestock farm at the mouth of the Big Sandy Creek in Scott County. He died in 1842 and left a large estate and land and lead mining deposits to his children.

The land on which the Eldred House would be built was originally owned by Richard Robley, one of the early settlers of Bluffdale, Illinois. Robley was one of a group of idealistic New Englanders who came west to Greene County in the 1820s. Several Vermont families, including the Robleys, Spencers, Brushes, and Russells, built the settlement of Bluffdale, where they hoped to bring education and enlightenment to the people of the western frontier. Robley first purchased 80 acres of land just north of the future site of the house in 1823. He later bought more land to the east. One section had been designated for schools in 1829, but later amended the law to allow the sale of the land in 1831. Two years later, Robley purchased 310 acres of that land from the Illinois School Commissioner, Samuel Smith, but apparently deferred payment. In 1836, he sold the land to Hiram R. Brown, who lived there with his wife, Hanna.

During this time, Ward Eldred's family lived just across the road on a small section of his extensive land holdings. Ward's first two wives had died before he purchased this section of ground. He married twice more in the 1840s, while raising cattle and growing crops on the land. All four of his wives died in childbirth. Ward died in 1851, after contracting an acute skin disease called erysipelas while driving cattle during a flood in the Illinois River bottoms. He left behind five sons and a seven-year-old daughter named Evaline.

After his father's death, James Eldred purchased his brother's interest in the land across the road from Ward Eldred's farm. James had married Emeline Smead, the sister of his father's fourth wife, in February 1851. Around that same time, the Eldreds had completed a new four-story limestone barn west of the house. Ward had need of such a structure because, at the time of his death, he owned 194 head of cattle, 70 dairy cows, 58 calves, 30 horses, five oxen, and a herd of goats. He sold cheese to markets in St. Louis and grew both wheat and corn. James inherited his father's cheese business and raised a variety of livestock and crops. The farm flourished and James and Emeline had four children -- Alice, Eva, Ward, and Alma -- by 1860. They also supported James's sister, Evaline, and had two domestic servants and three laborers for the farm.

By this time, James and Emeline's growing brood had outgrown Ward's old house and they decided to construct a new home in 1861. The new house became the most elegant structure in the area, despite the rather odd architectural combinations that had created it. While unquestionably in the Greek Revival-style, it was also a product of the Illinois River bluffs, mixing traditional architecture with local materials. Eldred created a country estate home that soon became the centerpiece of the area's social life in the 1860s and 1870s. In addition to raising their children and managing the farm and business, James and Emeline regularly hosted lavish parties that included the social elite of a multiple county region.

In the midst of gaiety and success, though, tragedy stalked the family. All three of the Eldred daughters died in the house. In 1861, the family was shattered by the death of Alma, who was only four-years-old at the time. In 1870, they lost their youngest daughter, Eva, and then Alice, in 1876. Both girls perished from tuberculosis, a terrible illness that was tragically common in America at the time. The deaths of the three girls stunned James and Emeline and they never really recovered.

And this was not the only bad luck that plagued the family. Due to the unpredictability of farm life, James's finances often suffered. In 1870, for example, a private tutor of the Eldred children sued James for his payment. He faced another lawsuit in 1900, owing money to John Snyder of Carrollton involving a lease on the Eldred property that was settled out of court. James was now sharing the farming duties with his son, Ward, now 25, and a cousin, Albon. E. Wilson, who was also a teacher at the Columbiana School at the Illinois River ferry landing on the Greene County side of the river. Wilson had discussed purchasing the land from James as early as 1880, apparently to help him settle a debt. Even though ready to sell at the time, James was getting older and five decades of farm work was starting to wear on him. Wilson remained a constant presence on the farm,

Members of the James Eldred family outside of their home

especially after he moved to Carrollton and started a grocery business. James finally began selling some of his land in 1883, when spring floods wreaked havoc on many local farms, damaging homes and threatening crops. Even more of his land was seized by county officials, presumably to pay off debt. This was a common occurrence for many local farmers in the spring of 1883.

That spring, Albon Wilson left the grocery business and purchased the title to the majority of James's remaining land. Wilson had recently married Cassie Robertson, who came from a wealthy family, and he used his newfound wealth to buy up land and make improvements to the various properties. The couple moved out to the old Ward Eldred home to manage the Bluffdale area farms. He allowed James and Emeline to continue to live in their own home until 1910, when they moved to Carrollton. Both of them died in 1911. Their son, Ward, was left to carry on the family name with two sons of his own.

By the time that James and Emeline passed away, Albon and Cassie were also living back in Carrollton. Albon himself died in 1912 and left all of the property to Cassie. She continued to maintain the Eldred House and the farms, with help from manager Lawrence Wagener, until her death in 1936.

After Cassie Wilson's death, the property went up for sale. It was purchased by Robert H. Levis of Godfrey, Illinois, who bought and sold a number of land parcels in the area during the 1930s and 1940s. The house and the immediate property remained in his hands until 1995. He ran it as Bluffdale Farms, Inc. with on-site tenants as managers. They did not use the Eldred House as a residence; they lived across the road in a modern 1918 house. The only occupation of the house during those years seems to have been a pair of families seeking refuge from a flood in 1943, and archaeologists during the nearby Koster Site excavations in the 1970s. For the most part, the once grand house became a storage unit for farm equipment and tools.

In 1995, Bluffdale Farms and the Levis family donated the property to the Illinois Valley Cultural Heritage Association (IVCHA), which began making plans to restore the house and create an information and visitor's center for the area. By then, the house was in deplorable condition. The structure was sound, but the stone was crumbling, the detail work had been erased by time and the elements, and the interior woodwork had largely vanished. Soon, though, a valiant effort began to be organized to not only save the house, but to restore it to how it looked in 1860, when it was built by James Eldred. Not long after work began, the volunteers who made up the majority of the work force, began to notice that strange things were happening at the ramshackle house: people were hearing voices and whispers, they were being touched and tapped on the shoulder, tools were vanishing and turning up in other places.

The Eldred House, it seemed, was haunted.

In the middle 2000s, American Hauntings, through efforts made by Loren Hamilton, began offering fundraising ghost hunting events at the Eldred House, with proceeds from each of the events going to help restore the house. Those who attended, looking for ghostly activity, were rarely disappointed. As of this writing, the events – and the restoration of the house – continue and the Eldred House has become a property that has been "saved by its ghosts."

But who are the spirits that still linger at the house?

In addition to members of the Eldred family, who are believed to have remained at the place where they experienced their greatest happiness and greatest sorrows, there are at least two other ghosts thought to inhabit the place. One of them, a Native American spirit, was here long before the Eldred family ever came to Illinois. A number of years ago, the Center for American Archaeology discovered prehistoric residence sites at the base of the bluff where the house now stands. They resembled those found at the Koster Site, a short distance from the Eldred House and the scene of ongoing excavations. Later, the remains of an Early American were discovered on the house's property. Workers were digging a trench for a new water line to service houses on the bluff and the bones were uncovered on the grounds. They were removed from the ground and left lying in the grass, where they were found the next day by IVCHA members. A call was made to local law enforcement, as well as to the Center for American Archaeology, and it was determined that they had come from a Native American burial site. Every effort was made to carefully and respectfully return the bones to the ground, but the damage had already been done. Apparently, when the remains had been disturbed, the spirit of the man they belonged to was also disturbed. Sightings of a shadowy figure began being reported on the grounds and they continue to this day. It is believed that rest still eludes the man whose body was unearthed, despite the efforts to bring him peace.

Another spirit of the house is said to be that of a peddler, or traveling salesman, who apparently visited the Eldreds one day and never left. During the time when the family lived in the house, it was common for peddlers to travel from town to town, selling their wares to farmers and those in rural areas. Legend states that just such a salesman called on the Eldred family one day and was invited to stay for supper. Later in the evening, seeing how tired and poorly the man seemed to be, they offered to let him stay the night. The next day, they discovered that he had died in the front parlor. The cause of his death remains a mystery, as does the reason why he chose to remain behind at the Eldred House. Over the years, scores of people who have stayed late in the house have experienced the sound of someone knocking at the front door. When the door is opened, there is never anyone there – never anyone who can be seen anyway. It's thought that perhaps the peddler is reliving his final night over and over again.

The most active spirits in the house, though, seem to be members of the Eldred family. Many ghost hunters and enthusiasts have collected recordings that they believe have captured the low voice of James Eldred. Others have not only recorded what they believe is the sound of Emeline's voice, but also the sound of a woman weeping. This is thought to be the terrible sorrow experienced by Emeline after the death of all three of her daughters in the house.

Others believe that they have actually seen the spirit of Emeline in the house and on the grounds. Some of them have been volunteers doing work on the house, ghost hunters attending events, and even neighbors who live near the isolated old mansion. Some of the locals say that they have seen a woman in period costume standing on the lawn. She always vanishes. Others say they have seen her looking out the window. Cindy Moscardelli, a Macoupin County resident, spotted the same woman peering out of the attic window of the house one night. The problem was that, at that time, there were no floors in the upper stories of the house – the woman was looking out the window but had nothing to stand on.

During an American Hauntings event on Halloween night 2009, Macoupin County investigators Chad and Debbie Musgrave were among those spending the entire night inside of the house. At that time, no one had slept inside of the Eldred House since the 1960s. As the group was crowded into the kitchen, listening to some of the history of the house, the Musgraves stepped out into the dining room. At the same time, they heard a sound on the stairs. When they looked up, they saw a shadowy figure lean over the handrail and look at the group that was gathered in the kitchen. A moment later, the shadow pulled back and the Musgraves heard the sound of footsteps going upstairs. Dan hurriedly followed, dashing up the steps to see who was on the second floor. The upper floor was completely empty. Had this been the ghost of Emeline Eldred, curious over the crowd that was in her kitchen? Or perhaps she was simply coming to join the party, since the Eldreds were so well known in the area for all of their grand social events.

There is probably no one who has experienced more ghostly phenomena in the Eldred House than Kelly Davis. She and her husband, Dan, have been instrumental in the rescue of the dilapidated house and have spent countless hours doing fundraising work and manual labor to make sure that the house continues its recovery. Since first coming to the Eldred House in 2007, she has spent many, many hours on investigations, all-night vigils, and tours at the property. She has had many experiences over the last decade, including walking into unexplained cold spots, capturing inexplicable recordings of what seem to be the voices of the dead, and even having stones tossed at her in the cellar of the house. One night, during one of many investigations, she set up a video camera that recorded the sounds of a man's heavy boots as they walked down the stairs – in front of a number of startled witnesses.

But Kelly seems to have the closest connection with the spirit of Alma, the little girl that died in the house in 1861. At first, she had no idea who this playful spirit might be, but after a long process of elimination, the identity of the ghost was revealed. Kelly has never claimed to be a psychic – she doesn't "speak to dead people" – but she does admit to having strange and often uncomfortable sensations in the house. She realized that the tiny ghost was Alma through games of "hide and seek." She began by walking around the house, calling out to each of the Eldred daughters until she got a response. The game has continued for years and Kelly will insist that when she plays, she will hear the soft and sweet laughter of a child somewhere nearby.

And she has not been the only one. Alma – and perhaps the other daughters, as well – have been experienced by many of the visitors to the house. They have heard and recorded the disembodied laughter of a young girl and have even seen a shape move past a doorway in the dim light of the evening, and the shape stood no higher than a young child.

The Eldred House remains today as one of the most haunted houses in Illinois. Based on the sheer numbers of ghostly incidents that have been documented at the old stone mansion, there is no doubt that few ghost seekers ever leave this place without finding what they came for.

House of Spirits
Tales of Frank Lloyd Wright's Dana House

The spectacular Dana House, designed by architect Frank Lloyd Wright, is located in the heart of Springfield's historical district. The impressive mansion was built for one of Springfield's leading citizens – all because she wanted to please the spirit of her father. The house's owner, Susan Lawrence Dana, was a fascinating and complex woman that was born into the highest echelons of the city's society. She lived a life of privilege, wealth, social status, and tragedy. Two of her husbands died and her third marriage ended in divorce. Both of her children died young, one living only a few hours and the other only two months. Her wanton lifestyle and unusual ways were beyond the limits of polite society for her day, especially for a woman, and after her health declined, she was eventually found to be insane.

For many years, the "official" status of the house was that it was not haunted. However, no one could deny the strange things that had occurred in the sprawling mansion – often things of Susan Lawrence Dana's creation – and could they could also not deny the fact that the house had once served as a link between this world and the next.

The Dana House was started in 1902, and upon its completion became a symbol of culture and high society in the city. Following in the wake of a series of tragic losses by Susan Lawrence Dana, the house provided her with both a distraction and a life's purpose. It was also a memorial to the man whose money had created the place, her father, R.D. Lawrence.

Rheuna Drake Lawrence was a successful businessman and contractor who came to Springfield in 1856. A few years later, he married Mary Agnes Maxcy and they had a child that same year that lived for only a short time. A second child was born in October 1862, and she was named Sue C. Lawrence. Her middle initial later transformed her name into "Susie" and, eventually, into Susan.

Lawrence's business interests thrived after the Civil War and he invested heavily in expanding railroad lines into the city. He also built a prominent Italianate villa at the corner of Fourth and Wright Streets downtown. By 1883, the year that Susie was married the first time, Lawrence was an extremely wealthy man. On December 4, he saw his daughter married to Edwin Ward Dana, a real estate investor from Lincoln, Illinois.

After the wedding, the newlyweds moved to Minneapolis, where Edwin tried to develop his own business. Unfortunately, things went badly and they moved to Chicago in 1893, where he started the Western Business Agency and named himself president. He claimed that the company had branches in nine western cities – which was untrue – but he didn't fool anyone. Within a year, his scheme had fallen apart. Disgraced, he borrowed money from his father-in-law so that he could move back to Springfield.

Sympathetic, Lawrence quickly put Edwin to work. He sent the couple to Oregon so that Edwin could manage some of the mines he owned. Edwin closed down one of the mines and moved to Leland, Oregon, leaving Susie in Grant's Pass, where living conditions were better. Within a month, Susie was on her way back to Illinois, bringing her husband's body with her. He had been hoisting ore at one of the mines when a harness snapped, causing a pulley arm to spin in reverse. He was struck in the chest and instantly killed. Susie was devastated. During her short marriage, she had buried not only her husband, but two infants, as well. A few years later, she would also bury her beloved father.

On February 17, 1901, R.D. Lawrence died in his Springfield home. His death was another tragic blow to Susie, but it also left her with her freedom and a financial windfall. As the new head of the household, Susie decided to build a grand home for the remaining family, which included her mother, a grandmother who died in August 1902, and her cousin, Flora Lawrence. In a search for a prestigious architect, Susie left Springfield and traveled to Chicago. There, she found the vitality that she was looking for in a young designer who was just starting to make a name for himself, Frank Lloyd Wright.

Wright, born in 1867, was an innovative designer and an architect ahead of his time. He is now considered one of America's greatest architects, but he was just becoming famous when Susie Lawrence Dana sought him out. Wright was the founder of the Prairie School of architecture – of which the Dana house would be a prime example – and it was a style created in 1900 when most Americans were still living in the box-shaped Victorian homes of the period. In time, the sprawling prairie houses would be altered into the "ranch" style homes of the modern era.

Frank Lloyd Wright was raised and educated in Wisconsin and spent his childhood on his mother's family farm. It was there where he learned to love nature and the outdoors, and he would someday combine his fascination with architecture with the natural world. In the 1880s, Wright moved to Chicago and studied under Louis Sullivan before opening his own firm in 1893. By the end of the century his studio in Oak Park, Illinois, had become famous in Chicago's social circles.

Wright and his staff were intrigued by the ideas that Susie brought to the studio. The original intention had been to incorporate the old villa into the new house and provide a home and gallery for living and entertainment. But the finished design turned out to be so much more. Only one room of the original house was ever used. Wright used the opportunity to create a Prairie house, which he believed was the home of the future. It would be long and horizontally-spaced with large, open spaces inside. He also designed all of the furniture for the house and designed the windows to capture natural light in a way that it would not be obstructed by anything in the house.

Work began in 1902, and it took two years to complete. Wright designed every aspect of the house, including the lights and furniture. In 1905, he added to the design by creating the Lawrence Memorial Library, which was connected to the house by a raised walkway. The Dana house became the first of Wright's designs to contain two-story rooms like the gallery, dining room, and hall. The gallery was a reception room for entertaining, connected to the main body of the house by a covered passage that doubled as a conservatory.

The principal common rooms were located on the main floor, while the bedrooms were upstairs. The staircases were all hidden, so as not to distract from the home's design and every room featured built-ins and specially constructed furniture. The interior walls were all cream-colored and were trimmed with fabulous woodwork. The library was constructed with built-in bookcases that had glass fronts. Beneath the walkway to the gallery were a billiards room and a bowling alley. The house was truly unique, trend-setting, and, at the time, there was not another one like it in the world.

That made it perfect for Susan, as she had started calling herself in 1903. She was exhausted at the completion of the house, but was exhilarated by the new and different design – at first. Soon, doubts began to creep in. The house was breathtakingly unusual and she worried what people might say, and worried about the exorbitant costs of the construction. To ease her fears, she decided to do what so many other members of American high society were doing at that time – she decided to host a séance. She had decided that she would contact the spirit of her dead father and make sure that he was happy about what she had done. She had always tried hard to please her father in life. Why would it be any different after death?

During the séance, Susan wrote a letter to her father, which read: "Papa, do you know all about the new home and are you pleased with it? Did I handle your will the way you wanted me to? I did the best I could. Susie."

Susan Lawrence Dana

She received a reply through the spirit medium that she had invited to the séance. Lawrence was delighted by the new house. He told her: "Susie, I love the new house – Ed [her late husband] and I often visit there together. You handled the will all right. Lovingly and devotedly. Father."

It was on this night that Susan began to realize the endless possibilities of Spiritualism and communication with the dead. And she wasn't alone in this realization in America at the time.

In the early twentieth century, the Spiritualist movement was a prominent force in America. Founded just over 50 years before, Spiritualism was based on the idea of life after death and that communication between the living and the dead could, and did, take place. Messages that came from the spirit world were passed along through a "medium," who could speak with the dead while in a trance and often produced messages and writings that came from the spirits. Other mediums claimed to be able to produce physical phenomena while in a trance state, including knockings, lights, sounds, music, ghostly voices, and even spirit materializations. Hundreds of these mediums flourished during the heyday of Spiritualism, offering their communications at séances. During these sittings, all sorts of strange events could take place from table lifting to ghosts appearing and speaking to loved ones left behind. The séances always took place in dark or dimly lighted rooms because, mediums claimed, darkness took away all of the distractions and made it easier for the spirits to manifest. During the heyday of the movement, it was a widely held and regarded system of beliefs and its leaders included some of the most respected and influential people of the nineteenth and early twentieth centuries, including Sir Arthur Conan Doyle, Sir William Barrett, Elizabeth Barrett Browning, James Fenimore Cooper, Washington Irving, Henry Longfellow, James Greenleaf Whittier, and many others.

In Springfield, Illinois, one of the most prominent believers in Spiritualism was Susan Lawrence Dana. After the many deaths that she had experienced in her life, she turned to the movement for comfort and managed to also achieve personal fulfillment from it. She began writing letters to her departed loved ones and received ghostly replies from the other side. Most of her letters seemed to seek insight into financial matters. She always sought approval from her father, and from her mother, after she passed away. She often signed the letters, "Your little girl, Susie." She would inquire as to whether or not she was "on the right path," when it came to money. In letters to her dead husband, she wrote of her loneliness: "I am so lonely, my poor heart aches until I almost die." The replies that she received from the spirits, through her medium, were supportive, offering loving words of comfort, but rarely offered solid advice. The reply letters through the medium were always sloppily written, scrawled missives, said to have been obtained while the medium was in a trance.

During the holiday season of 1904, Susan fought her loneliness by throwing lavish parties. She hosted the Women's Club, threw parties for local children and residents of orphanages, held dinners for residents of old-age homes, and offered a grand gala for the families of the workers who had built the house. She did everything to make sure that the house was noisy and boisterous. She had come to hate the lonely silences that plagued her life.

The busy holiday season took its toll on Susan and her mother. They traveled to the Caribbean that winter and relaxed in the Bahamas, and in Jacksonville and Palm Beach, Florida. They were on a train that was bound for Savannah, Georgia, when Mrs. Lawrence suffered a heart attack and died.

Susan was thrown into the pits of depression following her mother's death. Almost everyone she had ever loved had been lost to her. In desperation, she delved further into the spirit world. Séances now became a regular event in her home and many of the guests were esteemed members of local society. Susan no longer needed the mediums who had once carried message for her to and from the other side. She could now speak to the dead on her own. She practiced her spiritual powers through slate writing, where the dead sent messages in words that were inexplicably written on ordinary slates. According to Susan, her dead mother instructed her to meet with her in her old bedroom three times every week to receive wisdom and knowledge.

Most of Susan's spirit communications continued to be about finances and personal affairs. She urgently pleaded with her father to help her to understand finances, because she seemed unable to grasp it on her own. She was constantly spending more than her investments could make. For example, it was recorded in 1915 that she received about $10,000 in income from her father's rental properties. That same year, she borrowed $132,000 to cover her expenses.

But she never let a lack of money slow her down. She continued to host expensive parties and dinners, often scheduling several events on the same day. She kept a full staff of servants employed, despite the fact that only she and cousin Flora lived in the house. She needed the constant racket to fill the quiet hours.

In March 1912, Susan secretly married a concert singer from Denmark named Jorgen Constantin Dahl. As if Susan needed more gossip to be spread about her, it should be noted that he was half her age. Tragically, though, Dahl died just one year after they were married, leaving Susan alone again. In 1915, she married once more, this time to a Springfield man named Charles Gehrmann. Little is known about him, or their marriage, but Susan kept busy with her regular activities throughout their marriage. They were rarely seen together. Eventually, they separated and divorced in 1930.

Married or not, Susan was living exactly as she pleased. She spent vast amounts of money, became an advocate of women's rights, and was actively involved in the suffrage moment. She was named as the Illinois chairman for the National Women's Party, which was working for women's right to vote, and proudly pulled the voting lever when the Nineteenth Amendment was finally passed.

Susan also continued her interests in the paranormal. She collected a huge library of books on the occult, spirit contact, psychic healing, and metaphysics. She gathered her circle of local knowledge seekers in her home and dubbed them the "Springfield Society of Applied Psychology." They became the "Lawrence Metaphysical Center" in 1924, and three years later, moved their meetings to a building downtown.

Unknown to many people, the move was a quiet signal that Susan was now living in reduced circumstances. Her money had finally run out and there was no one left who would loan her anymore. She had to close down the grand house that Frank Lloyd Wright had built for her. She and cousin Flora, who was seriously ill, moved into the Lawrence cottage, which was located across the railroad tracks from the main house. Susan cared for Flora and took her meals at a boarding house across the street.

Flora died in 1928, leaving Susan completely alone. She was now in poor health and desperately sad. She consulted mediums, as she had always done, and at the request of the spirits, changed her name to Susan Zane Lawrence. Susan had friends who still cared for her and she kept in touch with Frank Lloyd Wright over the years. Sadly, their final meeting was canceled when Susan fell down the steps of the cottage and was injured. She wrote him a letter that stated a fraternal organization was thinking of buying the house. That sale never materialized.

By 1939, Susan's health was badly in decline and friends tried to get her to appoint a conservator for her estate. They had no success. Her financial affairs, always troubled, were now beyond repair. The Marine Bank in Springfield refused to foreclose on her, however, thanks to their love for Susan and respect for her father. Regardless, it was no secret that she owed them more than $167,000; they simply didn't talk about it. No one wanted to embarrass the woman who had been so generous to the people of the city.

In May 1942, Susan entered St. John's Hospital and would never leave it. No time was wasted and that same afternoon, a court petition was filed that declared Susan insane and unable to handle her affairs. The court appointed attorney Earl Bice as conservator of the estate and a cousin from Chicago, Farnetta Radcliffe, as caretaker of Susan herself.

An inventory showed that Susan, despite her debts and mortgages, had faithfully kept all of her father's properties intact, including the Springfield buildings, the house, and even the abandoned mines in Colorado and Oregon. She also had an enormous amount of personal property that was estimated to value around $75,000. The inventory list was 178 pages long, but foolishly handled. Things were given ridiculously low values by people who obviously had no idea what they were doing, appraising Frank Lloyd Wright furniture pieces for $10 and rare Japanese prints at $2.50. Susan's estate was worth far more than the auction papers claimed. It was a final, terrible injustice committed against a broken woman.

An auction was held in July 1943 and ran for six days. The sale drew tourists and curiosity-seekers and the newspapers wrote of Susan's eccentric collections. Sadly, her wonderful belongings, including rare artwork, photographic equipment, and her incredible book collection, brought little money. The house itself was treated as an eyesore and the appraiser deemed it "undesirable." He stated that if anyone could be found to buy it, it would sell for less than $20,000. Unfortunately, he was right.

Charles C. Thomas, a book publisher, purchased the house later that same year for $17,500. The good news was that Thomas was familiar with Wright's work and he wrote the architect in 1943 and assured him the house was in good hands. The house was turned into the headquarters for Thomas Publishing Co. and the roof, walls, and gutters were repaired before the company moved into the house in 1944.

Susan Lawrence passed away on February 20, 1946. It was reported that she was lucid at the time and completely aware of her surroundings. It is unknown if she was ever told about the sale of her wonderful house and cherished books and belongings.

Charles Thomas died in August 1968, but the company stayed in the house for another decade. They had saved the house from ruin, but when they left in 1981, the place was badly in need of restoration. A chain-link fence surrounded the front terrace, the garden pool was gone, the bowling alley had been cut into tops for tables, the sand-finished walls had been painted, and they had allowed collectors and museum curators to buy most of the original Wright pieces that had remained in the house. Luckily, the governor of Illinois at that time, James R. Thompson, was an antique lover and fan of Frank Lloyd Wright. He supported a bill to purchase the house and to begin its restoration. The state took possession of the place in 1981 and began a three-year project to restore it to its condition in 1910. In addition to the work done on the house, much of the original furniture was recovered, as well.

Today, the Dana House remains a tribute to both the architect Frank Lloyd Wright and the heiress, adventuress, women's rights advocate, and Spiritualist Susan Lawrence Dana, who remains an integral part of the haunted history of Central Illinois.

And that should be the end of the story, but it's not.

There is no question that the Dana House boasts a solid connection to the Spiritualist movement in Illinois and America, despite the repeated attempts to downplay that part of its history. Past directors have been brutal when it comes to anything to do with ghosts. I have strongly-worded, often offensive letters in my files from a past director who wanted me to retract the stories that I had written about Susan and her séances. At one point, he even banned me from returning to the house! But time has passed, tempers have cooled, and staff members now know there is no way that they can explain the unusual events that continue to occur in the house.

Or the ghosts that they have experienced there.

A number of years ago, an account in the *Springfield State Journal-Register* recalled an incident when staff members heard the sound of someone clapping in the empty house. A light sconce mysteriously unscrewed itself from the wall on the anniversary of Susan Dana's death. Candles that had been lit for a recreation of Susan's mother's funeral blew out during the service, startling not only the audience, but the minister who was performing the reenactment.

The strange events continue to occur. Motion alarms are frequently tripped in the house after hours. When staff members arrive to reset the alarms, weird happenings often occur. One night, the alarm was tripped by a heavy rainstorm and when a staff member entered the house to reset it, a fireplace grate suddenly began shaking back and forth, sending him quickly out of the house. On another occasion when an alarm was triggered, a staff member found that things had been moved around in the library. All of the curtains were off the windows and tossed on the floor. The curtain rods were still hanging on the windows and in order to get the curtains off the rods, someone would have had to have unscrewed several brackets, slid the curtains off the rods, and then reattached the brackets to the rods. There simply had not been time for anyone to have done this and, besides that, the house had been locked up and empty.

There are numerous doors throughout the house – perhaps as many as 100 between bedroom, closet, and cabinet doors – and all of them are kept closed for safety and security reasons. One morning, an employee came in and found that every single door in the house was standing open. Startled and unnerved by this incident, he waited until other staff members arrived, told them what he had found, and then they went around the house in pairs and closed all of the doors.

On another morning, a staff member was alone in the basement and heard someone come in the back kitchen door, which has its own alarm. Thinking that it was strange since that door is not used very often, he went to see who had come inside. He found that he was still alone in the house, even though the back kitchen door was standing open. Somehow, the alarm had not been tripped.

Objects have a habit of disappearing in the house, only to turn up somewhere else. Sometimes they vanish for days and then return with no explanation. One staff member was cutting ribbons one afternoon that were to be placed across antique chairs so that guests wouldn't sit on them. She placed the scissors and ribbon on a table and left the room for a moment. When she returned, both objects were gone. There was no one else in that part of the house who could have taken them. A little while later, both items turned up again. The ribbon was in place across the chair, just as the staff member planned, but the scissors had been shoved in the back of the chair.

Many staff members and guests have reported hearing voices in various rooms of the house. A simple glance will show that the rooms are empty. Some claim that they have heard the sound of heavy breathing in shadowy corners of the house. Others report the sound of music coming from the musician's balcony, an area that was once in heavy use during the many parties that Susan hosted in the house.

There are also those who believe they have come into contact with Susan herself, still wandering about the house that she loved so much during her lifetime. Some say they have seen the figure of a woman pass by doorways in the house, float down staircases, or peer out of the windows. Guests will sometimes ask their guides who the woman in costume is, only to be told that guides only appear in costumes for special events, never on a daily basis. Is it Susan Lawrence? Perhaps it is, or perhaps it is one of the other women linked to the house, like Susan's mother, grandmother, or even her cousin, Flora. The house has seen more than its share of sadness over the years, so who can say for sure what spirit remains within its walls?

If I were to hazard a guess, though, I would say that it is Susan Lawrence Dana who haunts this house, still clinging to a life that she once knew. It was a life of pain, sorrow, and grief, that often caused her heartbreak, and yet it was also a life of wealth, passion, and achievement. For every lonely night that she spent within the confines of the house, she spent at least three other nights surrounded by friends, admirers, and kindred spirits who shared her fascination with the spirit world. If ghosts can remain behind by choice, then I believe that Susan remained in her glorious house because she wanted to, relishing the life she once lived and holding onto one last chance to make her mark on history.

Nights at Norb Andy's
Hauntings at the Virgil Hickox House

Norb Andy's Tabarin in downtown Springfield has long been a place of legend. For more than 50 years, the tavern was the favorite watering hole for state politicians and for locals who always felt at home. Watched over by salty old Norbert Anderson, who opened the place in 1937, it was a Springfield tavern where "everybody knew your name," so to speak.

But Norb Andy's was only the latest incarnation of the house. It began as a family residence that was later used as an undertaking parlor, influenza hospital, speakeasy during Prohibition, and finally a saloon that catered to both the highest officials in the state and the average man off the street. It has always been regarded as a place where you could experience the history of the past, whether you were there to hoist a beer mug, have a good meal – or came in hopes of encountering one of the many ghosts rumored to linger in the building.

There is little doubt about it; Norb Andy's is a very haunted place.

The building that Norb Andy's calls home today was built in 1839 by Virgil Hickox, a Springfield businessman, developer, political figure, and friend to both Abraham Lincoln and Stephen Douglas. Hickox had been born in Jefferson County, New York, in 1806. He came west to Springfield as a young man in 1834, and started his own mercantile store, which was almost immediately successful. In 1839, he married Marie Catherine Cabanis and built a home for what would soon be a growing family on Capitol Avenue between Fifth and Sixth Streets. The house would see many renovations over the years, but it still stands as the oldest residential structure in downtown Springfield.

Hickox became a prominent businessman. In addition to his thriving store, he was also the president of Springfield's Savings Bank. He also helped to bring the city its first railroad line, an extension of the Chicago & Alton Railroad, and co-founded the city of Lincoln, Illinois. Even though he had only a grade-school education, he worked as an attorney and became an important political figure, even though the only political office he ever held was Canal Commissioner for the Chicago & Michigan Canal. He did chair the Democratic State Committee for 20 years and was an associate of both Lincoln and Douglas. Hickox served as Douglas's campaign manager in the 1858 Senate race against Abraham Lincoln. Hickox became the recipient of the last letter ever written by Stephen Douglas on May 10, 1861. In it, Douglas urged his support for Lincoln and the Union. He wrote that there could be only two political parties in America after the start of the Civil War – one of patriots and one of traitors. He advised his friends to lay down any views that would impede the preservation of the Union.

The Virgil Hickox House in Springfield

Hickox passed away in February 1880. His family moved out of the stately Capitol Avenue house soon after. By then, it had been remodeled several times and had largely taken on its present form, with an Italianate design featuring bracketed eaves and long, arched windows.

Seven years later, the Sangamo Club, a private men's club, opened in the building and remained there for 15 years. After World War I, the club moved to a new location and the house was taken over by the Sangamon County Coroner's office, who lived upstairs and operated a funeral home business in the basement. It was during this time, immediately after the war, that the office was pressed into use as a temporary hospital and morgue to combat the spread of sickness during the 1918 Spanish Influenza Epidemic.

The flu turned out to be a devastating epidemic that started at a military training camp in Kansas that was preparing soldiers to fight in World War I. They took the illness to Europe, where it spread rapidly, causing sickness and death, and may have even affected the outcome of the war. Some say that the Germans were too sick with influenza to stop the final Allied assault.

The second wave of the epidemic was much worse than the first. It was spread coast-to-coast by soldiers as they returned home at war's end. Thousands died, but little was done to curb the spread of the virus. Doctors warned local health departments to quarantine the sick and to restrict attendance at large public gatherings. However, most towns, in the grip of patriotic fervor, resisted the advice and held rallies and parades for returning soldiers. As the death toll climbed, it was realized that the greatest number of deaths came from children and young adults, who were normally in the healthiest of age groups. Nearly one-fourth of all Americans caught the flu between the fall of 1918 and the late winter of 1919. Even if sufficient numbers of doctors had been available, they could have done little to intercede. No flu vaccines existed at the time and caregivers could do little but encourage patients to drink plenty of fluids, hand out aspirin, and keep the dying comfortable. Emergency Red Cross hospitals were set up from coast to coast, but doctors and nurses were scarce, as the war effort had taken many of them into the military and to France. Despite frantic appeals, calls for more nurses went unanswered.

In many cases, entire families were incapacitated with illness, unaided by doctors and avoided by their neighbors, who refused to enter homes that had "Influenza" signs nailed to the front door. Because death rates were highest among people in their twenties, many of whom were parents, the flu produced thousands of young orphans around the country.

The epidemic was slowly brought under control and almost seemed to vanish as a few more months passed. By then, however, the damage was done. Millions were dead around the world, entire families were wiped out, towns had been laid waste and never recovered, and American history had been altered in a way that had never happened before. And all because of the flu...

In Springfield, the influenza raged for several weeks and reached its peak period between the middle of October and early November 1918. By the time public health officials issued an order to stop all public gatherings, there were over 300,000 confirmed cases of the flu in Illinois and several thousand of them were in Springfield.

In October, an order was issued stating that all schools, theaters, billiard rooms, and dance halls would be closed until further notice. This included all classes and sporting events at the colleges and at all of the public schools. The order also banned all church services and all meetings and gatherings of "social, patriotic, religious or educational nature." All children were told to stay inside of their homes and were not allowed to mingle with other children in the neighborhood.

On October 18, a similar order was issued by Illinois' Governor Lowden, who allowed for some gatherings to take place, but only those directly related to the war effort. However, the following rules had to be applied to any such meetings: "crowding would not be permitted... persons affected by colds would not be admitted... coughers, sneezers and spitters would be expelled... and the premises had to be ventilated, heated and cleaned."

Bans began to be lifted the following month, and on November 11, the Armistice was signed and the Great War was officially over. Reports of new outbreaks of the flu had dropped significantly, and it was believed safe for the public to gather once more. The people of Springfield celebrated into the early morning hours. Blowing whistles spread the news and people left their homes and ran out into the streets.

But things were more somber at the former Virgil Hickox house. With thousands of cases of influenza being reported in Springfield, and not nearly enough hospital beds to treat the sick in the quarantined city, many public officers had to be put into service as temporary medical stations. The coroner's office was among them. About 350 people died from the flu in Springfield in the fall of 1918 and their bodies were also brought to the coroner's office. Many of them were even embalmed downstairs in the basement. The building was overwhelmed by the influx of the dying and the dead, and this dark time in the city's history is believed to have left a psychic impression on the Virgil Hickox house.

Among the restless ghosts who haunt this house are those of children, who would ordinarily have no reason to linger at a place that is best-known for the tavern that occupies the basement. Among the scores of dead during the Spanish Flu epidemic were many children, all of whom were especially susceptible to the disease. Over the years, witnesses have claimed a variety of contacts with the spectral children who seem attached to the house. Some of them may have died within its walls, while others may have accompanied their dying parents to the place and then found themselves orphaned by the cruel illness. Has their grief and loneliness kept them at the place where their mothers and father choked out their final breaths? And if so, will they ever find peace, or will they continue to haunt this building for as long as it stands?

In the early 1920s, as America entered into the era of Prohibition, the basement of the Virgil Hickox house was turned into a "speakeasy" – an establishment that illegally sold alcohol. The term came from the fact that patrons often had to "speak easy" or stay quiet while they were drinking, since many of these establishments were hidden inside of, or behind, a legitimate business. Thousands of speakeasies operated across America during Prohibition – usually linked to organized crime – and were often raided by the police and Prohibition agents. Money placed in the right hands usually had them open again a short time later. Free-flowing alcohol, mobsters, and money usually led to violence, and murders commonly occurred in speakeasies around the country. Such violence, bloodshed, and danger have led to lingering spirits in many of these old locations – including, perhaps, the one in the basement of the Hickox house.

Visitors and ghost hunters have reported numerous unexplainable events in the basement, from disembodied footsteps to mysterious voices, eerie recordings, strange photographs, and more. Many believe that at least a few of the ghosts who have been encountered at this very haunted house are connected to the illegal operation that thrived in the basement in the late 1920s and early 1930s.

But if those ghosts do remain, they do not do so alone.

If there is any one ghost that is more closely connected to the house than any other, it is the rowdy spirit of Norbert Anderson himself, the man who opened Norb Andy's Tabarin in 1937. Norb, as everyone called him, was a local fixture. He gave life to the place, made everyone feel welcome, and loved to laugh and joke with the regular patrons. It was said that if you weren't a regular, thanks to Norb, you'd soon become one. He decorated the place with a nautical theme, simply because he always liked the fisherman décor found in taverns back east. The bar was made from knotty pine, while fishnets, buoys, a ship's wheel, and whale oil lamps gave the place character and warmth. Even long after Norb died, and many other operators tried their hand at saloon-keeping, the décor at Norb Andy's has stayed the same.

Norb's warm version of hospitality became a tradition at the tavern and it created a clientele that kept coming back for 50 years. The bartenders and staff knew the customers by name, greeted them affectionately, and thanked them for coming when they left. Patrons knew that they could always get a good meal and a stiff drink at Norb Andy's and just might bump into a well-known politician or former governor – like James Thompson, Adlai Stevenson, or Alan Dixon – on the way in or out of the door. Norb Andy's drew so many people from Springfield's political circles that a back room was set up so that they could hold meetings or chat unofficially with other politicians. The staff never revealed who used the room, when they met, or what they drank. Who knows how many deals were struck in the back room of Norb Andy's over the years that changed everything from taxes to benefits in the state of Illinois? The answer to that will always remain one of the mysteries of the tavern.

During Norb's tenure, the tavern became a Springfield institution. When he passed away, it was an end of an era for the neighborhood bar. But this wasn't the end of the story for Norb Andy's. When it reopened a number of years later, at the same location with the same nautical theme, people flocked back to the saloon, returning for food, drinks, and old friends. Just about everything that people had always liked about the bar was still there – including Norb Anderson.

It seems that the jovial bar owner returned to make sure that his customers still knew that he was around. His prank-playing ghost has long been believed responsible for the supernatural antics that continue to occur at the tavern. He is still around, and he's still looking after the old place, although these days, he seems interested in delivering some frights to go along with the "horseshoes" and cold drinks.

Most of the interviews that we have with staff members and patrons were conducted around 2012. It closed again for a time and reopened shortly before this writing, so the current status of the haunting is unknown. However, staff members at the time of the interviews had largely gotten used to Norb's pranks – but they were quick to assure us that, as far as they were concerned, there was little doubt that Norb was still around. Some of them claimed to have actually spotted his presence in the place, sitting at the north end of the bar, watching over the operation with a smile on his face, just as he did in life. Many claimed also to have heard the sound of doors opening when no one was around, saw items being moved about, and witnessed pictures falling off the walls for no reason. A few of them even stated that they would not go into the back area of the tavern unless they had to.

One of the cooks that was interviewed said that she had experienced a lot of activity in the kitchen. While she was alone in the room she had felt someone playfully tug on her hair. Other times, even when the kitchen was very hot, with the burners on the stove working overtime, she would experience this icy cold chill that came from nowhere. She also said that she once glanced over and spotted a man standing in the corner of the room with his arms crossed. When she looked back at him, he was gone. In addition, on a few occasions when she was alone in the tavern at night, she heard the sounds of footsteps and things moving around upstairs in the Virgil Hickox house when there was no one there. She said that she stopped working alone at night after that.

Customers who are sitting at the bar, engaged in conversation, will often reach for their drinks and find that they have been moved, or switched with another person's drink, when they're not looking. This is a frequent occurrence, as is when bartenders will fill drinks for waitresses, and place them at the server's station, only to find that they have disappeared before the server can pick them up. One bartender told us that liquor bottles would move about during her shift. Even though she always put them back where they had been, she never found them in the same place twice. She was working alone at the time.

One of the most frightening pranks that Norb likes to play involves the restrooms. Legend has it that the apparition of a man in a blue, polyester sports coat will sometimes appear standing behind people when they look into the mirror. Bartenders claimed that people, especially women, had been known to rush out of the restroom, scared and disheveled, because of an encounter with the ghost.

The appearance of Norb's ghost isn't normally as startling, but according to some, it can still be quite eerie. One bartender stated that she was just opening the tavern one afternoon and was getting things ready for the evening's business and noticed a man sitting on the stool at the end of the bar. She had only just unlocked the door and was sure that no one had come inside yet. She was a little startled, but thought little of it. She was on her way to the storage room to get a new bottle of liquor and told the man that she would be right with him.

The man, she recalled, was wearing an ugly blue sports coat.

When she returned from the back, though, the man was gone. Again, it was weird, but not overly strange. She assumed he had gone to the restroom, or maybe he didn't want to wait. And then she happened to glance over at a picture that was hanging on the wall. The man in the blue sports coat, who had just been sitting at her bar, was in the picture. It was Norbert Anderson – the dead man who had once owned the bar. He had been sitting just a few feet away from her and she later recalled that she could still smell his aftershave when she realized that she had just seen a ghost.

The spirit of Norb Andy's, it seems, lives on.

The Spirit of Villa Kathrine

On the highs overlooking the Mississippi River at Quincy stands a Moorish castle that overlooks the river. For travelers along the river, such a site often came as a surprise, but this is no figment of the imagination – it's a real-life, twentieth century castle that was created by an eccentric millionaire named George Metz, who abandoned the place after the death of his only companion, his dog, Bingo.

For years, the house stood as a tribute to one man's dreams of bringing the exotic regions of the world to the small river town of Quincy. It became a museum for all of the exotic wonders, souvenirs, and furnishing that Metz brought back from his travels to the Middle East and Africa. The castle captured the imaginations of the townspeople and of reporters, who wrote wild stories of the wealthy Metz, a man so rich that he never worked a day in his life and traveled the world instead. Speculative tales were written about Villa Kathrine, the origins of the house's name, and about Metz himself, the mysterious owner of the bizarre house.

In time, the house was abandoned and fell into a state of decay. Its strange history added fuel to the weird stories about the house, where now only the ghosts of the past still dwelled. Villa Kathrine, the current tenants of the place can assure you, is haunted. But it's a ghost unlike any that most have ever encountered before.

Villa Kathrine in Quincy, looking out over the Mississippi River

George Metz, son of wealthy Quincy businessman William Metz, also had the urge to travel. Without employment or responsibilities to keep him at home, he followed the same paths taken by other scions of robber barons and millionaires of the late nineteenth century and began to travel the world. According to the legend of Villa Kathrine, Metz's wanderings were motivated by his lifelong dream to find the perfect home. He found it in the centuries-old Villa Ben Ahben in Algeria. He later stated that he was struck by the golden color of the exterior. He told a reporter, "The marvelous domes of the villa appeared like large, inverted bowls, each a miniature heaven. I decided then to endeavor to fashion a similar villa in emulous rivalry."

Metz's dream of building his own version of the house back home in Quincy became an obsession. Villa Ben Ahben became the model for his design, but he needed to find suitable furnishings for the house so that he could feel the same stirring of adventure at home that he did in his travels. According to his story, he spent the next two years wandering North Africa with the "secretive Moors," haggling with caravan trains, persuading and buying. He bought thousands of items and pieces of furniture for the villa, including crescents for the domes and minarets of the villa, antique door knockers, Arabic symbols, divans, Egyptian lamps, and much more.

After two years of planning, sketching, and acquiring objects, Metz returned to Quincy to make his dream a reality. He assembled his hundreds of pages of notes and sketches and went looking for a sympathetic architect. Needless to say, he had a tough time finding one in his hometown. Eventually, he found a young man and recent college graduate named George Behrensmeyer, who agreed to take on Villa Kathrine as his very first commission.

Working together, they found a location in Quincy that was "so correct," Metz said, "that it exceeded my expectations." The site for the house was to be on a bluff that looked down on the Mississippi River. Like Villa Ben Ahben in Algiers, the surrounding homes and buildings were several hundred feet away. Working from Metz's drawings, Behrensmeyer began designs for the dream castle. He scaled the place down so that it would rest securely on the bluff and then, in 1900, the brick and stucco walls of Villa Kathrine began to rise.

Local builders, led by Herman Schachtsieck, worked alongside tile layers, plasterers, and craftsmen who labored to build a showcase for Metz's exotic collection. The foundation was made from locally quarried limestone, and the brick was made in Quincy. The interior and exterior grillwork and screens were framed in native lumber and sheet metal. A newly patented plaster covered the exterior.

Newspaper reports about the strange structure began to appear in the spring of 1900 and locals began to whisper about the place almost as soon as the work began. The favorite story seemed to be that Metz built the house in mourning over a lost love. It was said that he met a "fair-haired, blue-eyed" woman in Germany and together, they had discovered the beauty of Villa Ben Ahben and the exotic regions of North Africa. Metz planned to bring his love home with him to his villa on the banks of the Mississippi, but his bliss was short-lived. Sadly, she refused to come to Quincy. Broken-hearted, Metz retired to a reclusive life in the newly-completed villa. Metz's refusal to deny or confirm the story fueled the gossip and speculation ran rampant, but little record about Metz's world travels remains, except when it was related to the house. Metz became a part of the house itself, and a part of its legend. Its history would not only create George Metz, it would destroy him, too.

Metz later described the house to the *St. Louis Republic* as a "picture of grandeur," and he was right. When completed, the castle evoked images of Moorish homes in North Africa and Spain, but at its heart, Villa Kathrine was a modest, two-story home. It was the exterior, with its one-story side wing, two square towers, multiple porches, and the numerous setbacks and projections that gave it an exotic, castle-like appearance. The villa's unique square south tower was decorated on all sides with a diamond pattern, with inlaid, carved lattice woodwork. Another tower was topped by a Moslem minaret with swirling red and white stripes and a silver dome. It was a miniature replica of a dome on the famous Mosque of Thais in Tunisia. The north tower also had a dome that was topped with a Muslim crescent that Metz found in an ancient ruin in northern Africa.

The building was also characterized by an unusual variety of windows that included rounded and pointed arches, keyhole shapes, and diamonds that added to its exotic appearance. The larger windows were also fitted with grilles in Moorish patterns. A terrace surrounded the front entrance and one could reach the door through a Moorish arch. Over the front door was a tile that held a relief cast of a woman's hand that was adorned with a wedding ring and holding a dove. Some believe that it was a cast of the hand of Metz's lost love, but we will never know for sure. The wooden door was ornamented with antique brass door trimmings brought from an old house in Algiers.

The inside of the building continued the Moorish theme. Heavy wooden beams crossed the ceiling and keyhole niches were fitted into the walls. Shelves of exotic pottery, carved chairs and tables, wall hangings, and rugs added to the unusual atmosphere of the rooms. Inside the front door was the drawing room and up a short flight of steps and through glass doors was the interior court. The court was surrounded by a gallery that was supported by eight pointed arches embraced by spiral pillars. The pillars are copies of those in the Court of Dolls in Seville, Spain. Around the center court, on both floors, were small square rooms that bordered a central pool. Above the pool, the villa's atrium was open to the roof, where a winter glass cover would be replaced by a summer awning. The walls of the court appear to be covered in black and white tiles, but this is only an illusion. For some reason, Metz had the walls painted to look like tile, an odd, money-saving gesture that stands out amidst the wealth of the house. Metz furnished the court with chairs, rugs, settees, and stools and the area was normally kept dimly lit by oil lamps. In the dining room, though, he hung a huge chandelier that once graced the salon of a luxurious Mississippi River showboat. The dining room and smoking room were decorated with rugs, art objects, tapestries, and trophies that he had collected in the Sahara. The entire house was lavishly filled with live plants and Moorish treasures.

The stairs, with sea-green balustrades and dark-brown handrails, ascended from the court into the upper levels and the north tower. The court is surrounded by a decorative rail and around it is an upstairs gallery where the bedrooms were located. Entry to the summer dining room was gained from the north tower's stairs. Metz often dined there on summer nights, enjoying the cool air and the view of the passing boats on the river.

The villa was fitted with hot and cold running water and tiled bathrooms. The main bath held a sunken cooper tub. Heat was provided by fireplaces and stoves.

Metz lived at Villa Kathrine as a bachelor for 12 years, during which, he wrote, "There was never the slightest hint of scandal, although the exotic structure inspired many grotesque stories." He was not a total recluse, though. On September 30, 1904, Albert Hastings and Pansy Darnell, an old family friend of Metz, were married at Villa Kathrine with Metz playing the wedding march on his pipe organ.

Despite friends who often dined with him, however, his only constant companion in the house was his beloved dog, Bingo. Brought over from Demark by Metz after one of his trips, Bingo was a 212-pound Great Dane that was rumored to be the largest dog in America. Metz had a special addition built for the dog off the kitchen. When Bingo died, he was buried on the grounds of the estate. Faced with the loss of his longtime friend, a cloud descended over Metz's dream, plunging him into a terrible depression. Out of fear for his safety, and because of his age and his ability to climb stairs and care for the house, Metz's relatives urged him to sell the place. Finally, in 1912, he agreed.

One day, a visiting couple, who professed a great interest in the house, prevailed on him to sell to them. Their enthusiasm convinced Metz that they would be ideal occupants for the villa and he sold the house and all of its furnishings to them. Little did he know that the buyers were actually agents for the Alton-Quincy Interurban Railroad, who planned to tear down the house and build a railyard on the site. Word got out and vandals descended on the mysterious house and carried off the decorations and the furniture, turning the place into a ruin.

Metz returned to the house one time, in 1913, with a reporter from St. Louis. The house was overrun with vermin and birds, the tinted walls were stained and destroyed, and what little furniture remained was shredded. He left it, vowing "never to return to this ruin again." Nineteen years later, Metz did come back for one final visit, returning this time with a reporter from Decatur to find the villa crumbling with decay. "I wish this place were mine again," he said, "I'd tear it down."

George Metz never lost his love for the Mississippi River, or for Quincy. After leaving Villa Kathrine, he lived in a succession of apartments with a wide view of the river, first at the Hotel Newcomb, then on the second floor of a house, and finally at the Lincoln Douglas Hotel. He spent most of his spare time feeding the birds and squirrels in Quincy's parks. Poor health finally took him to St. Vincent Hospital, where he died from pneumonia in 1937.

Villa Kathrine survived the treachery of the Alton-Quincy Interurban Railroad and it passed into the lives of decades of owners, renters, and caretakers, many of whom spoke of odd happenings in the house. They told stories of lights that behaved strangely, doors that mysteriously slammed closed, objects that vanished, and the sound of footsteps pacing around and around the pool in the center of the villa. Many believed that George Metz's restless spirit had returned to watch over the place. Was he filled with despair because of the way the house had been ruined? Or did he simply love the villa so much that he never wanted to leave it?

Either of those suppositions could be true, but according to recent stories of the house, George Metz does not remain behind at this house alone? What good was the man, Metz always believed, without his faithful companion?

After many years of neglect and decay, the villa was finally saved by the Friends of the Castle, a non-profit group who leased the building from the Quincy Park District and began working to restore it. It has since been transformed into a tourist and cultural center and it is open today for a new generation of people to visit the weird castle for themselves -- and to possibly experience the lingering ghost.

Villa Kathrine is also home to the local tourist and convention office and staff members assured me a few years ago that there is a ghost that haunts this house. They don't believe that it's George Metz, however, but rather his faithful dog, Bingo. No one knows how or why he stayed behind at the villa after death. Perhaps it was George Metz's enduring affection for the dog that kept him from passing on to the other side, but whatever the reason for his presence, staff members have often reported hearing the clicking of Bingo's toenails on the tile floors of the house. They have often heard the sound in the quiet of the afternoon, or in the early evening, after visitors have departed for the day

It's definitely an unusual ghost to be left haunting a house, but perhaps it's fitting, based on the unusual legends and lore that surround one of the oddest homes in Central Illinois.

The Haunted House on the Prairie
Legends of Voorhies Castle

When several generations of people who grew up on the Central Illinois prairie were once asked to name the most haunted house in the region, one dwelling always came to mind -- Voorhies Castle. This lonely and isolated old house was the stuff from which decades of legends were born, from mysterious deaths, strange disappearances, haunted happenings, and a myriad of ghosts. The "Castle" became a wonderfully spooky place to visit for legions of area teenagers, all hoping to see a ghost.

But few of them actually knew the real story behind the building -- and subsequent abandoning -- of the house. If they had, they might have found the place to be even scarier.

The story of Voorhies Castle began in 1867 when a Swedish immigrant named Nels Larson arrived in America. He settled near Galesburg, Illinois, and went to work for a local farmer, soon earning a reputation as a hard and efficient worker. Larson saved every dollar that he made and within a short time, he moved south and settled in Piatt County, near the town of Bement. There, he went to work for a local farmer and landowner named William Voorhies.

Voorhies himself had returned to America in 1868. During the Civil War, he studied medicine in Germany and, at war's end, returned to his home state of Kentucky and married Ellen Duncan of Lexington. Two years later, he gave up practicing medicine and moved north to Illinois. He purchased three sections of prairie land in Piatt County and set aside a parcel for a homestead. He soon found the land to be rich and productive and eventually built a large home with a wide verandah on three sides. He loved to sit out there at the end of each day and look out over the land that he cultivated with great success. Although prosperous, Voorhies discovered that he had more land than he could handle and he began selling off small parcels to upstanding and hardworking men in the area. It would be one of these parcels of land that Nels Larson would purchase in 1885.

Before that time came, though, Nels Larson started out with very little. Even after going to work for William Voorhies, he only earned $30 a month in the summer and $40 per month in the fall and winter. He had to give back $9 each month for his room and board and provide his own clothing. He lived frugally and saved all of the money that he could. Finally, in 1872, he spent $325 for a good team of horses and went into debt for a harness, plows, and a wagon. He rented 60 acres of land from Voorhies and set out on his own. Later, he bought a large parcel of property from his former employer near Voorhies, a small community named in honor of the wealthy landowner. It was also in 1872 that Larson sent for his fiancée, Johannah Nilson, who was still living in Sweden at that time. Later that same year, they were married.

Larson continued to buy more land as he could, and lease other parcels. Larson soon had a number of farmers working for him, renting his property in exchange for a portion of the proceeds from the harvest. In addition to his own farm, he was a partial owner in many others. The small town of Voorhies, which Larson now owned, began to grow. The homes there were tenant houses, rented by Larson's workers, and he owned the general store. The town was also home to a church, a grain elevator, a corn crib and several barns, barber shop, jeweler, blacksmith and a post office. The post office had a license to sell money orders and tickets for travel on the Wabash passenger trains that passed through town. The rail station was also useful for the loading and unloading of grain and cattle. The grain elevator was added to the town in 1897 and was operated by Larson's son, George, who was also the postmaster.

There was no question that Larson was now the most powerful and wealthy landowner in the area, but he certainly wasn't liked by everyone. It was often stated that he expected more from his workers than most were willing to give and some described him as a "tyrant." A worker could be fired for the slightest infraction, often at Larson's whim. One night, the local general store was burned to the ground at a loss of more than $1,600. Although it was clearly a case of arson, Larson refused to allow an investigation of the crime. He knew that someone who hated him had burned it to the ground. He simply rebuilt the place, hiring a security guard to watch over the new building. There were other cases of vandalism, too, possibly by disgruntled employees, including the burning of several cattle guards and small outbuildings on his property. Larson just chose to ignore them.

The greatest animosity felt toward Larson probably came from his son, George, who was born in 1873. He was a graduate of both Bement High School and Brown Business College in Decatur, but could never get out from under his father's control. He always admitted that he was afraid of his father, and for this reason, stayed in Voorhies to act as postmaster and to handle the running of the grain elevator.

In 1903, George began courting a local girl named Naomi Shasteen. His parents disapproved of her and stated that she was only after the Larson family money. Nevertheless, the two of them were married in June of that year. They took a wedding trip to Chicago and then settled into a small cottage that was built just west of the Larson's main house. This arrangement was not a good one and dissension quickly grew, building toward a confrontation that took place one morning on the sidewalk between the two houses. Naomi, who was accustomed to gentlemen stepping off the sidewalk and allowing her to pass, refused to step off the walk when ordered to do so by Nels Larson. He demanded that the young woman move out of his way, but she refused. Infuriated, he screamed at her, leaving the girl in tears. Shortly after, George constructed a house for he and his wife a quarter-mile away and across the railroad tracks from Voorhies.

On the other hand, Larson's daughter, Ellen, was the pride of his life and his spoiled princess. Ellen was born in August 1880 and after graduating from Bement High School in 1901, stayed at home in the now-completed "castle." She had a room, tucked between the twin towers of the house, that was richly decorated and furnished with whatever the young woman desired. She reigned over the house and grounds, flirting with being an artist and rising late in the day. Her life in Voorhies was pleasant and filled with good memories, unlike her brother's sad life. Ellen later married James Lamb, a doctor from Cerro Gordo. She bore him four children but her heart developed a complication with the fourth pregnancy. After that, she was often confined to bed and was only allowed to leave the house occasionally for evening outings or Sunday afternoon drives. She withdrew more and more into seclusion, only visited by a few friends. During her infrequent day trips, she usually visited the castle, which was empty by that time. She disappeared inside and remained there for hours. Perhaps she was trying to recapture a little of the life she once knew there. Ellen passed away in 1955, just four months after the death of her husband.

It would be the Voorhies Castle that would create the true legend of the Larson family.

By 1900, Nels Larson was firmly entrenched as the ruler of his vast domain, which consisted of tenants, farms, land, various businesses, and even an entire village. He had lived in several houses around the area, but now decided that he needed a manor house from which to oversee his property. This house, later dubbed "Voorhies Castle," would be patterned after a chalet in his native Sweden. Larson contacted a Chicago architect to draw up plans to his specifications. A contractor was then hired and construction began in the summer of 1900.

The house was a strange mixture of styles and eccentricities. When first completed, the towers on the corners of the house were three stories high, looming one floor higher than the rest of the structure. Larson had thought one of them would make the perfect location for his office. Patterning himself after his former employer, William Voorhies, he wanted to be able to look out over all of the lands that he owned, just as Voorhies had gazed out from his verandah. However, when the towers

The Larson family and the "Castle" in 1902

were completed, they looked so strange that Larson reluctantly ordered the third floor of each tower removed. He was forced to rely on the front porch alone, with a frontage of 60 feet and a double platform swing, from which to look out on the fields and village.

The front door of the house was extra wide and commonly called a "casket door," as it allowed access for both coffin and pallbearers in the days when funerals were held in the homes of the deceased. The door was flanked by large windows that, like those in the rest of the house, were wider than normal for the time period. Each was designed with a large pane in the lower sash and a series of smaller ones in the top sash. The windows were hung with either lace curtains or velvet draperies, depending on the room.

Inside of the house was a large reception hall that was fitted with an oak fireplace. The mantel was carved with complicated leaves, bleeding heart flowers, and lion's heads. Larson had brought an artist from Sweden especially for the purpose of hand-carving the fireplace, along with two others in the house. Sliding pocket doors were fitted into each doorway leading to the adjoining rooms. The west parlor contained a cherry wood fireplace. It was also decorated with a large fern that was kept near the south window. Old photographs show the fern on a round, wooden pillar with fronds that are so long that they almost touch the floor. This parlor led into the west tower and the doorway was adorned with wooden scrollwork. The ceiling was papered and decorated with clouds and stars. It was in this room where Larson conducted most of his business affairs. On the opposite side of the reception hall was the east parlor, where Ellen's piano was kept. This room was designed for lady visitors and it contained emerald furniture, scrolled doorways, a bookcase secretary, and even a "fainting couch" for the lady whose corset stays might be too tight.

The house also boasted indoor plumbing and a bathroom with all of the latest innovations. It was located between the east parlor and the back room that served as Johannah's sewing room. The sewing room was also used as an extra bedroom. The bed in this room was a foldaway device and the room also contained an oak dresser, washstand, and walnut bureau. A heavy safe was kept hidden in the closet – Nels Larson did not trust the banks -- and the walls were undecorated except for a large map of Illinois.

The dining room was also located on the first floor and it boasted a beautiful parquet floor designed of maple, mahogany, birch, oak, and sycamore pieces. There was also a marble-topped sideboard and a dining room table that could be extended to seat 24 people. In the corner of the room was a gold couch where Larson napped each day following his lunch. The telephone and the doorbell, both battery-operated devices, were mounted on the wall of the dining room.

The kitchen was small, but filled to capacity. It had a tiled floor and contained a drop-leaf table and chairs, a high cupboard, a stove, a sink, and a water heater. The kitchen was further cramped by the five doors that exited off of it, going to the basement, the upstairs, the back porch, dining room, and to a small pantry that was lined from floor to ceiling with shelves and cupboards. Larson had this designed so that the kitchen staff could easily wait on family members with their access to all parts of the house.

The largest of the upstairs chambers was the master bedroom, which extended across the east end of the house. It was dominated by a huge rosewood bed and dresser that had to be moved into position before the house could be completed. The bedroom furniture had been acquired as part of a settlement between Larson and William Voorhies, the details of which have never been revealed. The tower room adjacent to this bedroom offered the best view of the land. It was from this room where Larson was said to look out over his holdings each morning after he got out of bed.

Only the finest materials were used in the construction of the house, which delayed its completion until 1904. On many occasions, Larson would return entire loads of lumber to the warehouse after discovering a few boards with knots in them.

The most eccentric addition to the estate came in 1910. It was a clock tower barn that Larson insisted be included on the property. The stories say that Larson had a fascination, or perhaps an obsession, with clocks. They could be found all over the house, from the large grandfather clock in the reception area to small timepieces scattered on the top of a wooden trunk in his bedroom. He constructed a large barn that could contain a clock tower. He ordered a Seth Thomas clock from a jeweler in Monticello and began construction on the new building, literally building the barn around the clock tower. The cattle pens, hay storage areas, and tool rooms in the barn were secondary to the tower and its clock. Work on the barn took almost five years to complete, even longer than it took to build the house. The new structure had to be equipped with a 68-foot-tall tower and had to be given enough support that it could hold the nearly two-ton clock mechanism.

The clock tower barn, Larson's most eccentric addition to the property

The clock mechanism was equipped with a deafening chime that would sound each hour. It was so loud that it could be heard for miles in every direction. Larson didn't care if the sound bothered the neighbors, residents of the village, or the livestock; only his own obsession with the clock mattered to him. Legend states that the clock mysteriously struck 13 times at the moment of Nels Larson's death, as though the man and the machine were somehow connected. The stories went on to add that the clock continued this odd activity for five decades, ringing out on the anniversary of its owner's passing. The clock tower remained an odd landmark on the prairie until the summer of 1976, when it was destroyed by a tornado. The stories say that a phantom clock still chimes every year on March 29, the day of Larson's death, at the exact moment that he passed from this world to the next.

The eerie stories of the Voorhies Castle began while the Larsons were still living in the house. The most mysterious event to occur in the house took place in 1914, when Johannah died. Many have speculated that she had a heart attack on the staircase, but the real cause of her death remains a mystery to this day. One of the field hands had gone to the house one afternoon to find her lying in a crumpled heap on the floor. Nels Larson was so stunned by this event that he left the house that night and went to Ellen's home in Cerro Gordo – and never returned. All of the clothing, furniture, and even his personal belongings were left behind. He never went back to his beloved house, abandoning everything that had been left there. The house seemed trapped in time with clothing in the closets, the table still set for dinner, Johannah's apron hanging over the back of a chair, and even food still sitting on the cold stove.

Johannah Larson had died, but stories from the era state that she never left the house, even after death. It was said that on certain nights, an eerie light could be seen coming from the east tower of the house. Those who were brave enough to venture onto the property claimed to see Johannah looking out the window of the tower room.

Nels Larson died in 1923 and his will specified that the house should remain in the family. The problem was that no one in the family wanted to live there because the house had no electricity. For all of his eccentric additions to the house – from running water, indoor plumbing, telephones, and countless clocks – Larson had a feel of electrical wiring. By the 1920s, the house was obsolete. Abandoned, it slowly began to sink into ruin.

As the years passed, attempts were made to rent out the crumbling Castle. Tenants moved into the house, but none stayed for long. It's likely that they were chased away by the deteriorating conditions of the house, and not by the ghosts. However, the rapid succession of tenants and the spooky atmosphere of the place combined to give the Castle a ghostly reputation. The stories grew and became more embellished as the years went by. It was said that someone died of fright in the house and the imprint of his or her body was still pressed into a couch in the living room. There was also said to be a pillar in the west parlor, which once held the large fern, which would inexplicably spin around under its own power. Reports said it spun so much that it eventually wore a circular pattern on the floor.

In 1967, the grandchildren of Nels Larson donated the Castle to the Illinois Pioneer Heritage Center in Monticello. The center opened the house as a tourist attraction, reportedly drawing up to 30,000 visitors each year. They came to view the unique architecture of the place and to soak up some of the ghostly ambiance. Unfortunately, the house became simply too expensive to take care of and it was closed down once again.

The Castle was empty with only caretakers to watch over the house on occasion. They added to the weird stories, which were widely reported in area newspapers every Halloween. According to their stories, the lights in the house – electricity had been added in the 1960s – refused to stay off and windows would open on their own. During an interview with the children of a former caretaker in 2009, I was told that they would often stop by the house in the evening to make sure things were secure, even though the children refused to go inside the dark and spooky old place. One night, after their father had gone inside, turning on lights to check out the house, he turned everything off and came back out to the car. Before they could drive away, though, all of the lights in the house turned back on by themselves. Their father drove away with plans to come back the next day.

Another caretaker had his own experiences. He locked up the house one night and discovered that several of the windows on the second floor had been mysteriously opened while he was on his way out the front door. He knew that they had all been closed just a few moments before. Thinking that someone was playing a prank on him, he went back inside, but found the place empty. He also told stories of hearing eerie sounds in the house, like footsteps on the stairs and the sound of piano keys clinking in the darkness. He finally quit working there after he was startled one night by a shadowy figure in the east tower. He was convinced that he had seen a ghost.

The odd stories about the house never seemed to stop and it became a favorite "haunt" for late night curiosity-seekers. Many of them claimed to have bizarre experiences and brushes with the supernatural. Many spoke of apparitions, seeing glowing balls of light, hearing sounds that had no explanation like whispers and ghostly footsteps, having flashlights that suddenly stopped working, and more.

The notoriety of the house began to fade by the middle 1970s. In 1972, Voorhies Castle was purchased by Milton and Sue Streenz, a Bloomington couple who set to work restoring the place. Over the course of the next six years, they repainted the entire house and did some extensive remodeling. They replaced 138 windowpanes and even added seven truckloads of flowers and trees to the estate. The couple remained in the house for the next six years, but in June 1978, Voorhies Castle was once again auctioned off. The elderly couple sadly admitted they were just not able to keep up with the physical work needed to maintain the old mansion anymore.

The house was eventually sold but over the course of the next few years, it was often vacant and began to deteriorate again. The decay of the mansion became the biggest problem that all of the new owners and tenants would face --- along with fending off the sightseers, for whom the ghostly landmark was still an attraction. Several of the more recent owners have made valiant attempts to restore the house and have done everything possible to discourage visitors from coming to the house. The most recent owners (as of this writing) have done further restoration and do occasionally open the house up for tours. Unauthorized visitors are still unwelcome, however. So much work has been done to the house that it's hardly recognizable anymore as the house that Nels Larson built.

Could this be one of the reasons that the stories of the resident ghosts have faded away?

The legends of Voorhies Castle, which began more than a century ago, are as haunting as the house has always been said to be. They leave us with many unanswered questions, but with the passage of time, it has become difficult for us to separate truth from fiction. If the house really was as haunted as so many people claim that it was, has the hauntings simply faded away over time? This seems possible, perhaps even likely. Is a house really haunted if no one remembers its ghosts? That's just one of the many questions that this story leaves us with.

But what if we do remember the people and the history that created the haunting in the first place? What if whatever was there still remains? What if it is just resting now, and waiting for some night, perhaps in the distant future, when the haunting will begin again?

EPILOGUE:

THE MAD GASSER OF MATTOON
An Unexplained Tale of Central Illinois

This is not a ghost story.

It's not a ghost story, but it involves a phantom of sorts – an unexplained enigma that has baffled those with an interest in the unexplained for more than 70 years. The legendary "Mad Gasser of Mattoon" wreaked havoc in the small Central Illinois town in 1944, and turned out to be so elusive that law enforcement officials eventually just declared him a figment of imagination, conjured up by nervous housewives, despite dozens of eyewitness reports and actual physical evidence that was left behind at the scene of some attacks.

What made things even more interesting was the fact that a series of nearly identical attacks that took place in Virginia in 1933 and 1934. The much more famous attacks in Illinois were written off as nothing more than mass hysteria, but how could the Mattoon residents have known anything about the events in Virginia, which were barely publicized, in order to duplicate them so closely?

Both of the series of attacks involved a mysterious figure, dressed in black, who came and went without warning, left little in the way of clues behind, and for some reason, sprayed a paralyzing gas into the windows of unsuspecting residents. The gas was never identified in either case and both cases involved fairly isolated areas where the attacks took place. The homes that were

attacked in Virginia were in a rural county and Mattoon, at that time, was a small, Central Illinois town with no large cities nearby. Also, police officials were totally stumped in both cases.

To this day, the mystery of the Mad Gasser remains unsolved, which is the reason that I decided to close this book of stories from Central Illinois with it. It's not a ghost story and perhaps for just that reason, it may be even scarier.

In 1933, Botetourt County, Virginia, was a quiet area of the state that had never really experienced much out of the ordinary. It was a fairly isolated part of the state, lying near the border with West Virginia, a couple of hours west of Richmond and southwest of Charlottesville. It was a working class area, made up of farmers, shopkeepers, and ordinary folks.

Nothing much had ever happened in the county, but that changed on December 22, when the home of Mr. and Mrs. Cal Huffman, near Haymakertown, was visited by a mysterious figure that was unlike anything seen, or even heard of, in the region before.

The phantom arrived around 10:00 that evening. After hearing a noise outside, Mrs. Huffman peered out the window and glimpsed a dark figure with some sort of metal contraption in his hand. It had a hose attached to it, which the figure pushed against the crack at the bottom of the window. An odd-smelling gas blew into the house and the figure outside ran away, vanishing into the darkness. A few moments later, Mrs. Huffman, who had called for her husband, Cal, began to feel sick to her stomach. She had no idea what had just occurred, but knew that she needed to lie down. She went to the bedroom, but her husband remained awake and alert, watching to see if the lurker with the gas might return. There had been stories in the newspapers about burglars who anesthetized their victims and then broke into homes while the occupants were asleep. Huffman prowled the house, watching outside, and then around 10:30, he stated that another wave of gas filled the house. Leaving his wife locked inside, he ran out and went to the home of his landlord, K.W. Henderson. The Huffman house was located on the Henderson property and was only a short distance away. When he arrived, he woke Henderson and asked him to call the police.

In a short time, a county patrol officer named Lemon arrived on the scene and stayed until nearly midnight, taking notes and examining the area around the house. Almost immediately after he left, the gasser returned. Another blast of noxious gas came in through an unguarded window, filling both floors of the Huffman cottage. All eight members of the Huffman family, along with Ashby Henderson, the landlord's wife, were sickened by the gas. Ashby and Cal Huffman had been keeping watch for the return of the prowler and both thought that they spotted a man running away from the house after the attack.

According to newspaper reports, the gas caused the victims to become very nauseated, caused headaches, and made mouth and throat muscles restrict. Alice, the Huffmans' 19-year-old daughter, was so stricken by the gas that she passed out and had to be given artificial respiration in order to revive her. For the next several days, she suffered from seizures. Her doctor, Dr. S.F. Driver, later reported that while part of her condition was caused by extreme nervousness over the attack, he had no doubt that the gas attack was responsible for the fact that her condition continued.

But what was the gas? No one knew. Dr. W.N. Breckenridge, who assisted with the police investigation, ruled out ether, tear gas, and chloroform. Investigators were also unclear as to how the attacker would have sprayed it into the house – or who the attacker might have been. The only clue that Officer Lemon found at the scene was the print of a woman's shoe in the dirt under the window where Mrs. Huffman had first seen the figure outside.

Whoever the phantom anesthetist was, he wasn't finished with Botetourt County. On December 24, he struck again in the small town of Cloverdale. Clarence Hall, his wife, and two children came home from a church service at around 9:00 p.m. Five minutes after they entered the house, they smelled a strange odor. Hall went into one of the back rooms of the house to investigate and came back moments later, staggering and swaying.

His wife, who also felt nauseated and weak, had to drag him outside. The effects of the gas did not linger with Mr. Hall, but Mrs. Hall experienced eye irritation for the next two days. Dr. Breckinridge again helped the police and he noted that the gas "tasted sweet" and that he detected a trace of formaldehyde in it. He still had no idea what the gas was, though, and investigators again found only one clue at the scene. Apparently, a nail had been pulled out from one of the window panes. It was possible that the attacker might have used this small hole to spray the gas inside.

A third attack occurred on December 27. Gas was sprayed into the window of a house owned by A.L. Kelly in Troutville. Kelly, a welder, lived there with his mother. Oddly, the police learned that a man and a woman in a 1933 Chevrolet had been seen driving back and forth in front of Kelly's house around the time of the attack. A neighbor managed to get a partial plate number on the car, but the police were unable to locate it.

The next two weeks were quiet, but the attacks resumed on January 10. The gasser struck at the home of Homer Hylton in Haymakertown. Hylton and his wife were upstairs asleep and their daughter, Mrs. Moore, whose husband was out of town on business, was sleeping downstairs. Around 10:00 p.m., she got up to attend to her baby and later recalled that she heard mumbling voices outside and someone fiddling with the window. Moments later, she said that the room filled with odd-smelling gas and as she grabbed her child, she experienced a "marked feeling of numbness." The window where the noises came from had been slightly broken for some time and this may have allowed the gasser access to the house. The police investigated, but stymied by the lack of clues, had already started to offer alternate causes for the weird events. It was suggested that Mrs. Moore imagined the voices outside, spooked by the sound of wind blowing through the crack in the glass, but how do we explain the gas? And how do we explain the fact that a neighbor, G.E. Poage, also heard voices outside at the same time?

On that same night, January 10, a Troutville man named G.D. Kinzie was also attacked. This case was not reported until later and was different from the others. Apparently, Dr. S.F. Driver, who had examined Alice Huffman on December 22, investigated this incident and stated that the gas used in the attack was chlorine. Investigators needed the gas being used in the attacks to be less mysterious than it was and Dr. Driver offered them a solution. After that, chlorine began to be mentioned in several subsequent incidents – until a Roanoke chemistry professor finally ruled it out as a possible source.

After a few quiet nights, the gasser returned on January 16, this time paying a visit to the home of F.B. Duval, near Bonsack. As the gas filled the downstairs rooms, Duval bolted out the house. He ran toward a neighbor's house to call the police and as he reached a nearby intersection, he spotted a man getting into a parked car and quickly driving away. With police officers, he spent the next several hours driving around, looking for the car, but found nothing. The next day, investigators again found the prints of a woman's shoes at the scene, this time near where the car had been parked.

On January 19, the gasser struck again. This time, gas was sprayed into the window of a Mrs. Campbell, a former judge's wife, near Cloverdale. She was sitting near a window and actually saw the shade move as the gas was forcibly sprayed inside. Moments later, she became sick.

A short time later, the gas attacks reached their peak with five incidents taking place over a period of just three nights. The first one occurred on January 21, when Howard Crawford and his wife returned to their rural home between Cloverdale and Troutville. Mr. Crawford went into the house first to turn on a lamp, but quickly came stumbling back out. He was overwhelmed by the gas, which Dr. Driver again pronounced was chlorine. Police officers were again able to find only a single clue at the house --- the crank of an old automobile. The metal crank seemed to have absolutely nothing to do with the attack, but it was simply too strange of an item to be left behind. On the other hand, it was also too common of an item in those days to be traced.

On January 22, three separate attacks occurred in Carvin's Cove. In just one hour's time, the gasser apparently covered a distance of about two miles, attacking in order in a line moving steadily southward, spraying gas at the homes of Ed Reedy, George C. Riley and Raymond Etter. At each of the houses, the occupants all claimed to experience numbness and nausea from some sort of gas. George Riley called his brother, a Roanoke police officer, and a blockade of the nearby roads was quickly put into place. Although the gasser managed to elude the authorities, one of Mr. Etter's sons claimed to see a figure running away from the direction of their house. He gave chase, and even fired a few shots at the man from a distance of 30 yards, but whoever he was, he got away.

On January 23, Mrs. R.H. Hartsell and her family spent the night with some neighbors and when they returned to their Pleasantdale Church home at 4:30 a.m., they discovered that the house had been filled with gas. For some bizarre reason, someone had also piled wood and brush up against their front door during the night. The only possible motive that I can see for this would have been to keep the family from easily escaping once the house was filled with gas. This means that the elusive gasser must have believed the family was home at the time of the attack.

This new series of gassings had the entire county in an uproar. Families who lived in more isolated areas began spending the night with friends and neighbors, hoping to find security in numbers. Local men began patrolling the roadways at night, armed with shotguns and rifles. The local newspaper, the *Roanoke Times,* stated that it was sure the gasser would be caught and it pleaded with the farmers not to shoot anyone.

The authorities were now growing more concerned. Prior to this, they had believed the gassings had been nothing more than pranks played by some mischievous boys. Now the county sheriff's office was forced to admit that if this had been the case, the boys would have already been caught. They had begun to investigate the idea that a mentally deranged person might be the culprit, perhaps even an unhinged gas victim from World War I.

On January 25, the gasser may have attempted to strike again, but this time was foiled. Around 9:00 p.m., a dog at the home of Chester Snyder began barking. Alerted, Snyder jumped up and grabbed his shotgun. Darting outside, he ran across the yard and fired a shot at a man that he saw creeping along a ditch that was about 20 feet from the house. The shot went wide and the gun was empty; Snyder had only loaded one shell. He ran back inside for more ammunition, but by the time he returned, the man was gone.

Snyder called the police and a deputy sheriff named Zimmerman investigated the scene. He managed to find footprints that led from the road to the ditch and signs that the prowler had hidden behind a tree on the property for some time before the dog sounded the alarm. More tracks led from the tree to the house and then stopped, marking the point where the man had retreated. Visitors who had left the Snyder home shortly before the incident recalled seeing a man walking about a half-mile away on the road. There was, of course, no real evidence to say that the prowler was actually the gasser, but based on the events that had been occurring, any sort of incident like this was immediately suspect.

On January 28, the gasser did manage to pull off another attack and he would actually return again to this same residence and attack again. The home belonged to Ed Stanley of Cloverdale. Stanley, his wife, and three other adults in the house were all affected by the still-mysterious gas. Frank Guy, a hired hand on the farm, ran outside immediately after the gas filled the house and stated that he saw four men running away in the direction of the Blue Ridge Mountains. He ran back inside to get his gun and when he returned to the yard, he couldn't see the fleeing figures, but could hear them in the woods. He fired several shots in the direction of the voices, but felt that it was unlikely that he hit anything.

Two nights later, the gasser – or, in this case, gassers – returned to the Stanley house. This time, however, the vigilant Stanley heard a sound outside the window before the gas attack took place. What happened after that remains a mystery as no further details were reported in the contemporary accounts.

The last of the likely authentic gas attacks took place in Nace, two miles from Troutville, on February 3. The house that was attacked belonged to A.P. Scaggs and he and his wife, along with five other adults, were all sprayed by the gas. The group was so badly affected by the gas that Sheriff Williamson would tell the skeptics who later emerged over the gassing cases that, "No amount of imagination in the world would make people as ill as the Skagges are."

This final incident was as dramatic as the first attack on the Huffman family, as if the gasser was marking his entrance and exit with large attacks. Another similarity to the Huffman attack was that it seemed as though the gas was sprayed into the house two times that evening, although one investigator stated that he believed lingering gas near the ceiling could have been responsible for what seemed to be a separate attack. The gas had some pretty strange effects on the people in the house. One of Scaggs' nephews began screaming hysterically that he was "trapped" in the house. The family dog was extremely sickened by the gas. Officer Lemon, who had been involved in the case since the beginning, returned to the house the following day to continue his investigation, and one of the children came in crying that the dog was dying. Lemon went out and saw that the animal was rolling over and over in the snow, just as dogs do when they are sprayed by a skunk. As no skunk odor was present, this certainly seemed odd. Witnesses later reported that the well-trained dog remained sick for some time and would not pay attention to commands for some time after the incident.

It was at this point that the entire story began to deteriorate. During the following week, there were 20 attacks reported in nearby Roanoke County and a number of other reports in Lexington, about 30 miles away. And while a few of the later "attacks" may have been genuine, they lacked the detail of the original incidents and most were likely hysterical reactions to ordinary odors or the result of hoaxes perpetrated by pranksters. In one of these hoaxes, a teenager threw a bottle of insecticide into a woman's window. A similar incident on February 9 gave the police and the newspapers the opportunity to declare that the gasser mystery was over.

The last "insecticide" case did have some interesting aspects to it, however. At the time when J.G. Shafer of Lithia believed his house was gassed on February 9, he went outside and scooped up some snow that contained a sweet-smelling substance. It was analyzed and was determined to contain sulfur, arsenic, and mineral oil, all of which was commonly used in insecticide sprays. This caused the police to dismiss the attack as a hoax, but was it really? Strangely, investigators found footprints leading from the front porch of the house to the barn, but no trail that led away from this building. It was as if whoever had been on the porch had then walked into the barn and simply vanished. Also, as with some of the other earlier cases, a "woman's tracks" led from the yard to the road.

The later cases that came along led the general public to swallow the unconvincing theory that faulty chimney flues and wild imaginations had caused the entire affair. Those who were attacked and police officers involved, like Officer Lemon, never accepted this explanation. However, the ongoing cases of panic did not help to convince the non-believers to reconsider. In hindsight, however, the later incidents actually helped prove that the original attacks were not the result of hysteria. None of the later incidents followed the pattern of the original attacks, they all occurred outside of the already established area, took place at no particular time, and the "gas" did not cause any lasting effects. It should also be noted that the original attacks, while taking place in Botetourt County, were spread out enough throughout the area that neighbors were unlikely to have infected one another with hysteria.

If we rule out hysteria in the Botetourt County incidents, then could a natural explanation have been to blame? This also seems unlikely. Pollution and faulty chimney flues can be ruled out when we examine the hard evidence in the case, including the selection of victims, times of the incidents, intense police investigations and, of course, the fleeing figure (or figures) that were spotted leaving the scene. Theories about hoaxes, and shell-shocked veterans, are not any more plausible. Even though a mysterious figure was often seen, there were never any useful clues left behind.

The identity of the Botetourt County Gasser was never discovered. It was almost as if the mysterious figure left Virginia and vanished without a trace. He never returned to Botetourt County again.

But did he surface once more in Central Illinois 11 years later?

Mattoon, which is located in the southeastern part of Central Illinois, is a fairly typical Midwestern town. The strange events that took place here in 1944, however, were anything but typical. These events would place the small city under the scrutiny of the entire nation and would one day become a textbook case of what authorities and psychologists called "mass hysteria." But was it really? Did the ominous phantom anesthetist of Botetourt County simply start over again in a new location?

The whirlwind of events began in the early morning hours of August 31. A Mattoon man was startled out of a deep sleep and complained to his wife that he felt sick. He questioned her about leaving the gas stove on in the kitchen because his symptoms seemed very similar to gas exposure. The woman tried to get out of bed and check the pilot light on the stove, but found to her surprise that she could not move. Just minutes later, according to published reports, a woman in a neighboring home also tried to get out of bed and discovered that she too was paralyzed.

The next evening, a woman named Mrs. Bert Kearney was awakened by a peculiar smell in her bedroom. The odor was sweet and overpowering, and as it grew stronger, she began to feel a peculiar prickling feeling in her legs and lower body. As she tried to get out of bed, she realized that her limbs were paralyzed. She began screaming, and drawing the attention of her neighbors, was able to alert the police. The following day, she complained of having burned lips and a parched mouth and throat from exposure to the gas. A hasty search of the yard by police officers, and her shaken neighbors, revealed nothing. But that would not be the last strange event to occur at this particular house.

Later on that evening, around midnight, Bert Kearney returned home from work, completely unaware of what had happened in his home that night. As he turned into his driveway, he spotted a man lurking near the house that would later fit the descriptions of the so-called "Mad Gasser." The stranger, according to Kearney, was tall and dressed in dark clothing and a tight-fitting black cap. He was standing near a window when Kearney spotted him, and when the odd character realized that he had been seen, he quickly ran away. Believing the dark-clothed man was a window peeper, Kearney ran after him, but the tall man sprinted away into the darkness.

These events soon became public knowledge and panic gripped the town. The story was badly handled by the authorities and the local newspaper reported the Kearney case, and subsequent others, in a wildly sensational manner. Years later, the newspaper would be blamed for everything that happened in the case and for manufacturing a scare by blowing a few isolated incidents out of proportion. The skeptics would call it "Gasser Hysteria," and would point fingers at the newspaper for the fear that swept through the community. The frightened citizens, according to these skeptics, took leave of their senses and began to imagine that a "mad gasser" was wreaking havoc in the town. This particular approach has been considered by many to be the simple explanation for the affair, but it certainly does not eliminate all of the evidence that points to something very bizarre taking place in Mattoon.

By the morning of September 5, the Mattoon police department had received reports of four more "gas attacks." The details in each of these attacks were eerily similar, even though none of the witnesses had compared notes or had time to check their stories. The newspapers had published a skewed version of the events, but the subsequent reports were not only almost identical to one another, but were accurate as to what had actually occurred. In each of the cases, the victims complained of a sickeningly sweet odor that caused them to become sick and slightly paralyzed for up to 30 minutes at a time.

Late on the night of September 5, the first real clues in the "Mad Gasser" case were discovered. They were found at the home of Carl and Beulah Cordes, but what these clues meant has yet to be discovered, even after all these years. The Cordes were returning home late that evening when they found a white cloth lying on their porch. Mrs. Cordes picked it up and noticed a strange smell coming from it. She held it up close to her nose and felt immediately nauseated and light-headed. She nearly fainted and her husband had to help her inside of the house. Within minutes, she was seized with a severe allergic reaction. Her lips and face began to swell and her mouth began to bleed. The symptoms began to subside in about two hours but, needless to say, she was terrified. Carl Cordes called the police and officers came out to investigate. They took the cloth into evidence, along with a skeleton key and an empty tube of lipstick that was found on the porch. They decided the prowler was probably trying to break into the house but had failed.

The police surmised that the cloth was connected to the other gas attacks. It should be noted, however, that the odor on the cloth caused different symptoms in Mrs. Cordes than in the other victims. She did become sick to her stomach but there were no sensations of paralysis. This incident is also different because if this was the gasser at work, then it is the only time when he actually tried to gain access to the home of his victims. Could his intentions in this incident have been different?

The gasser attacked again that same night, but he was back to his old tricks and sprayed his gas into an open window. There would only be one other report that even hinted that the attacker tried to break into the house. The woman in this instance claimed that a "person" in dark clothing tried to force open her front door. Was it really the "Mad Gasser?"

The attacks continued and Mattoon residents began reporting fleeting glimpses of the gasser, always describing him as a tall, thin man in dark clothes and wearing a tight black cap. More attacks were reported and the harried police force tried to respond to the mysterious crimes that left no clues behind. Eventually, the authorities even summoned two FBI agents from Springfield to look into the case, but their presence did nothing to discourage the strange reports. Panic was widespread and rumors began to circulate that the attacker was an escapee from an insane asylum or a German spy who was testing out some sort of poisonous gas.

Armed citizens took to the streets, organizing watches and patrols to thwart any further attacks, but several took place anyway. The gas attacks were becoming more frequent and the attacker was leaving behind evidence like footprints and sliced window screens. This evidence would become particularly interesting after the revelations of the authorities in the days to come.

A local citizens' "vigilance group" did manage to arrest one suspect as the gasser, but after he passed a polygraph test, he was released. Local businessmen announced that they would be holding a mass protest rally on Saturday, September 10, to put more pressure on the already pressured Mattoon police force. Now, the gasser was becoming more than a threat to public safety -- he was becoming a political liability and a blot on the public image of the city.

The gasser, apparently not dissuaded by armed vigilantes and newspaper articles, resumed his attacks. The first incident took place at the home of Mrs. Violet Driskell and her daughter, Ramona. They awoke late in the evening to hear someone removing the storm sash on their bedroom window. They hurried out of bed and tried to run outside for help, but the fumes overcame Ramona and she began vomiting. Her mother stated that she saw a man running away from the house.

A short time later that night, the gasser sprayed fumes into the partially-opened window of a room where Mrs. Russell Bailey, Katherine Tuzzo, Mrs. Genevieve Haskell, and Mrs. Haskell's young son were sleeping. At another home, Miss Frances Smith, the principal of the Columbian Grade School, and her sister, Maxine, were also overwhelmed with gas and became ill. They began choking as they were awakened and felt partial paralysis in their legs and arms. They also said that as the sweet odor began to fill the room "as a thin, blue vapor," they heard a buzzing noise from outside and believed that it was the gasser's "spraying apparatus" in operation.

By September 10, "Mad Gasser" paranoia had peaked. FBI agents were trying to track down the type of gas being used in the attacks and the police force had to divide its time between looking for the gasser and keeping armed citizens off the streets. Neither law enforcement agency was having much luck. By the following Saturday night, several dozen well-armed farmers from the surrounding area had joined the patrols in Mattoon. In spite of this, six attacks took place anyway, including the three previously mentioned. Another couple, Mr. and Mrs. Stewart B. Scott, returned to their farm on the edge of Mattoon late in the evening to find the house filled with sweet smelling gas.

The report from the Scott farm seemed to mark a turning point in the case. It was almost as if the idea that the strange gas attacks could move from within the city of Mattoon to a rural farm tipped the scales of official acceptance of the story in the wrong direction. In the words of Thomas V. Wright, the City Commissioner of Public Health: "There is no doubt that a gas maniac exists and has made a number of attacks. But many of the reported attacks are nothing more than hysteria. Fear of the gas man is entirely out of proportion to the menace of the relatively harmless gas he is spraying. The whole town is sick with hysteria and last night it spread out into the country."

At this point, newspaper accounts of the affair began to take on a more skeptical tone, and despite claims by victims and material evidence left behind, the police began to dismiss new reports of attacks and suggested that local residents were merely imagining things. The episode had gone too far and that was really the only thing left for them to do. The gasser, if he existed at all, could not be caught, identified, or tracked down. Officials started to believe that if they ignored the problem, it would just go away. After all, if the man were real, how could he have possibly escaped detection for so long?

Psychology experts opined that the women of Mattoon had dreamed up the "Gasser" as a desperate cry for attention, as many of their husbands were overseas fighting in the war. This theory ignored the fact that many victims and witnesses were men and that this so-called "fantasy" was leaving behind evidence of his existence.

On the night of September 11, the police received a number of phone calls, but after half-hearted attempts to investigate, dismissed all of them as false alarms. Just days before, a crime specialist with the State Department of Public Safety named Richard T. Piper told reporters, "This is one of the strangest cases I have ever encountered in my years of police work." But now new calls were only worthy of perfunctory examination. This is in spite of the fact that a doctor who appeared on the scene shortly after one of the evening's attacks stated that there had been a "peculiar odor" in the room. The officials were just no longer interested.

The Mattoon police chief issued what he felt was the final statement on the gas attacks on September 12. He stated that large quantities of carbon tetrachloride gas were used at the local Atlas Diesel Engine Co. and that this gas must be causing the reported cases of illness and paralysis. It could be carried throughout the town on the wind and could have left the stains that were found on the rag at one of the homes. As for the "Mad Gasser" himself, well, he was simply a figment of their imaginations. The whole case, he said "was a mistake from beginning to end."

Not surprisingly, a spokesman for the Atlas Diesel Engine plant was quick to deny the allegations that his company had caused the concern in town, maintaining that the only use for that gas in the plant was in their fire extinguishers and any similar gases used there caused no ill effects in the air. Besides that, why hadn't this gas ever caused problems in the city before? And how exactly was this gas cutting the window screens on Mattoon homes before causing nausea and paralysis?

The official explanation also failed to explain how so many identical descriptions of the "Gasser" had been reported to the police. It also neglected to explain how different witnesses managed to report seeing a man of the gasser's description fleeing the scene of an attack, even when the witness had no idea that an attack had taken place.

The last "Gasser" attack took place on September 13, and while it was the last incident connected to the attacker in Mattoon, it was also possibly the strangest. It occurred at the home of Mrs. Bertha Bench and her son, Orville. They described the attacker as being a woman who was dressed in a man's clothing and who sprayed gas into a bedroom window. The next morning, footprints that appeared to have been made by a woman's high-heeled shoes were found in the dirt below the window. And while this report does not match any of the earlier attacks in Mattoon, readers will undoubtedly recognize the claims of a woman's shoe prints from several attacks in Botetourt County in 1933.

After this night, the "Mad Gasser of Mattoon" was never seen or heard from again.

The real story behind what happened in Mattoon and Botetourt County is still unknown and it's unlikely that we will ever know what was behind these strange events. It is certain that something did take place in both locations, however strange, and theories abound as to what it may have been. Was the "Mad Gasser" real? And if he was, who was he? And if he was real, could he have been the same figure in both cases? It's hard to ignore the similarities between the two cases, from his method of operation to the unusual form of attacks. In Virginia, though, the gasser was not always reported as being alone as he was in Mattoon, but then again, what about the identical reports of prints left by a woman's shoe?

Stories have suggested that Mattoon's Gasser was anything from a mad scientist to an ape-man (although who knows where that came from?) and researchers today have their own theories, some of which are just as wild.

Could he have been some sort of extraterrestrial visitor using some sort of paralyzing agent to further a hidden agenda?

Could he have been some sort of odd inventor who was testing a new apparatus? Interestingly, I was sent a letter in 2002 from a woman who explained to me that her father grew up in Mattoon during the time when the gas attacks were taking place. He told her that there had been two sisters living in town at the time who had a brother who was allegedly insane. A number of people in town believed that he was the Mad Gasser and so his sisters locked him in the basement until they could find a mental institution to put him in. After they locked him away, her father told her, the gas attacks stopped. Is this the answer to the mystery?

Or could the "Gasser" have been an agent of our own government, who came to an obscure Midwestern town to test some military gas that could be used in the war effort? It might be telling that once national attention came to Mattoon, the authorities began a policy of complete denial and the attacks suddenly ceased. Coincidence?

Whoever, or whatever, he was, the "Mad Gasser" has vanished into time and, real or imagined, is only a memory in the world of the unknown. Perhaps he was never here at all. Perhaps he was, as Donald M. Johnson wrote in the 1954 issue of the *Journal of Abnormal and Social Psychology*, simply a "shadowy manifestation of some unimaginable unknown."

But was he really? How do we explain the sightings of the "Mad Gasser" that were made by people who did not even know the creature was alleged to exist? Or identical sightings from independent witnesses who could not have possibly known that others had just spotted the same figure? Was the "Gasser," as some have suggested, a visitor from a dimension outside of our own, thus explaining his ability to appear or disappear at will? Was he a creature so outside the realm of our imaginations that we will never be able to comprehend his motives or understand the reason why he came to Mattoon?

Perhaps this is the solution to the mystery – that this is a mystery that we'll never understand. If you think about that long enough, it can make your head hurt. It's a solution that simply causes more questions to be asked. And, in keeping with that, here's one:

If the rules of physics don't actually apply to a phantom attacker like the Mad Gasser, and he is capable of traveling from one dimension to another, coming and going without explanation, where might he appear the next time?

Think about that one when you turn off the lights and get into bed at night.
I told you: this is no ghost story. But maybe, just maybe, it's much scarier.

BIBLIOGRAPHY
Sources, Notes & Recommended Reading

Since my book *Haunted Illinois* was first published in 1999 (followed by subsequent, updated editions) it has been a great source of material by a lot of writers who followed in my wake. There have been a lot of bad writers who have used my work and ideas and a lot of good ones who, frankly, often made the stories better. I have never minded the stories being used, as long as they were properly credited, which some writers just didn't bother to do. I won't give attention to list the names of those who blatantly used the material without attribution, but I will make a note of really good writers like my friends Jim Graczyk, Luke Naliborski, and – even though he's never liked me very much – Michael Kleen, who has always, always listed his sources. Check out their books if you get a chance – you won't be sorry!

Adams, Joseph. "A Lost Village" *Historic Illinois*, August 1999
Bain, Donald - *War in Illinois*; 1978
Banton, O.T. *History of Macon County, Illinois*; 1976
Cole, Charles Arthur – *Illinois: End of the Civil War Era; 1919*
Coleman, E.T. – *History of Macon County;* 1929
Coleman, Loren - *Mysterious America*; 2000
Davis, James E. *Frontier Illinois*; 1998
DeNeal, Gary - *Knight of Another Sort*; 1998
Dickensen, Fred – *Album of Famous Mysteries*
Doyle, Don Harrison – *Social Order of a Frontier Community: Jacksonville;* 1983
Drury, John. *Old Illinois Houses*; 1948
Eames, Charles M. – *Historic Morgan & Classic Jacksonville;* 1885
Fliege, Stu. *Tales and Trails of Illinois*; 2002
Holst, Erika – *Wicked Springfield; 2010*
Howard, Robert. *Illinois – A History of the Prairie State*; 1972
Hughes, Linda Clark – *Tales of Old Decatur;* 1976
Hynd, Alan – *Murder, Mayhem & Mystery;* 1958
Illinois Valley Cultural Heritage Association Archives
Kleen, Michael – *Ghostlore of Illinois Colleges and Universities;* 2015
----------------- - *Legends and Lore of Illinois;* 2013
------------------ - *Paranormal Illinois*; 2010
Levins, Peter – *Album of Famous Mysteries*
Lewis, Chad and Terry Fisk – *Illinois Road Guide to Haunted Locations; 2007*
Lewis, Lloyd. *Myths After Lincoln*; 1929
Lisman, Gary L. – *Bittersweet Memories;* 2005
McCarthy, Stephanie E. – *Haunted Peoria: Peoria's Haunted Memories;* 2009
Moreno, Richard – *It Happened in Illinois*; 2011
Moffett, Garrett – *Haunted Springfield, Illinois;* 2011
-------------------- – *Myths and Mysteries of Illinois;* 2013
Norman, Michael, and Beth Scott. *Haunted America*; 1994
----------------- *Historic Haunted America*; 1995

Parrish, Randall. *Historic Illinois*; 1905
Pease, Theodore Calvin – *Illinois: The Frontier State;* 1918
Pensoneau, Taylor – *Brothers Notorious*; 2002
Russell, Dorotha. *Squire of Voorhies*; 1967
Scott, Beth, and Michael Norman. *Haunted Heartland*; 1985
Shoemaker, Michael T. - The Mad Gasser of Botetourt - *Fate Magazine*; June 1985
Shults, Sylvia – *Fractured Spirits*; 2012
Speer, Bonnie Stahlman - *The Great Abraham Lincoln Hijack*; 1990
Taylor, Troy - *Bloody Illinois*; 2008
------------ - *Flickering Images; 2011*
------------ - *Ghosts of Springfield;* 1997
------------ - *Haunted Decatur*; 2009
------------ - *Haunted Illinois* 1999; 2002; 2004
----------- - *Haunted President*; 2009
----------- - *Illinois Hauntings*; 2011
----------- - *Mysterious Illinois*; 2006
----------- - *Weird Illinois*; 2005
----------- - *Wicked Decatur*; 2011
----------- - *Wicked Northern Illinois*; 2011
Taylor, Troy & Lisa Taylor Horton – *Haunted Jacksonville;* 2014

Personal Interviews and Correspondence

Newspapers, Periodicals & Journals

Chicago American
Chicago Daily Herald
Chicago Daily News
Chicago Herald & Examiner
Chicago Tribune
Decatur Bulletin-Sentinel
Decatur Evening Bulletin
Decatur Herald
Decatur Review
Decatur Tribune
Fate Magazine
Fortean Times Magazine
Historic Illinois: Newsletter of the Illinois Historic Preservation Agency
Illinois Times
Jacksonville Journal-Courier
Peoria Journal-Star
Peoria Times-Observer
Springfield State Journal - Register

Note: Although American Hauntings Ink, Troy Taylor and all affiliated with this book have carefully researched all sources to insure the accuracy and completeness of all information contained here, we assume no responsibility for errors, inaccuracies or omissions.

Special Thanks to:

April Slaughter: Cover Design and Artwork
Lois Taylor: Editing and Proofreading
Lisa Taylor Horton & Lux
Haven & Helayna Taylor
Orrin Taylor
Rene Kruse
Rachael Horath
Elyse & Thomas Reihner
Bethany Horath
Mary DeLong
Kaylan Schardan
John Winterbauer
Adam White
Len Adams
Luke Naliborski
Julie Ringering
Sandy Guire
Bobbi Brooks
Steve Mangin
Sonny Ervin
Rest of the Staff & Crew from American Hauntings
And, of course, all of the people who supported my fledgling efforts at book writing and ghost tours back in 1994. It all continues to be possible, thanks to you!

CPSIA information can be obtained
at www.ICGtesting.com
Printed in the USA
LVHW020905070723
751641LV00004B/25